FROM MINIATURES BY JEHAN DE GRISE († 1344) IN BODLEIAN MS. 264 (*Li romans d'Alixandre*)

THE MEDIAEVAL STAGE

BY

E. K. CHAMBERS

VOLUME II

OXFORD UNIVERSITY PRESS

Oxford University Press, Amen House, London E.C.4
GLASGOW NEW YORK TORONTO MELBOURNE WELLINGTON
BOMBAY CALCUTTA MADRAS KARACHI LAHORE DACCA
CAPE TOWN SALISBURY NAIROBI IBADAN ACCRA
KUALA LUMPUR HONG KONG

FIRST EDITION 1903
REPRINTED LITHOGRAPHICALLY IN GREAT BRITAIN
BY LOWE & BRYDONE, PRINTERS, LTD., LONDON
FROM SHEETS OF THE FIRST EDITION
1925, 1948, 1954, 1963

CONTENTS

Volume I

BOOK IV. THE INTERLUDE

APPENDICES

BOOK III

RELIGIOUS DRAMA

heȝe vpon a doune,
    þer al folk hit se may,
a mile from þe toune,
    aboute þe midday,
þe rode is vp arered;
his frendes aren afered,
    ant clyngeþ so þe clay;
þe rode stond in stone,
marie stont hire one,
    ant seiþ 'weylaway'!

CHAPTER XVIII

LITURGICAL PLAYS

[*Bibliographical Note.*— The liturgical drama is fully treated by W. Creizenach, *Geschichte des neueren Dramas* (vol. i, 1893), Bk. 2; L. Petit de Julleville, *Les Mystères* (1880), vol. i. ch. 2; A. d'Ancona, *Origini del Teatro Italiano* (2nd ed. 1891), Bk. 1, chh. 3–6; M. Sepet, *Origines catholiques du Théâtre moderne* (1901), and by L. Gautier in *Le Monde* for Aug. and Sept. 1872. The studies of W. Meyer, *Fragmenta Burana* (1901), and C. Davidson, *English Mystery Plays* (1892), are also valuable. A. W. Ward, *History of English Dramatic Literature* (2nd ed. 1899), vol. i. ch. 1 deals very slightly with the subject. A good popular account is M. Sepet, *Le Drame chrétien au Moyen Âge* (1878). Of older works, the introduction to E. Du Méril's *Origines latines du Théâtre moderne* (1849, facsimile reprint, 1896) is the best. The material collected for vol. ii of C. Magnin's *Origines du Théâtre* is only available in the form of reviews in the *Journal des Savants* (1846–7), and lecture notes in the *Journal général de l'Instruction publique* (1834–6). Articles by F. Clément, L. Deschamps de Pas, A. de la Fons-Melicocq, and others in A. N. Didron's *Annales archéologiques* (1844–72) are worth consulting; those of F. Clément are reproduced in his *Histoire de la Musique religieuse* (1860). There are also some notices in J. de Douhet, *Dictionnaire des Mystères* (1854).—The texts of the *Quem quaeritis* are to be studied in G. Milchsack, *Die Oster- und Passionsspiele*, vol. i (all published, 1880), and C. Lange, *Die lateinischen Osterfeiern* (1887). The former compares 28, the latter no less than 224 manuscripts. The best general collection of texts is that of Du Méril already named: others are T. Wright, *Early Mysteries and other Latin Poems* (1838); E. de Coussemaker, *Drames liturgiques du Moyen Age* (1860), which is valuable as giving the music as well as the words; and A. Gasté, *Les Drames liturgiques de la Cathédrale de Rouen* (1893). A few, including the important *Antichristus*, are given by R. Froning, *Das Drama des Mittelalters* (1891). The original sources are in most cases the ordinary service-books. But a twelfth-century manuscript from St. Martial of Limoges (*Bibl. Nat. Lat.* 1139) has four plays, a *Quem quaeritis*, a *Rachel*, a *Prophetae*, and the *Sponsus*. Facsimiles are in E. de Coussemaker, *Histoire de l'Harmonie au Moyen Age* (1852). A thirteenth-century manuscript from Fleury (*Orleans MS.* 178) has no less than ten, a *Quem quaeritis*, a *Peregrini*, a *Stella* in two parts, a *Conversio Pauli*, a *Suscitatio Lazari* and four *Miracula S. Nicholai*. Two later plays and fragments of three others are found in the famous thirteenth-century manuscript from Benedictbeuern (*Munich MS.* 19,486, printed in J. A. Schmeller, *Carmina Burana*, 3rd ed. 1894, with additional fragments in W. Meyer, *Fragmenta Burana*, 1901). This is probably the repertory of travelling goliardic clerks. The twelfth-century manuscript which preserves the three plays of Hilarius (*Bibl. Nat. Lat.* 11,331, printed in J. J. Champollion-Figeac, *Hilarii Versus et Ludi*, 1838) is of a similar character.—The tropes are fully dealt with by L. Gautier, *Hist. de la*

Poésie liturgique au Moyen Age, vol. i (all published, 1886), and W. H. Frere, *The Winchester Troper* (1894). I have not been able to see A. Reiners, *Die Tropen-, Prosen- und Präfations-Gesänge des feierlichen Hochamtes im Mittelalter* (1884). Antiquarian data are collected by H. J. Feasey, *Ancient English Holy Week Ceremonial* (1897), and A. Heales, *Easter Sepulchres*, in *Archaeologia*, vol. xlii. I have printed an important passage from the *Regularis Concordia* of St. Ethelwold (965–75) in Appendix O. The *Planctus Mariae* are treated by A. Schönbach, *Die Marienklagen* (1874), and E. Wechssler, *Die romanischen Marienklagen* (1893). W. Köppen, *Beiträge zur Geschichte der deutschen Weihnachtsspiele* (1893), and M. Sepet, *Les Prophètes du Christ* (1878), contain valuable studies of the evolution of the *Stella* and the *Prophetae* respectively. The relation of dramatic to iconic art in the Middle Ages is brought out by P. Weber, *Geistliches Schauspiel und kirchliche Kunst* (1894). A rather primitive bibliography is F. H. Stoddard, *References for Students of Miracle Plays and Mysteries* (1887).—Authorities forEnglish facts given without references in the present volume will be found in Appendices W and X.]

THE discussions of the first volume have often wandered far enough from the history of the stage. But two or three tolerable generalizations emerge. The drama as a living form of art went completely under at the break-up of the Roman world : a process of natural decay was accelerated by the hostility of Christianity, which denied the theatre, and by the indifference of barbarism, which had never imagined it. If anything of a histrionic tradition survived, it took the shape of pitiable farce, one amongst many heterogeneous elements in the *spectacula* of disreputable mimes. For the men of the Middle Ages, however, peasants or burghers, monks or nobles, such *spectacula* had a constant attraction : and the persistence of the deep-rooted mimetic instinct in the folk is proved by the frequent outcrops of primitive drama in the course of those popular observances which are the last sportive stage of ancient heathen ritual. Whether of folk or of minstrel origin, the *ludi* remained to the last alien and distasteful to the Church. The degradation of Rome and Constantinople by the stage was never forgotten ; nor the association with an heathenism that was glossed over rather than extinct : and though a working compromise inevitably tended to establish itself, it remained subject to perpetual protest from the austerer spirit in the counsels of the clergy.

It is the more remarkable that the present volume has to describe a most singular new birth of the drama in the very bosom of the Church's own ritual. One may look at the event as one will, either as an audacious, and at least partly successful, attempt to wrest the pomps of the devil to a spiritual service, or as an inevitable and ironical recoil of a barred human instinct within the hearts of its gaolers themselves. From either point of view it is a fact which the student of European culture cannot afford to neglect. And apart from its sociological implications, apart from the insight which it gives into the temper of the folk and into the appeal of religion, it is of the highest interest as an object lesson in literary evolution. The historian is not often privileged to isolate a definite literary form throughout the whole course of its development, and to trace its rudimentary beginnings, as may here be done, beyond the very borders of articulate speech.

The dramatic tendencies of Christian worship declared themselves at an early period[1]. At least from the fourth century, the central and most solemn rite of that worship was the Mass, an essentially dramatic commemoration of one of the most critical moments in the life of the Founder[2]. It is

[1] On these tendencies generally, see Davidson, 130; Ward, i. 32; R. Rosières, *Société française au Moyen Age*, ii. 228; E. King, *Dramatic Art and Church Liturgy* (*Dublin Review*, cxxv. 43). Mediaeval liturgiologists such as Belethus, Durandus, and Honorius of Autun (*P.L.* clxxii), lay great stress on the symbolical aspect of ritual and ceremonial. J. M. Robertson, *The Gospel Mystery-Play* (*The Reformer*, N.S. iii (1901), 657), makes an ingenious attempt to show that the earlier gospel narratives of the Passion, those of Saints Matthew and Mark, are based upon a dramatic version. This, he thinks, to have been on classical lines, and to have been performed liturgically until about the second century, when it was dropped in deference to the ascetic views of the stage then prevalent (cf. vol. i. p. 11). But the narrative, with its short speeches, its crowd of characters and its sufferings 'coram populo' cannot, on the face of it, be derived from a *classical* drama. A nearer parallel would be the Graeco-Jewish Ἐξαγωγή of Ezechiel (first century B.C., cf. Ward, i. 3). The Gospel narrative is, no doubt, mainly 'a presentation of dramatic action and dialogue'; but this may be because it was built up around *Logia*. Of external evidence for Mr. Robertson's view there is none. The ritual of the first two centuries was probably a very simple one; cf. F. E. Warren, *Liturgy of the Ante-Nicene Church*, 54. The earliest liturgical dramas, even in the Greek churches, and those only guessed at, are of the fourth (cf. p. 206). Mr. Robertson claims support from *Galatians*, iii. 1 οἷς κατ' ὀφθαλμοὺς Ἰησοῦς Χριστὸς προεγράφη ἐσταυρωμένος. Lightfoot, however, declares that the meaning of προγράφειν is 'write up in public,' 'placard,' 'proclaim.' If it cannot, as he says, mean 'paint,' still less can it mean 'represent dramatically.'

[2] Duchesne, 47: A. V. G. Allen, *Christian Institutions*, 515.

his very acts and words that day by day throughout the year the officiating priest resumes in the face of the people. And when the conception of the Mass developed until instead of a mere symbolical commemoration it was looked upon as an actual repetition of the initial sacrifice, the dramatic character was only intensified. So far as the Canon of the Mass goes, this point needs no pressing. But the same liturgical principle governs many other episodes in the order of the mediaeval services. Take, for example, the ritual, of Gallican origin, used at the dedication of a church [1]. The bishop and his procession approach the closed doors of the church from without, but one of the clergy, *quasi latens*, is placed inside. Three blows with a staff are given on the doors, and the anthem is raised *Tollite portas, principes, vestras et elevamini, portae aeternales, et introibit Rex gloriae*. From within comes the question *Quis est iste rex gloriae?* and the reply is given *Dominus virtutum ipse est Rex gloriae*. Then the doors are opened, and as the procession sweeps through, he who was concealed within slips out, *quasi fugiens*, to join the train. It is a dramatic expulsion of the spirit of evil. A number of other instances are furnished by the elaborate rites of Holy week. Thus on Palm Sunday, in commemoration of the entry into Jerusalem, the usual procession before Mass was extended, and went outside the church and round the churchyard or close bearing palms, or in their place sprigs of yew, box, or withies, which the priest had previously blessed [2].

[1] Duchesne, 393, 469, with the *Ordo dedicationis Ecclesiae* from a ninth-century Metz *Sacramentary* there printed; Maskell, *Monum. Rit. Eccl. Angl.* (1882) I. cccxxvi, 196, with text from *Sarum Pontifical*. The ceremonies are symbolically explained by Hugo of St. Victor, *de Sacramentis*, ii. 5. 3 (*P. L.* clxxvi, 441), who says, 'Interrogatio inclusi, ignorantia populi.'

[2] Duchesne, 236; Martene, iii. 71; Gasté, 69; Feasey, 53; *Use of Sarum*, i. 59; *Sarum Missal*, 258; *Sarum Processional*, 47; *York Missal*, i. 84; *York Processional*, 148. The custom is described in the *Peregrinatio Silviae* (Duchesne, 486) as already in use at Jerusalem in the fourth century. 'Etiam cum coeperit esse hora undecima, legitur ille locus de evangelio, ubi infantes cum ramis vel palmis occurrerunt Domino, dicentes: *Benedictus qui venit in nomine Domini*. Et statim levat se episcopus et omnis populus porro: inde de summo monte Oliveti totum pedibus itur. Nam totus populus ante ipsum cum ymnis vel antiphonis, respondentes semper: *Benedictus qui venit in nomine Domini*. Et quotquot sunt infantes in hisdem locis, usque etiam qui pedibus ambulare non possunt, quia teneri sunt, in collo illos parentes sui tenent,

The introduction of a *Palmesel* might make the ceremony more dramatic still[1]. Some of the texts used were of a prophetic character, and the singer of these was occasionally dressed as a prophet[2]. At the doors of the church the procession was greeted by boys stationed upon the roof of the porch, and certain French uses transferred to the occasion the dedication solemnity of *Tollite portas* just described[3]. The reading of the gospel narratives of the Passion, which on Palm Sunday, on the Monday or Tuesday, and the Wednesday in Holy week and on Good Friday preceded the Gospel proper, was often resolved into a regular oratorio. A tenor voice rendered the narrative of the evangelist, a treble the sayings of Jews and disciples, a bass those of Christ himself[4]. To particular episodes of these Passions special dramatic action was appropriated. On Wednesday, at the words *Velum templi scissum est*, the Lenten veil, which since the first Sunday in Lent had hidden the sanctuary from the sight of the people, was dropped to the ground[5]. On Good Friday the

omnes ramos tenentes, alii palmarum, alii olivarum; et sic deducitur episcopus in eo typo quo tunc Dominus deductus est. Et de summo monte usque ad civitatem, et inde ad Anastase per totam civitatem, totum pedibus omnes, sed et si quae matronae sunt aut si qui domini, sic deducunt episcopum respondentes, et sic lente et lente, ne lassetur populus; porro iam sera pervenitur ad Anastase.'

[1] Cf. ch. xiv.

[2] Collier, i. 82; Feasey, 68, 75, quoting payments 'for the prophets.' their 'raiment,' 'stages' for them, &c., from sixteenth-century Revels and churchwardens' accounts. The *Sarum Processional*, 50 (from eds. 1508, 1517), has 'finito evangelio, unus puer ad modum prophetae indutus, stans in aliquo eminenti loco, cantat lectionem propheticam modo quo sequitur.' Then come alternating passages between the 'propheta' and 'tres clerici.' Perhaps the latter were also sometimes disguised, but the *Sarum Processional*, as well as the thirteenth-century *Consuetudinary* and the *York Missal* (*MS. D*), all specify that the clergy, other than the prophet, shall be 'habitu non mutato.' Several of the London records given by Mr. Feasey mention an 'angel,' and one of them a 'chylde that playde a messenger.' A Coutances Order of 1573 (Gasté, 74) forbids 'spectacula . . . cum habitibus inhonestis' at the Gospel during Mass on Palm Sunday.

[3] Martene, iii. 72; Gasté, 72; R. Twigge, *Mediaeval Service Bks. of Aquitaine* (*Dublin Review*, cxv. 294; cxvii. 67); Pearson, ii. 296.

[4] *Sarum Missal*, 264. The *York Missal*, i. 102, says, for Good Friday, 'Diaconus legat Passionem,' but *MS. D.* adds 'vel legatur a tribus Presbyteris, si sic ordinatum erit.' Payments for the singers of the Passion are quoted from churchwardens' accounts (1447-1562) by Feasey, 81. The singing was sometimes done from the rood loft.

[5] Feasey, 17; *Use of Sarum*, i. 140 'quarta autem feria ante pascha dum passio domini legitur ad prolacionem ipsius clausulae *Velum*

words *Partiti sunt vestimenta* were a signal for a similar bit of by-play with a linen cloth which lay upon the altar [1]: Maundy Thursday had its commemorative ceremony of the washing of feet [2]; while the *Tenebrae* or solemn extinction, one after another, of lights at the Matins of the last three days of the week, was held to symbolize the grief of the apostles and others whom those lights represented [3].

These, and many other fragments of ceremonial, have the potentiality of dramatic development. Symbolism, mimetic action, are there. The other important factor, of dialogued speech, is latent in the practice of antiphonal singing. The characteristic type of Roman chant is that whereby the two halves of the choir answer one another, or the whole choir answers the single voice of the *cantor*, in alternate versicle and respond [4]. The antiphon was introduced into Italy by St. Ambrose of Milan. It had originated, according to tradition, in Antioch, had been in some relation to the histrionic tendencies of Arianism, and was possibly not altogether uninfluenced by the traditions both of the Greek tragic chorus and of Jewish psalmody [5].

templi scissum est: praedictum velum in area presbiterii decidat.' The same rubric is in the Wells *Ordinale* (H. E. Reynolds, *Wells Cathedral*, 42).

[1] J. W. Legg, *Westminster Missal* (H.B.S.), 1469; G. F. Aungier, *Hist. and Antiq. of Syon Monastery*, 350; Lanfranc, *Decreta pro Ord. S. Bened.* (*P.L.* cl. 465) 'Ubi dicitur *Partiti sunt vestimenta mea sibi*, sint duo de indutis iuxta altare, hinc et inde trahentes ad se duos pannos qui ante officium super altare missi fuerant, linteo tamen remanente subtus missale'; *Leofric's Missal* (Exeter, eleventh century), 261 'hac expleta statim duo diaconi nudant altare sindone quae prius fuerit sub evangelio posita in modum furantis. Aliqui vero, antequam legatur passio domini, praeparant sindones duas sibi coherentes et in eo versu ubi legitur: *Partiti sunt vestimenta*, scindunt hinc inde ipsas sindones desuper altare in modum furantis, et secum auferunt'; *York Missal*, i. 102 'hic distrahantur linteamina super altare connexa'; *Sarum Missal*, 323 'hic accedant duo ministri in superpelliceis, unus ad dextrum et alius ad sinistrum cornu altaris; et inde duo linteamina amoveant quae ad hoc super altare fuerunt apposita.' I find the custom in Aquitaine (*Dublin Review* (1897), 366), and in Hungary (Dankó, *Vetus Hymnarium Eccles. Hungariae*, 534).

[2] Martene, iii. 99; Feasey, 107; Wordsworth, 184.

[3] Feasey, 84; Wordsworth, 290.

[4] Strictly speaking the *Antiphon* is begun by one half of the choir and finished by the other; the *Responsorium* is a solo with a short refrain sung by the choir, like the secular *carole*; cf. ch. viii, and *Use of Sarum*, i. 307; Dankó, *Vetus Hymnarium Eccl. Hung.* 11.

[5] Duchesne, 108; Davidson, 134; F. E. Warren, *Liturgy of the Ante-Nicene Church*, 74.

At any rate, it lent itself naturally to dialogue, and it is from the antiphon that the actual evolution of the liturgical drama starts. The course of that evolution must now be followed.

The choral portions of the Mass were stereotyped about the end of the sixth century in the *Antiphonarium* ascribed to Gregory the Great [1]. This compilation, which included a variety of antiphons arranged for the different feasts and seasons of the year, answered the needs of worship for some two hundred years. With the ninth century, however, began a process, which culminated in the eleventh, of liturgical elaboration. Splendid churches, costly vestments, protracted offices, magnificent processions, answered especially in the great monasteries to a heightened sense of the significance of cult in general, and of the Eucharist in particular [2]. Naturally ecclesiastical music did not escape the influence of this movement. The traditional *Antiphonarium* seemed inadequate to the capacities of aspiring choirs. The Gregorian texts were not replaced, but they were supplemented. New melodies were inserted at the beginning or end or even in the middle of the old antiphons. And now I come to the justification of the statement made two or three pages back, that the beginnings of the liturgical drama lie beyond the very borders of articulate speech. For the earliest of such adventitious melodies were sung not to words at all, but to vowel sounds alone. These, for which precedent existed in the Gregorian *Antiphonarium*, are known as *neumae* [3]. Obviously the next stage was to write texts, called generically 'tropes,' to them; and towards the end of the ninth century three more or less independent schools of trope-writers grew up. One, in northern France, produced Adam of St. Victor; of another,

[1] Frere, vi. The Gregorian *Liber Antiphonarius* is in *P.L.* lxxviii. 641.

[2] Radulphus Glaber, *Hist. sui Temporis* († 1044), iii. 4 (Bouquet, *Rerum Gallic. et Francic. Script.* x. 29) 'Igitur infra supradictum millesimum tertio iam fere imminente anno, contigit in universo pene terrarum orbe, praecipue tamen in Italia et in Galliis, innovari Ecclesiarum Basilicas, licet pleraeque decenter locatae minime indiguissent. Aemulabatur tamen quaeque gens Christicolarum adversus alteram decentiore frui. Erat enim instar ac si mundus ipse excutiendo semet, reiecta vetustate, passim candidam ecclesiarum vestem indueri t.'

[3] Ekkehardus, *Vita B. Notkeri Balbuli*, c. xvi (Goldast, *Rerum Alaman. Script.* i. 235) 'Iubilus, id est neuma . . . si autem tristitiae fuerit oratio, ululatus dicitur, si vero gaudii, iubilus.'

at the Benedictine abbey of St. Gall near Constance, Notker and Tutilo are the greatest names; the third, in northern Italy, has hitherto been little studied. The *Troparia* or collections of tropes form choir-books, supplementary to the *Antiphonaria*. After the thirteenth century, when trope-writing fell into comparative desuetude, they become rare; and such tropes as were retained find a place in the ordinary service-books, especially the later successor of the *Antiphonarium*, the *Graduale*. The tropes attached themselves in varying degrees to most of the choral portions of the Mass. Perhaps those of the *Alleluia* at the end of the *Graduale* are in themselves the most important. They received the specific names, in Germany of *Sequentiae*, and in France of *Prosae*, and they include, in their later metrical stages, some of the most remarkable of mediaeval hymns. But more interesting from our particular point of view are the tropes of the *Officium* or *Introit*, the antiphon and psalm sung by the choir at the beginning of Mass, as the celebrant approaches the altar [1].

Several *Introit* tropes take a dialogue form. The following is a ninth-century Christmas example ascribed to Tutilo of St. Gall [2].

'Hodie cantandus est nobis puer, quem gignebat ineffabiliter ante tempora pater, et eundem sub tempore generavit inclyta mater.

[1] Gautier, *Les Tropes*, passim; *Winchester Troper*, vi; Dankó, *Vetus Hymnarium Eccles. Hungariae*, 15; Julleville, *Myst.* i. 21; Creizenach, i. 47. Gautier, i, defines a trope, 'Qu'est-ce qu'un Trope? C'est l'interpolation d'un texte liturgique,' and M. Gerbert, *de cantu et musica sacra* (1774), i. 340 'Tropus, in re liturgica, est versiculus quidam aut etiam plures ante inter vel post alios ecclesiasticos cantus appositi.' Of earlier writers, cf. Durandus, iv. 5 'Est autem proprie tropus quidam versiculus qui in praecipuis festivitatibus cantatur immediate ante introitum quasi quoddam praeambulum et continuatio ipsius introitus.' Gautier, 111, describes a large number of Tropers; Frere, *Winchester Troper*, xxvii, xxx, those of English uses from Winchester, Canterbury, Worcester, St. Albans, Dublin; Pamelius, *Liturgicon* (1609), ii. 611 an English Troper in the library of St. Bavon's, Ghent. Amongst tropes in the wider sense are included the *farsurae* (vol. i. p. 277). Many of the later tropes are trivial, indecent, or profane. They are doubtless the work of *goliardi* (vol. i. p. 60).

[2] *St. Gall MS.* 484, f. 13 (ninth century); cf. Gautier, 34, 62, 139, 218; *Winchester Troper*, xvi; Meyer, 34. It is also in the Winchester Tropers (tenth-eleventh century), and the Canterbury Troper (fourth century), and is printed therefrom in *Winchester Troper*, 4, 102. Here it is divided between two groups of *Cantores*, and has the heading 'Versus ante officium canendi in die Natalis Domini.'

Int[errogatio].

quis est iste puer quem tam magnis praeconiis dignum vociferatis? dicite nobis ut collaudatores esse possimus.

Resp[onsio].

hic enim est quem praesagus et electus symmista dei ad terram venturum praeuidens longe ante praenotavit, sicque praedixit.'

The nature of this trope is obvious. It was sung by two groups of voices, and its closing words directly introduce the *Introit* for the third mass (*Magna missa*) on Christmas day, which must have followed without a break [1]. It is an example of some half a dozen dialogued *Introit* tropes, which might have, but did not, become the starting-point for further dramatic evolution [2]. Much more significant is another trope of unknown authorship found in the same St. Gall manuscript [3]. This is for Easter, and is briefly known as the *Quem quaeritis*. The text, unlike that of the *Hodie cantandus*, is based closely upon the Gospels. It is an adaptation to the form of dialogue of the interview between the three Maries and the angel at the tomb as told by Saints Matthew and Mark [4].

'Quem quaeritis in sepulchro, [o] Christicolae?

Iesum Nazarenum crucifixum, o caelicolae.

non est hic, surrexit sicut praedixerat.
ite, nuntiate quia surrexit de sepulchro.
Resurrexi [5].'

This is the earliest and simplest form of the *Quem quaeritis*.

[1] The *Introit* is: 'Puer natus est nobis, et filius datus est nobis: cuius imperium super humerum eius, et vocabitur nomen eius magni consilii angelus. *Ps.* Cantate domino canticum novum.'

[2] Gautier, 219, prints a dialogued trope for a feast of St. Peter from an eleventh-century troper of St. Martial of Limoges: the *Winchester Troper*, 6, 103, has one for St. Stephen's day (Winchester) and one for St. John the Evangelist's (Canterbury). Meyer, 35, calls attention to the dialogued Christmas *versus sacerdotales* in Hartker's tenth-century St. Gall *Antiphonarium* (J. M. Thomasius, *Opera*, iv. 187).

[3] *St. Gall MS.* 484, f. 11; printed and facsimiled by Gautier, 216, 220.

[4] *S. Matthew* xxviii. 1–7; *S. Mark* xvi. 1–7.

[5] The *Introit* is: 'Resurrexi et adhuc tecum sum, alleluia: posuisti super me manum tuam, alleluia; mirabilis facta est scientia tua, alleluia, alleluia. *Ps.* Domine, probasti me.'

It recurs, almost unaltered, in a tenth-century troper from St. Martial of Limoges[1]. In eleventh-century tropers of the same church it is a little more elaborate[2].

'TROPUS IN DIE.

Quem quaeritis in sepulchro, Christicolae?

Ihesum Nazarenum crucifixum, o caelicole.

non est hic, surrexit sicut praedixerat,
ite, nuntiate quia surrexit. Alleluia.

ad sepulchrum residens angelus nuntiat resurrexisse Christum:
en ecce completum est illud quod olim ipse per prophetam dixerat ad patrem taliter inquiens,
Resurrexi.'

Here the appended portion of narrative makes the trope slightly less dramatic. Yet another addition is made in one of the Limoges manuscripts. Just as the trope introduces the *Introit*, so it is itself introduced by the following words:

'Hora est, psallite. iube, dompnus, canere.
eia, eia, dicite.'

As M. Gautier puts it, the trope is troped[3].

In the Easter *Quem quaeritis* the liturgical drama was born, and to it I shall return. But it must first be noted that it was so popular as to become the model for two very similar tropes belonging to Christmas and to the Ascension. Both of these are found in more than one troper, but not earlier, I believe, than the eleventh century. I quote the Christmas trope from a St. Gall manuscript[4].

[1] Lange, 22, from *Bibl. Nat. Lat. MS.* 1240, f. 30[b]. As to date (923–34) and *provenance* of the MS., I follow H. M. Bannister in *Journal of Theological Studies* (April, 1901). Lange, 4, considers it an eleventh-century *Antiphonar* from Beaune.

[2] Printed by Frere, 176; cf. Gautier, 219. The version in Lange, 20, is incomplete. The Limoges Tropers (*Bibl. Nat.* 887, 909, 1084, 1118, 1119, 1120, 1121), all of the eleventh century, are described by Gautier, 111; cf. p. 29.

[3] *Bibl. Nat.* 1118, f. 40[v]; cf. Gautier, 226; Frere, 176.

[4] *Bodl. Douce MS.* 222, f. 6 (eleventh century; cf. Gautier, 136), printed and facsimiled by Gautier, 215, 219. Du Méril, *Or. Lat.* 149, gives it from a Limoges Troper (*B.N.* 909, f. 9): it is also in *B.N.* 1118, f. 8vo, and probably the other

'*In Natale Domini ad Missam sint parati duo diaconi induti dalmaticis, retro altare dicentes*

Quem quaeritis in praesepe, pastores, dicite?

Respondeant duo cantores in choro

salvatorem Christum Dominum, infantem pannis involutum, secundum sermonem angelicum.

Item diaconi

adest hic parvulus cum Maria, matre sua, de qua, vaticinando, Isaïas Propheta: ecce virgo concipiet et pariet filium. et nuntiantes dicite quia natus est.

Tunc cantor dicat excelsa voce

alleluia, alleluia. iam vere scimus Christum natum in terris, de quo canite, omnes, cum Propheta dicentes:

Puer natus est.'

The Ascension trope is taken from an English troper probably belonging to Christ Church, Canterbury[1].

'Quem cernitis ascendisse super astra, o Christicolae?

Ihesum qui surrexit de sepulchro, o caelicolae.

iam ascendit, ut praedixit, ascendo ad patrem meum et patrem vestrum, deum meum et deum vestrum.

alleluia:

regna terrae, gentes, linguae, conlaudate dominum:
quem adorant caeli cives in paterno solio:
deo gratias dicite eia.'

I return now to the Easter *Quem quaeritis*. In a few churches this retained its position at the beginning of Mass, either as an *Introit* trope in the strict sense, or, which comes to much the same thing, as a chant for the procession which

Limoges MSS. Frere, 145, gives it from the twelfth-century St. Magloire Troper (*B.N.* 13,252), and R. Twigge, in *Dublin Review* (1897), 362, from a fifteenth-century breviary of Clermont-Ferrand (*Cl. F. MS.* 67). Here it is sung by two boys, and near the altar after the Te Deum at Matins. According to Gautier, 123, it is also in the late eleventh-century Nevers Troper (*B.N.* 9449).

[1] Frere, 110, from *Cott. MS. Calig.* A. xiv (eleventh century). It comes between an illumination of the Ascension and the heading 'In Die Ascensionis Domini.' It is also in the St. Magloire Troper (*B.N.* 13,252, f. 10v) under the heading 'In Ascensione Tropi ad Processionem,' and in the St. Martial of Limoges Tropers (Gautier, 219; Lange, 20). Martene, iii. 193, describes it as sung in the procession before Mass at Vienne.

immediately preceded. This was the use of the Benedictine abbey of Monte Cassino at the beginning of the twelfth century, of that of St. Denys in the thirteenth [1], and of the church of St. Martin of Tours in the fifteenth [2]. Even in the seventeenth century the *Quem quaeritis* still appears in a Paris manuscript as a '*tropus* [3],' and Martene records a practice similar to that of Monte Cassino and St. Denys as surviving at Rheims in his day [4].

But in many tropers, and in most of the later service-books in which it is found, the *Quem quaeritis* no longer appears to be designed for use at the Mass. This is the case in the only two tropers of English use in which, so far as I know, it comes, the Winchester ones printed by Mr. Frere [5]. I reproduce the earlier of these from the Bodleian manuscript used by him [6].

[1] Martene, iv. 147 '"Post processionem," *addunt Dionysianae consuet.* [thirteenth century], "ascendant iuxta Sancta Sanctorum quidam bene cantantes, alii in dextro latere, alii in sinistro latere assistentes, bene et honorifice tropas scilicet: *Quem quaeritis*; coniubilantes, et sibi invicem respondentes; et cum intonuerint, *Quia surrexi*, dicens, *Patri*, mox Archicantor et duo socii eius assistentes in choro regias virgas in manibus tenentes, incipiant officium." Hunc ritum accepisse videntur a Cassinensibus, quorum Ordinarium [before 1105] haec habet: "Processione finita, vadat Sacerdos post altare, et versus ad chorum dicat alta voce, *Quem quaeritis?* et duo alii Clerici stantes in medio chori respondeant: *Iesum Nazarenum*; et Sacerdos: *Non est hic*; illi vero conversi ad chorum dicant: *Alleluia.* Post haec alii quatuor cantent tropos, et agatur missa ordine suo."' As usual in *Ordinaria* (cf. e. g. p. 309) only the opening words of the chants are given. A similar direction is contained in *MS. Casinense*, 199, a twelfth-century breviary (*Bibliotheca Casinensis*, iv. 124): cf. also Lange, 21, 23.

[2] Martene, iii. 173; Lange, 24 (Tours i).

[3] Lange, 26. Cf. the account of the Vienne *Quem quaeritis* (p. 26).

[4] Martene, iv. 148.

[5] Mr. Frere does not print any *Introit* tropes from the Worcester, St. Albans, and Dublin tropers: a leaf is unfortunately missing from the Canterbury troper (Frere, 107) where the *Quem quaeritis* might have come. It is not amongst the few tropes taken by Pamelius, *Liturgicon* (1609), ii. 611, from the English troper at St. Bavon's, Ghent (Frere, 142). As the *Concordia Regularis* was partly based on Ghent customs (cf. p. 307), I should gladly know more of this.

[6] *Bodl. MS.* 775; described by Frere, xxvii, as *MS. E* 'Its date lies between 979 and 1016, since Ethelred is mentioned as reigning sovereign in the Litany on f. 18^{v}, and in consequence it has sometimes been called "The Ethelred Troper." Also, as it has the Dedication Festival on the 24th of November, it is probably anterior to the re-dedication of the Cathedral on Oct. 20, 980, since this day became subsequently the Dedication Festival.' A facsimile from the MS. was published by the *Palaeographical Society* (Series ii. pl. iii), and it was suggested that it

'ANGELICA DE CHRISTI RESURRECTIONE.

Quem quaeritis in sepulchro, Christicolae?
Sanctarum mulierum responsio.
Ihesum Nazarenum crucifixum, o caelicola!
Angelicae voces consolatus.
non est hic, surrexit sicut praedixerat,
ite, nuntiate quia surrexit, dicentes:
Sanctarum mulierum ad omnem clerum modulatio:
alleluia! resurrexit Dominus hodie,
leo fortis, Christus filius Dei! Deo gratias dicite, eia!
Dicat angelus:
venite et videte locum ubi positus erat Dominus, alleluia! alleluia!
Iterum dicat angelus:
cito euntes dicite discipulis quia surrexit Dominus, alleluia! alleluia!
Mulieri una voce canant iubilantes:
surrexit Dominus de sepulchro,
qui pro nobis pependit in ligno.'

In this manuscript, which is dated by Mr. Frere in 979 or 980, the text just quoted is altogether detached from the Easter day tropes. Its heading is rubricated and immediately follows the tropes for Palm Sunday. It is followed in its turn, under a fresh rubric, by the ceremonies for Holy Saturday, beginning with the *Benedictio Cerei.* From the second, somewhat later Cambridge manuscript, probably of the early eleventh century, the Holy Saturday ceremonies have disappeared, but the *Quem quaeritis* still precedes and does not follow the regular Easter tropes, which are headed *Tropi in die Christi Resurrectionis*[1]. The precise position which the

is in an early eleventh-century hand, but possibly copied an earlier text. But surely it would have been brought up to date on such a matter as the Dedication Festival.

[1] *C.C.C. Cambridge MS.* 473, of the middle of the eleventh century, described by Frere, xxvii, as *MS. CC.* The text of the *Quem quaeritis* differs slightly from that of the *Bodl. MS.* and does not appear to be quite complete. It is facsimiled by Frere (pl. 26[a]). The printed text in Frere, 17, represents both versions; that in Manly, i. xxi, follows the *Bodl. MS.* Both Frere and Manly have 'Angelice uocis consolatio' where the *Bodl. MS.*, as I read it, has 'Angelice uoces consolatus' (clearly in error).

Quem quaeritis was intended to take in the Easter services is not evident from these tropers by themselves. Fortunately another document comes to our assistance. This is the *Concordia Regularis*, an appendix to the *Rule* of St. Benedict intended for the use of the Benedictine monasteries in England reformed by Dunstan during the tenth century. The *Concordia Regularis* was drawn up by Ethelwold, bishop of Winchester, as a result of a council of Winchester held at some uncertain date during the reign of Edgar (959–79); it may fairly be taken for granted that it fixed at least the Winchester custom. I translate the account of the *Quem quaeritis* ceremony, which is described as forming part, not of the Mass, but of the third Nocturn at Matins on Easter morning[1].

'While the third lesson is being chanted, let four brethren vest themselves. Let one of these, vested in an alb, enter as though to take part in the service, and let him approach the sepulchre without attracting attention and sit there quietly with a palm in his hand. While the third respond is chanted, let the remaining three follow, and let them all, vested in copes, bearing in their hands thuribles with incense, and stepping delicately as those who seek something, approach the sepulchre. These things are done in imitation of the angel sitting in the monument, and the women with spices coming to anoint the body of Jesus. When therefore he who sits there beholds the three approach him like folk lost and seeking something, let him begin in a dulcet voice of medium pitch to sing *Quem quaeritis.* And when he has sung it to the end, let the three reply in unison *Ihesu Nazarenum.* So he, *Non est hic, surrexit sicut praedixerat. Ite, nuntiate quia surrexit a mortuis.* At the word of this bidding let those three turn to the choir and say *Alleluia! resurrexit Dominus!* This said, let the one, still sitting there and as if recalling them, say the anthem *Venite et videte locum.* And saying this, let him rise, and lift the veil, and show them the place bare of the cross, but only the cloths laid there in which the cross was

[1] A full account of the *Concordia Regularis* and extracts from the Latin text are in Appendix O.

wrapped. And when they have seen this, let them set down the thuribles which they bare in that same sepulchre, and take the cloth, and hold it up in the face of the clergy, and as if to demonstrate that the Lord has risen and is no longer wrapped therein, let them sing the anthem *Surrexit Dominus de sepulchro*, and lay the cloth upon the altar. When the anthem is done, let the prior, sharing in their gladness at the triumph of our King, in that, having vanquished death, He rose again, begin the hymn *Te Deum laudamus*. And this begun, all the bells chime out together.'

The liberal *scenario* of the *Concordia Regularis* makes plain the change which has come about in the character of the *Quem quaeritis* since it was first sung by alternating half-choirs as an *Introit* trope [1]. Dialogued chant and mimetic action have come together and the first liturgical drama is, in all its essentials, complete.

I am not quite satisfied as to the relations of date between the *Concordia Regularis* and the Winchester tropers, or as to whether the *Quem quaeritis* was intended in one or both of these manuscripts for use at the Easter Matins [2]. But it is clear that such a use was known in England at any rate before the end of the tenth century. It was also known in France and in Germany: the former fact is testified to by the *Consuetudines* of the monastery of St. Vito of Verdun [3]; the

[1] I cannot understand why Mr. Frere, xvi, thinks that the *Quem quaeritis* was 'a dramatic dialogue which came to be used as a trope to the *Introit* of Easter: but at Winchester it kept its independent place.' It is used as a trope a century before the date of the *Concordia Regularis*.

[2] Why is the *Quem quaeritis* in the *Bodl. MS.* apparently on Good Friday? Perhaps this was an irregular use reformed by Bp. Ethelwold. If so the *C. R.* must be about 980 or later. This is not impossible (cf. App. O). In the later *C.C.C.C. MS.* the *Q. q.* might, I think, from its position be intended for Easter Matins. The version described in the *C. R.* differs slightly from that of the tropers.

[3] Martene, iv. 299 'Saeculo, ut aiunt, x scriptae': cf. Douhet, 849. Martene, iii. 173, cites another Matins version from a 'vetustissimum rituale' of Poitiers. If this is identical with the 'pontificale vetustissimum: annorum circiter 800' mentioned in his list of authorities (i. xxii) it may be earlier than the tenth century. It is certainly not the 'liber sacramentorum annorum 900 circiter' with which Douhet, 848, would identify it. The Pontificale was used by Martene in his edition of 1738; about the first edition of 1700–6, I cannot say. This version is not in Lange, and, as the omission of the usual first line is curious, I print it below (p. 29).

latter by the occurrence of the *Quem quaeritis* in a troper of Bamberg, where it has the heading *Ad visitandum sepulchrum* and is followed by the Matins chant of *Te Deum*[1].

The heading of the Bamberg version and the detailed description of the *Concordia Regularis* bring the *Quem quaeritis* drama into close relations with the Easter 'sepulchre'[2]. They are indeed the first historical notices of the ceremony so widely popular during the Middle Ages. Some account of the Easter sepulchre must accordingly be inserted here, and its basis shall be the admirably full description of St. Ethelwold[3]. He directs that on Good Friday all the monks shall go *discalceati* or shoeless from Prime 'until the cross is adored'[4]. In the principal service of the day, which begins at Nones, the reading of the Passion according to St. John and a long series of prayers are included. Then a cross is made ready and laid upon a cushion a little way in front of the altar. It is unveiled, and the anthem *Ecce lignum crucis* is sung. The abbot advances, prostrates himself, and chants the seven penitential psalms. Then he humbly kisses the cross. His example is followed by the rest of the monks and by the clergy and congregation. St. Ethelwold proceeds:—

'Since on this day we celebrate the laying down of the body of our Saviour, if it seem good or pleasing to any to follow on similar lines the use of certain of the religious, which is worthy of imitation for the strengthening of faith in the unlearned vulgar and in neophytes, we have ordered it on this wise. Let a likeness of a sepulchre be made in a vacant part of the altar, and a veil stretched on a ring which may hang there until the adoration of the cross is over. Let the deacons who previously carried the cross come and wrap it in a cloth

[1] Lange, 29; cf. Creizenach, i. 49.

[2] The Verdun *Consuetudines* do not. The burial and resurrection of the cross clearly formed no part of the Good Friday and Easter rites. The dialogue takes place 'in subterraneis specubus,' i.e. the crypt, and the representatives of the Maries return to the choir 'cruce vacua nuntiantes: *Surrexit Dominus*' (Martene, iv. 299).

[3] Appendix O.

[4] Bare feet continued to be the rule for the *Adoratio Crucis*. An exception is at Exeter, where, according to Pearson, ii. 296, they were forbidden, cf. Feasey, 115.

in the place where it was adored [1]. Then let them carry it back, singing anthems, until they come to the place of the monument, and there having laid down the cross as if it were the buried body of our Lord Jesus Christ, let them say an anthem. And here let the holy cross be guarded with all reverence until the night of the Lord's resurrection. By night let two brothers or three, or more if the throng be sufficient, be appointed who may keep faithful wake there chanting psalms.'

The ceremony of the burial or *Depositio Crucis* is followed by the *Missa Praesanctificatorum*, the Good Friday communion with a host not consecrated that day but specially reserved from Maundy Thursday; and there is no further reference to the sepulchre until the order for Easter day itself is reached, when St. Ethelwold directs that 'before the bells are rung for Matins the sacristans are to take the cross and set it in a fitting place.'

In the *Concordia Regularis*, then, the *Depositio Crucis* is a sequel to the *Adoratio Crucis* on Good Friday. The latter ceremony, known familiarly to the sixteenth century as 'creeping to the cross,' was one of great antiquity. It was amongst the Holy week rites practised at Jerusalem in the fourth century [2], and was at an early date adopted in Rome [3]. But the sepulchre was no primitive part of it [4]; nor is it

[1] St. Ethelwold's Latin is atrocious, but I think that the sepulchre was made on the altar, not in the hollow of it, and covered from sight until wanted by a veil let down all round it from a circular support above. Cf. the Latin text in Appendix O: perhaps it is corrupt.

[2] *Peregrinatio Silviae* in Duchesne, 490. The object of adoration was a fragment of the true Cross, 'sanctum lignum crucis.' The Invention of the Cross by St. Helena is put by tradition †326. Doubtless many other churches obtained a fragment, and used it for the same purpose: cf. Feasey, 116. Thus the cross used at Rome was 'lignum pretiosae crucis' (Duchesne, 465: cf. his ed. of the *Liber Pontificalis*, i. 374).

[3] Duchesne, 238. For the mediaeval ceremony, cf. Feasey, 114; Pearson, ii. 293; Milchsack, 121; Rock, iii. 2. 241; Martene, iii. 129; iv. 137; *Sarum Missal*, 328; *York Missal*, i. 105; *York Manual*, 156, and the Durham extract in Appendix P: for that of modern Rome, Malleson and Tuker, ii. 271.

[4] The *sepulchrum* is not in the *Sacramentarium Gelasianum* (†seventh century, ed. H. A. Wilson, 77); nor the *Sacramentum Gregorianum* (†eighth century, *P. L.* lxxviii. 86), 'qua salutata et reposita in loco suo'; nor in the Roman *Ordines* collected by Mabillon (*P. L.* lxxviii) nor in those added by Duchesne, 451, 464. The *Ordines* of 954 and 963 repeat the Gregorian formula,

possible to trace either the use which served St. Ethelwold as a model[1], or the home or date of the sepulchre itself. It is unlikely, however, that the latter originated in England, as it appears almost simultaneously on the continent, and English ritual, in the tenth century, was markedly behind and not in advance of that of France and Germany[2]. St. Ethelwold speaks of it as distinctively monastic but certainly not as universal or of obligation amongst the Benedictine communities for whom he wrote. Nor did the *Concordia Regularis* lead to its invariable adoption, for when Ælfric adapted St. Ethelwold's work for the benefit of Eynsham about 1005 he omitted the account of the sepulchre[3], and it is not mentioned in Archbishop Lanfranc's Benedictine *Constitutions* of 1075[4]. At a later date it was used by many

which is expanded by those of 1215 and 1319 into 'in suo loco super altare.' There is no mention of the *sepulchrum* in the Gallican liturgical books collected by Mabillon (*P. L.* lxxii). Of English books Leofric's *Exeter Missal* (tenth century, ed. F. E. Warren) has no *Sepulchrum*; nor the *Missal* of St. Augustine's Canterbury (†1100, ed. M. Rule), 'reposita in loco solito'; nor the *Missal* of Robert of Jumièges (ninth and tenth century, ed. H.A. Wilson for *H. B. Soc.*). Pearson, ii. 316, suggests that the cross used for adoration was the great rood usually placed in the rood-loft, but sometimes 'super altare.'

[1] Ethelwold's *Concordia Regularis* was largely founded on that of Benedict of Aniane (†817; cf. Miss Bateson in *E. H. Review*, ix. 700), but there is no Easter week *ordo* in this (*P. L.* ciii. 701) nor in the same writer's *Memoriale* or *Ordo Monasticus* (*P. L.* lxvi. 937: cf. his *Vita*, c. viii, in *Acta SS.* Feb. ii. 618). Ethelwold also borrowed customs from Fleury and Ghent (Appendix O). The *sepulchrum* is not mentioned in the *Consuetudines Floriacenses* (tenth century, ed. De Bosco, *Floriac. Vet. Bibl.* (1605), 390); cf. Creizenach, i. 49: nor in the description of a thirteenth-century *coutumier* in Rocher, *Hist. de l'Abbaye de St.-Benoît-sur-Loire*, 323. The only Fleury *Quem quaeritis* is of a late type in a thirteenth-century MS.; cf. p. 32. At Ghent, however, an inventory of treasures remaining at St. Bavon's after a Norman invasion (1019–24) includes 'tabulas de sepulchro 23,' which appear to be distinct from *reliquiae* 'de sepulchro Domini' and 'de operculo ligneo quod super corpus ipsius positum fuit in sepulchro' (*Neues Archiv*, viii. 374). Did the possession of these 'reliquiae' suggest to the monks of St. Bavon's the construction of an Easter sepulchre?

[2] It is merely a guess to say St. Gall. Schübiger, *Sängerschule St. Gallens*, 69, mentions the sepulchre there, but gives no very early notice. The sepulchre was known in the Eastern, as well as the Western Church, and for all I know may have come from Jerusalem (Feasey, 177). As to date, Weber, 32, suggests that pictorial representations of the Maries at the tomb show the influence of the dramatic *Visitatio Sepulchri* as far back as the ninth century. His chief point is that the Maries carry *turribula* (cf. p. 25, n. 5).

[3] *E. H. Review*, ix. 706.

[4] *P. L.* cl. 465 'adorata ab omni-

Benedictine houses, notably by the great Durham Priory[1]; but the Cistercians and the Carthusians, who represent two of the most famous reforms of the order, are said never to have adopted it, considering it incompatible with the austerity of their rule[2]. On the other hand it was certainly not, in mediaeval England, confined to monastic churches. The cathedrals of Salisbury[3], York[4], Lincoln[5], Hereford[6], Wells[7], all of which were served by secular canons, had their sepulchres, and the gradual spread of the Sarum use probably brought a sepulchre into the majority of parish churches throughout the land[8].

There are naturally variations and amplifications of the sepulchre ceremonial as described by St. Ethelwold to be recorded. The *Depositio Crucis*, instead of preceding the *Missa Praesanctificatorum*, was often, as in the Sarum use,

bus cruce, portitores eius elevantes eam incipiant antiphonam *Super omnia ligna cedrorum*, et sic vadant ad locum ubi eam collocare debent.' This does not exclude a sepulchre, but probably the *locus* was an altar which might serve as a *statio* for the processions 'ad crucifixum' ordered on Easter Saturday after vespers and thrice a day through Easter week. Such processions continued in later ritual to visit the cross after its *Elevatio* on Easter morning: cf. *York Manual*, 177.

[1] See the description of the ceremony by a sixteenth-century eye-witness in Appendix P. The *sepulchrum* was also used by the Bridgettines of Sion monastery, an order of reformed Benedictine nuns (G. F. Aungier, *Hist. of Syon Monastery*, 350).

[2] J. D. Chambers citing J. B. Thiers, *De Expositione S. Sacramenti*, iii. 19.

[3] See the extracts from Sarum service-books in Appendix Q.

[4] *York Missal*, i. 106; *York Manual*, 163, 170.

[5] Wordsworth, 278.

[6] *Hereford Missal* (ed. Henderson), 96.

[7] H. E. Reynolds, *Wells Cathedral*, 32.

[8] The fullest accounts of the Easter sepulchre in England are those by H. J. Feasey, *Ancient English Holy Week Ceremonial*, 129, and A. Heales, *Easter Sepulchres: their Object, Nature, and History* in *Archaeologia*, xlii. 263; cf. also *Monumenta Vetusta* (Soc. of Antiquaries), iii. pll. xxxi, xxxii; Parker, *Glossary of Architecture*, s.v. Sepulchre; M. E. C. Walcott, *Sacred Archaeology*, s.v. Easter Sepulchre; T. F. Dyer, *Church Lore Gleanings*, 219; W. Andrews, *Old Church Lore*, iii; J. D. Chambers, *App.* xxiv; Micklethwaite, 52; Rock, iii. 2. 92, 240, 251. Continental *ordines* and notices may be found in Martene, iii. 131, 172, 178; iv. 141, 145; Milchsack, 41, 121; Pearson, ii. 295; Wetzer and Welte, *Kirchen-Lexicon*, s.v. Grab; J. Dankó, *Vetus Hymn. Eccl. Hungariae*, 535, 579. I have not seen this writer's *Die Feier des Osterfestes* (Wien, 1872). On representations of the sepulchre in mediaeval art, cf. P. Weber, 32, and the miniature from Robert of Jumièges' *Missal* (ed. F. E. Warren for *H. B. Soc.* pl. viii).

transferred to the end of Vespers, which on Good Friday followed the *Missa* without a break[1]. The *Elevatio* regularly took place early on Easter morning before Matins. The oldest custom was doubtless that of the *Regularis Concordia*, according to which the cross was removed from the sepulchre secretly by the sacristans, since this is most closely in agreement with the narrative of the gospels. But in time the *Elevatio* became a function. The books of Salisbury and York provide for it a procession with the antiphons *Christus resurgens* and *Surrexit Dominus*. Continental rituals show considerable diversity of custom[2]. Perhaps the most elaborate ceremonials are those of Augsburg and Würzburg, printed by Milchsack. In these the *Tollite portas* procession, which we have already found borrowed from the dedication of churches for Palm Sunday, was adapted to Easter day[3]. But the old tradition was often preserved by the exclusion or only partial admission of the populace to the *Elevatio*. In the Augsburg ritual just quoted, all but a few privileged persons are kept out until the devil has been expelled and the doors solemnly opened[4]. A curious light is thrown upon this by a decree of the synod of Worms in 1316, which orders that the 'mystery of the resurrection' shall be performed before the *plebs* comes

[1] At Exeter on the other hand Vespers on both Good Friday and Easter Eve were sung before the Sepulchre; and so with the Hours at Tours (Feasey, 130).

[2] Martene, iii. 179; Milchsack, 122; Lange, 135. The latter gives a Passau fifteenth-century version which ends 'quibus finitis stantes ante altare, mutua caritate se invicem deosculentur, dicentes: *Surrexit dominus vere. Et apparuit symoni.* Dicatur una oratio de resurrectione. Statim fiat pulsatio.' The Easter greeting and kiss of peace were in use, either before or after Matins at many churches (Martene, iii. 171, 180) and do not depend upon the sepulchre.

[3] Milchsack, 128, 135; cf. Meyer, 64. The *Ordo Augustensis* of 1487 directs that a procession shall go from the sepulchre 'per ambitum vel cimeterium . . . usque ad ultimam ianuam, quae claudatur.' Here the *Tollite portas* dialogue is held with the 'levita iunior, vel alius in figura diaboli grossa voce.' On the other hand, in the *Ordo Wirceburgensis* of 1564 the procession knocks at the door from inside, and the respondent 'loco Sathanae' is without.

[4] 'Sacerdos . . . antequam congregetur chorus, cum processione sibi paucorum adiunctorum . . . foribus ecclesiae clausis, secretius tollat sacramentum de sepulchro'; cf. the fifteenth-century Passau *Breviary* (Lange, 135) 'clam surgitur' and the *Ordo Sepulturae* in the *Missalis Posoniensis* of 1341 (Dankó, 579) 'laicis exclusis.' I have not noticed any such limitation in English rubrics later than the *Concordia Regularis*.

into the church, and gives as a reason the crowds caused by a prevalent superstition that whoever saw the crucifix raised would escape for that year 'the inevitable hour of death' [1].

A widespread if not quite universal innovation on the earlier use was the burial, together with the cross or crucifix, of a host, which was consecrated, like that used in the *Missa Praesanctificatorum*, on Maundy Thursday. This host was laid in a pyx [2], monstrance [3], or cup [4], and sometimes in a special image, representing the risen Christ with the cross or *labarum* in his hands, the breast of which held a cavity covered with beryl or crystal [5]. Within the sepulchre both the host and the crucifix were laid upon or wrapped in a fine linen napkin.

The actual structure of the sepulchre lent itself to considerable variety. St. Ethelwold's *assimilatio quaedam sepulchri* upon a vacant part of the altar may have been formed, like that at Narbonne several centuries later, by laying together some of the silver service-books [6]. There are other examples of a sepulchre at an altar, and it is possible that in some of

[1] Milchsack, 119 'quum a nostris antecessoribus ad nos pervenerit, ut in sacra nocte dominicae resurrectionis ad sustollendam crucifixi imaginem de sepulchro, ubi in parasceve locata fuerat, nimia virorum et mulierum numerositas, certatim sese comprimendo, ecclesiam simul cum canonicis et vicariis introire nitantur, opinantes erronee, quod si viderent crucifixi imaginem sustolli, evaderent hoc anno inevitabilem mortis horam. His itaque obviantes statuimus, ut resurrectionis mysterium ante ingressum plebis in ecclesiam peragatur': cf. Pearson, ii. 298.

[2] A Finchale inventory of 1481 (J. T. Fowler, *Trans. of Durham and North. Arch. Soc.* iv. 134) includes 'Item 1 pixis argentea cum coopertorio et ymagine crucifixi in summitate coopertorii pro corpore x[i] deferendo in passione x[i].' A pyx was also used in the Sarum rite (Appendix Q).

[3] Feasey, 165; Dankó, *Vet. Hymn. Eccl. Hung.* 535.

[4] *York Manual*, 174 'cuppa in qua est sacramentum.'

[5] At Durham (Appendix P) and at Lincoln (Wordsworth, 278); cf. Feasey, 164; Heales, 307. The image 'cum corona spinea' used at York (*York Manual*, 170) was of course the crucifix. A Reformation record of 1566 at Belton, Lincolnshire, speaks of 'a sepulker with little Jack broken in pieces' (Feasey, 165). Either a mere image or a mechanical puppet (cf. p. 158) may be meant. The *labarum* is the sign of the risen Christ in the later versions of the *Quem quaeritis*; cf. p. 35. It figures in nearly all paintings of the Resurrection.

[6] Narbonne *Ordinarium* (†1400) 'levent cum filo pannum, qui est super libros argenti super altare in figura sepulcri' (Martene, iii. 172; Lange, 65); Le Mans, *Ordinarium* 'Tunc tres clerici accedentes ad altare cum reverentia sublevent palium cum quo sepulchrum fuerit coopertum' (Lange, 66); cf. Pearson, ii. 293.

these the altar itself may have been hollow and have held the sacred deposit. Sometimes the high altar was used, but a side-altar was naturally more convenient, and at St. Lawrence's, Reading, the 'sepulchre awlter' was in the rood-loft[1]. The books were a primitive expedient. More often the sepulchre was an elaborate carved shrine of wood, iron, or silver. If this did not stand upon the altar, it was placed on the north side of the sanctuary or in a north choir aisle. In large churches the crypt was sometimes thought an appropriate site[2]. Often the base of the sepulchre was formed by the tomb of a founder or benefactor of the church, and legacies for making a structure to serve this double purpose are not uncommon in mediaeval wills. Such tombs often have a canopied recess above them, and in these cases the portable shrine may have been dispensed with. Many churches have a niche or recess, designed of sole purpose for the sepulchre[3]. Several of these more elaborate sepulchres are large enough to be entered, a very convenient arrangement for the *Quem quaeritis*[4]; a few of them are regular chapels, more than one of which is an exact reproduction of the Holy Sepulchre at Jerusalem, and is probably due to the piety of some local pilgrim[5]. Wood, metal, or stone, permanent or movable, the sepulchre was richly adorned with paintings and carvings of the Passion and the Resurrection, with Easter texts, with figures of censer-swinging angels and sleeping knights[6]. A seal was, at least

[1] Feasey, 131. In versions of the *Quem quaeritis* given by Lange, 24, 25, 26, the action is at the altar. A Senlis *Breviary* (fourteenth century) has 'elevantes palium altaris' (Lange, 27), and a Sens thirteenth-century MS. 'Sublevans tapetum altaris, tamquam respiciens in sepulchrum' (Lange, 64). But I am not sure that there was a genuine sepulchre in all these cases: cf. p. 26.

[2] Würzburg *Breviary* (fourteenth century) 'descendunt in criptam ad visitandum sepulcrum' (Lange, 53): cf. the Verdun *Consuetudines* (p. 16), where there may or may not have been a regular sepulchre.

[3] I have seen a beautiful one at Tarrant Hinton, Dorset, which is not amongst those mentioned by Heales or Feasey.

[4] The performers are sometimes directed to enter the sepulchre; cf. e.g. Lange, 28.

[5] Feasey, 149. There is such a chapel beneath the choir of the *Jérusalem* church at Bruges. The Winchester sepulchre is a chapel, but not of the Jerusalem type. At St. Gall the sepulchre was († 1583) in the 'sacellum S. Sebastiani' (Lange, 69).

[6] J. Britton, *Redcliffe Church*, 47, prints a contemporary description of a sepulchre given in 1470 by 'Maister Canynge' to St. Mary Redcliffe, Bristol, with, amongst

at Hereford and in Hungary, set upon it[1]. A canopy was hung over it and upon it lay a pall, also a favourite object for a pious legacy. Similar legacies might meet the expense of the 'sepulchre light,' which was kept burning from Good Friday to Easter morning, and was only extinguished for a few minutes on Easter Saturday to be re-lit from the freshly blessed 'new fire[2].' Or the light might be provided by one of the innumerable guilds of the Middle Ages, whose members, perhaps, also undertook the devout duty of keeping the two nights' vigil before the sepulchre[3]. This watch was important. The Augsburg ritual already quoted makes the possibility of arranging it a condition of setting up the sepulchre at all[4]. The watchers sang psalms, and it is an example of the irrepressible mediaeval tendency to *mimesis* that they were sometimes accoutred like the knights of Pilate[5]. After the *Elevatio*, the crucifix seems to have been placed upon a side-altar and visited by processions in Easter, while the host was reserved in a tabernacle. The Sarum *Custumary* directs that the empty sepulchre shall be daily censed at Vespers and removed

other adornments, 'Heaven made of timber and stain'd clothes' and 'Hell, made of timber and iron-work thereto, with Divels to the number of 13.' This is apparently not a Chatterton forgery. Feasey, 166, gives a somewhat similar London specification, and also (p. 145) describes a fourteenth-century wooden sepulchre from Kilsby, Northants, believed to be the only one in existence. I have a suspicion that the wooden so-called 'watcher's chamber' to the shrine of St. Frideswide in Christ Church, Oxford, is really a sepulchre. It is in the right place, off the north choir aisle, and why should a watcher of the shrine want to be perched up in a wooden cage on the top of a tomb?

[1] Dankó, 536, 580. Two instances are given. In one the sepulchre was sealed, in the other the pyx, 'sigillo vel clavi ecclesiae.' At Hereford 'episcopus . . . cereo claudat sepulchrum' (Feasey, 159, from *Harl. MS.* 2983).

[2] Cf. vol. i. p. 126.

[3] Wordsworth, 279; Feasey, 161; Heales, 272, 299.

[4] Milchsack, 127.

[5] G. Gilpin, *The Bee-Hive of the Romish Church* (1579) (translated from Isaac Rabbotenu of Louvain, 1569) 'They make the graue in a hie place in the church, where men must goe up manie steppes, which are decked with blacke cloth from aboue to beneath, and upon everie steppe standeth a siluer candlesticke with a waxe candle burning in it, and there doe walke souldiours in harnesse, as bright as Saint George, which keep the graue, till the Priests come and take him up; and then commeth sodenlie a flash of fire, wherwith they are all afraid and fall downe; and then up startes the man, and they begin to sing Alleluia, on all handes, and the clocke striketh eleuen.' Feasey, 168, quotes De Moleon for a statement that the watchers at Orleans were dressed as soldiers.

on the Friday in Easter week before Mass [1]. Naturally there was some division of opinion at the Reformation as to the precise spiritual value of the Easter sepulchre. While Bishop Hooper and his fellow pulpiters were outspoken about the idolatrous cult of a 'dead post [2],' the more conservative views which ruled in the latter years of Henry VIII declared the ceremony to be 'very laudable' and 'not to be contemned and cast away [3].' The Cromwellian *Injunctions* of 1538 sanctioned the continued use of the sepulchre light, and by implication of the sepulchre itself. The Edwardine *Injunctions* of 1547 suppressed the sepulchre light and were certainly interpreted by Cranmer and others as suppressing the sepulchre [4]. The closely related 'creeping to the cross' was forbidden by proclamation in 1548; and in 1549, after the issue of the first Act of Uniformity and the first Prayer Book of Edward VI, the disallowance of both ceremonies was legalized, or renewed by *Articles* for the visitation of that year [5]. Payments for the breaking up of the sepulchre now appear in many churchwardens' accounts, to be complicated before long by payments for setting the sepulchre up again, in consequence of an order by Queen Mary in 1554 [6]. In the same year the crucifix and pyx were missing out of the sepulchre at St. Pancras' Church in Cheapside, when the priests came for the *Elevatio* on Easter morning, and one Marsh was committed to the Counter for

[1] Appendix Q.

[2] Hooper, *Early Writings* (Parker Soc.), 45 'The ploughman, be he never so unlearned, shall better be instructed of Christ's death and passion by the corn that he soweth in the field, and likewise of Christ's resurrection, than by all the dead posts that hang in the church, or are pulled out of the sepulchre with *Christus resurgens.* What resemblance hath the taking of the cross out of the sepulchre and going a procession with it, with the resurrection of Christ? None at all: the dead post is as dead when they sing *Iam non moritur*, as it was when they buried it with *In pace factus est locus eius*': cf. Ridley, *Works* (Parker Soc.), 67.

[3] *Articles devised by the King's Majesty*, 1536 (Burnet, i. 1. 435; i. 2. 472; cf. Froude, ii. 486); Strype, *Eccles. Memorials*, i. 1. 546; i. 2. 432.

[4] Dixon, ii. 82, 432, 513, 516; iii. 37; Hardy and Gee, *Doc. illustrative of English Church History*, 278; Cardwell, *Documentary Annals of the Reformation*, i. 7; Froude, iv. 281. There certainly were sepulchres in 1548 (Feasey, 175).

[5] Dixon, iii. 37; Wilkins, iv. 32. The *Act of* 2 *and* 3 *Edward VI*, c. 10 (Froude, iv. 495), against images and paintings, was probably also held to require the demolition of many sepulchres: cf. Ridley's *Visitation Articles* of 1550, quoted by Heales, 304.

[6] Dixon, iv. 129.

the sacrilege[1]. The Elizabethan *Injunctions* of 1559, although they do not specifically name the sepulchre, doubtless led to its final disappearance[2]. In many parts of the continent it naturally lasted longer, but the term 'visiting sepulchres' seems in modern times to have been transferred to the devotion paid to the reserved host on Maundy Thursday[3].

I now return to the *Quem quaeritis* in the second stage of its evolution, when it had ceased to be an *Introit* trope and had become attached to the ceremony of the sepulchre. Obviously it is not an essential part of that ceremony. The *Depositio* and *Elevatio* mutually presuppose each other and, together, are complete. For the dramatic performance, as described by St. Ethelwold, the clergy, having removed the cross at the beginning of Matins, revisited the empty sepulchre quite at the close of that service, after the third respond[4], between which and the normal ending of Matins, the *Te Deum*, the *Quem quaeritis* was intercalated. The fact that the Maries bear censers instead of or in addition to the scriptural spices, suggests that this *Visitatio* grew out of a custom of censing the sepulchre at the end of Matins as well as of Evensong[5]. But the *Visitatio* could easily be omitted, and in fact it was omitted in many churches where the *Depositio* and *Elevatio* were in use. The Sarum books, for instance, do not in any way prescribe it. On the other hand, there were probably a few churches

[1] Dixon, iv. 157; S. R. Maitland, *Essays on the Reformation* (ed. 1899), 186.

[2] Hardy and Gee, *op. cit.* 428. Art xxiii forbids 'monuments of ... idolatry and superstition.' The Elizabethan *Visitation Articles* collected in the *Second Report* of the *Ritual Commission* make no mention of sepulchres. They generally follow pretty closely the wording of the *Injunctions*. But the *Articles* of Bentham, Bishop of Lichfield and Coventry (1565), specify 'monuments of idolatry and superstition' as including 'Sepulchres which were used on Good Friday' (Heales, 307). Notices of the destruction of sepulchres become numerous, being found, for instance, in the case of 50 out of 153 Lincolnshire churches (Feasey, 142), and pious legacies begin to direct tombs 'whereas the sepulchre was wonte to stande.'

[3] Davidson, 140; Malleson and Tuker, ii. 263, 267, 272. The latest examples of the *Quem quaeritis* are of the eighteenth century from Cologne and Angers (Lange, 36, 39) and Venice (*Z. f. d. A.* xli. 77).

[4] This respond begins *Dum transisset Sabbatum*.

[5] Cf. p. 18, n. 2. The Sarum *Custumary* provides for censing on feasts (*a*) at the anthem 'super Magnificat' at Vespers, (*b*) during or after the *Te Deum* at Matins (*Use of Sarum*, i. 113, 121). The sepulchre is included only at Vespers (cf. Appendix Q), but the variation I suggest would not be great.

which adopted the *Visitatio* without the more important rite. Bamberg seems to have been one of these, and so possibly were Sens, Senlis, and one or two others in which the *Quem quaeritis* is noted as taking place at an altar [1]. However, whether there was a real sepulchre or not, the regular place of the *Quem quaeritis* was that prescribed for it by St. Ethelwold, between the third respond and the *Te Deum* at Matins. It has been found in a very large number of manuscripts, and in by far the greater part of them it occupies this position [2]. In the rest, with the exception of a completely anomalous example from Vienne [3], it is either a trope [4], or else is merged

[1] Cf. p. 22, n. 1. The Bamberg *Agenda* of †1597 (Lange, 93) has an *Ordo visitandi sepulchrum* which opens with directions for the construction of a sepulchre, which would obviously not be the case if the *Depositio* and *Elevatio* had preceded. Lange rarely prints more than the *Visitatio*, but of one group of texts he notes (p. 135) that the MSS. generally have also the *Elevatio*.

[2] Lange's collection from 224 MSS. supersedes those of Du Méril, Coussemaker, Milchsack, &c. He supplemented it by versions from Meissen, Worms, Venice, and Grau in Hungary in *Z. f. d. A.* (1896), xli. 77; and has not got those from the (*a*) Winchester *Tropers* (cf. p. 12); (*b*) Autun and Nevers *Tropers* of the eleventh century (Gautier, 126, 219); (*c*) St. Magloire, twelfth-century *Troper* (cf. p. 11); (*d*) Dublin *Processionals* (Appendix R); (*e*) Laon twelfth-century *Ordinary* (Chevalier, *Ordinaires de Laon*, 118); (*f*) Clermont-Ferrand fifteenth-century *Breviary* (cf. p. 11); (*g*) Poitiers *Ritual* (Martene, iii. 173); (*h*) Verdun tenth-century *Consuetudinary* (Martene, iv. 299; cf. p. 15). The MSS. extend from the tenth to the eighteenth century. The majority of them are Breviaries; some are Ordinaries, Antiphoners, Processionals; a few are late Tropers, in which, besides the Tropes proper, the Holy week *Ordo* is included (cf. Gautier, 81); two (*B. N. Lat.* 1139 from Limoges, and *Orleans MS.* 178, from Fleury) are special books of dramatic *repraesentationes*; cf. p. 1.

[3] Martene, iii. 180, from an undated *Caeremoniale*. Lange, 26, only gives a portion of the text containing the *Quem quaeritis* proper, which was sung as a processional trope before the *Missa maior*. The procession had immediately before gone to the sepulchre and sung other anthems. But the sepulchre played a part at two other services. Before Matins the clergy had in turn entered the sepulchre, found it empty, came out and given each other the kiss of peace and Easter greeting. No *Elevatio* is described; perhaps it was still earlier 'clam.' After Lauds, the *Missa matutinalis* was sung 'ad sepulchrum' and the *prosa* or Alleluia trope was thus performed: 'Prosa *Victimae Paschali*. Finito ℣ *Dicat nobis Maria*, clericulus stans in sepulcro cum amictu parato et stola, dicat ℣. *Angelicos testes*. Chorus respondeat *Dic nobis Maria*. Clericulus dicat *Angelicos testes*. Clericus dicat *Surrexit Christus*. Chorus *Credendum est magis* usque ad finem.' On this prose and its relation to the *Quem quaeritis* cf. p. 29. At St. Mark's, Venice (*Z. f. d. A.* xli. 77), the position of the *Quem quaeritis* is also abnormal, coming just before Prime, but this version dates from 1736.

[4] Cf. p. 12.

with or immediately follows the *Elevatio* before Matins[1]. The evidence of the texts themselves is borne out by Durandus, who is aware of the variety of custom, and indicates the end of Matins as the *proprior locus*[2].

No less difficult to determine than the place and time at which the Easter sepulchre itself was devised, are those at which the *Quem quaeritis*, attached to it, stood forth as a drama. That the two first appear together can hardly be taken as evidence that they came into being together. The predominance of German and French versions of the *Quem quaeritis* may suggest an origin in the Frankish area: and if the influence of the Sarum use and the havoc of service-books at the Reformation may between them help to account for the comparative rarity of the play in these islands, no such explanation is available for Italy and Spain. The development of the religious drama in the peninsulas, especially in Italy, seems to have followed from the beginning lines somewhat distinct from those of north-western Europe. But between France and Germany, as between France and England, literary influences, so far as clerkly literature goes, moved freely: nor is it possible to isolate the centres and lines of diffusion of that gradual process of accretion and development through which the *Quem quaeritis* gave ever fuller and fuller expression to the dramatic instincts by which it was prompted. The *clerici vagantes* were doubtless busy agents in carrying new motives and amplifications of the text from one church to another. Nor should it be forgotten that, numerous as are the versions preserved, those which have perished must have been more numerous still, so that, if all

[1] Lange, 28 (Parma), 30 (Laon), 47 (Constance), 68 (Rheinau), 69 (St. Gall). At Rheinau, the *Elevatio* takes place in the course of the *Quem quaeritis*: at Parma, and probably in the other cases, the 'sacrista pervigil' has already removed the 'Corpus Christi.'

[2] Durandus, lib. vi. c. 87. He describes the normal *Visitatio*, in terms much resembling those of Belethus (cf. p. 31), and adds 'quidam vero hanc presentationem faciunt, antequam matutinum inchoent, sed hic est proprior locus, eo quod *Te deum laudamus* exprimit horam, qua resurrexit. Quidam etiam eam faciunt ad missam, cum dicuntur sequentia illa *Victimae paschali*, cum dicitur versus *Dic nobis* et sequentes.' Ioannes Abrincensis, *de Offic. eccles.* (*P.L.* cxlvii. 54), briefly notes the 'officium sepulchri' as 'post tertium responsorium,' and says no more.

were before us, the apparent anomaly presented by the occurrence of identical features in, for instance, the plays from Dublin and Fleury, and no others, would not improbably be removed. The existence of this or that version in the service-books of any one church must depend on divers conditions; the accidents of communication in the first place, and in the second the laxity or austerity of governing bodies at various dates in the licensing or pruning of dramatic elaboration. The simplest texts are often found in the latest manuscripts, and it may be that because their simplicity gave no offence they were permitted to remain there. A Strassburg notice suggests that the ordering of the *Quem quaeritis* was a matter for the discretion of each individual parish, in independence of its diocesan use [1]; while the process of textual growth is illustrated by a Laon *Ordinarium*, in which an earlier version has been erased and one more elaborate substituted [2].

Disregarding, however, in the main the dates of the manuscripts, it is easy so to classify the available versions as to mark the course of a development which was probably complete by the middle of the twelfth and certainly by the thirteenth century. This development affected both the text and the dramatic interest of the play. The former is the slighter matter and may be disposed of first [3].

The kernel of the whole thing is, of course, the old St. Gall trope, itself a free adaptation from the text of the Vulgate, and the few examples in which this does not occur must be regarded as quite exceptional [4]. The earliest additions were taken from anthems, which already had their place

[1] Strassburg *Agenda* of 1513 (Lange, 50) 'Haec prescripta visitatio sepulcri observetur secundum consuetudinem cuiuslibet ecclesiae.' Meyer, 33, quotes a passage even more to the point from the Bamberg *Agenda* of 1587 'Haec dominicae resurrectionis commemoratio celebrioribus servit ecclesiis, unde aliarum ecclesiarum utpote minorum et ruralium rectores et parochi ex ordine hic descripto aliquid saltem desumere possunt, quod pro loci et personarum illic convenientium qualitate commodum fore iudicaverint.'

[2] Laon *Ordinarium* of twelfth century (U. Chevalier, *Ordinaires de Laon*, 118). The change consisted mainly in the introduction of the *Victimae paschali*: cf. p. 29.

[3] Cf. the full discussion, mainly from the textual point of view, throughout Lange's book, with that of Meyer, and Creizenach, i. 47; Froning, 3; Wirth, 1.

[4] The Bohemian fourteenth-century version (Lange, 130) is nearly

in the Easter services, and which in some manuscripts of the Gregorian *Antiphonarium* are grouped together as suitable for insertion wherever may be desired[1]. So far the text keeps fairly close to the words of Scripture, and even where the limits of the antiphonary are passed, the same rule holds good. In time, however, a freer dramatic handling partly establishes itself. Proses, and even metrical hymns, beginning as choral introductions, gradually usurp a place in the dialogue, and in the latest versions the metrical character is very marked. By far the most important of these insertions is the famous prose or sequence *Victimae paschali*, the composition of which by the monk Wipo of St. Gall can be pretty safely dated in the second quarter of the eleventh century[2]. It goes as follows:

'Victimae paschali laudes immolant Christiani.
agnus redemit oves, Christus innocens patri reconciliavit peccatores.
mors et vita duello conflixere mirando, dux vitae mortuus regnat vivus.

all narrative sung by the Ebdomarius: the only dialogue is from the *Victimae paschali*. Martene, iii. 173, gives, from a 'vetustissimum Rituale,' this Poitiers version, not in Lange, 'Finitis matutinis, accedunt ad sepulchrum, portantes luminaria. Tunc incipit Maria: *Ubi est Christus meus?* Respondet angelus *Non est hic*. Tunc Maria aperit os sepulchri, et dicit publica voce: *Surrexit Christus*. Et omnes respondent *Deo gratias*.' Possibly Maria here is the Virgin, who is not usually included in the *Visitatio*. But the same anthem opens a twelfth-century Limoges version, headed 'Oc est de mulieribus' in *B. N. Lat. MS.* 1139, a collection of ritual plays. The full text is 'Ubi est Christus meus dominus et filius excelsus?' which is not really appropriate to any other speaker: cf. Milchsack, 38. A frequent variant on 'Quem quaeritis in sepulchro, o Christicolae?' is 'Quem quaeritis, o tremulae mulieres, in hoc tumulo plorantes?'; nor can the two forms be localized (Lange, 84).

[1] Lange, 32. These MSS. are of the eleventh and twelfth centuries. I find no such section in the normal text of the Gregorian *Liber responsalis*, which is the antiphonary for the office (*P. L.* lxxviii. 769). The 'antiphonae de resurrectione domini ubicumque volueris' of the *B. N. Lat. MS.* 17,436 include the 'Cito euntes dicite, &c.,' 'Currebant duo simul, &c.,' 'Ardens est cor meum, &c.,' and others which are regularly introduced into the play. Another commonly used is the *Christus resurgens* with its verse, 'Dicant nunc Iudaei, &c.,' which the Sarum books assign to the *Elevatio* (Appendix Q): cf. Lange, 77.

[2] Text in Daniel, *Thesaurus Hymnologicus*, ii. 95; Kehrein, *Lateinische Sequenzen des Mittelalters*, 81, and with facsimile and setting in A. Schübiger, *Die Sängerschule St. Gallens*, 90, &c.; cf. Lange, 59; Meyer, 49, 76; Milchsack, 34; Chevalier, *Repertorium Hymnologicum*, s. vv.; A. Schübiger, *La Séquence de Pâques Victimae Paschali et son auteur* (1858).

dic nobis, Maria, quid vidisti in via ?
sepulchrum Christi viventis et gloriam vidi resurgentis;
angelicos testes, sudarium et vestes.
surrexit Christus, spes mea, praecedet suos in Galilaeam.
credendum est magis soli Mariae veraci, quam Iudaeorum turbae fallaci.
scimus Christum surrexisse a mortuis vere: tu nobis, victor, rex, miserere.'

Originally written as an *Alleluia* trope or sequence proper, a place which it still occupies in the reformed Tridentine liturgy [1], the *Victimae paschali* cannot be shown to have made its way into the *Quem quaeritis* until the thirteenth century [2]. But it occurs in about a third of the extant versions, sometimes as a whole, sometimes with the omission of the first three sentences, which obviously do not lend themselves as well as the rest to dramatic treatment. When introduced, these three sentences are sung either by the choir or by the Maries: the other six fall naturally into dialogue.

The *Victimae paschali* is an expansion of the text of the *Quem quaeritis*, but it does not necessarily introduce any new dramatic motive. Of such there were, from the beginning, at least two. There was the visit of the Maries to the sepulchre and their colloquy with the angel; and there was the subsequent announcement of the Resurrection made by them in pursuance of the divine direction. Each has its appropriate action: in the one case the lifting of the pall and discovery of the empty sepulchre, in the other the display by the Maries of the cast-off grave-clothes, represented by a *linteum*, in token of the joyful event. It is to this second scene, if the term may be used of anything so rudimentary, that the *Victimae paschali* attaches itself. The dialogue of it is between the Maries and the choir, who stand for the whole body of disciples, or sometimes two singers, who are their spokesmen [3]. A new scene is, however, clearly added to

[1] Malleson-Tuker, ii. 27. It is used throughout Easter week.

[2] Lange, 60. It was interpolated during the thirteenth century in a twelfth-century Laon version (Chevalier, *Ordinaires de Laon*, 118).

[3] Narbonne, †1400 (Lange, 65) 'duo canonici, tanquam apostoli'; cf. Lange, 75.

the play, when these two singers not only address the Maries, but themselves pay a visit to the sepulchre. Now they represent the apostles Peter and John. In accordance with the gospel narrative John outstrips Peter in going to the sepulchre, but Peter enters first: and the business of taking up the *linteum* and displaying it to the other disciples is naturally transferred to them from the Maries. The apostle scene first makes its appearance in an Augsburg text of the end of the eleventh century, or the beginning of the twelfth [1]. It occurs in rather more than half the total number of versions. These are mainly German, but the evidence of Belethus is sufficient to show that it was not unknown in twelfth-century France [2]. The addition of the apostle scene completed the evolution of the Easter play for the majority of churches. There were, however, a few in which the very important step was taken of introducing the person of the risen Christ himself; and this naturally entailed yet another new scene. Of this type there are fifteen extant versions, coming from one Italian, four French, and four German churches [3]. The earliest is of the twelfth century, from a Prague convent. The new scene closely follows the Scripture narrative. Mary

[1] Augsburg *liber liturgicus* of eleventh or twelfth century (Lange, 82).

[2] Belethus, c. cxiii (*P. L.* ccii. 119) 'fit enim in plerisque Ecclesiis ut cantato ultimo responso, cum candelis cereis et solemni processione eant ex choro ad locum quemdam, ubi imaginarium sepulcrum compositum est, in quod introducuntur aliquot in personis mulierum et discipulorum Ioannis et Petri, quorum alter altero citius revertitur, sicut Ioannes velocius cucurrit Petro, atque item alii quidam in personis angelorum qui Christum resurrexisse dixerunt a mortuis. Quo quidem facto personae eae redeunt ad chorum, referuntque ea quae viderint et audierint. Tunc chorus, audita Christi resurrectione, prorumpit in altam vocem, inquiens, *Te Deum laudamus*.' It is to be observed that Belethus knows no *Depositio* and *Elevatio*. After the *Adoratio*, he has, like the older Roman liturgies, 'crucifixus in suum locum reponi debet' (c. xcviii). Durandus, vi. 87, has an account very similar to that of Belethus, but says 'Si qui autem habent versus de hac representatione compositos, licet non authenticos non improbamus'; cf. also p. 27.

[3] Engelberg (1372), Cividale (fourteenth century), Nuremberg (thirteenth century), Einsiedeln (thirteenth century), Prague (six, twelfth to fourteenth centuries), Rouen (two, thirteenth and fifteenth centuries), Mont St.-Michel (fourteenth century), Coutances (fifteenth century), Fleury (*Orleans MS.* 178, thirteenth century); all printed by Lange, 136 sqq. Gasté, 58, 63, also gives the Rouen and Coutances versions, the latter more fully than Lange. Meyer, 80, discusses the interrelations of the texts.

Magdalen remains behind the other Maries at the sepulchre. The Christ appears; she takes him for the gardener, and he reveals himself with the *Noli me tangere*. Mary returns with the new wonder to the choir. This is the simplest version of the new episode. It occurs in a play of which the text is purely liturgical, and does not even include the *Victimae paschali*. A somewhat longer one is found in a Fleury play, which is in other respects highly elaborate and metrical. Here the Christ appears twice, first disguised *in similitudinem hortolani*, afterwards *in similitudinem domini* with the *labarum* or resurrection banner. The remaining versions do not depart widely from these two types, except that at Rouen and Mont St.-Michel, the Christ scene takes place, not at the sepulchre but at the altar, and at Cividale in a spot described as the *ortus Christi*[1].

The formal classification, then, of the versions of the *Quem quaeritis*, gives three types. In the first, the scenes between the Maries and the angel, and between the Maries and the choir, are alone present; in the second the apostle scene is added to these; the third, of which there are only fifteen known examples, is distinguished by the presence of the Christ scene. In any one of these types, the *Victimae paschali* and other proses and hymns may or may not be found[2]. And it must now be added that it is on the presence of these that the greater or less development of lyric feeling, as distinct from dramatic action, in the play depends. The metrical hymns in particular, when they are not merely choral overtures, are often of the nature of *planctus* or laments put in the mouths of the Maries as they approach the sepulchre or at some other appropriate moment. These *planctus* add greatly to the vividness and humanity of the play, and are thus an important step in the dramatic evolution. The use of them

[1] Lange, 138. In this text the Maries have a *locus suus*. The MS. is a *Processional*, and it may be that the play was given not in the church, but in the open square, as was the Annunciation play in the same MS. (Coussemaker, 284; cf. p. 67). It is none the less liturgical. Rouen had probably an 'ortus Christi' out of which came the apparition 'in sinistro cornu altaris,' for at Easter, 1570, divine service was performed in a 'paradis dressé avec la plus grande solennité dans la chapelle Notre-Dame, derrière le chœur' (Gasté, 58).

[2] These are of course the 'versus' spoken of with tolerance in the passage just quoted from Durandus.

may be illustrated by that of the hymn *Heu! pius pastor occiditur* in the Dublin version found by Mr. Frere and printed, after a different text from his, in an appendix [1]. This play has not the Christ scene, and belongs, therefore, to the second type of *Quem quaeritis*, but, in other respects, including the *planctus*, it closely resembles the Fleury version described above. Another *planctus*, found in plays of the third type from Engelberg, Nuremberg, Einsiedeln, and Cividale, is the *Heu nobis! internas mentes* [2]; a third, the *Heu! miserae cur contigit*, seems to have been interpolated in the *Heu! pius pastor* at Dublin; a fourth, the *Omnipotens pater altissime*, with a refrain *Heu quantus est dolor noster!* is found at places so far apart as Narbonne and Prague [3]: and a fifth, *Heu dolor, heu quam dira doloris angustia!* is also in the Fleury text [4].

Another advance towards drama is made in four Prague versions of the third type by the introduction of an episode for which there is no Scriptural basis at all. On their way to the sepulchre, the Maries stop and buy the necessary spices of a spice-merchant or *unguentarius*. In three thirteenth-century texts the *unguentarius* is merely a *persona muta*; in one of the fourteenth he is given four lines [5]. The *unguentarius* was destined to become a very popular character, and to afford much comic relief in the vernacular religious drama of Germany. Nor can it be quite confidently said that his appearance in these comparatively late liturgical plays is a natural development and not merely an instance of reaction by the vernacular stage.

[1] Appendix R. The *Heu! pius pastor occiditur* does not seem to have been found outside the Fleury and Dublin plays (Chevalier, *Repert. Hymn.* n°. 7741).

[2] Lange, 136, 141; Milchsack, 35, 66.

[3] Lange, 64, 74.

[4] Ibid. 162.

[5] Ibid. 151. The fourteenth-century text runs:

Tres Mariae:
'aromata preciosa querimus,
Christi corpus ungere volumus,
holocausta sunt odorifera
sepulturae Christi memori.'

Ungentarius:
'dabo vobis ungenta optima,
salvatoris ungere vulnera,
sepulturae eius ad memoriam
et nomen eius ad gloriam.'

The earlier texts have 'aromata... memori,' preceded by 'Mariae cantantes "aromata" procedant ad unguentarium pro accipiendis ungentis' and followed by 'quibus acceptis accedant ad sepulchrum.' Meyer, 58, 91, 106, calls this scene, in which he finds the first introduction of non-liturgical verse, the *Zehnsilberspiel*, and studies it at great length.

The scenic effect of the *Quem quaeritis* can be to some extent gathered from the rubrics, although these are often absent and often not very explicit, being content with a general direction for the performers to be arrayed *in similitudinem mulierum* or *angelorum* or *apostolorum*, as the case may be. The setting was obviously simple, and few properties or costumes beyond what the vestments and ornaments of the church could supply were used. The Maries had their heads veiled [1], and wore surplices, copes, chasubles, dalmatics, albs, or the like. These were either white or coloured. At Fécamp one, presumably the Magdalen, was in red, the other two in white [2]. The thuribles which, as already pointed out, they carried, were sometimes replaced by boxes or vases representing the ointment and spices [3]. Sometimes also they carried, or had carried before them, candles. Two or three rubrics direct them to go *pedetemptim*, as sad or searching [4]. They were generally three in number, occasionally two, or one only. The angels, or angel, as the case might be, sat within the sepulchre or at its door. They, too, had vestments, generally white, and veiled or crowned heads. At Narbonne, and probably elsewhere, they had wings [5]. They held lights, a palm, or an ear of corn, symbolizing the Resurrection [6]. The apostles are rarely described; the ordinary priestly robes doubtless sufficed. At Dublin, St. John, in white, held a palm, and St. Peter, in red, the keys [7]. In the earliest Prague version of the Christ scene, the Christ seems to be represented by one of the angels [8]. At Nuremberg the *dominica persona* has a crown and bare feet [9]. At Rouen he holds a cross, and

[1] Lange, 24, 51, 64 'coopertis capitibus' (Tours, fifteenth century), 'capita humeralibus velata' (Rheinau), 'amictibus in capitibus eorum' (Narbonne, †1400).

[2] Lange, 36 (fourteenth century).

[3] Ibid. 27, 36, 53, 64, &c.; Appendix R.

[4] Lange, 51, 160; cf. *Conc. Regularis* (Appendix O).

[5] Lange, 64 'induti albis et amictibus cum stolis violatis et sindone rubea in facie eorum et alis in humeris' (Narbonne, †1400).

[6] Lange, 40, 155, 158, 162 'palmam manu tenens, in capite fanulum largum habens' (Toul, thirteenth century), 'tenens spicam in manu' (Rouen, fifteenth century), 'tenens palmam in manu et habens coronam in capite' (Mont St.-Michel, fourteenth century), 'vestitus alba deaurata, mitra tectus caput etsi deinfulatus, palmam in sinistra, ramum candelarum plenum tenens in manu dextra' (Fleury, thirteenth century).

[7] Appendix R.

[8] Lange, 147.

[9] Ibid. 143 'quae sit vestita

though there is a double appearance, there is no hint of any change of costume[1]. But at Coutances and Fleury the first appearance is as *hortulanus*, indicated perhaps by a spade, which is exchanged on the second for the cross[2].

It must be borne in mind that the *Quem quaeritis* remained imperfectly detached from the liturgy, out of which it arose. The performers were priests, or nuns, and choir-boys. The play was always chanted, not spoken[3]. It was not even completely resolved into dialogue. In many quite late versions narrative anthems giving the gist of each scene are retained, and are sung either by the principal actors or by the choir, which thus, as in the hymns or proses which occur as overtures[4], holds a position distinct from the part which it takes as representing the disciples[5]. Finally the whole performance ends in most cases with the *Te Deum laudamus*, and thus becomes a constituent part of Matins, which normally comes to a close with that hymn. The intervention of the congregation, with its Easter hymn *Christ ist erstanden*, seems to lie outside the main period of the evolution of the *Quem quaeritis*. I only find one example so early as the thirteenth century[6].

dalmatica casulamque complicatam super humeros habeat; coronamque capiti superimpositam, nudis pedibus.'

[1] Lange, 156 'albatus cum stola, tenens crucem.'

[2] Ibid. 159, 164 'in habitu ortolani . . . redeat, indutus capa serica vel pallio serico, tenens crucem' (Coutances); 'praeparatus in similitudinem hortolani . . . is, qui ante fuit hortulanus, in similitudinem domini veniat, dalmaticatus candida dalmatica, candida infula infulatus, phylacteria pretiosa in capite, crucem cum labaro in dextra, textum auro paratorium in sinistra habens' (Fleury). The *labarum* is the banner of Constantine with the Chi-Ro monogram (cf. Gibbon-Bury, ii. 567): but the banner usually attached to the cross in mediaeval pictures of the Resurrection itself bears simply a large cross; cf. Pearson, ii. 310.

[3] A study of the music might perhaps throw light on the relation of the versions to each other. I am sorry that it is beyond my powers: moreover Lange does not give the notation; Coussemaker gives it for half a dozen versions.

[4] For such overtures cf. Lange, 36, 62, 64; Milchsack, 37, 38, 40. On the doubtful use of the *Gloriosi et famosi* at Einsiedeln, cf. p. 54.

[5] In the Prague versions (Lange, 151). The choir, or rather 'conventus,' introduces the scenes with the three following anthems: (i) 'Maria Magdalena et alia Maria ferebant diluculo aromata, dominum querentes in monumento,' (ii) 'Maria stabat ad monumentum foris plorans; dum ergo fleret, inclinavit se et prospexit in monumentum,' (iii) 'Currebant duo simul et ille alius discipulus praecucurrit cicius petro et venit prior ad monumentum.'

[6] Lange, 146 (Nuremberg); for later examples cf. Lange, 99 sqq.

It is in quite late texts also that certain other Easter motives have become attached to the play. The commonest of these are the whispered greeting of *Surrexit Christus* and the kiss of peace, which have been noted elsewhere as preceding Matins[1]. At Eichstädt, in 1560, is an amusing direction, which Mr. Collins would have thought very proper, that the *pax* is to be given to the *dominus terrae, si ibi fuerit*, before the priest. The same manuscript shows a curious combination of the *Quem quaeritis* with the irrepressible *Tollite portas* ceremony[2]. Another such is found at Venice[3]. But this is as late as the eighteenth century, to which also belongs the practice at Angers described by De Moleon, according to which the Maries took up from the sepulchre with the *linteum* two large Easter eggs—*deux œufs d'autruche*[4].

Besides the *Quem quaeritis*, Easter week had another liturgical drama in the *Peregrini* or *Peregrinus*[5]. This was established by the twelfth century. It was regularly played at Lichfield[6], but no text is extant from England, except a late transitional one, written partly in the vernacular[7]. France affords four texts, from Saintes[8], Rouen[9],

The hymn generally comes just before the *Te Deum*. A fourteenth-century Bohemian version from Prague (Lange, 131) has a similar Bohemian hymn 'Buoh wssemohuczy.' At Bamberg in 1597 'potest chorus populo iterum praecinere cantilenas pascales Germanicas' (Lange, 95). At Rheinau in 1573 it is suggested that the *Quem quaeritis* itself may as an alternative be sung in German (Lange, 68) 'hisce aut Germanicis versibus cantatis.' At Aquileja in 1495 'Populus cantet *Christus surrexit*,' apparently in Latin (Lange, 106); and at Würzburg in 1477, 'Populus incipit Ymnum suum: *Te Deum*' (Lange, 67).

[1] Lange, 39, 119, 122, 124; cf. Martene, iii. 171.

[2] Lange, 41.

[3] *Z. f. d. A.* xli. 77.

[4] Lange, 39.

[5] Creizenach, i. 56; Julleville, i. 67.

[6] *Lichfield Statutes of Hugh de Nonant*, 1188-98 (*Lincoln Statutes*, ii. 15, 23) 'Item in nocte Natalis representacio pastorum fieri consuevit et in diluculo Pasche representacio Resurreccionis dominicae et representacio peregrinorum die lune in septimana Pasche sicut in libris super hijs ac alijs compositis continetur . . . De officio succentoris . . . et providere debet quod representacio pastorum in nocte Natalis domini et miraculorum in nocte Pasche et die lune in Pascha congrue et honorifice fiant.'

[7] Cf. p. 90.

[8] Text in *Bibl. de l'École des Chartes*, xxxiv. 314, from *B. N. Lat.* 16,309 (thirteenth-century Saintes *Breviary*), *begins* 'Quando fiunt Peregrini, non dicitur prosa, sed peregrini deforis veniunt canendo ista'; *ends* with *Magnificat* and *Oratio*, 'Deus qui sollempnitate paschali.'

[9] Text in Gasté, 65; Du Méril,

Beauvais [1], and Fleury [2]. The play is also recorded at Lille [3]. In Germany it is represented by a recently-discovered fragment of the famous early thirteenth-century repertory of the *scholares vagantes* from the Benedictbeuern monastery [4]. The simplest version is that of Saintes, in which the action is confined to the journey to Emmaus and the supper there. The Rouen play is on the same lines, but at the close the disciples are joined by St. Mary Magdalen, and the *Victimae paschali* is sung. The Benedictbeuern play similarly ends with the introduction of the Virgin and two other Maries to greet the risen Christ. But here, and in the Beauvais and Fleury plays, a distinct scene is added, of which the subject is the incredulity of Thomas and the apparition to him. It is, I think, a reasonable conjecture that the *Peregrini*, in which the risen Christ is a character, was not devised until he had already been introduced into the later versions of the *Quem quaeritis*. Indeed the Fleury *Peregrini*, with its double appearance and change of costume for Christ, seems clearly modelled on the Fleury *Quem quaeritis*. But the lesser play has its own proper and natural place in the Easter week services. It is attached to the *Processio ad fontes*, which is a regular portion, during that season, of Vespers [5]. The Christ with the Resurrection cross is personated by the priest who

117, from Rouen *Ordinarium* (fourteenth century), *begins* 'Officium Peregrinorum debet hic fieri hoc modo'; *ends* 'Et processio, factis memoriis, redeat in choro et ibi finiantur vesperae.' Gasté, 68, quotes an order of 1452 'Domini capitulantes concluserunt quod in istis festis Paschae fiat misterium representans resurrectionem Christi et apparitionem eius suis discipulis, eundo apud castrum de Emaux, amotis et cessantibus indecenciis.'

[1] Text in G. Desjardins, *Hist. de la Cath. de Beauvais* (1865), 115, 269, *begins* 'Ordo ad suscipiendum peregrinum in secunda feria Paschae ad vesperas'; *ends* with *Oratio de Resurrectione*. Meyer, 133, describes the MS. as of the first half of the twelfth century.

[2] Text in Du Méril, 120, from *Orleans MS.* 178 (thirteenth century), *begins* 'Ad faciendam similitudinem dominicae apparitionis in specie Peregrini, quae fit in tertia feria Paschae ad Vesperas'; *ends* 'Salve, festa dies.'

[3] E. Hautcœur, *Documents liturgiques de Lille*, 55, from *Ordinarium* of thirteenth century, 'Feria ii. . . . in vesperis . . . post collectam fit representatio peregrinorum. Qua facta cantatur Christus resurgens, et itur in chorum.'

[4] W. Meyer, *Fragmenta Burana*, 131, with text and facsimile. The play begins 'Incipit exemplum apparicionis domini discipulis suis ⟨iuxta⟩ castellum Emaus, ubi illis apparuit in more peregrini,' &c.

[5] *Use of Sarum*, i. 157; *Sarum Breviary*, i. dccccxxix.

normally accompanies the procession *cum cruce*. At Rouen the play was a kind of dramatization of the procession itself[1]; at Lille it seems to have had the same position; at Saintes and Beauvais it preceded the *Magnificat* and *Oratio* or *Collecta*, after which the procession started. In the remaining cases there is no indication of the exact time for the *Peregrini*. The regular day for it appears to have been the Monday in Easter week, of the Gospel for which the journey to Emmaus is the subject; but at Fleury it was on the Tuesday, when the Gospel subject is the incredulity of Thomas. At Saintes, a curious rubric directs the Christ during the supper at Emmaus to divide the 'host' among the *Peregrini*. It seems possible that in this way a final disposal was found for the host which had previously figured in the *Depositio* and *Elevatio* of the sepulchre ceremony.

A long play, probably of Norman origin and now preserved in a manuscript at Tours, represents a merging of the *Elevatio*, the *Quem quaeritis*, and the *Peregrini*[2]. The beginning is imperfect, but it may be conjectured from a fragment belonging to Klosterneuburg in Germany, that only a few lines are lost[3]. Pilate sets a watch before the sepulchre. An angel sends lightning, and the soldiers fall as if dead[4]. Then come the Maries, with *planctus*. There is a scene with the *unguentarius* or *mercator*, much longer than that at Prague, followed by more *planctus*. After the *Quem quaeritis*, the soldiers announce the event to Pilate. A *planctus* by the

[1] The *Peregrini* start 'a vestiario . . . per dextram alam ecclesiae usque ad portas occidentales, et subsistentes in capite processionis.' Then the *Sacerdos*, 'nudus pedes, ferens crucem super dextrum humerum' comes 'per dextram alam ecclesiae' to meet them. They lead him 'usque ad tabernaculum, in medio navis ecclesiae, in similitudinem castelli Emaux praeparatum.'

[2] Text in Milchsack, 97; Coussemaker, 21, from *Tours MS.* 927 (twelfth or thirteenth century); cf. Creizenach, i. 88; Julleville, i. 62; Meyer, 95; and on the MS. which also contains the 'Ordo representacionis Adae,' and is not native to Tours, cf. p. 71.

[3] Milchsack, 105; Creizenach, i. 90. The beginning and end of the Klosterneuburg play were printed from a thirteenth-century MS., now lost, by B. Pez, *Thesaurus novus Anecd.* ii. 1. liii. It began 'Primo producatur Pilatus cum responsorio: *Ingressus Pilatus*,' and ended with 'Christ, der ist erstanden'; cf. Meyer, 126.

[4] 'Modo veniat angelus et iniciat eis fulgura; milites cadunt in terram velut mortui.'

Magdalen leads up to the apparition to her. The Maries return to the disciples. Christ appears to the disciples, then to Thomas, and the *Victimae paschali* and *Te Deum* conclude the performance. A fragment of a very similar play, breaking off before the *Quem quaeritis*, belongs to the Benedictbeuern manuscript already mentioned [1].

It is clear from the rubrics that the Tours play, long as it is, was still acted in church, and probably, as the *Te Deum* suggests, at the Easter Matins [2]. Certainly this was the case with the Benedictbeuern play. In a sense, these plays only mark a further stage in the process of elaboration by which the fuller versions of the *Quem quaeritis* proper came into being. But the introduction at the beginning and end of motives outside the events of the Easter morning itself points to possibilities of expansion which were presently realized, and which ultimately transformed the whole character of the liturgical drama. All the plays, however, which have so far been mentioned, are strictly plays of the Resurrection. Their action begins after the Burial of Christ, and does not stretch back into the events of the Passion. Nor indeed can the liturgical drama proper be shown to have advanced beyond a very rudimentary representation of the Passion. This began with the *planctus*, akin to those of the *Quem quaeritis*, which express the sorrows of the Virgin and the Maries and St. John around the cross [3]. Such *planctus* exist both in Latin and

[1] Meyer, 97, 125, with text and facsimile, 'Incipit ludus immo exemplum Dominice resurrectionis.' The episode of the Resurrection with the dismay of the soldiers is found not only in the Tours and Benedictbeuern MS., but also in the simpler Coutances *Quem quaeritis*. Lange, 157, omits this passage, but Gasté, 63, gives it; 'Si Mariae debeant representari, finito responsorio quatuor clerici armati accedentes ad sepulcrum Domini pannis sericis decenter ornatum et secum dicant personagia sua. Quo facto, duo pueri induti roquetis veniant ad monumentum ferentes duas virgas decorticatas in quibus sunt decem candelae ardentes; et statim cum appropinquaverint ad sepulcrum praedicti milites, procidant quasi mortui, nec surgant donec incipiatur *Te Deum*, ... &c.' There is no actual appearance of the Rising Christ in any of these three plays as originally written. But a later hand has inserted in the Benedictbeuern MS. directions for the Christ to appear, discourse with the angels, and put on the 'vestem ortulani.'

[2] Creizenach thinks the play (like Adam) was outside the church, because the Maries appear 'ante ostium ecclesiae.' But 'ante' may be inside. Mary Magdalen at one point is 'in sinistra parte ecclesiae stans,' and most of the action is round the *sepulchrum*.

[3] E. Wechssler, *Die romani-*

the vernacular. The earliest are of the twelfth century. Several of them are in dialogue, in which Christ himself occasionally takes part, and they appear to have been sung in church after Matins on Good Friday [1]. The *planctus* must be regarded as the starting-point of a drama of the Passion, which presently established itself beside the drama of the Resurrection. This process was mainly outside the churches, but an early and perhaps still liturgical stage of it is to be seen in the *ludus breviter de passione* which precedes the elaborated *Quem quaeritis* of the Benedictbeuern manuscript, and was probably treated as a sort of prologue to it. The action extends from the preparation for the Last Supper to the Burial. It is mainly in dumb-show, and the slight dialogue introduced is wholly out of the Vulgate. But at one point occurs the rubric *Maria planctum faciat quantum melius potest*, and a later hand has inserted out of its place in the text the most famous of all the laments of the Virgin, the *Planctus ante nescia* [2].

schen Marienklagen (1893); A. Schönbach, *Die Marienklagen* (1873); cf. Creizenach, i. 241; Julleville, i. 58; Sepet, 23; Milchsack, 92; Coussemaker, 285, 346; Meyer, 67; Pearson, ii. 384.

[1] A *planctus* ascribed to Bonaventura (thirteenth century) has the titles 'Officium de compassione Mariae' (Wechssler, 14), and 'Officium sanctae crucis' (*Bibl. de l'École des Chartes*, xxxiv. 315). Another, the 'Surgit Christus cum trophaeo,' is headed in thirteenth- and fourteenth-century MSS. 'Sequentia devota antiquorum nostrorum de resurrectionis argumentis. Sanctarum virginum Mariae ac Mariae Magdalene de compassione mortis Christi per modum dyalogi sequentia.' The chorus begins, and 'tres bene vociferati scholares respondent' (text in Milchsack, 92; cf. Wechssler, 14). A third, 'O fratres et sorores,' is headed 'Hic incipit planctus Mariae et aliorum in die Parasceves' (text from fourteenth-century Cividale MS. in Coussemaker, 285; Julleville, i. 58; cf. Wechssler, 17). Ducange, s. v. *Planctus*, quotes a (thirteenth-century) Toulouse rubric, 'planctum beatissimae Virginis Mariae, qui dicitur a duobus puerulis post Matutinum et debent esse monachi, si possunt reperiri ad hoc apti.' This *planctus* was sung from the 'cathedra praedicatorii.' On the use of vernacular Italian *planctus* by the *laudesi* in churches through Lent, cf. Wechssler, 30. The vernacular German 'ludus passionis' printed by O. Schönemann, *Der Sündenfall und Marienklage* (1855), 129, from a Wolfenbüttel fifteenth-century, MS., seems to have still been meant for liturgical use, as it has the rubric 'debet cantari post *crux fidelis* et sic finiri usque ad vesperam lamentabiliter cum caeteris sicut consuetum est fieri.' It incorporates the *Depositio*.

[2] Meyer, *Fragmenta Burana*, 64, 122, with text and facsimile. The piece ends 'et ita inchoatur ludus de resurrectione. Pontifices: *O domine recte meminimus*,' which is the opening of the Easter play already described.

CHAPTER XIX

LITURGICAL PLAYS (*continued*)

THE 'Twelve days' of the Christmas season are no less important than Easter itself in the evolution of the liturgical drama. I have mentioned in the last chapter a Christmas trope which is evidently based upon the older Easter dialogue. Instead of *Quem quaeritis in sepulchro, o Christicolae?* it begins *Quem quaeritis in praesepe, pastores, dicite?* It occurs in eleventh- and twelfth-century tropers from St. Gall, Limoges, St. Magloire, and Nevers. Originally it was an *Introit* trope for the third or 'great' Mass. In a fifteenth-century breviary from Clermont-Ferrand it has been transferred to Matins, where it follows the *Te Deum*; and this is precisely the place in the Christmas services occupied, at Rouen, by a liturgical drama known as the *Officium Pastorum*, which appears to have grown out of the *Quem quaeritis in praesepe?* by a process analogous to that by which the Easter drama grew out of the *Quem quaeritis in sepulchro*[1]*?* A *praesepe* or 'crib,' covered by a curtain, was made ready behind the altar, and in it was placed an image of the Virgin. After the *Te Deum* five canons or vicars, representing the shepherds, approached the great west door of the choir. A boy *in similitudinem angeli* perched *in excelso* sang them the 'good tidings,' and a number of others *in voltis ecclesiae* took up the *Gloria in excelsis*. The shepherds, singing a hymn, advanced to the *praesepe*. Here they were met with the *Quem quaeritis* by two priests *quasi obstetrices*[2]. The dia-

[1] Printed by Du Méril, 147; Gasté, 25; Davidson, 173, from Rouen *Ordinaria* (*Rouen MSS.* Y. 108 of fifteenth century, Y. 110 of fourteenth century); Coussemaker, 235, with notation, from Rouen *Gradual* (*Bibl. Nat. Lat.* 904); it is also in *B. N. Lat.* 1213 (fifteenth century) and *Bibl. Mazarin.* 216 (Du Méril, 148).

[2] The 'obstetrices' figure in the *Protevangelium Iacobi*, chh. 18 sqq. (Tischendorf, *Evangelia Apocrypha*, 33), and the *Pseudo-Matthaei Evan-*

logue of the trope, expanded by another hymn during which the shepherds adore, follows, and so the drama ends. But the shepherds 'rule the choir' throughout the *Missa in Gallicantu* immediately afterwards, and at Lauds, the anthem for which much resembles the *Quem quaeritis* itself[1]. The *misterium pastorum* was still performed at Rouen in the middle of the fifteenth century, and at this date the shepherds, *cessantibus stultitiis et insolenciis*, so far as this could be ensured by the chapter, took the whole 'service' of the day, just as did the deacons, priests, and choir-boys during the *triduum*[2].

If the central point of the *Quem quaeritis* is the *sepulchrum*, that of the *Pastores* is the *praesepe*. In either case the drama, properly so called, is an addition, and by no means an invariable one, to the symbolical ceremony. The *Pastores* may, in fact, be described, although the term does not occur in the documents, as a *Visitatio praesepis*. The history of the *praesepe* can be more definitely stated than that of the *sepulchrum*. It is by no means extinct. The Christmas 'crib' or *crèche*, a more or less realistic representation of the Nativity, with a Christ-child in the manger, a Joseph and Mary, and very often an ox and an ass, is a common feature in all Catholic countries at Christmas time[3]. At Rome, in particular, the *esposizione del santo bambino* takes place with great ceremony[4]. A tradition ascribes the first *presepio* known in Italy to St. Francis, who is said to have invented it at Greccio in 1223[5]. But this is a mistake. The custom is

gelium, ch. 13 (Tischendorf, 77). In the latter they are named Salome and Zelomi.

[1] Gasté, 31 'Archiepiscopus, vel alius sacerdos versus ad Pastores dicat: *Quem vidistis, pastores, dicite; annunciate nobis in terris quis apparuit.* Pastores respondeant: *Natum vidimus et choros angelorum collaudantes Dominum. Alleluia, alleluia*, et totam antiphonam finiant': cf. Meyer, 39; *Sarum Breviary*, clxxxviii; Martene, iii. 36; Durandus, vi. 13, 16 'in laudibus matutinis quasi choream ducimus, unde in prima antiphona dicimus; *Quem vidistis, pastores?* &c. Et ipsi responderunt: *Natum vidimus.*'

[2] Gasté, 33.

[3] Tille, *D. W.* 309; Pollard, xiii; Durandus-Barthélemy, iii. 411; E. Martinengo-Cesaresco, *Puer Parvulus* in *Contemporary Review*, lxxvii (1900), 117; W. H. D. Rouse, in *F. L.* v. 6; J. Feller, *Le Bethléem Verviétois*, 10. I find a modern English example described in a letter of 1878 written by Mr. Coventry Patmore's son Henry from a Catholic school at Ushaw (*Life of C. Patmore*, i. 308).

[4] Malleson-Tuker, ii. 212.

[5] P. Sabatier, *Life of St. Francis*

many centuries older than St. Francis. Its Roman home is the church of S. Maria Maggiore or *Ad Praesepe*, otherwise called the '*basilica* of Liberius.' Here there was in the eighth century a permanent *praesepe*[1], probably built in imitation of one which had long existed at Bethlehem, and to which an allusion is traced in the writings of Origen[2]. The *praesepe* of S. Maria Maggiore was in the right aisle. When the Sistine chapel was built in 1585–90 it was moved to the crypt, where it may now be seen. This church became an important station for the Papal services at Christmas. The Pope celebrated Mass here on the vigil, and remained until he had also celebrated the first Mass on Christmas morning. The bread was broken on the manger itself, which served as an altar. At S. Maria Maggiore, moreover, is an important relic, in some boards from the *culla* or cradle of Christ, which are exposed on the *presepio* during Christmas[3]. The *presepio* of S. Maria Maggiore became demonstrably the model for other similar chapels in Rome[4], and doubtless for the more temporary structures throughout Italy and western Europe in general.

In the present state of our knowledge it is a little difficult to be precise as to the range or date of the *Pastores*. The only full mediaeval Latin text, other than that of Rouen, which has come to light, is also of Norman origin, and is still unprinted[5]. In the eighteenth century the play survived at Lisieux and Clermont[6]. The earliest Rouen manuscript is of the thirteenth century, and the absence of any reference to

(Eng. transl.), 285, from Thomas of Celano, *Vita Prima*, 84, and Bonaventura, *Vita*, 149; cf. D'Ancona, i. 116.

[1] Usener, i. 280. It is called 'oratorium sanctum quod praesepe dicitur' (†731–41) and 'camera praesepii' (†844–7).

[2] Origen, *adv. Celsum*, i. 51; cf. Usener, i. 283, 287.

[3] Usener, i. 281; Tille, *D. W.* 54; Malleson-Tuker, ii. 210.

[4] Usener, i. 280. Gregory IV (827–43) 'sanctum fecit praesepe ad similitudinem praesepii S. dei genetricis quae appellatur maior,' in S. Maria in Trastevere.

[5] Gasté, 33, citing *Montpellier MS*. H. 304. The play occurs, with an *Officium Stellae*, in an anonymous treatise *De ratione divini officii*. The Amiens *Ordinarium* of 1291 (Grenier, 389) gives directions for a *Pastores* during the procession after the communion at the midnight mass. In preparation lights were lit at the *praesepe* during first vespers 'dum canitur versus *praesepe iam fulget tuum*.' At the end of the first nocturn the figure of a child was placed there. At the first lesson of the second nocturn the cry of *noël* was raised.

[6] Du Méril, 148.

the *Officium Pastorum* by John of Avranches, who writes primarily of Rouen, and who does mention the *Officium Stellae*, makes it probable that it was not there known about 1070[1]. Its existence, however, in England in the twelfth century is shown by the Lichfield *Statutes* of 1188–98, and on the whole it is not likely to have taken shape later than the eleventh. Very likely it never, as a self-contained play, acquired the vogue of the *Quem quaeritis*. As will be seen presently, it was overshadowed and absorbed by rivals. I find no trace of it in Germany, where the *praesepe* became a centre, less for liturgical drama, than for carols, dances, and 'crib-rocking[2].'

Still rarer than the *Pastores* is the drama, presumably belonging to Innocents' day, of *Rachel*. It is found in a primitive form, hardly more than a trope, in a Limoges manuscript of the eleventh century. Here it is called *Lamentatio Rachel*, and consists of a short *planctus* by Rachel herself, and a short reply by a consoling angel. There is nothing to show what place it occupied in the services[3].

The fact is that both the *Pastores* and the *Rachel* were in many churches taken up into a third drama belonging to the Epiphany. This is variously known as the *Tres Reges*, the *Magi*, *Herodes*, and the *Stella*. It exists in a fair number of different but related forms. Like the *Quem quaeritis* and the *Pastores*, it had a material starting-point, in the shape of a star, lit with candles, which hung from the roof of the church, and could sometimes be moved, by a simple mechanical device, from place to place[4]. As with the *Quem quaeritis*,

[1] Ioannes Abrincensis, *De officiis ecclesiasticis* (*P. L.* cxlvii. 41, 43). Neither Belethus nor Durandus mentions the *Pastores*.

[2] Cf. vol. i. p. 272. The *praesepe* is of course in the *Stella*, which is found at Strassburg, Bilsen, and Einsiedeln, but even this is more characteristic of France than of Germany.

[3] Text ed. C. Magnin (*Journal des Savants* (1846), 93), from *Bibl. Nat. Lat.* 1139.

[4] Gasté, 50 'Corona ante crucem pendens in modum stellae accendatur' (Rouen); Du Méril, 153 'stellam pendentem in filo, quae antecedit eos' (Limoges). The churchwardens' accounts of St. Nicholas, Yarmouth, from 1462–1512 (*Norfolk Archaeology*, xi. 334), contain payments for 'making a new star,' 'leading the star,' 'a new balk line to the star and ryving the same star.' Pearson, ii. 325, lays stress on the prominence of the star in the German vernacular mysteries. J. T. Micklethwaite, *Ornaments of the Rubric*, 44, says that the 'star' was called a 'trendle' or 'rowell.' Its use does not necessarily imply the presence of a drama.

the development of the *Stella* must be studied without much reference to the relative age of the manuscripts in which it happens to be found. But it was probably complete by the end of the eleventh century, since manuscripts of that date contain the play in its latest forms[1].

The simplest version is from Limoges[2]. The three kings enter by the great door of the choir singing a *prosula*. They show their gifts, the royal gold, the divine incense, the myrrh for funeral. Then they see the star, and follow it to the high altar. Here they offer their gifts, each contained in a gilt cup, or some other *iocale pretiosum*, after which a boy, representing an angel, announces to them the birth of Christ, and they retire singing to the sacristy. The text of this version stands by itself: nearly all the others are derived from a common tradition, which is seen in its simplest form at Rouen[3]. In the Rouen *Officium Stellae*, the three kings, coming respectively from the east, north, and south of the church, meet before the altar. One of them points to the star with his stick, and they sing:

'1. Stella fulgore nimio rutilat,
2. Quae regem regum natum demonstrat
3. Quem venturum olim prophetiae signaverant.'

[1] The account of the *Stella* here given should be supplemented from Creizenach, i. 60; Köppen, 10. The latter studies the verbal relation of the texts much more fully than can be done here. Meyer, 38, argues for their origin in an archetype from Germany. There are doubtless many other texts yet unprinted. Ch. Magnin, *Journal de l'Instruction publique*, Sept. 13, 1835, mentions such in Soleures, Fribourg, and Besançon *Rituals*.

[2] Text in Du Méril, 151; Martene, iii. 44, from Limoges *Ordinarium* of unspecified date. The version is partly metrical, and the action took place 'cantato offertorio, antequam eant ad offerendum.

[3] Text in Gasté, 49; Du Méril, 153; Davidson, 176; from *Rouen MS*. Y. 110 (fourteenth-century *Ordinarium*); Coussemaker, 242, from *Bibl. Nat. Lat. MS*. 904 (thirteenth-century *Gradual*, with notation); *P. L.* cxlvii. 135, from *B.N.* 904 and *B.N.Lat.* 1213 (fifteenth-century *Ordinarium*); cf. Gasté, 3. The rubric begins 'Officium regum trium secundum usum Rothomagensem. Die epyphaniae, tercia cantata.' John of Avranches (†1070) describing the Epiphany service, probably of Rouen, says, after mentioning the *Evangelium genealogiae*, which follows the ninth *responsorium* of Matins, 'Deinde stellae officium incipiat' (*P. L.* cxlvii. 43). Gasté, 53, quotes some Rouen chapter orders. In 1379 Peter Chopillard, painter, was paid 'pro pingendo baculos quos portant Reges die Apparitionis.' In 1507 the chapter after 'matura deliberatio' ordered the 'representatio trium Regum' to be held. In 1521 they suppressed it.

They kiss each other and sing an anthem, which occurs also in the Limoges version: *Eamus ergo et inquiramus eum, offerentes ei munera; aurum thus et myrrham.* A procession is now formed, and as it moves towards the nave, the choir chant narrative passages, describing the visit of the *Magi* to Jerusalem and their reception by Herod. Meanwhile a star is lit over the altar of the cross where an image of the Virgin has been placed. The *Magi* approach it, singing the passage which begins *Ecce stella in Oriente.* They are met by two in dalmatics, who appear to be identical with the *obstetrices* of the Rouen *Pastores.* A dialogue follows:

'Qui sunt hi qui, stella duce, nos adeuntes inaudita ferunt.

Magi respondeant:

nos sumus, quos cernitis, reges Tharsis et Arabum et Saba, dona ferentes Christo, regi nato, Domino, quem, stella deducente, adorare venimus.

Tunc duo Dalmaticati aperientes cortinam dicant:

ecce puer adest quem queritis, Iam properate adorate, quia ipse est redemptio mundi.

Tunc procidentes Reges ad terram, simul salutent puerum, ita dicentes:

salve, princeps saeculorum.

Tunc unus a suo famulo aurum accipiat et dicat:

suscipe, rex, aurum.

Et offerat.

Secundus ita dicat et offerat:

tolle thus, tu, vere Deus.

Tercius ita dicat et offerat:

mirram, signum sepulturae.'

Then the congregation make their oblations. Meanwhile the *Magi* pray and fall asleep. In their sleep an angel warns them to return home another way. The procession returns up a side aisle to the choir; and the Mass, in which the *Magi*, like the shepherds on Christmas day, 'rule the choir,' follows.

In spite of the difference of text the incidents of the Rouen and Limoges versions, except for the angelic warning introduced at Rouen, are the same. There was a dramatic advance when the visit to Jerusalem, instead of being merely narrated by the choir, was inserted into the action. In the play performed at Nevers [1], Herod himself, destined in the fullness of time to become the protagonist of the Corpus Christi stage, makes his first appearance. There are two versions of the Nevers play. In the earlier the new scene is confined to a colloquy between Herod and the *Magi*:

'[*Magi.*] Vidimus stellam eius in Oriente, et agnovimus regem regum esse natum.

[*Herodes.*] regem quem queritis natum stella quo signo didicistis? Si illum regnare creditis, dicite nobis.

[*Magi.*] illum natum esse didicimus in Oriente stella monstrante.

[*Herodes.*] ite et de puero diligenter investigate, et inventum redeuntes mihi renuntiate.'

The later version adds two further episodes. In one a *nuntius* announces the coming of the *Magi*, and is sent to fetch them before Herod: in the other Herod sends his courtiers for the scribes, who find a prophecy of the birth of the Messiah in Bethlehem. Obviously the Herod scene gives point to the words at the end of the Rouen play, in which the angel bids the *Magi* to return home by a different way.

At Compiègne the action closes with yet another scene, in which Herod learns that the *Magi* have escaped him [2].

'*Nuncius.* Delusus es domine, magi viam redierunt aliam.

[*Herodes.* incendium meum ruina extinguam [3].]

[1] Texts ed. L. Delisle, in *Romania*, iv (1875), 1. The earlier version is from *Bibl. Nat. Lat.* 9449 (†1060, a *Gradual*, or, according to Gautier, *Les Tropes*, 123, a *Troper*). The text is headed 'Versus ad Stellam faciendam.' The later is from *B. N. Lat.* 1235 (twelfth-century *Gradual*). It is headed 'Ad Comm[unionem].' Of the first part, down to the end of the interview with Herod, there are two alternative forms in this MS. The one, a free revision of the normal text, is headed:

'Sic speciem veteres stellae struxere parentes,
quatinus hos pueri versus psallant duo regi.'

[2] Text in K. A. M. Hartmann, *Über das altspanische Dreikönigsspiel* (Leipzig Diss. 1879), 43, from eleventh-century *B. N. Lat. MS.* 16,819.

[3] This line is not actually in the Compiègne text. But it is in most

Armiger. decerne, domine, vindicari iram tuam, et stricto mucrone quaerere iube puerum, forte inter occisos occidetur et ipse.

Herodes. indolis eximiae pueros fac ense perire.

Angelus. sinite parvulos venire ad me, talium est enim regnum caelorum.'

In a Norman version which has the same incidents as the Compiègne play, but in parts a different text, the *armiger* is the son of Herod, and the play ends with Herod taking a sword from a bystander and brandishing it in the air [1]. Already he is beginning to tear a passion to tatters in the manner that became traditionally connected with his name. Another peculiarity of this Norman version is that the *Magi* address Herod in an outlandish jargon, which seems to contain fragments of Hebrew and Arabic speech.

The play of the *Stella* must now, perhaps, be considered, except so far as mere amplifications of the text are concerned, strictly complete. But another step was irresistibly suggested by the course it had taken. The massacre of the Innocents, although it lay outside the range of action in which the *Magi* themselves figured, could be not merely threatened but actually represented. This was done at Laon [2]. The cruel suggestion of Archelaus is carried out. The Innocents come in singing and bearing a lamb. They are slain, and the play ends with a dialogue, like that of the distinct Limoges *planctus*, between the lamenting Rachel and an angelic *consolatrix*.

The absorption of the motives proper to other feasts of the Twelve nights into the Epiphany play has clearly begun. A fresh series of examples shows a similar treatment of the *Pastores*. At Strassburg the *Magi*, as they leave Herod, meet the shepherds returning from Bethlehem :

of the later versions of this scene, and is interesting, as being a classical tag from Sallust, *Catilina*, c. 32; cf. Köppen, 21; Creizenach, i. 63. Reminiscences of *Aeneid*, viii. 112; ix. 376, are sometimes put into Herod's mouth in the scene with the *Magi* (Du Méril, 164, 166).

[1] The version is described, but unfortunately not printed by Gasté, 53. It is from the *De ratione divini officii* in *Montpellier MS.* H. 304.

[2] Text, headed 'Ordo Stellae' in U. Chevalier, *Ordinaires de l'église de Laon*, xxxvi, 389 from *Laon MS.* 263 (thirteenth-century *Trophonarium*).

'Pastores, dicite, quidnam vidistis?
infantem vidimus.'

This, however, is not taken from the *Pastores* itself, but from the Christmas Lauds antiphon [1]. Its dramatic use may be compared with that of the *Victimae paschali* in the *Quem quaeritis*. In versions from Bilsen [2] near Liège and from Mans [3], on the other hand, although the meeting of the *Magi* and the shepherds is retained, a complete *Pastores*, with the angelic tidings and the adoration at the *praesepe*, forms the first part of the office, before the *Magi* are introduced at all.

The Strassburg, Bilsen, and Mans plays have not the *Rachel*, although the first two have the scene in which the *nuntius* informs Herod that the *Magi* have deceived him. A further stage is reached when, as at Freising and at Fleury, the *Pastores*, *Stella* and *Rachel* all coalesce in a single, and by this time considerable, drama. The Freising texts, of which there are two, are rather puzzling [4]. The first closely resembles the plays of the group just described. It begins with a short *Pastores*, comprising the angelic tidings only. Then the scenes between the *Magi* and Herod are treated at great length. The meeting of the *Magi* and the shepherds is followed by the oblation, the angelic warning, and the return of the

[1] Text printed by Lange in *Zeitsch. f. deutsch. Alterthum*, xxxii. 412, from *B. M. Add. MS.* 23,922 (*Antiphoner* of †1200). The play was 'In octava Epiphaniae' after the *Magnificat* at Vespers. The 'rex' who presided and possibly acted Herod (cf. p. 56) was, I suppose, an Epiphany king or 'rex fatuorum.'

[2] Text in C. Cahier and A. Martin, *Mélanges d'Archéologie*, i. (1847–9), 258; Clément, 113, from eleventh-century *Evangeliarium*, now in a Bollandist monastery in Brussels (Meyer, 41). It is a revision of the normal text. The author has been so industrious as even to put many of the rubrics in hexameters. The opening is

'*Ordo*. Post Benedicamus puerorum splendida coetus
ad regem pariter debent protendere gressu,
praeclara voce necnon istic resonare.'

[3] Translation only in P. Piolin, *Théâtre chrétien dans le Maine* (1891), 21. The exact source is not given.

[4] The first text in Du Méril, 156; Davidson, 174, from *Munich MS.* 6264[a] (eleventh century). Apparently it begins with a bit of dumb show, 'Rex sedens in solio quaerat consilium: exeat edictum ut pereant continuo qui detrahunt eius imperio.' Then comes 'Angelus, in primis.' Second text, headed 'Ordo Rachaelis' in Du Méril, 171; Froning, 871, from *Munich MS.* 6264 (eleventh century). It is mainly metrical.

messenger to Herod. In the second Freising text, which is almost wholly metrical, the *Pastores* is complete. It is followed by a quite new scene, the dream of Joseph and his flight into Egypt. Then come successively the scene of fury at court, the massacre, the *planctus* and consolation of Rachel. Clearly this second text, as it stands, is incomplete. The *Magi* are omitted, and the whole of the latter part of the play is consequently rendered meaningless. But it is the *Magi* who are alone treated fully in the first Freising text. I suggest, therefore, that the second text is intended to supplement and not to replace the first. It really comprises two fragments: one a revision of the *Pastores*, the other a revision of the closing scene and an expansion of it by a *Rachel*.

As to the Fleury version there can be no doubt whatever[1]. The matter is, indeed, arranged in two plays, a *Herodes* and an *Interfectio Puerorum*, each ending with a *Te Deum*; and the performance may possibly have extended over two days. But the style is the same throughout and the episodes form one continuous action. It is impossible to regard the *Interfectio Puerorum* as a separate piece from the *Herodes*, acted a week earlier on the feast of the Innocents; for into it, after the first entry of the children with their lamb, *gaudentes per monasterium*, come the flight into Egypt, the return of the *nuntius*, and the wrath of Herod, which, of course, presuppose the *Magi* scenes. Another new incident is added at the end of the Fleury play. Herod is deposed and Archelaus set up; the Holy Family return from Egypt, and settle in the parts of Galilee[2].

I have attempted to arrange the dozen or so complete Epiphany plays known to scholars in at least the logical order of their development. There are also three fragments, which fit readily enough into the system. Two, from a Paris manuscript and from Einsiedeln, may be classed respectively with the

[1] Texts in Du Méril, 162, 175; Davidson, 175; Coussemaker, 143; Wright, 32, from *Orleans MS.* 178. The first part begins with the rubric 'Parato Herode et ceteris personis . . .'; the second with 'Ad interfectionem Puerorum . . .'

[2] Wordsworth, 147, suggests that the name 'Le Galilee,' given at Lincoln to a room over the south porch and also found elsewhere, may be 'derived from some incident in the half-dramatic Paschal ceremonies.' For another liturgical drama in which 'Galilee' is required as a scene, cf. p. 60.

Compiègne and Strassburg texts [1]. The third, from Vienne, is an independent version, in leonine hexameters, of the scene in which the *Magi* first sight the star, a theme common to all the plays except that of Limoges [2]. I do not feel certain that this fragment is from a liturgical drama at all.

The textual development of the *Stella* is closely parallel to that of the *Quem quaeritis*. The more primitive versions consist of antiphons and prose sentences based upon or in the manner of the Scriptures. The later ones, doubtless under the influence of wandering scholars, become increasingly metrical. The classical tags, from Sallust and Virgil, are an obvious note of the scholarly pen. With the exception of that from Limoges, all the texts appear to be derived by successive accretions and modifications from an archetype fairly represented at Rouen. The Bilsen text and the Vienne fragment have been freely rewritten, and the process of rewriting is well illustrated by the alternative versions found side by side in the later Nevers manuscript. With regard to the place occupied by the *Stella* in the Epiphany services, such manuscripts as give any indications at all seem to point to a considerable divergence of local use. At Limoges and Nevers, the play was of the nature of a trope to the Mass, inserted in the former case at the *Offertorium*, in the latter at the *Communio* [3]. At Rouen the *Officium* followed Tierce, and preceded the ordinary procession before Mass. At Fleury the use of the *Te Deum* suggests that it was at Matins; at Strassburg it followed the *Magnificat* at Vespers, but on the octave of Epiphany, not Epiphany itself. Perhaps the second part of the Fleury play was also on the octave. At Bilsen the play followed the *Benedicamus*, but with this versicle nearly all the Hours end [4]. I do not, however, hesitate to

[1] *B.N. Lat.* 1152 (eleventh century) in *Bibl. de l'École des Chartes*, xxxiv. 657. Einsiedeln fragment (eleventh–twelfth century) printed by G. Morel in *Pilger* (1849), 401; cf. Köppen, 13.

[2] Text in Du Méril, 151, from *Vienne MS.* 941 (fourteenth century). It is entitled 'Ad adorandum filium Dei per Stellam invitantur Eoy.' The first three lines, headed 'Stella,' are an address to the 'exotica plebs'; each of the remaining ten lines is divided between three speakers, 'Aureolus,' 'Thureolus,' 'Myrrheolus.'

[3] On the use of tropes at these points in the Mass, cf. Frere, xix.

[4] *Use of Sarum*, i. 280.

say that the Limoges use must have been the most primitive one. The kernel of the whole performance is a dramatized *Offertorium*. It was a custom for Christian kings to offer gold and frankincense and myrrh at the altar on Epiphany day[1]; and I take the play to have served as a substitute for this ceremony, where no king actually regnant was present.

There is yet one other liturgical play belonging to the Christmas season, which for the future development of the drama is the most important of all. This is the *Prophetae*[2]. It differs from the *Quem quaeritis*, the *Peregrini*, the *Pastores*, and the *Stella* by the large number of performers required, and by the epical mode of its composition. Its origin, in fact, is to be sought in a narrative, a *lectio*, not a chant. The source was the pseudo-Augustinian *Sermo contra Iudaeos, Paganos et Arianos de Symbolo,* probably written in the sixth century, but ascribed throughout the Middle Ages to the great African[3]. A portion of this sermon was used in many churches as a lesson for some part or other of the Christmas offices[4]. The passage chosen is in a highly rhetorical vein. *Vos, inquam, convenio, O Iudaei* cries the preacher, and calls upon the Jews to bear witness out of the mouths of their own prophets to the Christ. Isaiah, Jeremiah, Daniel, Moses, David, Habakkuk, Simeon, Zacharias and Elisabeth, John the Baptist;—each in turn is bidden to speak, and each testimony is triumphantly quoted. Then: *Ecce, convertimur*

[1] Martene, iii. 44; in England the royal offering is still made, by proxy, at the Chapel Royal, St. James's (Ashton, 237).

[2] I follow the epoch-making *étude* of M. Sepet, *Les Prophètes du Christ*, in *Bibl. de l'École des Chartes*, xxviii. (1867), 1, 210, xxix. (1868), 205, 261, xxxviii. (1877), 397 (I am sorry not to be able to cite the separate edition printed at Paris, 1878); cf. also Creizenach, i. 67; Julleville, *Myst.* i. 35; and, especially, Weber, 41. But none of these writers could make use of the Laon version discovered by M. Chevalier. Meyer, 53, suggests that Sepet has exaggerated the importance of the *Prophetae* in the development of the O.T. dramatic cycle.

[3] Text in *P. L.* xlii. 1117; on the date cf. Weber, 41. The *lectio* is printed by Sepet, xxviii. 3.

[4] At Arles it was the sixth *lectio* at Matins on Christmas day (Sepet, xxviii. 2); at Rome the fourth lesson at Matins on Christmas eve (Martene, iii. 31); at Rouen it was read at Matins two days earlier (Martene, iii. 34); in the *Sarum Breviary*, i. cxxxv, it makes the fourth, fifth, and sixth *lectiones* at Matins on the fourth Sunday in Advent.

ad gentes. Virgil—*poeta facundissimus*—is pressed into the service, for the famous line of his fourth eclogue:

> 'iam nova progenies caelo demittitur alto[1],'

Nebuchadnezzar, who saw four walking in the furnace, and finally the Erythraean Sibyl, whose acrostic verses on the 'Signs of Judgement' first appear in the writings of Eusebius[2].

The dramatic form of this *lectio* possibly led to its being chanted instead of read, and distributed between several voices in the manner of the Passions from Palm Sunday to Good Friday[3]. At any rate in the eleventh century there appears in a Limoges manuscript a metrical adaptation in which it has been wholly converted into a dramatic dialogue[4]. This Limoges *Prophetae* follows the sermon pretty closely in its arrangement. A *Precentor* begins:

> 'Omnes gentes congaudentes, dent cantum laetitiae!
> deus homo fit, de domo David, natus hodie.'

He addresses a couplet each *Ad Iudaeos*, *Ad Gentes*, and then calls in turn upon each of the prophets, who reply, Virgil pronouncing his line, the Sibyl the *Iudicii Signum*, and the others a couplet or quatrain apiece. They are nearly identical with the personages of the sermon: Israel is added, Zacharias disappears, and the order is slightly different. Finally the *Precentor* concludes:

> 'Iudaea incredula,
> cur manens adhuc inverecunda?'

Two later versions, belonging respectively to Laon[5] and to

[1] *Bucol.* iv. 7.

[2] Eusebius, *Orat. Const. Magn. ad Sanctorum Coetum*, c. 18 (*P.G.* xx. 1288). On the *Iudicii Signum* and the *Dit des quinze Signes* (Text in Grass, *Adamsspiel*, 57) derived from it, cf. Sepet, xxviii. 8; Du Méril, 185. According to Martene, iii. 34, the *Versus Sibyllae* were often sung at Matins on Christmas day, apparently apart from the *sermo*. Thus at Limoges they were sung after the sixth *responsorium*.

[3] Sepet, xxviii. 13; cf. p. 5.

[4] Text in Du Méril, 179; Coussemaker, 11; Wright, 60; from *Bibl. Nat. Lat.* 1139 (eleventh or twelfth century). Weber, 51, gives an interesting account of the *Prophetae* in art, and points out that the play seems to have influenced such representations in Italy early in the eleventh century.

[5] Text in U. Chevalier, *Ordinaires de l'Église de Laon*, xxxvi, 385, from *Laon MS.* 263 (thirteenth century *Trophonarium*). It is headed 'Ordo Prophetarum.'

Rouen[1], diverge far more from the model. They are at much the same stage of development. In both the play is ushered in with the hymn *Gloriosi et famosi*, the verses of which are sung by the prophets, and the refrain by the choir[2]. The costumes and symbols of the prophets are carefully indicated in the rubrics. The *Precentor* of Limoges is represented by two singers, called at Laon *Appellatores*, and at Rouen *Vocatores*. The dialogue is amplified beyond that of Limoges. *Sex Iudaei* and *sex Gentiles*, for instance, take parts: and the *Vocatores* comment with the choir in an identical form of words on each prophecy. The Laon text is a good deal the shorter. The prophets are practically the same as at Limoges, with one remarkable exception. At the end is introduced Balaam, and to his prophecy is appended a miniature drama, with the angel and the ass: thus—

'*Hic veniat Angelus cum gladio. Balaam tangit asinam, et illa non praecedente, dicit iratus:*

quid moraris, asina,
obstinata bestia?
iam scindent calcaria
costas et praecordia.

Puer sub asina respondet:

[1] Text in Gasté, 4, from *Rouen MS.* Y. 110 (fourteenth-century *Ordinarium*). The opening is 'Nota, Cantor; si *Festum Asinorum* fiat, processio ordinetur post Terciam. Si non fiat Festum, tunc fiat processio, ut nunc praenotatur. Ordo *Processionis Asinorum* secundum Rothomagensem usum. Tercia cantata, paratis Prophetis iuxta suum ordinem, fornace in medio navis ecclesiae lintheo et stuppis constituta, processio moveat de claustro, et duo clerici de secunda sede, in cappis, processionem regant, hos versus canentes: *Gloriosi et famosi*. . . . Tunc processio in medio ecclesiae stet.' At the end the 'Prophetae et ministri' rule the choir. Unfortunately the MS., like other *Ordinaria*, only gives the first words of many of the chants.

[2] The *Gloriosi et famosi* hymn occurs in a twelfth-century Einsiedeln MS. (Milchsack, 36) as an overture to the *Quem quaeritis*. It is arranged for 'chorus' and 'Prophetae,' and was therefore borrowed from Christmas. It is followed by another hymn, more strictly Paschal, the *Hortum praedestinatio*, and this, which is also used with the Sens *Quem quaeritis* (Milchsack, 58), is sung at the end of the Rouen *Prophetae* by 'omnes prophetae et ministri [? = vocatores] in pulpito'—a curious double borrowing between the two feasts. Meyer, 51, argues that the Einsiedeln MS., which is in a fragmentary state, contained a *Prophetae*, to which, and not to the *Quem quaeritis*, the *Gloriosi et famosi* belonged.

angelus cum gladio,
quem adstare video,
prohibet ne transeam;
timeo ne peream.'

The Rouen text adds quite a number of prophets. The full list includes Moses, Amos, Isaiah, Aaron, Jeremiah, Daniel, Habakkuk, Balaam, Samuel, David, Hosea, Joel, Obadiah, Jonah, Micah, Nahum, Zephaniah, Haggai, Zechariah, Ezekiel, Malachi, Zacharias, Elisabeth, John the Baptist, Simeon, Virgil, Nebuchadnezzar, and the Sibyl. In this version, also, the part of Balaam is expanded into a drama.

'*Duo missi a rege Balac dicant:*
Balaam, veni et fac.
Tunc Balaam, ornatus, sedens super asinam, habens calcaria, retineat lora et calcaribus percutiat asinam, et quidam iuvenis, habens alas, tenens gladium, obstet asinae. Quidam sub asina dicat:
cur me cum calcaribus miseram sic laeditis.
Hoc dicto, Angelus ei dicat:
desine regis Balac praeceptum perficere.'

Here, too, another little drama is similarly introduced. This is the story of Shadrach, Meshach, and Abednego, which, with an *imago* for the brethren to refuse to worship and a *fornax* for them to be cast into, attaches itself to the *vocatio* of Nebuchadnezzar.

In the Limoges manuscript the *Prophetae* is followed by the words *Hic inchoant Benedicamus*[1]. As has been pointed out in the case of the Bilsen *Pastores*, this is not conclusive as to the hour at which the performance took place. The day was probably that of Christmas itself. But even the day would naturally vary with the variable position of the *lectio* out of which the *Prophetae* grew. At Lincoln it was likewise Christmas day. But at Rouen the *processio asinorum* was on Christmas eve, and took the place of the ordinary festal procession after Tierce and before Mass[2]. And at St. Martin

[1] Sepet, xxviii. 25.

[2] So says Gasté, 4. But I think he must be wrong, for the *Introit* with which the text concludes is *Puer natus est*, which belongs to the *Magna missa* of the feast-day, and not to the eve.

of Tours the *Prophetae* was on New Year's day, performances being given both at Matins and Vespers [1].

The question naturally suggests itself: What was the relation of these liturgical plays of the Christmas season to the Feast of Fools and other ecclesiastical *ludi* of the Twelve nights, which were discussed in the first volume? At Rouen, the *Prophetae* received the name of *processio asinorum* and took place at a *festum asinorum*, a name which we know to have been elsewhere synonymous with *festum fatuorum*. At Tours, it was played at a reformed *festum novi anni*, with a Boy Bishop and at least traces of expelled disorder. So, too, with the other plays. The Rouen *Pastores* was infected by the fifteenth century with the *stultitiae et insolentiae* of the *triduum*. At Bilsen the *Stella* was performed before a *rex*, who can hardly have been any other than a *rex fatuorum* of Epiphany. At Autun the *regnum Herodis* was considered a Feast of Fools [2]. Probably in both churches the *rex* acted Herod in the play. I think it must be taken for granted that the plays are the older institution of the two. They seem all to have taken shape by the eleventh century, before there is any clear sign that the Kalends had made their way into the churches and become the Feast of Fools. The plays may even have been encouraged as a counter-attraction, for the congregation, to the Kalends outside. On the other hand, I do not hold, as some writers do, that the riotous Feasts of Asses were derived from the pious and instructive ceremony so called at Rouen [3]. On the contrary, Balaam and his ass are an interpolation in the *Prophetae* both at Rouen

[1] Martene, iii. 41, from a fourteenth-century *Rituale*: 'dicto versiculo tertii nocturni, accenditur totum luminare, et veniunt Prophetae in capitulo revestiti, et post cantant insimul *Lumen Patris*, et clericus solus dicit *In gaudio*, et post legitur septima lectio. Post nonam lectionem ducunt prophetas de capitulo ad portam Thesaurarii cantilenas cantando, et post in chorum, ubi dicunt cantori prophetias, et duo clericuli in pulpito cantando eos appellant. Post dicitur nonum [responsorium?] in pulpito...... Post [primam] recitatur miraculum [Martene conjectures *martyrologium*] in claustro ... [Ad vesperas] dictis psalmis et antiphonis, ducunt ad portam Thesaurarii prophetas, sicut ad matutinum et reducunt in chorum similiter, et habent clerici virgas plenas candelis ardentibus, vocant eos clerici duo sicut ad vesperas [? matutinum].' Presently follows the *Deposuit*: cf. vol. i. p. 309.

[2] Cf. vol. i. p. 313.

[3] Gasté, 20.

and, more obviously, at Laon. Balaam, alone of the Laon performers, is not from the pseudo-Augustine sermon. Is he not, therefore, to be regarded as a reaction of the Feast of Fools upon the *Prophetae*, as an attempt to turn the established presence of the ass in the church to purposes of edification, rather than of ribaldry[1]? I think the explanation is the more plausible one. And I find a parallel reaction of the turbulence of the Feast of Fools upon the *Stella*, in the violence of speech and gesture which permanently associated itself at a very early stage with the character of Herod. The view here taken will be confirmed, when we come to consider certain ecclesiastical criticisms passed upon the liturgical plays in the twelfth century.

Whatever the exact relation of the divine and profane *ludi* at Easter and Christmas may be, it seems to have been, in the main, at these two great seasons of festivity that what may be called the spontaneous growth of drama out of liturgy took place. There are yet a fair number of Latin plays to be spoken of which are in a sense liturgical. That is to say, they were acted, certainly or probably, in churches and during intervals in the services. But of these such a spontaneous growth cannot be asserted, although it cannot also, in the present state of the evidence, be confidently denied. Their metrical and literary style is parallel to that of the Easter and Christmas plays in the latest stages of development; and, until further data turn up, it is perhaps permissible to conjecture that they were deliberately composed on the model of the *Quem quaeritis* and the *Stella*, when these had become widespread and popular. Indeed, some such derivation of the *Peregrini* from the *Quem quaeritis* and of the *Stella* itself, at least in part, from the *Pastores*, has already appeared probable.

In dealing with this new group of plays, we come, for the first and only time, upon an individual author. As might be expected, this author is a *scholaris vagans*, by name Hilarius.

[1] Sepet, xxviii. 219, suggests that Balaam, when first introduced into the *Prophetae*, merely prophesied, as he does in the *Adam* (Grass, 46). Possibly, yet his introduction at the end of the Laon play (unknown to Sepet) looks as if he were an appendix for the sake of his ass.

It would even be doing him no great injustice to call him a goliard. What little is known of Hilarius is gathered from his writings, which exist in a single manuscript. He may have been an Englishman, for a large proportion of his verses are addressed to English folk. He was a pupil, about 1125, of the famous Abelard at his oratory of Paraclete in a desert near Nogent-sur-Seine. Afterwards he made his way to Angers. Many of his verses are of the familiar goliardic type, amorous and jocund; but amongst them are three plays[1]. Two of these are comparatively short, and contain each a few stanzas of French interspersed amongst the Latin. The subject of one is a miracle wrought by St. Nicholas[2]; of the other, the *Suscitatio Lazari*[3]. The third play, wholly in Latin, falls into two parts, and gives at considerable length the story of *Daniel*[4]. I take it that these plays were not written for any church in particular, but represent the repertory of a band of wandering clerks. At the end, both of the *Daniel* and of the *Suscitatio Lazari*, is a rubric or stage-direction, to the effect that, if the performance is given at Matins, the *Te Deum* should follow; if at Vespers, the *Magnificat*. Evidently the connexion with the church service, so organic in the plays of the more primitive type, has become for Hilarius almost accidental. As to the place of the plays in the calendar, the manuscript gives no indication, and probably Hilarius and his friends would be willing enough to act them whenever they got a chance. But the St. Nicholas

[1] Champollion-Figeac, *Hilarii Versus et Ludi* (1838), from *B. N. Lat. MS.* 11,331. The plays are also printed by Du Méril, *Or. Lat.* On the life cf. *Hist. Litt. de la France*, xx. 627; *D.N.B.* s.v. Hilary; Morley, *English Writers*, iii. 107.

[2] Du Méril, 272 'Ludus super iconia Sancti Nicolai.' There is a 'persona iconie.' A *Barbarus* speaks partly in French.

[3] Du Méril, 225 'Suscitatio Lazari: ad quam istae personae sunt necessariae: Persona Lazari, duarum Sororum, quatuor Iudaeorum, Iesu Christi, duodecim Apostolorum, vel sex ad minus . . . (ends). Quo finito, si factum fuerit ad Matutinas, Lazarus in piat: *Te Deum laudamus*: si vero ad Vesperas: *Magnificat anima mea Dominum.*'

[4] Du Méril, 241 'Historia de Daniel repraesentanda,' with a list of the 'personae necessariae' and a final rubric as in the 'Suscitatio Lazari': cf. Sepet, xxviii. 232, on this and similar plays and their relation to the *Prophetae*. From the names 'Hilarius,' 'Iordanus,' 'Simon,' attached to parts of the *Daniel* in the MS., it would seem that Hilarius had collaborators for this play (Sepet, xxviii. 248).

play would come most naturally on the day of that saint, December 6. The *Suscitatio Lazari* would be appropriate enough as an addition to the *Quem quaeritis* and the *Peregrini* in Easter week. The story is told, indeed, in the Gospel for Friday in the fourth week in Lent; but that does not seem a very likely date for a play. The *Daniel* perhaps grew, as we have seen a *Balaam* and a *Nebuchadnezzar* growing, out of a *Prophetae*; and may have been a substitute for a *Prophetae* at Christmas.

These dates are borne out, or not contradicted, by other similar plays, which have more of a local habitation. For no one of Hilarius' three stands quite alone. Of Latin plays of St. Nicholas, indeed, quite a little group exists; and the great scholastic feast evidently afforded an occasion, less only than Easter and Christmas, for dramatic performances. The earliest texts are from Germany. Two are found in a Hildesheim manuscript of the eleventh century[1]; a third in an Einsiedeln manuscript of the twelfth[2]. The thirteenth-century Fleury playbook contains no less than four, two of which appear to be more developed forms of the Hildesheim plays. The theme is in every case one of the miraculous deeds which so largely make up the widespread legend of the saint[3]. Nicholas restores to life the three clerks

'quos causa discendi literas
apud gentes transmisit exteras,'

and whom the greed of an innkeeper has slain[4]. He provides with a dowry the daughters of a poor gentleman, who are threatened with a life of shame[5]. He brings back from captivity the son of his wealthy adorer[6]. His image preserves

[1] E. Dümmler, in *Z. f. d. Alterthum*, xxxv. 401; xxxvi. 238, from *B. M. Addl. MS.* 22,414 ('Liber Sancti Godehardi in Hild[esheim]'). On the group of Nicholas plays cf. Creizenach, i. 105.

[2] G. Morel, in *Anzeiger für Kunde der deutschen Vorzeit*, vi. (1859), 207, from *Einsiedeln MS.* 34.

[3] *Golden Legend*, ii. 109; Wace, *Vie de Saint-Nicolas* (ed. Delius, 1850).

[4] Du Méril, 262; Coussemaker, 100. The play ends with the *Te Deum*. The same subject is treated in the Einsiedeln play, and one of those from Hildesheim.

[5] Du Méril, 254; Coussemaker, 83. The play ends with the anthem 'O Christi pietas,' used at second Vespers on St. Nicholas' day (*Sarum Breviary*, iii. 38). The same subject is treated in the other Hildesheim play.

[6] Du Méril, 276; Coussemaker, 123; begins 'Ad repraesentandum

from housebreakers the riches of a Jew[1]. Alone of the extant Latin plays, these of St. Nicholas are drawn from outside the Biblical story. Each of the Fleury versions introduces at the end one of the anthems proper to St. Nicholas' day, and their connexion with the feast is therefore clear.

A second Lazarus play, which includes not only the *Suscitatio* but also the episode of Mary Magdalen in the house of Simon, is likewise in the Fleury playbook[2]. A second *Daniel*, composed by the *iuventus* of Beauvais, occurs in the same manuscript which contains the Office of the Circumcision for that cathedral[3]. It was perhaps intended for performance on the day of the *asinaria festa.* Other plays seem, in the same way as the *Daniel*, to have budded off from the *Prophetae.* A fragment is preserved of an *Isaac and Rebecca* from Kloster Vorau in Styria[4]. A twelfth-century mention of an *Elisaeus*[5] and an eleventh-century one of a *Convivium Herodis*[6], which suggests rather the story of John the Baptist than that of the *Magi*, point to an activity in this direction of which all the traces have possibly not yet been discovered.

quomodo Sanctus Nicolaus, &c....': ends with anthem 'Copiosae caritatis' used at Lauds on St. Nicholas' day (*Sarum Breviary*, iii. 37).

[1] Du Méril, 266; Coussemaker, 109; begins 'Aliud miraculum de Sancto Nicolao, &c. . . .': ends with anthem 'Statuit ei Dominus,' not in *Sarum Breviary*, but used at Rome as *Introit* on feasts of Pontiffs. This is the subject of Hilarius' play.

[2] Text in Du Méril, 213; Coussemaker, 220. The play contains a Paschal sequence and ends with a *Te Deum.* Part of the action is in a *platea*; Simon has a *domus*, which afterwards 'efficiatur quasi Bethania.' Other 'loci' represent 'Ierusalem' and 'Galilaea' (cf. p. 50), and the 'Suscitatio' takes place at a 'monumentum' (probably the Easter sepulchre).

[3] Text in Coussemaker, 49, and Danjou, *Revue de la Musique religieuse*, iv. (1848), 65. Cf. Sepet, xxviii. 232, and on the MS., vol. i. p. 284. As in the Beauvais *Officium Circumcisionis*, there are many processional chants or *conductus*, in one of which are the terms 'celebremus Natalis solempnia' and 'in hoc Natalitio' which attach the play to Christmas, or at least the Christmas season. The text begins 'Incipit Danielis ludus,' and ends with the *Te Deum.* The following quatrain serves as prologue:

'Ad honorem tui, Christe,
Danielis ludus iste
in Belvaco est inventus
et invenit hunc iuventus.'

Meyer, 56, finds relations between the Beauvais *Daniel* and that of *Hilarius.*

[4] Text in *Anzeiger für Kunde d. deutschen Vorzeit* (1877), 169, from late twelfth-century MS.; cf. Creizenach, i. 74.

[5] Cf. p. 99.

[6] Creizenach, i. 6, 71. The unauthentic *Annales* of Corvei mention also a play on *Joseph* under the year 1264 (Creizenach, i. 75).

Three plays, each more or less unique in character, complete the tale. The Fleury playbook has a *Conversio Beati Pauli Apostoli*, doubtless designed for the feast on January 25[1]. The shorter, but highly interesting collection from Limoges, has a play of the wise and foolish virgins, under the title of *Sponsus*[2]. This has attracted much attention from scholars, on account of the fact that it is partly in French, or more strictly in a dialect belonging to the Angoumois, and slightly affected by Provençal. As it is therefore of the nature of a transitional form, it may be well to give a somewhat full account of it. It opens with a Latin chorus beginning

'Adest sponsus qui est Christus: vigilate, virgines!'

The angel Gabriel then addresses the virgins, and warns them in four French stanzas to expect 'un espos, Sauvaire a nom.' Each stanza has a refrain, probably sung chorally:

'gaire noi dormet:
aici 's l'espos que vos or atendet!

Then comes a lyric dialogue, in which the *Fatuae*, who have wasted their oil, attempt in vain to get some, first from the *Prudentes*, and then from some *Mercatores*, whose presence here recalls the *unguentarius* in the Prague versions of the *Quem quaeritis*[3]. This dialogue is in Latin, but with a French refrain:

'dolentas, chaitivas, trop i avem (*or* avet) dormit.'

[1] Text in Du Méril, 237; Coussemaker, 210; begins 'Ad repraesentandam conversionem beati Pauli apostoli, &c....': ends with *Te Deum*. Four 'sedes' are required, and a 'lectus' for Ananias.

[2] Latest text, with long introduction, mainly philological, by W. Cloetta, in *Romania*, xxii. (1893), 177; others by Du Méril, 233; Coussemaker, 1; E. Boehmer, in *Romanische Studien*, iv. 99; K. Bartsch, *Lang. et Litt. françaises*, 13; cf. also Julleville, *Les Myst.* i. 27; E. Stengel, *Z. f. rom. Phil.* iii. 233; E. Schwan, *Z. f. rom. Phil.* xi. 469; H. Morf, *Z. f. rom. Phil.* xx. 385. The manuscript is *Bibl. Nat. Lat.* 1139. MM. Cloetta (p. 221) and G. Paris (*Litt. fr. au moyen âge*[2], 237, 246) assign the *Sponsus* to the earlier half or second third of the twelfth century, and the former, with the delightful diffidence of a philologist, thinks, on linguistic grounds, that it was written at Saint Amant de Boixe (sixteen *kilomètres* north of Angoulême). It only remains for some archivist to find a clerk of St. Martial of Limoges whose native place was this very village.

[3] Cf. p. 33.

Then comes the *Sponsus*, to whom the *Fatuae* finally appeal:

'audi, sponse, voces plangentium:
aperire fac nobis ostium
cum sociis ad dulce prandium;
nostrae culpae praebe remedium!
dolentas, chaitivas, trop i avem dormit.

Christus.

amen dico, vos ignosco, nam caretis lumine,
quod qui perdunt procul pergunt huius aulae limine.
alet, chaitivas, alet, malaüreias!
a tot jors mais vos son penas livreias,
e en efern ora seret meneias!

Modo accipiant eas daemones et praecipitentur in infernum.'

This stage direction, together with an allusion in the opening lines of the *Sponsus* to the 'second Adam,' link this remarkable, and, I venture to think, finely conceived little piece to the Christmas play of *Adam* to be discussed in the next chapter. It has essentially an Advent theme, and must have been performed either in Advent itself or at the Christmas season, with which Advent is prophetically connected [1].

Finally, there is a play which was almost certainly performed at Advent [2]. This is the Tegernsee play of *Antichristus* [3]. It is founded upon the prophecy in St. Paul's second epistle to the Thessalonians of the *homo peccati*, *filius perditionis*, who shall sit in the temple of God until the Christ shall slay him with the breath of his mouth, and destroy him with the glory of his advent [4]: and it is an elaborate spectacle, requiring for

[1] H. Morf, *loc. cit.*, considers the *Sponsus* an Easter play.

[2] Creizenach, i. 77. An Italian dramatic *Lauda* on the same subject is headed 'In Dominica de Adventu' (D'Ancona, i. 141).

[3] Text in Froning, 206, from edition of Zezschwitz, *Vom römischen Kaisertum deutscher Nation* (1877). The earliest edition is by Pez, *Thesaurus Anecd. Noviss.* (1721-9), ii. 3, 187. This writer introduced confusion by giving the play the title *Ludus paschalis de adventu et interitu Antichristi*. It has nothing to do with Easter. The latest and best edition is that by W. Meyer, in *Sitzungsberichte d. hist.-phil. Classe d. königl. bayr. Akad. d. Wiss.* (Munich), 1882, I. The unique MS. is *Munich MS.* 19,411 (twelfth-thirteenth century), formerly in Kloster Tegernsee. Both Zezschwitz and Meyer have long and valuable introductions; cf. also Froning, 199; Creizenach, i. 78. T. Wright prints the play from Pez, in *Chester Plays*, ii. 227.

[4] 2 *Thessalonians*, ii. 3-12. According to *York Missal*, i. 10, part

its proper performance a large number of actors and a spacious stage, with a temple of God and seven royal *sedes*, together with room for much marching and counter-marching and warfare[1]. It must have taken up the whole nave of some great church. It begins with a procession of Emperor, Pope, and Kings, accompanied by personages emblematic of *Gentilitas*, *Sinagoga* and *Ecclesia* with her attendants *Misericordia* and *Iustitia*. The first part of the action represents the conquest of the four corners of Christendom by the Emperor and his championship of Jerusalem against the King of Babylon. *Ecclesia*, *Gentilitas*, and *Synagoga* punctuate the performance with their characteristic chants. Then come the Hypocrites, *sub silentio et specie humilitatis inclinantes circumquaque et captantes favorem laicorum*. They are followed by Antichrist himself, who instructs Hypocrisy and Heresy to prepare the way for his advent. Presently Antichrist is enthroned in the temple and gradually saps the Empire, winning over the King of the Greeks by threats, the King of the Franks by gifts, and the King of the Teutons, who is incorruptible and invincible, by signs and wonders. He marks his vassals on the brow with the first letter of his name. Then the Hypocrites attempt to persuade *Synagoga* that Antichrist is the Messiah; but are refuted by the prophets Enoch and Elijah. Antichrist has the rebels slain; but while he is throned in state, thunder breaks suddenly over his head, he falls, and *Ecclesia* comes to her own again with a *Laudem dicite deo nostro*.

The author of the *Antichristus* is not only a skilled craftsman in rhyming Latin metres; he is also capable of carrying a big literary scheme successfully to a close. His immediate source was probably the tenth-century *Libellus de Antichristo*

of this passage is read at Mass on Saturday in the *Quatuor Tempora* of Advent.

[1] 'Templum domini et vii sedes regales primum collocentur in hunc modum:
Ad orientem templum domini; huic collocantur sedes regis Hierosolimorum et sedes Sinagogae.
Ad occidentem sedes imperatoris Romani; huic collocantur sedes regis Theotonicorum et sedes regis Francorum.
Ad austrum sedes regis Graecorum.
Ad meridiem sedes regis Babiloniae et Gentilitatis.'
Other than this direction the play has no heading, but in later stage-directions it is incidentally called a 'ludus.'

of Adso of Toul[1]. Into this he has worked the central theme of the *Prophetae* and the debating figures from that very popular *débat* or 'estrif,' the *Altercatio Ecclesiae et Synagogae*[2]. His work differs in several obvious respects from the comparatively simple, often naive, liturgical dramas which have been considered. It is ambitious in scope, extending to between four and five hundred lines. It introduces allegorical figures, such as we shall find, long after, in the moralities. It has a purpose other than that of devotion, or even amusement. It is, in fact, a *Tendenzschrift*, a pamphlet. The instinct of the drama, which sways the imaginations of men perhaps more powerfully than any other form of literature, to mix itself up with politics is incorrigible: *Antichristus* is a subtle vindication, on the one hand, of the Empire against the Papacy, on the other of the *rex Teutonicorum* against the *rex Francorum*. It probably dates from about 1160, when Frederick Barbarossa was at the height of his struggle with Alexander III, who enjoyed the sympathies of Louis VII of France. And it is anti-clerical. The Hypocrites who carry out the machinations of Antichrist are the clerical reformers, such as Gerhoh of Reichersberg[3], who were the mainstay of the papacy in Germany.

It is improbable that the few and scattered texts which have come to light represent all the liturgical plays which had made their appearance by the middle of the twelfth century. Besides the lost *Elisaeus* and *Convivium Herodis*, there is evidence, for example, of scholars' plays in honour, not only of St. Nicholas, but of their second patron, the philosophical St. Catharine of Alexandria. Such a *ludus de Sancta Katarina* was prepared at Dunstable in England by one Geoffrey, a Norman clerk who had been invited to England as schoolmaster to the abbey of St. Albans. For it he borrowed certain

[1] Printed in *P. L.* ci. 1291.

[2] Pseudo-Augustine, *De altercatione Ecclesiae et Synagogae dialogus* in *P. L.* xlii. 1131. On this theme and the *débats* based thereon cf. *Hist. Litt.* xxiii. 216; G. Paris, § 155; Pearson, ii. 376. P. Weber, *Geistliches Schauspiel und kirchliche Kunst* (1894), is mainly occupied with this motive and its place in the religious drama and religious art. It is a most valuable study, but I find no ground for the conjecture (Weber, 31, 36) that the *Altercatio*, like the *Prophetae*, had already, before the *Antichrist*, been semi-dramatically rendered in the liturgy.

[3] Cf. p. 98.

choir copes belonging to the abbey, and had the misfortune to let these be burnt with his house. Deeply repentant, he took the religious habit, and in 1119 became abbot of St. Albans. From this date that of the *ludus* may be judged to be early in the twelfth century[1].

It cannot, of course, be assumed that every play, say in the fifteenth century, which although probably or certainly written in the vernacular was performed in a church, had a Latin prototype[2]. Many such may have been written and acted for the first time on existing models, when the vernacular drama was already well established. But there are certain feasts where it is possible to trace, on the one hand, the element of mimetic ceremony in the services, and on the other, perhaps, some later representation in the dramatic cycles, and where a Latin text might at any time turn up without causing surprise. With a few notes on some of these this chapter must conclude. A highly dramatic trope for Ascension day, closely resembling the *Quem quaeritis*, has already been quoted from the tropers of Limoges[3]. An *Ordinarium* of St. Peter's of Lille directs that, after the respond *Non vos relinquam*, the officiant shall mount a pulpit and thence appear to ascend towards heaven from the top of a mountain[4]. Fifteenth-century *computi* speak of this or of a more elaborate performance as a *mysterium*, and include amongst other items payments for painting the scars on the hands of the performer[5]. On Whit-

[1] *Representations*, s.v. Dunstable.

[2] At Rouen, e.g., a confraternity played a *misterium* on the feast of the Assumption in a waxen 'hortus' set up in their chapel; and this between 1446 and 1521 required reformation from various 'derisiones,' especially a 'ludus de marmousetis' (Gasté, 76). But I know of no evidence for a Latin Assumption play, although such may quite well have existed. The Lincoln Assumption play was given in the cathedral, as a wind-up to a cycle (*Representations*, s.v. Lincoln).

[3] Cf. p. 11.

[4] Ducange, s.v. *Festum Ascensionis*, 'qui . . . officio hac die praeerat, cum modicum panis et vini degustasset, cantato responsorio *Non vos relinquam*, ambonem ascendebat, ubi ex monte efficto coelum petere videbatur; tunc pueri symphoniaci veste angelica induti decantabant *Viri Galilaei*, etc.'

[5] Julleville, *Les Myst.* ii. 9; *Annales archéologiques*, xviii. 173 'pro pingendo cicatrices in manibus D. Iohannis Rosnel, facientis mysterium in die Ascensionis' (1416), 'pro potandum cum discipulis,' 'vicariis representantibus Crucifixum cum suis discipulis et ibidem simul manducantibus et bibentibus vinum,' 'pro pingendo vulnera,' 'pro faciendo novas nubes,' 'pro pictura dictarum nubium,' 'pro cantando non vos.' In Germany (Naogeorgos

Sunday it was the custom at St. Paul's in London and many other churches, during the singing of the hymn *Veni Creator Spiritus* at Tierce, to open a hole in the roof and let down symbols of the Pentecost; a dove, a globe of fire, bits of burning tow to represent tongues of fire, a censer, flowers, pieces of flaky pastry [1]. This same hole in the roof sometimes served a similar purpose at a mimetic representation of the Annunciation. The Gospel for the day was recited by two clerks dressed as Mary and the angel, and at the words *Spiritus Sanctus supervenit in te* a white dove descended from the roof. This can hardly be called a drama, for, with the exception of a short fifteenth-century text from Cividale, only the words of the Gospel itself seem to have been used; but obviously it is on the extreme verge of drama. A curious variant in the date of this ceremony is to be noted. In several

in Stubbes, i. 337) the crucifix was drawn up by cords and an image of Satan thrown down. For England, see the end of Lambarde's account, below.

[1] Grenier, 388 (Amiens, 1291, and elsewhere in Picardy); Hautcœur, *Documents liturgiques de Lille*, 65 (thirteenth century), and *Histoire de l'Église de Lille*, i. 427; Gasté, 75 (Bayeux, thirteenth century, Caen, Coutances); D'Ancona, i. 31 (Parma), i. 88 (Vicenza, 1379, a more elaborate out-of-door performance); Naogeorgos in Stubbes, i. 337 (Germany); Ducange, s.v. *nebulae*. I have three English examples: Hone, *E. D. Book*, i. 685 (*Computus* of St. Patrick's, Dublin, for 1509), 'we have iv[s] vii[d] paid to those playing with the great and little angel and the dragon; iii[s] paid for little cords employed about the Holy Ghost; iv[s] vi[d] for making the angel censing (*thurificantis*), and ii[s] ii[d] for cords of it—all on the feast of Pentecost'; *Lincoln Statutes*, i. 335; ii. cxviii. 165 (1330) 'in distributione autem Pentecostali percipiet . . . clericus ducens columbam vj denarios'; W. Lambarde, *Alphabetical Description of the Chief Places in England and Wales* (1730, written in sixteenth century), 459, s.v. Wytney, 'The like Toye I myselfe (beinge then a Chyld) once saw in *Poules* Church at *London*, at a Feast of *Whitsontyde*, wheare the comynge downe of the *Holy Gost* was set forthe by a white Pigion, that was let to fly out of a Hole, that yet is to be sene in the mydst of the Roofe of the great Ile, and by a longe Censer, which descendinge out of the same Place almost to the verie Grounde, was swinged up and downe at suche a Lengthe, that it reached with thone Swepe almost to the West Gate of the Churche, and with the other to the Quyre Staires of the same, breathynge out over the whole Churche and Companie a most pleasant Perfume of suche swete Thinges as burned thearin; with the like doome Shewes also, they used every whear to furnishe sondrye Partes of their Churche Service, as by their Spectacles of the Nativitie, Passion, and Ascension of *Christe*.' From further notices in W. S. Simpson, *St. Paul's and Old City Life*, 62, 83, it appears that the censing was on Monday, Tuesday, and Wednesday in Whitweek, that the Lord Mayor attended, and that the ceremony was replaced by sermons in 1548.

Italian examples, of which the earliest dates from 1261, and in one or two from France, it belongs to the feast of the Annunciation proper on March 25[1]. But in later French examples, and apparently also at Lincoln[2], it has been transferred to the Advent season, during which naturally the Annunciation was greatly held in remembrance, and has been attached to the so-called 'golden' Mass celebrated ten days before Christmas during the *Quatuor Tempora*[3]. It thus became absorbed into the Christmas dramatic cycle.

[1] Creizenach, i. 76; D'Ancona, i. 90, 92, 114 (Padua, Venice, Trevigi), and i. 29 (Parma *Ordinarium* of fifteenth century) 'ad inducendum populum ad contritionem, . . . ad confirmandum ipsum in devotione Virginis Mariae . . . fit reverenter et decenter Repraesentatio Virginis Mariae . . . cum prophetis et aliis solemnitatibus opportunis'; Coussemaker, 280 (Cividale *Processionalia* of fourteenth and fifteenth centuries). In the fourteenth century there was a procession to the market-place, where 'diaconus legat evangelium in tono, et fit repraesentatio Angeli ad Mariam.' In the fifteenth century 'In Annuntiatione B. M. Virginis Repraesentatio' was a similar procession and 'cantatur evangelium cum ludo, quo finito, revertendo ad ecclesiam, cantatur Te Deum.' The text goes slightly beyond the words of the Gospel (Luke i. 26–38) having a part for 'Helisabeth.' Gasté, 79, describes the foundation of a *mystère* of the Annunciation during vespers on the eve of the feast at Saint-Lo, in 1521.

[2] I gather this from the *consuetudo* of giving gloves to Mary, the Angel, and the Prophets at Christmas (*Representations*, s.v. Lincoln). Here, as at Parma, the *Prophetae* appear in connexion with the Annunciation ceremony.

[3] See the curious and detailed document in Appendix S as to the Tournai ceremony founded by Peter Cotrel in the sixteenth century. A precisely similar foundation was that of Robert Fabri at Saint Omer in 1543 (*Bull. arch. du Comité des travaux historiques* (1886), 80; *Mém. de la Soc. des Antiquaires de la Morinie*, xx. 207). The inventory of the 'ornementz et parementz' in a 'coffre de cuir boully' includes 'ung colomb de bois revestu de damas blancq.' Alike at Tournai, St. Omer, and Besançon (Martene, iii. 30) the ceremony was on the Wednesday in the *Quatuor Tempora* of Advent. For the 'golden Mass' of this day the Gospel is the same as that of the Annunciation; cf. *York Missal*, i. 6; Pfannenschmidt, 438.

CHAPTER XX

THE SECULARIZATION OF THE PLAYS

[*Bibliographical Note.*—The best general account of the vernacular religious drama of Europe is that of W. Creizenach, *Geschichte des neueren Dramas* (vol. i. 1893), Books 2–4; and this may be supplemented by K. Hase, *Das geistliche Schauspiel* (1858, trans. A. W. Jackson, 1880); R. Proelss, *Geschichte des neueren Dramas* (1880–3), vol. i. ch. 1; C. Davidson, *English Mystery Plays* (1892), and G. Gregory Smith, *The Transition Period* (1900), ch. 7. There is also the cumbrous work of J. L. Klein, *Geschichte des Dramas* (1865–86). The nearest approach to a general bibliography is F. H. Stoddard, *References for Students of Miracle Plays and Mysteries* (1887).—For Germany may be added R. Froning, *Das Drama des Mittelalters* (1890–1); K. Pearson, *The German Passion Play* (in *The Chances of Death and Other Studies in Evolution*, 1897, vol. ii); L. Wirth, *Die Oster- und Passionsspiele bis zum 16. Jahrhundert* (1889); J. E. Wackernell, *Altdeutsche Passionsspiele aus Tirol*, 1897; R. Heinzel, *Beschreibung des geistlichen Schauspiels im deutschen Mittelalter* (1898), and the articles by F. Vogt on *Mittelhochdeutsche Literatur*, § 73, and H. Jellinghaus on *Mittelniederdeutsche Literatur*, § 5, in H. Paul, *Grundriss der germanischen Philologie*, vol. ii (2nd ed. 1901). F. Vogt gives a few additional recent references. Older works are F. J. Mone, *Schauspiele des Mittelalters* (1846); H. Reidt, *Das geistliche Schauspiel des Mittelalters in Deutschland* (1868), and E. Wilken, *Geschichte der geistlichen Spiele in Deutschland* (1872). Many of the books named print texts. Lists of others are given by Pearson and by Heinzel, and full bibliographical notices by K. Goedeke, *Grundriss zur Geschichte der deutschen Dichtung* (2nd ed.), vol. i (1884), §§ 67, 92, and vol. ii (1886), § 145.—For France, L. Petit de Julleville, *Les Mystères* (1880), is excellent and exhaustive, and contains many bibliographical references, although the 'Liste des ouvrages à consulter' intended as part of the work seems never to have been printed. M. de Julleville is also the writer of the article on *Théâtre religieux* in the *Hist. de la Langue et de la Littérature françaises*, vol. ii (1896). G. Gröber's article on *Französische Litteratur*, §§ 129, 362 in his *Grundriss der romanischen Philologie*, vol. ii (1901–2), brings the subject up to date and adds some recent authorities. Mortensen, *Medeltidsdramat i Frankrike* (1899), is beyond my range. G. Paris, *La Littérature française au moyen âge* (2nd ed., 1890), is a brief summary, and L. Clédat, *Le Théâtre au moyen âge* (1897), a useful popular account. G. Bapst, *Essai sur l'Histoire du Théâtre* (1893), is good on matters of stage arrangement. Older works are O. Le Roy, *Études sur les Mystères* (1837), and J. de Douhet, *Dictionnaire des Mystères* (1854). Only fragments of C. Magnin's investigations are available in the *Journal des Savants* (1846–7) and the *Journal général de l'Instruction publique* (1834–6). Texts are in A. Jubinal, *Mystères du 15e siècle* (1837); Monmerqué et Michel, *Théâtre français au moyen âge* (1842); E. Fournier, *Le Théâtre français avant la Renaissance* (1872), and the series published by the *Société des Anciens Textes français*. The most recent text of *Adam* is that by K. Grass, *Das Adamsspiel* (1891). M. Wilmotte, *Les Passions allemandes du Rhin dans leur Rapport avec l'ancien Théâtre français* (1898), deals with the interrelations of the French and German texts. C. Hastings, *Le Théâtre français et anglais* (1900, trans.1901), is a compilation of little merit.—For Italy there is A. D'Ancona, *Origini del Teatro italiano* (2nd ed. 1891), with texts in the same writer's *Sacre Rappresentazioni* (1872), in Monaci, *Appunti per la Storia del Teatro italiano* (*Rivista di Filologia Romana*, vols. i, ii), and in F. Torraca, *Il Teatro italiano dei Secoli xiii, xiv, e xv* (1885).—For Spain, A. F. von Schack, *Geschichte der dramatischen Litteratur und Kunst in Spanien* (1845–54), and G. Baist, *Spanische Litteratur*, §§ 19, 63, in Gröber's *Grundriss*, vol. ii (1897).—For the minor Romance dramatic literatures, Provençal, Catalan, Portuguese, I must be content to refer to the last-named authority, and for that of Holland to the similar *Grundriss* of H. Paul.]

THE evolution of the liturgic play described in the last two chapters may be fairly held to have been complete about the middle of the thirteenth century. The condition of any further advance was that the play should cease to be liturgic. The following hundred years are a transition period. During their course the newly-shaped drama underwent a process which, within the limits imposed by the fact that its subject-matter remained essentially religious, may be called secularization. Already, when Hilarius could write plays to serve indifferently for use at Matins or at Vespers, the primitive relation of *repraesentatio* to liturgy had been sensibly weakened. By the middle of the fourteenth century it was a mere survival. From ecclesiastical the drama had become popular. Out of the hands of the clergy in their naves and choirs, it had passed to those of the laity in their market-places and guild-halls. And to this formal change corresponded a spiritual or literary one, in the reaction of the temper of the folk upon the handling of the plays, the broadening of their human as distinct from their religious aspect. In their origin *officia* for devotion and edification, they came, by an irony familiar to the psychologist, to be primarily *spectacula* for mirth, wonder, and delight.

It is, however, the formal change with which I am here mainly concerned; and of this it will be the object of the present chapter to trace as briefly as possible the outlines. The principal factor is certainly that tendency to expansion and coalescence in the plays which has been already seen at work in the production of such elaborate pieces as the *Quem quaeritis* of the Tours or that of the Benedictbeuern manuscript, the Fleury *Stella*, the Rouen *Prophetae* and the *Antichristus*. This culminates in the formation of those great dramatic cycles of which the English Corpus Christi plays are perhaps the most complete examples. But before we can approach these, we must consider a little further the independent development of the Easter and Christmas groups.

It is noteworthy that, during the period now under discussion, the importance of Christmas falls markedly into the background when compared with that of Easter; and a reason for this will presently suggest itself. The *Stella*, indeed, as such, appears to have almost reached its term [1]; for such further growth as there is we must look chiefly to the *Prophetae*. The process by which little episodic dramas, as of Balaam and Nebuchadnezzar at Rouen, bud out from the stem of the *Prophetae*, is one capable of infinite extension. By 1204 the play had found its way to Riga, on the extreme border of European civilization, and the *ludus prophetarum ordinatissimus* there performed included scenes from the wars of Gideon, David, and Herod [2]. The text of the Riga play is unfortunately not preserved, but the famous Norman-French *Ordo repraesentationis Adae* is an example of a *Prophetae*, in which the episodes, no longer confined to the stories of the prophets in the stricter sense, have outgrown and cast into the shade the original intention [3]. Most things about the *Adam*

[1] Creizenach, i. 154, 317, 346. A slight addition to the *Stella* is made by two Provençal plays of †1300 (ed. P. Meyer in *Romania*, xiv. 496) and 1333 (*dramatis personae* only in *Revue des Sociétés savantes*, viii. 259) which introduce episodes from the life of the Virgin previous to the Nativity.

[2] Creizenach, i. 70, quoting *Gesta Alberti Livoniensis episcopi* (†1226) in Gruber, *Origines Livoniae* (1740), 34 'Eadem hyeme factus est ludus prophetarum ordinatissimus, quam Latini Comoediam vocant, in media Riga, ut fidei Christianae rudimenta gentilitas fide etiam disceret oculata. Cuius ludi et comoediae materia tam neophytis, quam paganis, qui aderant, per interpretem diligentissime exponebatur. Ubi autem armati Gedeonis cum Philistaeis pugnabant; pagani, timentes occidi, fugere coeperunt, sed caute sunt revocati . . . In eodem ludo erant bella, vtpote Dauid, Gedeonis, Herodis. Erat et doctrina Veteris et Novi Testamenti.'

[3] Text edited by V. Luzarche (Tours, 1854); L. Palustre (Paris, 1877); K. Bartsch, *Chrestomathie*, ed. 1880, 91); K. Grass (Halle, 1891); cf. the elaborate study by Sepet, xxix, 105, 261, and Julleville, *Les Myst.* i. 81; ii. 217; Creizenach, i. 130; Clédat, 15. The manuscript

are in dispute. Scholars differ as to whether the manuscript belongs to the twelfth or the thirteenth century, and as to whether it is the work of a Norman or of an Anglo-Norman scribe. The piece is manifestly incomplete, but how far incomplete it is hard to say. What we have consists of three sections. There is a long play of nearly six hundred lines on the Fall and Expulsion from Paradise, in which the speakers are Adam and Eve, the *Figura* of God and the *Diabolus*. Then comes a much shorter one of Cain and Abel; and finally a *Prophetae*, which breaks off after the part of Nebuchadnezzar. Of the general character of this interesting piece something further will be said presently, but the point to notice here is that, although Adam and Abel may of course be regarded as prophetic types of Christ, if not exactly prophets, yet there is a real extension of the dramatic content of the *Prophetae* in the prefixing to it of a treatment of so momentous a subject as the Fall[1]. For with the addition of the Fall to the already dramatized Redemption, the framework of a structural unity was at once provided for the great cosmic drama of the future. And the important motive seems to have been still further emphasized in a lost play performed at Regensburg in 1195, which treated, besides the Prophets and the Creation and Fall of Man, the Creation of the Angels and the Fall of Lucifer[2].

is *Tours MS.* 927, formerly belonging to the Benedictines of Marmoutier. Grass, vi, summarizes the opinions as to its date. In any case the text is probably of the twelfth century, and Grass, 171, after an elaborate grammatical investigation, confirms the opinion of Luzarche, doubted by Littré and others, that it is of Anglo-Norman rather than Norman origin. But, even if the writer was an Anglo-Norman clerk, the play must have been written for performance in France. I doubt if it was ever actually played or finished. It is followed in the MS. by a Norman (not Anglo-Norman) poem on the Fifteen Signs of Judgement (text in Grass, 57), which looks like material collected for an unwritten Sibyl prophecy. The remaining contents of the first part of the MS., which may be of the twelfth century, are some hymns and the Latin Tours *Quem quaeritis* (p. 38).

[1] Sepet, xxix, 112, 128, points out that certain *lectiones* and *responsoria* which accompany the *Adam* and *Cain and Abel* are taken from the office for Septuagesima. Possibly an independent liturgical drama of the Fall arose at Septuagesima and was absorbed by the *Prophetae*. But mention of the 'primus Adam' is not uncommon in the Nativity liturgy; cf. Sepet, xxix, 107, and the *Sponsus* (p. 61).

[2] *Annales Ratisponenses* (*M.G.H. Scriptores*, xvii. 590) 'Anno Domini 1194. Celebratus est in Ratispona ordo creacionis angelorum et ruina[e]

Yet another step towards the completion of the Christmas cycle was taken when the *Prophetae* and the *Stella* were brought together in a single drama. Such a merging is represented by two related texts from German sources [1]. One is from a fourteenth-century manuscript now at St. Gall [2]. The structure is of the simplest. The setting of the pseudo-Augustine sermon has altogether disappeared. Eight prophets deliver a speech apiece, announcing their own identities after a naïve fashion—*Ich bin der alte Balaam*, and so forth—which strongly recalls the 'folk' or 'mummers'' plays. Then follows without break a *Stella*, whose scenes range from the Marriage of the Virgin to the Death of Herod. Far more elaborate is the Christmas play found in the famous repertory of the *scholares vagantes* from Benedictbeuern [3]. A peculiarity of this is that for the first time Augustine appears *in propria persona*. He presides over the prophecies, taking the place of the *Precentor* of the Limoges *Prophetae*, and the *Appellatores* or *Vocatores* of Laon and Rouen. The only prophets are Isaiah, Daniel, the Sibyl, Aaron, and Balaam, and there is once more a special episode for Balaam's ass.

'*Quinto loco procedat Balaam sedens in asina et cantans:*
vadam, vadam, ut maledicam populo huic.
Cui occurrat Angelus evaginato gladio dicens:
cave, cave ne quicquam aliud quam tibi dixero loquaris.
Et asinus cui insidet Balaam perterritus retrocedat. Postea recedat angelus et Balaam cantet hoc:
orietur stella ex Iacob, etc.'

A long *disputatio* follows between Augustine, an *Archisynagogus*, and the prophets, in which at one point no less a person intervenes than the *Episcopus Puerorum*, affording an inter-

Luciferi et suorum, et creacionis hominis et casus et prophetarum . . . septima Idus Februarii.'

[1] Köppen, 35, discusses the textual relation between the St. Gall and Benedictbeuern plays and their common source, the Freising *Stella*.

[2] Text in Mone, *Schauspiele des Mittelalters*, i. 143; cf. Creizenach, i. 123.

[3] Text in Schmeller, *Carmina Burana*, 80; Du Méril, 187; Froning, 877, from a Munich MS. of thirteenth to fourteenth century formerly in the abbey of Benedictbeuern in Bavaria; cf. Creizenach, i. 96; Sepet, xxxviii, 398. The title 'Ludus scenicus de nativitate Domini' given by Schmeller is not in the MS.

esting example of that interrelation between the religious plays and the festivities of the *triduum* and the Feast of Fools, about which something has already been said[1]. Presently the prophets retire and sit *in locis suis propter honorem ludi*. The *Stella* extends from the Annunciation to the Flight into Egypt. Here the original play seems to have ended; but a later writer has added a scene in Egypt, in which the idols fall at the approach of the Holy Family, and some fragments adapted from the *Antichristus*, and hardly worked up into anything that can be called a scene.

The form of Christmas play, then, characteristic of the transition century, consists of a version of the *Prophetae* extended at the beginning by a dramatic treatment of the Fall, or extended at the end by the absorption of the *Stella*. It so happens that we do not, during the period in question, find examples in which both extensions occur together. But this double amplification would only be the slightest step in advance, and may perhaps be taken for granted. The Rouen *Mystère de l'Incarnation et la Nativité* of 1474 offers, at a much later date, precisely the missing type[2].

The Easter cycle, also, received memorable accretions during the period. The *Quem quaeritis* of the Tours manuscript, it will be remembered, included a series of scenes beginning with the Setting of the Watch before the Sepulchre, and ending with the Incredulity of Thomas. Important additions had still to be made, even within the limits of this *cadre*. One was a more complete treatment of the Resurrection itself through the introduction of the figure of Christ stepping with the *labarum* out of the sepulchre, in place of a mere symbolical indication of the mystery by the presence of angels with lighted candles and the dismay of the soldiers[3]. Another, closely related to the Resurrection, was the scene known as the Harrowing of Hell. This was based upon the account of the *Descensus Christi ad Inferos*, the victory over Satan, and the freeing from limbo of Adam and the other Old

[1] Cf. p. 56. The Balaam in *Adam* is 'sedens super asinam,' but no further notice is taken of the animal.

[2] Text ed. Le Verdier (*Soc. des Bibliophiles normands*); cf. Julleville, *Les Myst.* ii. 36, 430.

[3] Cf. p. 38.

Testament Fathers, which forms part of the apocryphal *Gospel of Nichodemus*[1]. The narrative makes use of that *Tollite portas* passage from the twenty-fourth Psalm, which we have already found adapted to the use of more than one semi-dramatic ceremonial[2], and naturally this found its way into the Harrowing of Hell, together with the so-called *canticum triumphale*, a song of welcome by the imprisoned souls:

'Advenisti, desirabilis, quem exspectabamus in tenebris, ut educeres hac nocte vinculatos de claustris.
te nostra vocabant suspiria.
te larga requirebant lamenta.
tu factus es spes desperatis, magna consolatio in tormentis.'

I cannot share the view of those who look upon the East Midland English *Harrowing of Hell* as intended for dramatic representation. The prologues found in two of the three manuscripts leave it clear that it was for recitation. It is in fact of the nature of an 'estrif' or *débat*, and may be compared with an Anglo-Saxon poem of the eighth or tenth century on the same subject[3]. But there is evidence that the scene had found its way into the Easter cycle at least by the beginning of the thirteenth century, for it occurs amongst the fragments of a play of that date from Kloster Muri; and in later versions it assumed a considerable prominence[4].

[1] Tischendorf, *Evangelia Apocrypha* (1876), 389.

[2] Cf. pp. 4, 5, 20. One of the anthems for Easter Saturday in the *Sarum Breviary* is *Elevamini, portae*.

[3] Text in Pollard, 166; K. Böddeker, *Altenglische Dichtungen des MS. Harl.* 2253 (1878), 264; E. Mall, *The Harrowing of Hell* (1871); cf. Ten Brink, ii. 242; Ward, i. 90; Creizenach, i. 158. There are three MSS.: (*a*) *Bodl. Digby MS.* 86 (late thirteenth century); (*b*) *Harl. MS.* 2253 († 1310); (*c*) *Edin. Advoc. Libr.* (*Auchinleck*) *MS.* W. 41 (early fourteenth century). The Digby version has a prologue beginning:

'Hou ihesu crist herewede helle
Of hardegates ich wille telle.'

The Harleian has:

'Alle herkneth to me nou,
A strif will I tellen ou.'

The Auchinleck prologue lacks the beginning, but the end agrees with the Harleian. Böddeker, who accepts the dramatic character of the piece, thinks that the prologues were prefixed later for recitation. In any case this poem became a source for a play in the *Ludus Coventriae* cycle (Pollard, xxxviii).

[4] Text of Muri fragments in Froning, 228; cf. Creizenach, i. 114; Wirth, 133, 281. A French fragment († 1300–50) also introducing this theme is printed by J. Bédier, in *Romania*, xxiv. (1895), 86. Pez, *Script. rerum austriacarum*, ii. 268, describes a vision of the thirteenth-century recluse

The liturgical drama proper abstained in the main from any strictly dramatic representation of the Passion. The nearest approach to such a thing is in the dialogued versions of the *Planctus Mariae* and in the Benedictbeuern *Ludus breviter de Passione*, which extends very slightly beyond these. The central event of the transition period is, therefore, the growth side by side with the *Quem quaeritis* of a Passion play, which in the end rather absorbs than is absorbed by it. A marked advance in this direction is shown in an Anglo-Norman fragment, probably written in the twelfth century, which includes, not indeed the Crucifixion itself, but the Descent from the Cross, the Healing of Longinus, and the Burial of Christ [1]. The first recorded Passion play is in Italy. It took place at Siena about 1200 [2]. In 1244 the Passion and Resurrection were played together at Padua [3]. The earliest text of a Passion play is contained in the Benedictbeuern manuscript [4]. It opens with the Calling of Andrew and Peter, the Healing of the Blind, Zacchaeus and the Entry into Jerusalem. Then follows a long episode of Mary Magdalen. She is represented with her lover, buying cosmetics of a *Mercator*—we have had the *Mercator* in the *Quem quaeritis* and in the *Sponsus*—and with a profane song upon her lips:

Wilbirgis: 'Item quadam nocte Dominicae Resurrectionis, cum in Monasterio ludus Paschalis tam a Clero quam a populo ageretur, quia eidem non potuit corporalitèr interesse, coepit desiderare, ut ei Dominus aliquam specialis consolationis gratiam per Resurrectionis suae gaudia largiretur. Et vidit quasi Dominum ad Inferos descendentem et inde animas eruentem, quae quasi columbae candidissimae circumvolantes ipsum comitabantur, et sequebantur ab inferis redeuntem.' Meyer, 61, 98, deals fully with the development of the Resurrection and Harrowing of Hell themes in the early vernacular plays.

[1] Text in Monmerqué et Michel, *Théâtre fr. au moyen âge*, 10, from *Bibl. Nat. fr.* 902; cf. Creizenach, i. 135; Julleville, *Les Myst.* i. 91; ii. 220; Clédat, 59. The MS. is of the fourteenth century, but the Norman-French, which some writers, as with the *Adam*, think Anglo-Norman, is assigned to the end of the twelfth century.

[2] D'Ancona, i. 90. The original authority for the statement, taken from a MS. treatise on the *Commedia italiana* by Uberto Benvoglienti, is not given.

[3] D'Ancona, i. 87, quoting several chronicles: 'hoc anno in festo Pascae facta fuit Reppraesentatio Passionis et Resurrectionis Christi solemniter et ordinate in Prato Vallis.'

[4] Text in Schmeller, *Carmina Burana*, 95; Du Méril, 126; Froning, 284; cf. Creizenach, i. 92; Wirth, 131, 278. The only heading to the play in the MS. is 'Sancta Maria assit nostro principio! amen.'

'Mundi delectatio dulcis est et grata,
cuius conversatio suavis et ornata.'

She is converted in a dream, puts on black, buys ointments from the same *Mercator*, and adores the Lord in the house of Simon. Then come, far more briefly treated, the Raising of Lazarus, the Betrayal by Judas, the Last Supper, the Mount of Olives, the Passion itself, from the Taking in Gethsemane to the Crucifixion. The introduction here of some *planctus Mariae* points to the *genesis* of the drama, which closes with the Begging of the Body of Christ by Joseph of Arimathaea. And so, at a blow, as it were, the content of the Easter play is doubled. Certain episodes, such as the Conversion of Mary Magdalen and the Raising of Lazarus had, as we know, received an independent dramatic treatment; but in the main the play before us, or its source, bears the character of a deliberate composition on the lines of the pre-existing *Quem quaeritis*. That it was to be followed in representation by a *Quem quaeritis* may perhaps be taken for granted. Indeed there is one personage, the wife of the *Mercator*, who is named in a list at the beginning, but has no part in the text as it stands [1]. She may have come into the Benedictbeuern *Quem quaeritis*, of which a fragment only survives, and this may have been intended for use, as might be convenient, either with the *Ludus breviter de Passione*, or with the longer text now under consideration. At all events, Passion and Resurrection are treated together in two slightly later texts, one from the south of France [2], the other from St. Gall [3]. The St. Gall Passion play takes the action back to the beginning of the missionary life of Christ, giving the Marriage at Cana, the Baptism, and the Temptation. It also includes a Harrowing of Hell.

Certain forms of the Passion play, as the conjoint Passion and Resurrection may now be termed, show an approximation to the type of the Christmas play. It is obvious that the

[1] Scenes between the *Mercator*, his wife, and their lad Rubin play a large part in the later German Passion plays; cf. Wirth, 168.

[2] Creizenach, i. 155. Two fourteenth-century texts exist, one in Provençal, one in Catalan.

[3] Text in Mone, *Schauspiele des Mittelalters*, i. 72; cf. Creizenach, i. 121; Wirth, 135, 282.

Fall and the *Prophetae* would be as proper a prologue to the Passion which completes the Atonement as to the Nativity which begins it. And the presence of Adam and other Old Testament characters in the Harrowing of Hell would be the more significant if in some earlier scene they had visibly been haled there. The first trace of these new elements is in the St. Gall play, where the Augustine of the *Prophetae* is introduced to speak a prologue. A long Frankfort play of the fourteenth century, of which unfortunately only the stage directions and actors' cues are preserved, carries the process further [1]. Again Augustine acts as presenter. A *Prophetae* begins the performance, which ends with the Ascension, a *Disputatio Ecclesiae et Synagogae* and the baptizing of the incredulous Jews by Augustine. On the other hand, the Fall forms the first part of an early fourteenth-century Passion play from Vienna [2]. Both the Fall of Lucifer and that of Adam and Eve are included, and there is a supplementary scene in hell, into which the souls of a usurer, a monk, a robber, and a sorceress are successively brought. Lucifer refuses to have anything to do with the monk, an early use of the Tomlinson motive.

The dramatic evolution is now within measurable distance of the 'cosmic' type finally presented by the English Corpus Christi plays. Two further steps are necessary: the juxtaposition of the Nativity and Passion scenes behind their common Old Testament prologue, and the final winding up of the action by the extension of it from the Ascension to the second coming of the Christ in the Last Judgement. The eschatological scenes of the *Sponsus* and the *Antichristus* are already available for such an epilogue. That the whole of this vast framework was put together by the beginning of the fourteenth century may be inferred from the notices of two performances, in 1298 and 1303 respectively, at Cividale [3]. The

[1] Text in Froning, 340 (begins 'Incipit ordo sive registrum de passione domini'); cf. Creizenach, i. 219; Wirth, 137, 295.

[2] Text in Froning, 305 (begins 'Ad materiae reductionem de passione domini. Incipit ludus pascalis'); cf. Creizenach, i. 92, 120; Wirth, 134, 293.

[3] Giuliano da Cividale, *Cronaca Friulana* (D'Ancona, i. 91; Muratori, *Rer. Ital. Script.* xxiv. 1205, 1209): 'Anno domini MCCLXXXXVIII die vii exeunte Maio,

first included the Passion, Resurrection, Ascension, Advent of the Holy Spirit, and Advent of Christ to Judgement: the second added to these the Creation, Annunciation, Nativity, with much else, and the Antichrist. Any further development could now be merely episodic. The text could be amplified at the fancy of the individual writer, or upon the suggestion of the great epic narratives, such as the *Cursor Mundi*, the *Passional*, the *Erlösung*[1]. An infinity of new scenes could be added from the Old Testament[2], from the apocryphal gospels and acts, from the historic narratives of the vengeance of the Crucified One upon Rome and Jewry[3]. But beyond the limits of the fixed *cadre* it was now impossible to go, for these were coincident with the span of time and eternity.

It is now necessary to consider briefly some modifications in the general character of the religious plays which accompanied or resulted from this great expansion of their scope.

videlicet in die Pentecostes et in aliis duobus sequentibus diebus, facta fuit Repraesentatio Ludi Christi, videlicet Passionis, Resurrectionis, Ascensionis, Adventus Spiritus Sancti, Adventus Christi ad iudicium, in curia Domini Patriarchae Austriae civitatis, honorifice et laudabiliter, per Clerum civitatensem . . . Anno MCCCIII facta fuit per Clerum, sive per Capitulum civitatense, Repraesentatio: sive factae fuerunt Repraesentationes infra scriptae: In primis, de Creatione primorum parentum; deinde de Annunciatione Beatae Virginis, de Partu et aliis multis, et de Passione et Resurrectione, Ascensione et Adventu Spiritus Sancti, et de Antichristo et aliis, et demum de Adventu Christi ad iudicium. Et predicta facta fuerunt solemniter in curia domini Patriarchae in festo Pentecostes cum aliis duobus diebus sequentibus, praesente r. d. Ottobono patriarcha aquileiensi, d. Iacobo q. d. Ottonelli de Civitate episcopo concordiensi, et aliis multis nobilibus de civitatibus et castris Foroiulii, die xv exeunte Maio.' Still earlier, some dramatic fragments not later than the mid-thirteenth century from Kloster Himmelgarten near Nordhausen, include scenes from both the early and late life of Christ (Text, ed. Sievers, in *Zeitsch. f. d. Phil.* xxi. 393; cf. Creizenach, i. 124); but these might conceivably belong to a set of plays for different dates, such as those of the Sainte Geneviève MS. (Julleville, *Les Myst.* ii. 379). Besides the English cosmic cycles, there are several fifteenth-century French ones described by Julleville, *Les Myst.* ii. 394 sqq.: in Germany plays of this scope are rare.

[1] Pearson, ii. 312; Köppen, 49; Ten Brink, i. 287.

[2] Cf. Sepet, xxxviii, 415; Creizenach, i. 260; G. Smith, 253; Julleville, *Les Myst.* ii. 352. *Le Mistère du viel testament*, printed +1510 (ed. Rothschild, 1878–91, for *Soc. des anciens textes français*), is a fifteenth-century compilation of O. T. plays from various sources.

[3] French versions of the *Vengeance de Notre Seigneur*, of which the chief episode is the Siege of Jerusalem, appear in the fifteenth century (Julleville, *Les Myst.* ii. 12, 415, 451). A late Coventry play on the same theme is unfortunately lost.

These all tend towards that process of secularization, that relaxing of the close bonds between the nascent drama and religious worship, which it is the especial object of this chapter to illustrate. Of capital importance is the transference of the plays from the interior of the church to its precincts, to the graveyard or the neighbouring market-place. This must have been primarily a matter of physical necessity. The growing length of the plays, the increasing elaboration of their setting, made it cumbrous and difficult to accommodate them within the walls. It is a big step from the early *Quem quaeritis*, *Pastores* or *Stella*, with their simple *mises-en-scène* of *sepulchrum* and *praesepe* to the complicated requirements, say, of the Fleury group, the *tabernaculum in similitudinem castelli Emaus* for the *Peregrini*, the half-dozen *loca*, *domus*, or *sedes* demanded by the *Suscitatio Lazari* or the *Conversio Pauli*. Still more exigent is the *Antichristus* with its *templum domini* and its seven *sedes regales*, and its space in between for marchings and counter-marchings and the overthrowing of kings. Yet for a long time the church proved sufficient. The Tours *Quem quaeritis* and some, if not all, of the Fleury plays were demonstrably played in the church. So was the Rouen *Prophetae*, and an allusion of Gerhoh of Reichersberg makes it extremely probable that so was the *Antichristus*[1]. One must conceive, I think, of the performances as gradually spreading from choir to nave, with the *domus*, *loca*, or *sedes* set at intervals against the pillars, while the people crowded to watch in the side aisles. It is in the twelfth century that the plays first seek ampler room outside the church. Of the transition plays dealt with in the present chapter, the *Adam*, the Benedictbeuern Christmas play, the Anglo-Norman *Resurrection*, were certainly intended for the open, and the contrary cannot be affirmed in any case with the same assurance. Again, the Riga *Prophetae* of 1204 was *in media Riga*, the Padua Passion play of 1244 was in a meadow, the *Pratum Vallis*, while in England an early thirteenth-century biographer of St. John of Beverley records a miracle wrought at a Resurrection play in the churchyard of the minster.

[1] Cf. p. 99.

Of the type of performance now rendered possible, a very good notion is given by the full stage directions of the *Adam.* These are so valuable a document for the history of stage management that I must take leave to excerpt from them somewhat liberally. The opening rubric recalls at once the minute stage directions of Ibsen and the counsel to the players in *Hamlet.*

'A Paradise is to be made in a raised spot, with curtains and cloths of silk hung round it at such a height that persons in the Paradise may be visible from the shoulders upwards. Fragrant flowers and leaves are to be set round about, and divers trees put therein with hanging fruit, so as to give the likeness of a most delicate spot. Then must come the Saviour clothed in a dalmatic, and Adam and Eve be brought before him. Adam is to wear a red tunic and Eve a woman's robe of white, with a white silk cloak; and they are both to stand before the Figure, Adam the nearer with composed countenance, while Eve appears somewhat more modest. And the Adam must be well trained when to reply and to be neither too quick nor too slow in his replies. And not only he, but all the personages must be trained to speak composedly, and to fit convenient gesture to the matter of their speech. Nor must they foist in a syllable or clip one of the verse, but must enounce firmly and repeat what is set down for them in due order. Whosoever names Paradise is to look and point towards it.'

After a *lectio* and a chant by the choir, the dialogue begins. The *Figura* instructs Adam and Eve as to their duties and inducts them into Paradise.

'Then the Figure must depart to the church and Adam and Eve walk about Paradise in honest delight. Meanwhile the demons are to run about the stage (*per plateas*), with suitable gestures, approaching the Paradise from time to time and pointing out the forbidden fruit to Eve, as though persuading her to eat it. Then the Devil is to come and address Adam.'

The *diabolus* thinks he is prevailing upon Adam. He joins the other demons and make sallies about the *plateae.* Then he returns *hylaris et gaudens* to the charge. But he fails.

'Then, sadly and with downcast countenance, he shall leave Adam, and go to the doors of hell, and hold council with the other demons. Thereafter he shall make a sally amongst the people, and then approach Paradise on Eve's side, addressing her with joyful countenance and insinuating (*blandiens*) manner.'

Eve, too, is hard to persuade, and is scolded by Adam for listening to the *diabolus*. But when a *serpens artificiose compositus* rises hard by the trunk of the forbidden tree, she lends her ear, is won over, takes the apple and gives it to Adam.

'Then Adam is to eat part of the apple; and after eating it he shall immediately recognize his sin and debase himself. He must now be out of sight of the people, and shall put off his solemn raiment, and put on poor raiment sewn together of fig-leaves, and with an air of extreme dolour shall begin his lament.'

When the Figure 'wearing a stole' comes again, Adam and Eve hide in a corner of Paradise, and when called upon stand up, 'not altogether erect, but for shame of their sin somewhat bowed and very sad.' They are driven out, and an angel with a radiant sword is put at the gate of Paradise. The Figure returns to the church.

'Then Adam shall have a spade and Eve a hoe, and they shall begin to till the soil and sow corn therein. And when they have sown, they shall go and sit down a while, as if wearied with toil, and anon look tearfully at Paradise, beating their breasts. Meanwhile shall come the devil and shall plant thorns and thistles in their tillage, and avoid. And when Adam and Eve come to their tillage and see the thorns and thistles sprung up, they shall be smitten with violent grief and shall throw themselves on the earth and sit there, beating their breasts and thighs and betraying grief by their gestures. And Adam shall begin a lament.'

Now the last scene is at hand.

'Then shall come the devil and three or four devils with him, carrying in their hands chains and iron fetters, which they shall put on the necks of Adam and Eve. And some shall push and others pull them to hell; and hard by hell shall be other devils ready to meet them, who shall hold high revel (*tripudium*) at their fall. And certain other devils shall point them out as they come, and shall snatch them up and carry them into hell; and there shall they make a great smoke arise, and call aloud to each other with glee in their hell, and clash their pots and kettles, that they may be heard without. And after a little delay the devils shall come out and run about the stage; but some shall remain in hell.'

The shorter play of Cain and Abel is similarly conceived. The sacrifices are offered on two great stones 'which shall have been made ready for the purpose'; and at the end of the performance the devils hale off Cain and Abel also to hell 'beating Cain often; but Abel they shall lead more gently.' The prophets, who have been prepared in a secret spot, now advance one by one and deliver their prophecies. Their appearance is described much as in the earlier *Prophetae*, and it is noted that each in turn at the finish of his harangue is to be led off to hell by the devils.

Unless the *Adam* extended much beyond the text left to us, a comparatively small number of *loca* would suffice for its representation. The contemporary Anglo-Norman Resurrection play required thirteen, as is set out at length in a versified prologue:

'En ceste manere recitom
La seinte resurreccion.
Primerement apareillons
Tus les lius e les mansions:
Le crucifix primerement
E puis apres le monument.
Une jaiole i deit aver
Pur les prisons emprisoner.
Enfer seit mis de cele part,
E mansions de l'altre part,
E puis le ciel; et as estals
Primes Pilate od ces vassals.
Sis u set chivaliers aura.
Caïphas en l'altre serra;
Od lui seit la jeuerie,
Puis Joseph, cil d'Arimachie.
El quart liu seit danz Nichodemes.

Chescons i ad od sei les soens.
El quint les deciples Crist.
Les treis Maries saient el sist.
Si seit pourvéu que l'om face
Galilée en mi la place;
Jemaüs uncore i seit fait,
U Jhesu fut al hostel trait;
E cum la gent est tute asise,
E la pés de tutez parz mise,
Dan Joseph, cil d'Arimachie,
Venge a Pilate, si lui die.'

I have ventured to arrange these *lius* (*loca*) and *mansions* (*domus*) or *estals* (*sedes*), upon the indications of the prologue, in the following plan :

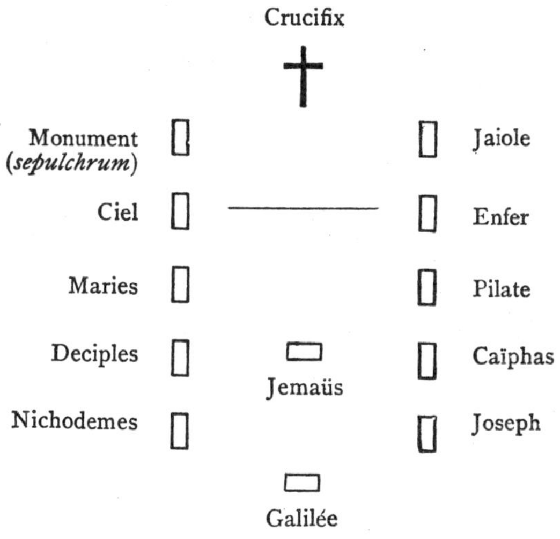

And I would point out that such a scheme is simply a continuation of the arrangement down the choir and nave of a church suggested above[1]. The crucifix is where it would stand in the church, above the altar. The place of the monument corresponds to that most usual for the *sepulchrum* on the north side of the chancel. The positions of heaven and hell are those in the former case of the stairs up to the

[1] Cf. p. 79.

rood-loft, in the latter of the stairs down to the crypt; and what, in a church, should serve for hell and heaven but crypt and rood-loft[1]? The Galilee answers to the porch at the west end of the church, which we know to have been so called[2]; and the castle of Emmaus stands in the middle of the nave, just as it did in the Fleury *Peregrini*. With my conjectural

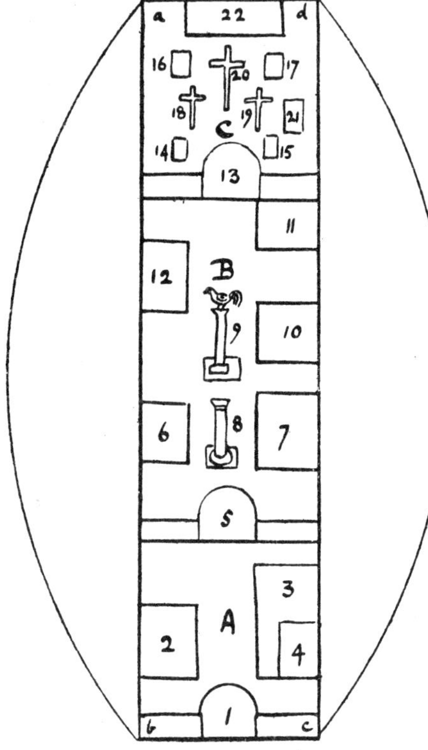

A. B. C. The three divisions of the stage, corresponding to the nave, choir, and sanctuary of a church.
1. The first door.
2. Hell.
3. The Garden of Gethsemane.
4. Mount Olivet.
5. The second door.
6. Herod's palace.
7. Pilate's palace.
8. The pillar of scourging.
9. The pillar for the cock.
10. The house of Caiaphas.
11. The house of Annas.
12. The house of the Last Supper.
13. The third door.
14, 15, 16, 17. Graves from which the dead arise.
18, 19. Crosses of the two thieves.
20. Cross of Christ.
21. The Holy Sepulchre.
22. Heaven.

PLAN OF DONAUESCHINGEN PASSION-PLAY STAGE (*sixteenth century*).

plan may be compared this actual plan of a sixteenth-century stage from Donaueschingen, in which a similar principle is apparent, the three divisions formed by cross-barriers corresponding to the three divisions of a church—sanctuary, choir, nave[3].

[1] Pearson, ii. 315; and cf. the angels aloft in the Rouen *Pastores* (p. 41).

[2] Cf. p. 50.

[3] Plan in Mone, ii. 156; Froning, 277; Davidson, 199; Pearson, ii.

The Anglo-Norman Resurrection play was pretty clearly out of doors[1]; and the double line of *sedes* may be thought of as stretching from the west door of the church right across the market-place. In *Adam* the *Figura* comes and goes from and to the church, which thus serves for a *ciel*; in the Benedictbeuern Christmas play, the chair of Augustine is set *in fronte ecclesiae*. This arrangement, also, can be paralleled from later plays, both French and German. At Freiburg in 1504 the stage was built across the cathedral yard from the south door to the Kaufhaus, a space of some 110 feet long[2]. At Rouen, in 1474, the *establies* went across the market-place from the Axe and Crown to the Angel[3]. It must not, however, be supposed that the rectangular stage survived as the invariable type. In particular a round type was sometimes preferred. The Cornish guary-plays were given in rounds, and a round is figured in a fifteenth-century miniature by Jean Fouquet, representing a play of Saint Apollonia[4].

I have spoken of a stage, but I am not sure that there was any stage in the sense of a platform. There is certainly no such scaffold in Fouquet's miniature, and the *plateae* of the Fleury *Suscitatio Lazari* and the *Adam* are probably only the open spaces kept free for the actors between the *sedes*[5]. In the *Adam* the devils are able to make sallies from the *plateae* amongst the spectators. The latter probably crowded upon barriers between the *sedes*. In the miniature, however, the *sedes* stand close together and are considerably raised, with

320; Könnecke, *Bilderatlas*, 55: on the play, cf. Creizenach, i. 224; Wirth, 139, 327. Another sixteenth-century plan from Lucerne is given by Leibing, *Die Inscenierung des 2-tägigen Osterspiels*, 1869; cf. Creizenach, i. 168.

[1] See the mention of 'en mi la place' in the prologue; but 'place' might be only the French equivalent of 'platea' as used in the Fleury *Suscitatio Lazari*.

[2] Pearson, ii. 322.

[3] Julleville, *Les Myst.* ii. 37.

[4] Reproduced in Clédat, 4; Bapst, 33, from *Horae* of †1460; cf. Jusserand, *Lit. Hist.* i. 470.

[5] D'Ancona, i. 191, however, describes the Italian *devozioni* as taking place on *talami* or platforms in the naves of churches. In France, minor religious plays at least took place on scaffolds, built up sometimes against the wall of a church (Bapst, 23, 29). A raised stage, with *sedes* along the back of it, is shown by the miniatures in the MS. of the Valenciennes *Passion* (reproduced in Jusserand, *Shakespeare in France*, 63; cf. Julleville, *Les Mystères*, ii. 153); but this is as late as 1547.

ladders running up to them. The spectators stand beneath. The prologue to the Anglo-Norman *Resurrection* speaks of *la gent* as seated, and possibly raised scaffolds for the audience were already in use. These were certainly known later, and the descriptions of some of them as no less than nine stories high have given rise to an erroneous theory that the plays were performed upon a many-storied stage[1]. It is clear that this was not really the case. All the *sedes* were on the same level, except that, for greater dignity, the Calvary, the Heaven, the Paradise might be, as in *Adam*, *loco eminentiore*, and that the *infernum* or hell, conventionally represented by the head and open gullet of a monstrous dragon, was low down, as if in the bowels of the earth[2]. It should be added that, as early as the first quarter of the twelfth century, plays had begun to make their way from the church, if not into the open, at any rate into buildings of domestic use. The authority for this is Gerhoh of Reichersberg, who speaks of performances in the refectory of Augsburg, when he was *magister scholae* there about 1123[3]. Some of the Fleury or other early plays may conceivably have been intended for the refectory.

The expansion of the cycles caused difficulties of time, as well as of space. Without a compression of manner alien to the long-winded Middle Ages, it was sometimes impossible to get the whole of the matter to be treated within the limits of a single day. The problem was amenable to more than one solution. The performance could be spread over two or more sittings. The first recorded example of such an arrangement is at Cividale in 1298[4], but it is one that would naturally suggest itself, especially for the Easter cycle, which fell naturally enough into the two dramas of Passion and Resurrection, from which, indeed, it sprang. In the Frankfort cue-book of the fourteenth century, it is carefully noted, that

[1] Julleville, *Les Myst.* i. 386; Bapst, 28.

[2] Cf. p. 137. Amongst the 'establies' required for the Rouen play of 1474 was 'Enfer faict en maniere d'une grande gueulle se cloant et ouvrant quant besoing en est' (Julleville, *Les Myst.* ii. 37). Just such an 'enfer' is represented in the Fouquet and Valenciennes miniatures.

[3] Cf. p. 98.

[4] Cf. p. 77.

if the audience are being kept too long, the *rectores* of the play shall defer the Resurrection to a second day[1]. Another device, which does not occur so early, was to divide the cycle into parts and play them in successive years. This method was adopted with the play of the Seven Joys of Mary at Brussels[2], and English examples will be found in a later chapter[3].

The cycles required in many cases a larger number of actors than the ecclesiastical bodies, even with the aid of wandering clerks and the cloister schools, could supply. It was necessary to press the laity into the service. The Easter play, of which the thirteenth-century anchoress Wilburgis was disappointed, was acted *tam a clero quam a populo*[4]. It was a further step in the same direction when the laity themselves took over the control and financing of plays. For this one must look mainly to that most important element in mediaeval town life, the guilds. Just as the Feast of Fools passed from the hands of the clergy into those of the *sociétés joyeuses*, so did the religious drama into those of more serious confraternities. The *burgenses* of Cahors, who in 1290 and 1302 played a *ludum de miraculis beati Marcialis* in the graveyard of St. Martial of Limoges, not improbably belonged to a guild formed to do honour to the patron[5]. The primary purpose of such guilds as these was devotional, and if they acted plays, it was doubtless with the countenance and assistance of the clergy to whose church they were affiliated. But those more secular and literary guilds, the *puys*, also undertook to act religious plays no less than *sotties* and farces; and in them

[1] Froning, 363 'Et notandum, quod optime congruit, ne populus nimiam moram faciendo gravetur, et ut resurrectio domini gloriosius celebretur, ut ulterior ordo ludi in diem alterum conservetur; quod si apud rectores deliberatum fuerit, Augustinus coram populo proclamet dicens sine rigmo, ut in die crastino revertatur.'

[2] Creizenach, i. 340.

[3] Cf. p. 130.

[4] Cf. p. 74. By the fifteenth century lay performers appear even in the ritual *Quem quaeritis*. An Augsburg version of 1487 (Milchsack, 129) concludes 'Permittitur tamen aliis, qui forsan huiusmodi personas [i.e. 'sacerdotes' et 'cantores'] non habent, ut cum aliis personis et etiam moribus honestis tamen et discretis, huiusmodi visitationem sepulchri exequantur.' See also the jest of Tyll Ulenspiegel with the parson's concubine who played the angel, quoted by Pearson, ii. 308.

[5] Julleville, *Les Myst.* ii. 2. For plays by German guilds cf. Pearson, ii. 364.

it may be suspected that the influence of the clergy would have to contend shrewdly with that of the minstrels[1]. It is not surprising to come in time upon signs of a rivalry between lay and clerical actors. Thus, in 1378, the scholars of St. Paul's are said to have presented a petition to Richard II, praying him to prohibit a play by some 'unexpert people' of the History of the Old Testament, a subject which they themselves had prepared at great expense for the ensuing Christmas. It may have been some similar dispute which led about the same date to the formation of the Parisian *Confrérie de la Passion*, which received from Charles VI a privilege to perform in and about the city, and became a model for many similar *confréries* throughout France. The charter bears the date of 1402. In 1398 the provost of Paris seems to have been moved to forbid dramatic performances without special sanction in the city or suburbs, a prohibition which, by the way, was flouted on the day of its proclamation at Saint-Maur. Exactly what led to this interposition of authority is not clear; but it probably induced the *confrérie*, who may have had a previous less formal existence, to apply for their privilege[2]. The *confrérie de la Passion* seem to have acted, as a rule, in closed rooms. It is not unlikely that the *puys* did the same.

The altered conditions of representation naturally reacted upon the style and temper of the plays themselves. This is not a subject that can be discussed in detail here, but a few points may be briefly noted. The first is the gradual substitution of vernacular tongues for the Latin of the liturgical drama. This was almost inevitable, where laymen performed to a lay audience. But the liturgical drama itself did not absolutely exclude the vernacular. In the *Sponsus*, and in the *Suscitatio Lazari* and the Nicholas play of Hilarius, fragments of French are inserted, just as they are in the 'farced' epistles used at the feasts of certain saints, notably at that of St. Stephen[3]. It was a step further when in the fourteenth

[1] Creizenach, i. 137; Julleville, *Les Myst.* i. 115; *Les Com.* 43. Probably the 'Jeu de Nicholas' of Jean Bodel, and the fourteenth-century 'Miracles de Notre Dame,' belong to the *répertoires* of *puys*.

[2] Julleville, *Les Myst.* i. 412; *Les Com.* 55.

[3] Du Méril, 410, 414, prints examples of such *épîtres farcies* for

century the nuns of Origny Ste.-Benoîte rewrote their liturgical *Quem quaeritis*, leaving indeed some of the more solemn parts, such as the dialogue of the Maries with the angel, or that of the Magdalen with the risen Christ, in Latin, but turning the rest into French[1]. Such an arrangement as this of Origny Ste.-Benoîte became in the transition plays, intended for out-of-door performance to a popular audience, the rule. There was naturally some local variation. Of the two longer scholars' plays in the Benedictbeuern manuscript, the Christmas play is wholly, the Passion play mainly, in Latin. A large proportion of Latin seems to have been retained in the Frankfort Passion play of the fourteenth century. But on the whole, as the texts grow, and especially as they draw upon the apocryphal books or the great mediaeval vernacular epics for matter not in the liturgical plays, the vernacular steadily gets the upper hand, until in the latest versions the traces of Latin must be regarded as mere survivals.

In some cases where Latin and vernacular appear together, the latter is of the nature of a translation, or rough and often much expanded paraphrase, of the former. This type of mixed and obviously transitional text can, as it happens, be illustrated from French, German, and English sources. It occurs, for instance, in the *Adam*. Here the Adam and Eve and Cain and Abel scenes are wholly, but for the preliminary *lectio* and the interpolated chants by the choir, in Norman-French. The prophecies, however, are given in the double form. Thus Isaiah says:

'Egredietur virga de radice Jesse, et flos de radice eius ascendet, et requiescet super eum spiritus domini.

'Or vus dirrai merveillus diz:
Jessé sera de sa raïz.
Verge en istra, qui fera flor,
Qui ert digne de grant unor.

the feasts of St. Stephen and St. Thomas of Canterbury: cf. the numerous references in D'Ancona, i. 66, and vol. i. p. 277.

[1] Text in Coussemaker, 256, from *Bibl. St. Quentin MS.* 75 (fourteenth century); cf. Julleville, *Les Myst.* i. 64. The *Quem quaeritis* includes the *Hortulanus* scene and has, like the Prague versions, the *Mercator*. It was probably written later than 1286, as the *Ordinarius* of that year (Coussemaker, 337) directs a shorter version in Latin.

> Saint espirit l'avra si clos,
> Sor ceste flor iert sun repos.'

There are many similar examples in German plays, of which the most complete is a *Quem quaeritis* in a fourteenth-century manuscript at Trèves[1]. In England Professor Skeat discovered at Shrewsbury a fragmentary text of this type in a manuscript of the early fifteenth century[2]. It is written in a northern, probably Yorkshire, dialect, and contains the part, with cues, of a single actor in three plays, a *Pastores*, a *Quem quaeritis*, and a *Peregrini*. In the first he played the Third Shepherd, in the second the Third Mary, in the last probably Cleophas. The fragment shows clearly enough the way in which the Latin text was first sung by a group of performers together, and then expanded by them separately in the vernacular. The two documents last quoted mark not only the transition from Latin to the vernacular, but also that from the sung drama of the liturgies to the spoken drama of the great cycles. In Professor Skeat's Shrewsbury fragments the Latin alone is musically noted. In the Trèves *Quem quaeritis* the Latin and portions of the German are noted, and a careful distinction is made between the lines to be spoken and those to be sung by the use of the terms *cantat* and *dicit* in the rubrics[3].

Again, the laicization of the drama was accompanied by a further development of the secular and even comic elements, of which the germs already existed in the plays. A more human and less distinctively ecclesiastical handling became possible[4]. The figure of Herod offered a melodramatic type of ranting tyrant which the tradition of the stage did not readily forget. The life of the unconverted Magdalen *in gaudio* gave the dramatist his opportunity to paint scenes of wholly secular luxury and romance. Naturally the comic developments attached themselves largely to personalities not

[1] Text in Froning, 49, from *Trier MS.* 75 (begins 'incipit ludus de nocte paschae, de tribus Mariis et Maria Magdalena' . . . ends 'explicit ludus'); cf. Creizenach, i. 112; Davidson, 149; Wirth, 120, 235.

[2] Cf. *Academy* for Jan. 4 and 11, 1890, where Prof. Skeat prints the text from *Shrewsbury MS. Mus.* iii. 42 f. 48 (a book of anthems). Manly, i. xxviii, also gives it with some valuable notes of his own.

[3] Creizenach, i. 109.

[4] Ibid. i. 99, 202; Pearson, ii. 271, 302, 394; Wirth, 168, 201, 215; D'Ancona, i. 62.

already defined in the Testament narratives. The *Mercator*, for instance, whose domesticities with his wife and his apprentice do so much to enliven the later German plays, is a thoroughly characteristic production of the mediaeval folk spirit, for the delectation of which Rutebeuf wrote the *Dit de l'Erberie*[1]. It is not, perhaps, altogether unjustifiable to trace a relation between him and the inveterate quack doctor of the spring folk drama itself[2]. This would not be the only point of contact between the *ludi* of the Church and those of the folk. The significance, from this point of view, of Balaam's ass has already been touched upon[3]. And in the growth of the devil scenes, from their first beginnings in the *Sponsus* or in the devil-deacon of the *Tollite portas*[4], to their importance in the *Adam* or the various treatments of the Fall of Lucifer and the Harrowing of Hell, may we not trace the influence of those masked and blackened demon figures who from all time had been a dear scandal of the Kalends and the Feast of Fools[5]? It is certain that the imps who sallied amongst the spectators and haled the Fathers off to their limbo of clashed kettles and caldrons must have been an immensely popular feature of the *Adam*; and it is noteworthy that in more than one place the *compagnies joyeuses* who inherited the Feast of Fools joined forces with more serious *confréries* and provided comic actors for the religious plays[6].

In yet another way the coming of the vernacular affected the character of the religious drama. It had been cosmopolitan; it was to be national: and from the fourteenth century, in spite of a few lendings and borrowings, and of a certain uniformity in the general lines of development, it really requires separate treatment in each of the European countries[7]. In Italy the divergence from the common type was perhaps most marked of all, although I think that Signor D'Ancona and others have perhaps pushed the doctrine of the independence and isolation of Italian drama to an extreme. They

[1] Cf. vol. i. p. 83.
[2] Cf. vol. i. pp. 185, 207, 213.
[3] Cf. p. 56.
[4] Cf. p. 4.
[5] Cf. vol. i. pp. 258, 268, 327.
[6] Julleville, *Les Myst.* ii. 412; *Les Com.* 149, 237 (Chaumont), 239 (Chauny).
[7] Creizenach, i. 356; cf. p. 146.

consider that it almost began afresh with the religious stirrings of the Umbrian Flagellants in 1260. The *compagnie* or associations of *disciplinati*, who were the outcome of this thoroughly folk movement, were wont, as they lashed themselves, to sing hymns of praise, *laudes*, whence they got the secondary name of *laudesi*. The lauds were mostly sung in the chapels of the *compagnie* after mass and a sermon on Sundays. Several fourteenth-century collections are extant, and contain examples intended for use throughout the circle of the ecclesiastical year. Many of them were dialogued, and appear to have been recited in costume with scenic accessories. The dramatic lauds were specifically known as *devozioni*, and by the end of the fourteenth century were in some cases performed rather elaborately upon a *talamo* or stage in the nave of a church, with *luoghi deputati* for the accommodation of the chief actors. According to Signor D'Ancona, the *devozioni*, which were composed by poor folk, were taken direct from the liturgy and owed little more than the initial hint or impulse to the liturgical drama; while at the other end of these developments, they became the source of the out-of-door and splendidly-staged *sacre rappresentazioni* which originated in Florence in the fifteenth century and thence spread to other Italian cities[1]. On this theory it must be observed that the *devozioni* have not been shown to be independent of the liturgical drama, and that the derivation of the *sacre rappresentazioni* from the *devozioni* is purely conjectural[3]. The *sacre rappresentazioni* were out of doors and produced by the clergy or laity; the *devozioni*, which have not been traced to Florence, were produced indoors by religious guilds of a very distinct type. The *sacre rappresentazioni*, moreover, included subjects, such as the *profeti*, which are not within the cycle of the

[1] D'Ancona, i. 87 sqq.; F. Torraca, *Discussioni e ricerche* (1888), 92; Creizenach, i. 299 sqq.; J. A. Symonds, *Renaissance in Italy*, iv. 242 sqq.; G. Smith, 297; Wechssler, 30; Gaspary, i. 138, 357; I. S. A. Herford, *The Confraternities of Penance, their Dramas and their Lamentations* in *E. H. Review*, vi. (1891), 646. A first instalment of dramatic Lauds was published by Monaci, *Appunti per la storia del teatro italiano* in *Rivista di Filologia Romana*, i. 235, ii. 29. For other collections cf. D'Ancona, i. 153; Gaspary, i. 361. D'Ancona has published *Sacre Rappresentazioni* (1872). A selection of Lauds, Devozioni, and Rappresentazioni is in F. Torraca, *Il teatro italiano dei Secoli xiii, xiv, e xv* (1885).

devozioni, but do belong to the liturgical drama. It is at least a tenable view, that the *devozioni* were merely a back-water of the drama, and that the *sacre rappresentazioni* were derived, like the fifteenth-century plays of other countries, from the liturgical drama through the medium of such transitional types as those already noted at Padua, Siena, and Cividale. The fact that the only transitional texts preserved are those of the *devozioni* has perhaps led to an exaggerated estimate of the importance of these. Even liturgical dramas are rare in Italy, although there are sufficient thoroughly to establish their existence. The chroniclers, however, mention one or two events which point to another dramatic tradition in Italy than that of the *devozioni*. At Florence itself, in 1306, there was a show of Heaven and Hell upon the Arno, which though merely pantomimic, may have been based on some dramatic representation of the Last Judgement[1]. At Milan, in 1336, was a *Stella*, in which the *Magi* rode through the streets, and Herod sat by the columns of San Lorenzo[2]. Both of these performances, like those at Padua and Cividale

[1] D'Ancona, i. 94.

[2] Galvano Flamma, *de rebus gestis a Vicecomitibus* (D'Ancona, i. 97; Muratori, *Rer. Ital. Script.* xii. 1017). The ceremony was 'in die Epifanie in conventu fratrum Praedicatorum . . . Fuerunt coronati tres Reges in equis magnis, vallati domicellis, vestiti variis, cum somariis multis et familia magna nimis. Et fuit stella aurea discurrens per aera, quae praecedebat istos tres Reges, et pervenerunt ad columnas Sancti Laurentii, ubi erat rex Herodes effigiatus, cum scribis et sapientibus. Et visi sunt interrogare regem Herodem, ubi Christus nasceretur, et revolutis multis libris responderunt, quod deberet nasci in civitate Bethleem in distantia quinque milliariorum a Hierusalem. Quo audito, isti tres Reges coronati aureis coronis, tenentes in manibus scyphos aureos cum auro, thure et myrrha, praecedente stella per aera, cum somariis et mirabili famulatu, clangentibus tubis, et bucinis praecedentibus, simiis, babuynis, et diversis generibus animalium, cum mirabili populorum tumultu, pervenerunt ad ecclesiam Sancti Eustorgii. Ubi in latere altaris maioris erat praesepium cum bove et asino, et in praesepio erat Christus parvulus in brachiis Virginis matris. Et isti Reges obtulerunt Christo munera; deinde visi sunt dormire, et Angelus alatus ei dixit quod non redirent per contratam Sancti Laurentii, sed per portam Romanam: quod et factum fuit. Et fuit tantus concursus populi et militum et dominarum et clericorum, quod nunquam similis fere visus fuit. Et fuit ordinatum, quod omni anno istud festum fieret.' This is precisely the liturgic *Stella* translated into an out-of-door *spectacle*, which in its turn becomes the model for many a Quattrocento painting; cf., e.g., Botticelli's *Magi* in the Uffizi, or Gentile da Fabriano's, with the baboons done to the life, in the Accademia.

and the *sacre rappresentazioni* themselves, were out of doors. It is true that the *sacre rappresentazioni* fell less into big cycles than did the contemporary plays of other countries: but cycles were not unknown [1], and it must be borne in mind that the extreme beauty and elaboration of the Florentine *mise-en-scène* made a limited scheme, on grounds both of time and expense, almost imperative.

With out-of-door plays climatic conditions began to be of importance. Even in sunny France, Christmas is not exactly the season to hang about the market-place looking at an interminable drama. It is not to be denied that Christmas plays continued to be occasionally acted well through the fifteenth century [2], but the number of these, compared with the Passions, is small [3]. Even Easter weather is not invariably genial. Nor, as the cycles lengthened, was the attachment of them to any one of the feasts, whose events they commemorated, a matter of first-rate importance. A tendency set in towards playing them as far as possible in the long warm days of the summer months. The first Whitsuntide performances are those at Cividale in 1298 and 1303; and Whitsuntide became a very favourite date [4]. At Florence the great patronal feast and procession of St. John the Baptist on June 24 was a natural occasion for *sacre rappresentazioni* [5].

[1] D'Ancona, i. 94, 301, considers, however, that the late fifteenth-century *Passio* of Revello was not a native growth, but modelled on contemporary cyclic plays from France.

[2] The Rouen play of 1474 (Julleville, *Les Myst.* ii. 36) was one, and cf. pp. 119, 122.

[3] Creizenach, i. 242; cf. the lists in Julleville, *Les Myst.* ii. 183.

[4] Julleville, *Les Myst.* ii. 9 sqq.

[5] D'Ancona, i. 218; Guasti, *Le feste di San Giovanni Baptista in Firenze* (1884). *Rappresentazioni* on St. John's day were known to the late fourteenth-century Florentine historian Goro di Stagio Dati. An account of the feast in 1407 makes no mention of them, but they appear in that of 1439, and are elaborately described in the *Storia* of Matteo di Marco Palmieri about 1454 (D'Ancona, i. 228). Early in the morning of June 22 started a procession of clergy, *compagnie*, *edifizii*, and *cavalleria*. These stopped in the Piazza della Signoria, and *rappresentazioni*, forming a complete cycle from the Fall of Lucifer to the Last Judgement, and lasting sixteen hours, were given upon the *edifizii*. D'Ancona suggests that the dumb show type of *rappresentazioni* preceded the dialogued one, 'come più semplice.' But this seems equally inconsistent with his view that the *rappresentazioni* grew out of *devozioni*, and mine that they were an adaptation of earlier cyclical plays to the conditions of the Florentine feast.

Another high day for the cyclical drama from the fourteenth century onwards, notably in England[1] and Spain[2], and to a much less degree in Germany[3] and France[4], was the recently-established feast of Corpus Christi. This, the most materialistic of all the Church's celebrations, is in honour of the mystery of the transubstantiated sacrament. It originated locally in an alleged revelation to Juliana, a Cistercian religious of Liège. Pope Urban IV designed in 1264 to make it a universal festival, but he died in the same year, and the bull which he had issued remained inoperative until it was confirmed by Clement V at the council of Vienne in 1311. Corpus Christi day was the Thursday after Trinity Sunday. An office was compiled for it by St. Thomas Aquinas, and the leading ceremony was a great procession in which the host, escorted by local dignitaries, religious bodies and guilds, was borne through the streets and displayed successively at out-of-door stations[5]. When the plays were transferred to Corpus Christi day, they became more or less attached to this procession. Sometimes, perhaps, the procession served as a mere preliminary parade for the actors, such as sometimes preceded plays at other times[6]. The play itself would follow on a fixed stage of the ordinary type. But the method of the great English cycles seems to point to a more complete merging of play and procession than this. The *domus*, *loci*, or *sedes* were set upon wheels, and known as 'pageants[7]'; and the performance was gone through during the procession,

[1] Cf. ch. xxi.

[2] D'Ancona, i. 243; Schack, ii. 103; Ticknor, *Hist. of Spanish Lit.* ii. 249. The *Autos Sacramentales* are so named from their connexion with this day.

[3] Creizenach, i. 170, 227. The earliest German mention is at the council of Prague in 1366 (Höfler, *Concilia Pragensia*, 13, in *Abhandl. d. königl. böhmischen Gesellsch. der Wiss.* series v. vol. 12) 'omnibus . . . clericis et laicis . . . mandatur ut ludos theatrales vel etiam fistulatores vel ioculatores in festo corporis Christi in processionibus ire quovis modo permittant et admittant.' Extant *Frohnleichnamsspiele* are those of Innsbruck, †1391 (Text in Mone, *Altteutsche Schauspiele*, 145), and of Künzelsau, †1479 (ed. H. Werner, in *Germania*, iv. 338). Cf. the description (†1553) of Naogeorgos (transl. Googe) in Stubbes, i. 337.

[4] Julleville, ii. 208.

[5] Ward, i. 44; Davidson, 215; Malleson-Tuker, ii. 227.

[6] See e.g. the 'Processio huius ludi' at the end of the text of the Alsfeld Passion of 1501 (Froning, 858); cf. Pearson, ii. 365. As to the general relations of processions and plays, cf. p. 160.

[7] Cf. p. 136.

being repeated at the various stations made by the host. If the cycle was a very long one, time could be saved by making an early play at one station coincident with a later play at that in front of it. It is, however, easy to see that with the arrangement here suggested the popularity of the pageants might throw the strictly religious aspect of the procession rather into the shade. The two would then be severed again, but the play might still retain its processional character. This is not, I think, an unreasonable conjecture as to how the type of play found, say at York, may have come into existence[1]. To Chester, where the plays were not on Corpus Christi day, but at Whitsuntide, the method must have been transferred at a later date.

During this brief survey of the critical period for the religious drama between the middle of the thirteenth and the middle of the fourteenth century, I have attempted to bring into relief the tendencies that were at work for its remodelling. But it must not be supposed that either the tendency to expansion or the tendency to secularization acted universally and uniformly. The truth is quite otherwise. To the end of the history of the religious drama, the older types, which it threw out as it evolved, co-existed with the newer ones[2]. The Latin tropes and liturgical dramas held their place in the church services. And in the vernaculars, side by side with the growing Nativities and Passions, there continued to be acted independent plays of more than one sort. There were the original short plays, such as the *Stella*, the *Annunciation*, the *Sponsus*, the *Antichrist*, by the running together of which the cycles came into being. There were plays, on the other hand, which originated as episodes in the cycles, and only subsequently attained to an independent

[1] The closest merging of play and procession is suggested by an order at Draguignan in 1558 (Julleville, *Les Myst.* ii. 209), where it was ordered 'Le dit jeu jora avec la procession comme auparadvant et le plus d'istoeres et plus brieves que puront estre seront et se dira tout en cheminant sans ce que personne du jeu s'areste pour eviter prolixité et confusion tant de ladite prosession que jeu, et que les estrangiers le voient aisement.' Perhaps the short speeches of the Innsbruck play were similarly delivered while the procession was moving. The nearest continental approach to the English type is the Künzelsau play, which was divided into three parts and played at three different stations (Creizenach, i. 227).

[2] Creizenach, i. 218.

existence. The majority of these were Old Testament plays, budded off, like the *Daniel*, from the *Prophetae*. And finally there were numerous plays drawn from hagiological legends, many of which never came into connexion with the cycles at all. Thus in the transition period we find, not only plays on St. Nicholas and St. Catherine for which liturgical models existed, but also the great French series of Miracles of the Virgin, and plays on Saints Theophilus, Dorothy, Martial, and Agnes[1]. The natural tendency of great churches to magnify their own patron saints led to further multiplication of themes. In the same way, long after the lay guilds and corporations had taken up the drama, performances continued to be given or superintended by the clergy and their scholars[2]. Priests and monks supplied texts and lent vestments for the lay plays. To the last, the church served from time to time as a theatre. All these points, as well as the traces of their liturgical origin lingering in the cycles, will be fully illustrated, so far as England is concerned, in the following chapters.

The question presents itself: What was the official attitude of the high ecclesiastical authorities towards the growing religious plays? It is not precisely answered, as the history of the Feast of Fools has shown, by the fact that the chapters and inferior clergy encouraged and took part in them. The liturgical drama had its motive, as St. Ethelwold is careful to point out, in a desire for devotion and the edification of

[1] Creizenach, i. 128, 137 sqq., 156; Julleville, *Les Myst.* i. 95, 107, 115, 185; ii. 2, 4, 5, 221, 226, 345; *Les Com.* 49; Sepet, 202, 242; Clédat, 63, 73, 105.

[2] Creizenach, i. 130, 165, 176; Julleville, *Les Myst.* i. 347; *Les Com.* 291; D'Ancona, i. 57; Pearson, ii. 303; Wirth, 144. A play could be given outside the church without wholly losing its connexion with the liturgy. It became a sort of procession: cf. pp. 32, 67. D'Ancona, i. 59, quotes from *Bibl. de l'École des Chartes*, iii. 450, a licence given by the Bishop of Langres in 1408 'Ut in quadem platea vel plateis congruis et honestis, infra vel extra villam, prope et supra rippariam loci, coram clero et populo, alta et intelligibili voce, lingua latina et materna, cum magna reverentia et honore ac diversis personacium et habituum generibus ad hoc congruis et necessariis, solemniter et publice vitam et miracula egregii confessoris et pontificis Machuti, recitare et exponere, missamque solemnem in pontificalibus, in platea seu plateis supradictis super altare portatili consecrato per alterum vestrum canonicorum vel alium ydoneum sacerdotem celebrare . . . licentiam et auctoritatem impertimus per praesentes.' Cf. the examples of plays at the Feasts of Fools and of the Boy Bishop (vol. i. pp. 295, 296, 299, 304, 306, 309, 313, 342, 348, 349, 380).

the vulgar[1]. The hope of affording a counter-attraction to the spring and winter *ludi* of hard-dying paganism probably went for something. Herrad of Landsberg, in the twelfth century, utters a regret that the *Stella* rightly instituted at Epiphany by the Fathers of the Church had given place to a shameless revel[2]. But a contrary opinion to Herrad's arose almost contemporaneously amongst the reforming anti-imperial clergy of Germany. This finds expression more than once in the writings of Gerhoh of Reichersberg[3]. He scoffs at the monks of Augsburg who, when he was *magister scolae* there about 1122, could only be induced to sup in the refectory, when a representation of Herod or the Innocents or some other quasi-theatrical spectacle made an excuse for a feast[4]. And he devotes a chapter of his *De Investigatione Antichristi*, written about 1161, to an argument that clergy who turn the churches into theatres are doing the work of that very Antichrist of whom they make a show[5]. Evidently Gerhoh has

[1] Cf. p. 16.

[2] Cf. vol. i. p. 318. Pearson, ii. 285, translates: 'The old Fathers of the Church, in order to strengthen the belief of the faithful and to attract the unbeliever by this manner of religious service, rightly instituted at the Feast of Epiphany or the Octave religious performances of such a kind as the star guiding the Magi to the new-born Christ, the cruelty of Herod, the dispatch of the soldiers, the lying-in of the Blessed Virgin, the angel warning the Magi not to return to Herod, and other events of the birth of Christ. But what nowadays happens in many churches? Not a customary ritual, not an act of reverence, but one of irreligion and extravagance conducted with all the license of youth. The priests having changed their clothes go forth as a troop of warriors; there is no distinction between priest and warrior to be marked. At an unfitting gathering of priests and laymen the church is desecrated by feasting and drinking, buffoonery, unbecoming jokes, play, the clang of weapons, the presence of shameless wenches, the vanities of the world, and all sorts of disorder. Rarely does such a gathering break up without quarrelling.'

[3] On Gerhoh (1093–1169) see the article in the 2nd ed. of Wetzer and Welte's *Kirchenlexicon*. He took a strong reforming and anti-imperial line in the controversies of his day.

[4] Gerhohus, *Comm. in Ps. cxxxii* (*P. L.* cxciv. 890) 'Cohaerebat ipsi Ecclesiae claustrum satis honestum, sed a claustrali religione omnino vacuum, cum neque in dormitorio fratres dormirent, neque in refectorio comederent, exceptis rarissimis festis, maxime in quibus Herodem repraesentarent Christi persecutorem, parvulorum interfectorem, seu ludis aliis aut spectaculis quasi theatralibus exhibendis comportaretur symbolum ad faciendum convivium in refectorio aliis pene omnibus temporibus vacuo.'

[5] Gerhohus, *de Inv. Ant.* lib. i. c. 5, *de spectaculis theatricis in ecclesia Dei exhibitis* (*Gerhohi Opera Inedita*, ed. Scheibelberger, i. 25) 'Et sacerdotes, qui dicuntur, iam non ecclesiae vel altaris ministerio dediti

been stung by the lampooning of his party as the *Hypocritae* in the pro-imperialist *Antichristus* which is still extant. But he includes in his condemnation plays of a less special and polemical character, referring especially to the Nativity cycle and to a lost play of *Elisaeus.* He repeats some of the old patristic objections against *larvae* and *spectacula,* and tells tales, such as Prynne will tell after him, of how horrors mimicked by actors have been miraculously converted into verities [1]. Literary historians occasionally commit themselves to the statement that Innocent III forbade the clergy to participate in miracle-plays [2]. It is more than doubtful

sunt, sed exercitiis avaritiae, vanitatum et spectaculorum, adeo ut ecclesias ipsas, videlicet orationum domus, in theatra commutent ac mimicis ludorum spectaculis impleant. Inter quae nimirum spectacula adstantibus ac spectantibus ipsorum feminis interdum et antichristi, de quo nobis sermo est, non ut ipsi aestimant imaginariam similitudinem exhibent sed in veritate, ut credi potest iniquitatis ipsius mysterium pro parte sua implent. Quidni enim diabolus abutatur in serium rebus sibi exhibitis in vanitatis ludicrum, sicut Dominus quoque Iesus convertens in seria ludibria, quibus apud Iudaeos vel Pilatum in passione sua affectus est? . . . Quid ergo mirum si et isti nunc antichristum vel Herodem in suis ludis simulantes eosdem non, ut eis intentioni est, ludicro mentiuntur sed in veritate exhibent, utpote quorum vita ab antichristi laxa conversatione non longe abest? . . . Contigit, ut comperimus, aliquando apud tales, ut eum quem inter ludicra sua quasi mortuum ab Elisaeo propheta suscitantem exhiberent peracta simulatione mortuum invenirent. Alius item antichristo suo quasi suscitandus oblatus intra septem dies vere mortuus, ut comperimus, et sepultus est. Et quis scire potest an et cetera simulata antichristi scilicet effigiem, daemonum larvas, herodianam insaniem in veritate non exhibeant? . . . Exhibent praeterea imaginaliter et salvatoris infantiae cunabula, parvuli vagitum, puerperae virginis matronalem habitum, stellae quasi sidus flammigerum, infantum necem, maternum Rachelis ploratum. Sed divinitas insuper et matura facies ecclesiae abhorret spectacula theatralia, non respicit in vanitates et insanias falsas, immo non falsas sed iam veras insanias, in quibus viri totos se frangunt in feminas quasi pudeat eos, quod viri sunt, clerici in milites, homines se in daemonum larvas transfigurant . . .'

[1] Prynne, *Histriomastix*, 556, refers to 'the visible apparition of the Devill on the Stage at the Belsavage Play-house, in Queene Elizabeth's dayes (to the great amazement both of the Actors and Spectators) whiles they were there prophanely playing the History of Faustus (the truth of which I have heard from many now alive, who well remember it), there being some distracted with that fearefull sight.'

[2] Pollard, xxiv. I do not know how Ward, i. 43, gets at the very different theory that in 1210 (*sic* for 1207) Innocent III ordered plays 'to be represented outside the church as well as inside.' Mr. Pollard, by the way, assigns the prohibition to 'Pope Gregory,' a further mistake, due, I suppose, to the fact that it was subsequently included in the Gregorian *Decretals.*

whether this was so. The prohibition in question is familiar to us, and it is clear that the *ludi theatrales* which Innocent barred from the churches were primarily the Feasts of Fools, and the like[1]. And as a matter of fact the *glossa ordinaria* to the decretal by Bernard de Bottone, which itself dates from about 1263, so interprets the words of the Pope as expressly to allow of Christmas and Easter representations calculated to stimulate devotion[2]. Yet there would have been no need for the gloss to have been written had not an opposite interpretation also been current. It was perhaps on the strength of the decree that another reformer, Robert Grosseteste, justified his action when in 1244 he directed his archdeacons to exterminate, so far as they could, the *miracula*, which he put on the same level as May-games and harvest-Mays, or the *scotales* of the folk[3]. And it is certainly appealed to before the end of the thirteenth century in the *Manuel des Péchés* of the Anglo-Norman William of Waddington[4]. Robert

[1] Cf. vol. i. p. 279.

[2] Quoted by Creizenach, i. 101, 'Non tamen hic prohibetur repraesentare praesepe Domini, Herodem, magos et qualiter Rachel ploravit filios suos, etc., quae tangunt festivitates illas, de quibus hic fit mentio, cum talia ad devotionem potius inducant homines quam ad lasciviam vel voluptatem, sicut in pascha sepulcrum Domini et alia repraesentantur ad devotionem excitandam': cf. vol. i. p. 342. J. Aquila, *Opusculum Enchiridion appellatum ferme de omni ludorum genere*, f. 14 (Oppenheim, 1516), after referring to the canon, says, 'Demonstrationes quae fiunt ad honorem dei puta passionis Christi aut vitae alicuius sancti non prohibentur in sacris locis ac temporibus fieri.' Both canon and gloss are cited in *Dives and Pauper*, a book of fifteenth-century English morality (F. A. Gasquet, *Eve of Reformation*, 317): cf. also D'Ancona, i. 54.

[3] Cf. vol. i. p. 91. An anchoress of Tarrant Keynston (*Ancren Riwle*, †1150, C. S. 318) was bound to confess if she 'eode oðe pleouwe ine chircheie: biheold hit ⁊ oðe wrastlinge ⁊ oðer fol gomenes': but 'pleouwe,' like *ludus* (vol. i. p. 393), may have a very general meaning.

[4] Manning, 146:—

Un autre folie apert
Vnt les fols clercs cuntroue,
Qe 'miracles' sunt apele;
Lur faces vnt la deguise
Par visers, li forsene,—
Qe est defendu en decree;
Tant est plus grand lur peche.
Fere poent representement,—
Mes que ceo seit chastement
En office de seint eglise
Quant hom fet la deu servise,—
Cum iesu crist le fiz dee
En sepulcre esteit pose,
Et la resurrectiun,
Pur plus auer deuociun.
Mes, fere foles assemblez
En les rues des citez,
Ou en cymiters apres mangers,
Quant venent les fols volunters,—
Tut dient qe il le funt pur bien,—
Crere ne les deuez pur rien
Qe fet seit pur le honur de dee,
Einz del deable, pur verite,
Seint ysidre me ad testimone
Qe fut si bon clerc lettre;
Il dist qe cil qe funt sepectacles

Grosseteste presumably, and William of Waddington specifically, objected to *miracula* even out of doors, which is surely stretching the words of Innocent III beyond what they will reasonably bear. In any case the austere view of the matter was not that which prevailed. The lax discipline of the 'Babylonish captivity' at Avignon, which allowed the Feast of Fools to grow up unchecked through the fourteenth century, was not likely to boggle at the plays. The alleged indulgence, not without modern parallels [1], of Clement VI to the spectators of the Chester plays and the performance of a *Stella* given by the English bishops in honour of their continental colleagues at the council of Constance in 1417 [2] are two out of

Cume lem fet en miracles,
Or ius qe nus nomames einz —
Burdiz ou turneinens, —
Lur baptesme vnt refusez,
E deu de ciel reneiez,' &c.

Robert Mannyng of Brunne (1303) translates:—

'Hyt ys forbode hym, yn the decre,
Myracles for to make or se;
For myracles, ȝyf þou begynne,
Hyt ys a gaderyng, a syghte of synne,
He may yn þe cherche þurghe þys resun
Pley þe resurrecyun,
Þat ys to seye, how Gode ros,
God and man yn myȝt and los,
To make men be yn beleue gode
That he has ros wyþ flesshe and blode:
And he may pleye wyþoutyn plyghte
Howe god was bore yn ȝole nyght,
To make men to beleue stedfastly
Þat he lyghte yn þe vyrgyne Mary.
Ȝuf þou do hyt in weyys or greuys,
A syghte of synne truly hyt semys.
Seynt Ysodre, y take to wytnes,
For he hyt seyþ þat soþ hyt es;
Þus hyt seyþ yn hys boke,
Þey foresake þat þey toke—
God and here crystendom—
Þat make swyche pleyys to any man
As myracles and bourdys,
Or tournamentys of grete prys,' &c.

The reference to 'Seynt Ysodre' is to Isidore of Seville, *Etymologiarum* xviii. 59, *de horum* [*ludorum*] *exsecratione* (*P.L.* lxxxii. 660). The saint is speaking of course of the Roman *spectacula*.

[1] On the 'pardon' or 'Ablass' given to actors at Oberammergau, and the meaning, or want of meaning, to be attached to it, see an amusing controversy in the *Nineteenth Century* for January and February, 1901.

[2] L'Enfant, *Hist. du Concile de Constance* (1727), ii. 404; Hardt, *Magnum Oecumenicum Constantiense Concilium* (1700), iv. 1089; K. Schmidt, *Die Digby-Spiele*, 12. The performance, which was possibly a dumb show, took place at a banquet on Jan. 24, 141$\frac{7}{8}$, and was repeated on the following Sunday before the emperor, who had arrived in the interval. Hardt quotes the German of one Dacher, an eyewitness: 'Am 24ten tag des Monats Januarii, das vvar auff Timotheus tag, da luden die Bischöff aus Engeland, der Bischoff Salisburgensis, der Bischoff von Londen, und demnach funff Bischoff von Engeland, alle Räht zu Costniz und sonst viel ehrbar Bürger daselbst, in Burchart Walters Haus, das man vorzeiten nennt zu dem Burgthor, itzt zu dem gulden Schvvert, allernächst bey S. Laurenz. Und gab ihnen fast ein köstlich mahl, ie 2. Gericht nach einander, jedes Gericht besonder mit 8 Essen: Die trug man allvveg eins mahl dar, deren allvveg

many proofs that the later mediaeval Church found no difficulty in accommodating itself to the somewhat disconcerting by-product of its own liturgy[1]. Such opposition to the religious drama as can be traced after the thirteenth century came not from the heads of the Church but from its heretics. It is chiefly represented by a curious *Tretise of miraclis pleyinge* which dates from the end of the fourteenth century and may safely be referred to a Wyclifite origin[2]. The burden of it is the sin of making 'oure pleye and bourde of tho myraclis and werkis that God so ernestfully wrouȝt to us.' On this note the anonymous preacher harps rather monotonously, and

waren 4 verguld oder versilbert. In dem mahl, zvvischen dem Essen, so machten sie solch bild und geberd, als unser Frau ihr Kind unsern Herrn und auch Gott gebahr, mit fast köstlichen Tüchern und Gevvand. Und Joseph stellten sie zu ihr. Und die heiligen 3 Könige, als die unser Frauen die Opffer brachten. Und hatten gemacht einen lauteren guldnen Stern, der ging vor ihnen, an einem kleinen eisern Drat. Und machten König Herodem, vvie er den drey Königen nachsandt, und vvie er die Kindlein ertodtet. Das machten sie alles mit gar köstlichem Gevvand, und mit grossen guldenen und silbernen Gürteln, und machten das mit grosser Gezierd, und mit grosser Demuht.'

[1] The provincial *C. of Sens* (1460), c. 3 (Labbé, xiii. 1728), while confirming the Basle decree, allowed 'aliquid iuxta consuetudines ecclesiae, in Nativitate Domini, vel Resurrectione . . . fiat cum honestate et pace, absque prolongatione, impedimento, vel diminutione servitii, larvatione et sordidatione faciei'; cf. the Toledo decree of 1473 quoted vol. i. p. 342. The *C. of Compostella* (1565), c.c. 9-11 (Aguirra *Conc. Hispan.* v. 450, 460), forbade 'actus sive repraesentationes' during service in church; they might take place with leave of the bishop, or in his absence the chapter, before or after service. Devotional 'actus' were allowed in Passion week on similar conditions. The Corpus Christi procession 'semel tantum subsistat, causa horum actuum vel representationum in eo loco extra ecclesiam quem Praelatus aut [capitulum] idoneum iudicabit.' On the other hand the *C. of Seville* (1512), c. 21 (Aguirra, v. 370), had forbidden priests or monks to perform or give a 'locus' for such 'actus': 'Sumus informati, quod in quibusdam Ecclesiis nostri Archiepiscopatus et Provinciae permittitur fieri nonnullas repraesentationes Passionis Domini nostri Iesu Christi, et alios actus, et memoriam Resurrectionis, Nativitatis Salvatoris nostri, vel alias repraesentationes. Et quia ex talibus actibus orta sunt, et oriuntur plura absurda, et saepe saepius scandala in cordibus illorum qui non sunt bene confirmati in nostra sancta fide Catholica, videntes confusiones, et excessus, qui in hoc committuntur . . .' Cf. also the Langres licence of 1408 (p. 97).

[2] Text in *Reliquiae Antiquae*, ii. 42; Hazlitt, 73; from late fourteenth-century volume of homilies formerly in library of St. Martin's-in-the-Fields. There is also in *Rel. Ant.* i. 322 a satirical English poem from *Cott. MS. Cleop.* B. ii (fifteenth century), against the miracle plays of the 'frer mynours,' apparently at Rome. But the Minorite in *Pierce the Ploughman's Crede* (†1394, ed. Skeat), 107, says of his order, 'At marketts & myracles · we medleþ vs nevere.'

adds that 'myraclis pleyinge . . . makith to se veyne siȝtis of degyse, aray of men and wymmen by yvil continaunse, eyther stiryng othere to letcherie and of debatis.' Like Gerhoh of Reichersberg, he thinks the plays 'gynnys of the dyvul to drawen men to the byleve of Anti-Crist.' He elaborately confutes the views that they are for the worship of God, or the more compassion of Christ, or lead to conversion. He will not allow that 'summe recreatioun men moten han, and bettere it is or lesse yvele that thei han theyre recreacoun by pleyinge of myraclis than bi pleyinge of other japis.' The analysis of the piece need not, perhaps, be pushed further. The opinions expressed do not appear to have had any weight either of popular or of ecclesiastical sentiment behind them; but they curiously antedate the histriomastic tracts of many a sixteenth and seventeenth-century Puritan.

This chapter may be fitly closed by a few words on the subject of nomenclature[1]. The old classical terms of *tragoedia* and *comoedia* are not of course normally used of the religious plays until the Renaissance influences come in towards the end of the fifteenth century. Their mediaeval sense, in fact, implies nothing distinctively dramatic[2]. The liturgical plays have often a purely liturgical heading, such as *Processio Asinorum*[3], or *Officium Sepulchri*[4], or *Ordo Rachaelis*[5]. Perhaps *officium* may be taken to denote the thing itself, the special service or section of a service; *ordo* rather the book, the written directions for carrying out the *officium*. Or they have

[1] Creizenach, i. 157, 162: Julleville, *Les Myst.* i. 107, 187; G. Smith, 251; Pollard, xix; Ward, i. 41.

[2] Cf. ch. xxv.

[3] Cf. p. 54 (Rouen, *Prophetae*, fourteenth century).

[4] Cf. pp. 37, 41, 45; Lange, 130, 155; 'officium sepulchri,' 'officium peregrinorum,' 'officium pastorum,' 'officium regum trium,' 'stellae officium' (Rouen, eleventh century–fifteenth century); 'resurrectionis domini aguntur officia' (Prague, fourteenth century). At Melk in 1517, 'acturus officium angeli' (Lange, 110), 'officium' has rather the sense of 'part.'

[5] Cf. pp. 37, 48, 49, 53, 71, 77; Lange, 48, 93, 95, 146; 'Ordo visitationis sepulchri' (Strassburg, 1513), 'Ordo visitandi sepulchrum' (Bamberg, 1597), 'Ordo ad visitandum sepulchrum' (Prague, twelfth century, Haarlem, thirteenth century), 'Ordo sepulchri' (Würzburg, thirteenth century), 'Ordo ad suscipiendum peregrinum' (Beauvais), 'Ordo stellae' (Laon, thirteenth century), 'Ordo [stellae]' (Bilsen, eleventh century), 'Ordo Rachaelis' (Freising, eleventh century), 'Ordo Prophetarum' (Laon, thirteenth century), 'Ordo creacionis, etc.' (Regensburg, 1194), 'Ordo, sive registrum de Passione domini' (Frankfort, fourteenth century).

a title derived from their subject, such as *Visitatio Sepulchri*[1], or *Suscitatio Lazari*[2]. Or they are introduced in terms which cannot be said to have a technical signification at all, *ad faciendam similitudinem*[3], *ad suscipiendum*[4], *ad repraesentandum*[5]. *Similitudo* I do not find outside Fleury, nor the corresponding *exemplum* outside the Benedictbeuern manuscript[6]. From *ad repraesentandum*, however, a technical term does arise, and *repraesentatio* must be considered, more than any other word, as the mediaeval Latin equivalent of 'dramatic performance[7].' This the Italian vernacular preserves as *rappresentazione*. A synonym for *repraesentatio*, which naturally came into use when the intention of recreation began to substitute itself for devotion, is *ludus*, with its vernacular renderings, all in common use, of *jeu*, *Spiel*, 'play.' But *ludus*, as already pointed out[8], is a generic term for 'amusement,' and the special sense of 'dramatic play' is only a secondary one[9]. 'Clerks' play' as a variant for miracle-play is occasionally found[10]. Yet another synonym which makes its appearance in the twelfth century, is *miraculum*; and this, originally a mere convenient shorthand for *repraesentatio miraculi*, came, especially in England, to stand for 'religious play' in general[11]. *Mystère*, or 'mystery,' on the other hand, is not

[1] See last note.

[2] Cf. p. 58.

[3] Cf. pp. 36, 37, 47; Lange, 160 'ad faciendam similitudinem domini sepulchri,' 'ad faciendam similitudinem domini apparitionis' (Fleury, thirteenth century), 'versus ad stellam faciendam' (Nevers, †1060), 'fiunt peregrini' (Saintes, thirteenth century).

[4] Cf. p. 103, n. 5 above.

[5] Cf. pp. 58, 60; Lange, 157; 'ad repraesentandum quomodo sanctus Nicolaus' (Fleury, thirteenth century), 'historia de Daniel repraesentanda' (Hilarius, twelfth century), 'si Mariae debeant repraesentari' (Coutances, fifteenth century).

[6] Cf. pp. 37, 39.

[7] Cf. pp. 45, 107; Lange, 136; 'in resurrectione domini repraesentatio' (Cividale, fourteenth century), 'repraesentatio trium Regum' (Rouen, 1507, 1521), 'repraesentacio pastorum . . . resurreccionis . . . peregrinorum' (Lichfield, †1190).

[8] Cf. vol. i. p. 393.

[9] Cf. pp. 63, 73, 'ludus super iconia Sancti Nicolai' (Hilarius, twelfth century); cf. the Antichrist and Benedictbeuern Nativity, and note 11 below.

[10] Cf. pp. 140, 202.

[11] Cf. vol. i. p. 91; vol. ii. pp. 60, 380; 'miraculum de Sancto Nicolao' (Fleury, thirteenth century), 'repraesentationes miraculorum' (Fitz-Stephen, †1180), 'miraculum in nocte Paschae' (Lichfield, †1190; cf. note 7 above), 'ludum . . . quem Miracula vulgariter appellamus' (Matthew Paris, thirteenth century), 'ludos quos vocant miracula' (Grosseteste, 1244). The vernacular 'miracles,' 'myraclis,' is found in the *Handlyng Synne*, and the *Tretise of miraclis pleyinge*.

English at all, in a dramatic sense[1], and in France first appears as *misterie* in the charter given by Charles VI in 1402 to the Parisian *confrérie de la Passion*[2]. This term also acquires a very general signification by the end of the fifteenth century. Its radical meaning is still matter of dispute. Probably it is derived from *ministerium*, should be spelt *mistère*, and is spelt *mystère* by a natural confusion with the derivative of *μυστήριον*. Even then the question remains, what sort of *ministerium*? M. Petit de Julleville would explain it as a 'religious function,' and thus equate it precisely with *officium*[3]. Only it does not appear in connexion with the liturgical plays[4], and perhaps it is more plausible to regard it as denoting the 'function' of the guild of actors, just as its doublet *menestrie*, the English 'minstrelsy,' denotes the 'function' of the minstrels[5], or its doublet *métier*, which in English becomes in fact 'mystery,' denotes the 'function' of the craft guilds. Perhaps the theory of M. de Julleville finds a little support from the term *actio*, which appears, besides its meaning in connexion with the Mass[6], to be once at least used for a play[7]. At any rate *actus* is so used as a Latin equivalent of the Spanish *auto*[8].

[1] Pollard, xix; Ward, i. 41. The first English use of the term 'mystery' is in the preface to Dodsley's *Select Collection of Old Plays* (1744). The distinction between 'mysteries' which 'deal with Gospel events only' and 'miracles,' which 'are more especially concerned with incidents derived from the legends of the Saints of the Church' is a not very happy invention of the literary historians.

[2] Julleville, *Les Myst.* i. 417 'Licence de faire et jouer quelque Misterre que ce soit, soit de la dicte Passion, et Résurreccion, ou autre quelconque tant de saincts comme des sainctes.'

[3] Julleville, *Les Myst.* i. 189.

[4] Except after its dramatic sense was already well established; cf. pp. 42, 65, 'mysterium in die Ascensionis' (Lille, 1416), 'misterium Pastorum' (Rouen, 1457).

[5] Cf. Appendix B.

[6] Walafridus Strabo, *de rebus eccles.*, c. 22, in the ninth century, gives the name 'actio' to the 'canon' or unchangeable portion of the Mass (Maskell, *Ancient Liturgy of the Church of England*, 112).

[7] Cf. *Representations*, s.v. Shipton.

[8] Cf. supra, p. 102, note 1.

CHAPTER XXI

GUILD PLAYS AND PARISH PLAYS

[*Bibliographical Note.*— The English miracle play has been often, fully, and admirably studied from the point of view of dramatic literature; perhaps less so from that of stage history. The best accounts are those of B. Ten Brink, *History of English Literature*, bk. v, chs. 2-6 (trans. W. C. Robinson, vol. ii, 1893); A. W. Ward, *History of English Dramatic Literature* (2nd ed., 1899), vol. i, ch. 1; W. Creizenach, *Geschichte des neueren Dramas*, vol. i (1893); and the introduction to A. W. Pollard, *English Miracle Plays, Moralities and Interludes* (3rd ed., 1898). These supersede J. P. Collier, *History of English Dramatic Poetry* (2nd ed., 1879), vol. ii, and J. L. Klein, *Geschichte des englischen Dramas* (1876), vol. i. Other useful books are J. A. Symonds, *Shakspere's Predecessors in the English Drama* (1884), ch. 3; K. L. Bates, *The English Religious Drama* (1893), and J. J. Jusserand, *Le Théâtre en Angleterre* (1881), ch. 2. The substance of this last is incorporated in the same writer's *Literary History of the English People*, vol. i (1895), bk. iii, ch. 6. W. J. Courthope, *History of English Poetry*, vol. i (1895), ch. 10, should also be consulted, as well as the valuable detailed investigations of A. Hohlfeld, *Die altenglischen Kollektivmisterien*, in *Anglia*, vol. xi (1889), and C. Davidson, *Studies in the English Mystery Plays* (1892). I do not think that S. W. Clarke, *The Miracle Play in England* (n.d.), and C. Hastings, *Le Théâtre français et anglais* (1900, trans. 1901), add very much. A. Ebert, *Die englischen Mysterien*, in *Jahrbuch für romanische und englische Literatur*, vol. i (1859), is an early manifestation of German interest in the subject, and the still earlier native learning may be found in T. Warton, *History of English Poetry* (ed. W. C. Hazlitt, 1871), §§ 6, 33; E. Malone, *Historical Account of the English Stage*, in *Variorum Shakespeare* (1821), vol. iii; W. Hone, *Ancient Mysteries Described* (1823). The antiquarianism of T. Sharp, *Dissertation on the Pageants or Dramatic Mysteries Anciently Performed at Coventry* (1825), is still a mine of material on the *Realien* of the stage.—The four great cycles have been edited as follows, in most cases with important introductions: the *Chester Plays* by T. Wright (*Shakespeare Society*, 1843-7) and by H. Deimling (*E. E. T. S.*, part only issued in 1893); the *York Plays* by L. T. Smith (1885); the *Towneley* or *Wakefield Plays* by an uncertain editor (*Surtees Society*, 1836), and by G. England and A. W. Pollard (*E. E. T. S.* 1897); the *Ludus Coventriae*, by J. O. Halliwell [-Phillipps] (*Shakespeare Society*, 1841). A miscellaneous collection of late plays from one of the *Bodleian Digby MSS.* has been printed by T. Sharp (*Abbotsford Club*, 1835), and F. J. Furnivall (*New Shakespeare Society*, 1882, *E. E. T. S.* 1896). The Cornish cycle is in E. Norris, *The Ancient Cornish Drama* (1859). Good selections of typical plays are in A. W. Pollard's book, and J. M. Manly, *Specimens of the Pre-Shakespearean Drama* (1897), vol. i. Older books of the same kind are J. P. Collier, *Five Miracle Plays, or Scriptural Dramas* (1836), and W. Marriott, *A Collection of English Miracle Plays or Mysteries*

(Basle, 1838). The bibliographies given by Miss Bates and by F. H. Stoddard, *References for Students of Miracle Plays and Mysteries* (1887), may be supplemented from my *Appendices* of *Representations* and *Texts*, which I have tried to make as complete as possible.]

THERE is no reason to doubt that England had its full share in the earlier development of the religious drama. Texts of the liturgical period are, indeed, rare. The tenth-century version of the *Quem quaeritis* from Winchester and the fourteenth-century version from Dublin stand, at least for the present, alone. But the wholesale destruction of liturgical books at the Reformation is sufficient to account for such a sparseness, and a few stray notices gathered from the wreckage of time bear sufficient witness to the presence in this country of several amongst the more widespread types of liturgical play. The Lichfield statutes (1188–98) provide for *repraesentationes* of the *Pastores*, the *Resurrectio*, the *Peregrini*; those of York (†1255) for the *Pastores* and the *Tres Reges*; a Salisbury inventory of 1222 includes 'crowns' or more probably 'stars' (*coronae*) *ad repraesentationes faciendas*; while Lincoln account books of the early fifteenth century appear to add the *Annuntiatio* and the *Prophetae*, a *visus* called *Rubum quem viderat* in 1420 perhaps forming a Moses scene in the latter. So late as 1518 the *Quem quaeritis* was performed in Magdalen College chapel, and plays of the Nativity and the Resurrection by the clerks of the chapel are contemplated at about the same date in the household regulations of the Earl of Northumberland at Leconfield. Nor were dramatic versions of the legends of saints unknown. I do not trace a St. Nicholas cycle in England, although Hilarius, in whose repertory a St. Nicholas play is included, is thought to have been an Englishman by birth. But the memory of a play of St. Catherine prepared by Geoffrey the Norman at Dunstable early in the twelfth century was preserved, owing to the accident which led to Geoffrey ultimately becoming abbot of St. Albans; and towards the close of the same century William Fitzstephen records the representations of the miracles of holy confessors and the passions of martyrs which took the place of minstrelsy in London. For the most part such early plays are found in close connexion with the cathedrals and great monasteries. But a document of about 1220, the interpretation of which must, however, be considered doubtful, would seem to suggest that plays (*actiones*) were habitually given at no less than five chapelries within the single parish of Shipton in Oxfordshire, and that the profits thereof formed an appreciable part of the income derived from that living by the prebendaries of Salisbury cathedral.

Examples of the transitional forms by which the liturgical drama grew into the popular religious drama of the great cycles can also be found in England. At Beverley a Resurrection play is described as taking place in the graveyard of the minster about 1220. The intrusion of the vernacular is represented by the curious bilingual text of a single actor's parts in the *Pastores*, *Quem quaeritis* and *Peregrini*, printed by Professor Skeat from a manuscript found at Shrewsbury. These are probably still liturgical in character, and it is to be observed that their subjects are precisely those of the three plays known to have been used in the neighbouring cathedral of Lichfield. It must remain a moot point whether the religious drama passed directly, in this country, from Latin to English, or whether there was a period during which performances were given in Norman-French. Scholars are inclined to find an Anglo-Norman dialect in that very important monument of the transition, the *Repraesentatio Adae*, as well as in an early example of the expanded Easter play. But even if the authors of these were, like Hilarius, of English birth, it hardly follows that their productions were acted in England. Nor do the probable borrowings of the Chester and other cycles from French texts much affect the question[1]. That the disfavour with which the austerer section of the clergy looked upon the vernacular religious plays had its spokesmen in England, was sufficiently illustrated in the last chapter.

The English miracle-play reaches its full development with the formation of the great processional cycles almost immediately after the establishment of the Corpus Christi festival in 1311. The local tradition of Chester, stripped of a certain

[1] Cf. p. 146.

confusion between the names of two distinct mayors of that city which has clung about it, is found to fix the foundation of the Chester plays in 1328. The date has the authority of an official municipal document, forms part of a quite consistent story, several points in which can be independently corroborated, and is on *a priori* grounds extremely plausible. Unfortunately, owing to the comparative scarcity of archives during this period, the first fifty years of the history of municipal drama are practically a blank. A mention, about 1350, of a *ludus filiorum Israelis*, in connexion with a guild of Corpus Christi at Cambridge, spans a wide gulf. There is no actual record of plays at Chester itself until 1462. Those of Beverley are first mentioned in 1377, those of York in 1378, and those of Coventry in 1392. But it must be added that the Beverley plays were an *antiqua consuetudo* in 1390, and that those of York were to take place at stations *antiquitus assignatis* in 1394. It is in 1378 that the earliest notice of plays in London, since the days of William Fitzstephen, comes to light. The fuller records which are from this time onward available reveal, during the next hundred and fifty years, a vigorous and widespread dramatic activity throughout the length and breadth of the land. It manifests itself at such extreme points as the Cinque Ports in the east, Cornwall in the west, and Newcastle in the north. It penetrates to Aberdeen and to Dublin. And though naturally it finds its fullest scope in the annually repeated performances of several amongst the greater cities, yet it is curious to observe in what insignificant villages it was from time to time found possible to organize plays. Performers from thirteen neighbouring places, many of them quite small, made their way to New Romney between 1399 and 1508; whilst the churchwardens of Chelmsford, in the twelve years after their own play in 1562, reaped a profit by hiring out their stock of garments to the men of some seventeen aspiring parishes. On the other hand, there were several important towns in which, so far as we can judge from documents, such as craft ordinances, which would almost certainly have referred to the plays of the crafts, if these had existed, the normal type of municipal drama failed to establish itself. London is one, although here the want was supplied in another way; others are Northampton, Nottingham, Bristol, Oxford, and Reading. And occasionally plays, which had once been annual, were allowed to fall into desuetude and decay. The corporation of Canterbury, for instance, called upon the crafts about 1500 to revive a Corpus Christi play which for some time had been 'left and laid apart.' Certainly, by the sixteenth century, if there was still pride and interest taken in many of the municipal plays, signs were not wanting that they were an institution which had almost outlived its day. A reason for this need hardly be sought beyond the *Zeitgeist*. No doubt the plays were a financial burden upon the poorer crafts and the poorer members of crafts. There was much grumbling at Beverley in 1411 because certain well-to-do persons (*generosi*), who did not practise any trade or handicraft, had hitherto escaped the payment of contributions to the civic function; and municipal authorities were constantly called upon to adjust and readjust the responsibility for this and that pageant with the fluctuations of prosperity amongst the various occupations. But on the other hand, the plays were the cause of much and profitable resort to those fortunate towns which possessed them. The mercers' guild at Shrewsbury found it necessary to impose a special fine upon those of its members whose business avocations required them 'to ride or goe to Coventrie Faire' at Corpus Christi tide, and so to miss the procession of guilds at home[1]. And although the mayor of Coventry wrote to Thomas Cromwell, in 1539, that the poor commoners were put to such expense with their plays and pageants that they fared the worse all the year after, yet against this may be set the statement made to Dugdale by 'some old people who had in their younger days been eye-witnesses of these pageants' that 'the confluence of people from farr and neare to see that shew was extraordinary great, and yeilded noe small advantage to this cittye.' Moreover the levy upon individuals was a trifling one; the whole of the company of smiths at Coventry only paid 3*s.* 4*d.* amongst them for 'pagent pencys' in 1552. A *leitourgia* is always an unpopular institution, and these

[1] *Trans. of Shropshire Antiq. Soc.* viii. 273.

complaints resemble nothing so much as the groans of an opulent London tradesman in the twentieth century over an extra penny on the education rate. In the smaller places it is clear that plays, far from being a source of expense, were a recognized method of raising funds for public purposes. Even in 1220 the *emolumentum actionum* from the chapelries of Shipton went to swell the purses of the Salisbury prebendaries. In 1505 the churchwardens of Kingston-on-Thames made £4 towards their new steeple by getting up a play for which they secured the patronage of royalty. At Braintree, in Essex, funds were similarly raised by Nicholas Udall and others, between 1523 and 1534, for the repair of the church. I have little doubt that when the mayor of Coventry said economy he meant Protestantism, just as when, under Elizabeth, the corporation of London wished to make a Puritanic attack upon the theatres, they were always smitten with a terrible dread of the infection of the plague [1].

Certainly the spirit of Protestantism, although it came to be willing to use the religious drama for its own purposes [2], was inclined to see both profanity and superstition in the ordinary miracle-plays [3]. Here, as elsewhere, it inherited the hostile tradition which such reforming clerics as Gerhoh of Reichersberg in the twelfth century and Robert Grosseteste in the thirteenth had handed down to Wyclif and his Lollards. At Bungay in 1514 certain ill-disposed persons 'brake and threw down five pageants' usually borne about the town on Corpus Christi day. One may fairly suspect, even at this early date, a Lollardist intention in the outrage, and perhaps also in the interposition of the authority of the warden of the Cinque Ports to suppress the play of New Romney in 1518. With the progress of the new ideas the big cycles began to be irregularly performed or to undergo textual modification. The plays of York, for example, were shorn in 1548 of the pageants representing the Death, Assumption, and Coronation

[1] *Analytical Index to Remembrancia of City of London*, 330 sqq.; 350 sqq.

[2] Cf. ch. xxv.

[3] For the general Puritan attitude to the stage, see S. Gosson, *Schoole of Abuse*, 1579 (ed. Arber); W. Prynne, *Histriomastix* (1633), with the authorities there quoted; and the tracts in W. C. Hazlitt, *The English Drama and Stage*.

of the Virgin. On the other hand, religious plays sometimes became a rallying-point for those who favoured the old order of things. There is extant a letter from Henry VIII to the justices of York, in which he refers to a riot promoted by certain papists at a play of St. Thomas the Apostle, and warns them not to suffer upon such occasions any language likely to tend to a breach of the peace. The brief Marian reaction led to the resumption of the plays in more than one town which had dropped them. The Lincoln corporation ordered 'St. Anne's Gild with Corpus Cristi play' to be brought forward again in 1554 and 1555. In London Henry Machyn records during 1557 a Passion play at the Grey Friars, and another in the church of St. Olave's, Silver Street, on the festival of the patron. The New Romney play was elaborately revived, after forty-two years' interval, in 1560. But the process of decay soon set in again. Even where the plays survived, they were Protestantized, and as Corpus Christi day was no longer observed, the performances had to be transferred to some other date. At York the text of the Corpus Christi play was 'perused and otherwise amended' in 1568. In 1569 it was acted upon Whit-Tuesday. Then it lay by until 1579, when the book was referred to the archbishop and dean for further revision, and apparently impounded by them. The Creed play was suppressed, by advice of the dean, in 1568, as unsuitable to 'this happie time of the gospell.' The *Paternoster* play was revised and played in 1572. Then this text also fell into the hands of the archbishop, and the corporation seem to have been unable to recover it. So ended the religious drama in York. In Chester the municipal authorities stood out gallantly for their plays. John Hankey and Sir John Savage, mayors in 1572 and 1575 respectively, were called before the privy council for sanctioning performances in spite of inhibitions from the archbishop of York and other persons of authority. They had revised the text, and had a new and Protestant version of the preliminary 'banns' prepared. Copies of the text appear to have been got ready for yet another performance in 1600, but the local annalists record that Henry Hardware, then mayor, 'would not suffer any Playes.' In one or two cities, new plays, dealing with apocryphal or other merely semi-religious themes, were substituted for the old ones. Thus at Lincoln a 'standing play' of the story of Tobit was given in 1564 and 1567; and in Coventry, where the old cycle had been 'laid down' in 1580, an Oxford scholar was hired in 1584 to write a semi-religious semi-historical drama of the Destruction of Jerusalem. In 1591, the Conquest of the Danes and the History of King Edward the Confessor were proposed as alternatives for this. By the end of the sixteenth century all the cycles of which most is known had come to an end. The smaller places—Chelmsford in 1574, Braintree in 1579, Bungay in 1591—had sold off their stock of playing-garments. For such dramatic entertainment as the provinces were still to get, they must look to travelling companies taking their summer vacation from the metropolis. Miracle-plays during the seventeenth century were a mere survival. They lingered in distant Cornwall and at Kendal in the hill country of the north; and had been replaced by morals, themselves almost equally obsolete, at Manningtree. The last religious play recorded in England is a quite exceptional one, given at the end of James I's reign before Gondomar, the Spanish ambassador, and an audience which numbered thousands at Ely Place in Holborn.

In giving some account of the distribution of the various types of religious play throughout England during the fifteenth and sixteenth centuries, I am dispensed from any obligation to be exhaustive by the fact that the greater municipal dramas at least have already been the subject of more than one fairly adequate discussion. All I shall attempt will be a brief general summary of the main points which emerge from the more or less detailed local notices collected in a lengthy appendix.

The characteristic English type of play was the long cycle given annually under the superintendence of the corporation or governing body of an important city and divided into a number of distinct scenes or 'pageants,' each of which was the special charge of one or more of the local 'crafts,' 'arts,' or 'occupations.' Such cycles, organized upon very similar lines, can be studied in the records available from Chester,

York, Beverley, Coventry, Newcastle, Lincoln, and Norwich; and the same general model is known or conjectured—sometimes, it is true, on the slightest indication—to have been followed in the plays of Lancaster, Preston, Kendal, Wakefield, Leicester, Worcester, Louth, Bungay, Canterbury, Dublin, and Aberdeen. As in all matters of municipal custom, the relative functions of the corporations and the crafts were nicely adjusted. The direction and control of the plays as a whole were in the hands of the corporations. They decided annually whether the performance should be given, or whether, for war, pestilence, or other reason, it should be withheld. They sent round their officers to read the proclamation or 'banns' of the play. They kept an official version of the text, at Chester an 'original,' at York a 'register' copied from the 'originals' belonging to the crafts. Agreements and disputes as to the liability of this or that craft to maintain or contribute to a particular pageant were entered or determined before them. They maintained order at the time of the play and inflicted fines on the turbulent, or upon crafts neglectful or unskilful in carrying out their responsibilities. In particular they required the provision of properly qualified actors. Thus Robert Greene and others were admonished before the leet of Coventry in 1440, that they should play *bene et sufficienter* so as not to cause a hindrance in any *iocus*. Similarly, Henry Cowper, 'webster,' was fined by the wardens of Beverley in 1452, *quod nesciebat ludum suum*. An order at York, in 1476, directed the choice of a body of 'connyng, discrete, and able players' to test the quality of all those selected as actors. All 'insufficiant personnes, either in connyng, voice or personne' they were to 'discharge, ammove, and avoide'; and no one was to perform more than twice in the course of the day. Sometimes the actual oversight of the plays was delegated to specially appointed officers. At Beverley the wardens themselves 'governed' the Corpus Christi plays, but the Paternoster play was in the hands of 'aldermen of the pageants.' At Aberdeen the Haliblude play was undertaken in 1440 by the local lord of misrule, known as the Abbot of Bon Accord; for the Candlemas play 'bailyes' represented the corporation. At

Lincoln the 'graceman' of the guild of St. Anne was responsible, and had the aid of the mayor. At Leicester a number of 'overseers' with two 'bedalls' were chosen to have the 'gydyng and rule' of the play.

The corporations do not appear to have themselves incurred much expenditure over the performances. They provided sitting-room and refreshments for their own members, and for distinguished guests. Richard II was elaborately entertained with a special *pagina* when he visited York on Corpus Christi day, 1397. Sixty years later a collation, including 'ij cofyns of counfetys and a pot of grene gynger,' was made ready for Queen Margaret on her visit to Coventry. At York and Beverley, but not at Coventry, the corporations paid the minstrels, and occasionally made a special contribution to the funds of a particularly poor pageant. At York the corporation could well afford to do this, for they claimed the right to fix certain 'stations' at which, as well as at two or three traditional ones, the plays should be given, and they made a considerable annual profit out of payments by well-to-do citizens who aspired to have one of these at their doors. The stations were marked by banners broidered with the arms of the city. At Leicester the 'playyng germands' seem to have belonged to the corporation. At Beverley in 1391 they owned all the 'necessaries,' pageant garments and properties, of the play of Paradise, and lent the same upon security to the craft charged therewith. The pageants may also have been originally corporation property in York, for it was stipulated in 1422 that one of them, like the banners at the stations, should bear the arms of the city, to the exclusion of those of the craft.

As a rule, the cost of the plays fell almost wholly upon the crafts. The ordinances of the craft-guilds provide for their maintenance as a *leitourgia* or fraternal duty, in the same way as they often provide for a 'serge' or light to be burnt in some chapel or carried in the Corpus Christi procession, or, at Beverley, for the *castellum* in which the craft sat to do honour to the procession of St. John of Beverley in Rogation week. At Coventry, where the burden upon the crafts was perhaps heaviest, they were responsible for the provision, repairing, ornamenting, cleaning, and strewing with rushes of the pageant, for the 'ferme' or rent of the pageant house, for the payment of actors, minstrels, and prompter, for the revision of play-book and songs and the copying of parts, for the 'drawing' or 'horsing' of the pageant on the day of the performance, for costumes and properties, and above all for copious refreshments before and after the play, at the stations, and during the preliminary rehearsals. The total cost of the smiths' pageant in 1490 was £3 7*s.* 5½*d.* In 1453 they had contracted with one Thomas Colclow to have 'the rewle of the pajaunt' for twelve years at an annual payment of £2 6*s.* 8*d.*, and other examples of 'play lettine' can be traced at Newcastle and elsewhere. But it was more usual for the crafts to retain the management of the pageants in their own hands; at York each guild appointed its 'pageant-masters' for this purpose. The expense to the craft primarily in charge of a pageant was sometimes lightened by fixed contributions from one or more minor bodies affiliated to it for the purpose. Part of it was probably met from the general funds of the craft; the rest was raised by various expedients. A levy, known as 'pagent pencys' at Coventry and as 'pajaunt silver' at York, was made upon every member. The amount varied with the numbers of the craft and the status of the craftsman. At York it ranged from 1*d.* to 8*d.* At Beverley the journeymen paid 8*d.* to light, play, and castle, and 6*d.* only in years when there was no play. At Coventry the ordinary members of more than one craft paid 1*s.*; others apparently less. To the proceeds of the levy might be added fines for the breach of craft ordinances, payments on the taking out of freedom by strangers and the setting up of shop or indenturing of apprentices by freemen. At York, the mercers are found granting free admission to a candidate for their fraternity on condition of his entering into a favourable contract for the supply of a new pageant. At Coventry, in 1517, one William Pisford left a scarlet and a crimson gown to the tanners for their plays, together with 3*s.* 4*d.* to every craft charged with the maintenance of a pageant. Besides the levy, certain personal services were binding upon the craftsmen. They had to attend upon the play, to do it honour; the Coventry cappers expected their journeymen to do the 'horsing' of the pageant.

In some cities, the crafts received help from outside. At Coventry, in 1501, the tilers' pageant got a contribution of 5*s*. from the neighbouring tilers of Stoke. At Chester, vestments were borrowed from the clergy; at Lincoln from the priory and the local gentry. A 'gathering' was also made in the surrounding districts. The only trace of any charge made to the spectators, other than the fees for 'stations' at York, is at Leicester, where, in 1477, the players paid over to the 'pachents' certain sums they had received for playing.

The majority of the crafts in a big city were, of course, already formed into guilds for ordinary trade purposes, and in their case the necessary organization for the plays was to hand. But no citizen could wholly escape his responsibility in so important a civic matter. At Coventry it was ordered in 1494 that every person exercising any craft must become contributory to some pageant or other. At York the innholders, who do not appear to have been a regular guild, were organized in 1483 for the purposes of a pageant on the basis of a yearly contribution of 4*d*. from each man. The demand at Beverley in 1411 for the appropriation of a play to the *generosi* has already been alluded to. In a Beverley list of 1520 the 'Gentylmen' are put down for the 'Castle of Emaut.' It may be suspected that some of the other crafts named in the same list, such as the 'Husbandmen' and the 'Labourers,' were not regular guilds; not to speak of the 'Prestes,' who played the 'Coronacion of Our Lady.' This participation of religious bodies in the craft plays can be paralleled from other towns. At York the hospital of St. Leonard took the Purification in 1415; at Lincoln the cathedral clergy, like the priests at Beverley, were responsible for the Coronation or Assumption of the Virgin, a play which at Chester was given by the 'worshipfull wyves of this town,' and at York by the innholders. Both at York and Chester this scene was dropped at the Reformation. Possibly its somewhat exceptional position may be accounted for by its having been a comparatively late addition in all four cycles. Some endeavour after dramatic appropriateness is visible in the apportioning of the other plays amongst the crafts. Thus Noah is given to the shipwrights (York, Newcastle), the watermen (Beverley, Chester), the fishers and mariners (York); the *Magi* to the goldsmiths (Beverley, Newcastle, York); the Disputation in the Temple to the scriveners (Beverley), the Last Supper to the bakers (Beverley, Chester, York); the Harrowing of Hell to the cooks (Beverley, Chester).

A somewhat anomalous position is occupied amongst towns in which the plays were in the hands of the crafts by Lincoln. Here the task of supervision was shared with the corporation by a special guild, religious and social rather than industrial in character[1], of St. Anne. Perhaps this guild had at one time been solely responsible for the plays, and there had been a crisis such as took place at Norwich in 1527. Before that date the charge of the plays had been borne, fittingly enough, by the guild of St. Luke, composed of painters and metal-workers. But in 1527 this guild was 'almost fully decayed,' and upon the representation of its members the corporation agreed that in future the pageants should be distributed amongst the various crafts as was customary elsewhere. The Lincoln plays were on St. Anne's day, but one does not find a position comparable to that of the St. Anne's guild held by Corpus Christi guilds in other towns. As a rule such guilds concerned themselves with the Corpus Christi procession, but not with the plays. At Ipswich, indeed, the Corpus Christi guild had the whole conduct of the plays, and the craft-guilds as such were not called upon; but this Ipswich guild arose out of a reorganization of the old merchant-guild, included all the burgesses, and was practically identical with the corporation. Other towns, in which the corporation managed the plays itself, without the intervention of the craft-guilds, are Shrewsbury, New Romney, and Lydd.

On the other hand, where neither the corporation nor the crafts undertook plays, it was no uncommon thing for a guild of the religious or social type to step into the breach. A series of London plays recorded in 1384, 1391, 1409, and 1411 may all be not unreasonably ascribed to a guild of

[1] On such guilds cf. Cutts, *Parish Priests*, 476; Rock, ii. 395; F. A. Gasquet, *The Eve of the Reformation*, 351.

St. Nicholas, composed of the 'parish clerks' attached to the many churches of the city. At a later date the performances of this guild seem to have become annual and they are traceable, with no very great certainty, to the beginning of the sixteenth century. They were cyclical in character, but not processional, and took place hard by the well known indifferently as Skinners' well or Clerkenwell, amongst the orchards to the north of London. Chaucer says of his 'parish clerk,' the 'joly Absolon,' that

> 'Somtyme, to shewe his lightnesse and maistrye,
> He pleyeth Heródës, on a scaffold hye[1].'

These London plays may have had some original connexion with the great fair of the neighbouring priory of St. Bartholomew upon August 24; but they are recorded at various dates during the summer, and extended over four, five, or even seven days. Whether the guild of St. Nicholas bore any relation to the clerks of St. Paul's, who petitioned Richard II in 1378 against the rivalry of certain 'unexpert people' in the production of an Old Testament play, must be matter for conjecture. The performance contemplated at St. Paul's was to be at Christmas. The Cambridge guild of Corpus Christi was responsible for a *ludus Filiorum Israelis* about 1350, and this is more likely to have formed part of a cycle than to have stood alone. An unverified extract of Warton's from a Michael-House *computus* suggests that some of the Cambridge colleges may have assisted in dramatic undertakings. At Abingdon the hospital of Christ held their feast on Holy Cross day (May 3), 1445, 'with pageantes and playes, and May games.' At Sleaford, in 1480, a play of the Ascension was performed by the guild of the Holy Trinity. At Wymondham a guild seems to have existed in the sixteenth century for the express purpose of holding a 'watch and play' at Midsummer. The proceedings were directed by officers designated 'husbands.' The one example of an isolated play under the management of a craft-guild is at Hull. Here an annual play of Noah, with a ship or ark which went in procession, was in the hands of the

[1] *C. Tales*, 3383 (*Miller's Tale*).

Trinity House, a guild of master mariners and pilots. The records extend from 1421 to 1529. There is no sign of a dramatic cycle at Hull. The Noah play was given on Plough Monday, and it is possible that one may trace here a dramatized version of just such a ship procession as may be found elsewhere upon the coasts in spring[1]. After the performance the 'ship' was hung up in the church. The text of the play was perhaps borrowed from that of the watermen of the neighbouring city of Beverley.

Where there were craft-plays, social and religious guilds sometimes gave supplementary performances. The 'schaft' or parochial guild of St. Dunstan's, Canterbury, owned a play of Abraham and Isaac in 1491. This may have been merely a contribution towards the craft-cycle on Corpus Christi day. On the other hand, the play of St. George, contemplated by the guild of that saint at New Romney in 1490, was probably an independent undertaking. The town play here was a Passion play. At York there were two rivals to the Corpus Christi plays. One was the *Paternoster* play, for the production of which a guild of the Lord's Prayer was in existence at least as early as 1378. By 1488 this guild was absorbed into the Holy Trinity guild of the mercers, and in the year named the play was given, apparently at the charges of the mercers, instead of the ordinary cycle. All the crafts contributed to similar performances in 1558 and 1572. But by this time the supervision, under the corporation, of the play had passed to one of the few religious guilds in York which had escaped suppression, that of St. Anthony. The other extraordinary York play was a Creed play, bequeathed to the guild of Corpus Christi in 1446. This was stationary, and was acted decennially about Lammas-tide (August 1) at the common hall. In 1483, it was 'apon the cost of the most onest men of every parish,' who were, it may be supposed, members of the guild. In 1535 the crafts paid for it instead of their usual cycle. Upon the suppression of the guild, the play-book passed into the custody of the hospital of St. Thomas.

In the same way there are instances in which the clergy,

[1] Cf. vol. i. p. 121.

who elsewhere lent help to the craft-plays, gave independent exhibitions of their own. At Chester, before the Reformation, they eked out the Whitsun cycle by a supplementary performance on Corpus Christi day. The priors of St. John of Jerusalem, Holy Trinity, and All Saints contributed their share to the somewhat incongruous blend of religious and secular entertainments provided by the traders of Dublin for the earl of Kildare in 1528. The so-called *Ludus Coventriae* has often been supposed to be the play-book of a cycle acted by the Grey Friars or Franciscans of Coventry. This theory hardly survives critical examination. But in 1557, during the Marian reaction, a Passion play was given at the Grey Friars in London, and the actors were possibly restored brethren. Miracle-plays must often have been performed in choir schools, especially upon their traditional feast-days of St. Nicholas, St. Catherine, and the Holy Innocents. But there are only two examples, besides that of St. Paul's in 1378, actually upon record. In 1430 the *pueri eleemosynae* of Maxstoke acted on Candlemas day in the hall of Lord Clinton's castle; and in 1486 those of St. Swithin's and Hyde abbeys combined to entertain Henry VII with the Harrowing of Hell as he sat at dinner in Winchester.

Many minor plays, both in towns and in country villages, were organized by the clergy and other officials of parish churches, and are mentioned in the account books of churchwardens. At London, Kingston, Oxford, Reading, Salisbury, Bath, Tewkesbury, Leicester, Bungay, and Yarmouth, such parochial plays can be traced, sometimes side by side with those provided by craft or other guilds. The parochial organization was the natural one for the smaller places, where the parish church had remained the centre of the popular life[1]. The *actiones* in the chapelries of Shipton in Oxfordshire during the thirteenth century may have been plays of this type. The municipal records of Lydd and New Romney mention visits of players to the towns between 1399 and 1508 from no less than fourteen neighbouring places in

[1] On the economics of a mediaeval parish and the functions of the churchwardens cf. Hobhouse, *Churchwardens' Accounts*, xi (Somerset Record Soc.).

Kent and Sussex, many of which must have been then, as they are now, quite insignificant. They are Hythe, Wittersham, Herne, Ruckinge, Folkestone, Appledore, Chart, Rye, Wye, Brookland, Halden, Bethersden, Ham, and Stone. A few other village plays are to be traced in the fifteenth century. In the sixteenth century they are fairly numerous, especially in the eastern counties. In Essex they are found at Chelmsford, Braintree, Halstead, Heybridge, Malden, Saffron Walden, Billericay, Starford, Baddow (by 'children'), Little Baddow, Sabsford, Boreham, Lanchire, Witham, Brentwood, Nayland, Burnham, High Easter, Writtle, Woodham Walter, and Hanningfield; in Cambridgeshire at Bassingbourne; in Lincolnshire at Holbeach; in Norfolk at Harling, Lopham, Garboldisham, Shelfhanger, and Kenninghall; in Suffolk at Boxford, Lavenham, and Mildenhall; in Leicestershire at Foston; in Somersetshire at Morebath; and in Kent once more at Bethersden. The latest instance is a 'Kynge play' at Hascombe in Surrey in 1579.

Parochial plays, whether in town or country, appear to have been in most cases occasional, rather than annual. Sometimes, as at Kingston and Braintree, they became a means of raising money for the church, and even where this object is not apparent, the expenses were lightened in various ways at the cost of neighbouring villages. 'Banns' were sent round to announce the play; or the play itself was carried round on tour. Twenty-seven villages contributed to a play at Bassingbourne in 1511. The Chelmsford play of 1562 and 1563 cost about £50, of which a good proportion was received from the spectators. The play was given at Malden and Braintree as well as at Chelmsford, and for years afterwards the letting out of the stock of garments proved a source of revenue to the parish. This same practice of hiring garments can be traced at Oxford, Leicester, and elsewhere. The parochial plays were always, so far as can be seen, stationary. At Leicester, Braintree, Halstead, and Heybridge they were in the church. That of Harling was 'at the church gate,' that of Bassingbourne in a 'croft'; that of Chelmsford in a 'pightell.' At Reading performances in the market-place and in an open piece of ground called (then and now) the 'Forbury' are mentioned.

There remain a certain number of plays as to the organization of which nothing definite can be said. Such are the minor plays, on the legends of saints, recorded by the annalists of London, Coventry, and Lincoln; those referred to in the corporation accounts of King's Lynn, as given by unspecified players between 1385 and 1462; and those which took place, as late as the seventeenth century, in 'rounds' or amphitheatres at St. Just, Perranzabulo, and elsewhere in Cornwall.

CHAPTER XXII

GUILD PLAYS AND PARISH PLAYS (*continued*)

THE last chapter occupied itself mainly with the diffusion of the vernacular religious plays in England, with their organization, and with their part in municipal and village life. That study must be completed by at least the outline of another, dealing with the content and nature of the performances themselves. Here again it is variety rather than uniformity which requires attention; for the records and texts of the fifteenth and sixteenth centuries bear witness to the effective survival of all the diverse types of play, to which the evolution of the dramatic instinct gave birth in its progress from liturgical office to cosmic cycle.

The term of the evolution—the cosmic cycle itself—is represented by five complete texts, and one fragment sufficiently substantial to be ranked with these. There are the plays of the York and Chester crafts. The manuscript of the former dates from the middle of the fifteenth century; those of the latter from the end of the sixteenth and beginning of the seventeenth: but in both cases it may be assumed that we possess the plays, with certain modifications, additions, and omissions, as they were given in the palmy days of their history. There are also, in a fifteenth-century manuscript, the so-called 'Towneley' plays, as to whose origin the most likely theory is that they are the craft-plays of Wakefield. There is the *Ludus Coventriae*, also of the fifteenth century, which has probably nothing to do with Coventry, but is either, as scholars generally hold, the text of a strolling company, or, as seems to me more probable, that of a stationary play at some town in the East Midlands not yet identified. If I am right, the *Ludus Coventriae* occupies a midway position between the three northern craft cycles, which are all processional plays, split up into a number of distinct pageants, and the fifth text, which is Cornish. This is probably of the fourteenth century, although extant in a fifteenth-century manuscript, and doubtless represents a stationary performance in one of the 'rounds' still to be seen about Cornwall. The fragment, also Cornish, is not a wholly independent play, but a sixteenth-century expansion of part of the earlier text.

A study of the table of incidents printed in an appendix will show the general scope of the cyclical plays[1]. My comments thereon must be few and brief. The four northerly cycles have a kernel of common matter, which corresponds very closely with just that dramatic stuff which was handled in the liturgical and the earliest vernacular dramas. It includes the Fall of Lucifer, the Creation, Adam and Eve, Cain and Abel; then the Annunciation and the group of scenes, from the *Pastores* to the Massacre of the Innocents, which went to make up the *Stella*; then the Passion in the narrower sense, centring in the *planctus Mariae* and extending from the Conspiracy of the Jews to the Descent from the Cross; then the Resurrection scenes, centring in the *Quem quaeritis* and ending with the *Peregrini* and Incredulity of Thomas; then the Ascension, the Pentecost, and finally the *Iudicium* or Doomsday. Almost equally invariable is something in the way of a *Prophetae*. But at York this is thrown into narrative instead of dramatic form; and at Chester the typical defile of prophets, each with his harangue, is deferred to almost the close of the cycle (Play xxiii), and in its usual place stand two independent episodes of Balaam and of Octavian and the Sibyl. Two other groups of scenes exhibit a larger measure of diversity between the four cycles. One is that drawn from the history of the Old Testament Fathers, out of which the Deluge and the Sacrifice of Isaac are the only incidents adopted by all four. The other is the series taken from the missionary life of Christ, where the only common scenes are the Raising of Lazarus and the Feast in the House of Simon the Leper, both of which can be traced back to the liturgical drama[2].

[1] Cf. Appendix T.

[2] Cf. pp. 58, 60.

The principal source of the plays belonging to this common kernel is, of course, the biblical narrative, which is followed, so far as it goes, with considerable fidelity, the most remarkable divergence being that of the *Ludus Coventriae*, which merges the Last Supper with the scene in the House of Simon. But certain embroideries upon scripture, which found their way into the religious drama at an early stage of its evolution, are preserved and further elaborated. Thus each of the four cycles has its Harrowing of Hell, which links the later scenes with the earlier by introducing, as well as the devils, such personages as Adam and Eve, Enoch and Elijah, John the Baptist and others [1]. Similarly the Suspicion of Joseph and the *obstetrices* at the Virgin Birth finds a place in all four [2], as does the Healing of Longinus, the blind knight, by the blood-drops from the cross [3]. Other apocryphal or legendary elements are confined to one or more of the cycles [4]. The Chester plays, for example, have a marked development of the eschatological scenes. Not only is the *Iudicium* itself extremely long and elaborate, but it is preceded by two distinct plays, one a section of the split-up *Prophetae* ending with the Fifteen Signs, the other an Antichrist, in which, as in the Tegernsee *Antichristus* [5], Enoch and Elijah appear as disputants. The most legendary of the northerly cycles is without doubt the *Ludus Coventriae*. It has the legend of Veronica, which is only hinted at in the corresponding York play. And it has so long a series of scenes drawn from the legends of the Virgin as to make it probable that, like the Lincoln plays and another East Midland cycle of which

[1] Cf. p. 73.

[2] Cf. p. 41.

[3] Cf. p. 75.

[4] I can only give the most general account of the legendary content of the plays. For full treatment of this in relation to its sources cf. the authorities quoted in the bibliographical note to chapter xxi, and especially L. T. Smith, *York Plays*, xlvii; P. Kamann, in *Anglia*, x. 189; A. Hohlfeld, in *Anglia*, xi. 285. Much still remains to be done, especially for the Chester plays and the *Ludus Coventriae*. The chief earlier sources are probably the *Evangelium Pseudo-Matthaei* and the *Evangelium Nicodemi* (including the *Gesta Pilati* and the *Descensus Christi ad Inferos*), both in Tischendorf, *Evangelia Apocrypha*, and the *Transitus Mariae* in Tischendorf, *Apocalypses Apocryphae*. The later sources include the *Legenda Aurea* of Jacobus de Voragine († 1275) and the *Cursor Mundi* (ed. R. Morris for E.E.T.S.), a Northumbrian poem of the early fourteenth century.

[5] Cf. p. 63.

a fragment is extant, it was performed not on Corpus Christi day but on that of St. Anne. Before the Annunciation it inserts the episodes of Joachim and Anne, Mary in the Temple, and the Betrothal of Mary. To the common episode of the Suspicion of Joseph it adds the Purgation of Mary. In the Resurrection scene is a purely legendary Apparition of Christ to the Virgin; while the Death, Burial, Assumption, and Coronation of Mary intervene between the Pentecost and the *Iudicium*. This matter from the after-history of the Virgin belongs also to the York plays, which add the Apparition to St. Thomas of India.

The Cornish plays, although in many respects they are parallel to those of the north, have yet some very marked features of their own. They have episodes of the miraculous Release of Nicodemus and Joseph of Arimathea from Prison, and of the Death of Pilate and the Interview of Veronica with Tiberius[1]. But their most remarkable legendary addition is an elaborate treatment of the history of the Holy Rood, which provides the motives for the scenes dealing with Seth, Moses, David, Solomon, Maximilla, and the Bridge upon Cedron[2]. On the other hand the Cornish plays close with the Ascension and entirely omit the sub-cycle of the Nativity, passing direct, but for the Holy Rood matter, from the Sacrifice of Isaac to the Temptation.

[1] Cf. the *Mors Pilati* in Tischendorf, *Evang. Apocr.* 456.

[2] The 'Holy Rood' episodes are those numbered 6, 13, 14, 16–20, 61 in the table. The fullest accounts of the legend in its varied literary forms are given by W. Meyer, *Die Geschichte des Kreuzholzes vor Christus* (*Abhandlungen der k. bayer. Akad. der Wiss.* I. Cl. xvi. 2. 103, Munich, 1881), and A. S. Napier, *History of the Holy Rood-tree* (E.E.T.S. 1894). Roughly, the story is as follows: Seth went to Paradise to fetch the oil of mercy. An angel gave him three pips from the tree of knowledge. These were laid beneath the tongue of Adam at his burial, and three rods, signifying the Trinity, sprang up. Moses cut the rods, and did miracles with them. At his death they were planted in Mount Tabor. An angel in a dream sent David to fetch them. They grew into one tree, in the shade of which David repented of his sin with Bathsheba. When the Temple was building, a beam was fashioned from the tree, but it would not fit and was placed in the Temple for veneration. The woman Maximilla incautiously sat upon it and her clothes caught fire. She prophesied of Christ, and the Jews made her the first martyr. The beam was cast into the pool of Siloam, to which it gave miraculous properties, and was finally made into a bridge. At the Passion, a portion of it was taken for the Rood.

It is not improbable that the majority of the Corpus Christi and other greater English plays reached the dimensions of a cosmic cycle. But in only a few cases is any definite evidence on the point available. Complete lists are preserved from Beverley and Norwich. The Beverley series seems to have been much on the scale of the four extant cycles. It extended in thirty-six pageants from the Fall of Lucifer to Doomsday. Like the Cornish cycle, it included the episode of Adam and Seth; and it presented an exceptional feature in the insertion of a play of the Children of Israel after the Flight into Egypt. The Norwich cycle, which began with the Creation and ended with Pentecost, was a short one of twelve pageants [1]. The small number is due, partly to the grouping of several episodes in a single play, partly to the omission of the Passion proper. The Resurrection followed immediately upon the Baptism. Of other plays, the chroniclers record that in 1391 the London performance covered both the Old and New Testament, that in 1409 it went from the Creation to the Day of Judgement, and that in 1411 it was 'from the begynnyng of the worlde.' The fragmentary indications of the records preserved show that the Chelmsford play stretched at least from the Creation to the Crucifixion, the Newcastle play at least from the Creation to the Burial of the Virgin [2], the Lincoln play at least from the Deluge to the Coronation of the Virgin. On the other hand the range of the Coventry plays can only be shown to have been from the Annunciation to Doomsday, although it may be by a mere accident that no Old Testament scenes are here to be identified [3].

Examples, though unfortunately no full texts, can also be traced of the separate Nativity and Easter cycles, the merging of which was the most important step in the formation of the complete Corpus Christi play. Both, if I read the evidence aright, existed at Aberdeen. There was a 'Haliblude' play

[1] The Norwich play of the Fall is extant in two sixteenth-century versions.

[2] The Newcastle play of the Building of the Ark is extant.

[3] Two Coventry plays are extant, the Shearmen and Taylors' play, extending from the Annunciation to the Massacre of the Innocents, and the Weavers' play of the Purification and Christ in the Temple.

on Corpus Christi day, which I conceive to have been essentially a Passion and Resurrection, and a play at Candlemas, which seems to have included, as well as the Purification, a *Stella*, a Presentation in the Temple, and something in the way of a *Prophetae*. There were performances of Passions in Reading in 1508, in Dublin in 1528, at Shrewsbury in 1567, and in London in 1557 and as late as between 1613 and 1622. I do not suppose that in any of these cases 'Passion' excludes 'Resurrection.' The New Romney town play, also, seems to have been a Passion in the wider sense. The records of Easter plays at Bath (1482), Leicester (1504–7), Morebath (1520–74), Reading (1507, 1533–5), and Kingston (1513–65), are too slight to bear much comment. They may relate to almost anything from a mere Latin *Quem quaeritis* to a full vernacular Passion and Resurrection.

One interesting text falls to be considered at this point. This is a fifteenth-century Burial and Resurrection of northern *provenance*. It is very lyrical in character, and apparently the author set out to write a 'treyte' to be read, and shortly after the beginning changed his mind and made a play of it. There are two scenes. The first is an elaborate *planctus*, 'to be playede on gud-friday after-none.' The second, intended for 'Esterday after the resurrectione, In the morowe' is a *Quem quaeritis*. An Ascension play was performed by the Holy Trinity guild at Sleaford in 1480. A 'Christmasse play' is recorded at Tintinhull in 1451. How much it included can hardly be guessed. But the *Stella* maintained its independent position, and is found at Yarmouth (1462–1512), Reading (1499, 1539), Leicester (1547), Canterbury (1503), Holbeach (1548), and Hascombe (1579)[1].

The plays just enumerated may be regarded as of pre-cyclical types. But there are a few others which, although they occur independently, would have their more natural position in cycles of less or greater range. In some of these cases it is probable that the independence is only apparent,

[1] Probably these smaller plays, chiefly Paschal, were in English. The Nativity and Resurrection plays in Lord Northumberland's chapel and the Resurrection play in Magdalen College chapel may have been in Latin (cf. p. 107).

a mere matter of incomplete evidence. There are two fifteenth-century plays, both on the subject of Abraham and Isaac, one of which is preserved in the 'Book of Brome' from Suffolk, the other in a manuscript now at Dublin, but probably of South Midland *provenance*. It is of course not impossible that these represent isolated performances, but it is on the whole more likely that they are fragments of lost cycles. A third play, of Midland origin, preserved in the Digby manuscript, occupies an exceptional position. It deals with the Massacre of the Innocents and the Purification, and allusions in a prologue and epilogue make it clear that it belonged to a cycle in which it was preceded by a *Pastores* and a *Magi,* and followed by a Christ in the Temple. This cycle, however, was not played all at once, but a portion was given year by year on St. Anne's day. One of the groups of plays brought together in the *Ludus Coventriae* was evidently intended for performance under similar conditions. It is probable that the *ludus Filiorum Israelis* of the Cambridge Corpus Christi guild about 1350, the Abraham and Isaac of the 'schaft' of St. Dunstan's, Canterbury, between 1491 and 1520, and the Adam and Eve (1507) and 'Cayme's pageaunt' 1512-5) of St. Lawrence's, Reading, formed parts of Corpus Christi cycles given in those towns.

Isolated performances of plays picked out of a cycle, or upon subjects usually treated in a cycle, are, however, not unknown. One or more of the Chester plays occasionally formed part of the civic entertainment of a royal or noble personage. When Henry VII visited Winchester in 1486, the schoolboys of the two great abbeys of Hyde and St. Swithin's gave a *Christi Descensus ad Inferos* before him at dinner. At York the acting of an 'interlude of St. Thomas the Apostle' on a St. Bartholomew's eve towards the end of the reign of Henry VIII became the occasion for a papist demonstration. This might have been either the Incredulity of Thomas (Play xlii) or the Apparition of the Virgin to St. Thomas in India (Play xlvi) from the Corpus Christi cycle. At York, also, there was, in the hands of a Corpus Christi guild, a distinct play, frequently performed between 1446 and the Reformation, called the Creed play. This was apparently an expansion of a motive found in the Pentecost scene at Chester and probably at Coventry, but not at York itself, wherein, after the coming of the Holy Ghost, each of the apostles in turn enunciates one of the articles of the so-called Apostles' creed. At Hull, where I find no trace of a cycle, the Trinity guild of sea-faring men had their play of Noah. At Lincoln, a play of Tobit, which does not actually, so far as I know, form part of the Old Testament section of any English cycle [1], was substituted for the regular Corpus Christi play after the Reformation. Naturally such exceptional performances became more common in the decadence of the religious drama [2]. Thus the very scratch series of plays shown before the earl of Kildare at Dublin, in the Christmas of 1528, included, besides other contributions both sacred and secular, an Adam and Eve by the tailors and a Joseph and Mary by the carpenters. The choice of these subjects was evidently motived by their appropriateness to the craft representing them. Similarly, when John Bale was bishop of Ossory in 1553, he had performed at the market-cross of Kilkenny, on the day of the proclamation of Queen Mary, a short fragment of a cycle consisting of a *Prophetae*, a Baptism, and a Temptation. One fancies that this strange protagonist of the Reformation must have had in his mind some quaint verbal analogy between 'John Bale' and 'John Baptist,' for he states that he also wrote a dramatic *Vita D. Ioannis Baptistae* in fourteen books. Nor is this the only example of the treatment of a subject, merely episodic in the Corpus Christi cycles, in a distinct and elaborate play. The invaluable Digby manuscript contains a similar expansion, from the East or West Midlands, of the story of Mary Magdalen. It follows the narrative of the *Golden Legend*, and introduces the familiar scenes of the Raising of Lazarus, the Feast in the House of Simon the Leper, the *Quem quaeritis*, and the *Hortulanus*, preceding these with episodes of the life of the Magdalen *in gaudio*, and following them with the Conversion of the

[1] 'Thobie' is included in the French collection of mysteries known as the *Viel Testament* (Julleville, *Les Myst.* ii. 354, 370).

[2] On the way in which the later local miracle-play and the scriptural interlude merge into each other, cf. p. 191.

King and Queen of Marseilles, and of Mary's Life in the Wilderness and Death. As offshoots from the Corpus Christi cycle may also be regarded the Deaths of the Apostles played in the Dublin series of 1528, Thomas Ashton's *Julian the Apostate* at Shrewsbury in 1565, and the *Destruction of Jerusalem*, written by John Smith in 1584 to take the place of the traditional plays at Coventry [1].

The Mary Magdalen and the rest of the group just described may be considered as standing halfway between the plays of and akin to the Corpus Christi cycle and those founded on the legends of saints. Of regular saint-plays there are unfortunately only two texts available from these islands. The Digby manuscript contains an East Midland Conversion of St. Paul, which, however, is almost wholly biblical and not legendary. It will be remembered that the subject was one known even to the liturgical drama [2]. There is also a Cornish play of St. Meriasek or Mereadocus, the patron saint of Camborne, written at the beginning of the sixteenth century. Other such plays are, however, upon record. It is perhaps curious that no mention should be found of any English parallel to either the Saint Nicholas plays or the *Miracles de Nostre Dame* of France. It can hardly be doubted that the former at least existed in connexion with the widespread revel of the Boy Bishop [3]. The most popular English saint for dramatic purposes appears to have been St. George. A play of St. George was maintained by the town of Lydd, and was probably copied by a neighbouring guild at New Romney. Another, on an elaborate scale, was given by a group of villages at Bassingbourne in 1511. These seem to have been genuine dramas, and not mere 'ridings' or folk-plays such as occur elsewhere [4]. A St. George play, described by Collier at Windsor in 1416, can be resolved into a cake.

[1] The Destruction of Jerusalem, together with the Visit of Veronica to Tiberius and the Death of Pilate, which are scenes in the Cornish cycle, forms the subject-matter of a French *Vengeance de Nostre Seigneur*, printed in 1491. Another *Vengeance de Nostre Seigneur* is attached to the Passion of Eustache Mercadé (†1414). A representation of a Vengeance, following close on one of a Passion, is recorded at Metz in 1437, and there are several later examples (Julleville, *Les Myst.* ii. 12, 175, 415, 451).

[2] Cf. p. 61.

[3] Cf. p. 97.

[4] Cf. vol. i. p. 221.

St. Thomas of Canterbury was only honoured with a dumb show in his own city, but there was a play upon him at King's Lynn in 1385. Of quite a number of other saint-plays the barest notices exist. London had hers on St. Catherine; Windsor on St. Clotilda; Coventry on St. Catherine and St. Crytyan; Lincoln on St. Laurence, St. Susanna, St. Clara, and St. James; Shrewsbury on St. Feliciana and St. Sabina; Bethersden in Kent on St. Christina; Braintree in Essex on St. Swithin, St. Andrew, and St. Eustace. The Dublin shoemakers contributed a play on their patron saints Crispin and Crispinian to the Dublin festival of 1528. In London, the plays on the days of St. Lucy and St. Margaret at St. Margaret's, Southwark, may have been on the stories of those saints; and during the Marian reaction a 'goodly' stage-play was given at St. Olave's church on St. Olave's day.

Quite unique, as dealing with a contemporary 'miracle,' is the play of the Blessed Sacrament, performed at one of the many places bearing the name of Croxton, in the latter half of the fifteenth century. According to the manuscript, the event upon which it was based, the marvellous conversion of a Jew who attempted an outrage upon a host, took place at Heraclea in Spain, in 1461. There is, curiously enough, a late French play, quite independent of the English one, upon an exactly parallel miracle assigned to Paris and the thirteenth century [1].

The variation in the types of English miracle-plays naturally implies some variation also in the manner of representation. The normal craft cycles of the greater towns were processional in character. They were not played throughout by a single body of actors and upon a single stage; but the action was divided into a number of independent scenes, to each of which was assigned its own group of performers and its own small movable stage or 'pageant.' And each scene was repeated at several 'stations' in different parts of the city, pageant succeeding pageant in regular order, with the general effect of a vast procession slowly unrolling itself along the streets [2].

[1] Julleville, *Les Myst.* ii. 574.

[2] Archdeacon Rogers thus describes the Chester plays (*Digby Plays*, xix) 'They first beganne at ye Abbaye gates; & when the firste pagiente was played at ye Abbaye

This method of playing was convenient to the distribution of the *leitourgia* among the guilds, and was adopted in all those places, Chester, York, Beverley, and Coventry, from which our records happen to be the fullest. But it was not the primitive method and, as has been pointed out in a previous chapter, it probably arose from an attempt about the beginning of the fourteenth century to adapt the already existing miracle-plays to the distinctive feature of the festival of Corpus Christi. To this point it will be necessary to recur [1]. The processional play was rare outside England, and even in England it at no period became universal. Two at least of the great cycles that survive, the Cornish one and the *Ludus Coventriae*, as well as several smaller plays, can be clearly shown from internal evidence to have been intended for stationary performance. They do not naturally cleave asunder into distinct scenes. The same personages appear and reappear: the same properties and bits of scenery are left and returned to, often at considerable intervals. Moreover stationary performances are frequently implied by the records. At Lincoln, after the suppression of the old *visus* of St. Anne's processional play, the corporation ordered the performance of a 'standing' play 'of some story of the Bible.' At Newcastle, although pageants of the plays went in the procession, the actual performance seems to have been given in a 'stead.' This arrangement is exactly parallel to that of the Florentine *rappresentazioni* on St. John's day in 1454 [2]. Elsewhere there was commonly enough no 'pageant' at all. The 'standing' plays may be traced at various removes from their original scene, the floor of the church [3]. Indeed, the examples of Braintree in 1523 and 1525, of Halstead in 1529, of Heybridge in 1532, seem to show that, quite apart from the survival of ritual plays proper, the miracle-play, even at the very moment of its extinction, had not been always and everywhere excluded from the church itself. The Beverley

gates, then it was wheeled from thence to the pentice at ye highe crosse before ye Mayor; and before that was donne, the seconde came, and ye firste wente in-to the water-gate streete, and from thence vnto ye Bridge-streete, and soe all, one after an other, tell all ye pagiantes weare played.'

[1] Cf. pp. 95, 160.

[2] D'Ancona, i. 228.

[3] Cf. p. 83.

repraesentatio dominicae resurrectionis about 1220 had got as far as the churchyard. At Bungay in 1566 they played in the churchyard, and at Harling in 1452 'at the cherch gate.' The latest of all the village plays, that of Hascombe in 1579, was at, but perhaps not in the church. The next step brought the plays to the market-place, which itself in many towns lay just outside the church door. At Louth the Corpus Christi play was in the 'markit-stede,' and so were some at least of the Reading plays. A neighbouring field might be convenient; the Bassingbourne play was in a 'croft,' that of Chelmsford in a 'pightell.' Certain places had a bit of waste ground traditionally devoted to the entertainment of the citizens. Such were the 'Forbury' at Reading and the 'Quarry' at Shrewsbury. The Aberdeen Haliblude play took place *apud ly Wyndmylhill.* Edinburgh constructed its 'playfield' in the Greenside at considerable cost in 1554, while in Cornwall permanent amphitheatres were in use. A writer contemporary with the later performances describes these as made of earth in open fields with an enclosed 'playne' of some fifty feet in diameter. If they are correctly identified with the 'rounds' of St. Just and Perranzabulo, these examples at least were much larger. The St. Just round is of stone, with seven tiers of seats, and measures 126 feet in diameter; the earthen one at Perranzabulo is 130 feet, and has a curious pit in the centre, joined to the edge by a trench. The disposition of these rounds at the time of performance can be studied in the diagrams reproduced from the fifteenth-century manuscript of the plays by Mr. Norris. Within a circular area is arranged a ring of eight spots which probably represent structures elevated above the general surface of the 'playne.' They have labels assigning them to the principal actors. Thus for the *Origo Mundi* the labels are *Celum*, *Tortores*, *Infernum*, *Rex Pharao*, *Rex Dauid*, *Rex Sal*[*omon*], *Abraham*, *Ortus.* From the stage directions it would appear that the raised portions were called *pulpita* or *tenti*, and by Jordan at a later date 'rooms'; that the 'playne' was the *platea*; and that the action went on partly on the *pulpita*, partly on the *platea* between them. Except that it is circular instead of oblong, the scheme corresponds exactly to that of the continental plays shown in an earlier chapter to have been determined by the conditions of performance within a church[1]. Those plays also had their *platea*; and their *domus*, *loca*, or *sedes* answer to the *pulpita* and *tenti* of Cornwall. Judging by the somewhat scanty indications available, the disposition of other English 'standing' plays must have been on very similar lines. In some cases there is evidence that the level *platea* was replaced by a raised 'platform,' 'scaffold,' or 'stage.' Thus Chaucer's 'joly Absolon' played Herod 'on a scaffold hye[2].' But the 'stages' or 'scaffolds' mentioned in accounts are sometimes merely for the spectators and sometimes equivalent to the *loca* of leading actors. In the Digby play of St. Mary Magdalen, a practicable ship moves about the *platea*. Possibly a similar bit of realism was used elsewhere for the ever popular 'Noy schippe,' and, if so, this may explain the pit and trench of the Perranzabulo 'round[3].'

As to the 'pageant' or movable stage of the processional plays, a good deal of information is preserved. Dugdale describes it at Coventry as a 'Theater . . . very large and high, placed upon wheels'; Rogers at Chester as 'a highe place made like a howse with ij rowmes, beinge open on ye tope: the lower rowme they apparelled and dressed them selues; and in the higher rowme they played; and they stood vpon 6 (*v.l.* 4) wheeles.' According to an inventory of 1565 the grocers' pageant at Norwich was 'a Howse of Waynskott paynted and buylded on a Carte w^t^ fowre whelys.' It had a square top or canopy; on it were placed a gilt griffin and two large and eighty-three small vanes; and about it were hung three painted cloths. Similar adornments of the pageant were in use at Coventry. At York it bore the arms of the city or of the guild. M. Jusserand has unearthed from a Bodleian manuscript two fourteenth-century miniatures which apparently represent pageants. These have draperies covering the whole of the lower 'room' down to the

[1] Cf. p. 83.

[2] *C. T.* 3384 (*Miller's Tale*). This 'scaffold' may have been merely a throne or *sedes* for Herod. But plays on platforms or scaffolds are found at Chelmsford, Kingston, Reading, Dublin.

[3] Cf. M. Jusserand, in *Furnivall Miscellany*, 186, and the pit for *La Mer* on the 1547 Valenciennes Passion play stage figured in his *Shakespeare in France*, 63.

ground and resemble nothing so much as the ambulant theatre of a Punch and Judy show [1]. The pageants were probably arranged so that the action might be visible from every side. The scenery would therefore be simple—a throne, a house. Certain plays, however, necessitate a divided scene, such as the inside and outside of a temple [2]. For the 'hell,' the traditional monstrous head on a lower level, with practicable chains and fire, was required [3]. The pageant used for the Flood scene was doubtless shaped like an ark. The 'shipp' belonging to the Trinity guild of Hull cost £5 8*s.* 4*d.* The ordinary pageant may have been less expensive. That of the Doom at York was made 'of newe substanciale' for seven marks, the old pageant and a free admission into the guild. At Lincoln three times as much was charged for housing the ship as for any other pageant.

The origin of the pageant is capable of a very easy explanation [4]. Like the *edifizio* of the Italian *rappresentazioni*, it

[1] *Furnivall Miscellany*, 192, 194, from *Bodl. MS.* 264, ff. 54[b], 76[a].

[2] The directions to the Coventry Weavers' play refer to the 'for pagand' and the 'upper part'; those of the Grocers' play at Norwich to the 'nether parte of y[e] pageant.' For the purposes of the dramas these are distinct localities.

[3] Cf. p. 86. The Digby St. Mary Magdalen play has the stage direction, 'a stage, and Helle ondyrneth that stage.' At Coventry the Cappers had a 'hell-mouth' for the Harrowing of Hell and the Weavers another for Doomsday.

[4] Every conceivable spelling of the word 'pageant' appears in the records. The *Promptorium Parvulorum*, ii. 377 († 1440, ed. A. Way for Camd. Soc.), has 'Pagent, *Pagina*,' and this is the usual Latin spelling, although *pagenda* and *pagentes* (acc. pl.) occur at Beverley. The derivation is from *pagina* 'a plank.' The *Catholicon Anglicum* (1483, ed. S. J. H. Herrtage for E. E. T. S.) has 'A Paiande; *lusorium*,' and there can be little doubt that 'playing-place,' 'stage' is the primary sense of the word, although as a matter of fact the derivative sense of 'scene' or 'episode' is the first to appear. Wyclif so uses it, speaking of Christmas in his *Ave Maria* (*English Works*, E. E. T. S. 206) 'he that kan best pleie a pagyn of the deuyl, syngynge songis of lecherie, of batailis and of lesyngis . . . is holden most merie mon.' In *Of Prelates* (*loc. cit.* 99) he says that false teachers 'comen in viserid deuelis' and 'pleien the pagyn of scottis,' masking under St. George's 'skochen.' The elaborate pageants used in masks and receptions (cf. p. 176, and vol. i. p. 398) led to a further derivative sense of 'mechanical device.' This, as well as the others, is illustrated in the passages quoted by the editors of the *Prompt. Parv.* and the *Cath. Angl.* from W. Horman, author of *Vulgaria* (1519) 'Alexander played a payante more worthy to be wondred vpon for his rasshe aduenture than for his manhede . . . There were v coursis in the feest and as many paiantis in the pley. I wyll haue made v stagȝ or bouthis in this playe (*scenas*). I wolde haue a place in the middyl of the pley (*orchestra*) that I myght

is simply the raised *locus*, *sedes*, or *domus* of the stationary play put upon wheels. Just as the action of the stationary play took place partly on the various *sedes*, partly in the *platea*, so Coventry actors come and go to and from the pageant in the street. 'Here Erode ragis in the pagond & in the strete also,' says a stage direction. It should be observed that the plays at Coventry were exceptionally long, and that scaffolds seem to have been attached to the pageant proper in order to get sufficient space.

The number of 'stations' at which the plays were given varied in the different towns. At York there were from twelve to sixteen; at Beverley six; at Coventry not more than three or four can be identified. The many scenes and frequent repetitions naturally made the processional plays very lengthy affairs. At Chester they were spread over three days; at York they were got through in one, but playing began at half-past four in the morning. At Newcastle, on the other hand, the plays were in the afternoon. The banns of the *Ludus Coventriae* promise a performance 'at vj of the belle,' but whether in the morning or evening is not stated.

The normal occasion for the greater plays was the feast of Corpus Christi on the Thursday after Trinity Sunday. A few exceptions are, however, to be noted. At Chester, Norwich, New Romney, and apparently Leicester, the date chosen was Whitsuntide. Yet at Chester the play is called the 'Corpus Christi play' in craft documents of the fifteenth century, and even in the municipal 'White Book' of the sixteenth; from which it must be inferred either that the term was used of all cyclical plays without regard to their date, or, more probably, that at Chester a performance originally given on Corpus Christi day had been for some reason transferred to Whitsuntide. The motive may have been a desire to avoid clashing between the plays and the great Corpus Christi procession in which the crafts everywhere

se euery paiaunt. Of all the crafty and subtyle paiantis and pecis of warke made by mannys wyt, to go or moue by them selfe, the clocke is one of the beste.' Synonyms for 'pageant' in the sense of 'stage' are 'cariadge' (Chester) and 'karre' (Beverley); in the sense of 'scene,' *iocus* (Coventry), *visus* (Lincoln), *processus* or 'processe' (Towneley and Digby plays, Croxton *Sacrament* and Medwall's morality of *Nature*).

took a prominent part. A difficulty arose on this score at York in 1426, and a Franciscan preacher, one William Melton, tried to induce the citizens to have the plays on the day before Corpus Christi. Ultimately the alternative was adopted of having the procession on the day after. At Lincoln the plays were on St. Anne's day (July 26) and the last pageant was acted by the clergy in the nave of the cathedral. At Aberdeen there appear to have been two cycles, a processional Nativity at Candlemas and a Haliblude play on Windmill Hill at Corpus Christi.

The oversight of the actors was, as pointed out in the last chapter, an important element in the civic control of the craft-plays. The mention at York of a commission of 'connyng, discrete and able players' must not be taken to imply that these were in any sense professionals. All the actors received fees, on a scale proportionate to the dignity of their parts. Thus at Coventry one Fawston got *4d.* 'for hangyng Judas,' and *4d.* more 'for coc croyng.' The payment to the performer of God was *3s. 4d.* A 'sowle,' whether 'savyd' or 'dampnyd,' got *20d.*, and a 'worme of conscyence' only *8d.* At Hull, Noah was generally paid *1s.*, God and Noah's wife a trifle less. But there is nothing to show that the performers were drawn from the minstrel class: they were probably, like 'joly Absolon,' members of the guilds undertaking the plays. The Chester men describe themselves in their banns as not 'playeres of price' but 'Craftes men and meane men.' The epilogue to the Conversion of St. Paul in the Digby manuscript similarly deprecates unkindly criticism of folk 'lackyng lytturall scyens . . . that of Retoryk haue non intellygens.' A characteristic of the acting which greatly impressed the imagination of the audience seems to have been the rant and bombast put from very early times in the mouths of such royal or pseudo-royal personages as Herod and Pilate.[1] In the Chester

[1] Cf. p. 90, and *Hamlet*, iii. 2. 9 'O, it offends me to the soul to hear a robustious periwig-pated fellow tear a passion to tatters, to very rags, to split the ears of the groundlings, who for the most part are capable of nothing but inexplicable dumb-shows and noise: I would have such a fellow whipped for o'erdoing Termagant; it outherods Herod.' The Miller in *Cant. Tales*, 3124, cries out 'in Pilates vois.' The torturers also seem to have been favourite performers;

plays fragments of French, as in a liturgical play fragments of gibberish [1], are used to enhance this effect. In the Cornish plays, as in the modern music hall, each performer at his first appearance displays himself in a preliminary strut about the stage. *Hic pompabit Abraham*, or *Moses*, or *David*, say the stage directions. As is usually the case with amateurs, the function of the prompter became an exceedingly important one. If the Cornish writer Richard Carew may be trusted, the local players did not learn their parts at all, but simply repeated them aloud after the whispers of the 'ordinary [2].' Probably this was exceptional; it certainly was not the practice at Beverley, where there is a record of an actor being fined *quod nesciebat ludum suum*. But it may be taken for granted that the 'beryng of the boke,' which is so frequently paid for in the accounts, was never a sinecure. Another functionary who occasionally appears is the stage-manager. In the later Cornish plays he is called the 'conveyour.' The great Chelmsford performance of 1562 was superintended by one Burles who was paid, with others, for 'suing' it, and who probably came from a distance, as he and his boy were boarded for three weeks.

The professional assistance of the minstrels, although not called in for the acting, was welcome for the music. This was a usual and a considerable item in the expenses. At the Chelmsford performance just mentioned the waits of Bristol and no less than forty other minstrels were employed. There is no sign of a musical accompaniment to the dialogue of the existing plays, which was spoken, and not, like that of their liturgical forerunners, chanted. But the York and Coventry texts contain some noted songs, and several plays have invitations to the minstrels to strike up at the conclusion or between the scenes. Minstrels are also found accompanying the proclaimers of the banns or preliminary announcements of plays. These banns seem to have been

cf. the *Poem on the Evil Times of Edward II* (T. Wright, *Political Songs*, C. S. 336):
'Hii ben degised as turmentours
that comen from clerkes plei.'

[1] Cf. p. 48.

[2] In Jean Fouquet's miniature representing the French mystery of St. Apollonia (cf. p. 85) a priest, with a book in one hand and a wand in the other, appears to be conducting the play.

versified, like the plays themselves. They are often mentioned, and several copies exist. Those of Chester were proclaimed by the city crier on St. George's day; those of the Croxton play and the *Ludus Coventriae* were carried round the country-side by *vexillatores* or banner-bearers. Minstrelsy was not the only form of lighter solace provided for the spectators of the plays. Two of those in the Digby manuscript were accompanied with dances. At Bungay a 'vyce' was paid 'for his pastyme before the plaie, and after the plaie.' There were 'vices' too at Chelmsford, and 'fools,' by which is meant the same thing[1], at Heybridge and New Romney. But these examples are taken from the decadence of the miracle-play, rather than from its heyday.

The accounts of the Bassingbourne play in 1511 include a payment to 'the garnement man for garnements and propyrts and playbooks.' This was an occasional and not an annual play, and apparently at the beginning of the sixteenth century such plays were sufficiently frequent to render the occupation of theatrical outfitter a possible one. Certainly those lucky parishes, such as Chelmsford or St. Peter's, Oxford, which possessed a stock of 'game gear,' found a profit in letting it out to less favoured places. The guilds responsible for the greater plays naturally preserved their own costumes and properties from year to year, supplementing these where necessary by loans from the neighbouring gentry and clergy. The Middle Ages were not purists about anachronism, and what was good enough for an English bishop was good enough for Annas and Caiaphas. The hands of the craftsmen who acted were discreetly cased in the gloves, without which no ceremonial occasion was complete, and sometimes, at least, vizors or masks were worn. But, as a rule, the stage setting left a good deal to the imagination. The necessaries for the play of Paradise at Beverley in 1391 consisted of the 'karre' or pageant, eight hasps, eighteen staples, two vizors, a pair of wings for the angel, a fir-spar (the tree of knowledge), a worm (the serpent), two pairs of linen breeches, two pairs of shifts, and one sword. For a similar play the Norwich grocers possessed

[1] Cf. p. 203.

in 1565, besides the pageant and its fittings, sufficient 'cotes and hosen' for all the characters, that of the serpent being fitted with a tail, a 'face' and hair for the Father, hair for Adam and Eve, and—'a Rybbe colleryd Red.' A few other interesting details can be gathered from various records. At Canterbury the steeds of the *Magi* were made of hoops and laths and painted canvas. In the Doomsday scene at Coventry the 'savyd' and 'dampnyd' souls were distinguished by their white or black colour[1]. The hell mouth was provided with fire, a windlass, and a barrel for the earthquake. There were also three worlds to be set afire, one, it may be supposed, at each station. The stage directions to Jordan's Cornish Creation of the World are full of curious information. The Father appears in a cloud and when he speaks out of heaven, 'let ye levys open.' Lucifer goes down to hell 'apareled fowle wth fyre about hem' and the plain is filled with 'every degre of devylls of lether and spirytis on cordis.' In Paradise a fountain and 'fyne flowers' suddenly spring up, and a little later 'let fyshe of dyuers sortis apeare & serten beastis.' Lucifer becomes 'a fyne serpent made wth a virgyn face & yolowe heare upon her head.' Adam and Eve departing from Paradise 'shewe a spyndell and a dystaff.' For the murder of Abel, according to old tradition, a 'chawbone' is needed[2], and for the ark, timber and tools, including 'a mallet, a calkyn yren, ropes, masstes, pyche and tarr.' I have not space to dwell further on these archaeological *minutiae*. One point, however, seems to deserve another word. Many writers have followed Warton in asserting that Adam and Eve were represented on the stage in actual nakedness[3].

[1] *Hen. V*, ii. 3. 42 'Do you not remember, a' saw a flea stick upon Bardolph's nose, and a' said it was a black soul burning in hell-fire?'

[2] *Hamlet*, v. 1. 85 'Cain's jaw-bone, that did the first murder.'

[3] Warton, ii. 223 'In these Mysteries I have sometimes seen gross and open obscenities. In a play of *The Old and New Testament*, Adam and Eve are both exhibited on the stage naked, and conversing about their nakedness: this very pertinently introduces the next scene, in which they have coverings of fig-leaves. This extraordinary spectacle was beheld by a numerous assembly of both sexes with great composure: they had the authority of scripture for such a representation, and they gave matters just as they found them in the third chapter of Genesis. It would have been absolute heresy to have departed from the sacred text in personating

The statement is chiefly based upon a too literal interpretation of the stage directions of the Chester plays[1]. There is a fine *a priori* improbability about it, and as a matter of fact there can be very little doubt that the parts were played, as they would have been on any other stage in any other period of the world's history, except possibly at the Roman *Floralia*[2], in fleshings. Jordan is quite explicit. Adam and Eve are to be 'aparlet in whytt lether,' and although Jordan's play is a late one, I think it may be taken for granted that white leather was sufficient to meet the exigencies even of mediaeval realism.

The accounts of miracle-plays frequently contain entries of payments for providing copies of the text used. When the stock of the Chelmsford play was dispersed in 1574, the copies were valued at £4. Such copies were naturally of more than one kind. There was the authoritative text kept for reference by the guild or other body of presenters. This is sometimes called the 'play-book' or 'game-book.' The Cornish term is *ordinale*, a derivative from the *ordo* of the liturgical drama[3]. That in use elsewhere is more commonly 'original,' which appears in a variety of quaint spellings[4]. In the great towns where plays were given by the crafts under the general supervision of the corporation, each craft held the 'original' of its own play, but approved transcripts of these were also in the hands of the corporation officers. At Chester this transcript was itself called the 'original'; at York it was the *registrum*. Most of the extant manuscripts of plays appear to be of the nature of 'originals.' From York and probably from Wakefield we have *registra*. The Chester texts are, however, late transcripts due to the zeal of local antiquaries, perhaps in view of some frustrated revival. Specimens exist also of two other kinds of copy. There are single plays from both Chester and York which have all the appearance of having been folded up for the pocket of a

the primitive appearance of our first parents, whom the spectators so nearly resembled in simplicity.'

[1] Deimling, i. 30 'Statim nudi sunt . . . Tunc Adam et Eva cooperiant genitalia sua cum foliis.'

[2] Cf. vol. i. p. 5.

[3] Cf. p. 103. So the 'ordinary' or prompter (p. 140) is the man in charge of the *ordinale*.

[4] 'Oreginale de S. Maria Magdalena' (*Digby MS.*); 'originall booke,' 'regenall,' 'rygynall,' 'oraginall' (Chester); 'orygynall,' 'rygenale' (Coventry); 'regenell' (Louth); 'ryginall' (Sleaford).

prompter. And the nature of the 'parts' prepared for individual actors may be seen from the transition example edited by Professor Skeat from a manuscript found at Shrewsbury. They contained the actors' own speeches, with the 'cues' or closing words of the preceding speeches which signalled to him that his turn was at hand [1].

Indications of the authorship of plays are very scanty. John Bale has preserved a list of his own plays, some at least of which were acted in mediaeval fashion. It may perhaps be assumed that Nicholas Udall, afterwards author of *Ralph Roister Doister*, wrote the play performed at Braintree in 1534, while he was vicar there. At Bassingbourne in 1511 one John Hobarde, 'brotherhood priest,' was paid 'for the play-book.' In this and in several of the following cases it is impossible to determine whether an author or merely a copying scribe is in question. The corporation of Beverley employed Master Thomas Bynham, a friar preacher, to write 'banis' for their plays in 1423. At Reading we find Mr. Laborne 'reforming' the Resurrection play about 1533. The later Cornish play of the Creation of the World was 'wryten' by William Jordan in 1611, and that of St. Meriasek by 'dominus Hadton' in 1504. At Bungay William Ellys was paid in 1558 'for the interlude and game-book [2], and Stephen Prewett, a priest at Norwich, for some labour about the matter of a game-book in 1526. This same Stephen Prewett had a fee from the Norwich grocers 'for makyng of a new ballet' in 1534. One of the extant Coventry plays was 'nevly correcte' and the other 'nevly translate' by Robert Croo in 1535. The name 'Thomas Mawdycke' and the date 1591 are written at the head of some songs belonging to the former. In 1566 Thomas Nycles set a song for the drapers. Robert Croo or Crowe seems to have made himself generally useful in connexion with the Coventry plays. In 1563 the smiths paid him for 'ij leves of our pley boke.' In 1557 he wrote the 'boke' for the drapers, and between 1556 and 1562 further assisted them by playing God, mending the 'devell's cottes,'

[1] Cf. p. 90.

[2] As the price paid was only 'iiij^{d}' a *printed* play was probably bought, from which the 'partes,' at a cost of 'ij^{s},' were written; cf. p. 192.

and supplying 'iij worldys' for burning and a hat for the Pharisee. A later Coventry playwright was John Smith of St. John's College, Oxford, who wrote the 'new play' of the Destruction of Jerusalem in 1584 for a sum of £13 6*s*. 8*d*. The fifteenth-century Croxton play has the initials 'R. C.' One of the plays in the Digby manuscript 'Ihon Parfre ded wryte.' The three others have the initials 'M. B.,' and against the *Poeta* of the prologue to one of them a later hand has written in the margin 'Myles Blomfylde.' I repeat the caution that some at least of these names may be those of mere copyists. Miles Blomfield has been identified with a monk of Bury of that name. As he was born in 1525 he obviously was not the original author of the Digby plays, which are probably of the fifteenth century. A much greater monk of Bury, John Lydgate, has been claimed as the author of the *Ludus Coventriae*, but there does not seem to be any real evidence for this [1]. On the other hand I see no reason to doubt the old Chester tradition which connects the plays of that city with the name of Randulph Higden, author of the *Polychronicon*. The story is very fairly coherent, and the date (1328) which it assigns for the plays falls within the period of Higden's monastic life at St. Werburgh's abbey.

It must, of course, be borne in mind that the notion of authorship is only imperfectly applicable to the miracle-plays. The task of the playwrights was one less of original composition than of adaptation, of rewriting and rearranging existing texts so as to meet the needs of the particular performances in which they were interested. Obviously this was a process that could be carried out with more or with less individuality. There were slavish adapters and there were liberal adapters. But on the whole the literary problem of the plays lies in tracing the evolution of a form rather than in appreciating individual work. Even when written, the plays, if periodically performed, were subject to frequent revision, motived partly by the literary instinct for furbishing up, partly by changing conditions, such as the existence of a varying number of craft-

[1] Ritson, *Bibl. Poet.* 79, included in his list of Lydgate's works a 'Procession of pageants from the creation' which has not been identified. On the 'Procession of Corpus Christi,' which follows in the list, cf. p. 161.

guilds ready to undertake the responsibility for a scene[1]. Further alterations, on theological rather than literary grounds, were naturally called for at the Reformation. Thus Jordan's Cornish *Creation of the World* is clearly based upon the older play printed by Mr. Norris. The book of the Norwich grocers contains two versions of their play of Paradise, the later of which, 'newely renvid accordynge unto ye Skrypture,' was substituted for the earlier in 1565. The Towneley manuscript has two alternative versions of the *Pastores*. That of York has a fragmentary second version of the Coronation of the Virgin, and when read with the records affords much evidence of the dropping, insertion, and rearrangement of scenes, and of doctrinal revision during the sixteenth century. At Coventry the local annals mention 'new playes' in 1520, fifteen years before the existing texts were 'nevly correcte' and 'translate' by Robert Crowe.

The determination of the relations in which the plays stand towards one another is a field in which literary scholars, delayed by the want of trustworthy critical texts, are only just beginning to set foot. The question lies outside the scope of these pages. But I may call attention to Mr. Pollard's analysis of the various *strata* in the Towneley plays[2], and to the studies by Professor Hohlfeld[3] and Professor Davidson[4] upon the greater cycles in general and especially upon the influence exercised by York over the Towneley and other plays, as excellent examples of what may be looked for. The *Ludus Coventriae* will afford a good subject for investigation, when the manuscript has been properly re-edited. It is evidently a patchwork cycle, roughly put together and in parts easy to break up into its constituent elements. The problem is not confined to English literature. The Chester tradition represents Higden's work as an affair rather of translation than of anything else. It is not quite clear whether translation from the Latin or from the Norman-French is intended. In any case it is probable that the earlier English playwrights made use of French models, and certain parallels

[1] Ten Brink, ii. 235 'An incessant process of separating and uniting, of extending and curtailing, marks the history of the liturgical drama, and indeed of the mediaeval drama generally.'

[2] *Towneley Plays* (E. E. T. S.), xiv.

[3] *Anglia*, xi. 253.

[4] Davidson, 252.

have already been traced between English plays and others to be found in the French collection known as the *Viel Testament*. Here, as elsewhere, the international solidarity of mediaeval literature is to be taken into account.

Two chapters back I defined the change which took place in the character of the religious drama of western Europe during the thirteenth century as being, to a large extent, a process of secularization. 'Out of the hands of the clergy,' I said, 'in their naves and choirs, the drama passed to those of the laity in their market-places and guild-halls.' And I pointed to the natural result of these altered conditions in 'the reaction of the temper of the folk upon the handling of the plays, the broadening of their human as distinct from their religious aspect [1].' A study of the texts and records of the fully developed miracle-play as it existed in these islands from the fourteenth to the sixteenth century can only confirm this view. I have indeed shown, I hope, in the course of this imperfect summary, that the variety of mediaeval theatrical organization was somewhat greater than a too exclusive attention to the craft-cycles of the great towns has always allowed scholars to recognize. But, with all qualifications and exceptions, it is none the less true that what began as a mere spectacle, devised by ecclesiastics for the edification of the laity, came in time to appeal to a deep-rooted native instinct of drama in the folk and to continue as an essentially popular thing, a *ludus* maintained by the people itself for its own inexhaustible wonder and delight [2]. Literary critics have laid stress upon the emergence of the rude humour of the folk, with its love of farce and realism, in somewhat quaint juxtaposition to the general subject-matter of the plays. I only desire to add here that the instinct which made the miracle-plays a joy to the mediaeval burgher is the same instinct which the more primitive peasant satisfied in a score of modes of rudimentary folk-drama [3]. The popularity and elaboration

[1] Cf. p. 69.

[2] Thus at York, the Corpus Christi procession which the plays were originally designed to magnify, had become by 1426 a hindrance to them; cf. p. 139.

[3] There is but little of direct merging of the plays with folk-customs. At Aberdeen the 'Haliblude' play was under the local lord of misrule. At Norwich the play was on Whit-Monday; the lord of misrule

of the devil scenes in the plays is the most striking manifestation of this identity[1]. For your horned and blackened devil is the same personage, with the same vague tradition of the ancient heathen festival about him, whether he riots it through the cathedral aisles in the Feast of Fools, or hales the Fathers to limbo and harries the forward spectators in the market-place of Beverley or Wakefield.

One must not look for absolute breaches of continuity, even in a literary evolution. That the liturgical types of religious drama continued to exist side by side with their popular offshoots, that here the clergy continued to present plays, and in spite of a certain adverse current of ascetic feeling, to assist the lay guilds in divers ways, has already been there shown. It is to be added that the texts of the plays bear traces to the end of their liturgical origin. The music used is reminiscent of church melodies[2]. The dialogue at critical moments follows the traditional lines and occasionally even reverts to the actual Latin of the *repraesentationes*. More than one play—the Towneley *Iuditium*, the Croxton *Sacrament,* the Digby *St. Mary Magdalen*—closes with the *Te Deum* which habitually ended Matins when the dramatic interpolation of the office was over. And what are the *Expositor* of the *Ludus Coventriae*, the *Doctor* of the Brome play, or even *Balaeus Prolocutor* himself, but the lineal descendants, through the dramatized St. Augustine, of certain German plays and the *appellatores* or *vocatores* of the *Prophetae*, of the priest who read the pseudo-Augustinian Christmas *lectio* from which the *Prophetae* sprang? Survivals such as these impress upon the student the unity of the whole religious drama of the Middle Ages, from trope to Corpus Christi cycle.

held revel on Whit-Tuesday. At Reading there were plays on May-day. At Chelmsford and Wymondham they were attached to the Midsummer 'watch' or 'show.' Typically 'folk' personages, the 'wodmen' (cf. vol. i. p. 185), appear in the Aberdeen Candlemas procession, and at Hull the 'hobby-ship' (cf. vol. i. p. 121) becomes the centre of a play.

[1] Richard Carew lays stress on the delight taken by the spectators in the devils of the Cornish plays. Collier, ii. 187, quotes a jest about the devil in a Suffolk stage-play from *C. Mery Talys* († 1533). In the *Conversion of St. Paul* of the Digby MS., a later hand has carefully inserted a devil scene. On the whole subject of the representation of devils in the plays, cf. Cushman, 16; Eckhardt, 53.

[2] *York Plays*, 524.

CHAPTER XXIII

MORALITIES, PUPPET-PLAYS, AND PAGEANTS

[*Bibliographical Note*.—The English moralities are well treated from a literary point of view in the books by Ten Brink, Ward, Creizenach, Pollard, Collier, Klein, Symonds, Bates, Jusserand, and Courthope, named in the bibliographical note to Chapter xxi, and also in the Introduction to A. Brandl, *Quellen des weltlichen Dramas in England vor Shakespeare* (1898). Some texts not easily available elsewhere are given in the same book; others are in Dodsley's *A Select Collection of Old English Plays* (ed. W. C. Hazlitt, 1874-6), vol. i, and J. M. Manly, *Specimens of the Pre-Shakespearean Drama* (1897), vol. i. Extracts are given by Pollard. Lists both of popular moralities and of moral interludes will be found in Appendix X. The French plays of a similar type are dealt with by L. Petit de Julleville, *La Comédie et les Mœurs en France au Moyen Age* (1886) and *Répertoire du Théâtre comique en France au Moyen Age* (1886).—On puppet-plays, C. Magnin, *Histoire des Marionnettes en Europe* (1852), and A. Dieterich, *Pulcinella* (1897), may be consulted. The traditional text of the stock English play is printed, with illustrations by G. Cruikshank, in J. P. Collier, *Punch and Judy* (1870). English pageants at the Corpus Christi feast and at royal entries are discussed by C. Davidson, *English Mystery Plays* (1892), § xvii, and Sir J. B. Paul, in *Scottish Review*, xxx (1897), 217, and the corresponding French *mystères mimés* by L. Petit de Julleville, *Les Mystères* (1880).]

I HAVE endeavoured to trace from its ritual origins the full development of that leading and characteristic type of mediaeval drama, the miracle-play. I now propose to deal, very briefly, with certain further outgrowths which, in the autumn of the Middle Ages, sprang from the miracle-play stock; and a final book will endeavour to bring together the scattered threads of this discursive inquiry, and to touch upon that transformation of the mediaeval into the humanist type of drama, which prepared the way for the great Elizabethan stage.

The miracle-play lent itself to modification in two directions: firstly, by an extension of its subject-matter; and secondly, by an adaptation of its themes and the methods to other forms of entertainment which, although mimetic, were not, in the full sense of the term, dramatic. There are a few plays upon record which were apparently represented after the traditional manner of miracles, but differ from these in that they treat subjects not religious, but secular. Extant examples must be sought in the relics, not of the English, but of the continental drama. The earliest is the French *Estoire de Griselidis,* a version of the story familiar in Chaucer's *Clerkes Tale*, which was written and acted, according to the manuscript, in 1395 [1]. Slightly later is a Dutch manuscript which contains, amongst other things, probably the *répertoire* of some *compagnie joyeuse*, three plays on the subjects respectively of Esmoreit, Gloriant of Brunswick, and Lanseloet and Sanderijn [2]. Both the French and Dutch plays belong to what may be called the wider circle of chivalric romance. An obvious link between such pieces and the ordinary miracle-play is to be found in those of the *Miracles de Nostre Dame* which, like *Amis et Amiles* or *Robert le Diable*, also handle topics of chivalric romance, but only such as are brought technically within the scope of the miracle-play by the intervention of the Virgin at some point of the action [3]. Similarly, another French play, dating from about 1439, on the subject, drawn not from romance but from contemporary history, of the Siege of Orleans, may be explained by the sanctity already attributed in the national imagination to Joan of Arc, who is naturally its leading figure [4]. But the usual range

[1] Ed. Groeneveld (1888); cf. Creizenach, i. 362; Julleville, *Les Myst.* i. 180, ii. 342.

[2] I do not think that these Dutch plays have been printed. The MS., in the Royal Library at Brussels, is described by Hoffmann von Fallersleben, *Horae Belgicae*, vi, xxix; cf. Creizenach, i. 366. Besides the three chivalric plays, it contains a dramatized *estrif* of Summer and Winter (cf. vol. i. p. 187) included with them under the general title of 'abele Spelen,' and also a long farce or 'Boerd.' To each of the five plays, moreover, is attached a short farcical after-piece. A few notices of other fifteenth-century Dutch chivalric plays are preserved. The subjects are Arnoute, Ronchevale, Florys und Blancheflor, Gryselle (Griseldis); cf. Creizenach, i. 372.

[3] Julleville, *Les Myst.* ii. 284, 310.

[4] Ed. F. Guessard et E. de Certain (1862) in *Collection des documents historiques*; cf. Creizenach, i. 372; Julleville, *Les Myst.* ii. 576; H. Tivier, *Étude sur le Myst. du Siège d'O.* (1868). The play may have been designed for performance at the festival held at Orleans in memory of the siege on May 8. The passage quoted from Sir Richard Morrison on p. 221, suggests that a similar commemoration was held in the sixteenth century by the English at Calais of the battle of Agincourt in 1415.

of subject was certainly departed from when Jacques Millet, a student at Orleans, compiled, between 1450 and 1452, an immense *mystère* in 30,000 lines on the *Istoire de la destruction de Troye la grant*[1]. In England, the few examples of the mingling of secular elements with the miracle-plays which present themselves during the sixteenth century can hardly be regarded as mediaeval[2]. The only theme which need be noticed here is that of King Robert of Sicily. A play on this hero, revived at the High Cross at Chester in 1529, is stated in a contemporary letter to have been originally written in the reign of Henry VII. But a still earlier *ludus de Kyng Robert of Cesill* is recorded in the Lincoln *Annales* under the year 1453.

Far more important than this slight secular extension of miracle-plays is another development in the direction of allegory, giving rise to the 'moral plays' or 'moralities,' as they came to be indifferently called[3], in which the characters are no longer scriptural or legendary persons, but wholly, or almost wholly, abstractions, and which, although still religious in intention, aim rather at ethical cultivation than the stablishing of faith. The earliest notices of morals are found about the end of the fourteenth century, at a time when the influence of the *Roman de la Rose* and other widely popular works was bringing every department of literature under the sway of allegory[4]. That the drama also should be touched with the spirit of the age was so inevitable as hardly to call for comment. But it will be interesting to point out some at least of the special channels through which the new tendency established itself. In the first place there is the twelfth-century Latin play of *Antichristus*. In a sense the whole content of this may be called allegorical, and the allegory becomes formal in such figures as *Heresis* and *Ypocrisis*,

[1] Ed. Stengel (1883); cf. Creizenach, i. 374; Julleville, *Les Myst.* ii. 569.

[2] Cf. *Representations*, s.v. Dublin.

[3] Collier, ii. 183, thinks the term 'morality' a 'recent' one, but it was used in 1503: cf. p. 201.

[4] There is not much direct imitation of the *Roman de la Rose* in the moralities. Perhaps the French *Honneur des Dames* of Andrieu de la Vigne (Julleville, *Rép. com.* 73) comes nearest. But its leading episode, the siege of the fortress of Danger, is reflected in the siege of the Castle of Perseverance and that of the Castle of Maudleyn in the *Mary Magdalen* of the Digby MS. On the general place of allegory in contemporary literature cf. Courthope, i. 341.

Iustitia and *Misericordia*, and in those of *Ecclesia*, *Synagoga*, and *Gentilitas*, suggested to the clerkly author by a well-known *disputatio*. The same theme recurs in more than one later play [1]. Secondly, there is the theme of the Reconciliation of the Heavenly Virtues, which is suggested by the words of the eighty-fifth Psalm: 'Mercy and Truth are met together: Righteousness and Peace have kissed each other.' This is treated in two unprinted and little known French plays, also of the twelfth century, which I have not as yet had occasion to mention and of which I borrow the following analysis from Dr. Ward: 'These four virtues appear personified as four sisters, who meet together after the Fall of Man before the throne of God to conduct one of those disputations which were so much in accordance with the literary tastes of the age; Truth and Righteousness speak against the guilty Adam, while Mercy and Peace plead in his favour. Concord is restored among the four sisters by the promise of a Saviour, who shall atone to Divine Justice on behalf of man.' One of these pieces is ascribed to the Anglo-Norman poet, Guillaume Herman (1127–70), the other to Stephen Langton, afterwards archbishop of Canterbury. They are generally spoken of as literary exercises, not intended for representation [2]. But it is obvious that they might very well find their places in miracle-play cycles, as links between the scenes dealing respectively with the Fall and the Redemption. Further, precisely such an episode, in precisely such a position, does occur, three hundred years later, in the English cycle known as the *Ludus Coventriae*. Nor is this the only allegorical element which distinguishes a certain part of this patchwork cycle from nearly all the other English plays [3]. It is not, perhaps, of great importance that in the Assumption scene the

[1] Cf. pp. 63, 77.

[2] Ward, i. 105; *Archaeologia*, xiii. 232. A *débat* on precisely this theme is introduced into the *Chasteau d'Amour*, a theological work in the form of a romance, ascribed to Robert Grosseteste (1175–1253), on which cf. F. S. Stevenson, *Life of Grosseteste*, 38; Jusserand, *Eng. Lit.* i. 214. In the English version of the fourteenth century (R. F. Weymouth, *The Castel of Love*, 273) the passage begins—

'For now I chul tellen of þe stryf
Þat a-mong þe foure sustren liþ.'

[3] No stress is of course to be laid upon the late introduction of Dolor and Myserye into the Grocers' play at Norwich, when the text was rewritten in 1565.

risen Christ receives the name of *Sapientia*, or that *Contemplatio* is the 'exposytour in doctorys wede,' by whom several other scenes are introduced. But there is a striking passage at the end of the Slaughter of the Innocents, where 'Dethe, Goddys masangere,' intervenes to make an end of the tyrannic Herod [1], and here, I think, may clearly be traced yet a third stream of allegorical tendency making its way into the drama from that singular *danse macabre* or 'Dance of Death,' which exercised so powerful a fascination on the art of the Middle Ages. Death hobnobbing with pope and king and clown, with lord and lady, with priest and merchant, with beggar and fool, the irony is familiar in many a long series of frescoes and engravings. Nor are cases lacking in which it was directly adapted for scenic representation. An alleged example at Paris in 1424 was probably only a painting. But in 1449 a *certain jeu, histoire et moralité sur le fait de la danse macabre* was acted before Philip the Good at Bruges, and a similar performance is recorded at Besançon in 1453 [2].

The process of introducing abstractions into the miracle-plays themselves does not seem to have been carried very far. On the other hand, the moralities, if God and the Devil may be regarded as abstractions, admit of nothing else. Two at least of the motives just enumerated, the Dance of Death and the Reconciliation of the Heavenly Virtues, recur in them. But both are subordinate to a third, which may be called the Conflict of Vice and Virtue. This *débat*-like theme is of course familiar in every branch of allegorical literature. Prof. Creizenach traces one type of it, in which the conflict is conceived under the symbols of siege or battle, to the *Psychomachia* of Prudentius [3], and perhaps even further to the passage about the 'whole armour of God' in St. Paul's epistle to the Ephesians [4]. For the purposes of the stage it

[1] *Ludus Cov.* 106 (play xi, *Virtutes*), 70, 79, 89, 105, 124, 129, 289 (plays viii–xiii, xxix, *Contemplacio*), 184 (play xix, *Mors*), 386 (play xli, *Sapientia*); cf. Hohlfeld, in *Anglia*, xi. 278.

[2] Jusserand, *Théâtre*, 123; Pearson, i. 2; Creizenach, i. 461; *Captain Cox*, clxvi; W. Seelmann, *Die Totentänze des Mittelalters* (*Jahrb. d. Vereins f. niederdeutsche Sprachforschung*, xvii. 1). A bibliography of the Dance of Death is given by Goedeke, i. 322 (bk. iii. § 92).

[3] Prudentius, *Psychomachia* († 400 *P. L.* lx. 11); cf. Creizenach, i. 463.

[4] *Ephesians*, vi. 11.

is eminently suitable, both because it lends itself to many and various modes of representation, and because conflict is the very stuff out of which drama is wrought.

As the earliest notices of moralities are found in English records and as this particular development of the drama is thoroughly well represented in English texts, I may save space by confining my attention to these, merely noting as I pass the contemporary existence of precisely parallel records and texts on the continent and particularly in France[1]. The first English moralities seem to have been known as *Paternoster* plays. Such a play is mentioned by Wyclif about 1378 as existing at York, and at some date previous to 1389 a special guild *Orationis Domini* was founded in that city for its maintenance. The play, however, survived the guild, and was acted from time to time as a substitute for the ordinary Corpus Christi plays up to 1572. Similarly, at Beverley a *Paternoster* play was acted by the crafts, probably in emulation of that of York, in 1469, while a third is mentioned in Lincoln documents as played at various dates from 1397 to 1521. Although all these *Paternoster* plays are lost, their general character can be made clear. In that of York 'all manner of vices and sins were held up to scorn and the virtues were held up to praise,' while an incidental entry in a *computus* shows that one division of it was known as the *ludus accidiae*. The information to be derived from Beverley is even more explicit. There were eight pageants. One was assigned to 'Vicious,' probably a typical representative of frail humanity, the other seven to the seven deadly sins which beset him, 'Pryde: Invy: Ire: Avaryce: Sleweth (or Accidie): Glotony: Luxuria.' The *Paternoster* play seems, therefore, to have been in some fashion a dramatization of the struggle of the vices and the corresponding virtues for the soul of man,

[1] Creizenach, i. 470; Julleville, *La Com.* 44, 78. The earliest French notice is that of the 'Gieux des sept vertuz et des sept pechiez mortelz' at Tours in 1390. A 'mystère de Bien-Avisé et Mal-avisé' is said to have been played in 1396 (Julleville, *Rép. com.* 324). The extant play of that name, somewhat later in date, is a morality. Other early French morals on a large scale are *L'Homme juste et l'Homme mondain* (1508) and *L'Homme pécheur* († 1494) (Julleville, *Rép. com.* 39, 67, 72). All these are on variants of the Contrast of Vice and Virtue theme.

and the name given to it may be explained by the mediaeval notion that each clause of the Lord's Prayer was of specific merit against one of the deadly sins[1]. Here then is one version of just that theme of the Conflict of Vice and Virtue noted as dominant in the moralities.

Of the half dozen extant English moralities which can with any plausibility be assigned to the fifteenth century, two are based upon a motive akin to that of the Dance of Death. These are the fragmentary *Pride of Life*, which is the earliest of the group, and *Everyman*, which is by far the finest[2]. In the former Death and Life contend for the soul of *Rex Vivus*, the representative of humanity, who is only saved from the fiends by the intervention of the Virgin. In the latter, God sends Death to summon Everyman, who finds to his dismay that of all his earthly friends only Good Deeds is willing to accompany him. The Conflict of Vice and Virtue is resumed in the moral of *Mundus et Infans* and in the three morals of the Macro manuscript, the *Castle of Perseverance*, *Mind*, *Will and Understanding*, and *Mankind*. In all four plays the representative of humanity, *Infans* or *Humanum Genus* or *Anima* or Mankind, is beset by the compulsion or swayed this way and that by the persuasion of allegorized good and bad qualities. At the end of the *Castle of Perseverance* the motive of the Reconciliation of the Heavenly Virtues is introduced in a scene closely resembling that of the *Ludus Coventriae* or the earlier essays of Guillaume Herman and Stephen Langton.

A somewhat unique position between miracle-play and morality is occupied by the Mary Magdalen drama contained in the Digby manuscript. The action of this, so far as it is scriptural or legendary, has already been summarized[3]; but it must now be added that the episodes of the secular life of the Magdalen *in gaudio* are conceived in a wholly allegorical vein. The 'kyngs of the world and the flesch' and the 'prynse of dylles' are introduced with the seven

[1] Creizenach, i. 465, quoting a thirteenth-century German sermon.

[2] Cf. p. 201 and *Texts* (ii). It is not quite clear whether the English play of *Everyman* is the original or a translation of the Dutch *Elckerlijk*, or whether the two plays have a common source.

[3] Cf. p. 131.

deadly sins and a good and a bad angel. The castle of Magdala, like the castle of Perseverance, is besieged. The Magdalen is led into a tavern by *Luxuria* and there betrayed by Curiosity, a gallant. We have to do less with a mystery beginning to show morality elements than with a deliberate combination effected by a writer familiar with both forms of drama.

The manner of presentation of the fifteenth-century moralities did not differ from that of the contemporary miracle-plays. The manuscript of the *Castle of Perseverance* contains a prologue delivered by *vexillatores* after the fashion of the *Ludus Coventriae* and the Croxton *Sacrament*. There is also, as in the Cornish mysteries published by Mr. Norris, a diagram showing a circular 'place' bounded by a ditch or fence, with a central 'castel' and five 'skaffoldys' for the principal performers. Under the castle is 'Mankynde, is bed' and near it 'Coveytyse cepbord.' The scaffolds are the now familiar *loca* or *sedes*. The scantier indications of more than one of the other moralities proper suggest that they also were performed in an outdoor 'place' with *sedes*, and a similar arrangement is pointed to by the stage directions of the *Mary Magdalen*. Nor could the moralities dispense with those attractions of devils and hell-fire which had been so popular in their predecessors. Belial, in the *Castle of Perseverance*, is to have gunpowder burning in pipes in his hands and ears and other convenient parts of his body; *Anima*, in *Mind, Will and Understanding*, has little devils running in and out beneath her skirts; and in *Mary Magdalen*, the 'prynse of dylles' enters in 'a stage, and Helle ondyr-neth that stage.' The later moralities, of which the sixteenth century affords several examples, were presented under somewhat different conditions, which will be discussed in another chapter[1]. Allusions to the 'morals at Manningtree,' however, in the beginning of the seventeenth century, suggest that moralities may have continued in out-of-the-way places to hold the open-air stage, just as miracle-plays here and there did, to a comparatively late date. Actual examples of the more popular type of morality from the sixteenth century

[1] Cf. p. 199.

are afforded by Skelton's *Magnificence* and by Sir David Lyndsay's *Satyre of the Thrie Estaitis,* shown successively at Linlithgow in 1540, on the Castle-hill at Cupar of Fife in 1552, and in the Greenside at Edinburgh about 1554. This remarkable piece differs in many ways from the English moralities. The theme consists of the arraignment of the estates of the realm before *Rex Humanitas.* Various 'vycis' and allegorical personages appear and plead, and the action is enlivened by farcical interludes for the amusement of the vulgar, and wound up by a sermon of 'Folie,' which points rather to French than to English models[1]. The flight of time is also shown by the fact that the *Satyre* aims less at the moral edification with which the fifteenth-century plays contented themselves, than at the introduction of a sharp polemic against abuses in church and state. Skelton's *Magnificence* had also, not improbably, some political bearing. To this matter also I return in another chapter[2].

Miracle-plays and moralities ranked amongst the most widespread and coloured elements, century after century, of burgher and even of village life. It is not surprising that their subjects and their methods exercised a powerful influence upon other manifestations of the mediaeval spirit. The share which their vivid and sensuous presentations of religious ideas had in shaping the conceptions of artists and handicraftsmen is a fascinating topic of far too wide a scope to be even touched upon here[3]. But a few pages must be devoted to indicating the nature of their overflow into various pseudo-dramatic, rather than strictly dramatic, forms of entertainment.

One of these is the puppet-show. It has been pointed out, in speaking of the liturgical drama, that the use of puppets to provide a figured representation of the mystery of the Nativity, seems to have preceded the use for the same purpose of living and speaking persons; and further, that the puppet-show, in the form of the 'Christmas crib,' has outlived the drama founded upon it, and is still in use in all Catholic

[1] Cf. vol. i. p. 381.

[2] Cf. p. 218.

[3] See Pearson, ii. 260, and the interesting study of P. Weber, *Geistliches Schauspiel und kirchliche Kunst* (1894).

countries[1]. An analogous custom is the laying of the crucifix in the 'sepulchre' during the Easter ceremonies, and there is one English example of a complete performance of a Resurrection play by 'certain smalle puppets, representinge the Persons of Christe, the Watchmen, Marie and others.' This is described by a seventeenth-century writer as taking place at Witney in Oxfordshire 'in the dayes of ceremonial religion,' and one of the watchmen, which made a clacking noise, was 'comonly called Jack Snacker of Wytney[2].' This points to the use of some simple mechanical device by which motion was imparted to some at least of the puppets. A similar contrivance was produced by Bishop Barlow to point a sermon against idolatry at Paul's Cross in 1547 and was given afterwards to the boys to break into pieces[3]. More elaborate representations of miracle-plays by means of moving puppets or *marionnettes* make their appearance in all parts of Europe at a period when the regular dramatic performances of similar subjects were already becoming antiquated, nor can they be said to be even yet quite extinct[4]. Most of them belong to the repertory of the professional showmen, and it will be remembered that some form or other of *marionnette* seems to have been handed down continuously amongst the minstrel class from Roman times[5]. In England the puppet-shows were much in vogue at such places as Bartholomew Fair, where they became serious rivals of the living actors[6]. The earliest name for them was 'motions[7].' Italian players brought 'an instrument of strange motions' to London in 1574[8]. Autolycus, in *The Winter's Tale*, amongst his other shifts for a living,

[1] Cf. p. 42.

[2] W. Lambarde, *Alphabetical Description of the Chief Places in England and Wales* (1730, written in the sixteenth century), 459, s. v. Wytney.

[3] Gairdner, 253, quoting an unnamed chronicler, 'a picture of the Resurrection of Our Lord made with vices, which put out his legs of sepulchre, and blessed with his hand and turned his head.'

[4] Magnin, *Marionnettes*; J. Feller, *Le Bethléem verviétois* (*Bull. de la Soc. verviétoise d'Arch. et d'Hist.* 1900).

[5] Cf. vol. i. p. 71.

[6] Morley, *passim*; Hone, 229; Strutt, 164; T. Frost, *Old Showmen and Old London Fairs* (1874); W. B. Boulton, *Amusements of Old London*, ii. 49, 224.

[7] The term 'motion' is not, however, confined to puppet-plays. Bacon, Essay xxxvii, uses it of the dumb-shows of masquers, and Jonson, *Tale of a Tub*, v. 1, of shadow-plays.

[8] *P. C. Acts*, viii. 131.

'compassed a motion of the Prodigal Son[1].' Ben Jonson, in *Bartholomew Fair*, introduces one Lanthorn Leatherhead, a puppet-showman, who presents in his booth a curious rigmarole of a motion in which Hero and Leander, Damon and Pythias, and Dionysius are all mixed up[2]. It would appear to have been customary for the showman, like his brethren of the modern Punch and Judy, to 'interpret' for the puppets by reciting a suitable dialogue as an accompaniment to their gestures[3]. The repertory of Lanthorn Leatherhead contained a large proportion of 'motions' on subjects borrowed from the miracle-play. Similar titles occur in the notices of later performances at Bartholomew Fair[4] and of those given by the popular London showman, Robert Powell, during the reign of Queen Anne[5]. In more recent times all other puppet-shows have been outdone by the unique vogue of Punch and Judy[6]. The derivation of these personages from the Pontius Pilate and Judas Iscariot of the miracle-plays is the merest philological whimsy. Punch is doubtless the Pulcinella[7], who makes

[1] *Winter's Tale*, iv. 3. 102.

[2] *Bartholomew Fair*, v. 3; cf. v. 1. 8 'O, the motions that I, Lanthorn Leatherhead, have given light to in my time, since my master Pod died! Jerusalem was a stately thing, and so was Nineveh, and the City of Norwich, and Sodom and Gomorrah, with the rising of the prentices and pulling down the bawdy-houses there upon Shrove-Tuesday; but the Gunpowder Plot, there was a get-penny! I have presented that to an eighteen or twenty pence audience, nine times in an afternoon'; also *Every Man out of His Humour*, Induction:

'Will show more several motions in his face
Than the new London, Rome, or Nineveh.'

[3] Lanthorn Leatherhead says of his puppets, 'I am the mouth of them all'; cf. *Hamlet*, iii. 2. 256 'I could interpret between you and your love, if I could see the puppets dallying'; *Two Gentlemen of Verona*, ii. 1. 100 'O excellent motion! O exceeding puppet! Now will he interpret to her.'

[4] Morley, 179, 187, 190, 247, 261, 273, 304, 321, records 'Patient Grisel' (1655, 1677), 'Susanna' (1655), 'Sodom and Gomorrah' (1656), 'Judith and Holophernes' (1664), 'Jephtha's Rash Vow' (1697, 1698, 1701, 1704, 1733), 'The Creation of the World' (1701).

[5] Powell's performances of the 'Creation of the World' at Bath and 'Susanna' at Covent Garden are referred to in the *Tatler* for May 14, 1709, and the *Spectator* for March 16, 1711.

[6] Hone, 230, describes a 'gallantee show' of the Prodigal Son and of Noah's Ark with a scene of 'Pull Devil, Pull Baker,' showing the judgement upon a baker who gave short weight (cf. the cut in Morley, 356), seen by him in London in 1818. This was an exhibition of *ombres chinoises* rather than a puppet-play proper.

[7] A. Dieterich, *Pulcinella*, 234, considers Pulcinella a descendant of Maccus, derives the name from *pullicenus*, *pulcinus*, *pullus*, and

his appearance about 1600 as a stock figure in the impromptu comedy of Naples. Under other names his traditions may, for all one knows, go back far beyond the miracle-plays to the *fabulae Atellanae*. But the particular drama in which alone he now takes the stage, although certainly not a miracle-play, follows closely upon the traditional lines of the moralities[1].

Another kind of religious dumb-show, at once more ancient and more important than that of the puppets, was presented by living persons in the 'ridings' or processions which formed an integral part of so many mediaeval festivals. Like the miracle-plays themselves, these *tableaux* reached their highest point of elaboration in connexion with the ceremonies of Corpus Christi day; and, in order to understand their relation to the regular dramas, it is necessary to return for a moment to the early history of the great feast. It has already been suggested that the processional character of the great English craft-cycles, with their movable pageants and their 'stations,' may be explained on the hypothesis, that the performances were at one time actually given during the 'stations' or pauses before temporary street altars of the Corpus Christi procession itself. The obvious inconveniences of such a custom, if it really existed, might not unnaturally lead to its modification. Except at Draguignan, where the dialogue was reduced to the briefest limits, no actual traces of it are left[2]. In England the difficulty seems to have been solved at Newcastle by sending the pageants round with the pro-

connects the fowl-masks of Italian comedy with the cockscomb of the English fool (cf. vol. i. p. 385).

[1] Collier, *Punch and Judy* (1870), 11 sqq.; Frost, *The Old Showmen and the Old London Fairs*, 29. The earliest English notice of Punch in England is in the overseers' books of St. Martin's-in-the-Fields for 1666 and 1667, 'Rec[d] of Punchinello, y[e] Italian popet player, for his booth at Charing Cross.' In a Bartholomew Fair playbill of the early eighteenth century, 'the merry conceits of Squire Punch and Sir John Spendall' were attached to the puppet-show of the Creation of the World. Punch was also amongst the *dramatis personae* of Robert Powell. The nature of these earlier Punch plays is unknown. That now traditional in England is implied by the ballad of *Punch's Pranks* († 1790). Collier, who prints it as given by one Piccini in Drury Lane, with cuts by Cruikshank, considers it to be derived from *Don Juan*. But it seems to me to come still nearer to the morality plays. French Punch plays have many other themes.

[2] Julleville, *Les Myst.* ii. 208; cf. p. 95.

cession in the early morning and deferring the actual plays until the afternoon. At Coventry representatives of the *dramatis personae* appear to have ridden in the procession, the cumbrous pageants being left behind until they were needed. Herod, for instance, rode on behalf of the smiths. At other places, again, the separation between procession and play was even more complete. The crafts which produced the plays were as a rule also burdened by their ordinances with the duties of providing a light and of walking or riding in honour of the host; but the two ceremonies took place at different hours on the same day, and there was no external relation, so far as the evidence goes, between them. Even so there was still some clashing, and at York, after an unsuccessful attempt on the part of the clergy in 1426 to get the plays put off, the procession itself appears to have been transferred to the following day.

On the other hand the difficulty seems to have been met in certain towns by suppressing the plays and reducing them to dumb-show 'pageants' carried in the procession. Lists are extant of such pageants as they were assigned to the crafts at Dublin in 1498 and at Hereford in 1503, and although it is not of course impossible that there were to be plays later in the day, there is no proof that this was the case. For a similar procession of *tableaux* held in London, in the earlier part of the fifteenth century, a set of descriptive verses was written by John Lydgate, and the adoption of this method of 'interpreting' the dumb-show seems to put the possibility of a regular dramatic performance out of court[1].

[1] Printed by Halliwell, *Minor Poems of Lydgate* (Percy Soc.), 95, from Shirley's *Harl.* 2251, f. 293, as a *Processioune of Corpus Cristi*, with a note at the end that 'Shirley kowde fynde no more.' It is also, with the same note, in Shirley's *Trin. Coll. Camb. MS.* R. 3. 20, f. 348, with the heading, 'Ordenaunce of a p'cessyoun of the feste of Corpus Cristi, made in London by Daun John Lydegate' (E. P. Hammond, in *Anglia*, xxii. 364), and is copied thence by John Stowe in *B. M. Add. MS.* 29,729, f. 166. The piece is nº. 153 in the list of Lydgate's works given by Ritson, *Bibl. Poet.* 79. It may be doubted whether Ritson's nº. 152 'A Procession of pageants from the creation' is really distinct. Lydgate describes to his hearers 'figures shewed in your presence' which embody 'gracious mysteries grounded in Scripture.' Of course 'mysteries' has no technical dramatic sense here. Lydgate's method of 'interpreting' may have been based on the incorrect mediaeval notion of the methods of the classical stage,

There were pageants also in the Corpus Christi processions at Bungay and at Bury St. Edmunds, but the notices are too fragmentary to permit of more than a conjecture as to whether they were accompanied by plays. The *tableaux* shown at Dublin, Hereford, and London were of a continuous and cyclical character, although at Hereford St. Catherine, and at Dublin King Arthur, the Nine Worthies, and St. George's dragon were tacked on at the tail of the procession[1]. A continental parallel is afforded by the twenty-eight *remontrances*, making a complete cycle from the Annunciation to the Last Judgement, shown at Béthune in 1549[2]. But elsewhere, both in England and abroad, the shows of the Corpus Christi procession were of a much less systematic character, and Dublin was not the only place where secular elements crept in[3]. At Coventry, in addition to the representative figures from the craft-plays, the guild of Corpus Christi and St. Nicholas, to which, as to special Corpus Christi guilds elsewhere, the general supervision of the procession fell, provided in 1539 a Mary and a Gabriel with the lily, Saints Catherine and Margaret, eight Virgins and twelve Apostles.

which he adopts in his *Troy Book* (cf. p. 208). The 'figures' represented twenty-seven persons whose utterances revealed the mystery of the Mass. There were eight patriarchs, the Ecclesiast, four prophets, the Baptist, four evangelists, St. Paul, and seven Christian doctors.

[1] Sharp, 172, quotes from a contemporary writer a passage showing that the Dublin procession, like those of Coventry and Shrewsbury, lasted to a recent date: 'The Fringes was a procession of the trades and corporations, performed in Ireland on Corpus Christi day, even within the author's recollection. King Solomon, Queen of Sheba, with Vulcan, Venus, and Cupid, were leading persons upon this occasion.'

[2] Julleville, *Les Myst.* ii. 211; Davidson, 219.

[3] The following is from an account of a continental Corpus Christi procession in Barnabe Googe's translation of Naogeorgos' *Popish Kingdom* (1553), iv. 699 (Stubbes, i. 337):

'Christes passion here derided is,
with sundrie maskes and playes;
Faire Ursley with hir maydens
all, doth passe amid the wayes:
And valiant George, with speare
thou killest the dreadfull dragon
here;
The deuil's house is drawne about,
wherein there doth appere
A wondrous sort of damned
sprites, with foule and fearefull
looke;
Great Christopher doth wade and
passe with Christ amid the
brooke:
Sebastian full of feathred shaftes,
the dint of dart doth feele;
There walketh Kathren with hir
sworde in hande, and cruell
wheele:
The Challis and the singing Cake,
with Barbara is led,
And sundrie other Pageants
playde in worship of this bred,
&c.'

The Coventry procession, it may be added, outlived the Corpus Christi feast. In the seventeenth century Godiva had been placed in it and became the most important feature. By the nineteenth century the wool-combers had a shepherd and shepherdess, their patron saint Bishop Blaize, and Jason with the Golden Fleece [1]. At the Shrewsbury 'Show,' which also until a recent date continued the tradition of an older Corpus Christi procession, Saints Crispin and Crispinian rode for the shoemakers. At Norwich the grocers sent the 'griffin' from the top of their pageant and a 'tree' which may have been the tree of knowledge from their Whitsun play of Paradise, but which was converted by festoons of fruit and spicery into an emblem of their trade [2].

Aberdeen seems to have been distinguished by having two great mimetic processions maintained by the guilds. The interpretation of the data is rather difficult, but apparently the 'Haliblude' play, which existed in 1440 and 1479, had given way by 1531 to a procession in which pageants of the Crucifixion, the Resurrection, and the Coronation of the Virgin were eked out by others of Saints Sebastian, Laurence, Stephen, Martin, Nicholas, John, and George. The other procession seems originally to have been introduced as an episode in a play of the Presentation in the Temple on Candlemas day. Its 'personnes' or 'pageants' are such as might furnish out the action of a short Nativity cycle, together with 'honest squiares' from each craft, 'wodmen,' and minstrels. But in this case also the play seems to have vanished early in the sixteenth century, while the procession certainly endured until a much later date.

There are no other English religious dumb-shows, outside those of Corpus Christi day, so elaborate as the Aberdeen Candlemas procession. On the same day at Beverley the guild of St. Mary carried a pageant of the Virgin and Child with Saints Joseph and Simon and two angels holding a great

[1] Sharp, 217, records a play of the *Golden Fleece* provided by Robert Crowe for the Cappers' Candlemas Dinner in 1525; the London drapers had a pageant with the same title in 1522 (cf. p. 165).

[2] Cf. the Paradise show at the London reception of Henry VI in 1432 (p. 170).

candlestick[1]. The guild of St. Helen, on the day of the Invention of the Cross (May 3), had a procession with a boy to represent the saint, and two men bearing a cross and a shovel[2]. The guild of St. William of Norwich paraded a knave-child between two men holding candles in honour of the youthful martyr[3]. In the Whitsuntide procession at Leicester walked the Virgin and Saint Martin, with the twelve Apostles[4]. More interesting is the pageant of St. Thomas the Martyr on December 29 at Canterbury, with the saint on a cart and knights played by children and an altar and a device of an angel and a 'leder bag for the blode[5].' Probably this list could be largely increased were it worth while[6]. The comparatively modern elements in the Corpus Christi pageantry of Coventry, Shrewsbury, and Dublin may be paralleled from the eighteenth-century festival of the Preston guild merchant on or near St. John Baptist's day with its Crispin and Crispinian, Bishop Blaize, Adam and Eve, Vulcan, and so forth[7], or the nineteenth-century wool trade procession on St. Blasius' day (February 3), at Bradford, in which once more Bishop Blaize, with the Jason and Medea of the Golden Fleece, appears[8]. It is noticeable how, as such functions grow more civic and less religious, the pageants tend to become distinctively emblematic of the trades concerned. The same feature is to be observed in the choice of subjects for the plays given by way of entertainment to the earl of Kildare at Dublin in 1528.

The dumb-show pageants, which in many cities glorified the 'ridings' on the day of St. George (April 23), have been

[1] Toulmin Smith, *English Guilds*, 149.

[2] Ibid. 148.

[3] Ibid. 30.

[4] Kelly, 7, 11.

[5] Cf. *Representations*, s. v. Canterbury.

[6] The 'pagent's paynted and lemenyd with gold' of the Holy Trinity, Saints Fabian, Sebastian, and Botulph, 'and the last pagent of the terement, & gen'all obyte, of the brether'n and suster'n, that be passed to God,' which the London guild of the Holy Trinity had on a 'rolle of velom, cou'ed with a goldeskyn' in 1463 (Hone, 81), were probably not, as Davidson, 224, thinks, 'a description and representation of the pageants which were carried in procession by the guild,' but illuminated pages (*paginae*). For a similar misunderstanding cf. p. 401, n. 1. Abp. Thoresby († 1357) circulated a 'tretys in Englisce . . . in smale pagynes' (Shirley, *Fasciculi Zizaniorum*, xiii).

[7] *Representations*, s. v. Preston.

[8] Dyer, 60.

described in an earlier chapter[1]. These 'ridings,' of curiously mingled religious and folk origin, stand midway between the processions just mentioned and such seasonal perambulations as the 'shows' and 'watches' of Midsummer. Even in the latter, elements borrowed from the pageants of the miracle-plays occasionally form an odd blend with the 'giants' and other figures of the 'folk' tradition[2]. The 'wache and playe' went together at Wymondham, and also apparently at Chelmsford, in the sixteenth century. At York we find the pageants of some of the crafts borrowed for a play, though apparently a classical and not a religious one, at the Midsummer show of 1585. At Chester, when the Whitsun plays were beginning to fall into desuetude, the crafts were regularly represented in the Midsummer show by some of their *dramatis personae*, who, however, rode without their pageants. The smiths sent 'the Doctors and little God,' the butchers sent 'the divill in his fethers,' the barbers sent Abraham and Isaac, the bricklayers sent Balaam and the Ass, and so forth. These with the giants, a dragon, a man in woman's clothes, naked boys, morris-dancers and other folk elements, made up a singular cavalcade.

In London, pageants were provided for the Midsummer show by the guilds to which the lord mayor and sheriffs for the year belonged. Thus the drapers had a pageant of the Golden Fleece in 1522, and pageants of the Assumption and Saint Ursula in 1523[3]. To a modern imagination the type of civic pageantry is the annual procession at the installation of the lord mayor in November, known familiarly as the lord mayor's show. This show was important enough from the middle of the sixteenth century, and the pens of many goodly poets, Peele, Dekker, Munday, Middleton, and others, were employed in its service[4]. But its history cannot be taken much further back, and it is exceedingly probable that when the Midsummer show came to an end in 1538, the pageants were transferred to the installation procession. The earliest

[1] Cf. vol. i. p. 221.
[2] Cf. vol. i. pp. 118, 120.
[3] Cf. *Representations*, s.v. London.
[4] J. G. Nichols, *London Pageants* (1837); F. W. Fairholt, *Lord Mayor's Pageants* (1843-4, Percy Soc. nos. 38, 43), and *The Civic Garland* (Percy Soc. 1845).

clear notice is in 1540, when a pageant of the Assumption, perhaps that which had already figured at the Midsummer show of 1523, was used[1]. The ironmongers had a pageant when the lord mayor was chosen from their body in 1566. It was arranged by James Peele, father of the dramatist, and there were two 'wodmen' in it, but unfortunately it is not further described[2]. In 1568, Sir Thomas Roe, merchant tailor, had a pageant of John the Baptist[3]. William Smith, writing an account of city customs in 1575, mentions, as a regular feature of the procession, 'the Pagent of Triumph richly decked, whereupon, by certain figures and writings, some matter touching Justice and the office of a Magistrate is represented[4].' And about ten years later the series of printed 'Devices' of the pageants begins.

The influence of miracle-plays and moralities is also to be looked for in the municipal 'shows' of welcome provided at the state entries of royal and other illustrious visitors. A large number of these, chiefly at coronations, royal marriages and the like, are recorded in chronicles of London origin, and with the London examples in their chronological order I will briefly deal. The earlier features of such ceremonies include the riding of the mayor and corporation to meet the king at some place outside the gates, such as Blackheath, or, in the case of a coronation, at the Tower, and the escorting of him with joyous *tripudium* or *carole* to the palace of Westminster, the reading of loyal addresses and the giving of golden gifts, the decking of walls and balconies with costly robes and tapestries, the filling of the conduits with wine, white and red, in place of the accustomed water[5]. The first example

[1] Herbert, i. 457. The same writer quotes a payment from the drapers' accounts of 1516 of £13 4*s*.7*d*. for 'Sir Laurens Aylmer's Pageant.' But this cannot have been intended for a lord mayor's show, for Aylmer's only mayoralty was in 1507–8, and a grocer, not a draper, was mayor in 1515–6 and in 1516–7.

[2] Malcolm, *Londinium Redivivum*, ii. 42; W. C. Hazlitt, *Livery Companies* (1892), 310.

[3] Herbert, i. 199.

[4] W. Smith, *A breffe description of the Royall Citie of London* (1575), quoted by Nichols, 95.

[5] The *Annales Londonienses* record at the visit of the Emperor Otho to King John in 1207 'tota civitas Londoniae induit solempnitatem pallis et aliis ornamentis circumornata,' and at the entry of Edward II after his marriage in 1308 'tapeti aurei' and the city dignitaries 'coram rege et regina

of pageantry in the proper sense occurs about the middle of the thirteenth century, in certain 'devices and marvels' shown at the wedding of Henry III to Eleanor of Provence in 1236[1]. These are not described in detail; but when Edward I returned to London after the defeat of William Wallace at Falkirk in 1298, it is recorded by a chronicler, quoted in Stowe's *Annals*, that the crafts made 'great and solemne triumph' and that the fishmongers in particular 'amongst other pageantes and shewes' had, as it was St. Magnus's day, one of the saint accompanied by a thousand horsemen, and preceded by four gilded sturgeons, four salmons on horseback and 'sixe and fourtie knights armed, riding on horses made like luces of the sea[2].' It was the fishmongers again who on the birth of Edward III in 1313 went in a *chorea* to Westminster with an ingeniously contrived ship in full sail, and escorted the queen on her way to Eltham[3]. At the coronation of Richard II in 1377 an elaborate castle was put up at the head of Cheapside. On the four towers of this stood four white-robed damsels, who wafted golden leaves in the king's face, dropped gilt models of coin upon him and his steed, and offered him wine from pipes laid on to the structure. Between the towers was a golden angel, which by a mechanical device bent forward and held out a crown as Richard drew near[4]. Similar stages, with a *coelicus ordo* of singers and boys and maidens offering wine and golden crowns, stood in Cheapside when Richard again rode through the city in 1392, in token

karolantes' (*Chronicles of the Reigns of Edw. I and Edw. II*, R. S. i. 13, 152). At the coronation of Henry IV in 1399 was an 'equitatio magnifica' (*Annales Hen. IV*, R. S. 291), and the streets were hung with 'paremens,' and there were 'nœuf broucherons a manière de fontaines en Cep a Londres, courans par plusieurs conduits, jettans vin blanc et vermeil' (Froissart, *Chroniques*, ed. Kervyn de Lettynhove, xvi. 205).

[1] M. Paris, *Chronica Maiora* (R. S.), iii. 336 'quibusdam prodigiosis ingeniis et portentis.'

[2] Stowe, *Annals*, 207. The authority quoted in the margin is 'Chro. Dun.,' which I cannot identify. It is not the Dunstable Annals in the *Annales monastici* (R. S.), vol. iii.

[3] *Annales Londonienses* (*Chron. of Edw. I and Edw. II*, R. S.), i. 221 'quaedam navis, quodam mirabili ingenio operata, cum malo et velo erectis, et depictis de supradictis armis [of England and France] et varietate plurima'; cf. H. T. Riley, *Memorials of London*, 107, from *Corporation Letter Book D*. f. 168.

[4] T. Walsingham, *Hist. Anglica* (R. S.), i. 331.

of reconciliation with the rebellious Londoners. And at St. Paul's was a youth enthroned amongst a triple circle of singing angels; and at Temple Bar St. John Baptist in the desert surrounded by all kinds of trees and a menagerie of strange beasts [1]. No similar details of pageantry are recorded at the coronations of Henry IV or Henry V. But when the latter king returned to London after the battle of Agincourt in 1415 there was a very fine show indeed. The procession came to the city from Eltham and Blackheath by way of London Bridge. Upon the tower masking the bridge stood two gigantic figures, one a man with an axe in his right hand and the city keys in his left, the other a woman in a scarlet mantle. Beyond this were two columns painted to resemble white marble and green jasper, on which were a lion and an antelope bearing the royal arms and banner. Over the foot of the bridge was a tower with a figure of St. George, and on a house hard by a number of boys representing the heavenly host, who sang the anthem *Benedictus qui venit in nomine Dei.* The tower upon the Cornhill conduit was decked with red and had on it a company of prophets, who sent a flight of sparrows and other birds fluttering round the king as he passed, while the prophets chanted *Cantate Domino canticum novum.* The tower of the great Cheapside conduit was green, and here were twelve Apostles and twelve Kings, Martyrs and Confessors of England, whose anthem was *Benedic, anima, Domino*, and who, even as Melchisedek received Abraham with bread and wine, offered the king thin wafers mixed with silver leaves, and a cup filled from the conduit pipes. On Cheapside, the cross was completely hidden by a great castle, in imitation white marble and green and red jasper, out of the door of which issued a bevy of virgins, with timbrel and dance and songs of 'Nowell, Nowell,' like unto the daughters of Israel who danced before David after the slaying of Goliath. On the castle stood boys feathered like angels, who sang *Te Deum* and flung down gold coins and boughs of laurel. Finally, on the tower of the little conduit near St. Paul's, all blue as the sky,

[1] Fabyan, 538; H. Knighton, *Chronicon* (R. S.), ii. 320; Richard Maydiston, *De concordia inter regem Ricardum II et civitatem London* (*Political Poems*, R. S. i. 282).

were more virgins who, as when Richard II was crowned, wafted golden leaves out of golden cups, while above were wrought angels in gold and colours, and an image of the sun enthroned [1]. The details of the reception of Henry and Catherine of France, six years later, are not preserved [2]. Nor are those of the London coronation of Henry VI in 1429. But there was a grand dumb-show at the Paris coronation in 1431 [3], and it was perhaps in emulation of this that on his return to London in the following year the king was received with a splendour equal to that lavished on the victor of Agincourt. There is a contemporary account of the proceedings by John Carpenter, the town clerk of London [4]. As in 1415 a giant greeted the king at the foot of London Bridge. On the same 'pageant [5]' two antelopes upbore the arms of England and France. On the bridge stood a magnificent 'fabric,' occupied by Nature, Grace, and Fortune, who gave the king presents as he passed. To the right were the seven heavenly Virtues, who signified the seven gifts of the Holy Ghost, by letting fly seven white doves. To the left, seven other virgins offered the regalia. Then all fourteen, clapping their hands and rejoicing in *tripudia*, broke into songs of welcome. In Cornhill was the Tabernacle of Lady Wisdom, set upon seven columns. Here stood Wisdom, and here the seven liberal Sciences were represented by Priscian, Aristotle, Tully, Boethius, Pythagoras, Euclid, and Albumazar. On the conduit was the Throne of Justice, on which sat a king surrounded by Truth, Mercy, and Clemency, with two Judges and eight Lawyers. In Cheapside was a Paradise with a grove full of all manner of foreign fruits, and three wells from which

[1] Full contemporary accounts in *Gesta Henrici Quinti* (Eng. Hist. Soc.), 61, and a set of verses by John Lydgate printed in *London Chronicle*, 214, and H. Nicolas, *Hist. of Agincourt* (1833), 326; more briefly in *London Chronicle*, 103; T. Walsingham, *Hist. Anglic.* (R. S.), ii. 314; cf. C. L. Kingsford, *Henry V*, 156.

[2] T. Walsingham, *Hist. Anglica* (R. S.), ii. 336 'ludicis et vario apparatu.'

[3] Cf. p. 174.

[4] Printed from *Corp. Letter Book K.* f. 103v, by H. T. Riley, *Liber Albus* (R.S.), iii. 457; cf. descriptive verses by Lydgate, *Minor Works* (Percy Soc.), 2; *London Chronicle*, 119; Fabyan, 603; Gregory, 173.

[5] Carpenter uses the term *pagina*, which here occurs for the first time in connexion with these London receptions. Mr. Riley quite unnecessarily proposes to read *machina*.

gushed out wine, served by Mercy, Grace, and Pity. Here the king was greeted by Enoch and Elijah [1]. At the cross was a castle of jasper with a Tree of Jesse, and another of the royal descent; and at St. Paul's conduit a representation of the Trinity amongst a host of ministering angels. In 1445 Margaret of Anjou came to London to be crowned. Stowe records 'a few only' of the pageants. She entered by Southwark bridge foot where were Peace and Plenty. On the bridge was Noah's ship; in Leadenhall, 'madam Grace Chancelor de Dieu'; on the Tun in Cornhill, St. Margaret; on the conduit in Cheapside, the Wise and Foolish Virgins; at the Cross, the Heavenly Jerusalem; and at Paul's Gate, the General Resurrection and Judgement [2].

The rapid kingings and unkingings of the wars of the Roses left little time and little heart for pageantries, but with the advent of Henry VII they begin again, and continue with growing splendour throughout the Tudor century. Space only permits a brief enumeration of the subjects chosen for set pageants on a few of the more important occasions. Singing angels and precious gifts, wells of wine and other minor delights may be taken for granted [3]. As to the details of Henry VII's coronation in 1485 and marriage in 1486 the chroniclers are provokingly silent, and of the many 'gentlemanlie pageants' at the coronation of the queen in 1487 the only one specified is 'a great redde dragon spouting flames of fyer into the Thames,' from the 'bachelors' barge'

[1] A pun was concealed here, for John de *Welles*, grocer, was mayor, and the 'oranges, almonds, and the pomegranade' on the trees were the grocers' wares. Cf. the tree of the Norwich grocers in the Corpus Christi procession (p. 163).

[2] Stowe, *Annals*, 385; cf. *London Chronicle*, 134 'goodly sights ayenst her coming'; Fabyan, 617 'sumptuous and costly pagentes, and resemblaunce of dyuerse olde hystoryes'; Gregory, 186 'many notabylle devysys in the cytte.' According to Stowe, Lydgate wrote verses for these pageants.

[3] A memorandum of ceremonial *As ffor the ressaunge off a Quene and her Crownacion* of the reign of Henry VII (*Antiquarian Repertory*, i. 302) has the following direction for the riding from the Tower to Westminster, 'at the condit in Cornylle ther must be ordined a sight w[t] angelles singinge and freche balettes y[r]on in latene, engliche and ffrenche, mad by the wyseste docturs of this realme; and the condyt of Chepe in the same wyse; and the condit must ryn bothe red wyn and whit wyne; and the crosse in Chepe muste be araid in y[e] most rialle wyse that might be thought; and the condit next Poules in the same wyse.'

of the lord mayor's company as she passed up the river from Greenwich to the Tower[1]. At the wedding of Prince Arthur to Katharine of Aragon in 1501, 'vi goodly beutiful pageauntes' lined the way from London Bridge to St. Paul's. The contriver is said to have been none other than Bishop Foxe the great chancellor and the founder of Corpus Christi College in Oxford. The subject of the first pageant was the Trinity with Saints Ursula and Katharine; of the second, the Castle of Portcullis, with Policy, Nobleness, and Virtue; of the third, Raphael, the angel of marriage, with Alphonso, Job, and Boethius; of the fourth, the Sphere of the Sun; of the fifth, the Temple of God; and of the sixth, Honour with the seven Virtues[2]. As to Henry VIII's coronation and marriage there is, once more, little recorded. In 1522 came Charles V, Emperor of Germany, to visit the king, and the city provided eleven pageants 'very faire and excellent to behold[3].' The 'great red dragon' of 1487 reappeared in 1533 when yet another queen, Anne Boleyn, came up from Greenwich to enjoy her brief triumph. It stood on a 'foist' near the lord mayor's barge, and in another 'foist' was a mount, and on the mount Anne's device, a falcon on a root of gold with white roses and red. The pageants for the progress by land on the following day were of children 'apparelled like merchants,' of Mount Parnassus, of the falcon and mount once more, with Saint Anne and her children, of the three Graces, of Pallas, Juno, Venus, and Mercury with the golden apple, of three ladies, and of the Cardinal Virtues[4]. The next great show was at the coronation of Edward VI in 1547, and included Valentine and Orson, Grace, Nature, Fortune and Charity, Sapience and the seven Liberal Sciences, Regality enthroned with Justice, Mercy and Truth, the Golden Fleece, Edward the Confessor and St. George, Truth, Faith, and

[1] Contemporary account in Leland, *Collectanea* (ed. Hearne), iv. 218, and J. Ives, *Select Papers* (1773), 127.

[2] Minutely detailed contemporary account in *Antiquarian Repertory*, ii. 248; cf. Stowe, *Annals*, 483; Hazlitt-Warton, iii. 160.

[3] Stowe, *Annals*, 517; Hall, 638; cf. *Representations* (London).

[4] Minutely detailed contemporary account in *Antiquarian Repertory*, ii. 232; Hall, 801; Collier, ii. 353. Leland's and Udall's verses for the pageants are in *Ballads from MSS.*, i. 378 (Ballad Soc.).

Justice. There was also a cunning Spanish rope-dancer, who performed marvels on a cord stretched to the ground from the tower of St. George's church in St. Paul's churchyard [1]. Mary, in 1553, enjoyed an even more thrilling spectacle in 'one Peter a Dutchman,' who stood and waved a streamer on the weathercock of St. Paul's steeple. She had eight pageants, of which three were contributed by the Genoese, Easterlings, and Florentines. The subjects are unknown, but that of the Florentines was in the form of a triple arch and had on the top a trumpeting angel in green, who moved his trumpet to the wonder of the crowd [2]. There were pageants again when Mary brought her Spanish husband to London in 1554. At the conduit in Gracechurch Street were painted the Nine Worthies. One of these was Henry VIII, who was represented as handing a bible to Edward; and the unfortunate painter was dubbed a knave and a rank traitor and villain by Bishop Gardiner, because the bible was not put in the hands of Mary [3]. At the coronation of Elizabeth in 1559, with which this list must close, it was Time and Truth who offered the English bible to the queen. The same pageant had representations of a Decayed Commonwealth and a Flourishing Commonwealth, while others figured the Union of York and Lancaster, the Seat of Worthy Governance, the Eight Beatitudes, and Deborah the Judge. At Temple Bar, those ancient *palladia* of London city, the giants Gotmagot and Corineus, once more made their appearance [4].

I do not wish to exaggerate the influence exercised by the miracle-plays and moralities over these London shows. London was not, in the Middle Ages, one of the most dramatic of English cities, and such plays as there were were not in the hands of those trade- and craft-guilds to whom the glorifying of the receptions naturally fell. The functions carried out by the fishmongers in 1298 and 1313 are much of the nature of masked ridings or 'disguisings,' and must be held to have a folk origin. The ship of 1313 suggests a 'hobby ship [5].'

[1] Contemporary account in Leland, *Collectanea* (ed. Hearne), iv. 313.

[2] Stowe, *Annals*, 616; cf. *Texts*, s.v. John Heywood.

[3] Holinshed, iii. 1121.

[4] Contemporary account in Nichols, *Progresses of Elizabeth*, i. 38.

[5] Cf. vol. i. p. 121.

Throughout the shows draw notions from many heterogeneous sources. The giants afford yet another 'folk' element. The gifts of gold and wine and the speeches of welcome [1] need no explanation. Devices of heraldry are worked in. The choirs of boys and girls dressed as angels recall the choirs perched on the battlements of churches in such ecclesiastical ceremonies as the Palm Sunday procession [2]. The term 'pageant' (*pagina*), which first appears in this connexion in 1432 and is in regular use by the end of the century, is perhaps a loan from the plays, but the structures themselves appear to have arisen naturally out of attempts to decorate such obvious architectural features of the city as London Bridge, the prison known as the Tun, and the conduits which stood in Cornhill and Cheapside [3]. It is chiefly in the selection of themes for the more elaborate mimetic pageants that the reflection of the regular contemporary drama must be traced. Such scriptural subjects as John the Baptist of 1392 or the Prophets and Apostles of 1415 pretty obviously come from the miracle-plays. The groups of allegorical figures which greeted Henry VI in 1432 are in no less close a relation to the moralities, which were at that very moment beginning to outstrip the miracle-plays in popularity. And in the reign of Henry VII the humanist tendencies begin to suggest subjects for the pageants as well as to transform the drama itself.

Certainly one does not find in London or in any English city those *mystères mimés* or cyclical dumb-shows, with which the good people of Paris were wont to welcome kings, and which are clearly an adaptation of the ordinary miracle-play to the conditions of a royal entry with its scant time for long drawn-out dialogue. The earliest of these upon record was in 1313 when Philip IV entertained Edward II and Isabella. It is not quite clear whether this was

[1] Warton, iii. 158, says that 'Speakers seem to have been admitted into our pageants about the reign of Henry VI.' But there were songs, and for all we know, speeches also in 1377 and 1415. Verses such as Lydgate wrote for pageants were often fastened on them, and read or not read aloud when the visitor approached, as might be convenient.

[2] Cf. p. 5.

[3] Wheatley-Cunningham, *London Past and Present*, i. 373, 458; iii. 409.

a procession like the disguising called the *procession du renard* which accompanied it, or a stationary dumb-show on pageants. But there is no doubt about the *moult piteux mystere de la Passion de Nostre Seigneur au vif* given before Charles VI and Henry V after the treaty of Troyes in 1420, for this is said to have been on *eschaffaulx* and to have been modelled on the bas-reliefs around the choir of Notre-Dame. Very similar must have been the *moult bel mystere du Vieil testament et du Nouvel* which welcomed the duke of Bedford in 1424 and which *fut fait sans parler ne sans signer, comme ce feussent ymaiges enlevez contre ung mur. Sans parler*, again, was the *mystère* which stood on an *eschaffault* before the church of the Trinity when Henry VI was crowned, only a few weeks before the London reception already mentioned [1].

It may be added that in many provincial towns the pageants used at royal entries had a far closer affinity to the miracle-plays proper than was the case in London. The place most often honoured in this sort was Coventry. In 1456 came Queen Margaret and poor mad Henry VI. One John Wedurley of Leicester seems to have been employed to organize a magnificent entertainment. At Bablake gate, where stood a Jesse, the royal visitors were greeted by Isaiah and Jeremiah. Within the gate was a 'pagent' with Saint Edward the Confessor and St. John the Evangelist. On the conduit in Smithford Street were the four Cardinal Virtues. In the Cheaping were nine pageants for the Nine Worthies. At the cross there were angels, and wine flowed, and at another conduit hard by was St. Margaret 'sleyng' her dragon and a company of angels. The queen was so pleased that she returned next year for Corpus Christi day. It appears from the smiths' accounts that the pageants used at the reception were those kept by the crafts for the plays. The smiths' pageant was had out again in 1461, with Samson upon it, when Edward IV came after his coronation, and in 1474 when the young prince Edward came for St. George's feast. The shows then represented King Richard II and his court, Patriarchs and Prophets, St. Edward the Confessor, the Three Kings of Cologne and St. George slaying

[1] Julleville, *Les Myst.* i. 196; ii. 186.

the dragon. Prince Arthur, in 1498, saw the Nine Worthies, the Queen of Fortune, and, once more, Saint George. For Henry VIII and Katharine of Aragon in 1511 there were three pageants: on one the ninefold hierarchy of angels, on another 'divers beautiful damsels,' on the third 'a goodly stage play.' The mercers' pageant 'stood' at the visit of the Princess Mary in 1525, and the tanners', drapers', smiths', and weavers' pageants at that of Queen Elizabeth in 1565. I do not know whether it is legitimate to infer that the subjects represented on these occasions were those of the Corpus Christi plays belonging to the crafts named[1].

York was visited by Richard III in 1483, and there were pageants, the details of which have not been preserved, as well as a performance of the Creed play[2]. It was also visited by Henry VII in 1486, and there exists a civic order prescribing the pageants for that occasion. The first of these was a most ingenious piece of symbolism. There was a heaven and beneath it 'a world desolaite, full of treys and floures.' Out of this sprang 'a roiall, rich, rede rose' and 'an othre rich white rose,' to whom all the other flowers did 'lowte and evidently yeve suffrantie.' Then appeared out of a cloud a crown over the roses, and then a city with citizens with 'Ebrauk' the founder, who offered the keys to the king. The other pageants represented Solomon and the six Henries, the Castle of David, and Our Lady. There were also devices by which a rain of rose-water and a hailstorm of comfits fell before the king[3]. During the same progress which took Henry to York, he also visited Worcester, where there were pageants and speeches, 'whiche his Grace at that Tyme harde not' but which should have represented Henry VI and a *Ianitor ad Ianuam*. Thence he went to Hereford, and was greeted by St. George, King Ethelbert, and Our Lady; thence to Gloucester, where the chronicler remarks with some surprise that 'ther was no Pageant nor Speche ordeynede'; and finally to Bristol, where were King Bremmius, Prudence, Justice, 'the Shipwrights Pageannt,' without any speech,

[1] Sharp, 145.
[2] Davies, 162, 171, 282.
[3] J. Raine, *English Miscellanies* (Surtees Soc., vol. lxxxv), 53, from *Corporation House Book*, vi. 15.

and a 'Pageannte of an Olifaunte, with a Castell on his Bakk' and 'The Resurrection of our Lorde in the highest Tower of the same, with certeyne Imagerye smytyng Bellis, and all wente by Veights, merveolously wele done[1].' In 1503 Henry VII's daughter Margaret married James IV of Scotland, and was received into Edinburgh with pageants of the Judgement of Paris, the Annunciation, the Marriage of Joseph and Mary, and the Four Virtues[2]. Eight years later, in 1511, she visited Aberdeen, and the 'pleasant padgeanes' included Adam and Eve, the Salutation of the Virgin, the *Magi*, and the Bruce[3].

The facts brought together in the present chapter show how 'pageant' came to have its ordinary modern sense of a spectacular procession. How it was replaced by other terms in the sense of 'play' will be matter for the sequel. It may be added that the name is also given to the elaborate structures of carpenters' and painters' work used in the early Tudor masks[4]. These the masks probably took over from the processions and receptions. On the other hand, the receptions, by an elaboration of the spoken element, developed into the Elizabethan 'Entertainments,' which are often classified as a sub-variety of the mask itself. This action and reaction of one form of show upon another need not at this stage cause any surprise. A sixteenth-century synonym for 'pageant' is 'triumph,' which is doubtless a translation of the Italian *trionfo*, a name given to the *edifizio* by the early Renascence, in deliberate reminiscence of classical terminology[5].

[1] Contemporary account in Leland, *Collectanea* (ed. Hearne), iv. 185. A description of an earlier reception of Edward IV at Bristol with 'Wylliam conquerour,' 'a greet Gyaunt delyueryng the Keyes,' and St. George is in Furnivall, *Political, Religious, and Love Poems* (E. E. T. S.), 5.

[2] Leland, *Collectanea*, iv. 263.

[3] Cf. *Representations*, s. v. Aberdeen.

[4] Cf. vol. i. p. 398.

[5] Symonds, *Renaissance in Italy*, iv. 338.

BOOK IV

THE INTERLUDE

Patronage cannot kill art: even in kings' palaces the sudden flower blooms serene.

MODERN PLAY.

CHAPTER XXIV

PLAYERS OF INTERLUDES

[*Bibliographical Note.*—The *Annals of the Stage* in J. P. Collier, *History of English Dramatic Poetry* (new ed. 1879), although ill arranged and by no means trustworthy, now become of value. They may be supplemented from the full notices of Tudor *spectacula* in E. Hall, *The Union of Lancaster and York*, 1548, ed. 1809, and from the various calendars of State papers, of which J. S. Brewer and J. Gairdner, *Letters and Papers of the Reign of Henry VIII* (1862–1903), including the *Revels Accounts* and the *Kings Books of Payments*, is the most important. Some useful documents are in W. C. Hazlitt, *The English Drama and Stage* (1869). The French facts are given by L. Petit de Julleville, *Les Comédiens en France au Moyen Âge* (1889).]

THE closing section of this essay may fitly be introduced by a brief retrospect of the conclusions already arrived at. The investigation, however it may have lingered by the way, has not been altogether without its *logos* or rational framework. The first book began with a study of the conditions under which the degenerate stage of the Roman Empire ceased to exist. The most important of these were the indifference of the barbarians and the direct hostility of the Church. A fairly clean sweep was made. Scarcely a thread of dramatic tradition is to be traced amongst the many and diverse forms of entertainment provided by mediaeval minstrelsy. But the very existence of minstrelsy, itself a singular blend of Latin and barbaric elements, is a proof of the enduring desire of the western European peoples for something in the nature of *spectacula*. In the strength of this the minstrels braved the ban of the Church, and finally won their way to at least a partial measure of toleration from their hereditary foes. In the second book it was shown that the instinct for *spectacula* had its definitely dramatic side. The *ludi* of the folk, based upon ancient observances of a forgotten natural religion, and surviving side by side with minstrelsy, broke out at point after point into *mimesis*. Amongst the villages they developed into dramatic May-games and dramatic sword-dances: in their *bourgeois* forms they overran city and cathedral with the mimicries of the Feast of Fools and the Boy Bishop; they gave birth to a special type of drama in the mask; and they further enriched Tudor revels with the characteristic figures of the domestic fool or jester and the lord of misrule. Upon the folk *ludi*, as upon the *spectacula* of the minstrels, the Church looked doubtfully. But the mimetic instinct was irresistible, and in the end it was neither minstrels nor folk, but the Church itself, which did most for its satisfaction. The subject of the third book is a remarkable growth of drama within the heart of the ecclesiastical liturgy, which began in the tenth century, and became, consciously or unconsciously, a powerful counterpoise to the attraction of *ludi* and *spectacula*. So popular, indeed, did it prove that it broke the bonds of ecclesiastical control; and about the thirteenth century a process of laicization set in, which culminated during the fourteenth in the great Corpus Christi cycles of the municipal guilds. The subject-matter, however, remained religious to the end, an end which, in spite of the marked critical attitude adopted by the austerer schools of churchmen, did not arrive until that attitude was confirmed by successive waves of Lollard and Protestant sentiment. Nor was the system substantially affected by certain innovations of the fifteenth century, a tendency to substitute mere spectacular pageantry for the spoken drama, and a tendency to add to the visible presentment of the scriptural history an allegorical exposition of theological and moral doctrine.

It is the object of the present book briefly to record the rise, also in the fifteenth century, of new dramatic conditions which, after existing for a while side by side with those of mediaevalism, were destined ultimately to become a substitute for these and to lead up directly to the magic stage of Shakespeare. The change to be sketched is primarily a social rather than a literary one. The drama which had already migrated from the church to the market-place, was to migrate still further, to the banqueting-hall. And having passed from the hands of the clergy to those of the folk, it was now to pass, after an interval of a thousand years, not immediately but ultimately, into those of a professional class of actors. Simultaneously it was to put off its exclusively religious character, and enter upon a new heritage of interests and methods, beneath the revivifying breath of humanism.

A characteristic note of the new phase is the rise of the term *interludium* or 'interlude.' This we have already come across in the title of that fragmentary *Interludium de Clerico et Puella* which alone amongst English documents seemed to bear witness to a scanty dramatic element in the repertory of minstrelsy [1]. The primary meaning of the name is a matter of some perplexity. The learned editors of the *New English Dictionary* define it as 'a dramatic or mimic representation, usually of a light or humorous character, such as was commonly introduced between the acts of the long mystery-plays or moralities, or exhibited as part of an elaborate entertainment.' Another recognized authority, Dr. Ward, says [2]: 'It seems to have been applied to plays performed by professional actors from the time of Edward IV onwards. Its origin is doubtless to be found in the fact that such plays were occasionally performed in the intervals of banquets and entertainments, which of course would have been out of the question in the case of religious plays proper.' I cannot say that I find either of these explanations at all satisfactory. In the first place, none of the limitations of sense which they suggest are really borne out by the history of the word. So far as its rare use in the fourteenth century goes, it is not confined to professional plays and it does not exclude religious plays. The *Interludium de Clerico et Puella* is, no doubt, a farce, and something of the same sort appears to be in the mind of Huchown, or whoever else was the author of *Sir Gawain and the Green Knight*, when he speaks of laughter and song as a substitute for 'enterludez' at Christmas [3].

[1] Cf. vol. i. p. 86.

[2] Ward, i. 108. The limitation by Collier, ii. 299, of 'what may be properly, and strictly, called *Interludes*' to farces of the type affected by John Heywood has introduced a most inconvenient semi-technical term into literary nomenclature. I do not so limit the word.

[3] *Gawain and the G. K.* 472:

'Wel bycommes such craft vpon, cristmasse,
Laykyng of enterludez, to laȝe & to syng.'

But on the other hand, Robert Mannyng of Brunne, at the very beginning of the century, classes 'entyrludes' with 'somour games' and other forbidden delights of the folk[1], while the Wyclifite author of the *Tretise on Miriclis* at its close, definitely uses 'entirlodies' as a name for the religious plays which he is condemning[2]. In the fifteenth century, again, although 'interlude' is of course not one of the commonest terms for a miracle-play, yet I find it used for performances probably of the miracle-play type at New Romney in 1426 and at Harling in 1452, while the jurats of the former place paid in 1463 for 'the play of the interlude of our Lord's Passion[3].' The term, then, appears to be equally applicable to every kind of drama known to the Middle Ages. As to its philological derivation, both the *New English Dictionary* and Dr. Ward treat it as a *ludus* performed in the intervals of (*inter*) something else, although they do not agree as to what that something else was. For the performance of farces 'between the acts of the long miracle-plays' there is no English evidence whatever[4]. The farcical episodes which find a place in the Towneley plays and elsewhere are in no way structurally differentiated from the rest of the text. There are some French examples of combined performances of farces and miracles, but they do not go far enough back to explain the origin of the word[5]. A certain support is no doubt

[1] Cf. vol. i. p. 93.

[2] Hazlitt, *E. D. S.* 80 'How thanne may a prist pleyn in entirlodies?' In Barbour, *Bruce* († 1375), x. 145 'now may ȝe heir ... Interludys and iuperdys, þat men assayit on mony vis Castellis and pelis for till ta,' the sense is metaphorical, as in 'ioculando et talia verba asserendo interludia fuisse vanitatis' quoted by Ducange from *Vit. Abb. S. Alb.*', i.e. probably Thomas Walsingham († 1422), not Matthew Paris († 1249). The reading is doubtful in Anastasius Bibliothecarius (9th cent.), *Hist. Pontif.* (*P. L.* lxxx. 1352), 'quem iussit sibi praesentari in interludo noctu ante templum Palladis.'

[3] For probable 1385 cases, cf. *Representations*, s.v. King's Lynn.

[4] A 'vyce' made pastime before and after a play at Bungay, but this was not until 1566.

[5] Julleville, *Les Com.* 97. These performances were known as *les pois pilés* and began about the middle of the fourteenth century. The Anglo-French *entrelude*, asterisked by the *N. E. D.*, is found in 1427 (cf. p. 186). Collier's theory receives some support from the Spanish use of the term *entremes* for a comic piece played in conjunction with a serious *auto*. But the earlier sense of *entremes* itself appears to be for an independent farce played at banquets (Ticknor, *Hist. of Span. Lit.* (ed. 1888), i. 231; ii. 449).

given to the theory of the *New English Dictionary* by the 'mirry interludes' inserted in Sir David Lyndsay's morality *Ane Satyre of the Thrie Estaits*, but, once more, it is difficult to elucidate a term which appears at the beginning of the fourteenth century from an isolated use in the middle of the sixteenth. Dr. Ward's hypothesis is perhaps rather more plausible. No doubt plays were performed at court and elsewhere between the banquet and the 'void' or cup of spiced drink which followed later in the evening, and possibly also between the courses of the banquet itself[1]. But this fact would not differentiate dramatic *ludi* from other forms of minstrelsy coming in the same intervals, and the fact that miracle-plays are called interludes, quite as early as anything else, remains to be accounted for. I am inclined myself to think that the force of *inter* in the combination has been misunderstood, and that an *interludium* is not a *ludus* in the intervals of something else, but a *ludus* carried on between (*inter*) two or more performers; in fact, a *ludus* in dialogue. The term would then apply primarily to any kind of dramatic performance whatever.

In any case it is clear that while 'interlude' was only a subordinate name for plays of the miracle-type, it was the normal name, varied chiefly by 'play' and 'disguising,' for plays given in the banqueting-halls of the great[2]. These

[1] Cf. the accounts in Leland, *Collectanea*, iv. 228, 236, of the court of Henry VII. Douglas, *Palace of Honour*, ii. 410 'At eis they eit with interludis betwene,' dates from 1501. Horman, *Vulgaria* (1519), quoted on p. 137, speaks of the 'paiantis' of a play as corresponding in number to the courses of a feast. Much earlier Raoul de Presles (†1374) in his *Exposicion* to Augustine, *de Civ. Dei*, ii. 8 (Abbeville, 1486), says that comedies 'sont proprement apellez interludia, pour ce quilz se font entre les deux mengiers.' But the use of *interludere* by Ausonius, *Idyll*, x. 76, 'interludentes, examina lubrica, pisces,' and Ambrose, *Epist.* xlvii. 4, 'interludamus epistolis,' supports my view.

[2] For a curious distinction, probably neither original nor permanent, drawn about 1530 between 'stage playes' (presumably out of doors) in the summer and 'interludes' (presumably indoors) in the winter, cf. the documents printed by H. R. Plomer, in *Trans. of Bibliographical Society*, iv (1898), 153, and A. W. Pollard in *Fifteenth Century Prose and Verse*, 305, about a suit between John Rastell, lawyer, printer, and playwright, and one Henry Walton. Rastell, going on a visit to France about 1525, had left with Walton a number of players' garments. These are fully described. They were mostly of say or sarcenet, and the tailor, who with the help of Rastell's wife had made them, valued them at 20*s.* apiece. Walton failed to restore them, and for some

begin to claim attention during the fifteenth century. Dr. Ward's statement that religious plays could not have been the subject of such performances does not bear the test of comparison with the facts. A miracle of St. Clotilda was played before Henry the Sixth at Windsor Castle in 1429, a *Christi Descensus ad Inferos* before Henry the Seventh during dinner at Winchester in 1486; nor is it probable that the play performed by the boys of Maxstoke Priory in the hall of Lord Clinton at Candlemas, 1430, was other than religious in character[1]. The records of the miracle-plays themselves show that they were often carried far from home. There was much coming and going amongst the villages and little towns round about Lydd and New Romney from 1399 to 1508. One at least of the existing texts, that of the Croxton *Sacrament*, appears to be intended for the use of a travelling troupe, and that such troupes showed their plays not only in market-places and on village greens but also in the houses of individual patrons, is suggested by entries of payments to players of this and that locality in more than one *computus*[2].

years let them on hire, to his own profit. Evidence to this effect was given by John Redman, stationer, and by George Mayler, merchant tailor, and George Birche, coriar, two of the king's players. These men had played in the garments themselves and had seen them used in 'stage pleyes' when the king's banquet was at Greenwich [in 1527; cf. vol. i. p. 400]. They had been used at least twenty times in stage plays every summer and twenty times in interludes every winter, and Walton had taken, as the 'common custume' was, at a stage play 'sumtyme xl^d^., sometyme ij^s^., as they couth agree, and at an interlude viij^d^ for every tyme.' Rastell had brought a previous suit in the mayor's court, but could only receive 35*s.* 9*d.*, at which the goods had been officially appraised. But they were then 'rotten and torne,' whereas Rastell alleged that they were nearly new when delivered to Walton and worth 20 marks. Walton relied on the official appraisement, and had a counter-claim for 40*s.* balance of a bill for 50*s.* costs 'in making of stage for player in Restall's grounde beside Fyndesbury, in tymbre, bourde, nayle, lath, sprigge and other thyngs.' He held the clothes against payment of this amount, which Rastell challenged.

[1] In 1503 a *Magi* was given in Canterbury guildhall. Some of the crafts of Coventry (1478–1568) and Newcastle (1536) had plays at their guild feasts. The indoor performances of Chester plays in 1567 and 1576 are late and exceptional.

[2] Cf. Appendix E, ii (Maxstoke), iii (Thetford), vii (Howard), viii (Tudor Court). 'Moleyn's wedding' attended by Lord Howard, is the first of many at which the players are recorded to have made the mirth. Some of the entries may imply visits *to* the plays, rather than *of* the plays, and this I suppose to be the case with Henry VII's payment 'to the players *at* Myles End.' It is perhaps a little arbitrary to

Thus Maxstoke Priory, between 1422 and 1461, entertained *lusores*[1] from Nuneaton, Coventry, Daventry, and Coleshill; while Henry the Seventh, between 1492 and 1509, gave largess, either at court or abroad, to 'pleyers' from Essex, Wimborne Minster, Wycombe, London, and Kingston. The accounts of the last-named place record an ordinary parochial play in the very year of the royal 'almasse.'

It is obvious that this practice of travelling must have brought the local players into rivalry with those hereditary gentlemen of the road, the minstrels. Possibly they had something to do with provoking that *querelosa insinuatio* against the *rudes agricolae et artifices diversarum misterarum* which led to the formation of the royal guild of minstrels in 1469. If so, the measure does not seem to have been wholly successful in suppressing them. But the minstrels had a better move to make. Their own profession had fallen, with the emergence of the *trouvère* and the spread of printing, upon evil days. And here were the scanty remnants of their audiences being filched from them by unskilled rustics who had hit upon just the one form of literary entertainment which, unlike poetry and romance in general, could not dis-

assume, as I have done, that players locally named are never professional. Thus the *lusores de Writhill* paid by the duke of Buckingham on Jan. 6, 1508, are almost certainly identical with the *lusores Dñi de Wrisell* (his brother-in-law, the earl of Northumberland) paid by him at Xmas, 1507 (*Archaeologia*, xxv. 318, 324), although it happens curiously enough that the Chelmsford wardrobe was drawn upon by players of Writtle in 1571–2. The local designation of members of the minstrel class is exceptional; but cf. the York example in the next note. The locally named *lusores* may, however, sometimes have acted not a miracle, but a May-game or sword-dance; e.g., at Winchester College in 1400 when they came 'cum tripudio suo' (App. E, iv).

[1] I have taken *lusores* in the *computi* as always meaning performers of a dramatic *ludus*. This is often demonstrably correct and never demonstrably incorrect, except that when Colet in his *Oratio ad Clerum* of 1511 quotes the canon 'ne sit publicus lusor' he seems to use the term in its canonical sense of 'gambler.' The English version (1661) has 'common gamer or player.' A similar ambiguity is, I think, the only one which attaches itself to 'player' where it is a technical term after the middle of the fourteenth century. Lydgate in his *Interpretacyon of the names of Goddys and Goddesses* (quoted by Collier, i. 31) uses it of an actor, although an older sense is preserved by the *Promptorium Parvulorum* (1440), 'Bordyoure or pleyere, *ioculator*.' The sense of *ludentes*, I think, is wide. The *ludentes 'de Donyngton'* and *'de Wakefield'* paid by the York corporation in 1446 (*York Plays*, xxxviii) are more likely to have been minstrels

pense with the living interpreter [1]. What could they do better than develop a neglected side of their own art and become players themselves? So there appear in the *computi*, side by side with the local *lusores*, others whose methods and status are precisely those of minstrels [2]. The generosity of Henry the Sixth at the Christmas of 1427 is called forth equally by the *entreludes* of the *jeweis de Abyndon* and the *jeues et entreludes* of *Jakke Travail et ses compaignons*. By 1464 'players in their enterludes' were sufficiently recognized to be included with minstrels in the exceptions of the Act of Apparel [3]. Like other minstrels, the players put themselves under the protection of nobles and persons of honour. The earliest upon record are those of Henry Bourchier, earl of Essex, and those of Richard, duke of Gloucester, afterwards Richard the Third. Both companies were rewarded by Lord Howard in 1482. The earls of Northumberland, Oxford, Derby, and Shrewsbury, and Lord Arundel, all had their players before the end of the century [4]. The regulations of the *Northumberland Household Book*, as well as entries in

whom the corporation did provide for the plays than actors whom they did not. On the other hand about *interludentes* and *interlusores*, neither of them very common terms, there can be no doubt. *Lusiatores* occurs as a synonym for *lusores* at Shrewsbury only. *Mimi* and *histriones* I have uniformly treated as merely minstrels. At a late date they might, I suppose, be actors, but it is impossible to differentiate.

[1] Plays were sometimes read, even in the fifteenth century. The prologue of *The Burial and Resurrection* has 'Rede this treyte,' although it was also converted into 'a play to be playede'; and the epilogue of the Digby *St. Mary Magdalen* has 'I desyer the redars to be my frynd.' Thomas Wylley in 1537 describes some of his plays to Cromwell as 'never to be seen, but of your Lordshyp's eye.' Prynne, 834, asserts that 'Bernardinus Ochin his Tragedy of Freewil, Plessie Morney his Tragedie of Jeptha his daughter, Edward the 6 his Comedie de meretrice Babilonica, Iohn Bale his Comedies de Christo et de Lazaro, Skelton's Comedies, de Virtute, de Magnificentia, et de bono Ordine, Nicholaus Grimoaldus, de Archiprophetae Tragedia . . . were penned only to be read, not acted'; but this is incorrect as regards Bale and Skelton and probably as regards others. The earliest printed plays are perhaps *Mundus et Infans* (1522) and *Hickscorner* (n. d.) both by Wynkyn de Worde (1501–35), *Everyman* (n. d.) by Richard Pynson (1509–27). If a *Nigramansir*, by Skelton, was really, as Warton asserts, printed by Wynkyn de Worde in 1504, it might take precedence.

[2] Cf. Appendix E.

[3] 3 *Edw. IV*, c. 5; cf. vol. i. p. 45. This was continued by 1 *Hen. VIII*, c. 14, 6 *Hen. VIII*, c. 1, and 24 *Hen. VIII*, c. 13.

[4] Cf. Appendix E; *Hist. MSS.* v. 548.

many *computi*, show that by the reign of Henry the Eighth the practice was widespread [1]. Naturally it received a stimulus when a body of players came to form a regular part of the royal household. Whether Richard the Third retained his company in his service during his brief reign is not upon record. But Henry the Seventh had four *lusores regis, alias, in lingua Anglicana, les pleyars of the Kyngs enterluds* at least as early as 1494. These men received an annual fee of five marks apiece, together with special rewards when they played before the king. When their services were not required at court, they took to the road, just as did the minstrels, *ioculator*, and *ursarius* of the royal establishment. In 1503 they were sent, under their leader John English, in the train of Margaret of Scotland to her wedding with James the Fourth at Edinburgh, and here they 'did their devoir' before the Scottish court [2]. Henry the Eighth increased their number to eight, and they can be traced on the books of the royal household through the reigns of Edward the Sixth and Mary, and well into that of Elizabeth [3].

[1] Percy, *N. H. B.* 22, 158, 339. An estimate for 1511–12 includes 'for rewardes to Players for Playes playd in Christynmas by Stranegers in my house after xx[d] every play by estimacion. Somme xxxiij[s] iiij[d].' Another of 1514–15 has 'for Rewards to Players in Cristynmas lxxij[s].' By 1522–3 the customary fee had largely grown, for a list of 'Al maner of Rewardis' of about that date has 'Item. My Lorde usith and accustometh to gif yerely when his Lordshipp is at home to every Erlis Players that comes to his Lordshipe bitwixt Cristynmas ande Candelmas If he be his [s]peciall Lorde and Frende ande Kynsman, xx[s] . . . to every Lordis Players, x[s].'

[2] Leland, *Collectanea* (ed. Hearne), iv. 265. The *computi* of James IV (*L. H. T. Accts.* ii. 131, 387; iii. 361) contain entries for plays before him by 'gysaris' including one at this wedding; but there is no evidence of a regular royal company at the Scottish court. In 1488 occurs a payment to 'Patrik Johnson and the playaris of Lythgow that playt to the King,' and in 1489 one to 'Patrick Johnson and his fallowis that playt a play to the kyng in Lythqow.' This Johnson or Johnstone, celebrated in Dunbar's *Lament for the Makaris*, seems to have held some post, possibly as a minstrel, at court (*L. H. T. Accts.* i. c, cxcviii, ccxliv, 91, 118; ii. 131; Dunbar, *Poems* (ed. S. T. S.), i. ccxxxvii).

[3] Collier, i. 44 and passim; Henry, *Hist. of Britain*, 454; cf. Appendix E, viii. The *Transactions of the New Shakspere Soc.* (1877–9), 425, contain papers about a dispute in 1529 between one of the company George Maller, glazier, and his apprentice, who left him and went travelling on his own account. From these it appears that 'the Kinge's plaierz' wore 'the Kinge's bage.' George Maller is the same player who appeared as a witness in the Rastell suit (cf. p. 184). There he is described as a merchant

The new conditions under which plays were now given naturally reacted upon the structure of the plays themselves. The many scenes of the long cyclical miracles, with their multitudinous performers, must be replaced by something more easy of representation. The typical interlude deals with a short episode in about a thousand lines, and could be handled in the hour or so which the lord might reasonably be expected to spare from his horse and his hounds [1]. Economy in travelling and the inconvenience of crowding the hall both went to put a limit on the number of actors. Four men and a boy, probably in apprenticeship to one of them, for the women's parts, may be taken as a normal troupe. In many of the extant interludes the list of *dramatis personae* is accompanied by an indication as to how, by the doubling of parts, the caste may be brought within reasonable compass [2]. The simplest of scenic apparatus and a few boards on trestles for a stage had of course to suffice. But some sort of a stage there probably was, as a rule, although doubtless the players were prepared, if necessary, to perform, like masquers, on the floor in front of the screen, or at best upon the dais where the lord sat at meals [3]. The pleasure-loving monks of Durham seem as far back as 1465 to have built at their cell of Finchale a special player-chamber for the

tailor; here as a glazier. That a king's player should have a handicraft, even if it were only nominal, at all, looks as if the professional actors were not invariably of the minstrel type. Perhaps the glamour of a royal 'bage' made even minstrelsy respectable. Arthur, prince of Wales, had his own company in 1498 (*Black Book of Lincoln's Inn*, i. 119), and Henry, prince of Wales, his by 1506.

[1] Medwall's *Nature* is divided into two parts, for performance on different days. But Medwall was a tedious person. Another interlude of his played in 1514 was so long and dull that Henry VIII went out before the end. *The Four Elements* was intended to take an hour and a half 'but if you list you may leave out much of the said matter . . . and then it will not be past three quarters of an hour of length.'

[2] This method begins with the Croxton *Sacrament*, which has twelve parts, but 'ix may play it at ease.' Bale's *Three Laws* claims to require five players and *Lusty Juventus* four. Several of the early Elizabethan interludes have similar indications.

[3] A Winchester *computus* of 1579 (Hazlitt-Warton, ii. 234) has 'pro diversis expensis circa Scaffoldam erigendam et deponendam, et pro domunculis de novo compositis cum carriagio et recarriagio ly joystes et aliorum mutuatorum ad eandem Scaffoldam, cum vj linckes et j° duodeno candelarum, pro lumine expensis, tribus noctibus in ludis comediarum et tragediarum xxv^{s} viij^{d}.'

purposes of such entertainments [1]. Henry the Eighth, too, in 1527 had a 'banket-house' or 'place of plesyer,' called the 'Long house,' built in the tiltyard at Greenwich, and decorated by none other than Hans Holbein [2]. But this was designed rather for a special type of disguising, half masque half interlude, and set out with the elaborate pageants which the king loved, than for ordinary plays. A similar banqueting-house 'like a theatre' had been set up at Calais in 1520, but unfortunately burnt down before it could be used [3]. Another characteristic of the interlude is the prayer for the sovereign and sometimes the estates of the realm with which it concludes, and which often helps to fix the date of representation of the extant texts [4].

Like the minstrels, the interlude players found a welcome not only in the halls of the great, but amongst the *bourgeois* and the village folk. In the towns they would give their first performance before the municipality in the guild-hall and take a reward [5]. Then they would find a profitable pitch in the courtyard of some old-fashioned inn, with its convenient

[1] Appendix E (i).

[2] Brewer, iv. 1390, 1393, 1394; Hall, 723; Collier, i. 98.

[3] Stowe, *Annals*, 511.

[4] The miracle-plays and popular morals have a more general prayer for the spiritual welfare of the 'sofereyns,' 'lordinges,' and the rest of their audience.

[5] Willis, *Mount Tabor* (1639, quoted Collier, ii. 196), describing the morality of *The Castle of Security* seen by him as a child, says 'In the city of Gloucester the manner is (as I think it is in other like corporations) that when Players of Enterludes come to towne, they first attend the Mayor, to enforme him what noble-mans servants they are and so to get licence for their publike playing: and if the Mayor like the Actors, or would show respect to their Lord and Master, he appoints them to play their first play before himselfe and the Aldermen and Common Counsell of the City; and that is called the Mayor's play, where every one that will comes in without money, the Mayor giving the players a reward as hee thinks fit, to show respect unto them. At such a play, my father tooke me with him, and made mee stand betweene his leggs, as he sate upon one of the benches, where we saw and heard very well.' In *Histriomastix*, a play of 1590–1610 (Simpson, *School of Shakespeare*, ii. 1), a crew of tippling mechanicals call themselves 'Sir Oliver Owlet's men and proclaim at the Cross a play to be given in the townhouse at 3 o'clock. They afterwards throw the town over to play in the hall of Lord Mavortius. In *Sir Thomas More* († 1590, ed. A. Dyce, for Shakespeare Society, 1844) 'my Lord Cardinall's players,' four men and a boy, play in the Chancellor's hall and receive ten angels. For similar scenes cf. the *Induction* to *The Taming of the Shrew*, and *Hamlet*, ii. 2; iii. 2.

range of outside galleries[1]. It is, however, rather surprising to find that Exeter, like Paris itself[2], had its regular theatre as early as 1348, more than two centuries before anything of the kind is heard of in London. This fact emerges from two mandates of Bishop Grandisson; one, already quoted in the previous volume, directed against the *secta* or *ordo*, probably a *société joyeuse*, of Brothelyngham[3], the other inhibiting a satirical performance designed by the youth of the city, in disparagement of the trade and mystery of the cloth-dressers. In both cases the 'theatre' of the city was to be the locality of the revels[4]. Much later, in 1538, but still well in anticipation of London, the corporation of Yarmouth

[1] The earliest record of plays at inns which I have noticed is in 1557, when some Protestants were arrested and their minister burnt for holding a communion service in English on pretence of attending a play at the Saracen's Head, Islington (Foxe, *Acts and Monuments*, ed. Cattley, viii. 444).

[2] Eustace Deschamps (+1415), *Miroir de Mariage* (*Œuvres*, in *Anc. Textes franç.* vol. ix), 3109 (cf. Julleville, *La Com.* 40):

Mais assez d'autres femmes voy,
Qui vont par tout sanz nul convoy
Aux festes, aux champs, au theatre,
Pour soulacier et pour esbatre:

. . . .

Elles desirent les cités,
Les douls mos a euls recités,
Festes, marchiés, et le theatre,
Lieux de delis pour euls esbatre.

This theatre was probably one established towards the end of the fourteenth century by the *confrérie de la Passion*. From about 1402 they performed in the *Hôpital de la Trinité*; cf. Julleville, *Les Com.* 61, *La Com.* 40.

[3] Cf. vol. i. p. 383.

[4] *Register of Bishop Grandisson* (ed. Hingeston-Randolph), ii. 1120. The letter, unfortunately too long-winded to quote in full, was written on Aug. 9, 1352, to the archdeacon of Exeter or his official. Grandisson says:—'Sane, licet artes mechanicas, ut rerum experiencia continue nos informat, mutuo, necessitate quadam, oporteat se iuvare; pridem, tamen, intelleximus quod nonnulli nostrae Civitatis Exoniae inprudentes filii, inordinate lasciviae dediti, fatue contempnentes quae ad ipsorum et universalis populi indigenciam fuerunt utiliter adinventa, quendam Ludum noxium qui culpa non caret, immo verius ludibrium, in contumeliam et opprobrium allutariorum, necnon eorum artificii, hac instanti Die Dominica, in Theatro nostrae Civitatis predictae publice peragere proponunt, ut inter se statuerunt et intendunt; ex quo, ut didicimus, inter praefatos artifices et dicti Ludi participes, auctores pariter et fautores, graves discordiae, rancores, et rixae, cooperante satore tam execrabilis irae et invidiae, vehementer pululant et insurgunt.' The *ludus* is to be forbidden under pain of the greater excommunication. At the same time the *allutarii* are to be admonished, since they themselves, 'in mercibus suis distrahendis plus iusto precio, modernis temporibus,' have brought about the trouble, 'ne exnunc, in vendendo quae ad eos pertinent, precium per Excellentissimum Principem et Dominum nostrum, Angliae et Franciae Regem illustrem, et Consilium suum, pro utilitate publica limitatum, exigant quovis modo.'

appear to have built a 'game-house' upon the garden of the recently surrendered priory [1].

In the villages the players probably had to content themselves with a stage upon the green; unless indeed they could make good a footing in the church. This they sometimes did by way of inheritance from the local actors of miracles. For while the great craft-cycles long remained unaffected by the professional competition and ultimately came to their end through quite different causes, it was otherwise in the smaller places. If the parson and the churchwardens wanted a miracle in honour of their patron saint and could readily hire the services of a body of trained actors, they were not likely to put themselves to the trouble of drilling bookless rustics in their parts. And so the companies got into the churches for the purpose of playing religious interludes, but, if the diatribes of Elizabethan Puritans may be trusted, remained there to play secular ones [2]. The rulers of the Church condemned the abuse [3], but it proved difficult to abolish, and even in 1602 the authorities of Syston in Leicestershire had to buy players off from performing in the church [4].

Even where the old local plays survived they were probably

[1] L. G. Bolingbroke, *Pre-Elizabethan Plays and Players in Norfolk* (*Norfolk Archaeology*, xi. 336). The corporation gave a lease of the 'game-house' on condition that it should be available 'at all such times as any interludes or plays should be ministered or played.' John Rastell's 50*s*. stage in Finsbury about 1520–5 (cf. p. 184), although not improbably used for public representations, is not known to have been permanent.

[2] At Rayleigh, Essex (1550), 20*s*. from the produce of church goods was paid to stage-players on Trinity Sunday (*Archaeologia*, xlii. 287). *An Answer to a Certain Libel* (1572, quoted Collier, ii. 72) accuses the clergy of hurrying the service, because there is 'an enterlude to be played, and if no place else can be gotten, it must be doone in the church'; cf. S. Gosson, *Third Blast of Retrait from Plaies and Theaters*, 1580 (Hazlitt, *E. D. S.* 134) 'Such like men, vnder the title of their maisters or as reteiners, are priuiledged to roaue abroad, and permitted to publish their mametree in euerie Temple of God, and that through England, vnto the horrible contempt of praier. So that now the Sanctuarie is become a plaiers stage, and a den of theeues and adulterers.' Possibly only the publication of the *banns* of plays in church is here complained of. Cf. also Fuller, *Church History* (1655), 391.

[3] Bonner's *Injunctions*, 17, of April, 1542 (Wilkins, iii. 864), forbade 'common plays games or interludes' in churches or chapels. Violent enforcers of them were to be reported to the bishop's officers; cf. the various injunctions of Elizabethan bishops in *Ritual Commission*, 409, 411, 417, 424, 436, and the 88th *Canon* of 1604.

[4] Kelly, 16 'Paid to Lord Morden's players because they should not play in the church, xij[d].'

more or less assimilated to the interlude type. It was certainly so with those written by John Bale and played at Kilkenny. It was probably so with the play of *Placidas* or *St. Eustace* given at Braintree in 1534, if, as is most likely, it was written by Nicholas Udall, who was vicar of Braintree at the time. And when we find the wardens of Bungay Holy Trinity in 1558 paying fourpence for an 'interlude and game-booke' and two shillings for writing out the parts, the conjecture seems obvious that what they had done was to obtain a copy of one of the printed interludes which by that time the London stationers had issued in some numbers. On the other hand the example of the travelling companies sometimes stirred up the folk, with the help, no doubt, of Holophernes the schoolmaster, to attempt performances of secular as well as religious plays on their own account. The rendering of *Pyramus and Thisbe* by the mechanicals of Athens, which is Stratford-upon-Avon, is the classical instance. But in Shropshire the folk are said to have gone on playing debased versions of *Dr. Faustus* and other Elizabethan masterpieces, upon out-of-door stages, until quite an incredibly late date [1].

I return to the atmosphere of courts. It must not be supposed that, under the early Tudors, the professional players had a monopoly of interludes. On the contrary, throughout nearly the whole of the sixteenth century, it remained doubtful whether the future of the drama was to rest in professional or amateur hands. The question was not settled until the genius of Marlowe and of Shakespeare came to the help of the players. Under the pleasure-loving Henries accomplish-

[1] Jackson-Burne, 493, citing Sir Offley Wakeman in *Shropshire Archaeological Transactions*, vii. 383. Such plays were performed on wagons at Shropshire wakes within the last century. The 'book' seems to have been adapted from the literary drama, if one may judge by the subjects which included 'St. George,' 'Prince Mucidorus,' 'Valentine and Orson,' and 'Dr. Forster' or 'Faustus.' But a part was always found for a Fool in a hareskin cap, with balls at his knees. He is described as a sort of presenter or chorus, playing 'all manner of megrims' and 'going on with his manœuvres all the time.' I have not been able to see a paper on *Shropshire Folk-plays* by J. F. M. Dovaston. G. Borrow, *Wild Wales*, chh. lix, lx (ed. 1901, p. 393), describes similar Welsh interludes which lasted to the beginning of the nineteenth century. The titles named suggest moralities. He analyses the *Riches and Poverty* of Thomas Edwards. This, like the Shropshire interludes, has its 'fool.'

ment in the arts of social diversion was as likely a road to preferment as another. Sir Thomas More won a reputation as a page by his skill in improvising a scene[1]. John Kite stepped almost straight from the boards to the bishopric of Armagh. His performances, not perhaps without some scandal to churchmen, were given when he was subdean of the Chapel Royal[2]. This ancient establishment, with its thirty-two gentlemen and its school of children, proved itself the most serious rival of the regular company. Both gentlemen and children, sometimes together and sometimes separately, took part in the performances, the records of which begin in 1506[3]. The rather exceptional nature of the repertory will be considered presently. Few noblemen, of course, kept a chapel on the scale of the royal one. But that of the earl of Northumberland was of considerable size, and was accustomed about 1523 to give, not only a Resurrection play at Easter and a Nativity play at Christmas, but also a play on the night of Shrove-Tuesday. The functionary to whom it looked for a supply of interludes was the almoner[4].

[1] Roper, *Life and Death of Sir Thomas More* († 1577, J. R. Lumby, *More's Utopia*, vi) 'would he at Christmas tyd sodenly sometymes stepp in among the players, and never studinge for the matter, make a parte of his owne there presently amonge them'; Erasmus, *Epist.* ccccxlvii 'adolescens comoediolas et scripsit et egit.' Bale, *Scriptores* (1557), i. 655, ascribes to him 'comoedias iuveniles. Lib. I.' In the play of *Sir Thomas More* (cf. p. 189) he is represented, even when Chancellor, as supplying the place of a missing actor with an improvised speech. Bale, ii. 103, says that Henry Parker, Lord Morley (1476–1556) 'in Anglica sermone edidit comoedias et tragoedias, libros plures.'

[2] The *Revels Account* for 1511 (Brewer, ii. 1496) notes an interlude in which 'Mr. Subdean, now my Lord of Armykan' took part. In his *Oratio ad Clerum* of the same year Colet criticizes the clerics who 'se ludis et iocis tradunt' (Collier, i. 64). A *Sermo exhortatorius cancellarii Eboracensis his qui ad sacros ordines petunt promoveri* printed by Wynkyn de Worde about 1525 also calls attention to the canonical requirement that the clergy should abstain 'a ludis theatralibus' (Hazlitt, *Bibl. Coll. and Notes*, 3rd series (1887), 274).

[3] Collier, i. 46 and *passim*; Bernard Andrew, *Annales Hen. VII* in Gairdner, *Memorials of Henry VII* (R. S.), 103; Hall, 518, 583, 723; Kempe, 62; *Revels Accounts*, &c., in Brewer, *passim*; cf. Appendix E (viii). The Chapel formed part of the household of Henry I about 1135 (*Red Book of Exchequer*, R. S. iii. cclxxxvii, 807); for its history cf. *Household Ordinances*, 10, 17, 35, 49; E. F. Rimbault, *The Old Cheque Book of the Chapel Royal* (C. S.); F. J. Furnivall, *Babees Book* (E. E. T. S.), lxxv.

[4] Percy, *N. H. B.* 44, 254, 345. In household lists for 1511 and 1520 comes the entry 'The Almonar, and if he be a maker of

The gentlemen of the Inns of Courts were always ready to follow in the wake of courtly fashion. Their interludes were famous and important in the days of Elizabeth, but, although Lincoln's Inn entertained external *lusores* in 1494 and 1498 [1], Gray's Inn is the only one in which amateur performances are recorded before 1556. A 'disguising' or 'plaie' by one John Roo was shown here in 1526, and got the actors into trouble with Wolsey, who found, or thought that he found, in it reflections on his own administration [2]. All 'comedies called enterludes' were stopped by an order of the bench in 1550, except during times of solemn Christmas [3]. In 1556 an elaborate piece for performance by all the Inns was in preparation by William Baldwin [4].

There were interludes, moreover, at universities and in schools. The earliest I have noted are at Magdalen College, Oxford, where they occur pretty frequently from 1486 onwards. They were given in the hall at Christmas, and overlap in point of time the performances of the *Quem quaeritis* in the chapel [5]. There was a play at Cardinal's College in 1530 [6]. Nicholas Grimald's *Christus Redivivus* was given at Brasenose about 1542. Possibly his *Archipropheta* was similarly given about 1546 at Christ Church, of which he had then become a member. Beyond these I do not know of any other Oxford representations before 1558. But in 1512 the University granted one Edward Watson a degree in grammar on condition of his composing a comedy [7]. At Cambridge

Interludys than he to have a Servaunt to the intent for Writynge of the Parts and ells to have non.' There were nine gentlemen and six children of the chapel. The 1522-3 list of 'Rewardes' has 'them of his Lordship Chappell and other his Lordshipis Servaunts that doith play the Play befor his Lordship uppon Shroftewsday at night, x[s],' and again, 'Master of the Revells . . . yerly for the overseyinge and orderinge of his Lordschip's playes interludes and Dresinge [? disguisinges] that is plaid befor his Lordship in his Hous in the xij days of Xmas, xx[s].' This latter officer seems to have been, as at court, distinct from the 'Abbot of Miserewll' (vol. i. p. 418).

[1] *Black Books of Lincoln's Inn*, i. 104, 119.

[2] Hall, 719; Collier, i. 103.

[3] R. J. Fletcher, *Pension Book of Gray's Inn*, xxxix, 496.

[4] *Hist. MSS.* vii. 613. The play was to comprehend a 'discourse of the world,' to be called *Love and Life*, and to last three hours. There were to be sixty-two *dramatis personae*, each bearing a name beginning with L.

[5] Cf. Appendix E (v).

[6] Brewer, iv. 6788.

[7] Boase, *Register of the University of Oxford* (O. H. S.), i. 298.

the pioneer college was St. John's, where the *Plutus* of Aristophanes was given in Greek in 1536 [1]. Christ's College is noteworthy for a performance of the antipapal *Pammachius* in 1545 [2]; and also for a series of plays under the management of one William Stevenson in 1550–3, amongst which it is exceedingly probable that *Gammer Gurton's Needle* was included [3]. Most of these university plays were however, probably, in Latin. The Elizabethan statutes of Trinity College [4] and Queens' College [5] both provide for plays, and in both cases the performances really date back to the reign of Henry VIII. At Trinity John Dee seems to have produced the *Pax* of Aristophanes, with an ingenious contrivance for the flight of the Scarabaeus to Zeus, shortly upon his appointment as an original fellow in 1546 [6].

The Westminster Latin play cannot be clearly shown to be pre-Elizabethan [7], and the Westminster dramatic tradition is,

[1] Mullinger, *Hist. of Cambridge*, ii. 73. Ascham, *Epist.* (1581), f. 126v, writing †1550 (quoted Hazlitt-Warton, iii. 304) says that Antwerp excels all other cities 'quemadmodum aula Iohannis, theatrali more ornata, seipsam post Natalem superat.' Speaking in *The Scholemaster* (ed. Mayor, 1863), 168, of his contemporaries at St. John's (†1530–54), Ascham highly praises the *Absalon* of Thomas Watson, which he puts on a level with Buchanan's *Jephthah*. Watson, however, 'would never suffer it to go abroad.' This play apparently exists in manuscript; cf. *Texts* (iv). Ascham himself, according to his *Epistles*, translated the *Philoktetes* into Latin (Hazlitt, *Manual*, 179). In *The Scholemaster*, he further says, 'One man in Cambrige, well liked of many, but best liked of him selfe, was many tymes bold and busie to bryng matters upon stages which he called Tragedies.' Ascham did not approve of his Latin metre. Possibly he refers to John Christopherson, afterwards bishop of Chichester, to whom Warton, iii. 303; Cooper, *Athenae Cantab.* i. 188; *D. N. B.* attribute a tragedy in Greek and Latin of *Jepthes* (1546). I can find no trace of this. It is not mentioned by Bahlmann.

[2] Cf. p. 220.

[3] J. Peile, *Christ's College*, 54; cf. p. 216.

[4] Mullinger, *Hist. of Cambridge*, ii. 627. *Statute* 24 of 1560, *De comoediis ludisque in Natali Christi exhibendis*, requires that 'novem domestici lectores . . . bini ac bini singulas comoedias tragoediasve exhibeant, excepto primario lectore quem per se solum unam comoediam aut tragoediam exhibere volumus.' A fine is imposed on defaulters, and the performances are to be in the hall 'privatim vel publice' during or about the twelve nights of Christmas. On an earlier draft of this statute cf. vol. i. p. 413.

[5] *Statute* 36 (*Documents relating to Cambridge*, iii. 54); cf. Mullinger, *op. cit.* ii. 73.

[6] Dee, *Compendious Rehearsall* (app. to Hearne, *Ioh. Glastoniensis Chronicon*, 501), after mentioning his election, says 'Hereupon I did sett forth a Greek comedy of Aristophanes' play named in Greek Εἰρήνη, in Latin *Pax*.'

[7] J. Sargeaunt, *Annals of Westminster*, 49; *Athenæum* (1903), i. 220.

therefore, less old than that of either Eton or St. Paul's. Professor Hales has, indeed, made it seem plausible that Udall's *Ralph Roister Doister* dates from his Westminster (? 1553–6) and not his Eton mastership (1534–41). But the Eton plays can be traced back to 1525–6 [1], and were a recognized institution when Malim wrote his *Consuetudinary* about 1561 [2]. In 1538 the Eton boys played, under Udall, before Cromwell [3]. A decade earlier, in 1527, John Ritwise had brought the boys of Colet's new foundation at St. Paul's to court. They acted an anti-Lutheran play before Henry and probably also the *Menaechmi* before Wolsey. Certainly they acted the *Phormio* before him in the following year [4]. The dramatic history of this school is a little difficult to disentangle from that of its near neighbour, the song-school of St. Paul's cathedral [5]. The song-school probably provided the children whom Heywood brought before the princess Mary in 1538 [6] and to court in 1553. But some doubt has been cast upon the *bona fides* of the account which Warton gives of further performances by them before the princess Elizabeth at Hatfield in 1554 [7]. Plays,

[1] Maxwell-Lyte, *Hist. of Eton* (3rd ed. 1899), 118 'pro expensis circa ornamenta ad duos lusus in aula tempore natalis Domini, x[s].'

[2] Printed in E. S. Creasy, *Memoirs of Eminent Etonians*, 91 'circiter festum D. Andreae ludimagister eligere solet pro suo arbitrio scaenicas fabulas optimas et quam accommodatissimas, quas pueri feriis natalitiis subsequentibus, non sine ludorum elegantia, populo spectante, publice aliquando peragant. Histrionum levis ars est, ad actionem tamen oratorum et gestum motumque corporis decentem tantopere facit, ut nihil magis. Interdum etiam exhibet Anglico sermone contextas fabulas, quae habeant acumen et leporem.'

[3] Brewer, xiv. 2. 334 'Woodall, the schoolmaster of Eton, for playing before my Lord, £5.'

[4] Brown, *Cat. of Venetian Papers*, iv. 3. 208, 225; Brewer, iv. 3563; Hall, 735; Cavendish, *Life of Wolsey* (ed. Singer), 201; Collier, i. 104.

[5] Lupton, *Life of Colet*, 154.

[6] *Texts*, s. v. Heywood.

[7] Warton speaks of a play by the 'children' or 'choirboys' of St. Paul's at a visit to Elizabeth by Mary and of another play of *Holophernes* 'perhaps' by the same children later in the year. But the dates given in his *Hist. of Poetry* (ed. Hazlitt), ii. 234, iii. 312, and his *Life of Sir Thomas Pope* (ed. 1780), 46, do not agree together, and the authority to which he refers (*Machyn's Diary*, then in MS.) does not bear him out. On his *bona fides* cf. H. E. D. Blakiston, in *E. H. Review*, for April, 1896. Ward, i. 153, rather complicates the matter by adding to *Holophernes* a second play called *The Hanging of Antioch*, but even in Warton's account this 'hanging' was only a curtain.

either in English or in Latin, of which Bale preserves a list, were also acted in the private school set up in 1538 by one Ralph Radclif in the surrendered Carmelite convent of Hitchin [1].

It will be seen that the non-professional dramatic activities of England, outside the miracle-plays, although of some importance in the sixteenth century, came late and hardly extended beyond courtly and scholastic circles. There is nothing corresponding to the plentiful production of farces by amateur associations of every kind which characterized fifteenth-century France. Besides the scholars and the *Basoche*, which corresponded roughly to the Inns of Court, but was infinitely more lively and fertile, there were the *Enfants sans Soucis* in Paris, and in the province a host of *puys* and *sociétés joyeuses*. All of these played both morals and farces, particularly the latter, for which they claimed a very free licence of satirical comment [2]. As a result,

[1] Bale, *Scriptores* (1557), i. 700 'Radulphus Radclif, patria Cestriensis, Huchiniae in agro Hartfordiensi, & in coenobio, quod paulo ante Carmelitarum erat, ludum literarium anno Domini 1538 aperuit, docuitque Latinas literas. Mihi quidem aliquot dies in unis & eisdem aedibus commoranti, multa arriserunt: eaque etiam laude dignissima. Potissimum vero theatrum, quod in inferiori aedium parte longe pulcherrimum extruxit. Ibi solitus est quotannis simul iucunda & honesta plebi edere spectacula, cum ob iuventutis, suae fidei & institutioni commissae, inutilem pudorem exuendum, tum ad formandum os tenerum & balbutiens, quo clare, eleganter, & distincte verba eloqui & effari consuesceret. Plurimas in eius museo vidi ac legi tragoedias & comoedias ... Scripsit de Nominis ac Verbi, potentissimorum regum in regno Grammatico, calamitosa &
Exitiali pugna, *Lib.* 2 ...
De patientia Grisilidis, *Com.* 1 ...
De Melibaeo Chauceriano, *Com.* 1 ...
De Titi & Gisippi amicitia, *Com.* 1 ...
De Sodomae incendio, *Tra.* 1 ...
De Io. Hussi damnatione, *Tra.* 1 ...
De Ionae defectione, *Com.* 1 ...
De Lazaro ac diuite, *Com.* 1 ...
De Iudith fortitudine, *Com.* 1 ...
De Iobi afflictionibus, *Com.* 1 ...
De Susannae liberatione, *Tra.* 1 ...
Claruit Radclifus, anno a Christi servatoris ortu 1552 ... Nescioque an sub Antichristi tyrannide adhuc vivat.' Bale, *Index*, 333, has fuller titles. Some of Radclif's plays were almost certainly in Latin, for Bale gives in Latin the opening words of each, and as Herford, 113, points out, those of the *Lazarus* and the *Griselda* clearly form parts of Latin verses. But he showed them 'plebi.' Professor Herford learnt 'that no old MSS. in any way connected with Radclif now remain at Hitchin, where his family still occupies the site of his school.'

[2] Julleville, *Les Com.*, *passim*. A collection of farces is in E. L. N. Viollet-le-Duc, *Ancien Théâtre français* (1854-7). For morals

although salaried *joueurs de personnages* begin to make their appearance in the account books of the nobles as early as 1392–3 [1], the professional actors were unable to hold their own against the unequal competition, and do not really become of importance until quite the end of the sixteenth century [2]. In England it was otherwise. The early suppression of the Feast of Fools and the strict control kept over the Boy Bishop afforded no starting-point for *sociétés joyeuses*, while the late development of English as a literary language did not lend itself to the formation of *puys*. We hear indeed of satirical performances by the guild of Brothelyngham at Exeter in 1348, and again by the *filii civitatis* in 1352 [3], but Bishop Grandisson apparently succeeded in checking this development which, so far as the information at present available goes, does not seem to have permanently established itself either at Exeter or elsewhere.

and farces at the Feasts of Fools and of the Boy Bishop abroad, and for the satirical tendency of such entertainments, cf. vol. i. p. 380. In 1427, after the feast of St. Laurent, Jean Bussières, chaplain of St. Remi de Troyes, 'emendavit quod fecerat certum perconnagium rimarum in cimiterio dicte ecclesie Sancti Remigii; de quibus rimis fuerat dyabolus et dixerat plura verba contra viros ecclesiasticos' (*Inv. des Arch. de l'Aube*, sér. G, i. 243). The fifteenth-century Dutch farces appear to have been played at the meetings of the *Rederijkerkammern*, and the German *Fastnachtsspiele*, which derive largely from folk *ludi*, by associations of handicraftsmen (Creizenach, i. 404, 407).

[1] Julleville, *Les Com.* 325.

[2] Ibid. 342. There is nothing to show the character of the French players who visited the English court in 1494 and 1495 (Appendix E, viii).

[3] Cf. p. 190 and vol. i. p. 383. The only known English *puy* is that of London (vol. i. p. 376).

CHAPTER XXV

HUMANISM AND MEDIAEVALISM

[*Bibliographical Note.*—The literary discussions and collections of texts named in the bibliographical note to chap. xxiii and the material on the annals of the stage in that to chap. xxiv remain available. W. Creizenach, *Geschichte des neueren Dramas*, vols. i–iii (1893–1903), is the best general guide on the classical drama and its imitations during the Middle Ages and the Renascence. W. Cloetta, *Beiträge zur Litteraturgeschichte des Mittelalters und der Renaissance*: i. *Komödie und Tragödie im Mittelalter* (1890); ii. *Die Anfänge der Renaissancetragödie* (1892), deals very fully with certain points. C. H. Herford, *Studies in the Literary Relations of England and Germany in the Sixteenth Century* (1886), has an admirable chapter on *The Latin Drama.* G. Saintsbury, *The Earlier Renaissance* (1901), chap. vi, may also be consulted. Useful books on the beginnings of the Elizabethan forms of drama are R. Fischer, *Zur Kunstentwicklung der englischen Tragödie von ihren ersten Anfängen bis zu Shakespeare* (1893); J. W. Cunliffe, *The Influence of Seneca on Elizabethan Tragedy* (1893); L. L. Schücking, *Studien über die stofflichen Beziehungen der englischen Komödie zur italienischen bis Lilly* (1901); F. E. Schelling, *The English Chronicle Play* (1902). The best bibliographies are, for the Latin plays, P. Bahlmann, *Die Erneuerer des antiken Dramas und ihre ersten dramatischen Versuche*, 1314–1478 (1896), and *Die lateinischen Dramen von Wimpheling's Stylpho bis zur Mitte des sechzehnten Jahrhunderts*, 1480–1550 (1893); and for English plays, W. W. Greg, *A List of English Plays written before 1643 and printed before 1700* (1900). This may be supplemented from W. C. Hazlitt, *A Manual for the Collector and Amateur of Old English Plays* (1892). A list of early Tudor interludes will be found in Appendix X.]

THE dramatic material upon which the interlude was able to draw had naturally its points of relation to and of divergence from that of the popular stage, whose last days it overlapped. It continued to occupy itself largely with the morality. The 'moral interludes' of the early Tudor period are in fact distinguished with some difficulty from the popular moralities by their comparative brevity, and by indications of the *mise en scène* as a 'room' or 'hall' rather than an open 'place[1].' The only clearly popular texts later than those

[1] The titles of the printed plays do not help, as they were probably added by the printers, and in any case 'enterlude' does not exclude a popular play.

of the fifteenth century, discussed in a previous chapter, are Sir David Lyndsay's Scottish *Satyre of the Thrie Estaitis*, and the *Magnificence*, which alone survives of several plays from the prolific pen of the 'laureate' poet, John Skelton. A somewhat intermediate type is presented by the *Nature* of Cardinal Morton's chaplain, Henry Medwall. This was certainly intended for performance as an interlude, but it is on the scale of the popular moralities, needing division into two parts to bring it within the limits of courtly patience; and like them it is sufficiently wide in its scope to embrace the whole moral problem of humanity. The conditions of the interlude, however, enforced themselves, and the later morals have, as a rule, a more restricted theme. They make their selection from amongst the battalions of sins and virtues which were wont to invade the stage together, and set themselves the task of expounding the dangers of a particular temperament or the advantages of a particular form of moral discipline. *Hickscorner* shows man led into irreligion by imagination and freewill. *Youth* concerns itself with pride, lechery, and riot, the specific temptations of the young. *The Nature of the Four Elements* and John Redford's somewhat later *Wit and Science* preach the importance of devotion to study. The distinction between the episodic and the more comprehensive moralities was in the consciousness of the writers themselves; and the older fashion did not wholly disappear. William Baldwin describes his play for the Inns of Court in 1556 as 'comprehending a discourse of the worlde[1]'; and mention is more than once made of an interesting piece called *The Cradle of Security*, which seems to have had a motive of death and the judgement akin to that found in *The Pride of Life* and in *Everyman*[2].

[1] *Hist. MSS.* vii. 613.

[2] Collier, ii. 196, quotes the description by Willis, *Mount Tabor* (1639), and refers to other notices of the play. In *Sir Thomas More* (†1590, ed. A. Dyce, from *Harl. MS.* 7368 for Shakes. Soc. 1844) 'my lord Cardinall's players' visit More's house and offer the following repertory:

'The Cradle of Securitie,
Hit nayle o' th' head, Impacient Pouertie,
The play of Foure Pees, Diues and Lazarus,
Lustie Juuentus, and the Mariage of Witt and Wisedom.'

The ascription of these plays to Wolsey's lifetime must not be pressed too literally. Of *Hit Nayle o' th' Head* nothing is known. Radclif (p. 197) wrote a *Dives and*

The morality was not, perhaps, quite such an arid type of drama as might be supposed, especially after the dramatists learnt, instead of leaving humanity as a dry bone of contention between the good and evil powers, to adopt a biographic mode of treatment, and thus to introduce the interest of growth and development [1]. But by the sixteenth century allegory had had its day, and the light-hearted court of Henry VIII and Katharine of Aragon might be excused some weariness at the constant presentation before it of argumentative abstractions which occasionally yielded nothing more entertaining than a personified *débat* [2]. Certainly it is upon record that Medwall's moral of 'the fyndyng of Troth,' played at the Christmas of 1513, appeared to Henry so long, that he got up and 'departyd to hys chambre [3].' The offenders on this occasion were English and his company of household players. They seem to have been unwisely wedded to the old methods. They pursued the princess Margaret to Scotland with a 'Moralite' in 1503, and in the reign of Edward VI they were still playing the play of *Self-Love* [4]. Perhaps this explains why they make distinctly

Lazarus. For the rest cf. p. 189; *Texts* (iv). The piece actually performed in *Sir Thomas More* is called *Wit and Wisdom*, but is really an adaptation of part of *Lusty Juventus*. A play of *Old Custome*, probably a morality, was amongst the effects of John, earl of Warwick, in 1545–50 (*Hist. MSS.* ii. 102).

[1] Cf. Brandl, xl. The performances of *Everyman* given in the courtyard of the Charterhouse in 1901, and subsequently in more than one London theatre, have proved quite unexpectedly impressive.

[2] John Rastell printed †1536 *Of gentylnes and nobylyte, A dyalogue . . . compilit in maner of an enterlude with divers toys and gestis addyd thereto to make mery pastyme and disport*; cf. *Bibliographica*, ii. 446. Heywood's *Witty and Witless* is a similar piece, and a later one, *Robin Conscience*, is in W. C. Hazlitt, *Early Popular Poetry*, iii. 221. In 1527 Rastell seems to have provided for the court a pageant of 'The Father of Hevin' in which a dialogue, both in English and Latin, of riches and love, written by John Redman, and also a 'barriers' were introduced (Brewer, iv. 1394; Collier, i. 98; Hall, 723; Brown, *Venetian Papers*, iv. 105). A dialogue of Riches and Youth, issuing in a 'barriers,' is described by Edward VI in 1552 (*Remains*, ii. 386). On the vogue during the Renascence of this dialogue literature, which derives from the mediaeval *débats*, cf. Herford, ch. 2.

[3] Collier, i. 69. This notice is said by Collier to be from a slip of paper folded up in the *Revels Account* for 1513–4. It is not mentioned in Brewer's *Calendar*.

[4] Leland, *Collectanea* (ed. Hearne), iv. 265; *Computus* for 1551–6 of Sir Thos. Chaloner (*Lansd. MS.* 824, f. 24) 'Gevyn on Shrove monday to the king's players who playd the play of Self-love . . . xx[s].'

less show in the accounts of Tudor revels than do their competitors of the Chapel. Unfortunately none of the pieces given by this latter body have been preserved. But, to judge by the descriptions of Hall, many of them could only be called interludes by a somewhat liberal extension of the sense of the term. There was perhaps some slight allegorical or mythological framework of spoken dialogue. But the real amusement lay in an abundance of singing, which of course the Chapel was well qualified to provide, and of dancing, in which the guests often joined, and in an elaborately designed pageant, which was wheeled into the hall and from which the performers descended. They were in fact masques rather than dramas in the strict sense, and in connexion with the origin of the masque they have already been considered[1].

The popular stage, as has been said, had its farcical elements, but did not, in England, arrive at any notable development of the farce. Nor is any marked influence of the overseas habit even now to be traced. The name is not used in England, although it is in Scotland, where at the beginning of the sixteenth century the relations with France were much closer[2]. Whether directly or indirectly through French channels, the farce is perhaps the contribution of minstrelsy to the nascent interlude. That some dramatic tradition was handed down from the *mimi* of the Empire to the *mimi* of the Middle Ages, although not susceptible of demonstration, is exceedingly likely[3]. That solitary mediaeval survival, the *Interludium de Clerico et Puella*, hardly declares its origin. But the farce, in its free handling of contemporary life, in the outspokenness, which often becomes indecency, of its language, in its note of satire, especially towards the priest and other institutions deserving of reverence, is the exact counter-

[1] Cf. ch. xvi.

[2] There was a 'farsche' at Edinburgh in 1554 (*Representations*, s. v.). In 1558 the Scottish General Assembly forbade 'farseis and clerke playis' (Christie, *Account of Parish Clerks*, 64). Julleville, *La Com.* 51, explains the term. *Farsa* is the L. L. past part. of *farcire* 'to stuff.' Besides its liturgical use (vol. i. p. 277) 'on appela *farce* au théâtre une petite pièce, une courte et vive satire formée d'éléments variés et souvent mêlée de divers langages et de différents dialectes. . . . Plus tard, ce sens premier s'effaça ; le mot de farce n'éveilla plus d'autre idée que celle de comédie très réjouissante.' *Farce* is, therefore, in its origin, precisely equivalent to the Latin *Satura*.

[3] Cf. vol. i. p. 83.

part of one of the most characteristic forms of minstrel literature, the *fabliau*. These qualities are reproduced in the interludes of John Heywood, who, though possibly an Oxford man, began life as a singer and player of the virginals at court, and belonged therefore to the minstrel class. He grew quite respectable, married into the family of Sir Thomas More and John Rastell the printer, and had for grandson John Donne. He was put in charge of the singing-school of St. Paul's, the boys of which probably performed his plays. Of the six extant, *Wit and Folly* is a mere dialogue, and *Love* a more elaborate disputation, although both are presented 'in maner of an enterlude.' But the others, *The Pardoner and the Friar*, *The Four P's*, *The Weather*, and *John, Tib and Sir John* are regular farces. And with them the farce makes good its footing in the English drama.

Those congeners of the French farce which took their origin from the Feast of Fools, the *Sottie* and the *Sermon joyeux*, are only represented in these islands by the Sermon of 'Folie' in Sir David Lyndsay's *Satyre of the Thrie Estaitis*[1]. But the 'fool' himself, as a dramatic character, is in Shakespeare's and other Elizabethan plays, and it must now be pointed out that he is in some of the earliest Tudor interludes. Here he has the not altogether intelligible name of the 'vice.' A recent writer, Professor Cushman of the Nevada State University, has endeavoured to show that the vice came into the interludes through the avenue of the moralities. Originally 'an allegorical representation of human weaknesses and vices, in short the summation of the Deadly Sins,' he lost in course of time this serious quality, and 'the term Vice came to be simply a synonym for buffoon[2].' This theory has no doubt the advantage of

[1] *Texts*, s. v. Lyndsay. The only other fragment of the Scottish drama under James IV is that ascribed to Dunbar (*Works*, ed. Scot. Text Soc., ii. 314). In one MS. this is headed '*Ane Littill Interlud of the Droichis Part of the* [*Play*] but in another *Heir followis the maner of the crying of ane playe.* Both have the colophon. *Finis off the Droichis Pairt of the Play.* From internal evidence the piece is a *cry* or *banes*. Ll. 138–41 show that it was for a May-game:

'ȝe noble merchandis ever ilkane
Address ȝow furth with bow and flane
In lusty grene lufraye,
And follow furth on Robyn Hude.'

[2] Cushman, 63, 68.

explaining the name. Unfortunately it proceeds by disregarding several plays in which the vice does occur, and reading him into many where there is none [1]. 'Vicious' had his pageant in the Beverley *Paternoster* play, and vices in the ordinary sense of the word are of course familiar personages in the morals, which generally moreover have some one character who can be regarded as the representative or the chief representative of human frailty. But the vice is not found under that name in the text, list of *dramatis personae*, or stage directions of any popular morality or of any pre-Elizabethan moral interlude except the Marian *Respublica*. The majority of plays in which he does occur are not morals, even of the modified Elizabethan type; and although in those which are he generally plays a bad part, even this is not an invariable rule. In *The Tide Tarrieth for No Man*, as in the tragedy of *Horestes*, he is Courage. Moreover, as a matter of fact, he comes into the interludes through the avenue of the farce. The earliest vices, by some thirty years, are those of Heywood's *Love*, in which he is 'Neither Loving nor Loved,' who mocks the other disputants, and plays a practical joke with fireworks upon them, and *The Weather*, in which he is 'Merry Report,' the jesting official of Jupiter. And in the later plays, even if he has some other dramatic function, he always adds to it that of a riotous buffoon. Frequently enough he has no other. It must be concluded then that, whatever the name may mean—and irresponsible philology has made some amazing attempts at explanation [2]—the character of the vice is derived from that of the domestic fool or jester. Oddly enough he is rarely called a fool, although the description of Medwall's *Finding of Truth* mentions 'the foolys part [3].' But the Elizabethan writers

[1] No play in the first two sections of the 'vice-dramas' tabulated by Cushman, 55, has a vice. Of the eleven plays (excluding *King John*, which has none) that remain, eight can be called morals. But to these must be added Heywood's *Love* and *Weather*, Grimald's *Archipropheta*, *Jack Juggler*, *Hester*, *Tom Tiler and His Wife*, none of which are morals, unless the first can be so called.

[2] Cushman, 68. It has been derived from *vis d'âne*, and from *vis*, 'a mask'; from the Latin *vice*, because the vice is the devil's representative; from *device*, 'a puppet moved by machinery,' and finally, by the ingenious Theobald, from 'O. E. *jeck*—Gk. εἰκαί, i.e. ϝικαῖ = ϝεικ = formal character.'

[3] Cf. *Texts*, s. v. Medwall. In

speak of his long coat and lathen sword, common trappings of the domestic fool[1]. Whether he ever had a cockscomb, a bauble, or an eared hood is not apparent. A vice seems to have been introduced into one or two of the later miracle-plays[2]. At Bungay in 1566 he 'made pastime' before and after the play, as Tarleton or Kempe were in time to do with their 'jigs' upon the London boards. And probably this was his normal function on such occasions.

From the moral the interlude drew abstractions; from the farce social types. The possibility of vital drama lay in an advance to the portraiture of individualities. The natural way to attain to this was by the introduction of historical, mythical, or romantic personages. The miracle-play had, of course, afforded these; but there is little to show that the miracle-play, during the first half of the sixteenth century, had much influence on the interlude[3]. The local players brought it to court, but, for the present, it was *démodé*. It was, however, to have its brief revival. The quarry of romantic narrative had hardly been opened by the Middle Ages. An old theme of Robert of Sicily, once used at Lincoln, was now remembered at Chester. Robin Hood had yielded dramatic May-games, and his revels were popular at Henry VIII's court[4]. New motives, however, now begin to assert themselves. Some at least of these were suggested by the study of Chaucer. Ralph Radclif's school plays at Hitchin included one on *Griselda* and one on *Meliboeus*[5]. Nicholas Grimald wrote one on *Troilus*, and another had been acted by the Chapel at court in 1516[6]. Radclif was also responsible for a *Titus and Gisippus*, while the king's players, shaking off their devotion to the moral, prepared in 1552 'a play of *Aesop's Crow*, wherein the most part of the actors were birds[7].' An extant piece on 'the

Misogonos († 1560) Cacurgus, the *Morio*, is a character, and is called 'foole' and 'nodye' but not 'vice.'

[1] Collier, ii. 191; Cushman, 69; cf. ch. xvi.

[2] Cf. *Representations*, s. vv. Bungay, Chelmsford.

[3] The 'pleyers with Marvells' at court in 1498 are conjectured to have played miracles. But they may have been merely *praestigiatores*.

[4] Cf. vol. i. p. 180.

[5] Cf. p. 197, n. 1.

[6] Cf. *Texts*, s. v. Grimald.

[7] W. B[aldwin], *Bell the Cat* (1553).

beauty and good properties of women' and 'their vices and evil conditions' is really a version through the Italian of the Spanish *Celestina*, one of the first of many English dramatic borrowings from South European sources.

So far I have written only of developments which were at least latent in mediaevalism. But the interlude had its rise in the very midst of the great intellectual and spiritual movement throughout Europe which is known as humanism; and hardly any branch of human activities was destined to be more completely transformed by the new forces than the drama. The history of this transformation is not, however, a simple one. Between humanism and mediaevalism there is no rigid barrier. As at all periods of transition, a constant action and reaction established themselves between the old and new order of ideas. Moreover, humanism itself held elements in solution that were not wholly reconcilable with each other. Many things, and perhaps particularly the drama, presented themselves in very different lights, according as they were viewed from the literary or the religious side of the great movement. Some brief indication of the in-and-out play of the forces of humanism as they affected the history of the interlude during the first half of the sixteenth century is, therefore, desirable.

The chief of these forces is, of course, the influence of classical comedy and tragedy. These, as vital forms of literature, did not long survive the fall of the theatres, with which, indeed, their connexion had long been of the slightest. In the East, a certain tradition of Christian book dramas begins with the anti-Gnostic dialogues of St. Methodius in the fourth century and ends with the much disputed Χριστὸς Πάσχων in the eleventh or twelfth [1]. It is the merest conjecture that some of these may have been given some kind of representation in the churches [2]. In the West the *Aulu-*

[1] Krumbacher, 534, 644, 653, 717, 746, 751, 766, 775. The Χριστὸς Πάσχων (ed. by J. G. Brambs, 1885; and in *P. G.* xxxviii. 131) was long ascribed to the fourth-century Gregory Nazianzen. Later scholars have suggested Joannes Tzetzes or Theodorus Prodromus, but Krumbacher thinks the author unidentified. A third of the text is a cento from extant plays, mainly of Euripides.

[2] Krumbacher, 645.

laria of Plautus was rehandled under the title of *Querolus* at the end of the fourth century, and possibly also the *Amphitruo* under that of *Geta*[1]. In the fifth, Magnus, the father of Consentius, is said by Sidonius, as Shakespeare is said by Ben Jonson, to have 'outdone insolent Greece, or haughty Rome[2].' Further the production of plays cannot be traced. Soon afterwards most of the classical dramatists pass into oblivion. A knowledge of Seneca or of Plautus, not to speak of the Greeks, is the rarest of things from the tenth century to the fourteenth. The marked exception is Terence who, as Dr. Ward puts it, led 'a charmed life in the darkest ages of learning.' This he owed, doubtless, to his unrivalled gift of packing up the most impeccable sentiments in the neatest of phrases. His vogue as a school author was early and enduring, and the whole of mediaevalism, a few of the stricter moralists alone dissenting, hailed him as a master of the wisdom of life[3]. At the beginning of the eleventh century, Notker Labeo, a monk of St. Gall, writes that he has been invited to turn the *Andria* into German[4]. Not long before, Hrotsvitha, a Benedictine nun of Gandersheim in Saxony, had taken Terence as her model for half a dozen plays in Latin prose, designed to glorify chastity and to celebrate the constancy of the martyrs. The dramaturgy of Hrotsvitha appears to have been an isolated experiment and the merest literary exercise. Her plays abound in delicate situations, and are not likely to have been intended even for cloister representation[5]. Nor is there much evidence for any representation of the Terentian

[1] Teuffel, ii. 372; Cloetta, i. 3, 70; Creizenach, i. 4, 20. The *Querolus* (ed. L. Havet, 1880) was ascribed by the Middle Ages to Plautus himself. The *Geta*, if it existed, is lost.

[2] Sidonius, *Carm.* xxiii. 134.

[3] Cloetta, i. 14; ii. 1; Creizenach, i. 1, 486; Bahlmann, *Ern.* 4; M. Manitius, in *Philologus*, suppl. vii. 758; Ward, i. 7, quoting Hrotsvitha, 'sunt etiam . . .
qui, licet alia gentilium spernant,
Terentii tamen fragmenta frequentius lectitant.'

[4] Creizenach, i. 2; Ward, i. 8; *Göttinger gelehrte Anzeigen* (1835), 911.

[5] Creizenach, i. 17; Cloetta, i. 127; Ward, i. 6; Pollard, xii; A. Ebert, *Gesch. d. Litt. d. Mittelalters* (1887), iii. 314; W. H. Hudson in *E. H. R.* iii. 431. The plays of Hrotsvitha (ed. K. A. Barack, 1858; ed. P. L. Winterfeld, 1901) are the *Gallicanus*, *Dulcitius*, *Callimachus*, *Abraham*, *Paphnutius*, *Sapientia*. They were discovered by Conrad Celtes and edited in 1501. It is not probable that he forged them.

comedies themselves. A curious fragment known as *Terentius et Delusor* contains a dialogue between the *vetus poeta* and a *persona delusoris* or mime. The nature of this is somewhat enigmatic, but it certainly reads as if it might be a prologue or *parade* written for a Terentian representation. In any case, it is wholly unparalleled [1]. In fact, although the Middle Ages continued to read Terence, the most extraordinary ideas prevailed as to how his dramas were originally produced. Vague reminiscences of the pantomimic art of later Rome led to the mistaken supposition that the poet himself, or a *recitator*, declaimed the text from a *pulpitum* above the stage, while the actors gesticulated voicelessly below [2]. By a further confusion the name of Calliopius, a third- or fourth-century grammarian through whose hands the text of Terence has passed, was taken for that of a *recitator* contemporary with the poet, and the *Vita Oxoniensis* goes so far as to describe him as a powerful and learned man, who read the comedies aloud in the senate [3]. The same complete ignorance of things scenic declares itself in the notions attached to the terms *tragoedia* and *comoedia*,

[1] Printed in Appendix U.

[2] Creizenach, i. 5; Cloetta, i. 38. One of the exceptionally learned men who really knew something about the classical drama was John of Salisbury († 1159), *Polycraticus*, i. 8 'comicis et tragoedis abeuntibus, cum omnia levitas occupaverit, clientes eorum, comoedi videlicet et tragoedi, exterminati sunt'; iii. 8 'comoedia est vita hominis super terram, ubi quisque sui oblitus personam exprimit alienam' (*P. L.* cxcix. 405, 488). For the popular notion cf. Lydgate, *Troy Book* (ed. 1555), ii. 11, perhaps translating Guido delle Colonne:

'In the theatre there was a smale aulter,
Amyddes sette that was half Circuler,
Which into East of custome was directe,
Upon the whiche a Pulpet was erecte,
And therin stode an auncient poete,
For to reherse by rethorykes swete,
The noble dedes that were hystoryall,
Of kynges & prynces for memoryall . . .
All this was tolde and red of the Poete,
And whyle that he in the pulpet stode,
With deadly face all deuoyde of blode,
Synging his ditees with muses all to rent,
Amyd the theatre shrowded in a tent,
There came out men gastfull of their cheres,
Disfygured their faces with viseres,
Playing by sygnes in the peoples syght,
That the Poet songe hath on heyght, . . .
And this was done in Apryll and in May.'

[3] Creizenach, i. 6; Cloetta, i. 35. See the miniature reproduced from a fifteenth-century MS. of Terence in P. Lacroix, *Sciences et Lettres au Moyen Âge* (1877), 534.

not only vulgarly, but in the formal definitions of lexicographers and encyclopaedists [1].

The characteristics which really differentiate the drama from other forms of literature, dialogue and scenic representation, drop out of account, the latter entirely, the former very nearly so. Both tragedy and comedy are regarded as forms of narrative. Tragedy is narrative which concerns persons of high degree, is written in a lofty style, and beginning happily comes to a sad conclusion. Comedy, on the other hand, concerns itself with ordinary persons, uses humble and everyday language, and resolves its complications in a fortunate ending [2]. Even these distinctions are not all consistently maintained, and the sad or happy event becomes the only fixed and invariable criterion [3]. The origin of such conceptions is to be found partly in the common derived classical use of *tragoedia* and *comoedia* to describe tragic and comic events as well as the species of drama in which these are respectively represented; partly in a misunderstanding of grammarians who, assuming the dialogue and the representation, gave definitions of tragedy and comedy in relation to each other [4]; and partly in the solecism of the fifth-century epic writer Dracontius, who

[1] Cloetta, i. 14, has accumulated a fund of learning on this subject; cf. Creizenach, i. 9.

[2] Johannes Januensis, *Catholicon* (1286), quoted by Cloetta, i. 28 'differunt tragoedia et comoedia, quia comedia privatorum hominum continet facta, tragoedia regum et magnatum. Item comoedia humili stilo describitur, tragoedia alto. Item comoedia a tristibus incipit sed cum laetis desinit, tragoedia e contrario.'

[3] Vincent of Beauvais, *Speculum maius triplex* († 1250), i. 109 'Comoedia poesis exordium triste laeto fine commutans. Tragoedia vero poesis a laeto principio in tristem finem desinens.' The Dante-commentator Francesco da Buti, quoted by Cloetta i. 48, illustrates this notion with an extraordinary explanation of the derivation of *tragedia* from *τράγος*; 'come il becco ha dinanzi aspetto di principe per le corna e per la barba, e dietro è sozzo mostrando le natiche nude e non avendo con che coprirle, così la tragedia incomincia dal principio con felicità e poi termina in miseria.' Krumbacher, 646, describes the very similar history of the terms *τραγῳδία* and *κωμῳδία* in Byzantine Greek.

[4] Boethius, who of course understood the nature of comedy and tragedy, says (*Cons. Philosoph.* ii. pr. 2. 36) 'quid tragoediarum clamor aliud deflet, nisi indiscreto ictu fortunam felicia regna vertentem?' This becomes in the paraphrase of his eleventh-century commentator Notker Labeo (ed. Hattemar, 52[b]) 'tragoediae sínt luctuosa carmina. álso díu sínt. díu sophocles scréib apud grecos. de euersionibus regnorum et urbium. úndesínt uuideruuártig tien comoediis. án dîen uuir îo gehórên laetum únde iocundum exitum.'

seems to have called his *Orestes* a tragedy, merely because it was from tragedies that the material he used was drawn [1]. The *comoedia* and *tragoedia* of the Latin writers, thus defined, was extended to all the varieties of narrative, in the widest sense of the word. The epics of Lucan and Statius, the elegies of Ovid, are *tragoediae*; the epistles of Ovid, the pastoral dialogues of Virgil, are *comoediae*; the satires of Horace, Persius, Juvenal, are one or the other, according to the point of view [2]. It is curious that, with all this wide extension of the terms, they were not applied to the one form of mediaeval Latin composition which really had some analogy to the ancient drama; namely to the liturgical plays out of which the vernacular mysteries grew. These must have been written by learned writers: some of them were probably acted by schoolboys trained in Terence; and yet, if Hrosvitha, as she should be, is put out of the reckoning, no inward or outward trace of the influence of classical tragedy or comedy can be found in any one of them. In the manuscripts, they are called *officium*, *ordo*, *ludus*, *miraculum*, *repraesentatio* and the like, but very rarely *comoedia* or *tragoedia*, and never before 1204 [3]. From the Latin the mediaeval notions of tragedy and comedy were transferred to similar compositions in the vernaculars. Dante's *Divina Commedia* is just a story which begins in Hell and ends in Paradise [4].

[1] Cloetta, i. 4; Teuffel, ii. 506. Blossius Aemilius Dracontius was a Carthaginian poet. The *Orestes* is printed in L. Baehrens, *Poet. Lat. Min.* (*Bibl. Teub.*), v. 218. There seems a little doubt whether the title *Orestis tragoedia* in the Berne MS. is due to the author or to a scribe. The Ambrosian MS. has *Horestis fabula*.

[2] Creizenach, i. 12.

[3] Ibid. i. 7; Cloetta, i. 49. The *ludus prophetarum* played at Riga in 1204 (p. 70) is called 'ludus ... quam Latini comoediam vocant.' Probably this is a bit of learning on the part of the chronicler; cf. the Michael-House instance (p. 344). For scraps from non-dramatic classical authors in liturgical plays, cf. p. 48. The 'theatricales ludi' of Innocent III and others (vol. i. p. 40; vol. ii. p. 99) seem to be not miracle-plays, but the Feast of Fools and similar mummings.

[4] Dante, *Dedicatio* of *Paradiso* to Can Grande (*Opere Latine*, ed. Giuliani, ii. 44) 'est comoedia genus quoddam poeticae narrationis ... Differt ergo a tragoedia in materia per hoc quod tragoedia in principio est admirabilis et quieta, in fine sive exitu est foetida et horribilis ... comoedia vero inchoat asperitatem alicuius rei, sed eius materia prospere terminatur.' P. Toynbee (*Romania*, xxvi. 542) shows that Dante substantially owed these definitions to the *Magnae Derivationes* of the late twelfth-century writer, Uguccione da Pisa.

Boccaccio[1], Chaucer[2], and Lydgate[3] use precisely similar language. And, right up to the end of the sixteenth century, 'tragedy' continues to stand for 'tragical legend' with the authors of the *Mirror for Magistrates* and their numerous successors[4]. Long before this, of course, humanistic research, without destroying their mediaeval sense, had restored to the wronged terms their proper connotation. There is a period during which it is a little difficult to say what, in certain instances, they do mean. When Robert Bower, in 1447, speaks of *comoediae* and *tragoediae* on the theme of Robin Hood and Little John, it is a matter for conjecture whether he is referring to dramatized May-games or merely to ballads[5]. Bale, in writing of his contemporaries, certainly applies the words to plays; but when he ascribes *tragoedias vulgares* to Robert Baston, a Carmelite friar of the time of Edward II, it is probable that he is using, or quoting a record which used, an obsolescent terminology[6]. What the *comoediae* of John Scogan, under Edward IV, may have been, must remain quite doubtful[7].

It is in the early fourteenth century and in Italy that a renewed interest in the Latin dramatists, other than Terence, can first be traced. Seneca became the subject of a commentary by the English Dominican Nicholas Treveth, and also attracted the attention of Lovato de' Lovati and the scholarly circle which gathered round him at Padua. The chief of these was Albertino Mussato, who about 1314 was moved by indignation at the intrigues of Can Grande of Verona to write his *Ecerinis* on the fate of that Ezzelino who, some eighty

[1] Boccaccio's *Ameto* bears the sub-title *Comedia delle Ninfe fiorentine*.

[2] Chaucer, *Monk's Prologue*, (*C. T.* 13,999):

'Or elles first Tragedies wol I telle
Of whiche I have an hundred in
  my celle.
Tragedie is to seyn a certeyn storie,
As olde bokes maken us memorie,
Of him that stood in greet pros-
  peritee
And is y-fallen out of heigh degree
Into miserie, and endeth wrecched-
  ly.'

Cf. the gloss in his *Boethius*, ii. pr. 2, 78, to the passage already quoted on p. 20[illegible]; and the description of *Troilus* in *T. C.* v. 1786.

[3] Lydgate, *Fall of Princes*, prol.:

'My maister Chaucer with his
  fressh commedies,
Is deed, alas, chefe poete of
  Bretayne:
That sometyme made full pitous
  tragedies.'

[4] W. F. Trench, *A Mirror for Magistrates; its Origin and Influence* (1898), 18, 76, 82, 120, 125.

[5] Cf. vol. i. p. 177.

[6] Bale, i. 370.

[7] Ibid. ii. 68.

years before, had tyrannized over Padua. This first of the Senecan tragedies of the Renascence stirred enthusiasm amongst the growing number of the *literati*. It was read aloud and Mussato was laureated before the assembled university. Two learned professors paid it the tribute of a commentary. The example of Mussato was followed in the *Achilleis* (1390) of Antonio de' Loschi of Vicenza and the *Progne* (†1428) of Gregorio Corraro of Mantua. Petrarch was familiar not only with Terence, but also with Seneca and Plautus, and his *Philologia*, written before 1331 and then suppressed, may claim to take rank with the *Ecerinis* as the first Renascence comedy. It was modelled, says Boccaccio, upon Terence. A fresh impulse was given to the study and imitation of Latin comedy in 1427 by the discovery of twelve hitherto unknown Plautine plays, including the *Menaechmi* and the *Miles Gloriosus*, and various attempts were made to complete the imperfect plays. In 1441 Leonardo Dati of Florence introduced a motive from the *Trinummus* into his, not comedy, but tragedy of *Hiempsal*[1].

It must be borne in mind that during these early stages of humanism classical models and neo-Latin imitations alike were merely read and not acted. There is no sign whatever that as yet the mediaeval misconception as to the nature of Roman scenic representation had come to an end. It was certainly shared by Nicolas Treveth and probably by both Petrarch and Boccaccio[2]. It was not indeed in these regular dramas that the habit of acting Latin first re-established itself, but in a mixed and far less classical type of play. It is probable that in schools the exercise of reciting verse, and amongst other verse dialogue, had never died out since the time of the Empire. In the fourth century the *Ludus Septem Sapientum* of the Bordeaux schoolmaster Ausonius, which consists of no more than a set of verses and a '*Plaudite!*' for each sage, was doubtless written for some such purpose[3]. Such also may have been the destiny of the 'elegiac' and

[1] Cloetta, ii. 4, 11, 91, 147; Creizenach, i. 487, 529, 572; Bahlmann, *Ern.* 9, 13, 15, 30, 40.

[2] Cloetta, ii. 69, 221; Creizenach, i. 490, 510, 580.

[3] The earliest printed text (†1473) of Claudian's *De Raptu Proserpinae* is from a version arranged as two pseudo-dramas (Cloetta, i. 135).

'epic' comedies and tragedies of which a fair number were produced, from the eleventh century to the thirteenth. These are comedies and tragedies, primarily, in the mediaeval sense. They are narrative poems in form. But in all of them a good deal of dialogue is introduced, and in some there is hardly anything else. Their subject-matter is derived partly from Terence and partly from the stock of motives common to all forms of mediaeval light literature. Their most careful student, Dr. Cloetta, suggests that they were intended for a half-dramatic declamation by minstrels. This may sometimes have been the case, but the capacity and the audience of the minstrels for Latin were alike limited, and I do not see why at any rate the more edifying of them may not have been school pieces[1]. By the fifteenth century it will be remembered, students, who had long been in the habit of performing miracle-plays, had also taken to producing farces, morals, and those miscellaneous comic and satiric pieces which had their origin in the folk-festivals. Many of these were in the vernaculars; but it is difficult to avoid classing with them a group of Latin dialogues and loosely constructed comedies, written in Terentian metres and presenting a curious amalgam of classical and mediaeval themes. Of hardly any of these can it be said positively that they were intended to be acted. This is, however, not unlikely in the case of the anonymous *Columpnarium*, which goes back to the fourteenth century. Pavia probably saw a performance of Ugolini Pisani's *Confabulatio coquinaria* (1435), which has all the characteristics of a carnival drollery, and certainly of Ranzio Mercurino's *De Falso Hypocrita*, which is stated in the manuscript to have been '*acta*' there on April 15, 1437. The *Admiranda* of Alberto Carrara was similarly '*acta*' at Padua about 1456. The exact way in which these pieces and others like them were performed must remain doubtful. Acting in the strict sense can only be distinctly asserted

[1] Cloetta, i, *passim*; Creizenach, i. 20; Peiper, *Die profane Komödie des Mittelalters*, in *Archiv f. Litteraturgeschichte*, v. 497. Some of the texts are in Müllenbach, *Comoediae Elegiacae* (1885), and T. Wright, *Early Mysteries and other Latin Poems* (1844). Cloetta gives references for the rest.

of Francesco Ariosto's dialogue of *Isis* which was given '*per personatos*' at the Ferrara carnival of 1444 [1].

All this pseudo-classic comedy was looked upon with scorn by the purists of humanism. But it made its way over the Alps and had a considerable vogue in Germany. In France it found an exponent in Jean Tissier de Ravisy (Ravisius Textor), professor of rhetoric in the College of Navarre at Paris, and afterwards rector of the Paris University, who wrote, in good enough Latin, but wholly in the mediaeval manner, a large number of morals, farces, and dialogues for representation by his pupils [2]. Two at least of these were turned into English interludes. The classical element predominates in the pseudo-Homeric *Thersites*, the production of which can be fixed to between October 12 and 24, 1537; the mediaeval in Thomas Ingelend's *The Disobedient Child*, which belongs to the very beginning of the reign of Elizabeth.

It was doubtless the study of Vitruvius which awakened the humanists to the fact that their beloved comedies had after all been acted after very much the fashion so long familiar in farces and miracle-plays. Exactly when the knowledge came is not clear. Polydore Vergil is still ignorant, and even Erasmus, at the date of the *Adagia*, uncertain. Alberti put a *theatrum* in the palace built on the Vatican for Nicholas V about 1452, but there is no record of its use for dramatic performances at that time, and the immediate successors of Nicholas did not love humanism. Such performances seem to have been first undertaken by the pupils of a Roman professor, Pomponius Laetus. Amongst these was Inghirami, who was protagonist in revivals of the *Asinaria* of Plautus and the *Phaedra* of Seneca. These took place about 1485. Several other representations both of classical plays and of neo-Latin imitations occurred in Italy before the end of the century; and the practice spread to other countries affected by the humanist wave, soon establishing itself as part of the regular sixteenth-century scheme of education. By this time, of course, Greek as well as Latin dramatic models were avail-

[1] Creizenach, i. 533, 548, 563, 581; Bahlmann, *Ern.* 13, 36, 38, 44, 48.

[2] Creizenach, i. 569; ii. 23, 43, 59; Bahlmann, *L. D.* 31; Julleville, *Les Com.* 298; J. Bolte, in *Vahlen-Festschrift* (1900), 589.

able. The Latin translation of the *Plutus* of Aristophanes by Leonardo Bruni (†1427) found several successors, and the play was acted at Zwickau in 1521. The study of Sophocles and Euripides began with Francesco Filelfo (†1481), but no representations of these authors are mentioned [1].

The outburst of dramatic activity in English schools and universities during the first half of the sixteenth century has already been noted. Wolsey may claim credit for an early encouragement of classical comedy in virtue of the performances of the *Menaechmi* and the *Phormio* given in his house by the boys of St. Paul's in 1527 and 1528 [2]. The master of St. Paul's from 1522 to 1531 was John Ritwise, who himself wrote a Latin play of *Dido*, which also appears to have been acted before Wolsey [3]. The *Plutus* was given at St. John's College, Cambridge, in 1536; the *Pax* at Trinity about a decade later [4]. A long series of English translations of classical plays begins with one of the *Andria* printed, possibly by John Rastell, under the title of *Terens in Englysh* [5].

A more important matter is the influence exercised by classical models upon the vernacular interludes. This naturally showed itself in school dramas, and only gradually filtered down to the professional players. Two plays compete for the honour of ranking as 'the first regular English comedy,' a term which is misleading, as it implies a far more complete break with the past than is to be discerned in either of them. One is Nicholas Udall's *Ralph Roister Doister*, the per-

[1] Creizenach, ii. 1, 71, 88, 370, 374; Heiland, *Dramatische Aufführungen*, in K. A. Schmid, *Enc. d. gesammten Erziehungs- und Unterrichtswesens* (2nd ed. 1876–87).

[2] Cf. p. 196.

[3] A. Wood, *Athenae* (ed. Bliss), i. 35, s. v. *Lilly*, says that Ritwise 'made the Tragedy of Dido out of Virgil; and acted the same with the scholars of his school before cardinal Wolsey with great applause.' The date of this performance is given in the *D. N. B.*, through a confusion with the anti-Lutheran play at court (cf. p. 196), as 1527. It is often identified with the *Dido* played before Elizabeth at Cambridge in 1564. But there is no reason to doubt the statement of Hatcher's sixteenth-century MS. account of King's College (transcript in *Bodl.* 11,614) that the author of this was Edward Halliwell, who, like Ritwise, was a fellow of the college.

[4] Cf. p. 195.

[5] For the translation of the *Philoktetes* of Sophocles by Roger Ascham, cf. p. 195. Bale, *Scriptores* (1557), i. 720, mentions a translation from Greek into Latin of *tragoedias quasdam Euripidis* by Thomas Keye or Caius († 1550).

formance of which can be dated with some confidence in 1553, by which time its author may already have been head master of Westminster; the other is *Gammer Gurton's Needle*, which was put on the stage at Christ's College, Cambridge, has been ascribed to John Still, afterwards bishop of Bath and Wells, and to John Bridges, afterwards bishop of Oxford, but is more probably the work of one William Stevenson, who was certainly superintending plays at Christ's College in 1550–3. Both plays adopt the classical arrangement by acts and scenes. But of the two *Gammer Gurton's Needle* is far closer to the mediaeval farce in its choice and treatment of subject. *Ralph Roister Doister*, although by no means devoid of mediaeval elements, is in the main an adaptation of the *Miles Gloriosus* of Plautus. A slighter and rather later piece of work, *Jack Juggler*, was also intended for performance by schoolboys, and is based upon the *Amphitruo*. The earliest 'regular English tragedy' on Senecan lines, or at least the earliest which oblivion has spared, is the *Gorboduc* or *Ferrex and Porrex* of 1561. This falls outside the strict scope of this chapter. But a fragment of a play from the press of John Rastell (1516–33) which introduccs 'Lucrcs' and Publius Cornelius, suggests that, here as elsewhere, the Elizabethan writers were merely resuming the history of the earlier English Renascence, which religious and political disturbances had so wofully interrupted.

Towards the end of Henry VIII's reign, the course of the developing interlude was further diverted by a fresh wave of humanist influence. This came from the wing of the movement which had occupied itself, not only with erudition, but also with the spiritual stirrings that issued in the Reformation. It must be borne in mind that the attitude of mere negation which the English Puritans, no doubt with their justification in 'antiquity,' came to adopt towards the stage, was by no means characteristic of the earlier Protestantism. The Lutheran reformers were humanists as well as theologians, and it was natural to them to shape a literary weapon to their own purposes, rather than to cast it aside as unfit for furbishing. About 1530 a new school of neo-Latin drama arose in Holland, which stood in much closer relations to mediaevalism than that which had had its origin in Italy. It aimed at applying the structure and the style of Terence to an edifying subject-matter drawn from the tradition of the religious drama. The English *Everyman* belongs to a group of related plays, both in Latin and in the vernaculars, on its moral theme. The *Acolastus* (1530, acted 1529) of William Gnaphaeus and the *Asotus* (1537, written †1507) of George Macropedius began a cycle of 'Prodigal Son' plays which had many branches. The movement began uncontroversially, but developed Protestant tendencies. It spread to Basle, where Sixt Birck, who called himself Xystus Betuleius, wrote a *Susanna* (1537), an *Eva* (1539), a *Judith* (1540), and to France, where the Scotchman George Buchanan added to the 'Christian Terence' a 'Christian Seneca' in the *Jephthes* (1554) and *Baptistes* (1564) performed, between 1540 and 1543, by his students at Bordeaux. In these, which are but a few out of many similar plays produced at this period, the humanists drew in the main upon such scriptural subjects, many of them apocryphal or parabolic, as were calculated, while no doubt making for edification, at the same time to afford scope for a free portrayal of human life. This on the whole, in spite of the treatment of such episodes as the Magdalen *in gaudio*, was a departure from the normal mediaeval usage[1].

A new note, of acute and even violent controversy, was introduced into the Protestant drama by the fiery heretic, Thomas Kirchmayer, or Naogeorgos. Kirchmayer wrote several plays, but the most important from the present point of view is that of *Pammachius* (1538), written during his pastorate of Sulza in Thuringia before his extreme views had led, not merely to exile from the Empire, but also to a quarrel with Luther. The *Pammachius* goes back to one of the most interesting, although of course not one of the

[1] Creizenach, ii. 74; Herford, 84; Ward, i. 120; Bahlmann, *L. D.* 39, 53, 66, 82. Many plays of this school are in *Comoediae et Tragoediae aliquot ex Novo et Vetere Testamento desumptae* (Brylinger, Basle, 1540) and *Dramata Sacra* (Oporinus, Basle, 1547).

most usual, themes of mediaeval drama, that of Antichrist; and it will readily be conceived that, for Kirchmayer, the Antichrist is none other than the Pope. It is interesting to observe that the play was dedicated to Archbishop Cranmer, whose reforming *Articles* of 1536 had roused the expectations of Protestant Germany. It was translated into English by John Bale, and was certainly not without influence in this country[1].

Both the merely edifying and the controversial type of Lutheran drama, indeed, found its English representatives. To the former belong the *Christus Redivivus* (1543) and the *Archipropheta* (1548) of the Oxford lecturer, Nicholas Grimald, one of which deals, somewhat exceptionally at this period, with the Resurrection, the other with John the Baptist. The *Absalon* of Thomas Watson, the *Jephthes* of John Christopherson (1546)[2], and the *Sodom*, *Jonah*, *Judith*, *Job*, *Susanna*, and *Lazarus and Dives* of Ralph Radclif (1546–56)[3], can only conjecturally be put in this class; and Nicholas Udall, who wrote an *Ezechias* in English, certainly did not commit himself irrecoverably in the eyes of good Catholics. John Palsgrave's *Ecphrasis* or paraphrase of *Acolastus* (1540) is supplied with grammatical notes, and is conceived wholly in the academic interest. On the other hand controversy is suggested in the titles of Radclif's *De Iohannis Hussi Damnatione*, and of the *De Meretrice Babylonica* ascribed by Bale to Edward VI[4], and is undeniably present in the *Christus Triumphans* (1551) of John Foxe, the martyrologist. This, like *Pammachius*, to which it owes much, belongs to the Antichrist cycle.

Nor was controversy confined to the learned language. As Protestantism, coquetted with by Henry VIII, and en-

[1] Creizenach, ii. 76; Herford, 119; Bahlmann, *L. D.* 71. The play is in Brylinger, 314. A recent edition is that by Bolte and Schmidt (1891).

[2] Cf. p. 195. Both Thomas Artour, of Cambridge (ob. 1532), who wrote a *Microcosmum, tragoediam*, and a *Mundum plumbeum, tragoediam* (Bale, i. 709), and John Hooker (ob. †1543), of Magdalen College, Oxford, who wrote a *comoediam, scilicet Piscatorem . . . alio titulo Fraus illusa vocatur* (Bale, i. 712), seem to have been Protestants, but nothing is known of the character of their plays, which may have been either English or Latin.

[3] Cf. p. 197.

[4] Bale, *Scriptores*, i. 674. It was written in his eleventh year (1547–8): cf. his *Remains*, i. xvi.

couraged by Cromwell, became gradually vocal in England and awakened an equally resonant reply, the vernacular drama, like every other form of literary expression, was swept into the war of creeds. This phase, dominating even the professional players, endured through the reigns of Edward VI and Mary, and still colours the early Elizabethan interludes. Its beginnings were independent of the Lutheran influences that so profoundly affected its progress. The morality already contained within itself that tendency to criticism which was perhaps the easiest way to correct its insipidity. Historically it was politics rather than religion with which the interlude first claimed to interfere. The story begins, harmlessly enough, at court, with an allegorical 'disguising' during the visit of the Emperor Charles V to London in 1523, in which the French king, typified by an unruly horse, was tamed by Amitie, who stood for the alliance between Charles and Henry [1]. In 1526 John Roo's morality, played at Gray's Inn, of 'Lord Governaunce' and 'Lady Publike-Wele' wrung Wolsey's withers, although as a matter of fact it was twenty years old [2]. Religion was first touched in 1527 in a piece of which one would gladly know more. It was played, as it seems, in Latin and French by the St. Paul's boys under John Ritwise, before ambassadors from France. The subject was the captivity of the Pope, and amongst the singular medley of characters named are found 'the herretyke, Lewtar' and 'Lewtar's wyfe, like a frowe of Spyers in Almayn [3].' This was, no doubt, all in the interests of orthodoxy; and a similar tone may be assumed in the comedies acted before Wolsey in the

[1] Hall, 641.

[2] Hall, 719; Collier, i. 103.

[3] Hall, 735; Collier, i. 104; Brewer, iv. 1603; Brown, *Venetian Papers*, iv. 208; Cavendish, *Life of Wolsey*, i. 136. The characters further included 'an oratur,' a Poet, Religion, Ecclesia, Veritas, Heresy, False Interpretation, 'Corrupcio Scriptoris,' St. Peter, St. Paul, St. James, a Cardinal, two Serjeants, the Dauphin and his brother, a Messenger, three 'Almayns,' 'Lady Pees,' 'Lady Quyetnes,' 'Dame Tranquylyte.' Brandl, lvi suggests that the play might have been related to the *Ludus ludentem Luderum ludens* of Johannes Hasenberg (1530), and the analysis of this piece given by Bahlmann, *L. D.* 48, shows that the two had several characters in common. Another anti-Luther play, the *Monachopornomachia* (1538) of Simon Lemnius (Bahlmann, *L. D.* 70), appears to be distinct.

following year on the release of the Pope[1]. But much water passed under the mill in the next few years, and in 1533 there was a comedy at court 'to the no little defamation of certain cardinals[2].' In the same year, however, a proclamation forbade 'playing of enterludes' 'concerning doctrines in matters now in question and controversie[3].' This is a kind of regulation which it is easier to make than to enforce. Its effect, if it had any, was not of long duration. In 1537 much offence was given to Bishop Gardiner, the Chancellor of Cambridge University, by the performance amongst the youth of Christ's College of a 'tragedie,' part at least of which was 'soo pestiferous as were intolerable.' This 'tragedie' was none other than the redoubtable *Pammachius* itself[4]. In the same year, strict orders were issued to stay games and unlawful assemblies in Suffolk, on account of a 'seditious May-game' which was 'of a king, how he should rule his realm,' and in which 'one played Husbandry, and said many things against gentlemen more than was in the book of the play[5].' These were exceptional cases. Both the students of Christ's and the Suffolk rustics had in their various ways overstepped the permitted mark. Certainly Henry was not going to have kingship called in question on a village green. But it is notorious that, in matters of religion, he secretly encouraged many obstinate questionings which he openly condemned. And there is evidence that Cromwell at least found the interlude a very convenient instrument for the encouragement of Protestantism. Bale tells us that he himself won the minister's favour *ob editas comedias*[6]; and there is extant amongst his papers a singular letter of this same year 1537, from Thomas Wylley, the vicar of Yoxford in Suffolk, in which he calls attention to three plays he has written, and asks that he may

[1] Brown, *Venetian Papers*, iv. 229.

[2] Herbert of Cherbury, *Life of Henry VIII* (Kennet, *Hist. of England*, ii. 173).

[3] Collier, i. 119, quoting Foxe, *Martyrologie* (1576), 1339.

[4] Herford, 129; Mullinger, *Hist. of Cambridge*, ii. 74; Cooper, *Annals of Cambridge*, i. 422; J. Peile, *Christ's College*, 48. The correspondence about the play between Gardiner and Parker is printed in full in J. Lamb, *Collection of Documents from C. C. C. C.* (1838), 49.

[5] Brewer, xii. 1. 557, 585.

[6] Bale, *Scriptores*, i. 702. Cf. also S. R. Maitland, *Essays on the Reformation*, 182.

have 'fre lyberty to preche the trewthe[1].' Cranmer, too, seems to have been in sympathy with Cromwell's policy, for in 1539 there was an enterlude at his house which a Protestant described as 'one of the best matiers that ever he sawe towching King John,' and which may quite possibly have been John Bale's famous play[2].

The position was altered after 1540, when Cromwell had fallen and the pendulum of Henry's conscience had swung back to orthodoxy. Foxe records how under the *Act Abolishing Diversity in Opinions* (1539), known as the *Act of the Six Articles*, one Spencer, an ex-priest who had become an interlude-player, was burned at Salisbury for 'matter concerning the sacrament of the altar'; and how, in London, one Shermons, keeper of the Carpenters' Hall in Shoreditch, 'was presented for procuring an interlude to be openly played, wherein priests were railed on and called knaves[3].' But the stage was by now growing difficult to silence. In 1542 the bishops petitioned the king to correct the acting of plays 'to the contempt of God's Word[4]'; and in 1543 their desire

[1] Brewer, xii. 1. 244; Collier, i. 128. 'The Lorde make you the instrument of my helpe, Lorde Cromwell, that I may have fre lyberty to preche the trewthe.

I dedycat and offer to your Lordeshype A Reverent Receyving of the Sacrament, as a Lenton matter, declaryd by vj chyldren, representyng Chryst, the worde of God, Paule, Austyn, a Chylde, a Nonne callyd Ignorancy; as a secret thyng that shall have hys ende ons rehersyd afore your eye by the sayd chyldren.

The most part of the prystes of Suff. wyll not reseyve me ynto ther chyrchys to preche, but have dysdaynyd me ever synns I made a play agaynst the popys Conselerrs, Error, Colle Clogger of Conscyens, and Incredulyte. That, and the Act of Parlyament had not folowyd after, I had be countyd a gret lyar.

I have made a playe caulyd A Rude Commynawlte. I am a makyng of a nother caulyd The Woman on the Rokke, yn the fyer of faythe a fynyng, and a purgyng in the trewe purgatory; never to be seen but of your Lordshyp's eye.

Ayde me for Chrystys sake that I may preche chryst.

Thomas Wylley
of Yoxforthe Vykar
fatherlesse and forsaken.'

[2] Brewer, xiv. 1. 22; Collier, i. 124.

[3] Foxe, *Acts and Monuments* (ed. Cattley), v. 443, 446.

[4] Brewer, xvii. 79; Wilkins, iii. 860. About the same date a *Discourse* (*Cotton MSS. Faustina*, C. ii. 5) addressed by Sir Richard Morison to Henry VIII is described by Brewer xvii. 707 as proposing 'a yearly memorial of the destruction of the bishop of Rome out of the realm, as the victory of Agincourt is annually celebrated at Calais, and the destruction of the Danes at Hoptide (*sic*: cf. vol. i. p. 154). It would be better that the plays of Robin Hood and Maid Marian should be forbidden, and others devised to set forth and declare lively before the people's

was met by the *Act for the Advauncement of true Religion and for the Abolishment of the Contrary*, which permitted of 'plays and enterludes for the rebukyng and reproching of vices and the setting forth of vertue'; but forbade such as meddled with 'interpretacions of scripture, contrary to the doctryne set forth or to be set forth by the kynges maiestie[1].' This led to a vigorous protest from John Bale, writing under the pseudonym of Henry Stalbridge, in his *Epistel Exhortatorye of an Inglyshe Christian.* Its repeal was one of the first measures passed under Edward VI[2].

Lord Oxford's men were playing in Southwark at the very hour of the dirge for Henry in the church of St. Saviour's[3]. Almost immediately 'the Poope in play' and 'prests in play' make their appearance once more[4]. Edward himself wrote his comedy *De Meretrice Babylonica.* In 1551 the English comedies 'in demonstration of contempt for the Pope' were reported by the Venetian ambassador to his government[5]. But the players were not to have quite a free hand. It was now the Catholic interludes that needed suppression. A proclamation of August 6, 1549, inhibited performances until the following November in view of some 'tendyng to sedicion[6].' The *Act of Uniformity* of the same year forbade interludes

eyes the abomination and wickedness of the bishop of Rome, the monks, friars, nuns and such like, and to declare the obedience due to the King.' In 1543 the Lord Mayor complained to the Privy Council of the 'licentious manner of players.' Certain joiners, who were the Lord Warden's players, were imprisoned and reprimanded for playing on Sunday (*P. C. Acts*, i. 103, 109, 110, 122).

[1] 34, 35 *Hen. VIII*, c. 1; Hazlitt, *E. D. S.* 3; Collier, i. 127. A proclamation of May 26, 1545 (Hazlitt, *E. D. S.* 6), states an intention to employ in the fleet 'all such ruffyns, Vagabonds, Masterles men, Comon players and euill disposed persons' as haunt 'the Banke, and such like naughtie places,' and forbids the retaining of servants, other than household servants or others allowed by law or royal licence. I have already (p. 185) called attention to the ambiguity of the term 'comon player,' and on the whole, in view of a reference in the proclamation to 'theft and falsehood in play' I think that gamblers are here in question. In any case the protected players were not suppressed.

[2] 1 *Edw. VI*, c. 12.

[3] *S. P. Dom. Edw. VI*, i. 5; Collier, i. 135.

[4] Kempe, 64, 74, with a list of personages for precisely such a play. W. Baldwin, on whom cf. pp. 194, 200, and *Modern Quarterly*, i. 259, was probably a dramatist of this temper.

[5] Brown, *Venetian Papers*, v. 347; cf. the letters between Gardiner and Somerset, quoted by Maitland, *Essays on the Reformation*, 228, from Foxe, vi. 31, 57.

[6] Hazlitt, *E. D. S.* 8; Collier, i. 142; Fuller, *Ch. Hist.* (1655), 391.

'depraving and despising' the *Book of Common Prayer*[1]. A more effective measure came later in a proclamation of 1551, requiring either for the printing or the acting of plays a licence by the king or the privy council[2]. Mary, at whose own marriage with Philip in 1554 there were Catholic interludes and pageants[3], issued a similar regulation in 1553, though naturally with a different intention[4]. But this was not wholly effectual, and further orders and much vigilance by the Privy Council in the oversight of players were required in the course of the reign[5].

Only a few texts from this long period of controversial drama have come down to us. On the Catholic side there is but one, the play of *Respublica* (1553). In this, and in the Protestant fragment of *Somebody, Avarice and Minister*, the ruling literary influence is that of Lyndsay's *Satyre of the Thre Estaitis*. Of the remaining Protestant plays, *Nice Wanton* (1560) and Thomas Ingelend's *The Disobedient Child* (n. d.) derive from the Dutch school of Latin drama and its offshoots. *Nice Wanton* is an adaptation of the *Rebelles* (1535) of Macropedius. *The Disobedient Child* has its relations, not only to the play of Ravisius Textor already mentioned, but also to the *Studentes* (1549) of Christopher Stymmelius. More distinctly combative in tendency is the *Lusty Juventus* (n. d.) of R. Wever, who may be reckoned as a disciple of John Bale. The activity of Bale himself can be somewhat obscurely discerned as the strongest impelling

[1] 2, 3 *Edw. VI*, c. 1.

[2] Hazlitt, *E. D. S.* 9; Collier, i. 144. In 1550 'il plaiers' were sought for in Sussex (*Remains* of Edward VI, ii. 280). In 1551 the council gave Lord Dorset a licence for his players to play in his presence only (*P. C. Acts*, iii. 307). In 1552 Ogle sent to Cecil a forged licence taken from some players (*S. P. Dom. Edw. VI*, xv. 33).

[3] Holinshed (1808), iv. 61.

[4] Hazlitt, *E. D. S.* 15; Collier, i. 155; *P. C. Acts*, iv. 426.

[5] *S. P. Dom. Mary*, viii. 50; *P. C. Acts*, v. 234, 237; vi. 102, 110, 118, 148, 168, 169. In Feb. 1556 the council sent Lord Rich to inquire into a stage-play to be given at Shrovetide at Hatfield Bradock, Essex, and directed him to stop such assemblies. An order against strolling players who spread sedition and heresy came in May. In June, 1557, performers of 'naughty' and 'lewd' plays were arrested in London and Canterbury. An order forbade plays throughout the country during the summer. In August a 'lewd' play called a 'Sackfull of News' was suppressed at the Boar's Head, Aldgate; and in September plays were forbidden in the city except, after licence by the ordinary, between All Saints and Shrovetide.

force on the Protestant side. He had his debts both to Lyndsay and to Kirchmayer, whose *Pammachius*, if not his other plays, he translated. But he is very largely original, and he is set apart from the other great figures of the Lutheran drama by the fact that all his plays were written *in idiomate materno.* Moreover, though not without classical elements, they were probably intended for popular performance, and approach more closely to the mediaeval structure than to that of the contemporary interlude. In his *Scriptores* he enumerates, under twenty-two titles, some forty-six of them. The five extant ones were probably all 'compiled' about 1538 while he was vicar of Thorndon in Suffolk. But some of them were acted at the market-cross of Kilkenny in 1553, and the others show signs of revision under Edward VI or even Elizabeth. In *God's Promises, John Baptist,* and *The Temptation,* Bale was simply adapting and Protestantizing the miracle-play. The first is practically a *Prophetae,* and they are all 'actes,' or as the Middle Ages would have said 'processes' or 'pageants,' from a scriptural cycle. Of similar character were probably a series of eleven plays extending from Christ in the Temple to the Resurrection. A *Vita D. Joannis Baptistae* in fourteen *libri* perhaps treated this favourite sixteenth-century theme in freer style. The polemics are more marked in *Three Laws,* which is a morality; and in *King John,* which is a morality varied by the introduction of the king himself as a champion against the Pope and of certain other historical figures. It thus marks an important step in the advance of the drama towards the treatment of individualities. With the *Three Laws* and *King John* may be grouped another set of lost plays whose Latinized titles point unmistakably to controversy. An *Amoris Imago* might be merely edifying; but it would be difficult to avoid meddling in matters of doctrine with such themes to handle as *De Sectis Papisticis, Erga Momos et Zoilos, Perditiones Papistarum, Contra Adulterantes Dei Verbum, De Imposturis Thomae Becketi.* A pair of plays *Super utroque Regis Coniugio,* must have been, if they were ever acted, a climax of audacity even for John Bale.

What then, in sum, was the heritage which the early

Elizabethan writers and players of interludes received from their immediate predecessors? For the writers there were the stimulus of classical method and a widened range both of intention and of material. Their claim was established to dispute, to edify, or merely to amuse. They stood on the verge of more than one field of enterprise which had been barely entered upon and justly appeared inexhaustible. 'Tragedy, comedy, history, pastoral, pastoral-comical, historical-pastoral, tragical-historical, tragical-comical-historical-pastoral'; they possessed at least the keys to them all. Their own work is a heterogeneous welter of all the dramatic elements of the past and the future. Belated morals and miracle-plays jostle with adaptations of Seneca and Plautus. The *dramatis personae* of a single play will afford the abstractions of the allegory and the types of the farce side by side with real living individualities; and the latter are drawn indifferently from contemporary society, from romance, from classical and from national history. These are precisely the dry bones which one day, beneath the breath of genius, should spring up into the wanton life of the Shakespearean drama. The players had made good their footing both in courts and amongst the folk. But their meddlings with controversy had brought upon them the hand of authority, which was not to be lightly shaken off. Elizabeth, like her brother, signalized the opening of her reign by a temporary inhibition of plays[1]; and her privy council assumed a jurisdiction, by no means nominal, over things theatrical. In their censorship they had the assistance of the bishop of London, as 'ordinary.' The lesser companies may have suffered from the statute of 1572 which confined the privilege of maintaining either minstrels or players of interludes to barons and personages of higher degree[2]. But the greater ones which had succeeded in establishing themselves in London, grew and flourished.

[1] The proclamation of 16 May 1559 is printed in Hazlitt, *E. D. S.* 19; Collier, i. 166; *N. S. S. Trans.* 1880–5, 17†. I do not think the proclamation loosely referred to by Holinshed (1587), iii. 1184, as at 'the same time' as another proclamation of 7 April is distinct from this. By 1 *Eliz.* c. 2 (the *Act of Uniformity*) the provision of 2, 3 *Edw. VI*, c. 1, against 'derogation, depraving or despising' the *Book of Common Prayer* in interludes was re-enacted with a penalty of 100 marks.

[2] Cf. vol. i. p. 54.

They lived down the competition of the amateurs which during the greater part of the century threatened to become dangerous, by their profitable system of double performances, at court and in the inn yards. Thus they secured the future of the drama by making it economically independent ; and the copestone of their edifice was the building of the permanent theatres. But for courtesy and a legal fiction, they were vagabonds and liable to whipping : yet the time was at hand when one player was to claim coat armour and entertain preachers to sack and supper at New Place, while another was to marry the daughter of a dean and to endow an irony for all time in the splendid College of God's Gift at Dulwich.

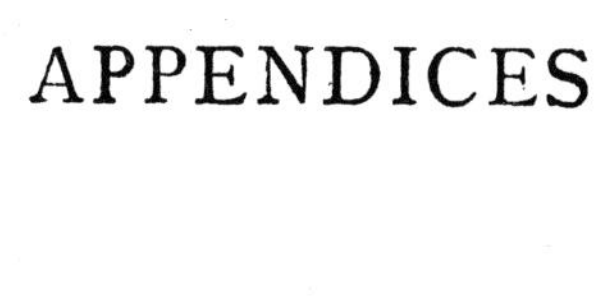

APPENDICES

APPENDICES

A

THE TRIBUNUS VOLUPTATUM

[The *tribunus voluptatum* was a municipal officer of the later Empire charged with the superintendence of the *spectacula*. He seems to have been appointed for life by the Emperor, and to have taken over functions formerly discharged by the praetors and quaestors. Mommsen, *Ostgothische Studien* (*Neues Archiv*, xiv. 495), says that he first appears in the fifth century. Possibly, therefore, Suetonius, *Tiberius*, 42, 'novum denique officium instituit a voluptatibus, praeposito equite R. T. Caesonio Prisco' refers to some other post. A *titulus*, 'de officio tribuni voluptatũ qđ a temelicis et scenariis,' which should be *C. Th.* i. 19, is missing from the text. *C. Th.* xv. 7, 13 (413), is addressed to the *tribunus voluptatum* of Carthage. The office was maintained in Italy under Theodoric (493–526). The *formula* of appointment here given is preserved by Cassiodorus, *Variae*, vii. 10; cf. *Var.* vi. 19 'cum lascivae voluptates recipiant tribunum.' The Senate is informed by *Var.* i. 43 (†509) of the promotion of Artemidorus, who had held the office, to be *praefectus urbanus*. The *tribunus voluptatum* of Rome is referred to in two inscriptions of 522 and 526 (Rossi, *Inscr. Christ.* i. Nos. 989, 1005). One Bacauda is appointed *tribunus voluptatum* in Milan by *Var.* v. 25 (523–6). Constantine Porphyrogenitus *de Caer.* i. 83 mentions an ἄρχων τῆς θυμέλης in the tenth-century court of Byzantium, who may be the same officer.]

Formula Tribuni Voluptatum.

Quamvis artes lubricae honestis moribus sint remotae et histrionum vita vaga videatur efferri posse licentia, tamen moderatrix providit antiquitas, ut in totum non effluerent, cum et ipsae iudicem sustinerent. amministranda est enim sub quadam disciplina exhibitio voluptatum. teneat scaenicos si non verus, vel umbratilis ordo iudicii. temperentur et haec legum qualitate negotia, quasi honestas imperet inhonestis, et quibusdam regulis vivant, qui viam rectae conversationis ignorant. student enim illi non tantum iucunditati suae, quantum alienae laetitiae et condicione perversa cum dominatum suis corporibus tradunt, servire potius animos compulerunt. Dignum fuit ergo moderatorem suscipere, qui se nesciunt iuridica conversatione tractare. locus quippe tuus his gregibus hominum veluti quidam tutor est positus. nam sicut illi aetates teneras adhibita cautela custodiunt, sic a te voluptates fervidae impensa maturitate frenandae sunt. age bonis institutis quod nimia prudentia constat invenisse maiores. leve desiderium etsi verecundia non cohibet, districtio praenuntiata modificat. agantur spectacula suis consuetudinibus ordinata, quia nec illi possunt invenire gratiam, nisi imitati fuerint aliquam disciplinam. Quapropter tribunum te voluptatum per illam indictionem nostra fecit electio, ut omnia sic agas, quemadmodum tibi vota civitatis adiungas, ne quod ad laetitiam constat inventum, tuis temporibus ad culpas videatur fuisse transmissum. cum fama diminutis salva tua opinione versare. castitatem dilige, cui subiacent prostitutae: ut magna laude dicatur: 'virtutibus studuit, qui voluptatibus miscebatur.' optamus enim ut per ludicram ammi-nistrationem ad seriam pervenias dignitatem.

B

TOTA IOCULATORUM SCENA

John of Salisbury, *Polycraticus* i. 8 (†1159, *P. L.* cxcix, 406), says, Satius enim fuerat otiari quam turpiter occupari. Hinc mimi, salii vel saliares, balatrones, aemiliani, gladiatores, palaestritae, gignadii, praestigiatores, malefici quoque multi, et tota ioculatorum scena procedit.' The specific terms belong to John of Salisbury's classical learning rather than to contemporary use; but his generic *ioculator* is the normal mediaeval Latin term for the minstrel in the widest sense. Classically the word, like its synonym *iocularis*, is an adjective, 'given to ioca,' 'merry.' Thus Cicero, *ad Att.* iv. 16. 3 'huic ioculatorem senem illum interesse sane nolui.' Similarly Firmicus Maternus (fourth century), *Mathesis*, viii. 22 'histriones faciat, pantomimos, ac scaenicos ioculatores,' and 4 *Conc. Carthag.* (398), c. 60 (*C. I. C. Decr. Gratiani*, i. 46. 6) 'clericum scurrilem et verbis turpibus ioculatorem ab officio retrahendum censemus.' Here the technical meaning is approached, which Gautier, ii. 12, declares to be complete in Salvian (fifth century), *de gubernatione Dei*. I cannot, however, find the word in Salvian, though I do find *iugulator*, 'cut-throat.' I have not come across *ioculator* as a noun before the eighth century (vol. i. p. 37), but thenceforward it is widely used for minstrels of both the *scôp* and the *mimus* type. A rarer form is *iocista. Iocul(ator* gives rise to the equally wide French term *jouglere, jougleur,* which seems to merge with the doublet *jogeler, jougler,* from *iocularis.* Similarly *ioca* becomes *jeu,* the equivalent of the classical and mediaeval Latin *ludus,* also in the widest sense. In Provençal *ioculator* becomes *joglar,* in English *jugelour, jugelere, jogeler,* &c. Thus *S. Eng. Leg.* i. 271 (†1290) 'Is iugelour a day bifore him pleide faste And nemde in his ryme and in is song þene deuel atþe laste'; King Horn (ed. Ritson), 1494 (†1300) 'Men seide hit were harperis, Jogelers, ant fythelers.' The incorrect modern French form *jongleur* seems due to a confusion between *jougleur* and *jangleur,* 'babbler,' and the English *jangler* has a similar use; cf. *Piers the Plowman,* B. Text, *passus* x. 31 (ed. Skeat, i. 286) 'Iaperes and Iogeloures, and Iangelers of gestes.' Here both words appear side by side. The English *jogelour* sometimes has the full sense of the French *jougleur,* as in the instances just given, but as a term for minstrels of the higher or *scôp* type it has to compete, firstly, with the native *gleeman,* from O. E. *gleoman, gligman,* and secondly, with *minstrel*; and as a matter of fact its commoner use is for the lower type of minstrel or buffoon, and in particular, in the exact sense of the modern *juggler,* for a conjuror, *tregetour* or *prestigiator.* The latter is the usual meaning of *jogelour,* with the cognate *jogelrye,* in Chaucer; for the former, cf. Adam Davie (†1312) 'the minstrels sing, the jogelours carpe.' In English documents the Latin *ioculator* itself to some extent follows suit; the *ioculator regis* of late fifteenth or early sixteenth-century accounts is not a minstrel or musician, but the royal *juggler* (cf. vol. i. p. 68). On the other hand the Provençal *joglar* is differentiated in the opposite sense, to denote a grade of minstrelsy raised above the mere *bufos* (vol. i. p. 63).

A street in Paris known at the end of the thirteenth century as the '*rue aus Jugléeurs,*' came later to be known as the *rue des Ménétriers* (Bernhard, iii. 378). This is significant of a new tendency in nomenclature which appears with the growth during the fourteenth century of the household entertainers at the expense of their unattached brethren of the road. *Minister* is classical Latin for 'inferior' and so 'personal attendant.' The *ministeriales* of the later Empire are officers personally appointed by the Emperor. Towards the end of the thirteenth century *minister,* with its diminutives *ministellus* and *ministrallus* (French *menestrel*), can be seen passing from the general sense of 'household attendant' to the special sense of 'household *ioculator.*' A harper was one of the *ministri* of Prince Edward in 1270 (vol. i. p. 49). Gautier, ii. 13, 51, quotes *li famles* (*famuli*) as a synonym for such *ioculatores*, and such doublets as 'menestrel et serviteur,' 'menestrel et varlet de chambre.' The *ministeralli* of Philip IV in 1288 include, with the musicians, the *rex heraudum* and the *rex ribaldorum*. From the beginning of the fourteenth century, however, *ministrallus*, with French *menestrel*, *menestrier*, and English *menestrel*, *mynstral*, is firmly established in the special sense. The antithesis between the *ministrallus* and the unattached *ioculator* appears in the terminology of the 1321 statutes of the Paris guild, 'menestreus et menestrelles, jougleurs et jougleresses'; but even this disappears, and the new group of terms becomes equivalent to the *ioculator* group in its widest sense. So too, *ministralcia*, *menestrardie*, *minstralcie*, although chiefly used, as by Chaucer, for music, are not confined to that; e. g. *Derby Accounts*, 109, 'cuidam tumblere facienti ministralciam suam.' The word is here approaching very near its kinsman *métier* (vol. ii. p. 105). Wright-Wülcker, 596, 693, quotes from the fifteenth-century glossaries, '*simphonia*, mynstrylsy,' and '*mimilogium*, mynstrisye.'

Ioculator and *ministrallus* are in their technical sense post-classical. But it is to be noted that the classical *histrio* and *mimus*, widened in connotation to an exact equivalent with these, remain in full use throughout the Middle Ages. They are indeed the more literary and learned words, as may be seen from the fact that they did not give rise to Romance or English forms; but they are not differentiated as to meaning. In particular, I do not find that *mimus* is used, as I have occasionally for convenience used it, to denote the lower minstrel of classical origin, as against the higher minstrel or *scóp*. Here are a few of many passages which go to establish this complete fourfold equivalence of *ioculator*, *ministrallus*, *mimus* and *histrio*; *Gloss.* in *B.N. MS.* 4883[a], f. 67[b] (Du Méril, *Or. Lat.* 23) 'istriones sunt ioculatores'; *Constit. regis Minorcae* (1337, Mabillon, *Acta SS. Bened. Ian.* iii. 27) 'In domibus principum, ut tradit antiquitas, mimi seu ioculatores licite possunt esse'; *Conc. Lateran.* (1215), c. 16 'mimis, ioculatoribus et histrionibus non intendant.' This triple formula, often repeated by ecclesiastics, is of course conjunctive, like 'rogues and vagabonds.' Guy of Amiens (†1068) calls Taillefer both *histrio* and *mimus* (vol. i. p. 43). At the beginning of the sixteenth century the royal minstrels are *histriones* in the accounts of Shrewsbury, *ministralli* in those of Winchester College (*App. E.* (*iv*)), *mimi* in those of Beverley (Leach, *Beverley MSS.* 171). The *ioculator regis*, as already said, is by this time distinct. The Scottish royal minstrels appear in the Exchequer

Rolls for 1433–50 as *mimi*, *histriones*, *ioculatores* (*L.H.T. Accounts*, i, cxcix). The town musicians of Beverley, besides their specific names of *waits* and *spiculatores*, have indifferently those of *histriones*, *ministralli*, *mimi* (Leach, *Beverley MSS. passim*). It is largely a matter of the personal taste of the scribe. Thus the Shrewsbury accounts have both *histriones* and *menstralles* in 1401, *histriones* in 1442, *ministralli* regularly from 1457 to 1479, and *histriones* regularly from 1483 onwards.

Many other names for minstrels, besides these dominant four, have been collected by scholars (Gautier, ii. 10; Julleville, *Les Com.* 17; Gröber, ii. 489; Bédier, 366). From the compliments exchanged in the *fabliau* of *Des Deux Bordeors Ribaux* (Montaiglon-Raynaud, i. 1) one may extract the equivalence of *menestrel*, *trouvère*, *ribaud*, *bordeor*, *jougleur*, *chanteur*, *lecheor*, *pantonnier*. Of such subordinate names many are specific, and have been dealt with in their turn in chh. iii, iv. Others, again, are abusive, and found chiefly in the mouths of ecclesiastics, or as distinctive of the lower orders of minstrels. There are *garcio*, *nebulo*, *delusor*, *saccularius*, *bufo*, *ribaud*, *harlot*. There are *bourdyour*, *japer*, *gabber*, *jangler* (vol. i. p. 84). There is *scurra*, an early and favourite term of this class; cf. Ælfric's gloss (Ducange, s.v. *Iocista*), '*Mimus*, *iocista*, *scurra*, gligmon'; Wright-Wülcker, 693 (fifteenth-century gloss), '*scurra*, harlot'; and vol. i. p. 32. There is *leccator*, *leccour* (cf. above and *App. F.* s.v. *Chester*). And finally, there are a few terms of general, but not very common, application. *Scenici* and *thymelici* come from the early Christian prohibitions (vol. i. pp. 12, 17, 24). More important are a group derived from *ludus*, which like *jeu* has itself the widest possible sense, covering every possible kind of amusement. The *Sarum Statutes* of 1319, in a *titulus* dealing with *histriones*, speak of those 'qui "menestralli" et quandoque "ludorum homines" vulgari eloquio nuncupantur' (vol. i. p. 40). In the fifteenth and sixteenth centuries appear such terms as *lusor*, *lusiator*, *ludens*, *interlusor*, *interludens*. The two latter of these are always specific, meaning 'actor'; the three former are usually so, although they may occasionally have the more general sense, and this is probably also true of the English *player*. This question is more fully discussed in vol. i. pp. 84, 393, and vol. ii. p. 185.

C

COURT MINSTRELSY IN 1306

[From *Manners and Household Expenses of England in the Thirteenth and Fifteenth Centuries*, 141 (Roxburghe Club, 1841), from Exchequer Roll (King's Remembrancer's Dept.) in Rolls Office. The Pentecost feast of 1306 was that at which Prince Edward, who became in the next year Edward II, was knighted. It is described in the *Annales Londonienses* (*Chronicles of Edward I and Edward II*, R. S. i. 146).]

Solutio facta diversis Menestrallis die Pentecostes anno xxxiiii^{to}.

[A.D. 1306.]

Le Roy de Champaigne Le Roy Capenny Le Roy Baisescue Le Roy Marchis Le Roy Robert	cuilibet v.*marc.*; summa, xvj.*li.* i.*marc.*
Phelippe de Caumbereye	lx.*s.*; summa, lx.*s.*
Robert le Boistous Gerard de Boloigne	cuilibet iiij.*marc.*; summa, c. vj.*s.* viij.*d.*
Bruant Northfolke	cuilibet xl.*s.*; summa, iiij.*li.*
Carltone Maistre Adam le Boscu Devenays	cuilibet xx.*s.*; summa, lx.*s.*
Artisien Lucat. Henuer	cuilibet xxx.*s.*; summa, iiij.*li.* [x.*s.*]
Le menestral Mons. de Montmaranci Le Roy Druet Janin le Lutour Gillotin le Sautreour Gillet de Roos Ricard de Haleford Le Petit Gauteron Baudec le Tabourer Ernolet Mahu qui est ove la dammoisele de Baar Janin de Brebant Martinet qui est ove le Conte de Warwike Gauteron le Grant	cuilibet xl.*s.*; summa, xxvj.*li.*

Le Harpour Levesque de Duresme — x.*s.*

Guillaume le Harpour qui est ove le Patriarke
Robert de Clou
Maistre Adam de Reve
Henri le Gigour
Corraud son compaignon
Le tierz Gigour
Gillot le Harpour
Johan de Newentone
Hugethun le Harpour lour compaignon
Adekin son compaignon
Adam de Werintone
Adam de Grimmeshawe
Hamond Lestivour
Mahuet qui est ove Mons. de Tounny
Johan de Mochelneye
Janin Lorganistre

} cuilibet ij.*marc.*; summa, xxj.*li.* di.*marc.*

Simond le Messager
Les ij. Trumpours Mons. Thomas de Brothertone
Martinet le Taborour
Richard Rounlo
Richard Hendelek
Janin de La Tour son compaignon
Johan le Waffrer le Roy
Pilk
Januche, Gillot } Trumpours Mons. le Prince
Le Nakarier
Le Gitarer
Merlin
Tomasin, Vilour Mons. Le Prince
Raulin qui est ove le Conte Mareschal
Esvillie qui est ove Mons. Pierres de Maule
Grendone
Le Taborer La Dame de Audham
Gaunsaillie
Guillaume sanz maniere
Lambyn Clay
Jaques Le Mascun
Son compaignon

} cuilibet j.*marc.*; summa, xl.*marc.*

Mahu du North
Le menestral ove les cloches
Les iij. menestraus Mons. de Hastinges
Thomelin de Thounleie
Les ij. Trompours le Comte de Hereforde
Perle in the eghe
Son compaignon
Janyn le Sautreour qui est ove Mons. de Percy
Les ij. Trumpours le Comte de Lancastre
Mellet
Henri de Nushom
Janyn le Citoler
Gilliame
Fairfax
Monet
Hanecocke de Blithe } cuilibet xx.*s.*; summa, iiij.*li.*

Summa totalis,—cxiiij.*li.* x.*s.*—Et issi demoerent des cc.*marc.*, pur partir entre les autres menestraus de la commune,—xviij.*li.* xvj.*s.* viij.*d.*—Et a ceste partie faire sunt assigne Le Roy Baisescu, Le Roy Marchis, Le Roy Robert, et Le Roy Druet, Gauteron le Graunt, Gauteron le Petit, Martinet le Vilour qui est ove le Conte de Warewike, et del hostiel Mons. le Prince, ij. scrjantz darmes . . . clerke.

[Five lines of which only a few words are legible.]

Richard le Harpour qui est ove le Conte de Gloucestre.
Wauter Bracon Trounpour
Wauter le Trounpour
Johan le Croudere
Tegwaret Croudere
Geffrai le Estiveur
Guillot le Taborer
Guillot le Vileur
Robert le Vilour
Jake de Vescy
Richard Whetacre

A ceux xj., por toute la commune, xvii.*li.* iiii.*s.* viii.*d.*

Denarii dati Menestrallis.

Vidulatori Dominae de Wak' . . . . . . v.*s.*
Laurentio Citharistae . . . . di.*marc.*
Johanni du Chat, cum Domino J. de Bur' . . . di.*marc.*

Mellers	v.*s.*
Parvo Willielmo, Organistae Comtissae Herefordiae .	v.*s.*
Ricardo de Quitacre, Citharistae	di.*marc.*
Ricardo de Leylonde, Citharistae	di.*marc.*
Carleton Haralde	v.*s.*
Gilloto Vidulatori Comitis Arundelliae	di.*marc.*
Amakyn Citharistae Principis	v.*s.*
Bolthede	v.*s.*
Nagary le Crouder Principis	v.*s.*
Matheu le Harpour	v.*s.*
Johanni le Barber	v.*s.*
ij. Trumpatoribus J. de Segrave	di.*marc.*
Ricardo Vidulatori Comitis Lancastriae . . .	v.*s.*
Johanni Waffrarario Comitis Lancastriae . . .	xl. *d.*
Sagard Crouther	xl. *d.*
William de Grymesar', Harpour	xl. *d.*
Citharistae Comitissae Lancastriae	xl. *d.*
ij. Menestrallis J. de Ber[wyke]	xl. *d.*
Henrico de Blida	xl. *d.*
Ricardo Citharistae	xl. *d.*
William de Duffelde	xl. *d.*
v. Trumpatoribus Principis, pueris, cuilibet ij.*s.* . .	x.*s.* in toto.
iiij[or]. Vigil' Regis, cuilibet di.*marc.*	xx.*s.*
Adinet le Harpour	
Perote le Taborer	
Adae de Swylingtone Citharistae	ij.*s.*
David le Crouther	xij.*d.*
Lion de Normanville	ij.*s.*
Gerardo	xij.*d.*
Ricardo Citharistae	ij.*s.*
Roberto de Colecestria	iij.*s.*
Johanni le Crouther de Salopia	xij.*d.*
Johanni le Vilour domini J. Renaude	xij.*d.*
Johanni de Trenham, Citharistae	ij.*s.*
Willielmo Woderove, Trumpatori	ij.*s.*
Johanni Citharistae J. de Clyntone	ij.*s.*
Waltero de Brayles	xij.*d.*
Roberto Citharistae Abbatis de Abbyndone . . .	xij.*d.*
Galfredo Trumpatori domini R. de Monte Alto . .	
Richero socio suo	ij.*s.*
Thomae le Croudere	ij.*s.*

Rogero de Corleye, Trumpatori . . . . . . ij.*s.*
Audoeno le Crouther . . . . xij.*d.*
Hugoni Daa Citharistae . . . . ij.*s.*
Andreae Vidulatori de Hor' . . . . . . ij.*s.*
Roberto de Scardeburghe . . . . xij.*d.*
Guilloto le Taborer Comitis Warrewici . . . iij.*s.*
Paul' Menestrallo Comitis Marescalli . . . . iij.*s.*
Matheo Waffraris domini R. de Monte Alto . . . ij.*s.*
iij. diversis menestrallis, cuilibet iij.*s.* . . . . ix.*s.*
Galfrido Citharistae Comitis Warrenniae . . . ij.*s.*
Matill' Makejoye . . . . xij.*d.*
Johanni Trumpatori domini R. de Filii Pagani . . xij.*d.*
Adae Citharistae domini J. Lestraunge. . . . xij.*d.*
Reginaldo le Menteur, Menestrallo domini J. de Buteturt xij.*d.*
Perle in the Eghe . . . . xij.*d.*
Gilloto Citharistae Domini P. de Malo Lacu . . x.*s.*
Roberto Gaunsillie . . . . xl.*d.* Item. xl.*d.*
Jacke de Vescy . . . . di.*marc.*
Magistro Waltero Leskirmissour et fratri suo, cuilibet iij.*s.* vj.*s.*

D

THE MINSTREL HIERARCHY

The term *rex* is not seldom applied as a distinction amongst minstrels. At the wedding of Joan of England in 1290 were present King Grey of England and King Caupenny of Scotland, together with Poveret, minstrel of the Marshal of Champagne (Chappell, i. 15). Poveret is perhaps the 'roy de Champaigne' of the 1306 list, which also includes the 'roys' Capenny, Baisescue, Marchis, Robert, and Druet (*Appendix C*). A 'rex Robertus,' together with 'rex Pagius de Hollandia,' reappears in accounts of the reign of Edward II (1307–27), while one of the minstrels of the king was William de Morlee, 'roy de North' (Percy, 416–8; cf. vol. i. p. 49). In France a list of the 'ministeralli' of Philip IV in 1288 includes the 'rex Flaiolatus,' 'rex Heraudum,' and 'rex Ribaldorum.' A certain Pariset, who was minstrel to the Comte de Poitiers in 1314, signs the statutes of the Paris guild in 1321 as 'Pariset, menestrel le roy,' and the various 'roys des menestreuls du royaume de France' who appear in and after 1338 may have been heads at once of the king's household minstrels and of the guild (*Appendix F*; cf. Bernhard, iii. 380). Further, the title is claimed by the authors of various pieces of minstrel literature. 'Adenet le roi' is the author of *Cleomadès* (Paris, 84; Percy, 416–8), and 'Huon le roi,' perhaps identical with 'Huon de Cambrai' and 'Huon Paucele,' of the *fabliau* of *Du Vair Palefroi* (Bedier, 438; Montaiglon-Raynaud, i. 3). The term *rex* is of course common enough in connexion with temporary or permanent associations of all sorts, and is probably of folk origin (vol. i. chaps. iv, viii). It is possible that some of these 'rois' may have been crowned by 'puis' (Lavoix, ii. 377), but it is more probable that they had some official pre-eminence amongst their fellows, and perhaps some jurisdiction, territorial or otherwise. Clearly this was the case with the 'roy des ministralx' at Tutbury. The appearance of the 'rex Flaiolatus' with the 'rex Heraudum' and the 'rex Ribaldorum' in the French list of 1288 is thus significant, for the latter had just such a jurisdiction over the riff-raff of the court (Ducange, s.v.), and I conceive the relation of the minstrel 'roys' to their fellows to have been much that of the 'Kings at arms' to the ordinary heralds. It seems that minstrels and heralds belonged to the same class of *ministri*. The order of the Emperor Henry II (vol. i. p. 52) couples 'ioculatores et armaturi' and 'Carleton Haralde' is actually rewarded in the 1306 list (*App. C*, p. 237). If one may quote a Celtic parallel, the *Arwyddfardd* or heralds formed a regular division (†1100) of Welsh minstrelsy (E. David, *La Poésie et la Musique dans la Cambrie*, 72–91). Under Richard II the head of the English royal minstrels was a *rex*, but from 1464 onwards the term used is *marescallus* (Rymer, xi. 512), and this again may be paralleled from the supreme position of the Earl Marshal in heraldry. At the head of the Earl of Lancaster's minstrels in 1308 was an *armiger*. I only find this term again in the burlesque account of the 'auncient minstrell' shown before Elizabeth at Kenilworth (*Appendix H*). He was 'a squier minstrel of Middilsex' and, as he bore the arms of Islington, presumably a 'wait.'

E

EXTRACTS FROM ACCOUNT BOOKS

I. Durham Priory.

[The entries, unless otherwise specified, are amongst the extracts (generally of *Dona Prioris*) from the Bursars' Rolls between 1278 and 1371, printed by Canon Fowler in vols. ii, iii of the *Durham Account Rolls* (Surtees Soc.). *D. H. B.* = *Durham Household Book* (Surtees Soc.), *F. P.* = *Inventories and Account Rolls of Finchale Priory* (Surtees Soc.). This was a cell of Durham Priory. The minstrelsy often took place at the *ludi Domini Prioris*, either in his *camera* (*D. A.* ii. 424) or at Beaurepaire, Witton, or other *maneria* of the Priory. There seem to have been in most years four *ludi ordinarii* (*D. A.* ii. 296), though occasionally only two or three are mentioned. These were at the feasts of Candlemas, Easter, St. John Baptist, and All Saints (*D. A.* i. 242, iii. 932). But the Prior, Sub-Prior, and brethren seem often to have been *ludentes*, *spatiantes*, or *in recreacione* (*D. A.* i. 118, 235), without much regard to fixed dates. In 1438–9 they were *ludentes* for as much as eleven weeks and four days at Beaurepaire (*D. A.* i. 71). See also *D. A.* i. 16, 116, 120, 129, 137, 138, 142, 166, 207, 263; ii. 287, 419, 456, 515; iii. 810, s.vv. *Ludi*, &c.; *D. H. B.* 9, 13, 54, 141, 240, 339; *F. P.* 30, ccxcv, ccccxxxvi.]

1278 Menestrallo Regis Scociae.
Menestrallo de Novo Castro.

1299. Roberto le Taburer.

1300–1. Cuidam hystrioni Regis.

1302–3. Histrionibus domini Regis.

1310–11. Hugoni de Helmeslaye stulto domini Regis.
Cuidam Iugulatori d'ni Regis.
Cuidam Cytharistae.

†1310. Histrionibus d'ni H. de Bello Monte.
In scissura tunicae stulti.

†1315. Histrionibus ad Natale.

1330–1. In uno garniamento pro Thoma fatuo empto.
Histrionibus ad Natale.
" in fest. S. Cuthberti in Marcio.
" ad fest. S. Cuthberti in Sept.
" d'ni Henrici de Beaumond.
Citharistae (in another roll 'citharatori') d'ni Roberti de Horneclyff ex precepto Prioris.

1333–4. Duobus histrionibus in die Veneris proximo post octavam beati Martini.

Histrionibus d'ni Regis quando d'nus noster Rex rediit de Novo Castro.

Stulto d'ni Episcopi.

Histrionibus comitis Warenne.

Histrionibus Regis Scociae.

1334–5. Histrionibus ad Natale.

1335–6. Histrionibus d'ni Regis Scociae.

Duobus histrionibus die Sci. Cuthberti.

Duobus histrionibus ex precepto Prioris.

Histrionibus Novi Castri ad fest. S. Cuthberti.

Histrionibus d'ni R. de Nevill, per Priorem.

In 1 Cythara empta pro Thom. Harpour. 3s.

Cuidam histrioni apud Beaurepaire per R. de Cotam ex dono Prioris.

Thomae fatuo ex precepto eiusdem.

†1335. Istrionibus d'ni Regis.

Istrionibus Reginae apud Pytingdon.

Istrionibus [die Dominica proxima post festum Epiphaniae, quo die d'nus Episcopus epulabatur cum Priore].

Will'o de Sutton, Citharaedo d'ni Galfridi Lescrop eodem die.

Istrionibus die Natalis Domini.

†1336. Duobus istrionibus d'ni Regis.

Edmundo de Kendall, Cytharaeto, de dono Prioris ad Pascha.

Menestrallis de dono [quando Episcopus epulabatur cum Priore].

†1337. In 1 pari sotularium pro Thoma fatuo.

1338–9. Several payments to 'istriones' and 'menestralli.'

In 4 ulnis burelli scacciati emptis pro garniamento Thomae Fole per preceptum Prioris.

1339–40. In panno empto in foro Dunelm. pro uno garniamento pro Thoma fatuo.

Willelmo Piper istrioni d'ni Radulphi de Nevill die Circumcisionis.

1341. Pelidod et duobus sociis suis histrionibus d'ni Regis post Natale Domini.

1341–42. In garniamentis emptis pro . . . Thoma fatuo (and similar entries, or for 'Russet,' 'pannus,' 'Candelwykstret' in other years).

†1343. Various payment to 'Istriones.'

1347–8. 'Istrionibus,' &c.

1350–51. Istrionibus ad Natale.
„ ad S. Cuthbertum in Sept.

1355–6. Will'o Pyper et aliis istrionibus ad Natale.
Item duobus istrionibus d'ni Episcopi et duobus istrionibus Comitis de Norhamton in festo Sci. Cuthberti in Marcio.
Item istrionibus d'ni Episcopi ad festum Paschae.
Item istrionibus in festo Sci. Cuthberti in Sept.

1356–7. In sepultura Thomae fatui et necessariis expensis circa corpus eius, per manus d'ni Prioris (similar entry in miscellaneous roll, 'Thomae Fole,' *D. A.* iii. 719).
Diversis ministrallis (*D. A.* iii. 718).

†1357. Et Will'o Blyndharpour ad Natale.
Et Ioh'i Harpour d'ni Ioh'is de Streuelyn et Will'o Blyndharpour de Novo Castro.
Et duobus Trompours Comitis de Norhamton apud Wyuestow.
Et cuidam Harpour vocato Rygeway.
Istrionibus d'ni Episcopi (and Harpers, &c.).

†1360. Petro Crouder apud Pityngton, per Capellanum.
Item eidem Petro pro uno quarterio ordii sibi dato per Priorem.
Duobus Istrionibus Episcopi in festo Assensionis Domini.
Et cuidam Istrioni Maioris villae Novi Castri per Capellanum.

1360–61. Will'o Pyper et aliis istrionibus ad Natale per manus Ioh'is del Sayles.
Cuidam Welsharpour d'ni Will'i de Dalton.
Item histrionibus aliorum dominorum.

1361–2. In uno viro ludenti in uno loyt et uxori eius cantanti apud Bewrpayr (*D. A.* i. 127, *Hostiller's Accounts*).

1362. Item cuidam histrioni harper episcopi Norwychiae in festo Transl. S^ci^. Cuthberti.
Cuidam Istrioni Jestour Jawdewyne in festo Natalis Domini.
Will'o ye kakeharpour ad idem festum.
Et Barry similem sibi ad id. festum.
Et cuidam ystrioni caecꝺ franco cum uno puero fratre suo.
Barry harper ex precepto Prioris in una tunica empta.

1363–4. Item cantoribus in Adventu Domini cum histrionibus ibidem ex dono Prioris.
Item cuidam histrioni die Dominica *Quasimodo geniti*.

1364–5. To two players of the Lord Duke at the said feast (of St. Cuthbert) (Raine, *St. Cuthbert*, 109, *Surtees Soc.*).

1365–6. Barry Harpour, ystrionibus, &c.

1366–8. Ministrallis, Istrionibus.

1368–9. Rob'o Trompour et Will'o Fergos ministrallo in die Sci. Cuthberti.

1373–4. Duobus Ministrallis cum uno Weyng.

1374. 12 ministrallis in festo S^{ci}. Cuthb.

1375–6. Ministrall. in die S. Cuthb. in Mar.

Cuidam ministrallo ludenti coram domino Priori in camera sua.

Tribus ministrallis Comitis del Marchie ludentibus coram domino Priore.

Cuidam ministrallo domini Regis veniente cum domino de Neuill.

12 ministrallis in festo Sci. Cuthb. in Sept.

4 ministrallis domini Principis in festo exaltacionis S^{ce}. Crucis.

Cuidam ministrallo in festo S^{ci}. Mathaei.

Ministrallis in festo S^{ci}. Cuthb. in Marcio anno Domini, &c. lxxv^{to}.

Duobus ministrallis in die Pasche.

1376–7. Willielmo Fergos et Rogero Harpour caeco ad Natale Domini.

Aliis ministrallis domini de Percy in eadem fest.

1377–8. Haraldis, histrionibus et nunciis, ut patet per cedulam.

1378–9. Histrionibus . . . dominorum Regis, Ducis, et aliorum dominorum.

1380–1. Iohanni Momford ministrallo domini Regis.

1381–2. Ministrallis domini de Neuill apud Beaurepaire cum domina de Lomly.

Ministrallo domini Ducis cum uno saltante in camera domini Prioris.

(and others.)

1384–5. Ministrallis domini Regis.

1394–5. Ministrallis in festo S. Cuthb., Henrici Percy, domini Ducis Lancastr., domini de Neuill, Ducis Eborac., de Scocia, comitis Canciae, ad Nat. Domini, de Hilton, Ric. Brome ministrallo, in fest. S. Cuthb. in Marc.

Uni Trompet domini Regis.

Uni Rotour de Scocia.

1395. Item, in vino, speciebus, in donis datis Confratribus, ministrallis et aliis diversis, ex curialitate (*F.P.* cxv).

1399–1400. Ministrallis.

1401–2. Ministrallis.

1416–7. Ministrallis.

Diversis pueris ludentibus coram eodem priore in festo S^ci^. Stephani hoc anno.

1441–2. Per . . . capellanum [et] . . . per bursarium ministrallis domini Regis et aliorum dominorum supervenientibus.

1446–7. Ministrallis.

1449–50. Ministrallis.

1464–5. Et solvit Iohanni Andrewson et sociis suis operantibus pro nova tectura unius camerae vocatae le Playerchambre (*F. P.* ccxcv).

1465. Item j por de ferro in camera Prioris, j in le plaer cha . . . (*F. P.* ccxcviii).

1496. Paid to Robert Walssch for two days playing John Gibson of Elvet 'herper' (*D. H. B.* 340).

1532–3. . . . bus lusoribus . . . Regis, in regardis, in auro, 15^s^.

Et custodi ursorum et cimearum dominae Principis.

Et capellano, per bursarium, pro 4 lusoribus domini Comitis de Darby, in auro, 7^s^. 6^d^. (*D. H. B.* 143, the last two items crossed out).

1536–7. In diversis donis datis ministrallis diversorum dominorum.

1538. Paid to the ministrels (*ministrallis*) at 'le musters' upon 'le Gelymore.'

1539–40. Paid to the players (*lusoribus*) of Auklande at Christmas before Master Hyndley, as a present (*D. H. B.* 340).

1554–5. [Cathedral Account.] Paid for two mynstralles.

II. Maxstoke Priory.

[Printed by Hazlitt-Warton, ii. 97, '*ex orig. penes me.*']

'In the Prior's accounts of the Augustine canons of Maxstoke in Warwickshire, of various years in the reign of Henry VI (1422–61), one of the styles or regular heads is *De Ioculatoribus et Mimis* . . . .

Ioculatori in septimana S. Michaelis, iv^d^.

Citharistae tempore natalis domini et aliis iocatoribus, iv^d^.

Mimis de Solihull, vi^d^.

Mimis de Coventry, xx^d^.

Mimo domini Ferrers, vi^d^.

Lusoribus de Eton, viii^d.
Lusoribus de Coventry, viii^d.
Lusoribus de Daventry, xii^d.
Mimis de Coventry, xii^d.
Mimis domini de Asteley, xii^d.
Item iiij mimis domini de Warewyck, x^d.
Mimo caeco, ii^d.
Sex mimis domini de Clynton.
Duobus mimis de Rugeby, x^d.
Cuidam citharistae, vi^d.
Mimis domini de Asteley, xx^d.
Cuidam citharistae, vi^d.
Citharistae de Coventry, vi^d.
Duobus citharistis de Coventry, viii^d.
Mimis de Rugeby, viii^d.
Mimis domini de Buckeridge, xx^d.
Mimis domini de Stafford, ii^s.
Lusoribus de Coleshille, viij^d. . . .
[1432] Dat. duobus mimis de Coventry in die consecrationis Prioris, xii^d.'

III. Thetford Priory.

[From Collier, i. 55, 84, on the authority of a 'MS. of the expenses of the Priory of Thetford, from 1461 to 1540, lately in the collection of Mr. Craven Orde, and now of the Duke of Newcastle.']

'The mention of "plays" and "players" does not begin until the 13th of Henry VII; but "Minstrels" and "Waytes" are often spoken of there as receiving rewards from the convent. The following entries, regarding "plays" and "players," occur between the 13th and 23rd of Henry VII:—

13 Henry VII [1497–8]. It^m. sol. in regard 12 capital plays, 4^s.
It^m. sol. to menstrell and players in festo Epiphaniae, 2^s.
19 Henry VII [1503–4]. It^m. sol. to the play of Mydenale, 12^d.
21 Henry VII [1505–6]. It^m. sol. in regard lusoribus et menstrall, 17^d.
23 Henry VII [1507–8]. It^m. sol. in regard lusoribus div. vices, 3^s 4^d.
It^m. sol. in regard to Ixworth play, 16^d.
It^m. sol. in regard to Schelfanger play, 4^d.

. . . From the 1st to the 31st Henry VIII, the King's players, the King's jugglers, the King's minstrels, and the King's bearwards were visitors of Thetford, and were paid various sums, from 4d to 6s 8d, by the Prior of the convent there, as appears by the entries in the account-book during that period. On one occasion, 16 Henry VIII, Cornyshe, "the master of the King's chapel," was paid 3s 4d by the prior; but he was then, probably, attendant upon the King, who is not unfrequently spoken of as having arrived, and being lodged at the Priory. Mr. Brandon and Mr. Smith are more than once rewarded as "Jugglers of the King." The Queen's players, the Prince's players, and the players of the Queen of France, also experienced the liberality of the Prior, as well as those of the Duke of Norfolk, the Duke of Suffolk, the Earl and Countess of Derby, Lord and Lady Fitzwater, the Lord Privy Seal, the Lord Chancellor, Sir Thomas Challoner and two gentlemen who are called Marks and Barney.'

IV. Winchester College.

[Extracts from *computi* partly by Hazlitt-Warton, ii. 98, and partly by M. E. C. Walcott, *William of Wykeham and his Colleges*, 206. The *satrapae* of 1466 and 1479 are said by Mr. Walcott to have been local notables, but a collation to them would not cost so little or be grouped with rewards to minstrels in the *computus*. Ducange says that the word is used 'pro quodam ministro vel satellite.' The Magdalen accounts use it for the 'serjeants' of the mayor of Oxford (Macray, *Register*, i. 15).]

1400. In dono lusoribus civitatis Wynton venient. ad collegium cum suo tripudio ex curialitate, xijd.

1412. In dat. Rico. Kent bochier tempore regno suo vocat. Somerkyng, xijd.

1415. In dat. diversis hominibus de Ropley venientibus ad coll. die Sanct. Innoc. et tripudiantibus et cantantibus in aula coram Epō. scholarium, xxd.

1422. Dat. histrioni dni epi Wynton et ioculatori ejusdem 5ti die Ianuarii, cuilibet, xxd.

1425. Dat. Gloucester ioculatori ludenti coram custode et sociis penultimo die Iulii, ob reverentiam ducis Exon. xijd.

1426. Dat. ministrellis d. epi Wynton tempore Nat. Dni. ex curialitate et honestate, ijs viiid.

Dat. ij ministrallis comitissae de Westmorland venient' ad coll. xxd.

1433. In dat. mimis dni cardinalis venient' ad collegium erga festum natale Dni iiijs.

1462. Dat' Epo Nicholatensi visitanti Dominum custodem in hospitio suo de nocte S^{ti}. Nicholai, iiij^{d}.

1464. Et in dat. ministrallis comitis Kanciae venient. ad coll. in mense Iulii, iiij^{s} iiij^{d}.

1466. Et in dat. satrapis Wynton venientibus ad coll. festo Epiphaniae, cum ij^{s} dat. iiij. interludentibus et J. Meke citharistae eodem festo, iiij^{s}.

1467. Et in datis iiij^{or} mimis dom. de Arundell venient. ad coll. xiij. die Febr. ex curialitate dom. custodis, ij^{s}.

In dat. Ioh. Pontisbery et socio ludentibus in aula in die circumcisionis, ij^{s}.

1471. In dat. uni famulo d^{ni} regis Angliae venienti ad collegium cum Leone mense Ianuarii, xx^{d}.

1472. Et in dat. ministrallis dom. Regis cum viij^{d}. dat. duobus Berewardis ducis Clarentiae, xx^{d}.

Et in dat. Iohanni Stulto quondam dom. de Warewyco, cum iiij^{d} dat. Thomae Nevyle taborario.

Et in datis duobus ministrallis ducis Glocestriae, cum iiij^{d}. dat. uni ministrallo ducis de Northumberland, viij^{d}.

Et in datis duobus citharatoribus ad vices venient. ad collegium viij^{d}.

1477. Et in dat. ministrallis dom. Principis venient. ad coll. festo Ascensionis Domini, cum xx^{d}. dat. ministrallis dom. Regis, v^{s}.

1479. Et in datis satrapis Wynton venientibus ad coll. festo Epiphaniae, cum xij^{d} dat. ministrallis dom. episcopi venient. ad coll. infra octavas epiphaniae, iii^{s}.

Dat. lusoribus de civitate Winton. venientibus ad collegium in apparatu suo mens. Iulii, v^{s} vij^{d}.

1481. Et in sol. ministrallis dom. regis venientibus ad collegium xv die Aprilis cum xij^{d} solut. ministrallis dom. episcopi Wynton venientibus ad collegium i^{o} die Iunii, iiij^{s} iiij^{d}.

Et in dat. ministrallis dom. Arundell ven. ad coll. cum viij^{d} dat. ministrallis dom. de la Warr, ij^{s} iij^{d}.

1483. Sol. ministrallis dom. regis, ven. ad coll. iij^{s} iiij^{d}.

1484. Et in dat. uni ministrallo dom. principis et in aliis ministrallis ducis Glocestriae v die Iulii, xx^{d}.

1536. In dat. ministrallis d^{ni} regis venientibus ad coll. xiij die April pro regardo, ij^{s}.

1573. In regardis dat' tibicinis dominae reginae cum vino, vij^{s} iiij^{d}.

In regardis dat. lusoribus dominae reginae, vj^{s} viij^{d}.

V. Magdalen College, Oxford.

[Extracts from account books made by J. R. Bloxam and W. D. Macray, *A Register of the Members of St. Mary Magdalen College, Oxford*, First Series, ii. 235; New Series, i. 3; ii. 3. The dates given below are for the year in which the account begins.]

1481. pro cerothecis pro chorustis, iiij^{d}.

1482. v^{o} die Decembris pro cerothecis episcopi in festo S. Nicholai iiij^{d}.

1483. pro cerothecis datis ad honorem Sancti Nicolai duobus choristis, viij^{d}.

1484. pro cerothecis Episcopi in festo Sancti Nicholai et eius crucem ferentis, viij^{d}.

1485. 'Ursarii' of Lord Stanley dined with the Fellows.

1486. pro factura sepulturae erga pascham, xij^{d}.

'Sex vagatores' dined with the servants.

Solut. vi^{o} die Ian. citharistis et mimis tempore ludi in aula in regardo, in tempore Nativitatis Domini, viij^{d}.

Solut. pro quodam ornamento lusorum vocato *ly Cape mayntenawnce*, ix^{d}.

1487. pro vestimentis lusorum tempore Nativ. Domini, consilio unius decani, ii^{s} ij^{d}.

pro clavis ad pannos in ornatum aulae pendendos, j^{d}.

1488. Sol. Iohanni Wynman pro scriptura unius libri de servicio episcopi pro die Innocencium, v^{d}.

1490. Singers from Abingdon, London and Hereford entertained.

1494. Sol. Pescode servanti quandam bestiam vocatam *ly merumsytt* ex consilio seniorum, quia Rex erat apud Woodstocke, xij^{d}.

1495. Sol. Henrico Mertyn pro lino, *alyn*, et aliis emptis pro ludo in die Paschae, xvij^{d} ob.

Sol. Pescod ducenti duo animalia nuncupata *mermosettes*.

1502. Sol. in expensis factis tempore Nativitatis Domini, in biberiis post interludia et alia, xiij^{s} iiij^{d}.

1506. To John Burgess, B.A., . . . x^{d} were paid for writing out a miracle-play ('scriptura lusi') of S^{t}. Mary Magd., and v^{s}. for some music; and viij^{d} to a man who brought some songs from Edward Martyn, M.A. For his diligence with regard to the above miracle-play, Kendall, a clerk, was rewarded with i^{s}.

pro expensis mimi, iiij^{s}, at Christmas.

1507. in quatuor refectionibus citharistae, at Epiphany.

1508. Sol. famulo Regis ducenti ursam ad collegium, ex mandato Vice-presidentis, xij^{d}.

1509. Sol. pane, cibo et aliis datis pueris ludentibus in die Paschae, mandato Vicepr. xvij^{d} ob.

1510. Sol. pro expensis factis in aula tempore Nativitatis Domini, xiij^{s} iiij^{d}.

Sol. cuidam mimo tempore Nativitatis Domini in regardo, viij^{d}.

1512. Sol. Petro Pyper pro pypyng in interludio nocte Sancti Iohannis, vj^{d}.

Sol. Iohanni Tabourner pro lusione in interludio Octavis Epiphaniae, vj^{d}.

Sol. Roberto Johnson pro una tunica pro interludiis, iiij^{s}.

1514. pro carnibus [? carbonibus] consumptis in capella tribus noctibus ante Pascha et in tempore Nativitatis, ij^{s}.

1518. To Perrot, the Master of the choristers, 'pro tinctura et factura tunicae eius qui ageret partem Christi et pro crinibus mulieribus, ij^{s} vj^{d}.'

1520. pro pane . . . datis clericis in vigiliis S^{ti}. Nicolai.

pro cerothecis puerorum in festo Sancti Nicolai.

1526. pro merendis datis episcopo capellanis clericis et aliis in vigilia S^{t}. Nicolai.

1529. pro . . . episcopo Nicholai.

1530. pro pueris in festo Sancti Nicholai.

1531. Solut. mimis dominae principisshae, xx^{d}.

Pro biberio dato sociis et scolaribus post interludia in tempore Natalis Domini, vj^{s} viij^{d}.

1532. To the Queen's players, by the President's order, xii^{d}.

pro biberio dato sociis post ludum baccalaureorum in magna aula, vj^{s} viij^{d}.

1535. pro merenda facta in vigilia Sancti Nicolai.

Actors at Christmas, iiii^{s} iiijd.

pro merenda facta post comediam actam, ix^{s} iij^{d}.

'ioculatoribus Regis,' by the President's order, xx^{d}.

1536. pro biberio in nocte Sancti Nicholai.

Sol. mimo pro solatiis factis sociis et scholasticis tempore Nativitatis Domini, viij^{s}.

1537. pro carbonibus consumptis in sacrario, per custodes sepulchri, et per pueros in festis hiemalibus, ij^{s} [and in other years].

1539. pro bellariis datis sociis cum ageretur comedia, viij^{s}.

1540. pro epulis datis sociis eo tempore quo agebatur tragedia, viij^{s} iiij^{d}.

pro bellariis datis sociis et clericis vigilia divi Nicolai, iiij^{s} viij^{d}.

pro pane et potu datis semicommunariis dum curabant publicam exhibere comediam, xx^{d}.

1541. A 'tympanista' was hired at Christmas and comedies acted.

1554. 30 Ian. in adventu [dom. Matravers] ad tragedias per duas noctes, xlij[s] viij[d] ob.

Pro epulis datis sociis post exactas tragedias, x[s] ix[d].

The only Elizabethan entry I need note is:—

1561. Sol. Joyner, pictori, depingenti portenta religiosorum in spectaculo Baulino, iij[s] iiij[d] . . . depingenti nomina haeresium in spectaculo (in aula) quod choristarum moderator [Richard Baull] ordinavit.

VI. Shrewsbury Corporation.

[Extracts from the Bailiffs' accounts by Owen and Blakeway, *Hist. of Shrewsbury* (1825), i. 262, 267, 275, 284, 290, 292, 325 sqq.; and by W. D. Macray in *Hist. MSS.* xv. 10. 25. It is not always clear to which calendar year an entry belongs. The accounts run from Michaelmas to Michaelmas, but Owen and Blakeway generally quote entries under one calendar year and sometimes under one regnal year.]

1401. 'Histriones' of the Prince and the Earl of Stafford.

'Menstralles' of the Earls of Worcester and Stafford.

1409. Players [i. e. in these early accounts, 'histriones,' not 'lusores'] of the countess and earl of Arundel, of Lord Powis, Lord Talbot, and Lord Furnivall.

Players 'in honorem villae' at the marriage of a cousin of David Holbache.

1437. Minstrels of earl of Stafford.

1438. Livery to two town minstrels, 'voc. *waytes*.'

1442. Some town minstrels called 'histriones.' In same year, 'histrionibus regis,' and in subsequent years 'histrionibus' of earl of Shrewsbury and others, including one 'voc. Trumpet.'

1450. Players and minstrels at coming of duke of York from Ireland.

1457. Denaria soluta uni ministrallo domini principis [Edward] pro honestate villae.

Quatuor ministrallis domini ducis de Bukyngham.

Duobus ministrallis d'ni de Powys.

1 lagenae vini de Ruyn dictis ministrallis.

Denaria data uni ministrallo d'ni principis et suo puero.

iiij. ministrallis d'ni ducis de Eboraco.

iv. ministrellis d'ni ducis de Excestro.

1474. Regardo ministrallis d'ni ducis de Clarence.

1478. Waltero Harper ministrallo d'ni principis.

Regardo dato uni ministrallo ducis Gloucestris vocato le Taborer.

Regardo sex ministrallis d'ni Regis.

1479. Soluta pro liberata ministrallorum vocatorum Wayts, quilibet eorum.

Soluta pro conductu unius ministralli vocati Wayt a villa de Norhampton usque Salop.

Soluta pro quodam regardo dato uni ministrallo d'ni Regis via elemosinaria causa eius paupertatis et aetatis.

[From this point *histriones* replaces *ministralli* in the accounts.]

1483. Soluta pro quodam regardo dato sex histrionibus domini Regis pro honestate villae.

Pro vino dato dictis histrionibus in praesencia ballivorum et aliorum proborum hominum pro honestate villae.

Pro liberatura communium histrionum vocatorum le Wayts villae.

Soluta ursenario domini Regis pro honestate villae.

1495. Pro vino dato domino Principi [Arthur] ad ludum in quarell.

1496. Wine given to the minstrels of our Lord the King.

To the King's minstrels.

To the Queen's minstrels.

To the Prince's players.

To the Earl of Derby's players.

To the Earl of Shrewsbury's players.

1503. In regardo dato ij Walicis histrionibus domini Regis.

1510. 'Lusoribus' in feast of Pentecost.

'Histrionibus' of Earl of Shrewsbury and King.

1516. In vino, pomis, waffers, et aliis novellis datis et expenditis super abbatem Salop et famulos suos ad ludum et demonstrationem martiriorum Felicianae et Sabinae in quarera post muros.

In regardo dato lusoris eiusdem martirii tunc temporis hoc anno.

1517. Regardo ursinario comitis Oxoniae.

In regardo dato ursinario domini Regis pro agitacione bestiarum suarum ultra denarios tunc ibidem collectos.

1518. In vino expendito super tres reges Coloniae equitantibus in interludio pro solacio villae Salop in festo Pentecost.

1520. Ralph Hubard, minstrel of Lord de 'Mountegyle.'

In regardo dato iiij^{or} interlusoribus comitis Arundele ostendentibus ballivis et comparibus suis diversa interludia.

Et in vino dato eis et aliis extraneis personis intuentibus interludia, ultra denarios collectos.

In regardo dato histrionibus Iohannis Talbot militis pro melodia eorum facta in presencia ballivorum.

In regardo dato iij histrionibus comitis Arundelle pro honestate villae Salop.

In regardo dato Benet & Welles histrionibus comitis Salop.

In regardo ij histrionibus comitissae de Derby pro honestate villae Salop.

Et in vino expendito per ballivos et compares suos audientes melodiam eorum.

Histrionibus domini Regis ex consuetudine.

In regardo dato et vino expendito super Willelmum More histrionem domini Regis eo quod est caecus et principalis citherator Angliae.

1521. Regardo dato M. Brandon ioculatori domini Regis pro honestate villae

Et in vino expendito par ballivos & compares suos videntes lusum et ioculationem dicti ioculatoris ultra ij denarios collectos de qualibet persona villae extraneis exceptis.

Soluta pro una roba nova depicta, sotularibus & aliis necessariis regardis & expensis factis super Ricardum Glasyer, abbatem de Marham, pro honestate & iocunditate villae.

In regardo dato portitori communis campanae circa villam pro proclamacione facta pro attendencia facienda super abbatem de Marham tempore Maii hoc anno.

In regardo dato iiij^or^ histrionibus domini Regis de consuetudine.

Histrionibus comitis Derby.

Regardo dato ursinario ducis Suffolke ultra 2^s. 3^d. de pecuniis collectis de circumstantibus ad agitacionem ursarum suarum.

Pro ursinario domini marchionis Dorsett.

1522. 'Ursenarius' of duke of Suffolk.

In regardo dato ioculatori domini Regis.

1524. 'Histrio' of Henry Knight.

'Histriones' of Earl of Derby.

'Histriones' of Lord Mount Egle.

1525. In regardo dato iiij histrionibus comitis Arundell.

Et in vino expendito super ballivos & compares suos audientes melodiam et ludentes inspicientes.

In regardo dato iiij^or^ interlusoribus ducis Suffolk.

Interluders of the Lady Princess, and wine spent at hearing their interludes.

1526. In regardo dato custodi cameli domini Regis ostendenti ballivis et comparibus suis ioca illius cameli.

Interlusoribus dominae principissae.

Ralph Hubard, minstrel of Lord de 'Mountegyle,' with one Lokkett.

1527. In regardo dato lusoribus villae tempore veris et mensis Maii pro iocunditate villae.

Interlusoribus dominae principissae.

Interluders of our Lord the King.

'Histriones,' of Sir John Talbot, Arthur Neuton and Sir John Lyngen.

1528. 'Ursenarius' of marquis of Exeter.

1530. 'Histrio' of baron of Burford.

1531. Data interlusoribus dominae principissae.

1533. Soluta Thomae Eton pro factura unius mansionis de duobus stagiis pro domino presidenti [Bishop of Exeter] et ballivis tempore ludi septimana Pentecostes.

Et in regardo dato lusoribus ad dictum lusum et pro reparacione ornamentorum suorum.

In vino dato domino presidenti & ballivis in mansione sua tempore lusi in Quarrera pone muros.

In regardo dato lusoribus & interlusoribus domini Regis ostendentibus & offerentibus ioca sua.

Et in vino expendito super eos et comitivam ballivorum & comparium suorum audientium & supervidentium lusum & melodiam eorum.

In expensis factis in garniamentis, liberatis et histrion[ibus] pro domino abbate de Marham tempore mensis Maii pro honestate villae hoc anno.

1535. In regardo m[agistro] Brandon, ioculatori domini Regis.

In regardo dato histrionibus extraneis melodiam et cantilenas eorum coram ballivis et comparibus pronunciantibus.

1538. Data in regardo lusoribus domini privati sigilli.

Data in regarda lusoribus domini principis [Edward].

Expendita super lusores domini principis, domini privati sigilli, domini visitatoris . . . pro honestate villae.

'Histriones' of Sir Thomas Cornewall and of Thomas Newport.

Rogero Philipps, goldsmyth, pro argento et emendacione colarium histrionum villae.

'Ursenarius' of marquis of Exeter.

1540. Data in regardo quibusdam interlusoribus de Wrexam ludentibus coram ballivis et comparibus suis in vino tunc expendito.

'Item, Mr. Bayleffes left on p^d^ more the same day at aft^r^ the play.

'Item, the vj men spend appon the kyng's pleyers in wyne.

'Item, there was left on p^d^ by Mr. Bayleffs w^t^ my Lorde Prinssys plears on Sonday after Seint Bartlaumew day.

'Item, there was sent them the nyght to supper a po^l^ of red and a po^l^ of claret.

'Item, Mr. Bayleffs left on p^d^ on Sonday after owre Lade day wyth my Lord Prinsys plears.'

Cuidam iugulatori ludenti coram ballivis.

1541. 'Ursenario ducis Norfoxiae.'

1542. In vino dato interlusoribus post interlusum in cimitirio sancti Cedde coram commissariis domini Regis ballivis et aliis.

Cuidem ursuario de la Northewiche.

Ursiatori praepotentis viri comitis Derby ad ij tempora.

Pro reparacione et pictura ornamentorum abbatis de Mayvole.

Et soluta pro una toga de nova facta dicto abbati de Mayvole.

Soluta Ricardo Glasier pro labore suo in ludendo abbatem de Mardall.

1548. Interlusoribus ludentibus cum domino abbate de Marall.

Soluta Iohanni Mason, peynter, pro pictura togae pro dicto domino de Marrall.

In regardo istrionibus ludentibus ante viros armatos.

Cuidam istrioni ludenti ante viros equiles equitantes ad Scociam.

1549. James Lockwood 'servienti et gestatori domini Regis.'

Interluders of Sir John Bridges and of Sir Edward Braye.

William Taylor, and others, interluders of the town of Salop, playing there in the month of May.

'Histriones' of William Sheldon and of Lord Ferrers [last use of term histrio].

1552. Interluders of Lord Russell.

Soluta domino de abbott Marram et pro apparatu eorum videlicet pro calciamentis tunicis et aliis vestibus.

1553. Expendita per ballivos et associatos suos die lunae in le Whitson wuck post visum lusum.

Pro tunicis et aliis vestimentis ac pistura eorundem pro Robyn Hood.

In vino dato eisdem interlusoribus.
In regardo le tomlers.

1554. In regardo Thomae Staney le jugler.
Wyett le gester.

1559. Regardo lusiatoribus domini Stafford.

1561. Item, gyvyn unto my lord Wyllybe's playarys in reward.
Item, spent at the gullet on the saem playarys.

1565. To Master Baly Pursell with the Quenes players.

1566. Yeven Mr. Justes Throgmerton's mynstrell.

1574. Paid and geven to my L. Sandwayes man, the berwart.
The players of noblemen and others and ber-wards of noblemen and mynstrells of noblemen, this yere, viii^{li} x^{s} $viij^{d}$.

1576. Leid out to my lord of Derby and my lord Staffart's musicions.

1582. Bestowed on her Majesty's players this yere.

1591. To my lord of Derby's musysyons, and to the erle of Woster's players . . . to my L. Beachem men, beinge players.

[From *Books of Council Orders* in *Hist. MSS.* xv. 13, 16, 18.]

1556. 16 May. The bailiffs to set forward the stage play this next Whitsontide for the worship of the town and not to disburse above £5 about the furniture of the play.

1570. 8 July. Lease of pasture 'behind the walles, exceptinge the Quarrell where the plases have bine accustomyd to be usyd.'

1575. 17 July. Five marks to be given to Mr. Churchyard for his pains taken in setting forth the show against the Queen's coming, being sent hither by the Lord President.

VII. The Howards of Stoke-by-Nayland, Essex.

[From accounts of Sir John Howard, in *Manners and Household Expenses* (Roxburghe Club, 1841), 325, 511.]

2 May, 1465. Item that he [my master] delyverd the pleyers at Moleyns [a servant of Sir John's] weddynge, ij^{s}.

12 Jan. 1466. And the sonday nexte after the xij day, I ȝafe to the pleyeres of Stoke, ij^{s}.

[From accounts of John, Lord Howard, afterwards Duke of Norfolk, in *Household Books of John, Duke of Norfolk, and Thomas, Earl of Surrey* (ed. Collier, Roxburghe Club, 1844), 104, 145, 146, 148, 149, 202, 336, 339.]

29 Aug. 1481. I paid to the pleirs of Turton [Thorington] Strete, xx^{d}.

26 Dec. 1481. Item, the xxvj day of December, my Lord toke the Plaiers of Kokesale [Coggeshall], iij^s^ iiij^d^.

27 Dec. 1481. Item, to the Plaiers of Hadley [Hadleigh], and the olde man and ij. children, vj^s^ viij^d^.

7 Jan. 1482. Item, to the Plaiers of Esterforde, iij^s^ iiij^d^.

9 Jan. 1482. Item, to Senclowe, that he paid to my Lord of Essex [Henry Bourchier] men, plaiers, xx^d^.

Thei are of Canans.

22 May, 1482. Item, that my Lord yaffe to the cherche on Whitson Monday at the pley, x^s^.

25 Dec. 1482. Item, on Crystemas day, my Lord gaff to iiij pleyers of my lord of Gloucestres, iij^s^ iiij^d^.

Item, the same day, my Lord gaff to iiij pleyers of Coksale, iij^s^ iiij^d^.

9 Jan. 1483. Item, the same day, my Lord paid to Garard, of Sudbury, for all suche stoffe as folewyth, that he bought for the Dysgysing [a schedule of paper, gunpowder, 'arsowde,' packthread, &c., follows]. Summe totall, xxj^s^ ob.

[From accounts of Thomas, Earl of Surrey, in *Household Books* (*ut supra*), 515, 517, 519.]

20 Dec. 1490. Payd for xviij yardes of lynen cloth, that M. Leynthorpe had for dysgysyng, at iiij^d^ the yard, . . . vj^s^ iiij^d^.

[Other expenses for the disguising follow.]

27 Dec. 1490. Item, payd to the playars of Chemsford, vj^s^. viij^d^.

2 Jan. 1491. Item, the said day, in reward to the panget [pageant (?)], iij^s^ iiij^d^.

Item, payd to ——, when he went to Bury to fach stuff for dygysers on Saynt Stevens day, xvj^d^.

8 Jan. 1492. Item, in reward to the players of Lanam [Lavenham], xl^s^.

[The Howard accounts also include many payments for minstrelsy, &c. The Duke of Norfolk kept singers, a harper, children of the chapel, and two fools, 'Tom Fool' and Richard, 'the fool of the kitchen.']

VIII. The English Court.

[From Rymer, *Foedera*, x. 387. A memorandum *de strenis, liberatis et expensis*, at Christmas, 1427.]

A Jakke Travail et ses compaignons feisans diverses jeuues et entreludes dedeins le feste de Noell devant notre dit sire le roi, 4 lib.

Et as autres jeweis de Abyndon feisantz autres entreludes dedeins le dit feste de Noel, 20 sol.

[Extracted by Collier, i. 50, from the *Household Book* of Henry VII, 1491–1505, and the *Book of King's Payments*, 1506–9. I cannot identify the former; the latter appears to be vol. 214 of the *Miscellanea of the Treasury of the Receipt of the Exchequer* (Scargill-Bird, *Guide to the Public Records*, 228). I omit, here and below, entries referring to minstrelsy, disguisings, and plays by the King's players and the Chapel. Probably some of the performances were given at London; others before the King on progress. I have corrected some of Collier's dates from the similar entries in Bentley, *Excerpta Historica*, 85, taken from a transcript in *B. M. Add. MS.* 7099.]

1 Jan. 1492. To my Lorde of Oxon pleyers, in rewarde, £1.

7 Jan. 1493. To my Lorde of Northumberlande Pleyers, in rewarde, £1.

1 Jan. 1494. To four Pleyers of Essex in rewarde, £1.

To the Pleyers of Wymborne Minster, £1.

6 Jan. 1494. To the Frenche Pleyers for a rewarde, £1.

31 Dec. 1494. To 3 Pleyers of Wycombe in rewarde, 13s 4d.

4 Jan. 1495. To the Frenshe Pleyers in rewarde, £2.

20 July, 1498. To the pleyers of London in rewarde, 10s.

14 June, 1499. To the pleyers with Marvells, £4.

6 Aug. 1501. To the Pleyers at Myles End, 3s 4d.

2 Jan. 1503. To the Pleyers of Essex in rewarde, £1.

20 May, 1505. To the Players of Kingeston toward the bilding of the churche steple, in almasse, 3s 4d.

1 Jan. 1506. To the players that played afore the Lord Stewarde in the Hall opon Sonday nyght, 6s 8d.

To my lorde Princes players that played in hall on new-yeres even, 10s.

25 Dec. 1506. To the Players that played affore the Lord Stewarde in the Hall opon Tewesday nyght, 10s.

2 Jan. 1509. To my lord of Buckingham's pleyers that playd in the Hall at Grenewich, 6s 8d.

[Extracted by Collier, i. 76, from the *Book of King's Payments* for 1509–17, now vol. 215 of the *Miscellanea of the Treasury of the Receipt of the Exchequer*. The document is more fully analysed in Brewer, ii. 1441. It is an account of the Treasurer of the Chamber.]

6 Jan. 1512. To the Players that cam out of Suffolke, that playd affore the Lorde Stewarde in the Kings Hall opon Monday nyght, 13s 4d.

1 Jan. 1515. To the Erle of Wiltyshires playres, that shulde have played in the Kings Hall oppon Thursday at nyght, in rewarde, $13^{s}\ 4^{d}$.

1 Jan. 1516. To the Erle of Wilshire's players, $13^{s}\ 4^{d}$.

[From *Accounts of Treasurer of Chamber* in *Trevelyan Papers* (C.S.), i. 146, 161, 174.]

1 Jan. 1530. To the Prince's plaiers.

1 Jan. 1531. To the Princes pleyers.

Item, paid to certain Players of Coventrye, as in wey of the Kinges rewarde, for playnge in the Corte this last Cristmas.

1 Jan. 1532. To the Princesse plaiers.

F

MINSTREL GUILDS

A. France.

1. *Arras*, †1105.

The famous *Pui d'Arras* (vols. i. p. 376, ii. p. 88) was in a sense a minstrel guild. According to tradition a plague was stayed by a simultaneous apparition of the Virgin in a dream to two minstrels, which led to the acquisition of 'le joyel d'Arras,' the miraculous 'cierge de notre Dame.' This was about 1105, and the result was the foundation of the *Confrérie* or *Carité de N. D. des Ardents*, which afterwards developed into the *pui*. This was not confined to minstrels, but they were predominant. The *Statutes* say, 'Ceste carité est estorée des jogleors, et les jogleors en sont signors[1].' The objects of the *pui*, however, were religious, social, and literary. It was not a craft guild, such as grew up two centuries later.

2. *Paris*, 1321.

Ordinances were made in 1321 'à l'acort du commun des menestreus et menestrelles, jougleurs et jougleresses' of Paris for the reformation of their 'mestier,' and registered with the provost of Paris in 1341. They chiefly regulate the employment of minstrels within the city. The 'mestres du dit mestier' are to be 'ii ou iii preudes hommes' appointed by the provost on behalf of the King. A number of 'guètes' and other minstrels sign, beginning with 'Pariset, menestrel le roy,' and ending with 'Jaque le Jougleur.' As a possible head of the 'mestier' is named 'li prevost de Saint-Julian.' This seems to contemplate the foundation of the *hospice et confrérie* under the

[1] Guy, xxvii.

patronage of SS. Julian and Genesius, and in close connexion with the 'mestier,' which actually took place 1328–35. But in the later Statutes of 1407 the head of the guild is called the 'roy des ménestriers,' and as by this time the guild seems to claim some authority over the whole of France, it is probable that this 'roy' was identical with the 'roy des menestreuls du royaume de France,' a title which occurs in various documents from 1338 onwards. He may also have been identical with the 'roy' of the King's household minstrels (cf. p. 239). The Paris guild lasted until the suppression of all such privileged bodies in 1776[1].

3. *Chauny.*

The corporation of 'les Trompettes jougleurs' of Chauny was founded during the fifteenth century. This town claimed to provide *bateleurs* for all the north of France[2].

B. England.

There are two early jurisdictions over minstrelsy, which are not strictly of the nature of guilds.

1. *Chester.*

Tradition has it that †1210 Randal Blundeville, Earl of Chester, besieged by the Welsh in Rhuddlan Castle, was relieved by Roger Lacy, constable of Cheshire, with a mob of riff-raff from Chester Midsummer fair. Randal gave to Lacy, and Lacy's son John gave to his steward Hugh de Dutton and his heirs the 'magistratum omnium leccatorum et meretricum totius Cestriae.' The fact of the jurisdiction is undoubted. It was reserved by the charter to the London guild in 1469, claimed by Laurence de Dutton in 1499, admitted upon an action of *quo warranto* as a right 'from time immemorial,' further reserved in the first Vagrant Act (1572) which specifically included minstrels, and in the successive Acts of 1597, 1603, 1628, 1641, 1713, 1740, 1744. It lapsed when this last Act was repealed in 1822. Up to 1756 the heir of Dutton regularly held his *curia Minstralciae* at Chester Midsummer fair, and issued licences to fiddlers in the city and county for a fee of $4\frac{1}{2}$*d.*, afterwards raised to 2*s.* 6*d.* Thomas Dutton (1569–1614), under puritan influences, inserted a proviso against piping and dancing on Sundays[3].

[1] B. Bernhard, *Rech. sur l'Hist. de la Corp. des Ménétriers ou Joueurs d'Instruments de la Ville de Paris* (*Bibl. de l'École des Chartes*, iii. 377; iv. 525; v. 254, 339).

[2] Julleville, *Les Com.* 238.

[3] Morris, 12, 346; Rymer, xi. 642; Ribton-Turner, 109, 129, 133, 148, 182, 201; Ormerod, *Hist. of Cheshire*, i. 36; *Memorials of the Duttons* (1901), 9, 209.

2. *Tutbury.*

Letters patent of John of Gaunt dated 1380 and confirmed by an 'inspeximus' of Henry VI in 1443 assigned 'le roy des ministralx' in the honour of Tutbury to arrest all minstrels within the honour not doing service on the feast of the Assumption. It was a custom that the prior of Tutbury should provide a bull for a bull-running by the assembled minstrels on this feast. The court was still held by an annual 'king of the fiddlers,' with the steward and bailiff of the honour (including Staffs., Derby, Notts., Leicester, and Warwick), at the end of the seventeenth century, and the minstrels claimed to be exempt, like those of Chester, from vagrancy legislation. But their rights were not reserved, either by the Charter of 1469 or the Vagrant Acts[1].

The first English craft guild of minstrels is later by a century and a half than that of Paris.

3. *London.*

A charter of Edward IV (1469), 'ex querelosa insinuatione dilectorum nobis Walteri Haliday, marescalli [and seven others] ministrallorum nostrorum,' declares that 'nonnulli rudes Agricolae et Artifices diversarum Misterarum Regni nostri Angliae finxerunt se fore Ministrallos. Quorum aliqui Liberatam nostram, eis minime datam, portarunt, seipsos etiam fingentes esse Ministrallos nostros proprios. Cuius quidem Liberatae ac dictae Artis sive Occupationis Ministrallorum colore in diversis Partibus Regni nostri praedicti grandes Pecuniarum Exactiones de Ligeis nostris deceptive colligunt et recipiunt.' Hence illegitimate competition with the real minstrels, decay of the art, and neglect of agriculture. The charter then does two things. It makes the royal minstrels a corporation with a marshall elected by themselves, and it puts them at the head of a 'Fraternitatem sive Gildam' of minstrels already existing in the chapel of the Virgin in St. Paul's, and in the royal free chapel of St. Anthony. All minstrels in the country are to join this guild or be suppressed. It is to have two *custodes* and to make statutes and ordinances. The jurisdiction of Dutton over Chester minstrels is, as already stated, reserved[2]. A 'serviens' or 'serjeant' seems to have been an officer of the guild[3]. With this exception nothing more is heard of it until 1594, when a dispute as to the office of the Master

[1] *Carta le Roy de Ministralx*, in Dugdale, *Monasticon* (1822), iii. 397, from *Tutbury Register* in Coll. of Arms; Plot, *Hist. of Staffs.* (1686), ch. x. § 69.

[2] Rymer (1710), xi. 642, (1741) v. 2. 169.

[3] Percy, 372.

of the Musicians' Company called for the intervention of the Lord Keeper[1].' In 1604 the Company received a new charter, which gave it jurisdiction within the city and a radius of three miles from its boundaries. It was further restricted to the city itself under Charles I. It still exists as the Corporation of the Master, Wardens, and Commonalty of the Art or Science of the Musicians of London[2].

The London guild would appear, from its peculiar relation to the royal household minstrels, and its claim to jurisdiction throughout the country, to have been modelled upon that of Paris. This claim was evidently not maintained, and in fact at least three other local guilds can be shown to have existed in the sixteenth century. A search, which I have not undertaken, would probably readily discover more.

4. *Canterbury.*

Ordinances, dated 1526, of the 'felowshyp of the craft and mystery of mynstrells' give the prerogative right to perform in the city to the members of this body, saving the privileges of the city waits, and 'the King's mynstrells, the Queane's, my Lord Prince's, or any honorable or wurshipfull mann's mynstrells of thys realme[3].'

5. *Beverley.*

An order of the Governors of the city (1555) recites an old custom 'since Athelstan' of the choice by minstrels between Trent and Tweed of aldermen of their fraternities during Rogation days, and renews orders for the 'fraternity of our Lady of the read arke in Beverley.' The statutes deal with the employment of minstrels in Beverley, and with their 'castells' at the Rogation-day procession. A new member must be 'mynstrell to some man of honour or worship or waite of some towne corporate or other ancient town or else of such honestye and conyng as shalbe thought laudable and pleasant to the hearers.' It is claimed that such are excluded from the 'Kyng's acts where they speake of vacabonds and valiant beggers.' Quite in the spirit of the London charter of 1469 it is ordered that 'no myler shepherd or of other occupation or husbandman or husbandman servant' shall assume the functions of a minstrel outside his own parish[4]. The earliest notice of this guild in the Beverley archives seems to be in 1557[5], but the terms of the order and the existence of pillars put up

[1] *Analytical Index to Remembrancia of the City of London*, 92.

[2] Grove, *Dict. of Music*, s.v. Musicians; W. C. Hazlitt, *Livery Companies of London*.

[3] Civis, No. xxi.

[4] Poulson, *Beverlac*, i. 302 (probably from *Lansd. MS.* 896, f. 180).

[5] Leach, *Beverley MSS.* 179.

by the minstrels in fifteenth-century churches in Beverley[1] point to some informal earlier association.

6. *York.*

A craft of Mynstrells certainly existed by 1561, in which year they undertook the pageant of Herod at the Corpus Christi plays[2].

G

THOMAS DE CABHAM

[The following extract from a *Penitential* formerly ascribed to John of Salisbury, but now to Thomas de Cabham, Bishop of Salisbury († 1313), is printed by B. Hauréau, *Notices et Extraits de Manuscrits*, xxiv. 2, 284, from *B.N. MSS. Lat.* 3218 and 3529[a], and by F. Guessard and C. Grandmaison, *Huon de Bordeaux*, vi, from *B. N. Sorbonne MS.* 1552, f. 71. The two texts differ in several points. According to Gautier, ii. 22, there are several similar thirteenth-century *Penitentials*, and it is difficult to say which was the original. The doctrine laid down about minstrels is often repeated in later treatises. See e.g. a passage from the fifteenth-century *Le Jardin des Nobles* in P. Paris, *Manuscrits français*, ii. 144.]

Tria sunt histrionum genera. Quidam transformant et transfigurant corpora sua per turpes saltus et per turpes gestus, vel denudando se turpiter, vel induendo horribiles larvas, et omnes tales damnabiles sunt, nisi reliquerint officia sua. Sunt etiam alii qui nihil operantur, sed criminose agunt, non habentes certum domicilium, sed sequuntur curias magnatum et dicunt opprobria et ignominias de absentibus ut placeant aliis. Tales etiam damnabiles sunt, quia prohibet Apostolus cum talibus cibum sumere, et dicuntur tales scurrae vagi, quia ad nihil utiles sunt, nisi ad devorandum et maledicendum. Est etiam tertium genus histrionum qui habent instrumenta musica ad delectandum homines, et talium sunt duo genera. Quidam enim frequentant publicas potationes et lascivas congregationes, et cantant ibi diversas cantilenas ut moveant homines ad lasciviam, et tales sunt damnabiles sicut alii. Sunt autem alii, qui dicuntur ioculatores, qui cantant gesta principum et vitam sanctorum, et faciunt solatia hominibus vel in aegritudinibus suis vel in angustiis, et non faciunt innumeras turpitudines sicut faciunt saltatores et saltatrices et alii qui ludunt in imaginibus inhonestis et faciunt videri quasi quaedam fantasmata per incantationes vel alio modo. Si autem non faciunt talia, sed cantant in instrumentis suis gesta principum et alia

[1] Crowest, 244.

[2] *York Plays*, xxxviii, 125; M. Sellers in *Eng. Hist. Review*, ix. 284.

talia utilia ut faciant solatia hominibus, sicut supradictum est, bene possunt sustineri tales, sicut ait Alexander papa. Cum quidam ioculator quaereret ab eo utrum posset salvare animam suam in officio suo, quaesivit Papa ab eo utrum sciret aliquod aliud opus unde vivere posset: respondit ioculator quod non. Permisit igitur Papa quod ipse viveret de officio suo, dummodo abstineret a praedictis lasciviis et turpitudinibus. Notandum est quod omnes peccant mortaliter qui dant scurris vel leccatoribus vel praedictis histrionibus aliquid de suo. Histrionibus dare nichil aliud est quam perdere.

H

PRINCELY PLEASURES AT KENILWORTH

[From *Robert Laneham's Letter* (ed. F. J. Furnivall for New Shakspere Society (1890); and in Nichols, *Progresses of Elizabeth*, i. 420) describing the entertainment of Elizabeth by the Earl of Leicester at Kenilworth, in July, 1575. G. Gascoigne, *The Princelye Pleasures at the Courte at Kenelworth* (1576, in Nichols, i. 502), leaves undescribed what he calls the 'Coventrie' (ed. 2, 'Countrie') shows.]

I. A Squire Minstrel.

Mary, syr, I must tell yoo: Az all endeuooour waz too mooue mirth & pastime (az I tolld ye): éeuen so a ridiculoous deuise of an auncient minstrell & hiz song waz prepared to haue been profferd, if méet time & place had béen foound for it. Ons in a woorshipfull company, whear, full appointed, he recoounted his matter in sort az it should haue been vttred, I chaunsed too be: what I noted, heer thus I tel yoo: A parson very méet séemed he for the purpoze, of a xlv. yéers olld, apparelled partly as he woold himself. Hiz cap of: his hed séemly roounded tonster wyze: fayr kemb, *that* with a spoonge deintly dipt in a littl capons greaz was finely smoothed too make it shine like a Mallard's wing. Hiz beard smugly shauen: and yet hiz shyrt after the nu trink, with ruffs fayr starched, sléeked, and glistening like a payr of nu shooz: marshalld in good order: wyth a stetting stick, and stoout, that euery ruff stood vp like a wafer: a side gooun of kendall green, after the freshnes of the yéer noow, gathered at the neck with a narro gorget, fastened afore with a white clasp and a keepar close vp to the chin: but easily for heat too vndoo when he list: Séemly begyrt in a red caddiz gyrdl: from that a payr of capped Sheffield kniuez hanging a to side: Out of hiz bozome drawne forth a lappet of his napkin, edged with a blu lace, & marked with a trulooue, a hart, and A. D. for Damian: for he was but a bachelar yet.

Hiz gooun had syde sleeuez dooun to midlegge, slit from the shooulder too the hand, & lined with white cotten. Hiz doobled sleeuez of blak woorsted, vpon them a payr of poynets of towny Chamblet laced a long the wreast wyth blu threeden points, a wealt toward the hand of fustian anapes: a payr of red neatherstocks: a pair of pumps on hiz féet, with a cross cut at the toze for cornz: not nu indéede, yet cleanly blakt with soot, & shining az a shoing horn.

Aboout hiz nek a red rebond sutable too hiz girdl: hiz harp in good grace dependaunt before him: hiz wreast tyed to a gréen lace, and hanging by: vnder the gorget of hiz gooun a fair flagon cheyn, (pewter, for) siluer, as a squier minstrel of Middilsex, that trauaild the cuntrée this soommer seazon vnto fairz & worshipfull mens hoousez: from hiz chein hoong a Schoochion, with mettall & cooller resplendant vpon hiz breast, of the auncient armez of Islington:

[Apparently the minstrel was got ready; but not shown. He was to have recited an Arthurian romance in verse.]

II. The Coventry Hock-Tuesday Show.

And héertoo folloed az good a sport (me thooght) prezented in an historicall ku, by certain good harted men of Couentrée, my Lordes neighboors thear: who, vnderstanding amoong them *the* thing that coold not bee hidden from ony, hoow carefull and studious hiz honor waz, that by all pleazaunt recreasions her highnes might best fynd her self wellcom, & bee made gladsum and mery, (the groundworke indeede, and foundacion, of hiz Lordship's myrth and gladnesse of vs all), made petition that they moought renu noow their olld storiall sheaw: Of argument, how the Danez whylom héere in a troubloous seazon wear for quietnesse born withall, & suffeard in peas, that anon, by outrage & importabl insolency, abuzing both Ethelred, the king then, and all estates euerie whear beside: at the greuoous complaint & coounsell of Huna, the king's chieftain in warz, on Saint Brices night, Ann. Dom. 1012 (Az the book sayz) that falleth yéerely on the thirtéenth of Nouember, wear all dispatcht, and the Ream rid. And for becauz the matter mencioneth how valiantly our English women for looue of their cuntrée behaued themseluez: expressed in actionz & rymez after their maner, they thought it moought mooue sum myrth to her Maiestie the rather.

The thing, said they, iz grounded on story, and for pastime woont too bee plaid in oour Citee yéerely: without ill exampl of mannerz, papistry, or ony superstition: and elz did so occupy the heads of a number, that likely inoough woold haue had woorz meditationz: had an auncient beginning, and a long continuauns: tyll noow of late laid dooun, they knu no cauz why, onless it wear by the zeal of certain theyr Preacherz: men very commendabl for their behauiour and learning, & swéet in their sermons, but sumwhat too sour in preaching awey theyr pastime: wisht therefore, that az they shoold continu their good doctrine in pulpet, so, for matters of pollicy & gouernauns of the Citie, they woold permit them to the Mair and Magistratez: and seyed, by my feyth, Master Martyn, they woold make theyr humbl peticion vntoo her highnes, that they might haue theyr playz vp agayn.

But aware, kéep bak, make room noow, heer they cum! And fyrst, . . . Captain Cox cam marching on valiantly before, cléen trust, & gartered aboue the knée, all fresh in a veluet cap (master Goldingham lent it him) floorishing with hiz tonswoord, and another fensmaster with him: thus in the foreward making room for the rest. After them proudly prickt on formost, the Danish launsknights on horsbak, and then the English: each with their allder poll marcially in their hand. Eeuen at the first entrée the méeting waxt sumwhat warm: that by and by kindled with corage a both sidez, gru from a hot skirmish vnto a blazing battail: first by speare and shield, outragious in their racez az ramz at their rut, with furious encoounterz, that togyther they tumbl too the dust, sumtime hors and man: and after fall too it with sworde & target, good bangz a both sidez: the fight so ceassing; but the battail not so ended: folloed the footmen, both the hostez, ton after toother: first marching in ranks: then warlik turning, then from ranks into squadrons, then in too trianglz; from that intoo rings, & so winding oout again: A valiant captain of great prowez, az fiers az a fox assauting a gooz, waz so hardy to giue the first stroke: then get they grisly togyther: that great waz the actiuitée that day too be séen thear a both sidez: ton very eager for purchaz of pray, toother vtterly stoout for redemption of libertie: thus, quarrell enflamed fury a both sidez. Twise the Danes had the better; but at the last conflict, beaten doun, ouercom, and many led captiue for triumph by our English wéemen.

This waz the effect of this sheaw, that, az it waz handled, made mooch matter of good pastime: brought all indéed intoo the great court, een vnder her highnes windo too haue been séen: but (az vnhappy it waz for the bride) that cam thither too soon, (and yet waz it a four a clok). For her highnes beholding in the chamber delectabl dauncing indéed: and héerwith the great throng and vnrulines of the people, waz cauz that this solemnitee of Brideale & dauncing, had not the full muster waz hoped for: and but a littl of the Couentrée plea her highnes also saw: commaunded thearfore on the Tuisday folloing to haue it ful oout: az accordingly it waz prezented, whearat her Maiestie laught well: they wear the iocunder, and so mooch the more becauz her highnes had giuen them too buckes, and fiue marke in mony, to make mery togyther: they prayed for her Maiesty, long, happily to reign, & oft to cum thither, that oft they moought sée héer: & what, reioycing vpon their ampl reward, and what, triumphing vpon the good acceptauns, they vaunted their play waz neuer so dignified, nor euer any players afore so beatified. . . .

Tuisday, according to commandement, cam oour Couentrée men: what their matter waz, of her highnes myrth and good acceptauns, and rewarde vntoo them, and of their reioysing thearat, I sheawd you afore, and so say the less noow.

I

THE INDIAN VILLAGE FEAST

[From Sir Walter Elliot, *On the Characteristics of the Population of Central India*, in *Journal of the Ethnological Society of London*, N. S. i. 94 (1869).]

In the north-east corner of the central mountainous region represented on the map, between the Mahanadi and Godavery rivers, is found a tribe which has preserved its normal character remarkably free from change and from external influence. The Konds, or, as they call themselves, the Kuingas, although only discovered within the last thirty-five years, are better known than most of the other barbarous tribes from the fact that for ages they have been in the habit of sacrificing human victims in great numbers to secure the favour of the deities presiding over their dwellings, fields, hills, &c., but especially of the earth-goddess.

The successful efforts employed to abolish this barbarous rite have made the subject familiar to all, and it is remarkable that such knowledge should have failed to attract attention to a practice precisely similar in its objects and in its details, which is observed in every village of Southern India, with this single difference, that a buffalo is substituted for a human victim. My attention was early drawn to this practice, which is called the festival of the village goddess (*Devi*, or *Grama Devati*), the descriptions of which led me to believe it might throw light on the early condition of the servile classes, and resolving to witness its celebrations, I repaired to the village of Serúr, in the Southern Mahratta country, in March, 1829. It would occupy too much time to describe the ceremony in full, which is the less necessary as the details vary in different places; but the general features are always the same.

The temple of the goddess is a mean structure outside the village. The officiating priests are the Parias, who, on this occasion, and on it alone, are exempt from the degrading condition which excludes them from the village, and from contact with the inhabitants. With them are included the Mangs or workers in leather, the Asádis or Dásaris, *paria* dancing-girls devoted to the service of the temple, the musician in attendance on them called Ràniga, who acts also as a sort of jester or buffoon, and a functionary called Pót-raj, who officiates as *pujári* to a rural god named also Pót-raj, to whom a small altar is erected behind the temple of the village goddess. He is armed with a long whip, which he cracks with great dexterity, and to which also at various parts of the ceremony divine honours are paid.

All the members of the village community take part in the festival with the hereditary district officers, many of them Brahmans. The shepherds or *Dhangars* of the neighbouring villages are also invited, and they attend with their priests called *Virgars* or *Irgars*, accompanied by the *dhol* or big drum peculiar to their caste. But the whole is under the guidance and management of the Parias.

The festival commences always on a Tuesday, the day of rest among the agricultural classes, both for man and beast. The most important and essential ceremonies take place on the second and fifth days. On the former, the sacred buffalo, which had been purchased by the Parias, an animal without a blemish, is thrown down before the goddess, its head struck off by a single blow and placed in front of the shrine with one fore-leg thrust into its mouth. Around are placed vessels containing the different cereals, and hard by a heap of mixed grains, with a drill plough in the centre. The carcase is then cut up into small pieces, and each cultivator receives a portion to bury in his field. The blood and offal are collected into a large basket, over which some pots of the cooked food which had been presented as a meat offering (*naivedya*) had previously been broken, and Pót-raj taking a live kid called the *hari-mariah*, hews it in pieces over the whole. The mess (*cheraga*) is then mixed together, and the basket being placed on the head of a naked Mang, he runs off with it, flinging the contents into the air, and scattering them right and left, as an offering (*bhut-bali*) to the evil spirits, and followed by the other Parias, and the village Paiks, with drawn swords. Sometimes the demons arrest the progress of the party, when more of the mess is thrown about, and fowls and sheep are sacrificed, till the spirits are appeased.

During the whole time of the sacrifice the armed paiks keep vigilant guard, lest any intruder should secrete a morsel of flesh or a drop of blood, which, if carried off successfully, after declaring the purpose, would transfer the merit of the offering to the strangers' village.

On the return of the party from making the circuit of the village another buffalo, seized by force wherever it can be found (*zulmi-khulga*), is sacrificed by decapitating it in the same manner as the former; but no particular importance is attached to it, and the flesh is distributed to be eaten.

The third and fourth days are devoted to private offerings. On the former all the inhabitants of caste, who had vowed animals to the goddess during the preceding three years for the welfare of their families, or the fertility of their fields, brought the buffaloes or sheep to the *paria pujári*, who struck off their heads. The fourth day was appropriated exclusively to the offerings of the Parias. In this way, some fifty or sixty buffaloes and several hundred sheep were slain, and the heads piled up in two great heaps. Many women on these days walked naked to the temple in fulfilment of vows, but they were covered with leaves and boughs of trees and surrounded by their female relations and friends.

On the fifth and last day (Saturday) the whole community marched in procession, with music, to the temple, and offered a concluding sacrifice at the Pót-raj altar. A lamb was concealed close by. The Pót-raj having found it after a pretended search, struck it simply with his whip, which he then placed upon it, and, making several passes with his hands, rendered it insensible; in fact, mesmerised it. When it became rigid and stiff he lifted it up and carried it about on the palm of his hand, to the amazement of the spectators, and then laid it down on the ground. His hands were then tied behind his back by the *pujári*, and the whole party began to dance round him with noisy shouts, the music and the shepherd's drum making a deafening noise. Pót-raj joined in the excitement, his eyes began to roll, his long hair fell loose over his shoulders, and he soon came fully under the influence of the *numen*. He was now led up, still bound, to the place where the lamb lay motionless. He rushed at it, seized it with his teeth, tore through the skin, and ate into its throat. When it was quite dead, he was lifted up, a dishful of the meat offering was presented to him; he thrust his bloody face into it, and it was then, with the remains of the lamb, buried beside the altar. Meantime his hands were untied, and he fled the place, and did not appear for three days. The rest of the party now adjourned to the front of the temple, where the heap of grain deposited the first day was divided among the cultivators, to be buried by each one in his field with the bit of flesh. After this a distribution of the piled-up heads was made by the hand of the Rániga. About forty sheep's heads were given to certain privileged persons, among which two were allotted to the Sircar! For the rest a general scramble took place, paiks, shepherds, Parias, and many boys and men of good caste, were soon rolling in the mass of putrid gore. The heads were flung about in all directions, without regard to rank or caste, the Brahmans coming in for an ample share of the filth. The scramble for the buffalo heads was confined to the Parias. Whoever was fortunate enough to secure one of either kind carried it off and buried it in his field. The proceedings terminated by a procession round the boundaries of the village lands, preceded by the goddess, and the head of the sacred buffalo carried on the head of one of the Mangs. All order and propriety now ceased. Rániga began to abuse the goddess in the foulest terms; he then turned his fury against the government, the head man of the village, and every one who fell in his way. The Parias and Asádis attacked the most respectable and gravest citizens, and laid hold of the Brahmans, Lingayats, and Zamindars without scruple. The dancing-women jumped on their shoulders, the shepherds beat the big drum, with deafening clangor, and universal license reigned.

On reaching a little temple, sacred to the goddess of boundaries (*polimera-amma*), they halted to make some offerings, and bury the sacred head. As soon as it was covered, the uproar began again. Rániga became more foul-mouthed than ever. In vain the head-men, the government officers, and others tried to pacify him by giving him small copper coins. He only broke out with worse imprecations and grosser abuse, till the circuit being completed, all dispersed; the Parias retired to their hamlet outside the town, resuming their humble, servile character, and the village reverted to its wonted peaceful appearance.

Next day (Sunday) the whole population turned out to a great hunting-party.

I found this remarkable institution existing in every part of India where I have been, and I have descriptions of it corresponding in all essential points, from the Dekhan, the Nizam's country, Mysore, the Carnatic, and the Northern Circars. The details vary in different places, but the main features agree in all, and correspond remarkably with the *Mariah* sacrifice of the Konds, which also varies considerably on minor points in different places.

J

SWORD-DANCES

I. Sweden (*Sixteenth Century*).

[From Olaus Magnus, *Historia de gentibus septentrionalibus* (1555), Bk. xv. chh. 23, 24.]

Ch. 23, *de chorea gladiatoria vel armifera saltatione.*

Habent septentrionales Gothi et Sueci pro exercenda iuventute alium ludum, quod inter nudos enses et infestos gladios seu frameas sese exerceant saltu, idque quodam gymnastico ritu et disciplina, aetate successiva, a peritis et praesultare sub cantu addiscunt: et ostendunt hunc ludum praecipue tempore carnisprivii, maschararum Italico verbo dicto. Ante etenim tempus eiusdem carnisprivii octo diebus continua saltatione sese adolescentes numerose exercent, elevatis scilicet gladiis sed vagina reclusis, ad triplicem gyrum. Deinde evaginatis itidemque elevatis ensibus, postmodo manuatim extensis, modestius gyrando alterutrius cuspidem capulumque receptantes, sese mutato ordine in modum figurae hexagoni fingendi subiiciunt, quam rosam dicunt: et illico eam gladios retrahendo elevandoque resolvunt ut super uniuscuiusque caput quadrata rosa resultet: et tandem vehementissima gladiorum laterali collisione, celerrime retrograda saltatione determinant ludum, quem tibiis vel cantilenis, aut utrisque simul, primum per graviorem, demum vehementiorem saltum et ultimo impetuosissimum moderantur. Sed haec speculatio sine oculari inspectione vix apprehenditur quam pulchra honestaque sit, dum unius parcissimo praecepto etiam armata multitudo quadam alacritate dirigitur ad certamen: eoque ludo clericis sese exercere et immiscere licet, quia totus deducitur honestissima ratione.

Ch. 24. Alia etiam iuvenum exercitatio est, ut certa lege arcualem choream ducant et reducant, aliis quidam instrumentis, sed eadem ut gladiatorum saltantium disciplina reducta. Arcubus enim seu circulis inclusis [inclusi?], primum modesto cantu heroum gesta referente vel tibiis aut tympanis excitati, gyrando incedunt seque dirigentis, qui rex dicitur, sola voce reducunt, tandem solutis arcubus aliquantulum celerius properantes mutua inclinatione conficiunt, veluti alias per gladios, rosam, ut formam sexangularem efficere videantur. Utque id festivius sonoriusque fiat, tintinnabula seu aereas campanulas genu tenus ligant.

II. Shetland (*Eighteenth Century*).

[From Sir Walter Scott's *Diary* for August 7, 1814, printed in Lockhart, *Life of Scott* (1837), iii. 162; (1878) i. 265.

At Scalloway my curiosity was gratified by an account of the sword-dance, now almost lost, but still practised in the Island of Papa, belonging to Mr. Scott. There are eight performers, seven of whom represent the Seven Champions of Christendom, who enter one by one with their swords drawn, and are presented to the eighth personage, who is not named. Some rude couplets are spoken (in *English*, not *Norse*), containing a sort of panegyric upon each champion as he is presented. They then dance a sort of cotillion, as the ladies described it, going through a number of evolutions with their swords. One of my three Mrs. Scotts readily promised to procure me the lines, the rhymes, and the form of the dance. . . . A few years since a party of Papa-men came to dance the sword-dance at Lerwick as a public exhibition with great applause. . . . In a stall pamphlet, called the history of Buckshaven [Fifeshire], it is said those fishers sprung from Danes, and brought with them their *war-dance* or *sword-dance*, and a rude wooden cut of it is given.

[A footnote by Lockhart adds:—]

Mr. W. S. Rose informs me that, when he was at school at Winchester, the morris-dancers there used to exhibit a sword-dance resembling that described at Camacho's wedding in *Don Quixote*; and Mr. Morritt adds that similar dances are even yet performed in the villages about Rokeby [Yorks, N.R.] every Christmas.

[The following account was inserted in a note to Scott's *The Pirate* (1821).]

To the Primate's account of the sword-dance, I am able to add the words sung or chanted, on occasion of this dance, as it is still performed in Papa Stour, a remote island of Zetland, where alone the custom keeps its ground. It is, it will be observed by antiquaries, a species of play or mystery, in which the Seven Champions of Christendom make their appearance, as in the interlude presented in *All's Well that ends Well.* This dramatic curiosity was most kindly procured for my use by Dr. Scott of Haslar Hospital [died 1875], son of my friend Mr. Scott of Melbie, Zetland. Dr. Hibbert has, in his *Description of the Zetland Islands*, given an account of the sword-dance, but somewhat less full than the following:—

'WORDS USED AS A PRELUDE TO THE SWORD-DANCE, A DANISH OR NORWEGIAN BALLET, COMPOSED SOME CENTURIES AGO, AND PRESERVED IN PAPA STOUR, ZETLAND.

PERSONÆ DRAMATIS[1].

(*Enter* MASTER, *in the character of* SAINT GEORGE.)

Brave gentles all within this boor[2],
If ye delight in any sport,
Come see me dance upon this floor,
Which to you all shall yield comfort.
Then shall I dance in such a sort,
As possible I may or can;
You, minstrel man, play me a Porte[3],
That I on this floor may prove a man.
[*He bows, and dances in a line.*
Now have I danced with heart and hand,
Brave gentles all, as you may see,
For I have been tried in many a land,
As yet the truth can testify;
In England, Scotland, Ireland, France, Italy, and Spain,
Have I been tried with that good sword of steel.
[*Draws, and flourishes.*
Yet I deny that ever a man did make me yield;
For in my body there is strength,
As by my manhood may be seen;
And I, with that good sword of length,
Have oftentimes in perils been,
And over champions I was king.
And by the strength of this right hand,
Once on a day I kill'd fifteen,
And left them dead upon the land.

[1] So placed in the old MS.

[2] *Boor*—so spelt to accord with the vulgar pronunciation of the word *bower*.

[3] *Porte*—so spelt in the original. The word is known as indicating a piece of music on the bagpipe, to which ancient instrument, which is of Scandinavian origin, the sword-dance may have been originally composed.

Therefore, brave minstrel, do not care,
But play to me a Porte most light,
That I no longer do forbear,
But dance in all these gentles' sight.
Although my strength makes you abased,
Brave gentles all, be not afraid,
For here are six champions, with me, staid,
All by my manhood I have raised. [*He dances.*
Since I have danced, I think it best
To call my brethren in your sight,
That I may have a little rest,
And they may dance with all their might;
With heart and hand as they are knights,
And shake their swords of steel so bright,
And show their main strength on this floor,
For we shall have another bout
Before we pass out of this boor.
Therefore, brave minstrel, do not care
To play to me a Porte most light,
That I no longer do forbear,
But dance in all these gentles' sight.

[*He dances, and then introduces his knights as under.*

Stout James of Spain, both tried and stour[1],
Thine acts are known full well indeed;
And champion Dennis, a French knight,
Who stout and bold is to be seen;
And David, a Welshman born,
Who is come of noble blood;
And Patrick also, who blew the horn,
An Irish knight amongst the wood.
Of Italy, brave Anthony the good,
And Andrew of Scotland King;
Saint George of England, brave indeed,
Who to the Jews wrought muckle tinte[2].
Away with this!—Let us come to sport,
Since that ye have a mind to war.
Since that ye have this bargain sought,
Come let us fight and do not fear.
Therefore, brave minstrel, do not care

[1] *Stour*—great.

[2] *Muckle tinte*—much loss or harm; so in MS.

To play to me a Porte most light,
That I no longer do forbear,
But dance in all these gentles' sight.
[*He dances, and advances to* JAMES *of Spain.*
Stout James of Spain, both tried and stour,
Thine acts are known full well indeed,
Present thyself within our sight,
Without either fear or dread.
Count not for favour or for feid,
Since of thy acts thou hast been sure;
Brave James of Spain, I will thee lead,
To prove thy manhood on this floor. [JAMES *dances.*
Brave champion Dennis, a French knight,
Who stout and bold is to be seen,
Present thyself here in our sight,
Thou brave French knight,
Who bold hast been;
Since thou such valiant acts hast done,
Come let us see some of them now
With courtesy, thou brave French knight,
Draw out thy sword of noble hue.
[DENNIS *dances, while the others retire to a side.*
Brave David a bow must string, and with awe
Set up a wand upon a stand,
And that brave David will cleave in twa [1]. [DAVID *dances solus.*
Here is, I think, an Irish knight,
Who does not fear, or does not fright,
To prove thyself a valiant man,
As thou hast done full often bright;
Brave Patrick, dance, if that thou can. [*He dances.*
Thou stout Italian, come thou here;
Thy name is Anthony, most stout;
Draw out thy sword that is most clear,
And do thou fight without any doubt;
Thy leg thou shake, thy neck thou lout [2],
And show some courtesy on this floor,
For we shall have another bout,
Before we pass out of this boor.

[1] Something is evidently amiss or omitted here. David probably exhibited some feat of archery.

[2] *Lout*—to bend or bow down, pronounced *loot*, as *doubt* is *doot* in Scotland.

Thou kindly Scotsman, come thou here;
Thy name is Andrew of Fair Scotland;
Draw out thy sword that is most clear,
Fight for thy king with thy right hand;
And aye as long as thou canst stand,
Fight for thy king with all thy heart;
And then, for to confirm his band,
Make all his enemies for to smart.

[*He dances.—Music begins.*'

'FIGUIR[1].

'The six stand in rank with their swords reclining on their shoulders. The Master (Saint George) dances, and then strikes the sword of James of Spain, who follows George, then dances, strikes the sword of Dennis, who follows behind James. In like manner the rest—the music playing—swords as before. After the six are brought out of rank, they and the Master form a circle, and hold the swords point and hilt. This circle is danced round twice. The whole, headed by the Master, pass under the swords held in a vaulted manner. They jump over the swords. This naturally places the swords across, which they disentangle by passing under their right sword. They take up the seven swords, and form a circle, in which they dance round.

'The Master runs under the sword opposite, which he jumps over backwards. The others do the same. He then passes under the right-hand sword, which the others follow, in which position they dance, until commanded by the Master, when they form into a circle, and dance round as before. They then jump over the right-hand sword, by which means their backs are to the circle, and their hands across their backs. They dance round in that form until the Master calls "Loose," when they pass under the right sword, and are in a perfect circle.

'The Master lays down his sword, and lays hold of the point of James's sword. He then turns himself, James, and the others, into a clew. When so formed, he passes under out of the midst of the circle; the others follow; they vault as before. After several other evolutions, they throw themselves into a circle, with their arms across the breast. They afterwards form such figures as to form a shield of their swords, and the shield is so compact that the Master and his knights dance alternately with this shield upon their heads. It is then

[1] *Figuir*—so spelt in MS.

laid down upon the floor. Each knight lays hold of their former points and hilts with their hands across, which disentangle by figuirs directly contrary to those that formed the shield. This finishes the ballet.

'EPILOGUE.

'Mars does rule, he bends his brows,
He makes us all agast[1];
After the few hours that we stay here,
Venus will rule at last.
Farewell, farewell, brave gentles all,
That herein do remain,
I wish you health and happiness
Till we return again. [*Exeunt.*'

The manuscript from which the above was copied was transcribed from *a very old one*, by Mr. William Henderson, jun., of Papa Stour, in Zetland. Mr. Henderson's copy is not dated, but bears his own signature, and, from various circumstances, it is known to have been written about the year 1788.

K

THE LUTTERWORTH ST. GEORGE PLAY

[From W. Kelly, *Notices Illustrative of the Drama, &c., . . . from . . . Manuscripts of the Borough of Leicester* (1865), 53. The version is that 'performed in some of the villages near Lutterworth, at Christmas 1863.']

THE CHRISTMAS MUMMERS' PLAY.

DRAMATIS PERSONAE.

1. CAPTAIN SLASHER, *in military costume, with sword and pistol.*
2. King of England, *in robes, wearing the crown.*
3. PRINCE GEORGE, *King's Son, in robes, and sword by his side.*
4. Turkish Champion, *in military attire, with sword and pistol.*
5. A Noble Doctor.
6. Beelzebub.
7. A Clown.

Enter Captain Slasher. I beg your pardon for being so bold,
I enter your house, the weather's so cold,
Room, a room! brave gallants, give us room to sport;
For in this house we do resort,—

[1] *Agast*—so spelt in MS.

Resort, resort, for many a day;
Step in, the King of England,
And boldly clear the way.

Enter King of England. I am the King of England, that boldly does appear;
I come to seek my only son,—my only son is here.

Enter Prince George. I am Prince George, a worthy knight;
I'll spend my blood for England's right.
England's right I will maintain;
I'll fight for old England once again.

Enter Turkish Knight. I am the Turkish Champion;
From Turkey's land I come.
I come to fight the King of England
And all his noble men.

Captain Slasher. In comes Captain Slasher,
Captain Slasher is my name;
With sword and pistol by my side,
I hope to win the game.

King of England. I am the King of England,
As you may plainly see,
These are my soldiers standing by me;
They stand by me your life to end,
On them doth my life depend.

Prince George. I am Prince George, the Champion bold,
And with my sword I won three crowns of gold;
I slew the fiery dragon and brought him to the slaughter,
And won the King of Egypt's only daughter.

Turkish Champion. As I was going by St. Francis' School,
I heard a lady cry 'A fool, a fool!'
'A fool,' was every word,
'That man's a fool,
Who wears a wooden sword.'

Prince George. A wooden sword, you dirty dog!
My sword is made of the best of metal free.
If you would like to taste of it,
I'll give it unto thee.
Stand off, stand off, you dirty dog!
Or by my sword you'll die.
I'll cut you down the middle,
And make your blood to fly.

[*They fight; Prince George falls, mortally wounded.*

Enter King of England. Oh, horrible! terrible! what hast thou done?
Thou hast ruin'd me, ruin'd me,
By killing of my only son!
Oh, is there ever a noble doctor to be found,
To cure this English champion
Of his deep and deadly wound?

Enter Noble Doctor. Oh yes, there is a noble doctor to be found,
To cure this English champion
Of his deep and deadly wound.

King of England. And pray what is your practice?

Noble Doctor. I boast not of my practice, neither do I study in the practice of physic.

King of England. What can you cure?

Noble Doctor. All sorts of diseases,
Whatever you pleases:
I can cure the itch, the pitch,
The phthisic, the palsy and the gout;
And if the devil's in the man,
I can fetch him out.
My wisdom lies in my wig,
I torture not my patients with excations,
Such as pills, boluses, solutions, and embrocations;
But by the word of command
I can make this mighty prince to stand.

King. What is your fee?

Doctor. Ten pounds is true.

King. Proceed, Noble Doctor;
You shall have your due.

Doctor. Arise, arise! most noble prince, arise,
And no more dormant lay;
And with thy sword
Make all thy foes obey. [*The Prince arises.*

Prince George. My head is made of iron,
My body is made of steel,
My legs are made of crooked bones
To force you all to yield.

Enter Beelzebub. In comes I, old Beelzebub,
Over my shoulder I carry my club,
And in my hand a frying-pan,

Pleased to get all the money I can.
Enter Clown. In come I, who 's never been yet,
With my great head and little wit:
My head is great, my wit is small,
I'll do my best to please you all.
Song (all join). And now we are done and must be gone,
No longer will we stay here;
But if you please, before we go,
We'll taste your Christmas beer. [*Exeunt omnes.*

L

THE PROSE OF THE ASS

[The text is taken from the following sources:—

i. *Beauvais, thirteenth century.*—(*a*) [Duc.]—Ducange, *Glossarium* (ed. 1733–6), s.v. *Festum*, from a lost MS.; copied incorrectly by Gasté, 23, and apparently also by Clément, 158: (*b*) [B[1]]—*Brit. Mus. Egerton MS.* 2615, f. 1, with music for singing in unison: (*c*) [B[2]]—Same *MS.* f. 43, with music harmonized in three parts; partly facsimiled in *Annales Archéologiques* (1856), xvi. 259, 300.

ii. *Sens, thirteenth century.*—[S]—*MS. Senonense*, 46[A], as printed by G. M. Dreves, *Analecta Hymnica*, xx. 217. The text has also been given from the MS. by F. Bourquelot, in *Bull. de la Soc. Arch. de Sens* (1858), vi. 79, and others. The version of Clément, 126 is probably, like the facsimile given by him in *Ann. Arch.* vii. 26, based on one 'calqué' from the MS. by a M. Amé, and, where it differs from that of Dreves, is the less trustworthy. Dreves, xx. 257 (cf. *infra*) and Millin, *Monum. Ant. Inédits*, ii. 348, also give the music of the opening lines. Modern settings are provided by B. De la Borde, *Essai sur la Musique* (1780), and Clément, in *Ann. Arch.* vii. 26, and *Chantes de la Sainte Chapelle.* An old French translation of the text is printed in Leber, ix. 368.

On these Beauvais and Sens MSS. cf. ch. xiii.

iii. *Bourges.*—[Bo.]—The first verse with the music and variants in the later verses are given by A. Gachet d'Artigny, *Nouveaux Mémoires* (1756), vii. 77, from a copy of a book given to Bourges cathedral by a canon named Jean Pastoris. Part of the Bourges music is also given by Millin, *loc. cit.*

I print the fullest version from Ducange, italicizing the lines not found elsewhere, and giving all variants, except of spelling, for the rest.

Outside Beauvais, Sens, and Bourges the only localized allusion to the prose that I have found is the Autun order of 1411 (vol. i. p. 312) 'nec dicatur cantilena quae dici solebat super dictum asinum.' It is not in the Puy *officium* for the Circumcision, which, though in a MS. of 1553, represents a ceremony as old as 1327 (U. Chevalier, *Prosolarium Ecclesiae Aniciensis*, 1894). The *officium* is full of *conductus* and *farsumina*, and the *clericuli* at second Vespers *tripudiant firmiter.* The *sanctum Praepucium* was a relic at Puy.

The following passage is from Theoph. Raynaudus, *Iudicium de puer-*

orum symphoniacorum processione in festo SS. Innocentium (*Opera Omnia*, 1665, xv. 209): 'Legi prosam quandam *de asino* e Metropolitanae cuiusdam Ecclesiae rituali exscriptam; quae super sacrum concinebatur in die S. Stephani, et dicebatur *prosa fatuorum*, qua nihil insulsius aut asino convenientius. Similis prosa *de bove*, quae canebatur in die S. Ioannis, intercidisse dicitur, haud magno sane dispendio. Itaque hae prosae erant particulae festi fatuorum, occoepti a die S. Stephani.' I have never come across the 'Prose of the Ox,' or any notice of it which appears to be independent of Raynaud's.]

I.

Orientis partibus
Adventavit Asinus,
Pulcher et fortissimus,
Sarcinis aptissimus.
Hez, Sire Asnes, car chantez,
Belle bouche rechignez,
Vous aurez du foin assez
Et de l'avoine a plantez.

II.

Lentus erat pedibus,
Nisi foret baculus,
Et eum in clunibus
Pungeret aculeus.
Hez, Sire Asnes, etc.

III.

Hic in collibus Sichen
Iam nutritus sub Ruben,
Transiit per Iordanem,
Saliit in Bethleem.
Hez, Sire Asnes, etc.

IV.

Ecce magnis auribus
Subiugalis filius
Asinus egregius
Asinorum dominus.
Hez, Sire Asnes, etc.

B[1] has heading *Conductus asi⟨ni ubi⟩ adducitur*; S, *Conductus ad tabulam.*

5–8 B[1,2] *Hez, hez, sire Asnes, hez*; S. *Hez, Sir asne, hez*; Bo. *He, he, he, Sire Ane. He.*

18. B[1,2]; S, *Enutritus.*

21–4. B[1] *Hez, hez* (and so in all verses but last); B[2] *Hez* (and so in all verses); S, *Hez, Sir asne, hez* (and so in all verses).

v.

Saltu vincit hinnulos,
Dammas et capreolos,
Super dromedarios
Velox Madianeos.
Hez, Sire Asnes, etc.

vi.

Aurum de Arabia,
Thus et myrrham de Saba
Tulit in Ecclesia
Virtus Asinaria.
Hez, Sire Asnes, etc.

vii.

Dum trahit vehicula,
Multa cum sarcinula,
Illius mandibula
Dura terit pabula.
Hez, Sire Asnes, etc.

viii.

Cum aristis hordeum
Comedit et carduum:
Triticum e palea
Segregat in area.
Hez, Sire Asnes, etc.

ix.

Amen dicas, Asine,
Iam satur de gramine,
Amen, Amen, itera,
Aspernare vetera.
Hez va, hez va! hez va, hez!
Bialx Sire Asnes, car allez:
Belle bouche, car chantez.

vi. $B^{1,2}$ omit; Bo. places after viii.
59. Duc. *a palea.*
65. Duc. adds (*hic genuflectebatur*).
66. Bo. *Iam satis de carmine.*

69–71. B^2 *Hez*; Clément,
Hez va! hez va! hez va! hez!
Bialx, sir asnes, car chantez,
Vous aurez du foin assez
Et de l'avoine a plantez.

I append the air of the Sens prose, as given by Dreves, *Analecta Hymnica*, xx. 257.

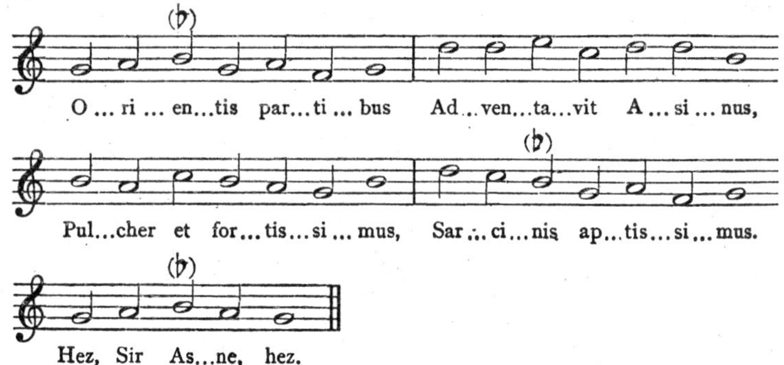

M

THE BOY BISHOP

I. The Sarum Office.

[From C. Wordsworth, *Ceremonies and Processions of the Cathedral Church of Salisbury* (1901), 52, which follows the practically identical texts of the printed *Processionals* of 1508 (ed. Henderson, 1882, 17) and 1555 and the printed *Breviary* (ed. Procter-Wordsworth, I. ccxxix). Mr. Wordsworth also found the office in two MS. breviaries (*Sarum Chapter MS.* 152 and *Peterhouse, Cambridge, MS.* 270). In the MS. (†1445) processional from Salisbury Cathedral (*Chapter MS.* 148), on which his book is mainly based, there is a *lacuna*, probably due to intentional mutilation, where the office should come. I find no allusion to the Boy Bishop in the printed *Sarum Missal* (ed. Dickinson, 67), or in the *Sarum Consuetudinary, Custumary*, or *Ordinal* (Frere, *Use of Sarum*).]

¶ *In die sancti Johannis.*

[De Episcopo Puerorum.]

Ad uesperas, post memoriam de S. Stephano eat processio Puerorum ad altare Innocencium, uel Sancte Trinitatis et Omnium Sanctorum quod dicitur Salue, *in capis sericis, cum cereis illuminatis et ardentibus in manibus, cantando, Episcopo Puerorum pontificalibus induto (executore officij, siue Episcopo presente) incipiente hoc responsorium.*

Solus Episcopus Innocencium, si assit, Christum Puerum, uerum et eternum, Pontificem designans, incipiat:

R. Centum quadraginta quattuor millia qui empti sunt de terra: hij sunt qui cum mulieribus non sunt coinquinati, uirgines enim permanserunt. Ideo regnant cum Deo et Agno, et Agnus Dei cum illis.

Tres pueri dicant hunc uersum.

V. Hij empti sunt ex omnibus, primicie Deo et Agno, et in ore illorum non est inventum mendacium. Ideo.

Omnes pueri dicant cantando simul hanc prosam

Sedentem in superne.

Chorus post vnumquemque uersum respondeat cantum prose super vltimam literam E.

V. Sedentem in superne maiestatis arce–e.

V. Adorant humillime proclamantes ad te–e.

V. Sancte · Sancte · Sancte · Sabaoth rex–e.

V. Plena sunt omnia glorie tue–e.

V. Cum illis vndeuiginti quinque–e.

V. Atque cum innocentissimo grege–e.

V. Qui sunt sine vlla labe–e.

V. Dicentes excelsa uoce–e.

V. Laus Tibi, Domine–e.

Rex eterne glorie–e.

Chorus respondeat Ideo regnant.

Ad hanc processionem non dicatur Gloria Patri *sed dum prosa canitur tunc Episcopus Puerorum thurificet altare: deinde ymaginem Sancte Trinitatis.*

Et postea dicat Sacerdos, modesta uoce, hunc uersum.

V. Letamini in Domino, et exvltate iusti.

R. Et gloriamini omnes recti corde.

Deinde dicat Episcopus Puerorum, sine Dominus uobiscum, *sed cum* Oremus, *oracionem.*

Deus, cuius hodierna die preconium innocentes martires non loquendo sed moriendo confessi sunt: omnia in nobis uitiorum mala mortifica, vt fidem tuam, quam lingua nostra loquitur, eciam moribus uita fateatur. Qui cum Deo Patre.

In redeundo precentor puerorum incipiat responsorium de S. Maria, uel aliquam antiphonam de eadem.

R. Felix namque es, sacra uirgo Maria, et omni laude dignissima. Quia ex te ortus est Sol iusticie, Christus Deus noster.

Et, si necesse fuerit, dicatur uersus:

V. Ora pro populo, interueni pro clero, intercede pro deuoto femineo sexu: senciant omnes tuum leuamen, quicumque celebrant tuam solempnitatem. Quia ex te Gloria · Quia ·

Et sic processio chorum intret, per ostium occidentale, vt supra. Et omnes pueri, ex vtraque parte chori, in superiori gradu se recipiant; et ab hac hora vsque post processionem diei proximi succedentis nullus clericorum solet gradum superiorem ascendere, cuiuscumque condicionis fuerit.

Ad istam processionem pro disposicione puerorum scribuntur canonici, ad ministrandum eisdem, maiores ad thuribulandum, et ad librum deferendum, minores ad candelabra deferenda.

Responsorio finito, cum suo uersu, Episcopus Puerorum in sede sua dicat uersum modesta uoce:

V. Speciosus forma pre filijs hominum:

R. Diffusa est gracia in labijs tuis.

Oracio. Deus qui salutis eterne beate Marie uirginitate fecunda humano generi premia prestitisti; tribue, quesumus, vt ipsam pro nobis intercedere senciamus, per quam meruimus Auctorem uite suscipere, Dominum nostrum Jesum Christum Filium tuum. *Que sic terminetur:* Qui Tecum uiuit et regnat in vnitate Spiritus Sancti Deus. Per omnia secula seculorum. Amen.

Pax uobis.

R. Et cum spiritu tuo.

Sequatur Benedicamus Domino, *a duobus uicarijs, uel a tribus, extra regulam.*

Tunc Episcopus Puerorum intret stallum suum, et in sede sua, benedicat populum.

Et interim cruciferarius accipiat baculum episcopi, conuersus ad Episcopum, et cum uenerit ad istum versum Cum mansuetudine *conuertat se ad populum et incipiat hanc antiphonam sequentem* (*que non dicatur Episcopo absente*)*: et cantet totam antiphonam vsque ad finem.*

Ant. Princeps ecclesie, pastor ouilis, cunctam plebem tuam benedicere digneris. *Hic conuertat se ad populum sic dicendo*:

Cum mansuetudine et caritate, humilitate uos ad benediccionem.

Chorus respondeat: Deo gracias.

Deinde retradat baculum Episcopo, et tunc Episcopus Puerorum, primo signando se in fronte, dicat, hoc modo incipiens:

Adiutorium nostrum in nomine Domini:

Chorus respondeat sic: Qui fecit celum et terram.

Item Episcopus, signando se in pectore, dicat sic:

Sit nomen Dei benedictum:

Chorus respondeat: Ex hoc nunc, et vsque in seculum.

Deinde Episcopus Puerorum, conuersus ad clerum, eleuet brachium suum, et dicat hanc benediccionem:

Crucis signo uos consigno:

Hic conuertat se ad populum, sic dicendo:

Nostra sit tuicio.

Deinde conuertat se ad altare, dicens:

Qui nos emit et redemit,

Postea ad seipsum reuersus ponat manum suam super pectus suum dicendo:

Sue carnis precio,

Chorus respondeat, vt sequitur, Amen.

His itaque peractis incipiat Episcopus Puerorum COMPLETORIUM *de die, more solito, post* Pater Noster *et* Aue Maria.

Et post Completorium dicat Episcopus Puerorum ad chorum conuersus sub tono supradicto.

Adiutorium nostrum in nomine Domini,

Chorus respondeat: Qui fecit celum et terram.

Episcopus Puerorum dicat:

Sit nomen Domini benedictum:

Chorus. Ex hoc nunc, et vsque in seculum.

Deinde dicat Episcopus:

Benedicat nos omnipotens Deus, Pater, et Filius, et Spiritus Sanctus.

Chorus: Amen.

¶ *In die SS. Innocencium*

si in DOMINICA euenerit:

Eodem modo processio fiat vt in die S. Stephani, excepto quod hac die tres pueri prosam in eundo dicant, in medio procedentes: que in ipsa stacione ante crucem ab eisdem terminetur.

In eundo, R. Centum quadraginta.

V. Hij empti.

Prosa. Sedentem in superne.

Sequatur. Gloria Patri, et Filio.

Ideo.

In introitu chori, de Natiuitate, vt supra.

AD MATUTINAS *in Die Innocencium*:

In tercio Nocturno, post lecciones et cetera, ad gradum altaris omnes pueri incipiant nonum Responsorium.

R. Centum quadraginta, *ut supra.*

Omnes simul dicant uersum:

V. Hij empti. Gloria Patri. Ideo.

V. Justi autem.

IN LAUDIBUS, *post Ps.* Laudate, *Episcopus Puerorum dicat modesta uoce, quasi legendo, Capitulum, loco nec habitu mutato, quia per totum diem capa serica vtitur* (Apoc. xix.)

Cap. Vidi supra montem Syon Agnum stantem, &c.

Ympnus. Rex gloriose martirum. *De Communi plurimorum martirorum* (Brev. Sarum, ii. 406).

V. Mirabilis Deus.

Ant. Hij sunt qui cum mulieribus, *et cetera, quam precentor dabit Episcopo.*

Ps. Benedictus.

Oracio. Deus, cuius hodierna, &c. Qui tecum uiuit.

Tunc omnes pueri dicant, loco Benedicamus, Verbum Patris (Brev. Sarum, i. p. cxc).

Chorus respondeat.

Consequenter dicat Episcopus Puerorum benediccionem super populum eodem modo quo ad uesperas precedentes.

Post tres Memorias (scilicet de Natiuitate Domini, de S. Stephano, et de S. Johanne) dicat Episcopus Puerorum benediccionem super populum, sicut et post Completorium supra dictum est.

Deinde tres de secunda forma dicant Benedicamus Domino, *more solito.*

Ad Vesperas. *Episcopus Puerorum incipiat*

Deus in adiutorium meum intende.

Ant. Tecum principium.

Ps. Dixit Dominus (*cix*).

Capitulum. Vidi supra montem.

R. Centum quadraginta.

Hoc Responsorium ab vno solo Puero, scilicet Cancellario, incipiatur ad gradum chori, in capa serica, et suus versus ab omnibus pueris cantetur in superpelliceis in stacione puerorum, cum prosa, si placet, et eciam cum Gloria Patri.

V. Hij empti sunt.

Ympnus. Rex gloriose martirum. *De Communi.*

V. Mirabilis Deus.

Episcopus Puerorum incipiat antiphonam:

Ant. Ecce vidi Agnum stantem.

Ps. Magnificat.

Oracio. Deus, cuius hodierna.

Dicta oracione, omnes pueri loco Benedicamus *dicant* Verbum Patris.

Ant. ad gradum altaris.

Et chorus totum respondeant.

¶ In Die S. Thomae Archiepiscopi Martyris.

Ad Vesperas, post memoriam de S. Johanne, accipiat cruciferarius baculum Episcopi Puerorum, et cantet antiphonam Princeps ecclesie, *sicut ad primas uesperas.*

Similiter Episcopus Puerorum benedicat populum supradicto modo.

Et sic compleatur seruicium (officium Puerorum) huius diei.

II. The York Computus.

[I have expanded the following document from the copy printed with all the contractions by Dr. E. F. Rimbault in *The Camden Miscellany* (C.S.), vii (1875), 31. The original roll was in the possession of the late Canon Raine.]

Compotus Nicholay de Newerk custodis bonorum Johannis de Cave Episcopi Innocencium Anno domini etc. nonagesimo sexto.

In primis receptum de xij denariis receptis in oblacione die Nativitatis domini. Et de xxiiij solidis j denario receptis in oblacione die Innocentium et j cochleare argenteum ponderis xx*d.* et j annulum argenteum cum bursa cerica eodem die ad missam. Et de xx*d.* rec. de Magistro Willelmo de Kexby precentore. Et de ij*s.* rec. de Magistro Johanne de Schirburne cancellario. Et de vj*s.* viij*d.* rec. de Magistro Johanne de Newton thesaurario ad Novam. Et de vj*s.* viij*d.* rec. de Magistro Thoma Dalby archidiacono Richmunde. Et de vj*s.* viij*d.* rec. de Magistro Nicholao de Feriby. Et de vj*s.* viij*d.* rec. de Magistro Thoma de Wallworthe. *Summa* lv*s.* v*d.* *Clausura.*

Item rec. de vj*s.* viij*d.* rec. de Domino Abbate Monasterii beatae Mariae virginis extra Muros Eboraci. Et de iij*s.* iiij*d.* rec. de Magistro Willelmo de Feriby Archidiacono Estridinge. *Villa.*

Summa x*s.*

Item de iij*s.* iiij*d.* rec. de domino Thoma Ugtreht milite. Et de ij*s.* rec. de priore de Kyrkham. Et de vj*s.* viij*d.* rec. de priore de Malton. Et de xx*s.* rec. de comitissa de Northumbria et j anulum aureum. Et de vj*s.* viij*d.* de priore de Bridlyngtone. Et de iij*s.* iiij*d.* de priore de Watton. Et de iij*s.* iiij*d.* de rectore de Bayntone. Et de iij*s.* iiij*d.* de Abbate de Melsa. Et de xx*d.* rec. de priore de Feriby. Et de vj*s.* viij*d.* rec. de domino Stephano de Scrope. Et de ij*s.* de priore de Drax. Et de vj*s.* viij*d.* de Abbate de Selby. Et de iij*s.* iiij*d.* rec. de priore de Pontefracte. Et de vj*s.* viij*d.* rec. de priore Sancti Oswaldi. Et de iij*s.* iiij*d.* rec. de priore de Munkbretton. Et de vj*s.* viij*d.* rec. de domino Johanne Depdene. Et de vj*s.* viij*d.* rec. de domina de Marmeon et j anulum aureum cum bursa cerica. Et de iij*s.* iiij*d.* de domina de Harsay. Et de vj*s.* viij*d.* de domina de Rosse. Et de ij*s.* rec. de Abbate Ryavalli. Et de ij*s.* rec. de Abbate *Patria.*

Bellalandi. Et de ij*s*. rec. de priore de Novoburgo. Et de xx*d*. rec. de priore de Marton. *Summa* v lib. x*s*.

Summa totalis Receptorum viij lib. xv*s*. v*d*.

De quibus dictus Nicholaus compotat.

Expensae infra civitatem.

Ad 'O virgo virginum.' In pane pro speciebus j*d*. In cervisia vj*d*. Item in sua Cena. In pane vij*d*. Et in pane dominico iiij*d*. In cervisia xxj*d*. In carne vitulorum et mutulorum ix*d*. obolus. In sawcetiis iiij*d*. In ij anatibus iiij*d*. In xij gallinis ij*s*. vj*d*. In viij wodkoks et j pluver ij*s*. ij*d*. In iij doș̃ et x feldfars xix*d*. In parvis avibus iij*d*. In vino ij*s*. iij*d*. In diversis speciebus xj*d*. In lx wardons v*d*. ob. In melle ij*d*. ob. In cenapio j*d*. In ij libris candelorum ij*d*. ob. In floure ij*d*. In focali j*d*. ob. Item coco vj*d*. *Summa* xv*s*. vj*d*. ob.

Item die Innocentium ad cenam. In pane iij*d*. In cervisia v*d*. In carne vitulorum et mutulorum vij*d*. In pipere et croco j*d*.

Diebus veneris et sabbati nichil quia non visitarunt.

Item dominica prima sequentibus diebus lunae Martis Mercurii nichil quia non visitarunt.

Die Jovis seu die Octavarum Innocentium inierunt versus Kexby ad dominum de Ugtrehte et revenerunt ad cenam. In pane ij*d*. In cervisia iiij*d*. In carne v*d*.

Diebus veneris et sabbati nichil quia non visitarunt.

Dominica ija seu die Sancti Willelmi devillaverunt. In pane ad Jantaculum ij*d*. In cervisia iij*d*. In carne v*d*.

Die lunae cum ebdomade sequente nichil quia extra villam.

Dominica iija cum ebdomade sequente extra villam.

Die sabbati revenerunt ad cenam. In pane j*d*. ob. In cervisia iij*d*. In lacte et piscibus iij*d*.

Dominica iiija nichil.

Die lunae inierunt ad scolas et post Jantaculum devillaverunt. In pane ij*d*. In cervisia iij*d*. ob. In carne vij*d*.

Die sabbati revenerunt ad cenam. In pane ij*d*. ob. In cervisia ij*d*. In piscibus vj*d*.

Dominica va usque ad finem Purificationis nichil.

Summa v*s*. vij*d*. ob.

Variae expensae per totam viam.

In primis. In zona empta pro episcopo iij*d*. In emendacione pilii sui j*d*. In pane equino ante arreptum itineris ij*d*. In oblacione apud Bridlyngtone ij*d*. In elemosina ibidem j*d*. In ferilay apud Melsam iiij*d*. In ferilay apud Drax iiij*d*. In pane equino apud Selby iiij*d*. Item barbitonsori j*d*. In j garth apud Bridlyngton j*d*. In emendacione j garth ibidem ob. In ij pectinibus equinis emptis apud

Bridlyngtone et Eboracum iiij*d.* In j garth apud Beverlacum j*d.* In ferracione equorum apud Feriby viij*d.* ob. In emendacione j garth ob. In cena apud Ledes xvij*d.* In feno et avena ibidem xiij*d.* Item in cena apud Riplay xvj*d.* In feno et avena ibidem xij*d.* ob. In ferracione equorum apud Fontans iiij*d.* In ferilay versus Harlsay iiij*d.* In bayting apud Allertone vj*d.* In vino pro episcopo viij*d.* In pane et feno equorum apud Helmslay vj*d.* In ferracione equorum apud Novumburgum iij*d.* *Summa* x*s.* vij*d.*

Variae expensae ad usum episcopi infra civitatem.

In primis. In j torchio empto ponderis xij lib. iiij*s.* iij*d.* In j pilio ix*d.* In j pari cirothecarum linearum iij*d.* In j pari manicarum iij*d.* In j pari cultellorum xiiij*d.* In j pari calcarium v*d.* Item pro factura robae xviij*d.* In furura agnina empta pro supertunica ij*s.* vj*d.* In fururis ex convencione vj*s.* In tortricidiis per totum tempus viij*d.* In carbone marino vij*d.* In carbone ligneo x*d.* In paris candelorum iiij*d.* ob. In xxviij paribus cirothecarum emptis pro vicariis et magistris scolarum iij*s.* iiij*d.* ob. Item pro emendacione capae cericae ij*d.*

Summa xxiij*s.* j*d.*

Stipendia servientium et equorum.

In primis Nicholao de Newsome tenori suo xiij*s.* iiij*d.* Et eidem pro suo equo conducto ij*s.* Item Roberto Dawtry senescallo vj*s.* viij*d.* Et pro predicationibus ejusdem in capella ij*s.* j*d.* ob. Item Johanni Baynton cantanti medium x*s.* Item Johanni Grene v*s.* Item Johanni Ellay iij*s.* iiij*d.* Item Johanni Schaptone servienti eidem cum ij equis suis x*s.* ij*d.* Item Thomae Marschale pro j equo iij*s.* iiij*d.* Item j sellare pro j equo iij*s.* vj*d.* Item pistori pro j equo iij*s.* vj*d.* Item Ricardo Fowler pro ij equis v*s.* *Summa* lxvij*s.* xj*d.* ob.

Feoda ministrorum in ecclesia ministrancium.

In primis succentori vicariorum ij*s.* Subcancellario xij*d.* Item cerae puerorum xij*d.* Item clericis de vestibus xij*d.* Item sacristis xij*d.* Item pro ornacione cathedrae episcopalis iiij*d.* Item in ligno pro stallis iiij*d.* Item in denariis communibus xviij*d.* Item custodi choristarum iij*s.* iiij*d.* *Summa* xj*s.* vj*d.*

Summa totalis Expensarum vj lib. xiiij*s.* x*d.* ob. Et sic Recepta excedunt expensas xl*s.* vj*d.* ob. ad usum Episcopi.

N

WINTER PROHIBITIONS

I. 190–200. Tertullian.

[From *De Idololatria* (*Tertulliani Opera*, ed. A. Reifferscheid and G. Wissowa, in *Corpus Script. Eccles.* xx; *P. L.* i. 674). Part of the argument of c. 15 is repeated in *De Corona Militari*, c. 13 (*P. L.* ii. 97). In *De Fuga in Persecutione*, c. 13 (*P. L.* ii. 119), bribes given by Christians to avoid persecution are called 'saturnalitia' given to soldiers.]

c. 10. [de ludimagistris]. Ipsam primam novi discipvli stipem Minervae et honori et nomini consecrat . . . quam Minervalia Minervae, quam Saturnalia Saturni, quae etiam serviculis sub tempore Saturnalium celebrari necesse est. Etiam strenuae captandae et septimontium, et Brumae et carae cognationis honoraria exigenda omnia, Florae scholae coronandae: flaminicea et aediles sacrificant creati; schola honoratur feriis; idem fit idolo natali: omnis diaboli pompa frequentatur. Quis haec competere Christiano existimabit, nisi qui putabit convenire etiam non magistris?

c. 14. *Quemadmodum*, inquit, *omnibus per omnia placeo*, nimirum Saturnalia et Kalendas Ianuarias celebrans hominibus placebat? . . . *Sabbata*, inquit, *vestra et numenias et ceremonias odit anima mea;* nobis, quibus sabbata extranea sunt et numeniae et feriae a deo aliquando dilectae, Saturnalia et Ianuariae et Brumae et Matronales frequentantur, munera commeant et strenae, consonant lusus, convivia constrepunt.

c. 15. Sed luceant, inquit, opera vestra; at nunc lucent tabernae et ianuae nostrae, plures iam invenias ethnicorum fores sine lucernis et laureis, quam Christianorum . . . ergo, inquis, honor dei est lucernae pro foribus et laurus in postibus? . . . certi enim esse debemus, si quos latet per ignorantiam litteraturae saecularis, etiam ostiorum deos apud Romanos, Cardeam a cardinibus appellatam et Forculum a foribus, et Limentinum a limine et ipsum Ianum a ianua . . . si autem sunt qui in ostiis adorantur, ad eos et lucernae et laureae pertinebunt; idolo feceris, quicquid ostio feceris . . . scis fratrem per visionem eadem nocte castigatum graviter, quod ianuam eius subito adnuntiatis gaudiis publicis servi coronassent. Et tamen non ipse coronaverat aut praeceperat; nam ante processerat et regressus reprehenderat factum . . . accendant igitur quotidie lucernas, quibus lux nulla est; affigant postibus lauros postmodum arsuras, quibus ignes imminent; illis competunt et testimonia tenebrarum et auspicia poenarum. Tu lumen es mundi et arbor virens semper; si templis renuntiasti, ne feceris templum ianuam tuam, minus dixi; si lupanaribus renuntiasti, ne induaris domui tuae faciem novi lupanaris.

II. 190–200. TERTULLIAN.

[*Apologeticus*, c. 42 in *P. L.* i. 492.]

Sed si ceremonias tuas non frequento, attamen et illa die homo sum. Non lavo sub noctem Saturnalibus, ne et noctem et diem perdam: attamen lavo et debita hora et salubri.

III. † 348. PRUDENTIUS.

[*Contra Symmachum*, i. 237 in *P. L.* lx. 139.]

Iano etiam celebri de mense litatur
auspiciis epulisque sacris, quas inveterato
heu! miseri sub honore agitant, et gaudia ducunt
festa Kalendarum.

IV. † 370. PACIANUS, BISHOP OF BARCELONA.

[Pacianus, *Paraenesis ad Poenitentiam* (*P. L.* xiii. 1081). Jerome, *de Viris illustribus*, c. 106 (*P. L.* xxiii. 703), says of Pacianus, 'scripsit varia opuscula, de quibus est Cervus.']

Hoc enim, puto, proximus Cervulus ille profecit, ut eo diligentius fieret, quo impressius notabatur. . . . Puto, nescierant Cervulum facere, nisi illis reprehendendo monstrassem.

V. 374–397. ST. AMBROSE.

[From *De Interpellatione Job et David*, ii. 1 (*P. L.* xiv. 813), concluding a passage on the *cervus* as a type of David and of Christ. The Benedictine editors think that if the allusion were to the *Cervulus*, St. Ambrose would have reprobated it. But in any case it is only a passing allusion.]

Sed iam satis nobis in exordio tractatus, sicut in principio anni, more vulgi, cervus allusit.

VI. 380–397. ST. CHRYSOSTOM.

[*Oratio Kalendis Habita* (*P. G.* xlviii. 953). A sermon preached at Antioch.]

'Αλλὰ πρὸς ἕτερα κατεπείγοντα ἡμῖν ὁ λόγος ὥρμηται, τὰ σήμερον ὑπὸ τῆς πόλεως ἁπάσης ἁμαρτηθέντα . . . καὶ γὰρ καὶ ἡμῖν πόλεμος συνέστηκε νῦν . . . δαιμόνων πομπευσάντων ἐπὶ τῆς ἀγορᾶς. αἱ γὰρ διαβολικαὶ παννυχίδες αἱ γινόμεναι τήμερον, καὶ τὰ σκώμματα, καὶ αἱ λοιδορίαι, καὶ αἱ χορεῖαι αἱ νυκτεριναί, καὶ ἡ καταγέλαστος αὕτη κωμῳδία, παντὸς πολεμίου χαλεπώτερον τὴν πόλιν ἡμῶν ἐξηχμαλώτισαν . . . περιχαρὴς ἡμῖν ἡ πόλις γέγονε καὶ φαιδρά, καὶ ἐστεφάνωται, καὶ καθάπερ γυνὴ φιλόκοσμος καὶ πολυτελής, οὕτως ἡ ἀγορὰ φιλοτίμως ἐκαλλωπίσατο σήμερον, χρυσία περιτιθεμένη, καὶ ἱμάτια πολυτελῇ, καὶ ὑποδήματα, καὶ ἕτερά τινα τοιαῦτα, τῶν ἐν τοῖς ἐργαστηρίοις ἑκάστου τῇ τῶν οἰκείων ἔργων ἐπιδείξει τὸν ὁμότεχνον παραδραμεῖν φιλονεικοῦντος. Ἀλλ' αὕτη μὲν ἡ φιλοτιμία, εἰ καὶ παιδικῆς ἐστι διανοίας, καὶ ψυχῆς οὐδὲν μέγα οὐδὲ ὑψηλὸν φανταζομένης, ἀλλ' ὅμως οὐ τοσαύτην ἐπισύρεται βλάβην. . . . Ἀλλ', ὅπερ ἔφην, οὐ τοσούτων ἐγκλημάτων ἀξία αὕτη ἡ φιλοτιμία· οἱ δὲ ἐν τοῖς καπηλείοις ἀγῶνες γινόμενοι τήμερον, οὗτοι μὲν μάλιστα ὀδυνῶσι, καὶ ἀσωτίας καὶ ἀσεβείας ἐμπεπλημένοι πολλῆς· ἀσεβείας μέν, ὅτι παρατηροῦσιν ἡμέρας οἱ ταῦτα ποιοῦντες, καὶ οἰωνίζονται, καὶ νομίζουσιν, εἰ τὴν νουμηνίαν τοῦ μηνὸς τούτου μεθ' ἡδονῆς καὶ εὐφροσύνης ἐπιτελέσαιεν, καὶ τὸν ἅπαντα τοιοῦτον ἕξειν ἐνιαυτόν· ἀσωτίας δέ, ὅτι ὑπὸ τὴν ἕω γυναῖκες καὶ ἄνδρες φιάλας καὶ ποτήρια πληρώσαντες μετὰ πολλῆς τῆς ἀσωτίας τὸν ἄκρατον πίνουσι. . . . Ταῦτα ἀπὸ νουμηνίας φιλοσόφει, ταῦτα ἀπὸ τῆς περιόδου τῶν ἐνιαυτῶν ἀναμιμνήσκου . . . Τὸ παρατηρεῖν ἡμέρας οὐ Χριστιανικῆς φιλοσοφίας, ἀλλ' Ἑλληνικῆς πλάνης ἐστίν. . . . Οὐδὲν ἔχεις κοινὸν πρὸς τὴν γῆν, ἔνθα ἡλίου δρόμοι, καὶ περίοδοι, καὶ ἡμέραι . . . Τὸ πρὸς ἡμέρας ἐπτοῆσθαι τοιαύτας, καὶ πλείονα ἐν αὐταῖς δέχεσθαι ἡδονήν, καὶ λύχνους ἅπτειν ἐπὶ τῆς ἀγορᾶς, καὶ στεφανώματα πλέκειν, παιδικῆς ἀνοίας ἐστίν. . . . Μὴ τοίνυν ἐπὶ τῆς ἀγορᾶς ἀνακαύσῃς πῦρ αἰσθητόν, ἀλλ' ἐπὶ τῆς διανοίας ἄναψον φῶς πνευματικόν . . . Μὴ τὴν θύραν τῆς οἰκίας στεφανώσῃς, ἀλλὰ τοιαύτην ἐπίδειξαι πολιτείαν, ὥστε τὸν τῆς δικαιοσύνης στέφανον σῇ κεφαλῇ παρὰ τῆς τοῦ Χριστοῦ δέξασθαι χειρός . . . Ὅταν ἀκούσῃς θορύβους, ἀταξίας καὶ πομπὰς διαβολικάς, πονηρῶν ἀνθρώπων καὶ ἀκολάστων τὴν ἀγορὰν πεπληρωμένην, οἴκοι μένε, καὶ τῆς ταραχῆς ἀπαλλάττου ταύτης, καὶ ἔμεινας εἰς δόξαν Θεοῦ.

VII. 380–397. St. Chrysostom.

[*Concio de Lazaro* I (*P. L.*, xlviii. 963). Preached at Antioch on the day after No. vi.]

Τὴν χθὲς ἡμέραν, ἑορτὴν οὖσαν σατανικήν, ἐποιήσατε ὑμεῖς ἑορτὴν πνευματικήν . . . Διπλοῦν τοίνυν οὕτω τὸ κέρδος ὑμῖν γέγονεν, ὅτι καὶ τῆς ἀτάκτου τῶν μεθυόντων ἀπηλλάγητε χορείας, καὶ σκιρτήματα ἐσκιρτήσατε πνευματικά, πολλὴν εὐταξίαν ἔχοντα· καὶ μετέσχετε κρατῆρος, οὐκ ἄκρατον ἐκχέοντος, ἀλλὰ διδασκαλίας πεπληρωμένου πνευματικῆς· καὶ αὐλὸς ἐγένεσθε καὶ κιθάρα τῷ Πνεύματι τῷ ἁγίῳ· καὶ τῶν ἄλλων τῷ διαβόλῳ χορευόντων, ὑμεῖς . . . ἐδώκατε τῷ Πνεύματι κροῦσαι τὰς ὑμετέρας ψυχάς.

VIII. 388. St. Jerome.

[*Comm. in Ephes.* vi. 4 in *P. L.* xxvi. 540.]

Legant episcopi atque presbyteri, qui filios suos saecularibus litteris erudiunt, et faciunt comoedias legere, et mimorum turpia scripta cantare, de ecclesiasticis forsitan sumptibus eruditos; et quod in corbonam pro peccato virgo aut vidua, vel totam substantiam suam effundens quilibet pauper obtulerat, hoc kalendariam strenam, et Saturnalitiam sportulam et Minervale munus grammaticus, et orator, aut in sumptus domesticos, aut in templi stipes, aut in sordida scorta convertit.

IX. †396. Asterius of Amasea.

[*Sermo adv. Kal. Festum*, in *P. G.* xl. 215.]

Δύο κατὰ ταυτὸν ἑορταὶ συνέδραμον ἐπὶ τῆς χθιζῆς καὶ τῆς ἐνεστώσης ἡμέρας, οὐ σύμφωνοί τε καὶ ἀδελφοί, πᾶν δὲ τοὐναντίον ἐχθρῶς τε καὶ ἐναντίως ἔχουσαι πρὸς ἀλλήλας. Ἡ μὲν γάρ ἐστι τοῦ ἔξωθεν συρφετοῦ, πολὺ συνάγουσα τοῦ μαμωνᾶ τὸ ἀργύριον . . . φιλεῖται μὲν τὸ στόμα, ἀγαπᾶται δὲ τὸ νόμισμα· τὸ σχῆμα διαθέσεως, καὶ τὸ ἔργον πλεονεξίας . . . τὰ δὲ ἄλλα πῶς ἄν τις εἴποι; μὴ καὶ ἐκκαλυψάμενος γυναικίζεται ὁ ἀριστεύς; κ.τ.λ.

X. 387–430. St. Augustine.

[*Sermo* cxcviii in *P. L.* xxxviii. 1024. In *Sermones* cxcvi and cxcvii Augustine also attacks the Calends, but in more general terms.]

Et modo si solemnitas gentium, quae fit hodierno die in laetitia saeculi atque carnali, in strepitu vanissimarum et turpissimarum cantionum, in conviviis et saltationibus turpibus, in celebratione ipsius falsae festivitatis, si ea quae agunt gentes non vos delectent, congregabimini ex gentibus. . . . Qui ergo aliud credit, aliud sperat, aliud amat, vita probet, factis ostendat. Acturus es celebrationem strenarum, sicut paganus, lusurus alea, et inebriaturus te: quomodo aliud credis, aliud speras, aliud amas? . . . Noli te miscere gentibus similitudine morum atque factorum. Dant illi strenas, date vos eleemosynas. Avocantur illi cantionibus luxuriarum, avocate vos sermonibus scripturarum: currunt illi ad theatrum, vos ad ecclesiam; inebriantur illi, vos ieiunate. Si hodie non potestis ieiunare, saltem cum sobrietate prandete. . . . Sed dicis mihi; quando strenas do, mihi accipio et ego. Quid ergo, quando das pauperi, nihil accipis? . . . Etenim illa daemonia delectantur canticis vanitatis, delectantur nugatorio spectaculo, et turpitudinibus variis theatrorum, insania circi, crudelitate amphitheatri, certaminibus animosis eorum qui pro pestilentibus hominibus lites et contentiones usque ad inimicitias suscipiunt, pro mimo, pro histrione, pro pantomimo, pro auriga, pro venatore. Ista facientes, quasi thura ponunt daemoniis de cordibus suis.

XI. †400. Severian.

[*Homilia de Pythonibus et Maleficis* (Mai, *Spicilegium Romanum*, x. 222). The author's name is given as Severian. A Severian was bishop of Gabala in Syria †400, a prolific preacher and an opponent of St. Chrysostom in Constantinople. It seems, however, a little hazardous to ascribe to him a Latin homily.]

Ecce veniunt dies, ecce kalendae veniunt, et tota daemonum pompa procedit, idolorum tota producitur officina, et sacrilegio vetusto anni novitas consecratur. Figurant Saturnum, faciunt Iovem, formant Herculem, exponunt cum venantibus suis Dianam, circumducunt Vulcanum verbis haletantem turpitudines suas, et plura, quorum, quia portenta sunt, nomina sunt tacenda; quorum deformitates quia natura non habet, creatura nescit, fingere ars laborat. Praeterea vestiuntur homines in pecudes, et in feminas viros vertunt, honestatem rident, violant iudicia, censuram publicam rident, inludunt saeculo teste, et dicunt se facientes ista iocari. Non sunt ioca, sed sunt crimina. In idola transfiguratur homo. Et, si ire ad idola crimen est, esse idolum quid videtur? . . . Namque talium deorum facies ut pernigrari possint, carbo deficit; et ut eorum habitus pleno cumuletur horrore, paleae, pelles, panni, stercora, toto saeculo perquiruntur, et quidquid est confusionis humanae, in eorum facie collocatur.

XII. 408–410. St. Jerome.

[*Comm. in Isaiam*, lxv. 11 (*P. L.* xxiv. 638).]

Et vos qui dereliquistis Dominum, et obliti estis montem sanctum meum. Qui ponitis fortunae mensam et libatis super eam. . . . Est autem in cunctis urbibus, et maxime in Aegypto, et in Alexandria idololatriae vetus consuetudo, ut ultimo die anni et mensis eorum qui extremus est, ponant mensam refertam varii generis epulis, et poculum mulso mixtum, vel praeteriti anni, vel futuri fertilitatem auspicantes. Hoc autem faciebant Israelitae, omnium simulacrorum portenta venerantes: et nequaquam altari victimas, sed huiusce modi mensae liba fundebant.

XIII. †412–†465. Maximus of Turin.

[*Homilia* ciii, *de Calendis Gentilium* (*P. L.* lvii. 491).]

Bene quodammodo Deo providente dispositum est, ut inter medias gentilium festivitates Christus Dominus oriretur, et inter ipsas tenebrosas superstitiones errorum veri luminis splendor effulgeret. . . . Quis enim sapiens, qui dominici Natalis sacramentum colit, non ebrietatem condemnet Saturnalium, non declinet lasciviam calendarum? . . . Sunt plerique, qui trahentes consuetudinem de veteri superstitione vanitatis, calendarum diem pro summa festivitate procurent; et sic laetitiam habere velint, ut sit magis illis tristitia. Nam ita lasciviunt, ita vino et epulis satiantur, ut qui toto anno castus et temperans fuerit, illa die sit temulentus atque pollutus; et quod nisi ita fecerit, putet perdidisse se ferias; quia non intelligit per tales se ferias perdidisse salutem. Illud autem quale est, quod surgentes mature ad publicum cum munusculo, hoc est, cum strenis unusquisque procedit; et salutaturus amicos, salutat praemio antequam osculo? . . . Adhuc et ipsam munificentiam strenas vocant, cum magis strenuum, quod——cogitur. . . . Hoc autem quale est quod, interposita die, tali inani exordio, velut incipientes vivere, aut auspicia colligant, omniaque perquirant; et exinde totius anni sibi vel prosperitatem, vel tristitiam metiuntur? . . . Hoc autem malis suis addunt, ut quasi de auspicatione domum redeuntes ramusculos gestent in manibus, scilicet pro omine, ut vel onusti ad hospitium redeant.

XIV. †412–†465. Maximus of Turin.

[*Homilia* xvi, *de Cal. Ian.* (*P. L.* lvii. 255).]

Quamquam non dubitem vos . . . universas calendarum supervenientium vanitates declinare penitus et horrere . . . necessarium, nec superfluum reor . . . precedentium patrum vobis repetantur alloquia. . . . Et illorum gravior atque immedicabilis languor est, qui superstitionum furore et ludorum suavitate decepti sub specie sanitatis insaniunt. An non omnia quae a ministris daemonum illis aguntur diebus falsa sunt et insana, cum vir, virium suarum vigore mollito, totum se frangit in feminam, tantoque illud ambitu atque arte agit, quasi poeniteat illum esse, quod vir est? Numquid non universa ibi falsa sunt et insana, cum se a Deo formati homines, aut in pecudes, aut in feras, aut in portenta transformant? Numquid non omnem excedit insaniam, cum decorem vultus humani Dei specialiter manibus in omnem pulchritudinem figuratum, squalore sordium et adulterina foeditate deturpant? . . . Post omnia, ad offensionis plenitudinem, dies ipsos annum novum vocant. . . . Novum annum Ianuarias appellant calendas, cum vetusto semper errore et horrore sordescant. Auspicia etiam vanissimi colligere se dicunt, ac statum vitae suae inanibus indiciis aestimantes, per incerta avium ferarumque signa imminentis anni futura rimantur.

XV. †412–†465. Maximus of Turin?

[*Sermo* vi, *de Cal. Ian.* (*P.L.* lvii. 543). The *Sermo* is ascribed to Maximus in three good MSS. and the style agrees with his. Other MSS. give it to St. Augustine or St. Ambrose, and it is printed in the Benedictine edition of the latter's works (*Sermo* vii. in *P. L.* xvii. 617). The editors, however, do not think it his.]

Est mihi adversus plerosque vestrum, fratres, querela non modica: de iis loquor qui nobiscum natale Domini celebrantes gentilium se feriis dediderunt, et post illud coeleste convivium superstitionis sibi prandium praepararunt. . . . Quomodo igitur potestis religiose Epiphaniam Domini procurare, qui Iani calendas quantum in vobis est devotissime celebratis? Ianus enim homo fuit unius conditor civitatis, quae Ianiculum nuncupatur, in cuius honore a gentibus calendae sunt Ianuariae nuncupatae; unde qui calendas Ianuarias colit peccat, quoniam homini mortuo defert divinitatis obsequium. Inde est quod ait Apostolus: *Dies observastis, et menses, et tempora, et annos; timeo ne sine causa laboraverim in vobis.* Observavit enim diem et mensem qui his diebus aut non ieiunavit, aut ad Ecclesiam non processit. Observavit diem qui hesterna die non processit ad ecclesiam, processit ad campum. Ergo, fratres, omni studio gentilium festivitatem et ferias declinemus, ut quando illi epulantur et laeti sunt, nunc nos simus sobrii, atque ieiuni, quo intelligant laetitiam suam nostra abstinentia condemnari.

XVI. *Fifth century.* St. Peter Chrysologus.

[*Sermo* clv in *P.L.* lii. 609.]

Ubi nostram Christus pie natus est ad salutem, mox diabolus divinae bonitati numerosa genuit et perniciosa portenta, ut ridiculum de religione componeret, in sacrilegium verteret sanctitatem. . . . Quorum formant adulteria in simulacris, quorum fornicationes imaginibus mandant, quorum titulant incesta picturis, quorum crudelitates commendant libris, quorum parricidia tradunt saeculis, quorum impietates personant tragoediis, quorum obscaena ludunt, hos qua dementia deos crederent, nisi quia criminum desiderio, amore scelerum possidentur, deos exoptant habere criminosos? . . . Haec diximus, quare gentiles hodie faciant deos suos talia committere, quae sustinemus, et faciant tales qui videntibus et horrori sunt et pudori; faciant ut eos aliquando et ipsi qui faciunt horreant et relinquant, et Christiani glorientur a talibus se liberatos esse per Christum: si modo non eorum ex spectaculis polluantur. . . . Et si tanta est de assensione damnatio, quis satis lugeat eos qui simulacra faciunt semetipsos? . . . Qui se deum facit, Deo vero contradictor existit; imaginem Dei portare noluit, qui idoli voluerit portare personam; qui iocari voluerit cum diabolo, non poterit gaudere cum Christo. . . . Abstrahat ergo pater filium, servum dominus, parens parentem, civem civis, homo hominem, Christianus omnes qui se bestiis compararunt, exaequarunt iumentis, aptaverunt pecudibus, daemonibus formaverunt.

XVII. 470–542. Caesarius of Arles?

[*Sermo Pseud.-Augustin.* cxxix *de Kal. Ian.* in *P. L.* xxxix. 2001. Parts of this sermon are reproduced 'mutatis mutandis' in the eighth-century Frankish *Homilia de Sacrilegiis* (§§ 23–26), edited by Caspari (cf. No. xxxix, below), and also in a MS. homily, *De Kalendis Ianuariis*, in *Cod Lat. Monac.* 6108 (tenth century), f. 48v. The rest of that homily is mainly from Maximus Taurinensis, *Hom.* 16 (No. xiv, above). And nearly the whole of the present *Sermo* is included in the *Homiliarium* of Burchardus of Würzburg and printed from his MS. by Eckart, *Francia Orientalis*, i. 837.

On the date and authorship of the *Sermo*, cf. Caspari, 67. It is ascribed to Augustine by a *Codex Colbertinus*. His editors, Blancpain and Coutant, treat it as not his (*a*) on account of the difference of style, (*b*) on account of the reference to the *ieiunium* prescribed by the *sancti antiqui patres* (i. e. amongst others, Augustine himself: cf. No. x). A *Codex Aceiensis* ascribes it to Faustinus (i.e. Faustus of Raji), and this is accepted by the Bollandists (*Acta SS. Ian.* i. 2), and by Eckart, *op. cit.* i. 433. Finally a *codex Navarricus* assigns it to Maxentius. This can hardly be the Scythian monk of that name († 520). Caspari suggests that there has been a scribal error. The *sermo* is headed 'De natali Domini. In calendis ianuariis.' There is nothing about the Nativity in it, and possibly a Nativity sermon and the author's name of the Kalends sermon which followed it have dropped out. He also thinks Maximus Taurinensis may be meant. However Caspari finally agrees with Blancpain and Coutant, that the style and the allusion to the *triduum ieiunii* so closely resembling that of the Council of Tours (No. xxii) point to a writer of the first half of the sixth century, and that he may very likely be Caesarius of Arles, who, as his *Vita* (cf. No. xx) states, did preach against the Kalends.]

Dies calendarum istarum, fratres carissimi, quas Ianuarias vocant, a quodam Iano homine perdito ac sacrilego nomen accepit. Ianus autem iste dux quidam et princeps hominum paganorum fuit: quem imperiti homines et rustici dum quasi regem metuunt, colere velut Deum coeperunt. . . . Diem ergo calendarum hodiernarum de nomine Iani, sicut iam dictum est, nuncuparunt: atque ut ei homini divinos honores conferre cupiebant, et finem unius anni et alterius initium deputarunt. Et quia apud illos Ianuariae calendae unum annum implere, et alterum incipere dicebantur, istum Ianum quasi in principio ac termino posuerunt, ut unum annum implere, alterum incipere diceretur. Et hinc est, quod idolorum cultores ipsi Iano duas facies figurarunt. . . . Hinc itaque est quod istis diebus pagani homines perverso omnium rerum ordine obscenis deformitatibus teguntur; ut tales utique se faciant qui colunt, qualis est iste qui colitur. In istis enim diebus miseri homines, et, quod peius est, aliqui baptizati, sumunt formas adulteras, species monstrosas, in quibus quidem sunt quae primum pudenda, aut potius dolenda sunt. Quis enim sapiens poterit credere, inveniri aliquos sanae mentis qui cervulum facientes, in ferarum se velint habitum commutare? Alii vestiuntur pellibus pecudum; alii assumunt capita bestiarum, gaudentes et exsultantes, si taliter se in ferinas species transformaverint, ut homines non esse videantur. . . . Iamvero illud quale et quam turpe est, quod viri nati tunicis muliebribus vestiuntur, et turpissima demum demutatione puellaribus figuris virile robur effeminant, non erubescentes tunicis muliebribus inserere militares lacertos: barbatas facies praeferunt, et videri feminae volunt. . . . Sunt enim qui calendis ianuariis auguria observant, ut focum de domo sua, vel aliud quodcumque beneficium, cuicumque petenti non tribuant. Diabolicas etiam strenas, et ab aliis accipiunt, et ipsi aliis tradunt. Aliqui etiam rustici, mensulas in ista nocte quae praeteriit, plenas multis rebus, quae ad manducandum sunt necessariae, componentes, tota nocte sic compositas esse volunt, credentes quod hoc illis calendae ianuariae praestare possint, ut per totum annum convivia illorum in tali abundantia perseverent. . . . Qui enim aliquid de paganorum consuetudine in istis diebus observare voluerint, timendum est ne eis nomen christianum prodesse non possit. Et ideo sancti antiqui patres nostri considerantes maximam partem hominum diebus istis gulae vel luxuriae deservire, et ebrietatibus et sacrilegis saltationibus insanire, statuerunt in universum mundum, ut per omnes Ecclesias publicum indiceretur ieiunium. . . . Ieiunemus ergo, fratres carissimi, in istis diebus. . . . Qui etiam in istis calendis stultis hominibus luxuriose ludentibus aliquam humanitatem impenderit, peccati eorum participem se esse non dubitet.

XVIII. ? 470–542. Caesarius of Arles ?

[*Sermo Pseud.-Augustin.* cxxx in *P.L.* xxxix. 2003. The authorship is generally taken to follow that of No. xvii, although a Fleury MS. ascribes it to Bp. Sedatus of Besiers † 589.]

Sic enim fit ut stultae laetitiae causa, dum observantur calendarum dies aut aliarum superstitionum vanitas, per licentiam ebrietatis et ludorum turpem cantum, velut ad sacrificia sua daemones invitentur. . . . Quid enim est tam demens quam virilem sexum in formam mulieris, turpi habitu commutare? Quid tam demens quam deformare faciem, et vultus induere, quos ipsi etiam daemones expavescunt? Quid tam demens quam incompositis motibus et impudicis carminibus vitiorum laudes inverecunda delectatione cantare? indui ferino habitu, et capreae aut cervo similem fieri, ut homo ad imaginem Dei et similitudinem factus sacrificium daemonum fiat? . . . Quicunque ergo in calendis ianuariis quibuscunque miseris hominibus sacrilego ritu insanientibus, potius quam ludentibus, aliquam humanitatem dederint, non hominibus, sed daemonibus se dedisse cognoscant. Et ideo si in peccatis eorum participes esse non vultis, cervulum sive iuvencam[1], aut alia quaelibet portenta, ante domos vestras venire non permittatis. . . . Sunt enim aliqui, quod peius est, quos ita observatio inimica subvertit, ut in diem calendarum si forte aut vicinis aut peregrinantibus opus sit, etiam focum dare dissimulent. Multi praeterea strenas et ipsi offerre, et ab aliis accipere solent. Ante omnia, fratres, ad confundendam paganorum carnalem et luxuriosam laetitiam, exceptis illis qui prae infirmitate abstinere non praevalent, omnes auxiliante Deo ieiunemus; et pro illis miseris qui calendas istas, pro gula et ebrietate, sacrilega consuetudine colunt, Deo, quantum possumus, supplicemus.

XIX. 470–542. Caesarius of Arles?

[*Sermo Pseud.-Augustin.* 265, *De Christiano Nomine cum Operibus non Christianis*, in *P.L.* xxxix. 2239.]

Licet credam quod illa infelix consuetudo . . . iam . . . fuerit . . . sublata; tamen, si adhuc agnoscatis aliquos illam sordidissimam turpitudinem de hinnicula vel cervula exercere . . . castigate.

XX. 470–542. Caesarius of Arles.

[Episcopi Cyprianus, Firminus et Viventius, *Vita S. Caesarii Arelatensis*, i. 5. 42; *P.L.* lxvii. 1021.]

Predicationes . . . contra calendarum quoque paganissimos ritus . . . fecit.

XXI. †554. Childebert.

[*Constitutio Childeberti, De Abolendis Reliquiis Idolatriae*, in Mansi, ix. 738; Boretius, i. 2.]

Noctes pervigiles cum ebrietate, scurrilitate, vel canticis, etiam in ipsis sacris diebus, pascha, natale Domini, et reliquis festivitatibus, vel adveniente die Dominico dansatrices per villas ambulare. Haec omnia, unde Deus agnoscitur laedi, nullatenus fieri permittimus.

XXII. 567. Council of Tours.

[Maassen, i. 121; Mansi, ix. 803.]

c. 18. [De ieiuniis monachorum]

Quia inter natale Domini et epyfania omni die festivitates sunt, idemque prandebunt excepto triduum illud, quod ad calcandam gentilium consuetudinem patris nostri statuerunt, privatas in kalendis Ianuarii fieri letanias, ut in ecclesia psalletur et ora octava in ipsis kalendis circumcisionis missa Deo propitio celebretur.

[1] *var. lect. anulas, agniculam, anniculam.*

c. 23. Enimvero quoniam cognovimus nonnullos inveniri sequipedes erroris antiqui, qui Kalendas Ianuarii colunt, cum Ianus homo gentilis fuerit, rex quidam, sed esse Deus non potuit; quisquis ergo unum Deum Patrem regnantem cum Filio et Spiritu Sancto credit, non potest integer Christianus dici, qui super hoc aliqua custodit.

XXIII. 572–574. Martin of Braga.

[Martin von Bracara, *De Correctione Rusticorum*, ed. C. P. Caspari, Christiania, 1883.]

c. 10. Similiter et ille error ignorantibus et rusticis hominibus subrepit, ut Kalendas Ianuarias putent anni esse initium, quod omnino falsissimum est. Nam, sicut scriptura dicit, viii. kal. Aprilis in ipso aequinoctio initium primi anni est factum.

c. 11. . . . Sine causa autem miser homo sibi istas praefigurationes ipse facit, ut, quasi sicut in introitu anni satur est et laetus ex omnibus, ita illi et in toto anno contingat. Observationes istae omnes paganorum sunt per adinventiones daemonum exquisitae.

c. 16. . . . Vulcanalia et Kalendas observare, menses ornare, lauros ponere, pedem observare, effundere [in foco] super truncum frugem et vinum, et panem in fontem mittere, quid est aliud nisi cultura diaboli?

XXIV. †560. Martin, Bishop of Braga.

[Quoted in the *Decretum Gratiani*, Pars ii, Causa 26, Quaestio 7, c. 13 (*C. I. Can.* ed. Friedberg, i. 1044), as from 'Martinus Papa,' or 'Martinus Bracarensis' [c. 74]. Mansi, ix. 857, gives the canon with a reference to *C. of Laodicea*, c. 39, which is a more general decree against taking part in Gentile feasts. Burchardus, x. 15, quotes it 'ex decreto Martialis papae.' Martin of Braga ob. 580. His *Capitula* are collected from the councils of Braga and the Great Councils. Caspari, *Martin von Bracara's De Con. Rusticorum*, xl, thinks that several of them, including c. 74, were his own additions.]

Non licet iniquas observationes agere calendarum, et otiis vacare gentilibus, neque lauro aut viriditate arborum cingere domos: omnis enim haec observatio paganismi est.

XXV. 573–603. Council of Auxerre.

[Maassen, i. 179.]

c. 1. Non licet kalendis Ianuarii vetolo aut cervolo facere vel streneas diabolicas observare, sed in ipsa die sic omnia beneficia tribuantur, sicut in reliquis diebus.

c. 5. Omnino inter supra dictis conditionibus pervigilias, quos in honore domini Martini observant, omnimodis prohibite.

c. 11. Non licet vigilia paschae ante ora secunda noctis vigilias perexpedire, quia ipsa nocte non licet post media nocte bibere, nec natale Domini nec reliquas sollemnitates.

XXVI. 6th cent. St. Samson, Bishop of Dôle.

[Anonymi *Vita S. Samsonis*, ii. 13 (*Acta S. S. Iulii*, vi. 590).]

Nam cum quodam tempore in Resia insula praedicaret, veniente per annuam vertiginem Kalenda Ianuaria, qua homines supradictae insulae hanc nequam solemnem inepte iuxta patrum abominabilem consuetudinem prae ceteris sane celebrare consueverant, ille providus spiritu ob duritiam eorum mitigandam, convenire eos omnes in unum fecit, ut, Deo revelante, sermo ad detestanda tam gravia mala sit. Tum hi omnes verum de eo amantes, pravos ritus anathematizaverunt, ac verum iuxta praecepta tenus sine suscipere spoponderunt. Ille nihilominus in Domino secundum Apostolos gaudens, omnes parvulos qui per insulam illam ob hanc nefariam diem discurrebant, vocavit ad se, eisque singulis per sobriam vocem mercedem nummismunculi auro quod est mensura domuit, praecipiens in nomine Domini, ne ulterius ab illis haec sacrilega consuetudo servaretur. Quod ita Deo operante factum est, ut usque hodie ibidem spiritales ioci eius solide et catholice remanserint.

XXVII. 588–659. St. Eligius of Rouen?

[*Sermo* in *Vita Eligii* of Audoënus of Rouen (*P. L.* lxxxvii. 524). According to E. Vacandard in *R. des Questions historiques*, lxiv. 471, this is largely a compilation from the sermons of St. Caesarius of Arles.]

Nullus in Kalendis Ianuarii nefanda et ridiculosa, vetulas aut cervulos, aut iotticos[1] faciat, neque mensas supra noctem componat, neque strenas aut bibitiones superfluas exerceat.

XXVIII. †636. St. Isidore of Seville.

[*De Ecclesiasticis Officiis*, i. 41; *De Ieiunio Kalendarum Ianuariarum* (*P. L.* lxxxiii. 774). This is the chief source of the similar passage in the ninth-century Pseudo-Alcuin, *De Div. Offic.* c. 4 (*P. L.* ci. 1177).]

1. Ieiunium Kalendarum Ianuariarum propter errorem gentilitatis instituit Ecclesia. Ianus enim quidam princeps paganorum fuit, a quo nomen mensis Ianuarii nuncupatur, quem imperiti homines veluti Deum colentes, in religione honoris posteris tradiderunt, diemque ipsam scenis et luxuriae sacraverunt.

2. Tunc enim miseri homines, et, quod peius est, etiam fideles,

[1] *var. lect.* ulerioticos. Ducange explains *jotticos* as '*ludi*, Gall. *jeux*.'

sumentes species monstruosas, in ferarum habitu transformantur: alii, femineo gestu demutati, virilem vultum effeminant. Nonnulli etiam de fanatica adhuc consuetudine quibusdam ipso die observationum auguriis profanantur; perstrepunt omnia saltantium pedibus, tripudiantium plausibus, quodque est turpius nefas, nexis inter se utriusque sexus choris, inops animi, furens vino, turba miscetur.

3. Proinde ergo sancti Patres considerantes maximam partem generis humani eodem die huiusmodi sacrilegiis ac luxuriis inservire, statuerunt in universo mundo per omnes Ecclesias publicum ieiunium, per quod agnoscerent homines in tantum se prave agere, ut pro eorum peccatis necesse esset omnibus Ecclesiis ieiunare.

XXIX. †685. St. Aldhelm.

[*Epist.* iii *in Eahfridum* (*P. L.* lxxxix. 93).]

Et ubi pridem eiusdem nefandae natricis ermuli[1] cervulique cruda fanis colebantur stoliditate in profanis, versa vice discipulorum gurgustia (imo almae oraminum aedes) architecti ingenio fabre conduntur.

XXX. 692. Quinisextine Council.

[*Conc. Quinisextinum* or *in Trullo*, held at Constantinople, *versio Latina*, c. 62 (Mansi, xi. 971).]

Kalendas quae dicuntur, et vota [Gk. βότα], et brumalia quae vocantur; et qui in primo Martii mensis die fit conventum ex fidelium universitate omnino tolli volumus: sed et publicas mulierum saltationes multam noxam exitiumque afferentes: quin etiam eas, quae nomine eorum, qui falso apud gentiles dii nominati sunt, vel nomine virorum ac mulierum fiunt, saltationes ac mysteria more antiquo et a vita Christianorum alieno, amandamus et expellimus; statuentes, ut nullus vir deinceps muliebri veste induatur, vel mulier veste viro conveniente. Sed neque comicas vel satyricas, vel tragicas personas induat; neque execrati Bacchi nomen, uvam in torcularibus exprimentes, invocent; neque vinum in doliis effundentes risum moveant, ignorantia vel vanitate ea, quae ab insaniae impostura procedunt, exercentes.

XXXI. 714. Gregory II.

[Gregorius II. *Capitulare datum episcopo et aliis in Bavariam ablegatis*, c. 9 (Mansi, xii. 260).]

Ut incantationes, et fastidiationes, sive diversae observationes dierum Kalendarum, quas error tradidit paganorum, prohibeantur.

[1] *Ermuli.* Ducange, s. v., would read *hinnuli.* He says that Archbishop Ussher thought that the passage referred to the Saxon god Irminsul.

XXXII. 731–741. Gregory III.

[*Iudicia*, c. 23 (*P. L.* lxxxix. 594). In *Epist.* 3 sent to Germany on the return of Boniface from Rome in 739, Gregory gives the more general direction 'abstinete et prohibete vosmetipsos ab omni cultu paganorum' (*P. L.* lxxxix. 579).]

Si quis . . . ut frater in honore Iovis vel Beli aut Iani, secundum paganam consuetudinem, honorare praesumpserit, placuit secundum antiquam constitutionem sex annos poeniteant. Humanius tres annos iudicaverunt.

XXXIII. † 742. St. Boniface (*alias* Winfrid).

[Bonifatius, *Epistola* xlix (*P. L.* lxxxix. 746). *Epistola* xlii (Jaffé, *Monumenta Moguntina*), *Epistola* l (Dummler, *Epistolae Merowingici et Karolini Aevi*, i. 301): cf. Kögel, i. 28; Tille, *Y. ad C.* 88. The letter is *Ad Zachariam Papam.*]

Quia carnales homines idiotae Alamanni, vel Bagoarii, vel Franci, si iuxta Romanam urbem aliquid fieri viderint ex his peccatis quae nos prohibemus, licitum et concessum a sacerdotibus esse putant; et dum nobis improperium deputant, sibi scandalum vitae accipiunt. Sicut affirmant se vidisse annis singulis in Romana urbe, et iuxta ecclesiam sancti Petri, in die vel nocte quando Kalendae Ianuariae intrant, paganorum consuetudine choros ducere per plateas, et acclamationes ritu gentilium, et cantationes sacrilegas celebrare, et mensas illa die vel nocte dapibus onerare, et nullum de domo sua vel ignem, vel ferramentum, vel aliquid commodi vicino suo praestare velle. Dicunt quoque se ibi vidisse mulieres pagano ritu phylacteria et ligaturas in brachiis et in cruribus ligatas habere, et publice ad vendendum venales ad comparandum aliis offerre. Quae omnia eo quod ibi a carnalibus et insipientibus videntur, nobis hic improperium et impedimentum praedicationis et doctrinae faciunt.

XXXIV. † 742. Pope Zachary.

[Zacharias Papa, *Epistola* ii (*P. L.* lxxxix. 918), *Epistola* li (Dümmler, *Epist. Merow. et Karol. Aevi*, i. 301). Written *Ad Bonifatium* in reply to No. xxxiii. The *constitutio* of Pope Gregory referred to appears to be No. xxxii.]

De Kalendis vero Ianuariis, vel ceteris auguriis, vel phylacteriis, et incantationibus, vel aliis diversis observationibus, quae gentili more observari dixisti apud beatum Petrum apostolum, vel in urbe Roma; hoc et nobis et omnibus Christianis detestabile et perniciosum esse iudicamus. . . . Nam et sanctae recordationis praedecessoris atque nutritoris nostri domini Gregorii papae constitutione omnia haec pie ac fideliter amputata sunt et alia diversa quam plura.

XXXV. 743. Council of Rome.

[Conc. Romanum, c. 9: Mansi, xii. 384. A slightly different version, headed 'Zacharias Papa in Conc. Rom. c. 9,' is in *Decretum Gratiani*, ii. 26. 7, c. 14 (*C. I. Can.* ed. Friedberg, i. 1045). This seems to be a result of Nos. xxxiii, xxxiv.]

Ut nullus Kalendas Ianuarias et broma ritu paganorum colere praesumpserit, aut mensas cum dapibus in domibus praeparare, aut per vicos et plateas cantiones et choreas ducere, quod maxima iniquitas est coram Deo: anathema sit.

XXXVI. †750. Priminius.

[*Dicta Abbatis Priminii*, c. 22 (Caspari, *Kirchenhistorische Anecdota*, i. 172).

Priminius was a German contemporary of Boniface.]

Nam Vulcanalia et Kalendas observare . . . quid aliut nisi cultura diabuli est? . . . Cervulos et vetulas in Kalendas vel aliud tempus nolite anbulare. Viri vestes femineas, femine vestes virilis in ipsis Kalandis vel in alia lusa quam plurima nolite vestire.

XXXVII. †766. Egbert.

[*Penitentiale Egberti*, viii. 4 (Haddan and Stubbs, iii. 424).]

Kalendas Ianuarias secundum paganam causam honorare, si non desinit, v annos poeniteat clericus, si laicus, iii annos poeniteat.

XXXVIII. †790–800. Lombard Capitulary.

[*Capit. Langobardicum*, c. 3; Boretius, i. 202; Gröber, *Zur Volkskunde aus Concilbeschlüssen und Capitularien* (1893), No. 11.]

De pravos homines qui brunaticus colunt et de hominibus suis subtus maida[1] cerias incendunt et votos vovent: ad tale vero iniquitas eos removere faciant unusquisque.

XXXIX. †*Eighth century*. Homilia de Sacrilegiis.

[C. P. Caspari, *Eine Augustin fälschlich beilegte Homilia de Sacrilegiis* (1886), § 17. Caspari (pp. 71, 73) assigns the homily to a Frankish clerk, probably of the eighth century. Later on (§§ 23–26) is another passage on the Kalends taken from the pseud-Augustine, *Sermo* cxxix, which is No. xvii, above.]

Quicumque in kalendas ienuarias mensas panibus et aliis cybis ornat et per noctem ponet et diem ipsum colit et [in eo] auguria aspicet vel arma in campo ostendit et feclum[2] et cervulum et alias miserias vel lusa

[1] *maida* G. explains as *Backtrog*, i. e. 'kneading-trough' (Gk. μάκτρα); cf. Diez, *Etym. Wörterbuch*, s.v. madia; Körting, *Lat.-Rom. Wörterbuch*, No. 4980.

[2] MS. *fectum*.

[facit] quę in ipso die insipientes solent facere, vel qui in mense februario hibernum credit expellere, vel qui in ipso mense dies spurcos ostendit, [et qui in kalendis ianuariis] aliquid auguriatur, quod in ipso anno futurum sit, non christianus, sed gentilis est.

XL. *Ninth century.* PSEUDO-THEODORE.

[*Penit. Pseudo-Theod.* c. xii (Wasserschleben, *ut infra*, 597; cf. Haddan and Stubbs, iii. 173). This *Penitential*, quoted by Tille, *Y. and C.* 98, and others as Theodore's, and therefore English, is really a Frankish one, partly based, but not so far as these sections are concerned, on the genuine *Penitential* of Theodore. I do not quote all the many Penitentials which copy from each other, often *totidem verbis*, prohibitions of the *Cervulus* and *Vetula*. They may be found in F. W. H. Wasserschleben, *Bussordnungen der abendländ. Kirche*, 368, 382, 395, 414, 424, 428, 480, 517; H. J. Schmitz, *Die Bussbücher und die Bussdisciplin der Kirche*, 311, 379, 479, 633. On the general character of these compilations and their filiation, see Schaff, vii. 371. Their ultimate authority for the particular prohibition of *cervulus* and *vetula*, under these names, is probably No. xxv.]

§ 19. Si quis in Kalendas ianuarii in cervolo aut vetula vadit, id est, in ferarum habitus se communicant et vestiuntur pellibus pecudum, et assumunt capita bestiarum: qui vero taliter in ferinas species se transformant, iii annos poeniteant, quia hoc daemoniacum est.

§ 24. Qui . . . kalendas Ianuarii, more paganorum, honorat, si clericus est, v annos poeniteat, laicus iii annos poeniteat.

XLI. †915. REGINO OF PRÜM.

[Regino von Prüm, *De synodalibus causis et disciplina ecclesiastica* (ed. Wasserschleben, 1840), i. 304.]

Fecisti aliquid quod pagani faciunt in Kalendis januariis in cervulo vel vetula tres annos poeniteas.

XLII. Before 1024. BURCHARDUS OF WORMS.

[*Collectio Decretorum*, xix. 5 (Grimm, iv. 1743; *P. L.* cxl. 960). The larger part of the book is from earlier Penitentials, &c., but the long chapter from which these extracts are taken appears to be based upon the writer's own knowledge of contemporary superstition. On the collection generally, cf. A. Hauck, in *Sitzb. Akad. Leipzig*, *phil.-hist. Kl.*, xlvi (1894), 65.]

Observasti Kalendas Ianuarias ritu paganorum, ut vel aliquid plus faceres propter novum annum, quam antea vel post soleres facere, ita dico, ut aut mensam tuam cum lapidibus vel epulis in domo tua praeparares eo tempore, aut per vicos et per plateas cantores et choros duceres, aut supra tectum domus tuae sederes ense tuo circumsignatus, ut ibi videres et intelligeres, quid tibi in sequenti anno futurum esset?

vel in bivio sedisti supra taurinam cutem, ut et ibi futura tibi intelligeres? vel si panes praedicta nocte coquere fecisti tuo nomine, ut, si bene elevarentur et spissi et alti fierent, inde prosperitatem tuae vitae eo anno praevideres?

Credidisti ut aliqua femina sit quae hoc facere possit, quod quaedam a diabolo deceptae se affirmant necessario et ex praecepto facere debere, id est, cum daemonum turba in similitudinem mulierum transformatam, quam vulgaris stultitia holdam [1] vocat, certis noctibus equitare debere super quasdam bestias, et in eorum se consortio annumeratam esse?

Fecisti quod quidam faciunt in Kalendis Ianuarii, i.e. in octava Natalis Domini; qui ea sancta nocte filant, nent, consuunt, et omne opus quodcunque incipere possunt, diabolo instigante propter novum annum incipiunt?

Fecisti ut quaedam mulieres in quibusdam temporibus anni facere solent, ut in domo tuo mensam praeparares, et tuos cibos et potum cum tribus cultellis supra mensam poneres, ut si venissent tres illae sorores quas antiqua posteritas et antiqua stultitia parcas nominavit, ibi reficerentur; et tulisti divinae pietati potestatem suam et nomen suum, et diabolo tradidisti, ita dico, ut crederes illas quas tu dicis esse sorores tibi posse aut hic aut in futuro prodesse?

O

THE REGULARIS CONCORDIA OF ST. ETHELWOLD

[The following extracts are taken from the text printed by W. S. Logemann in *Anglia*, xiii (1891), 365, from *Cotton MS. Tiberius A. III*, † 1020–1030. This MS. has Anglo-Saxon glosses. Other MSS. are in *Cotton MS. Faustina B. III*, and *Bodleian MS. Junius*, 52, ii. Earlier editions of the text are in Reyner, *De Antiquitate Ordinis Benedictinorum in Anglia*, App. iii. p. 77, and Dugdale, *Monasticum Anglicanum*, i. xxvii. The literary history is discussed by W. S. Logemann in *Anglia*, xv (1893), 20; M. Bateson, *Rules for Monks and Canons* in *English Hist. Review*, ix (1894), 700; and F. Tupper, *History and Texts of the Benedictine Reform of the Tenth Century*, in *Modern Language Notes*, viii. 344. The *Prooemium* of the document states that it was drawn up by the bishops, abbots, and abbesses of England upon the suggestion of King Edgar at a Council of Winchester, and that certain additions were made to it by Dunstan. The traditional ascription by Cotton's librarian and others of the authorship of the *Regularis Concordia* to Dunstan is probably based on this record of the revision which, as archbishop, he naturally gave it. The actual author is thought by Dr. Logemann, and by

[1] *Cod. Madrid*, Friga holdam; *var. lect.* unholdam.

Dr. Stubbs (*Memorials of Dunstan*, R. S. cx) to have been Ælfric, a monk, first of Abingdon and then of Winchester, who became abbot of Cerne, and in 1005 of Eynsham, and was a considerable writer in Anglo-Saxon. Dr. Logemann's view is based on a theory that the *Concordia* is the 'Regula Aluricii, glossata Anglice' which occurs amongst the titles of some tracts once in the library of Christ Church, Canterbury (*Anglia*, xv. 25). But the *Concordia* is more likely to have been the 'Consuetudines de faciendo servitio divino per annum, glossatae Anglice,' which is in the same list, and in fact the Canterbury copy is probably that in *Cotton MS. Faustina, B. III* (*E.H.R.* ix. 708). Perhaps the 'Regula Aluricii' was a copy of the letter to the monks of Eynsham, which Ælfric at some date after 1005 based upon the *Concordia* and the *De Ecclesiasticis Officiis* of Amalarius of Metz. This is printed, from *C. C. C. C. MS.* 265, by Miss Bateson, in Dean Kitchin's *Obedientiary Rolls of St. Swithin's, Winchester*, 173 (*Hampshire Record Soc.*). It omits the *Sepulchrum* and its *Visitatio*. In any case this letter makes it clear that Ælfric was not the author of the *Concordia*, for he says 'haec pauca de libro consuetudinum quem sanctus Aethelwoldus Wintoniensis episcopus cum coepiscopis et abbatibus tempore Eadgari felicissimi regis Anglorum undique collegit ac monachis instituit observandum.' The author, therefore, so far as there was a single author, was Ethelwold, whom I take to be the 'abbas quidam' of the *Prooemium*. He became Abbot of Abingdon about 954, and Bishop of Winchester in 963. In 965 Elfrida, who is also mentioned in the *Prooemium*, became queen. The date of the *Concordia* probably falls, therefore, between 965 and the death of Edgar in 975. There were Councils of Winchester in 969 and 975 (Wilkins, i. 247, 261): but the Council at which the *Concordia* was undertaken may be an earlier one, not otherwise recorded. The *Concordia* is said in the *Prooemium* to have been based in part upon customs of Fleury and of Ghent. It is worth pointing out that Ethelwold had already reformed Abingdon after the model of Fleury, and that Dunstan, during his banishment, had found refuge in St. Peter's at Ghent (Stephens-Hunt, *Hist. of the English Church*, i. 347, 349). Miss Bateson suggests that another source is to be found in the writings of an earlier Benedictine reformer, Benedict of Aniane (*E.H.R.* ix. 700).]

De Consuetudine Monachorum.

Prohemum Regularis Concordiae Anglicae Nationis Monachorum Sanctimonialiumque Orditur.

[The *Prooemium* opens with an account of the piety of King Edgar 'abbate quodam assiduo monente' and the purification of the English monasteries.]

. . . Regulari itaque sancti patris Benedicti norma honestissime suscepta, tam abbates perplurimi quam abbatissae cum sibi subiectis fratrum sororumque collegiis sanctorum sequi vestigia una fide non tamen uno consuetudinis usu certatim cum magna studuerunt hilaritate. Tali igitur ac tanto studio praefatus rex magnopere delectatus arcana quaeque diligenti cura examinans synoda le concilium Wintoniae fieri decrevit . . . cunctosque . . . monuit ut concordes aequali consuetudinis usu . . . nullo modo dissentiendo discordarent . . . Huius praecellentissimi regis sagaci monitu spiritualiter conpuncti non tantum episcopi verum etiam abbates et abbatissae . . . eius imperiis toto mentis conamine alacriter obtemperantes, sanctique patroni nostri Gregorii documenta quibus beatum Augustinum monere studuit, ut non solum Romanae verum etiam Galliarum honestos ecclesiarum usus rudi Anglorum ecclesia decorando constitueret, recolentes, accitis Floriacensibus beati Benedicti nec non praecipui coenobii quod celebri Gent nuncupatur vocabulo monachis quaeque ex dignis eorum moribus honesta colligentes, . . . has morum consuetudines ad vitae honestatem et regularis observantiae dulcedinem . . . hoc exiguo apposuerunt codicello . . . Hoc etenim Dunstanus egregius huius patriae archiepiscopus praesago afflatus spiritu ad corroborandum praefati sinodalis conventus conciliabulum provide ac sapienter addidit, ut videlicet

. . . .

[On Maundy Thursday] In qua missa sicut in sequentium dierum communicatio prebetur tam fratribus quam cunctis fidelibus reservata nihilominus ea die eucharistia quae sufficit ad communicandum cunctis altera die . . . .

In die Parascevae agatur nocturna laus [i. e. the *Tenebrae*] sicut supra dictum est. Post haec venientes ad primam discalceati omnes incedant quousque crux adoretur. Eadem enim die hora nona abbas cum fratribus accedat ad ecclesiam. . . . Postea legitur passio domini nostri Ihesu Christi secundum Iohannem . . . Post haec celebrentur orationes . . . Quibus expletis per ordinem statim preparetur crux ante altare interposito spatio inter ipsam et altare sustentata hinc et inde a duobus diaconibus. Tunc cantent . . . Deferatur tunc ab ipsis diaconibus ante altare, et eos acolitus cum pulvillo sequatur super quem sancta crux ponatur . . . Post haec vertentes se ad clerum nudata cruce dicant antiphonam *Ecce lignum crucis* . . . Ilico ea nudata veniat abbas ante crucem sanctam ac tribus vicibus se prosternat cum omnibus fratribus dexterioris chori scilicet senioribus et iunioribus et cum magno cordis suspirio vii^m poenitentiae psalmos cum orationibus sanctae cruci competentibus decantando peroret . . . Et eam humiliter deosculans surgat. Dehinc sinisterioris chori omnes fratres eadem mente devota peragant. Nam salutata ab abbate vel omnibus cruce redeat ipse abbas ad sedem suam usque dum omnis clerus ac populus hoc idem faciat. Nam quia ea die depositionem corporis salvatoris nostri celebramus usum quorundam religiosorum imitabilem ad fidem indocti vulgi ac neofitorum corroborandam equiparando sequi si ita cui visum fuerit vel sibi taliter placuerit hoc modo decrevimus. Sit autem in una parte altaris qua vacuum fuerit quaedam assimilatio sepulchri velamenque quoddam in gyro tensum quod dum sancta crux adorata fuerit deponatur hoc ordine. Veniant diaconi qui prius portaverunt eam et involvant eam sindone in loco ubi adorata est. Tunc reportent eam canentes antiphonas . . . donec veniant ad locum monumenti depositaque cruce ac si domini nostri Ihesu Christi corpore sepulto dicant antiphonam . . . In eodem loco sancta crux cum omni reverentia custodiatur usque dominicae noctem resurrectionis. Nocte vero ordinentur duo fratres aut tres aut plures si tanta fuerit congregatio, qui ibidem psalmos decantando excubias fideles exerceant. . . . [The *Missa de Praesanctificatorum* follows] . . . Sabbato sancto hora nona veniente abbate in ecclesiam cum fratribus novus ut supra dictum est afferatur ignis. Posito vero cereo ante altare ex illo accendatur igne. Quem diaconus more solito benedicens hanc orationem quasi voce legentis proferens dicat . . .

In die sancto paschae . . . eiusdem tempore noctis antequam matutinorum signa moveantur sumant editui crucem et ponant in loco sibi congruo. . . . Dum tertia recitatur lectio quatuor fratres induant se, quorum unus alba indutus ac si ad aliud agendum ingrediatur atque latenter sepulchri locum adeat, ibique manu tenens palmam quietus sedeat. Dumque tertium percelebratur responsorium residui tres succedant, omnes quidem cappis induti turribula cum incensu manibus gestantes ac pedetemptim ad similitudinem querentium quid veriant ante locum sepulchri. Aguntur enim haec ad imitationem angeli sedentis in monumento atque mulierum cum aromatibus venientium ut ungerent corpus Ihesu. Cum ergo ille residens tres velut erraneos ac aliquid querentes viderit sibi adproximare incipiat mediocri voce dulcisono cantare *Quem quaeritis*: quo decantato fine tenus respondeant hi tres uno ore *Ihesum Nazarenum*. Quibus ille, *Non est hic*: *surrexit sicut praedixerat. Ite nuntiate quia surrexit a mortuis.* Cuius iussionis voce vertant se illi tres ad chorum dicentes *Alleluia*: *resurrexit dominus.* Dicto hoc rursus ille residens velut revocans illos dicat antiphonam *Venite et videte locum*: haec vero dicens surgat et erigat velum ostendatque eis locum cruce nudatum sed tantum linteamina posita quibus crux involuta erat. Quo viso deponant turribula quae gestaverunt in eodem sepulchro sumantque linteum et extendant contra clerum, ac veluti ostendentes quod surrexerit dominus, etiam non sit illo involutus, hanc canant antiphonam, *Surrexit dominus de sepulchro*, superponantque linteum altari. Finita antiphona Prior, congaudens pro triumpho regis nostri quod devicta morte surrexit, incipiat hymnum *Te deum laudamus*: quo incepto una pulsantur omnia signa.

P

THE DURHAM SEPULCHRUM

[From *A Description or Breife Declaration of all the Ancient Monuments, Rites and Customes belonginge or beinge within the Monastical Church of Durham before the Suppression* (ed. J. Raine, Surtees Soc. xv). This anonymous tract was written in 1593. A new edition is in course of preparation for the Surtees Society.]

p. 9. The Quire—The Passion.

Within the Abbye Church of Durham, uppon Good Friday theire was marvelous solemne service, in the which service time, after the Passion was sung, two of the eldest Monkes did take a goodly large Crucifix, all of gold, of the picture of our Saviour Christ nailed uppon the crosse, lyinge uppon a velvett cushion, havinge St. Cuthbert's armes uppon it all imbroydered with gold, bringinge that betwixt them uppon the said cushion to the lowest greeces in the Quire; and there betwixt them did hold the said picture of our Saviour, sittinge of every side, on ther knees, of that, and then one of the said Monkes did rise and went a pretty way from it, sittinge downe uppon his knees, with his shooes put of, and verye reverently did creepe away uppon his knees unto the said Crosse, and most reverently did kisse it. And after him the other Monke did so likewise, and then they did sitt them downe on every side of the Crosse, and holdinge it betwixt them, and after that the Prior came forth of his stall, and did sitt him downe of his knees, with his shooes off, and in like sort did creepe also unto the said Crosse, and all the Monkes after him one after another, in the same order, and in the mean time all the whole quire singinge an himne. The seruice beinge ended, the two Monkes did carrye it to the Sepulchre with great reverence, which Sepulchre was sett upp in the morninge, on the north side of the Quire, nigh to the High Altar, before the service time; and there lay it within the said Sepulchre with great devotion, with another picture of our Saviour Christ, in whose breast they did enclose, with great reverence, the most holy and blessed Sacrament of the Altar, senceinge it and prayinge unto it upon theire knees, a great space, settinge two tapers lighted before it, which tapers did burne unto Easter day in the morninge, that it was taken forth.

The Quire—The Resurrection.

There was in the Abbye Church of Duresme verye solemne service uppon Easter Day, betweene three and four of the clocke in the morninge, in honour of the Resurrection, where two of the oldest

Monkes of the Quire came to the Sepulchre, being sett upp upon Good Friday, after the Passion, all covered with red velvett and embrodered with gold, and then did sence it, either Monke with a pair of silver sencers sittinge on theire knees before the Sepulchre. Then they both rising came to the Sepulchre, out of which, with great devotion and reverence, they tooke a marvelous beautifull IMAGE OF OUR SAVIOUR, representing the resurrection, with a crosse in his hand, in the breast wherof was enclosed in bright christall the holy Sacrament of the Altar, throughe the which christall the Blessed Host was conspicuous to the behoulders. Then, after the elevation of the said picture, carryed by the said two Monkes uppon a faire velvett cushion, all embrodered, singinge the anthem of *Christus resurgens*, they brought it to the High Altar, settinge that on the midst therof, whereon it stood, the two Monkes kneelinge on theire knees before the Altar, and senceing it all the time that the rest of the whole quire was in singinge the foresaid anthem of *Christus resurgens*. The which anthem beinge ended, the two Monkes tooke up the cushions and the picture from the Altar, supportinge it betwixt them, proceeding, in procession, from the High Altar to the south Quire dore, where there was four antient Gentlemen, belonginge to the Prior, appointed to attend theire cominge, holdinge upp a most rich CANNOPYE of purple velvett, tached round about with redd silke and gold fringe; and at everye corner did stand one of theise ancient Gentlemen, to beare it over the said image, with the Holy Sacrament, carried by two Monkes round about the church, the whole quire waitinge uppon it with goodly torches and great store of other lights, all singinge, rejoyceinge, and praising God most devoutly, till they came to the High Altar againe, whereon they did place the said image there to remaine untill the Ascension day.

p. 26. THE SOUTH ALLEY OF THE LANTERN.

Over the [second of the iij Alters in that plage] was a merveylous lyvelye and bewtiful Immage of the picture of our Ladie, so called the LADY OF BOULTONE, which picture was maide to open with gymmers from her breaste downdward. And within the said immage was wrowghte and pictured the immage of our Saviour, merveylouse fynlie gilted, houldinge uppe his handes, and houlding betwixt his handes a fair large CRUCIFIX OF CHRIST, all of gold, the which crucifix was to be taiken fourthe every Good Fridaie, and every man did crepe unto it that was in that church at that daye. And ther after yt was houng upe againe within the said immage.

Q

THE SARUM SEPULCHRUM

[I give the various directions and rubrics referring to the sepulchre from the *Consuetudinary* (†1210), *Ordinal* (†1270), *Customary* (first half of fourteenth century), *Processional* (1508, &c.), *Missal* (1526, &c.), and *Breviary* (1531). The printed sixteenth-century rubrics practically reproduce the later *Ordinal* of the middle of the fourteenth century.]

The Depositio.

[From the *Processional*, with which the *Missal* practically agrees.]

Finitis vesperis, exuat sacerdos casulam, et sumens secum unum, de praelatis in superpelliceis discalceati reponant crucem cum corpore dominico [scilicet in pixide, *Missal*] in sepulcrum incipiens ipse solus hoc responsorium *Aestimatus sum*, genuflectendo cum socio suo, quo incepto statim surgat. Similiter fiat in responsorio *Sepulto Domino*. Chorus totum responsorium prosequatur cum suo versu, genuflectendo per totum tempus usque ad finem servitii. Responsoria ut sic: *Aestimatus sum.* Chorus prosequatur *cum descendentibus in lacum* . . . Dum praedictum responsorium canitur cum suo versu, praedicti duo sacerdotes thurificent sepulcrum, quo facto et clauso ostio, incipiet idem sacerdos responsorium *Sepulto Domino*. . . . Item praedicti duo sacerdotes dicant istas tres antiphonas sequentes genuflectendo continue: *In pace* . . . *In pace factus est* . . . *Caro mea* . . . His finitis, et dictis prius orationibus ad placitum secrete ab omnibus cum genuflexione, omnibus aliis ad libitum recedentibus, ordine [non, *Missal*] servato, reinduat sacerdos casulam, et eodem modo quo accessit in principio servitii, cum diacono et subdiacono et ceteris ministris abscedat.

The Sepulchre Light.

[From the *Consuetudinary*.]

In die parasceues post repositum corpus domini in sepulcro, duo cerei dimidie libre ad minus in thesauraria tota die ante sepulcrum ardebunt. In nocte sequente et exinde usque ad processionem quae fit in die pasche ante matutinas, unus illorum tan-

[From the *Processional*, with which the *Missal* and *Customary* practically agree.]

Exinde [i.e. from the *Depositio*] continue ardebit unus cereus ad minus ante sepulcrum usque ad processionem quae fit in Resurrectione Dominica in die Paschae: ita tamen quod dum Psalmus *Benedictus* canitur et cetera quae sequuntur, in sequenti

tum, magnum eciam cereum paschalem.

nocte extinguatur: similiter et extinguatur in Vigilia Paschae, dum benedicitur novus ignis, usque accendatur cereus paschalis.

The Elevatio.

[From the *Consuetudinary.*]

In die pasche ante matutinas conueniant clerici ed ecclesiam accensis cunctis cereis per ecclesiam: duo excellenciores presbiteri in superpelliceis ad sepulchrum accedant prius incensato ostio sepulchri cum magna ueneratione, corpus dominicum super altare deponant: deinde crucem de sepulchro tollant, excellenciore presbitero inchoante antiphonam *Christus resurgens* et sic eant, per ostium australe presbiterii incedentes, per medium chori regredientes, cum thuribulario et ceroferariis precedentibus, ad altare sancti martini canentes praedictam antiphonam cum uersu suo. Deinde dicto uersiculo *Surrexit dominus de sepulchro*, et dicta oracione

[From the *Ordinal.*]

In Die Pasche

Ad Processionem ante Matutinas conueniant omnes clerici ad ecclesiam ac accendantur luminaria per ecclesiam. Episcopus uel decanus in superpelliceo cum ceroferariis thuribulariis et clero in sepulcrum accedant, et incensato prius sepulcro cum magna ueneracione corpus domini assumant et super altare ponant. Iterum accipientes crucem de sepulcro inchoet episcopus uel decanus Ant. *Christus resurgens.* Tunc omnes cum gaudio genua flectant et ipsam crucem adorent, idipsum canentes cum ℣. *Dicant nunc.* Tunc omnes campane in classicum pulsentur, et cum magna ueneracione deportetur crux ad

[From the *Breviary*, with which the *Processional*, although less full, practically agrees.]

In die sancto Paschae ante Matutinas et ante campanarum pulsationem conveniant Clerici ad ecclesiam, et accendantur luminaria per totam ecclesiam. Tunc duo excellentiores Presbyteri in superpelliceis cum duobus Ceroferariis, et duobus thuribulis, et clero ad sepulchrum accedant: et incensato a praedictis duobus Presbyteris prius sepulchro cum magna veneratione, videlicet genuflectendo, statim post thurificationem corpus Dominicum super altare privatim deponant: iterum accipientes crucem de sepulchro, choro et populo interim genuflectente incipiat excellentior persona Ant. *Christus resurgens.* Et Chorus prosequatur totam anti-ab excellenciore sacerdote post debitam campanarum pulsacionem inchoentur matutine.

locum ubi prouisum sit, clero canente predictam antiphonam. Quo facto dicat Sacerdos ℣. *Surrexit dominus de sepulcro.* Or. *Deus qui pro nobis.* Que terminetur sic, *Per eundem christum dominum nostrum.*

phonam sic, *ex mortuis . . . Alleluya.*

Et tunc dum canitur Antiphona, eat processio per ostium australe presbyterii incedens et per medium chori regrediens [per ostium presbyterii australe incedendo per medium chori, et ingrediens, *Processional*] cum praedicta cruce de sepulchro inter praedictos duos Sacerdotes super eorum brachia venerabiliter portata, cum thuribulis et Ceroferariis praecedentibus, per ostium presbyterii boreale exeundo, ad unum altare ex parte boreali ecclesiae, Choro sequente, habitu non mutato, minoribus [excellentioribus, *Processional*] praecedentibus: ita tamen quod praedicti duo excellentiores in fine processionis subsequantur, corpore Dominico super altare in pixide dimisso et sub Thesaurarii custodia [in subthesaurarii custodia, *Processional*], qui illud statim in praedicta pixide in tabernaculo deponat [dependat ut potest in ista statione praecedente, *Processional*]: et tunc pulsentur omnes campanae in classicum.

Finito Antiphona praedicta, sequatur a toto Choro

V. *Dicant nunc Iudei . . . Alleluya.*

Finita autem Antiphona cum suo Versu a toto Choro, dicat excellentior persona in sua statione ad altare conversus hunc Versum.

V. *Surrexit Dominus de sepulchro.*

R. *Qui pro nobis pependit in ligno. Alleluya.*

Oremus.

Oratio. *Deus, qui pro nobis . . . Per Christum Dominum nostrum.*

Et terminetur sub Dominicali tono ad processionem: nec praecedat nec subsequatur *Dominus vobiscum.*

Finita Oratione omnes cum gaudio genuflectent ibidem et ipsam crucem adorent, in primis digniores, et tunc secrete sine processione in chorum redeant.

His itaque gestis discooperiantur ymagines et cruces per totam ecclesiam: et interim pulsentur campanae, sicut in Festis principalibus, ad Matutinas more solito.

The Censing in Easter Week.

[From the *Customary.*]

Ad primas uesperas . . . post inchoacionem antiphone super psalmum *Magnificat* procedat executor officii cum alio sacerdote . . . ad thurificandum altare . . . In die tamen pasche et per ebdomadam thurificetur sepulchrum domini post primam thurificacionem altaris, scilicet antequam thurificator altaris circumeat.

The Removal of the Sepulchre.

[From the *Customary.*]

Die ueneris in ebdomada pasche ante missam amoueatur sepulchrum.

R

THE DUBLIN QUEM QUAERITIS

[From *Bodleian MS.* 15,846 (*Rawlinson Liturg.* D. 4), f. 130, a Sarum processional written in the fourteenth century and belonging in the fifteenth to the church of St. John the Evangelist, Dublin. A less good text from *Dublin, Abp. Marsh's Library, MS.* V. 3, 2, 10, another fourteenth century processional from the same church, is facsimiled by W. H. Frere, *Winchester Troper*, pl. 26^b, and printed therefrom by Manly, i. xxii. I give all the important variants of this version.]

[1] Finito iij ℟º cum suo ℣ et G*lo*ria p*at*ri uenient tres p*er*sone in s*up*erpell*iceis* et i*n* capis[1] s*er*icis capitib*us* uelatis quasi tres Marie querentes Ih*esu*m[2], si*n*gule portantes pixidem in manib*us* q*uas*i aromatib*us*, qua*rum* prima ad ingressu*m* chori usque sepulcru*m* procedat p*er* se[3] quasi lamentando dicat:

Heu! pius pastor occiditur,
Quem nulla culpa infecit:
O mors lugenda!

Factoq*ue* modico int*er*uallo, i*n*tret sec*un*da M*a*ria co*n*simili[4] modo et dicat:

Heu! nequam gens Iudaica,
Quam dira frendet uesania,
Plebs execranda!

Deinde iij Maria consimili m*odo* d*ica*t[5]:

Heu! uerus doctor obijt,
Qui uita*m* f*un*ctis contulit:
O res plangenda!

1—1 *Omitted by Frere, probably because it was inconvenient to facsimile part only of a page.*

2 *Christu*m.

3 et.

4 Sim*i*li.

5 *Omitted.*

Ad huc paululu*m* procede*n*do prima Maria dicat [1]:

Heu! misere cur contigit [2]
Uidere mortem Saluatoris?

Deinde secunda Maria d*icat* [3]:

Heu! Consolacio nostra,
Ut quid mortem sustinuit!

Tu*nc* [4] iij Maria:

Heu! Redempcio nostra,
Ut quid taliter agere uoluit!

Tu*nc* se co*n*iu*n*ga*n*t et procedant ad gradu*m* cho*ri* an*te* altar*e* si*mul* [5] dice*n*tes:

Iam, iam, ecce, iam properemus ad tumulum
Unguentes [6] Delecti [7] corpus sanctissimum

[8] Dei*n*de proceda*n*t si*mi*l*iter* p*ro*pe sepulchru*m* et p*ri*ma Maria d*ica*t p*er* se

Condumentis aromatu*m*
Ungam*us* corpus sanctissimu*m*
Quo preciosa [8].

Tu*nc* s*ecun*da Maria dicat p*er* se:

Nardi uetet commixtio,
Ne putrescat in tumulo
Caro beata!

Deinde iij Maria [9] dicat per se [9]:

Sed nequimus hoc patrare sine adiutorio.
Quis nam saxum reuoluet [10] a monumenti ostio?

Facto int*er*uallo, ang*elus* nix*us* sepulcru*m* apparuit [11] eis et dicat hoc modo:

Quem queritis ad sepulcrum, o Cristicole?

Deinde respo*n*deant tres Marie simul d*icentes* [12]:

Ih*esu*m Nazarenum crucifixum, o celicola!

Tu*nc* angelus dicet [13]:

Surrexit, non est hic, sicut dixit;
Uenite et uidete locum ubi positus fuerat.

Deinde p*redicte* M*a*rie sepulcru*m* intrent *et* [14] inclinantes se *et* prospicientes undiq*ue* intra sepulcru*m*, alta uoce quasi gaudentes [15] *et* admirantes *et* paru*m* a sepulcro recedentes sim*ul* dica*n*t [16]:

1 dicat hoc modo.
2 contingit.
3 *Omitted.*
4 Deinde.
5 *Omitted.*
6 Ungentes.
7 Dilecti.
8–8. *Omitted: but a later hand has written on a margin of the manuscript,* Condimentis aromatum vnguentes corpus *sanctissimum* quo p*re*ciosa.
9–9 *Omitted.*
10 reuoluit.
11 appariat.
12 *Omitted.*
13 dicat sic.
14 *Omitted.*
15 gaudendo.
16 dica*n*t sim*ul*.

Alleluya! resurrexit Dominus!
Alleluya! resurrexit Dominus hodie!
Resurrexit potens, fortis, *Christus*, Filius Dei!

Deinde ang*elus* ad eas[1]:

Et euntes dicite discipulis eius et Petro quia surrexit.

In quo reu*er*tant ad angelum quasi mandatu*m* suu*m* ad imple*n*du*m* parate simul dicentes[2]:

Eya! pergamus propere
Mandatum hoc perficere!

Int*er*im ueniant ad ingressu*m* cho*ri* due p*er*sone nude pedes sub personis ap*osto*lo*rum* Iohannis *et* Pet*ri* indute albis sine paruris cu*m* tunicis, quo*rum* Ioh*ann*es amictus tunica alba palma*m* in manu gestans, Petrus uero rubea tunica indutus claues in manu ferens[3]; *et* p*re*dicte mulieres de sepulcro reuertentes *et* quasi de choro simul exeuntes, dicat prima Maria [4]p*er* se[4] sequentiam:

Victime paschali laudes
Immolant *Christ*iani.
Agnus redemit oues:
Christus innocens Patri
Reconsiliauit peccatores.
Mors et uita duello
Conflixere mirando:
Dux uite mortuis[5]
Regnat uiuus.

Tu*n*c obuiantes eis in medio chori predicti discipuli, interrogantes simul dicant:

Dic nobis, Maria,
Quid uidisti in uia?

Tu*n*c p*ri*ma Maria respondeat quasi monstrando:

Sepulcrum *Christi* uiuentis
Et gloriam uidi resurgentis.

Tu*n*c ij Maria *respon*det si*mi*l*iter*[6] mo*n*strando:

Angelicos testes,
Sudarium et uestes.

Tunc iij[7] M*a*ria respondeat:

Surrexit *Christus*, spes nostra,
Precedet uos in Galileam.

Et sic p*ro*cedant sim*ul* ad ostium chori; int*er*im[8] currant duo ad

[1] eas dicens.
[2] dicentes simul.
[3] deferens.
[4–4] *Omitted. Lines* 3–5 *of the sequence are preceded by* Secu*n*da Maria, *and lines* 6–9 *by* Tercia Maria di*cat*.
[5] *Manly suggests* mortuus.
[6] respondeat quasi.
[7] Tercia.
[8] et interim.

monumentum; uerumptamen ille discipulus quem diligebat Ihesus uenit prior ad monumentum, iuxta euangelium: 'Currebant autem duo simul et ille alius discipulus precucurrit cicius Petro et uenit prior ad monumentum, non tamen introiuit.' Uidentes discipuli predicti[1] sepulcrum uacuum et uerbis Marie credentes reuertant se ad chorum dicentes[2]:

Credendum est magis soli Marie ueraci
Quam Iudeorum turbe fallaci!

Tunc audita[3] Christi resurreccione, chorus prosequatur alta uoce quasi gaudentes et exultantes sic dicentes[4]:

Scimus Christum surrexisse
A mortuis uere.
Tu nobis, uictor Rex, miserere!

Qua finita, executor officii incipiat:

Te Deum laudamus.

[5] Tunc recedant sanctae Marie apostoli et angelus[5].

S

THE AUREA MISSA OF TOURNAI

[Communicated from *Lille Bibl. Munic. MS.* 62 (sixteenth century) by L. Deschamps de Pas to the *Annales archéologiques*, xvii (1857), 167.]

Sequuntur ceremonie et modus observandus pro celebratione misse Missus est Gabriel Angelus, &c., vulgariter dicte Auree Misse quolibet anno in choro ecclesie Tornacensis decantande feria x[a] ante festum nativitatis Domini nostri Iesu-Christi, ex fundatione venerabilis viri magistri Petri Cotrel, canonici dicti ecclesie Tornacensis et in eadem archidiaconi Brugensis, de licentia et permissione dominorum suorum decani et capituli predicte ecclesie Tornacensis.—Primo, feria tercia, post decantationem vesperum, disponentur per carpentatorem ecclesie in sacrario chori dicte ecclesie Tornacensis, in locis iam ad hoc ordinatis et sibi oppositis, duo stallagia, propter hoc appropriata, que etiam ornabuntur cortinis et pannis cericeis ad hoc ordinatis per casularium iam dicte ecclesie, quorum alterum, videlicet quod erit de latere episcopi, serviet ad recipiendam beatam virginem Mariam, et alterum stallagium ab illo oratorio oppositum, quod erit de latere decani, serviat ad recipiendum et recludendum Angelum.—Item

[1] *Omitted.* [2] dicentes hoc modo. [3] audito. [4] dicant.
[5–5] *Omitted.*

similiter eodem die deputatus ad descendendum die sequenti columbam, visitabit tabernaculum in altis carolis dispositum, disponet cordas, et parabit instrumentum candelis suis munitum, per quod descendet Spiritus Sanctus in specie columbe, tempore decantationis ewangelii, prout postea dicetur, et erit sollicitus descendere cordulam campanule, et illam disponere ad stallagium Angeli, ad illam campanulam pulsandam suo tempore, die sequenti, prout post dicetur.—Item in crastinum durantibus matutinis, magistri cantus erunt solliciti quod duo iuvenes, habentes voces dulces et altas, preparentur in thesauraria, hostio clauso, unus ad modum virginis seu regine, et alter ad modum angeli, quibus providebitur de ornamentis et aliis necessariis propter hoc per fundatorem datis et ordinatis.—Item post decantationem septime lectionis matutinarum, accedent duo iuvenes, Mariam videlicet et Angelum representantes, sic parati de predicta thesauraria, ad chorum intrando per maius hostium dicti chori, duabus thedis ardentibus precedentibus: Maria videlicet per latus domini episcopi, in manibus portans horas pulchras, et Angelus per latus domini decani, portans in manu dextra sceptrum argenteum deauratum, et sic morose progredientur, cum suis magistris directoribus, usque ad summum altare, ubi, genibus flexis, fundent ad Dominum orationem. Qua facta, progredientur dicti iuvenes quilibet ad locum suum, Maria videlicet ad stallagium, de parte episcopi preparatum, cum suo magistro directore, et Angelus ad aliud stallagium de parte decani similiter preparatum, etiam cum suo alio magistro directore, et ubique cortinis clausis. Coram quibus stallagiis remanebunt predicte thede, ardentes usque ad finem misse.—Item clerici thesaurarie, durantibus octava et nona lectionibus matutinarum, preparabunt maius altare solemniter, ut in triplicibus festis, et omnes candele circumquaque chorum sacrarum de rokemes, et in corona nova existentes accendentur. Et clerici revestiarii providebunt quod presbyter, dyaconus, subdiaconus, choriste, cum pueris revestitis, sint parati, in fine hymni TE DEUM, pro missa decantanda, ita quod nulla sit pausa inter finem dicti himpni TE DEUM et missam. Et in fine praedicte misse sit paratus presbiter ebdomarius cantandi versum *Ora pro nobis*, et deinde, *Deus in adiutorium*, de laudibus illas perficiendo per chorum, et in fine psalmi *De profundis* dicendi, in fine matutinarum, more consueto, adiungetur collecta *Adiuva nos* pro fundatore ultra collectam ordinariam.—Item, cum celebrans accesserit ad maius altare, pro incipienda missa, et ante *Confiteor* immediate cortine circumquaque oratorium Virginis solum aperientur, ipsa Virgine attente orante et ad genua existente suo libro aperto, super pulvinari ad hoc ordinato, Angelo adhuc semper clauso in suo stallagio remanente.—Item cum cantabitur *Gloria in Excelsis Deo* tunc cortine stallagii, in quo erit Angelus, aperientur. In quo stallagio stabit dictus Angelus erectus, tenens in manibus suis suum sceptrum argenteum, et nichil aliud faciens, quousque fuerit tempus cantandi ewangelium, nec interim faciet Virgo aliquod signum videndi dictum angelum, sed, submissis oculis, erit semper intenta ad orationem.—Item cum appropinquarit tempus cantandi dictum ewangelium, diaconus cum subdiacono, pueris cum candelis et cruce precedentibus, progredientur ad locum in sacrario sibi preparatum, et cantabit ewangelium *Missus est Gabriel*, et etiam cantabunt partes suas Maria et Angelus, prout ordinatum et notatum est in libro ad hoc ordinato. —Item cum Angelus cantabit hec verba ewangelii, *Ave, gratia plena, Dominus tecum*, faciet tres ad Virginem salutationes; primo ad illud verbum *Ave*, humiliabit se tam capite quam corpore, post morose se elevando; et ad illa verba, *gratia plena*, faciet secundam humiliationem, flectendo mediocriter genua sua, se postea relevando; et ad illa verba, *Dominus tecum*, quae cantabit cum gravitate et morose, tunc faciet terciam humiliationem ponendo genua usque ad terram et finita clausula assurget, Virgine interim se non movente. Sed dum Maria virgo cantabit *Quomodo fiet istud*, assurget et vertet modicum faciem suam ad Angelum cum gravitate et modestia, non aliter se movendo. Et dum cantabit Angelus *Spiritus Sanctus superveniet in te*, etc., tunc Angelus vertet faciem suam versus columbam illam ostendendo, et subito descendet ex loco in altis carolis ordinato, cum candelis in circuitu ipsius ardentibus, ante stallagium sive oratorium Virginis, ubi remanebit, usque post ultimum *Agnus Dei*, quo decantato, revertetur ad locum unde descenderat.—Item magister cantus, qui erit in stallagio Angeli, sit valde sollicitus pro propria vice pulsare campanam in altis carolis, respondente in initio ewangelii, ut tunc ille qui illic erit ordinatus ad descendendum columbam sit preadvisatus et preparet omnia necessaria et candelas accendat. Et secunda vice sit valde sollicitus pulsare dictam campanulam, ita quod precise ad illud verbum *Spiritus Sanctus* descendat ad Virginem columbam ornatam candelis accensis, et remaneat ubi descenderit, usque ad ultimum *Agnus Dei* decantatum, prout dictum est. Et tunc idem magister cantus iterum pulsabit pro tercia vice eamdem campanulam, ut revertatur columba unde descenderit. Et sit ille disponendus vel deputandus ad descendendum dictam columbam bene preadvisatus de supra dicta triplici pulsatione et quid quilibet significabit ne sit in aliquo defectus.—Item predicti, diaconus, Maria, et Angelus complebunt totum ewangelium in eodem tono prout cuilibet sibi competit, et ewangelio finito reponet se Maria ad genua et orationem, et Angelus remanebit rectus, usque in finem misse, hoc excepto, quod in elevatione corporis Christi ponet se ad genua.—Item postea proficietur missa, Maria et Angelo in suis stallagiis usque in fine permanentibus.—Item missa finita, post *Ite, missa est*, Maria et Angelus descendent de suis stallagiis et revertentur cum reliquiis et revestitis usque ad revestiarium predictum eorum, flambellis precedentibus. In quo revestiario presbiter celebrans cum predictis revestitis Maria et Angelo dicet psalmum *De profundis*, prout in choro cum adiectione collecte *Adiuva* pro fundatore.—Item fiet missa per omnia, ut in die Annunciationis dominice cum sequentia sive prosa *Mittit ad virginem*, cum organis et discantu prout in triplicibus.

T

SUBJECTS OF THE CYCLICAL MIRACLES

[This comparative table is based on that drawn up by Prof. Hohlfeld in *Anglia*, xi. 241. The episodes are taken in their scriptural order, which is not always that of the plays. I have added the Cornish data, using O. P. R. to indicate the *Origo Mundi*, *Passio Domini*, and *Resurrectio Domini* of the older text, and J. for William Jordan's *Creation of the World*. I have quoted Halliwell's divisions of the *Ludus Coventriae*, really a continuous text, for convenience sake.]

Episodes.	*York.*	*Townley.*	*Chester.*	*Ludus Cov.*	*Cornwall.*
1. Fall of Lucifer . .	i	i	i	i	O. 48[1]: J. 114–334.
2. Creation and Fall of Man	ii–vi	i[2]	ii	i, ii	O. 1–437: J. 1–113, 335–1055.
3. Cain and Abel . .	vii	ii	ii	iii	O. 438–633: J. 1056–1317.
4. Wanderings of Cain	—	—	—	—	J. 1332–1393.
5. Death of Cain . .	—	—	—	iv	J. 1431–1726.
6. Seth in Paradise and Death of Adam	—	—	—	—	O. 634–916: J. 1318–1331, 1394–1430, 1727–2093, 2146–2210.
7. Enoch	—	—	—	—	J. 2094–2145.
8. Noah and the Flood	viii, ix	iii	iii	iv	O. 917–1258: J. 2211–2530[3].
9. Abraham and Melchisedec . .	—	—	iv	—	
10. Abraham and Isaac .	x	iv	iv	v	O. 1259–1394.
11. Jacob's Blessing .	—	v[2]	—	—	
12. Jacob's Wanderings .	—	vi	—	—	

[1] Only a stage-direction, *Hic ludit* [? *cadit*] *Lucifer de celo*.

[2] Imperfect.

[3] Jordan closes with an invitation to a *Redemptio* on the morrow.

Episodes.	*York.*	*Town-ley.*	*Ches-ter.*	*Ludus Cov.*	*Cornwall.*
13. Moses and the Exodus	xi	viii	—	vi	O. 1395–1714.
14. Moses in the Wilderness . . .	—	vii	v	vi	O. 1715–1898.
15. Balaam . . .	—	—	v	—	
16. David and the Rods	—	—	—	—	O. 1899–2104.
17. David and Bathsheba	—	—	—	—	O. 2105–2376.
18. Building of the Temple . . .	—	—	—	—	O. 2377–2628.
19. Prophecy of Maximilla . . .	—	—	—	—	O. 2629–2778.
20. Bridge over Cedron .	—	—	—	—	O. 2779–2824.
21. *Prophetae* . .	xii [1]	vii	—	vii	
22. Joachim and Anna .	—	—	—	viii	
23. Mary in the Temple	—	—	—	ix	
24. Betrothal of Mary .	—	x [1]	—	x	
25. Annunciation . .	xii	x	vi	xi	
26. Salutation of Elizabeth . . .	xii	xi	vi	xiii	
27. Suspicion of Joseph .	xiii	x	vi	xii	
28. Purgation of Mary .	—	—	—	xiv	
29. Augustus and Cyrenius . . .	—	ix	—	—	
30. Nativity . . .	xiv	—	vi	xv	
31. Conversion of Octavian . . .	—	—	vi	—	
32. *Pastores* . . .	xv	xii, xiii [2]	vii	xvi	
33. Purification . .	xli [3]	xvii [4]	xi	xviii	
34. *Magi* before Herod .	xvi, xvii [2]	xiv	viii	xvii	
35. Offering of *Magi* .	xvii	xiv	ix	xvii	
36. Flight into Egypt .	xviii	xv	x	xix	
37. Massacre of Innocents . . .	xix	xvi	x	xix	
38. Death of Herod .	—	—	—	xix	
39. Presentation in Temple . . .	xx	xviii [4]	—	xx	
40. Baptism . . .	xxi	xix	—	xxi	
41. Temptation . .	xxii	—	xii	xxii	P. 1–172.
42. Marriage in Cana .	[lost]	—	—	—	
43. Transfiguration .	xxiii				
44. Woman in Adultery	xxiv	—	xii	xxiii	
45. Healing of Blind in Siloam . . .	—	—	xiii	—	
46. Raising of Lazarus .	xxiv	xxxi [3]	xiii	xxiv	
47. Healing of Bartimaeus . . .	—	—	—	—	P. 393–454.
48. Entry into Jerusalem	xxv	—	xiv	xxvi	P. 173–330.
49. Cleansing of Temple	—	—	xiv	—	P. 331–392.
50. Jesus in House of Simon the Leper .	[lost]	xx [1]	xiv	xxvii	P. 455–552.
51. Conspiracy of Jews .	xxvi	xx	xiv	xxv	P. 553–584.

[1] Narrated. [2] Duplicates. [3] Misplaced. [4] Imperfect.

Episodes.	*York.*	*Townley.*	*Chester.*	*Ludus Cov.*	*Cornwall.*
52. Treachery of Judas .	xxvi	xx	xiv	xxvii	P. 585–616.
53. Last Supper . .	xxvii	xx	xv	xxvii	P. 617–930.
54. Gethsemane . .	xxviii	xx	xv	xxviii	P. 931–1200.
55. Jesus before Caiaphas	xxix	xxi	xvi	xxx	P. 1200–1504.
56. Jesus before Pilate .	xxx	—	xvi	xxx	P. 1567–1616.
57. Jesus before Herod .	xxxi	—	xvi	xxix, xxx	P. 1617–1816.
58. Dream of Pilate's Wife	xxx	—	—	xxxi	P. 1907–1968, 2193–2212.
59. Remorse and Death of Judas . .	xxxii	xxxii [1]	—	xxxii	P. 1505–1566.
60. Condemnation .	xxxiii	xxii	xvi	xxxii	P. 1817–2533.
61. Cross Brought from Cedron . .	—	—	—	—	P. 2534–2584.
62. Bearing of the Cross	xxxiv	xxii	xvii	xxxii	P. 2585–2662.
63. Veronica . . .	xxxiv	—	—	xxxii	—
64. Crucifixion . .	xxxv	xxiii	xvii	xxxii	P. 2663–2840.
65. Casting of Lots .	xxxv	xxiii, xxiv	xvii	—	P. 2841–2860.
66. *Planctus Mariae* [cf. p. 39] . . .	xxxvi	xxiii	xvii	xxxii	P. 2925–2954.
67. Death of Jesus. .	xxxvi	xxiii	xvii	xxxii	P. 2861–3098.
68. Longinus . .	xxxvi	xxiii	xvii	xxxiv	P. 3003–3030.
69. Descent from Cross.	xxxvi	xxiii	xvii	xxxiv	P. 3099–3201.
70. Burial . . .	xxxvi	—	—	xxxiv	P. 3202–3216.
71. Harrowing of Hell .	xxxvii	xxv	xviii	xxxiii, xxxv	P. 3031–3078: R. 97–306.
72. Release of Joseph and Nicodemus	—	—	—	—	R. 1–96, 307–334, 625–662.
73. Setting of Watch .	xxxviii	xxvi	xix	xxxv	R. 335–422.
74. Resurrection . .	xxxviii	xxvi	xix	xxxv	R. 423–678.
75. *Quem Quaeritis* .	xxxviii	xxvi	xix	xxxvi	R. 679–834.
76. *Hortulanus* . .	xxxix	xxvi	xix [2]	xxxvii	R. 835–892.
77. *Peregrini* . .	xl	xxvii	xx	xxxviii	R. 1231–1344.
78. Incredulity of Thomas	xlii	xxviii	xx	xxxviii	R. 893–1230, 1345–1586.
79. Death of Pilate .	—	—	—	—	R. 1587–2360.
80. Veronica and Tiberius . . .	—	—	—	—	R. 1587–2360.
81. Ascension . .	xliii	xxix	xxi	xxxix	R. 2361–2630.
82. Pentecost . .	xliv	[? lost]	xxii	xl	
83. Death of Mary. .	xlv	—	—	xli	
84. Burial of Mary .	[lost]	—	—	xli	
85. Apparition of Mary to Thomas . .	xlvi	—	—	—	
86. Assumption and Coronation . . .	xlvii [3]	—	[lost]	xli	
87. Signs of Judgement [cf. p. 53] . .	—	—	xxiii	—	
88. Antichrist [cf. p. 62].	—	—	xxiv	—	
89. Doomsday . .	xlviii	xxx	xxv	xlii [4]	

[1] Late addition. [2] Imperfect? [3] And later fragment. [4] Imperfect.

U

INTERLUDIUM DE CLERICO ET PUELLA

[Printed by Wright and Halliwell, *Reliquiae Antiquae* (1841), i. 145, from an early fourteenth-century MS., then belonging to the Rev. R. Yerburgh, of Sleaford. On the piece and its sources in the Latin, French, and English *fabliaux* of *Dame Siriz*, cf. Ten Brink, i. 255; ii. 295; Jusserand, *Lit. Hist.* i. 446. Ten Brink assigns the dramatic text, which is in the South Northumbrian dialect, to the reign of Edward I (1272–1307).]

Hic incipit Interludium de Clerico et Puella.

[Scene 1.]

Clericus. Damishel, reste wel.
Puella. Sir, welcum, by Saynt Michel!
Clericus. Wer esty sire, wer esty dame?
Puella. By Gode, es noner her at hame.
Clericus. Wel wor suilc a man to life,
That suilc a may mithe have to wyfe!
Puella. Do way, by Crist and Leonard,
No wily lufe, na clerc fayllard,
Na kepi herbherg, clerc, in huse no y flore
Bot his hers ly wit-uten dore.
Go forth thi way, god sire,
For her hastu losye al thi wile.
Clericus. Nu, nu, by Crist and by sant Jhon,
In al this land ne wis hi none,
Mayden, that hi luf mor than the,
Hif me mithe ever the bether be.
For the hy sory nicht and day,
Y may say, hay wayleuay!
Y luf the mar than mi lif,
Thu hates me mar than gayt dos chuief.
That es noute for mys-gilt,
Certhes, for thi luf ham hi spilt.
A, suythe mayden, reu ef me
That es ty luf, hand ay salbe.
For the luf of [the] y mod of efne;
Thu mend thi mode, and her my stevene.
Puella. By Crist of heven and sant Jone!
Clerc of scole ne kepi non;

For many god wymman haf thai don scam.
By Crist, thu michtis haf be at hame.
Clericus. Synt it nothir gat may be,
Jhesu Crist, by-tethy the,
And send neulit bot thar inne,
That thi be lesit of al my pyne.
Puella. Go nu, truan, go nu, go,
For mikel thu canstu of sory and wo.

[Scene 2.]

Clericus. God te blis, Mome Helwis.
Mome Helwis. Son, welcum, by san Dinis!
Clericus. Hic am comin to the, Mome,
Thu hel me noth, thu say me sone.
Hic am a clerc that hauntes scole,
Y hidy my lif wyt mikel dole;
Me wor lever to be dedh,
Than led the lif that hyc ledh,
For ay mayden with and schen,
Fayrer ho lond hawy non syen.
Tho hat mayden Malkyn, y wene;
Nu thu wost quam y mene,
Tho wonys at the tounes ende,
That suyt lif, so fayr and hende.
Bot if tho wil hir mod amende,
Neuly Crist my ded me send.
Men send me hyder, vyt uten fayle,
To haf thi help anty cunsayle.
Thar for amy cummen here,
That thu salt be my herand-bere,
To mac me and that mayden sayct,
And hi sal gef the of my nayct,
So that hever al thi lyf
Saltu be the better wyf.
So help me Crist! and hy may spede,
Rithe saltu haf thi mede.
Mome Ellwis. A, son, wat saystu? benedicite,
Lift hup thi hand, and blis the.
For it es boyt syn and scam,
That thu on me hafs layt thys blam.
For hic am an ald quyne and a lam.

Y led my lyf wit Godis love.
Wit my roc y me fede,
Cani do non othir dede,
Bot my pater noster and my crede,
Tho say Crist for missedede,
And my navy Mary,
For my scynne hic am sory,
And my de profundis,
For al that yn sin lys.
For cani me non othir think,
That wot Crist, of heven kync.
Ihesu Crist, of heven hey,
Gef that hay may heng hey,
And gef that hy may se,
That thay be henge on a tre,
That this ley as leyit onne me.
For aly wymam (*sic*) ami on.

V

TERENTIUS ET DELUSOR

[I follow the text of P. de Winterfeld, *Hrotsvithae Opera* (1902), xx; the piece was previously edited by C. Magnin in *Bibliothèque de l'École des Chartes*, i (1840), 517; A. de Montaiglon in *L'Amateur des Livres* (1849); A. Riese, in *Zeits. f. d. österreich. Gymn.* xviii. 442; R. Sabbadini (1894). The only manuscript is *B. N. Lat. MS.* 8069 of the late tenth or early eleventh century. Various scholars have dated the poem from the seventh to the tenth century; Winterfeld declares for the ninth. It might have been intended as a prologue to a Terentian revival or to a mime. The homage paid to the *vetus poeta* by the *delusor* in his asides rather suggests the former; cf. Cloetta, i. 2; Creizenach, i. 8.]

[Delusor.]

Mitte recordari monimenta vetusta, Terenti;
  cesses ulterius: vade, poeta vetus.
vade, poeta vetus, quia non tua carmina curo;
  iam retice fabulas, dico, vetus veteres.
dico, vetus veteres iamiam depone camenas,
  quae nil, credo, iuvant, pedere ni doceant.
tale decens carmen, quod sic volet ut valet istud;
  qui cupit exemplum, captet hic egregium.
huc ego cum recubo, me taedia multa capescunt:
  an sit prosaicum, nescio, an metricum.

dic mihi, dic, quid hoc est? an latras corde sinistro?
dic, vetus auctor, in hoc quae iacet utilitas?

Nunc TERENTIUS *exit foras audiens haec et ait*:

quis fuit, hercle, pudens, rogo, qui mihi tela lacessens
turbida contorsit? quis talia verba sonavit?
hic quibus externis scelerosus venit ab oris,
qui mihi tam durum iecit ridendo cachinnum?
quam graviter iaculo mea viscera laesit acuto!
hunc ubi repperiam, contemplor, et hunc ubi quaeram?
si mihi cum tantis nunc se offerat obvius iris,
debita iudicio persolvam dona librato.

Ecce persona DELUSORIS *praesentatur et hoc audiens inquit*:

quem rogitas ego sum: quid vis persolvere? cedo;
huc praesens adero, non dona probare recuso.

TERENTIUS.

tune, sceleste, meas conrodis dente Camenas?
tu quis es? unde venis, temerarie latro? quid istis
vocibus et dictis procerum me, a! perdite, caedis?
tene, superbe, meas decuit corrumpere Musas?

PERSONA DELUSORIS.

si rogitas, quis sum, respondeo: te melior sum:
tu vetus atque senex, ego tyro valens adulescens;
tu sterilis truncus, ego fertilis arbor, opimus.
si taceas, vetule, lucrum tibi quaeris enorme.

TERENTIUS.

quis tibi sensus inest? numquid melior me es? . . .
nunc, vetus atque senex quae fecero, fac adolescens.
si bonus arbor ades, qua fertilitate redundas?
cum sim truncus iners, fructu meliore redundo.

PERSONA *secum*.

nunc mihi vera sonat; set huic contraria dicam—
quid magis instigas? quid talia dicere certas?
haec sunt verba senum, qui cum post multa senescunt
tempora, tunc mentes in se capiunt pueriles.

TERENTIUS.

hactenus antiquis sapiens venerandus ab annis
inter et egregios ostentor et inter honestos.

sed mihi felicem sapientis tollis honorem,
qui mihi verba iacis et vis contendere verbis.

PERSONA.

si sapiens esses, non te mea verba cierent.
o bone vir, sapiens ut stultum ferre libenter,
obsecro, me sapias; tua me sapientia firmet.

TERENTIUS.

cur, furiose, tuis lacerasti carmina verbis?
me retinet pietas, quin haec manus arma cerebro
implicet ista tuo: pessumdare te miseresco.

PERSONA *secum.*

quam bene ridiculum mihi personat iste veternus.—
te retinet pietas? nam fas est credere, credo.
me, peto, ne tangas, ne sanguine tela putrescant.

TERENTIUS.

cur, rogo, me sequeris? cur me ludendo lacessis?

[PERSONA.]

sic fugit horrendum praecurrens damna leonem.

[TERENTIUS.]

vix ego pro superum teneor pietate deorum,
ad tua colla meam graviter lentescere palmam.

PERSONA.

vae tibi, pone minas: nescis quem certe minaris.
verba latrando, senex cum sis vetus, irrita profers.
i, rogo, ne vapules et, quod minitare, reportes;
nunc ego sum iuvenis: patiarne ego verba vetusti?

TERENTIUS.

o iuvenis, tumidae nimium ne crede iuventae:
saepe superba cadunt, et humillima saepe resurgunt.
o mihi si veteres essent in pectore vires,
de te supplicium caperem quam grande nefandum.
si mihi plura iacis et tali voce lacessis,
p. . . . .

W

REPRESENTATIONS OF MEDIAEVAL PLAYS

[I have attempted to bring together, under a topographical arrangement, the records of such local plays of the mediaeval type as I am acquainted with. Probably the number could be increased by systematic search in local histories and transactions of learned societies. But my list is a good deal longer than those of L. T. Smith, *York Plays*, lxiv; Stoddard, 53; or Davidson, 219. For convenience I have also noted here a few records of Corpus Christi processions, and of folk 'ridings' and other institutions. The following index-table shows the geographical distribution of the plays. The names italicized are those of places where plays have been reported in error or are merely conjectural.]

INDEX.

ABERDEEN, SCOTLAND.

I summarize the references to plays and pageants in the Burgh Records[1].

May 13, 1440. Richard Kintor, abbot of Boneacord, was granted 'unus burgensis futurus faciendus' (i.e. the fees on taking up the freedom), 'pro expensis suis factis et faciendis in quodam ludo de ly Haliblude ludendo apud ly Wyndmylhill.'

Sept. 5, 1442. 'Thir craftes vndirwritten sal fynd yerly in the offerand of our Lady at Candilmes thir personnes vnderwrittin; that is to say,

The littistares sal fynd,

The empriour and twa doctoures, and alsmony honeste squiares as thai may.

The smythes and hammermen sal fynd,

The three kingis of Culane, and alsmony honeste squiares as thai may.

[1] J. Stuart, *Extracts from the Council Register of the Burgh of Aberdeen*, vol. i. 1398–1570 (Spalding Club, 1844).

The talzoures sal fynd,

Our lady Sancte Bride, Sancte Helone, Joseph, and alsmony squiares as thai may.

The skynnares sal fynd,

Two bischopes, four angeles, and alsmony honeste squiares as thai may.

The webstares and walkares sal fynd,

Symon and his disciples, and alsmony honeste squiares, etc.

The cordinares sal fynd,

The messyngear and Moyses, and alsmony honeste squiares, etc.

The fleschowares sal fynd,

Twa or four wodmen, and alsmony honest squiares, etc.

The brethir of the gilde sall fynd,

The knyghtes in harnace, and squiares honestely araiit, etc.

The baxsteiris sal fynd,

The menstralis, and alsmony honest squyares as thai may.'

May 21, 1479. Order for the alderman 'to mak the expensis and costis of the comon gude apon the arayment, and uthris necessaris, of the play to be plait in the fest of Corpos Xristi nixttocum.'

Feb. 1, $148\frac{4}{5}$. Order for all craftsmen to 'beyr thare takyinis of thare craft apon thare beristis, and thare best aray on Canddilmes day at the Offerand.'

Feb. 3, $150\frac{2}{3}$. Fine imposed upon certain websters, because 'thai did nocht it that accordit thame to do one Candilmese day, in the Passioun [? Pr'ssioun, "Procession"],' owing to a dispute as to precedence with the tailors.

Jan. 30, $150\frac{5}{6}$. Order for continuance of 'the ald lovabile consuetud and ryt of the burgh' that the craftsmen 'kepit and decorit the procession one Candilmes day yerlie; . . . and thai sale, in order to the Offering in the Play, pass tua and ij togidr socialie; in the first the flesshoris, barbouris, baxturis, cordinaris, skineris, couparis, wrichtis, hat makars [and] bonat makars togidr, walcaris, litstaris, wobstaris, tailyeouris, goldsmiths, blaksmithis and hammermen; and the craftsmen sal furnyss the Pageants; the cordinaris, the Messing[er]; wobstaris and walcaris, Symeon; the smyths [and] goldsmiths, iij Kingis of Cullane; the litstaris, the Emperour; the masons, the Thrie Knichtis; the talyors, our Lady, Sanct Brid, and Sanct Elene; and the skynners, the Tua Bischopis; and tua of ilke craft to pass with the pageant that thai furnyss to keip thair geir.'

May 28, 1507. Order for precedence 'in ale processiounis, baitht in Candilmes play and utheris processionis.'

Jan. 30, 151$\frac{0}{1}$. The order of Jan. 30, 150$\frac{5}{6}$ repeated *verbatim.*

Feb. 3, 151$\frac{0}{1}$. Citizens fined 'becauss thai passt not in the procession of Candilmes day to decoir the samyn.'

Feb. 5, 152$\frac{3}{4}$. Johne Pill, tailor, to do penance, 'for the disobeing of David Anderson, bailze, becaus he refusit to pas in the Candilmess processioun with his taikin and sing of his craft in the place lemit to his craft, and in likewise for the mispersoning of the said Dauid Andersoun, the merchandis of the said guid town, in calling of thame Coffeis, and bidding of thame to tak the salt pork and herboiss in thair handis.'

May 22, 1531. Order for the craftsmen to 'keipe and decoir the processioun on Corpus Cristi dais, and Candilmes day . . . every craft with thair awin baner . . . And euery ane of the said craftis, in the Candilmes processioun, sall furneiss thair pageane, conforme to the auld statut, maid in the yeir of God jai v^{c} and x yeris . . .

The craftis ar chargit to furneiss thair panzeanis vnder writtin.

The flescharis, Sanct Bestian and his Tourmentouris.

The barbouris, Sanct Lowrance and his Tourmentouris.

The skynnaris, Sanct Stewin and his Tourmentouris.

The cordinaris, Sanct Martyne.

The tailzeouris, the Coronatioun of Our Lady.

Litstaris, Sanct Nicholes.

Wobstaris, walcaris, and bonet makaris, Sanct John.

Baxstaris, Sanct Georg.

Wrichtis, messonis, sclateris, and cuparis, The Resurrectioun.

The smithis and hemmirmen to furneiss The Bearmen of the Croce.'

June 13, 1533. A very similar order, but without the list of pageants, and so worded as to extend the obligation of furnishing pageants to the Corpus Christi, as well as the Candlemas procession:—'The craftismen . . . sall . . . keip and decoir the processionis on XXi day and Candelmes day . . . euery craft with thair avin banar . . . with thair pegane . . . And euery craft in the said processionis sall furneiss thair pegane and banar honestlie as effers, conforme to the auld statut maid in the yeir of God jaj v^{c} and tene yers.'

June 21, 1538. Dispute between goldsmiths and hammermen as to precedence 'in the processioun of Corpus Xri.'

June 25, 1546. Litsters ordered to 'haue thar banar and Pagane, as uther craftis of the said Burgh hes, ilk yeir, on Corpus Xhri day, and Candilmess dayis processiounis.'

June 4, 1553. Disputes as to ordering of Corpus Christi procession.

May 21, 1554. Similar disputes. A 'Pagane' in procession mentioned.

May 29, 1556. Order for observance of statute as to Corpus Christi procession.

The interpretation of these notices is not quite clear. Davidson, 220, seems to think that there was never more than a *mystère mimé* at Candlemas. But the 'play' is mentioned in 1506, 1507, and 1510. I conjecture that the Passion and Nativity cycles were not merged in Aberdeen. The Passion (Haliblude play) was performed, perhaps only occasionally, on Corpus Christi day; the Nativity annually, at Candlemas. The 'persones' of 1442 and the 'Pageants' of 150$\frac{5}{6}$ are practically identical, and would furnish a short play, with Moses and Octavian to represent the *Prophetae*, a *Stella*, and a *Presentation in the Temple*. But there was certainly also a procession in which the 'honest squiares' of 1442 figured. This may have preceded the play, but it may have been in some way introduced into it at 'the offerand' (of the Virgin in the Temple, or of the Magi?). The pageants in the list of 1531 are such as cannot all have formed part of a connected cycle. But some of them might come from the 'Haliblude' play, and I take it that this list was meant for the Corpus Christi procession only, the Candlemas procession being still regulated by the order of 1507.

Bon Accord.

The Haliblude play of 1440 was directed by the Abbot of Bon Accord. This was the Aberdeen name for the Lord of Misrule. There are many notices of him.

April 30, 1445. Order 'for letting and stanching of diuerse enormyteis done in time bygane be the abbotis of this burgh, callit of bone acorde, that in time to cum thai will giue na feis to na sic abbotis. Item, it is sene speidful to thame that for the instant yher thai will haue na sic abbot; but thai will that the alderman for the tyme, and a balyhe quhom that he will tak til him, sall supple that faute.'

August 17, 1491. Dispute as to fee of 'Abbat of Bonacord.'

May 8, 1496. Choice, 'for vphaldin of the auld lovable consuetud, honour, consolacioun, and pleasour of this burgh,' of two 'coniunctlie abbotis and priour of Bonacord,' with fee of five marks.

Nov. 30, 1504. All 'personis burges nichtbours, and burgyes sonnys' to ride with 'Abbot and Prior of Bonaccord' on St. Nicholas day annually when called on by them.

[In 1511 and 1515 this function of the Abbot has passed to the provost and baillies.]

May 16, 1507. 'All manere of youthis, burgeis and burges sonnys salbe redy everie halyday to pass with the Abbat and Prior of Bonacord.'

May 8, 1508. 'All personis that are abill within this burghe sall be ready with thair arrayment maid in grene and yallow, bowis, arrowis, brass, and all uther convenient thingis according thairto, to pass with Robyne Huyd and Litile Johnne, all tymes convenient tharto, quhen thai be requirit be the saidis Robyne and Litile Johnne.'

Nov. 17, 1508. Order for St. Nicholas riding 'with Robert Huyid and Litile Johne, quhilk was callit, in yers bipast, Abbat and Prior of Bonacord.'

April 13, 1523. Choice of 'Lordis of Bonaccord,' young men 'to rise and obey to thame.' They are also to be 'Mastris of Artuilyery.'

April 30, 1527. Grant of 'x marks of the fyrst fremen that hapynnis to be frathinfurht' to 'the Lord of Bonnacord and his fellow.'

Aug. 3, 1528. Similar grant to 'thair lovits, Jhone Ratray and Gilbert Malisoun, thair Abbatis out of ressoun.'

April 16, 1531. One of those chosen to be 'lords of Bonacord, to do plesour and blythnes to the toune in this sessoun of symmir incumming' protests against his appointment.

Oct. 11, 1533. Grant of fee to 'lordis of Bonaccord.'

April 30, 1535. Order 'that all the zoung abil men within this guid [toune] haue thair grene cottis, and agit men honest cottis, efferand to thame, and obey and decor the lordis of Bonaccord.'

April 4, 1539. 'The lordis of Bonacordis desyr' for their fee, and for 'all the yong able men within this guid towne to conwey ws euery Sunday and halyday, and wther neidfull tymes, aboulzeit as your M. has deuisit, and agit men to meit us at the crabstane or kirkyard' is granted.

June 23, 1539. Fee to 'lordis of Bonacord.'

April 17, 1541. Similar fee 'to help to the decoration and plesour to be done be thaim to this guid towne.'

April 17, 1542. Similar fee.

April 24, 1542. 'Alex. Kayn, accusit in gugment for his wyff . . . for the hawy strublens and vile mispersoning of Alex. Gray and Dauid Kintoir, lordis of Bonacord, and thair company present with thame for the tyme, sayand common beggaris and skafferis, thair meltyd was but small for all thair cuttit out hoyss, with moy oder inurious wordis, unleful to be expremit.'

July 24, 1545. Grant of 'compositioun siluer' as fee.

April 20, 1548. Similar fee.

April 14, 1552. 'The said day, the counsell, all in ane voce, havand respect and consideratioune that the lordis of Bonnacord in tymes bygane hase maid our mony grit, sumpteous, and superfleous banketing induring the tyme of thair regnn, and specialie in May, quhilks wes thocht nother profitabill nor godlie, and did hurt to sundry young men that wer elekit in the said office, becaus the last elekit did aye pretent to surmont in thair predecessouris in thair ryetouss and sumpteous banketing, and the causs principal and gud institutiounn thairof, quhilk wes in halding of the gud toun in glaidnes and blythtnes, witht danssis, farsiis, playis, and gamis, in tymes convenient, necleckit and abusit; and thairfor ordinis that in tyme cummin all sic sumpteous banketing be laid doun aluterlie except thre sobir and honest, vizt., upoun the senze day, the first Sonday of May, and ane [ ] upoun Tuisday efter Pasche day, and na honest man to pass to ony of thair banketis except on the said thre dais allanerlie; and in ane place of the forsaid superfleouss banketing to be had and maid yeirly to generall plais, or ane at the lest, with danssis and gammes usit and wont; and quha souer refuisis to accept the said office in tyme cumming, beand elekit thairto be the toun, to tyne his fredome, priuelege, takis, and profit he hes or ma haf of the toun, and neuer to be admittit frathinfurtht to office, honour, nor dingnete.'

May 27, 1552. Grant of fee, larger than usual, 'be ressoune that thai ar put to grytar coist this yeir nor utheris that bar office before thaim hes bene put to, and that be ressoune of cummyng of the quenis grace, my lord governor, and the maist of the lords and grit men of this realme, presently to this toun.'

[1555. Parliament 'statute and ordanit that in all tymes cumming na maner of persoun be chosin Robert Hude nor Lytill Johne, Abbot of vnressoun, Quenis of Maij, nor vtherwyse, nouther in Burgh nor to landwart in ony tyme to cum, and gif ony Prouest, Baillies, counsall, and communitie, chesis sic ane Personage as Robert Hude, Lytill Johne, Abbottis of vnressoun, or Quenis of Maij within Burgh, the chesaris of sic sall tyne thair fredome for the space of fyve zeiris, and vther wyse salbe punist at the Quenis grace will, and the acceptar of sicklyke office salbe banist furth of the Realme. And gif ony sic persounis sic as Robert Hude, Lytill Johne, Abbottis of vnresson, Quenis of Maij, beis chosin outwith Burgh and vthers landwart townis, the chesars sall pay to our Souerane Lady x pundis, and thair persounis put in waird, thair to remane during the Quenis grace plesoure. And gif ony wemen or vthers about simmer treis singand makis perturbatioun to the Quenis liegis in the passage throw Burrows and vthers landwart townis, the wemen perturbatouris for skafrie of money or vtherwyse salbe takin handellit and put upon the Cukstulis of everie Burgh or towne.]

May 4, 1562. 'John Kelo, belman, wes accusit in jugement for the passing throw the rewis of the toune with the hand bell, be oppin voce, to convene the haill communitie, or sa mony thairof as wald convene, to pass to the wood to bring in symmer upoun the first Sonday of Maii, contravinand the actis and statutis of the quenis grace, and lordis of consell, eppeirandlie to raise tumult and ingener discord betuix the craftismen and the fre burgessis of gild, and the saidis craftismen to dissobey and adtempt aganis the superioris of the toun, gif it stuid in thair power, as the saidis prowest and baillies ar informit, the said Johnne hawing na command of the saidis prowest and baillies to do the same; and inlykwyise, Alexander Burnat *alias* Potter wes accusit for passing throw the toun with ane swech, to the effect and occasioun aboun wryttin.'

May 14 *and* 18, 1565. Several citizens disfranchised for disobeying the proclamation made by 'Johnne Kelo, belman,' forbidding any persons 'to mak ony conventione, with taburne plaing, or pype, or fedill, or have anseinges, to convene the quenis legis, in chusing of Robin Huid, Litill Johnne, Abbot of Ressoune, Queyne of Maii, or sicklyk contraveyne the statutis of parliament, or mak ony tumult, scism, or conventione.'

Royal Entry.

The entertainment of Queen Margaret, wife of James IV, in May, 1511, seems to have included some of the pageants from the Nativity cycle. The following extract is from Dunbar's *The Quenis Reception at Aberdein*[1]:—

'Ane fair processioun mett hir at the Port,
  In a cap of gold and silk, full pleasantlie,
Syne at hir entrie, with many fair disport,
  Ressauet hir on streittis lustilie;
  Quhair first the salutatioun honorabilly
Of the sweitt Virgin, guidlie mycht be seine;
  The sound of menstrallis blawing to the sky;
Be blyth and blisfull, burgh of Aberdein.

And syne thow gart the orient kingis thrie
  Offer to Chryst, with benyng reuerence,
Gold, sence, and mir, with all humilitie,
  Schawand him king with most magnificence;

[1] Dunbar, *Works* (ed. J. Small, for Scottish Text Soc.), ii. 251.

Syne quhow the angill, with sword of violence,
Furth of the joy of paradice putt clein
Adame and Eve for innobedience;
Be blyth and blisfull, burgh of Aberdein.

And syne the Bruce, that euir was bold in stour,
Thow gart as roy cum rydand vnder croun,
Richt awfull, strang, and large of portratour,
As nobill, dreidfull, michtie campioun;
The [nobill Stewarts] syne, of great renoun,
Thow gart upspring, with branches new and greine,
Sa gloriouslie, quhill glaided all the toun:
Be blyth and blisfull, burgh of Aberdein.

Syne come thair four and twentie madinis ȝing,
All claid in greine of mervelous bewtie,
With hair detressit, as threidis of gold did hing,
With quhyt hattis all browderit rycht bravelie,
Playand on timberallis, and syngand rycht sweitlie;
That seimlie sort, in ordour weill besein,
Did meit the quein, hir saluand reverentlie:
Be blyth and blisfull, burgh of Aberdein.

The streittis war all hung with tapestrie,
Great was the press of peopill dwelt about,
And pleasant padgcanes playit prattelie;
The legeiss all did to thair lady loutt,
Quha was convoyed with ane royall routt
Off gryt barrounes and lustie ladyis [schene];
Welcum, our quein! the commoness gaif ane schout:
Be blyth and blisfull, burgh of Aberdein.

Abingdon, Berkshire.

Certain 'jeweis de Abyndon' were at Court at Xmas 1427 (Appendix E, viii).

A seventeenth-century account of the Hospital of Christ says that the fraternity held their feast on May 3 (Holy Cross day), 1445, with 'pageantes and playes and May games.' They employed twelve minstrels[1].

Appledore, Kent.

Appledore players were at New Romney in 1488.

[1] Hearne, *Liber Niger Scaccarii* (ed. 2), ii. 598.

BADDOW, ESSEX.

The Chelmsford (q.v.) wardrobe was hired by 'children of Badow' during 1564–6.

BASSINGBOURNE, CAMBRIDGESHIRE.

A play 'of the holy martyr St. George' was held in a field at Bassingbourne on the feast of St. Margaret, July 20, 1511. The churchwardens' accounts for the play show, besides payments for refreshments:—

'First paid to the garnement man for garnements and propyrts and playbooks, xx^{s}.

To a minstrel and three waits of Cambridge . . .

Item . . . for setting up the stages.

Item to John Beecher for painting of three Fanchoms and four Tormentors.

Item to Giles Ashwell for easement of his croft to play in, i^{s}.

Item to John Hobarde, Brotherhood Priest, for the play book, ii^{s}. viii^{d}.'

Twenty-seven neighbouring villages contributed to these expenses[1].

BATH, SOMERSETSHIRE.

The accounts of St. Michael's, Bath, for 1482, include 'pro potatione le players in recordacione ['rehearsing'?] ludorum diversis vicibus,' with other expenditure on players and properties. As one item is 'et Iohĩ Fowler pro cariando le tymbe a cimiterio dicto tempore ludi,' the play was perhaps a *Quem quaeritis*[2].

Chaucer's Wife of Bath, in her husband's absence at London during Lent, would make her 'visitaciouns'—

'To pleyes of miracles and mariages[3].'

BETHERSDEN, KENT.

The churchwardens' accounts record *ludi beatae Christinae*, in 1522. St. Christina's day was July 24[4]. Bethersden players were at New Romney in 1508.

BEVERLEY, YORKSHIRE.

A thirteenth-century *continuator* of the *Vita* of St. John of Beverley records a recent (†1220) miracle done in the Minster:—

[1] B. H. Wortham, *Churchwardens' Accounts of Bassingbourne* (*Antiquary*, vii. 25); Lysons, *Magna Britannia*, *Cambridgeshire*, 89; Dyer, 343, from *Antiquarian Repertory* (1808), iii. 320.

[2] C. B. Pearson, *Accounts of St. Michael's*, *Bath* (*R. Hist. Soc. Trans.* vii. 309).

[3] *Cant. Tales*, 6140 (*W. of B.'s Prol.* 558).

[4] L. T. Smith, *York Plays*, lxv.

'Contigit, ut tempore quodam aestivo intra saepta polyandri ecclesiae B. Ioannis, ex parte aquilonari, larvatorum, ut assolet, et verbis et actu fieret repraesentatio Dominicae resurrectionis. Confluebat ibi copiosa utriusque sexus multitudo, variis inducta votis, delectationis videlicet, seu admirationis causa, vel sancto proposito excitandae devotionis. Cum vero, prae densa vulgi adstante corona, pluribus, et praecipue statura pusillis, desideratus minime pateret accessus, introierunt plurimi in ecclesiam; ut vel orarent, vel picturas inspicerent, vel per aliquod genus recreationis et solatii pro hoc die taedium evitarent.' Some boys climbed into the *triforium*, in order that, through the windows, 'liberius personarum et habitus et gestus respicerent, et earundem dialogos auditu faciliori adverterent.' One of these fell into the church, but was miraculously preserved[1].

The Corpus Christi play is first mentioned in 1377. It was 'antiqua consuetudo' in 1390, when an 'ordinacio ludi Corporis Christi cum pena' was entered in the Great Guild Book, requiring the crafts or 'artes' to produce 'ludos suos et pagentes' under a penalty of 40*s*. The plays were held annually, subject to an order by the oligarchical town council of twelve *custodes* or *gubernatores* on St. Mark's day. The *custodes* 'governed' the play, and met certain general expenses. In 1423 they paid Master Thomas Bynham, a friar preacher, for writing 'banis'; also the waits ('*spiculatores*') who accompanied the 'banis.' In the same year they gave a breakfast to the Earl of Northumberland. In 1460 they put up a scaffold for their own use. Apparently the pageants and properties belonged to them, for in 1391 they handed over to John of Arras, on behalf of the 'hairers,' for his life and under surety, the necessaries for the play of Paradise; 'viz. j karre, viij hespis, xviij stapels, ij visers, ij wenges angeli, j fir-sparr, j worme, ij paria caligarum linearum, ij paria camisarum, j gladius.' Otherwise the expenses were met by the crafts, whose members paid a fixed levy towards the play, the 'serge' or light maintained by the craft in some chapel, and the wooden 'castle' erected at the procession of St. John of Beverley on Monday in Rogation week. Thus the Barbers' *Ordinances* in 1414 require their members to pay 2*s*. and a pound of wax on setting up shop, and 2*s*. on taking an apprentice. Certain fines also were in this company appropriated to the same purposes. In 1469 journeymen cappers paid 8*d*. for any year when there was a play, and 6*d*. when there was not. The town *Ordinances* of 1467 contemplate annual payments by all craftsmen. In 1449 the

[1] *Acta Sanctorum*, Maii, ii. 189; *Historians of the Church of York*, i. 328 (Rolls Series, lxxi); Rock, ii. 430; A. F. Leach in *Furnivall Miscellany*, 206.

custodes contributed 4*s*. to the Skinners' play as 'alms of the community.' If a craft failed to produce its play, the *custodes* exacted the whole or a part of the fine of 40*s*. specified in the *Ordinacio* of 1390. They also levied other disciplinary fines; as on John 'cordewainer' in 1423, for hindering the play, on Henry Cowper, 'webster,' in 1452, 'quod nesciebat ludum suum'; on the alderman of the 'paynetors,' in 1520–1 'because their play was badly and confusedly played, in contempt of the whole community, before many strangers'; and so forth. The order of 1390 specified thirty-eight crafts to play; 'viz. mercers et drapers, tannatores, masons, skynners, taillors, goldsmyths, smyths, plummers, bollers, turnors, girdelers, cutlers, latoners, brochemakers, horners, sponers, ladilers, furburs, websters, walkers, coverlidwevers, cartwrightes, coupars, fletchers, bowers, cordewaners, baksters, flesshewers, fysshers, chaundelers, barburs, vynters, sadilers, rapers, hayrers, shipmen, glovers, and workmen.' As elsewhere, changing conditions of social life led to alterations in this list, and consequent divisions and mergings of the plays. Thus in 1411 it seems to have been felt as a grievance that certain well-to-do inhabitants of Beverley, who belonged to no craft, escaped all charge for the plays, and it was agreed that in future the 'digniores villae' should appoint four representatives and contribute a play. In 1493 the Drapers formed a craft of their own apart from the Mercers, and consequently a play was divided, the Drapers taking 'Demyng Pylate,' and leaving to the Mercers 'Blak Herod.' On the fly-leaf of the *Great Guild Book* is a list of crafts and their plays, dated by Mr. Leach †1520, which differs considerably from that of 1390. It is as follows:—

'Gubernacio Ludi *Corporis Christi*.

Tylers: the fallinge of Lucifer.
Saddelers: the makinge of the World.
Walkers: makinge of Adam and eve.
Ropers: the brekinge of the Comaundments of God.
Crelers: gravinge and Spynnynge.
Glovers: Cayn.
Shermen: Adam and Seth.
Wattermen: Noe Shipp.
Bowers and Fletshers: Abraham and Isaak.
Musterdmakers and Chanlers: Salutation of Our Lady.
Husbandmen: Bedleem.
Vynteners: Sheipherds.
Goldsmyths: Kyngs of Colan.
Fyshers: Symeon.
Cowpers: fleyinge to Egippe.
Shomakers: Children of Ysraell.
Scryveners: Disputacion in the Temple.
Barbours: Sent John Baptyste.
Laborers: the Pynnacle.
The Mylners: rasynge of Lazar.
Skynners: ierusalem.
Bakers: the Mawndy.

Litsters: prainge at the Mownte.
Tailyours: Slepinge Pilate.
Marchaunts [i.e. *Mercers*]: Blak Herod.
Drapers: Demynge Pylate.
Bocheours: Scorgynge.
Cutlers and Potters: the Stedynynge.
Wevers: the Stanginge.
Barkers: the Takinge of the Crose.
Cooks: Haryinge of hell.
Wrights: the Resurrection.
Gentylmen: Castle of Emaut.
Smyths: Ascencion.
Prestes: Coronacion of Our Lady.
Marchaunts: Domesday.

The thirty-eight pageants of 1390 have become thirty-six in 1520. Besides the 'Gentylmen,' dating from 1411, the 'Prestes' are noticeable. These are probably the 'clerus Gildae Corporis Christi,' who in 1430 led the Corpus Christi procession in which many of the crafts with their lights took part. Procession and play, though on the same day, seem to have been in 1430 quite distinct. The play lasted only one day, and was given in 1449 at six stations; viz. at the North Bar, by the Bull-ring, between John Skipworth and Robert Couke in Highgate, at the Cross Bridge, at the Fishmarket (now called Wednesday Market), at the Minster Bow, and at the Beck. Poulson stated that the performances lasted into the reign of James I. Mr. Leach could find no trace of them in the municipal archives after 1520[1]. But the *Ordinances*, dated 1555, of the Minstrels' guild 'of our Lady of the read arke' provide that certain forfeits shall go to the 'comon place' (which I take to be 'common plays') of Beverley.

A second craft-play appears in 1469, when a number of crafts, thirty-nine in all, gave a Pater Noster play on the Sunday after St. Peter and Vincula (August 1). Copies of the text (*registra*) were made for the crafts. The stations were those of the Corpus Christi play. There were eight 'pagends' named after the eight principal 'lusores,' viz. 'Pryde: Invy: Ire: Avaryce: Sleweth (also called 'Accidie'): Glotony: Luxuria: Vicious.' A number of crafts united to furnish each of these; apparently the most important was that of 'Vicious,' provided by the 'gentilmen, merchands, clerks and valets.' Aldermen of the pageants were appointed[2].

Billericay, Essex.

The Chelmsford (q.v.) wardrobe was twice hired by men of 'Beleryca,' or 'Belyrica' during 1564–6.

[1] A. F. Leach, *Beverley Town Documents* (Selden Soc. xiv), l. lix. 33, 45, 75, 99, 109, 117; and in *Furnivall Miscellany*, 208; Poulson, *Beverlac*, i. 268 sqq., 302; *Lansdowne MS.* 896, f. 133 (Warburton's eighteenth-century collections for a history of Yorkshire).

[2] A. F. Leach, in *Furnivall Miscellany*, 220.

Bishop Auckland, Durham.

The *lusores* of 'Auklande' received a present from Durham Priory for playing before Master Hyndley, at Christmas, 1539. (App. E, i.)

Boreham, Essex.

'Casse of Boreham' hired the Chelmsford (q.v.) wardrobe in 1566 and 1573, and the 'players of Boreham,' at Twelfth Night, 1574.

Boxford, Suffolk.

A play appears in the churchwardens' accounts for 1535 [1].

Braintree, Essex.

The churchwardens' accounts of St. Michael's include the following:—

'*Anno* 1523. A Play of St Swythyn, acted in the Church on a Wednesday, for which was gathered 6 : 14 : 11½; Pd at the said Play, 3 : 1 : 4; due to the Church, 3 : 13 : 7½.

Anno 1525. There was a Play of St Andrew acted in the Church the Sunday before Relique Sunday; Rcd, 8 : 9 : 6; Pd, 4 : 9 : 9; Due to the Church, 3 : 19 : 8.

Anno 1529. A Play in Halstead Church.

Anno 1534. A Play of Placidas *alias* St Eustace. Rd, 14 : 17 : 6½; Pd, 6 : 13 : 7½; due, 8 : 2 : 8½.

Anno 1567. Rd of the Play money, 5 : 0 : 0.

Anno 1570. Recd of the Play money, 9 : 7 : 7; and for letting the Playing garments, 0 : 1 : 8.

Anno 1571. Rcd for a Playbook, 20d; and for lending the Play gere, 8 : 7d.

Anno 1579. For the Players Apparel, 50s [2].'

Nicholas Udall was vicar of Braintree, 1533–1537. The plays were probably in aid of the large expenditure on the fabric of the church between 1522 and 1535.

The Chelmsford (q.v.) play was given at Braintree in 1562.

Brentwood, Essex.

'Mr. Johnston of Brentwoode' hired the Chelmsford (q.v.) wardrobe in 1566.

Bristol, Gloucestershire.

A town-clerk's account of municipal customs, after describing the banquet on St. Katharine's Eve (Nov. 24), concludes:—

[1] Corrie, *Boxford Parish Accounts* (*Cambridge Antiq. Soc. Trans.* i. 266).

[2] Pearson, ii. 413; Morant, *History of Essex* (1768), ii. 399.

'And then to depart, euery man home: the Maire, Shiref, and the worshipfull men redy to receyue at theire dores Seynt Kateryns players, makyng them to drynk at their dores, and rewardyng theym for theire plays[1].' Were these plays more than a 'catterning' *quête* (vol. i. p. 253)?

There is no mention of plays amongst the records, including several craft-guild ordinances, in the *Little Red Book of Bristol* (ed. W. B. Bickley, 1901). But 'the Shipwrights Pageannt' was used at the reception of Henry VII in 1486 (p. 175).

Brookland, Kent.

Brookland players were at New Romney in 1494.

Bungay, Suffolk.

On the night after Corpus Christi day, June 16, 1514, certain persons 'brake and threw down five pageants of the said inhabitants, that is to saye, hevyn pagent, the pagent of all the world, Paradyse pagent, Bethelem pagent, and helle pagent, the whyche wer ever wont tofore to be caryed abowt the seyd town upon the seyd daye in the honor of the blissyd Sacrement.'

The churchwardens' accounts of St. Mary's show payments in 1526 for copying the game-book, and to Stephen Prewett, a Norwich priest, for his labour in the matter.

The accounts of Holy Trinity show payments: in 1558, to a man riding to Yarmouth for the 'game gear,' 'to William Ellys for the interlude and game booke, iiij^{d},' 'for writing the partes, ij^{s}'; in 1566, on occasion of 'the interlude in the churchyarde,' for apparel borrowed from Lord Surrey, 'for visors,' and 'to Kelsaye, the vyce, for his pastyme before the plaie, and after the playe, both daies, ij^{s}.' In 1577, a churchwarden gave a receipt to his predecessor for 'game pleyers gownes and coats, that were made of certayne peces of olld copes.' In 1591, 5*s*. was received for 'players cootes[2].'

Burnham, Essex.

'Wm Crayford of Burnam' hired the Chelmsford (q.v.) wardrobe in 1568.

Bury St. Edmund's, Suffolk.

The *Ordinances* of the Weavers (1477) assign half of certain fines to 'the sustentacione and mayntenaunce of the payent of the

[1] L. Toulmin Smith, *Ricart's Kalendar* (Camden Soc.), 80.

[2] L. G. Bolingbroke, in *Norfolk Archaeology*, xi. 336; *Eastern Counties Collectanea*, 272.

Assencione of oure Lord God and of the yiftys of the Holy Gost, as yt hath be customed of olde tyme owte of mynde yeerly to be had to the wurschepe of God, amongge other payenttes in the processione in the feste of Corpus Xr̃i.'

Journeymen weavers are to pay 'iiij^{d}' yearly to the 'payent' and all 'foreyne' as well as 'deyzin' weavers are to be contributory to it[1].

It is not clear whether the 'payent' had a *ludus* or was a dumb-show.

Camborne, Cornwall.

See Texts (i), *Cornish Plays*, *St. Meriasek*.

Cambridge, Cambridgeshire.

William de Lenne and Isabel his wife, joining the guild of Corpus Christi (†1350), spent half a mark '*in ludo Filiorum Israelis*[2].'

Warton says:—

'The oldest notice I can recover of this sort of spectacle [Latin plays] in an English University is in the fragment of an ancient accompt-roll of the dissolved college of Michael-House in Cambridge; in which, under 1386, the following expense is entered: 'Pro ly pallio brusdato et pro sex larvis et barbis in comedia[3].'

Canterbury, Kent.

A Burghmote order (†1500) directed 'a play called Corpus Christi play . . . maintained and played at the costs of the Crafts and Mysteries,' although 'of late days it hath been left and laid apart,' to be revived at Michaelmas[4].

A book of the play of Abraham and Isaac, belonging to the 'schaft' or parochial guild of St. Dunstan's, lay in the keeping of the church-wardens of that church from 1491 to 1520[5].

On Jan. 6, 1503, the corporation paid for a play of the *Three Kyngs of Coleyn* in the guildhall. The account mentions three 'bests' made of hoops and laths and painted canvas, 'heddyng of the Hensshemen,' a castle in the courthall, and a gilt star.

Annual accounts for 'the pagent of St. Thomas' on the day of his

[1] *Hist. MSS.* xiv. 8, 133; Arnold, *Memorials of St. Edmund's Abbey* (R. S.), iii. 361.

[2] Masters, *Hist. of C.C.C. Cambridge* (ed. 1753), i. 5.

[3] Hazlitt-Warton, iii. 302. The only reference given is 'MSS. Rawlins. Bibl. Bodl. Oxon.' Mr. F. Madan kindly informs me that the document cannot now be identified amongst the Rawlinson MSS.

[4] *Arch. Cantiana*, xvii. 147.

[5] *Ibid.* xvii. 80.

martyrdom (Dec. 29), appear amongst the financial records of the corporation from 1504–5 until 'far on in the reign of Queen Elizabeth.' I select some items:—

'1504–5.

Paied to Sampson Carpenter and hys man hewyng and squeryng of tymber for the Pagent.

For makyng St Thomas Carte with a peyer of whyles.

To iiij men to helpe to cary the Pagent.

For a newe myghter.

For two bagges of leder.

For payntyng of the awbe and the hedde.

For gunpowder.

For lynnen cloth bought for St Thomas garment.

For forgyng and makyng the knyghts harnes.

For the hyre of a sworde.

For wasshynge of an albe and an amys.'

In later years.

'Pro le yettyng sanguynem.

Pro le payntyng capitis Sci Thomae.

For them that holpe to dress the Pagent and for standyng of the same in the barne.

For a payer of new gloves for Seynt Thomas.

For payntyng of the hede and the Aungell of the pagent.

Paied to hym that turned the vyce.

Paied for wyre for the vyce of the Angell.

For 1 quarter of lambe and brede and drynke gevyn to the children that played the knyghtes, and for them that holpe to convey the Pagent abowte.

For a new leder bag for the blode.

For wasshyng of the albe and other clothys abowte the Auter, and settyng on agayn the apparell.'

Until 1529 the pageant stood in the barn of St. Sepulchre's convent; thenceforward in the archbishop's palace. In 1536–7 'Seynt Thomas' became 'Bysshop Bekket,' and the show was suppressed, to be revived with some added 'gyaunts' under Mary[1].

This pageant was probably a dumb-show of the martyrdom of Becket.

Chelmsford, Essex.

The Earl of Surrey rewarded the players of 'Chemsford' on Dec. 27, 1490 (Appendix E, vii).

[1] *Hist. MSS. Comm.* ix. 1, 147.

The churchwardens' accounts give minute details of a play held in 1562 and 1563. The following are the chief items:—

'Inprms paid unto the Mynstrolls for the Show day and for the play day.

Unto Willm. Hewet for makinge the vices coote, a fornet of borders, and a Jerken of borders.

To John Lockyer for making iiij shep hoks and for iron work that Burle occupied for the hell.

Item paide to Robt Mathews for a pair of wombes.

to Lawrence for watching in the Churche when the temple was a-dryenge.

for carrying of plonk for the stages.

for . . . the scaffold.

to M. Browne for the waightes of Bristowe.

for makyng the conysants.

forty Mynstrells meate and drinke.

to William Withers for making the frame for the heaven stage and tymber for the same.

for writtinge.

to William Withers for makynge the last temple, the waies, and his paynnes.

to John Wryght for makynge a cotte of lether for Christ.

to Solomon of Hatfild for parchmente.

to Mother Dale and her company for reaping flagges for the scaffold.

to Polter and Rosse for watching in the pightell on the play show.

for fyftie fadam of lyne for the cloudes.

for tenn men to beare the pagiante.

to Browne for keapinge the cornehill on the showe daye.

to Roistone for payntenge the Jeiants, the pagiante, and writing the plaiers names.

for paper to wright the Bookes.'

There are many other payments to workmen and for refreshments, and large sums to various people 'for suinge the play.' Is this 'showing,' 'stage-managing'? One Burles, who was twice paid for 'suinge,' was also boarded with his boy for three weeks.

An inventory of garments made in February, 1564, includes, with many velvet gowns and jerkins, &c.:—

'ij vyces coates, and ij scalpes, ij daggers (j dagger wanted).

v prophets cappes (one wantinge).

iij flappes for devils.

iiij shepehoks, iiij whyppes (but one gone).'

I infer that the play was a cyclical one, extending at least from Creation to Crucifixion. The temple, which required renewing, was probably rent in twain. There were heaven, hell, *Prophetae*, *Pastores*. The performance was not in the church, although the temple was put to dry there, but in a 'pightell' or enclosure, upon a scaffold, with stages for the spectators. It was held in connexion with a 'showe,' which was on Cornhill, and to which I assign the 'pagiante' and 'jeiantes.' The time was therefore probably Midsummer.

The accounts seem to cover two years and at least four performances. In 1562, Midsummer day with its show fell on a Saturday. The play was on Monday. On Tuesday it was repeated at Braintree, and later on at Malden, and possibly elsewhere. Then in 1563 it was again given in Chelmsford at Midsummer.

The total expenditure was over £50, although, unless the forty minstrels acted, nothing was paid to actors. Against this was received 'at the seconde play' £17 11*s*. 3*d*., and 'at the ij last plaies' £19 19*s*. 4*d*., and £2 19*s*. was realized by letting out the garments to the men of Sabsford in 1562 and 1563, and 16*s*. more for letting them to 'Mr William Peter, Knyght.' Nor did this source of income soon close. A second inventory of 1573 shows that the garments were carefully preserved. They became a valuable stock. In 1564–6 alone the hire of them brought in £10 14*s*. 3*d*. They were let to men of Colchester, Walden, Beleryca, Starford, Little Badow, and to 'children of Badow.' Further loans are noted as follows in later years:—

'Receipts, June 3, 1566.

Sabsforde men.
Casse of Boreham.
Somers of Lanchire.
Barnaby Riche of Witham.
Willm Monnteyne of Colchester.
M^r. Johnston of Brentwoode, the 10th Dec.
Richard More of Nayland.
Frauncis Medcalfe, the iiij of June, 1568.
Wm Crayford of Burnam, the ij of June, 1568.

1570–1572.

High Ester men.
Parker of Writtell.
Mrs Higham of Woodham Walter.

1572.

Parker of Writtell, Aprill.

The Earle of Sussex players.

John Walker of Hanfild.

1573.

Casse of Boreham.

1574.

Players of Boreham, till the mondaye after twelfe day.

In 1574 the 'playe books' were valued at £4, and in the same year all the garments, &c., included in the inventory of 1573 were sold to George Studley and others for £6 12*s.* 4*d.* In 1575 one Mr. Knott was paid 8*d.* 'for the makinge of two oblijacyons for the assurance of the players garments belonginge to the Pyshe [1].'

Chester, Cheshire.

[*Authorities.*—(i) Editions of the plays by Wright and Deimling, described on p. 408. (ii) Notices in Furnivall, *Digby Plays*, xviii, from (*a*) *Harl. MSS.* 1944, 1948, which are versions of a *Breviary of the City of Chester*, compiled in 1609 by David Rogers from the collections of his father, Robert Rogers, Archdeacon of Chester, who died in 1595; (*b*) local *Annales* in *Harl.* 2125 (Randle Holme's *Collections*), and Daniel King's *Vale-Royall* (1656). (iii) Notices in R. H. Morris, *Chester in the Plantagenet and Tudor Reigns* (1894), from (*a*) Corporation archives, (*b*) accounts of the Smiths' Company in *Harl.* 2054, (*c*) a copy in *Harl.* 2150 (cited in error as *Harl.* 2050) of part or all of the contents of a record known as the *White Book of the Pentice.* This was bound with other documents by Randle Holme, and indexed by him in 1669. I do not find any mention of such a 'White Book' in the calendar of extant Corporation archives by Mr. J. C. Jeaffreson, in *Hist. MSS.* viii. 1. 355, unless it is identical with the *Pentice Chartulary* compiled in 1575-6 on the basis, partly of an older 'Black Book,' 'translated oute of Laten and Frenche' in 1540, and partly of loose 'sceduls, papers and books' in the Treasure House.]

The Whitsun Plays: The Tradition.

The Chester plays are traditionally ascribed to the mayoralty of one John Arneway. As 'John Arneway,' 'de Arnewey,' 'Hernwey,' or 'Harnwey' served continuously as mayor from 1268 to 1277 [2], and as no other of the great English cycles of municipal plays can claim anything like this antiquity, it is worth while to examine the evidence pretty closely. I therefore put the versions of the tradition in chronological order.

(*a*) 1544. The following document is headed 'The proclamation for the Plaies, newly made by William Newhall, clarke of the Pentice, the first yere of his entre.' It is dated 'tempore Willi Sneyde, draper, secundo tempore sui maioritatis' [Oct. 9, 1543-1544], endorsed as made 'opon the rode ee' [Rood-eye], and stated on an accompanying

[1] Pearson, ii. 414; *Freemasons' Magazine and Magic Mirror*, Sept. 1861.

[2] Morris, 575.

sheet to be 'of laten into Englishe translated and made by the said William Newhall the yere aforesaid[1].'

'For as moche as of old tyme, not only for the Augmentacon and increase of [the holy and catholick] faith of our Savyour, Jhu' Crist, and to exort the mynds of the co'mon people to [good devotion and holsome] doctryne thereof, but also for the co'men Welth and prosperitie of this Citie a plaie [and declaration—] and diverse stories of the bible, begynnyng with the creacon and fall of Lucifer, and [ending with the general] jugement of the World to be declared and plaied in the Witson wek, was devised [and made by one Sir] Henry Fraunces, somtyme monk of this dissolved monastery, who obtayned and gate of Clement, then beyng [bushop of Rome, a thousand] daies of pardon, and of the Busshop of Chester at that time beyng xl^ti daies of pardon graunted from thensforth to every person resortyng in pecible maner with good devocon to here and se the sayd [plaies] from tyme to tyme as oft as they shalbe plaied within this Citie [*and that every person disturbing the same plaies in any manner wise to be accursed by thauctoritie of the said Pope Clement bulls unto such tyme as he or they be absolved therof* (*erased*)], which plaies were devised to the honour of God by John Arneway, then maire of this Citie of Chester, and his brethren, and holl cominalty therof to be brought forthe, declared and plead at the cost and charges of the craftsmen and occupacons of the said Citie, whiche hitherunto have frome tyme to tyme used and performed the same accordingly.

Wherfore Maister Maire, in the Kynges name, straitly chargeth and co'mandeth that every person and persons of what estate, degre or condicion soever he or they be, resortyng to the said plaies, do use [themselves] pecible without makyng eny assault, affrey, or other disturbance whereby the same plaies shalbe disturbed, and that no maner person or persons who soever he or they be do use or weare eny unlaufull wepons within the precynct of the said Citie duryng the tyme of the said plaies [*not only upon payn of cursyng by thauctoritie*

[1] Morris, 317. Canon Morris does not say where he found the document. He dates it in '24 Hen. VIII, 1531.' [The regnal year, 24 Hen. VIII, by the way, is 1532–3.] But the monastery is called 'dissolved,' which it was not until 1541. The list of Mayors (Morris, 582) gives William Snead (1516–7), William Sneyde (1531–2), William Sneyde, jun. (1543–4). Obviously two generations are concerned. The second mayoralty of the younger man was 1543–4. And the appointment of Newhall as clerk of the Pentice was in 1543 (Morris, 204). Oddly, Canon Morris's error was anticipated in a copy of the proclamation made on the fly-leaf of *Harl. MS.* 2013 of the plays (Deimling, 1), which states that it was 'made by W^m newall, Clarke of the pentice [in R]udio 24, H. 8 [1532–3].'

of the said Pope Clement Bulls, but also (*erased*)] opon payn of enprisonment of their bodies and makyng fyne to the Kyng at Maister Maires pleasure. And God save the Kyng and Mr. Maire, &c.[1]'

(*b*) †1544–7[2]. The documents concerning the plays copied for Randle Holme out of the 'White Book of the Pentice[3]' are (1) a list of the plays and the crafts producing them (cf. p. 408); (2) a note that 'On Corpus Xρi day the colliges and prestys bryng forth a play at the assentement of the Maire'; (3) a note that all the arrangements detailed are subject to alteration by the Mayor and his brethren; (4) a version, without heading, of Newhall's proclamation which entirely omits the allusions to Sir Henry Fraunces and the pardons, while retaining that to Arneway; (5) verses headed 'The comen bannes to be proclaymed and Ryddon with the Stewardys of every occupacon.' These are printed in Morris, 307. They give a list of the plays (cf. p. 408), and add that there will be a 'solempne procession' with the sacrament on Corpus Christi day from 'Saynt Maries on the Hill' to 'Saynt Johns,' together with 'a play sett forth by the clergye In honor of the fest.' The passage referring to Corpus Christi is marked by Randle Holme's copyist as 'Erased in the Booke[4].' The only historical statement in the Banns is that

'Sir John Arnway was maire of this citie
When these playes were begon truly.'

(*c*) †1551–1572. The later Banns, given most fully in Rogers's *Breauarye of Chester* (cf. Furnivall, xx), but also more or less imperfectly in MSS. *h* and *B* of the plays (Deimling, i. 2), were probably written for one or other of the post-Reformation performances, but not that of 1575, as they contemplate a Whitsun performance, while that of 1575 was after Midsummer. They state that

'some tymes there was mayor of this Citie
Sir John Arnway, Knyght, who most worthilye
contented hym selfe to sett out in playe
The devise of one done Rondall, moonke of Chester abbe.'

(*d*) 1609. The *Breauarye* itself, in an account probably due to

[1] I reproduce Canon Morris's text *literatim*. But he does not explain the square brackets, and I do not understand them.

[2] The 'proclamation' in the White Book is clearly a revision of the 1544 version. On the other hand, the Corpus Christi procession was suppressed in 1547. The 'Banns,' which include a pageant 'of our lady thassumpcon' not in the list of plays, are perhaps rather earlier.

[3] *Harl. MS.* 2150, ff. 85^b–88^b.

[4] It is this entry which shows that *Harl. MS.* 2150 is not the 'White Book,' but a copy. The official catalogue of the Harleian collection is in doubt on this point.

the elder Rogers, who may have himself seen some of the later performances, says (Furnivall, xviii):—'Heare note that these playes of Chester called ye whitson playes weare the woorke of one Rondoll, a monke of ye Abbaye of St Warburge in Chester, who redused ye whole history of the byble into Englishe storyes in metter, in ye englishe tounge; and this moncke, in a good desire to doe good, published ye same, then the firste mayor of Chester, namely Sir Iohn Arneway, Knighte, he caused the same to be played ["anno domini, 1329"][1].' In a list of Mayors contained in the same MS. is given (Furnivall, xxv), under the year 1328 and the mayoralty of Sir John Arneway, 'The whitson playes Inuented, in Chester, by one Rondoll Higden, a monke in Chester abbaye.'

(*e*) 1628. On the cover of MS. *H* of the plays (*Harl. MS.* 2124) is this note:—'The Whitsun playes first made by one Don Randle Heggenet, a Monke of Chester Abbey, who was thrise at Rome, before he could obtain leaue of the Pope to haue them in the English tongue.

The Whitsun playes were playd openly in pageants by the Cittizens of Chester in the Whitsun Weeke.

Nicholas the fift Then was Pope in the year of our Lord 1447.

Ano 1628.

Sir Henry ffrancis, sometyme a Monke of the Monestery of Chester, obtained of Pope Clemens a thousand daies of pardon, and of the Bishop of Chester 40 dayes pardon for every person that resorted peaceably to see the same playes, and that every person that disturbed the same, to be accursed by the said Pope untill such tyme as they should be absolued therof.'

(*f*) 1669. Randle Holme made a note upon his copy of the 'White Book of the Pentice' (*Harl.* 2150, f. 86 b), of the 'Whitson plaies . . . being first presented and putt into English by Rand. Higden, a monck of Chester Abbey.'

(*g*) *Seventeenth century*. A 'later hand' added to the copy of Newhall's proclamation on the fly-leaf of MS. *h* (1600) of the plays:

'Sir Io Arnway, maior 1327 and 1328, at which tyme these playes were written by Randall Higgenett, a monk of chester abby, and played openly in the witson weeke.'

(*h*) *Seventeenth century*. An account of the plays amongst Lord De Tabley's MSS.[2] assigns them to 'Randall Higden, a monk of Chester Abbey, A. D. 1269.'

[1] So printed by Furnivall, possibly as an addition to the text of *Harl.* 1944, from the shorter copy of the *Breauarye* in *Harl.* 1948.

[2] *Hist. MSS.* i. 49.

Up to a certain point these fragments of tradition are consistent and, *a priori*, not improbable. About 1328 is just the sort of date to which one would look for the formation of a craft-cycle. Randall or Randulf Higden[1], the author of the *Polychronicon*, took the vows at St. Werburgh's in 1299 and died in 1364. An accident makes it possible also to identify Sir Henry Francis, for he is mentioned as senior monk of Chester Abbey in two documents of May 5, 1377, and April 17, 1382. The occurrence of the name of this quite obscure person in a tradition of some 200 years later is, I think, evidence that it is not wholly an unfounded one. It is true that Newhall's proclamation states that Francis 'devised and made' the plays, whereas the Banns of 1575 and the later accounts assign the 'devise' to 'done Rondall.' But this discrepancy seems to have afforded no difficulty to the writer of 1628, who clearly thought that Heggenet 'made' the plays, and Francis obtained the 'pardon' for them. The Pope Clement concerned is probably Clement VI (1342–52), but might be the Antipope Clement VII (1378–94). The one point which will not harmonize with the rest is that about which, unfortunately, the tradition is most uniform, namely, the connexion of the plays with the mayoralty of Sir John Arneway. For neither Higden nor Francis could have worked for a mayor whose terms of office extended from 1268 to 1277. But even this difficulty does not appear to be insoluble. I find from Canon Morris's invaluable volume that a later mayor bearing a name very similar to Arneway's, one Richard Erneis or Herneys, was in office from 1327 to 1329, precisely at the date to which the tradition, in some of its forms, ascribes the plays. Is it not then probable that to this Richard Herneys the establishment of the plays is really due, and that he has been confused in the memory of Chester with his greater predecessor, the 'Dick Whittington' of the city, John Arneway or Hernwey? I am glad to be the means of restoring to him his long withheld tribute of esteem.

The Records.

If the plays were actually established in 1327–9, the first hundred years of their history is a blank. The earliest notice in any record is in 1462, when the Bakers' charter refers to their 'play and light of

[1] C. L. Kingsford in *D. N. B.* s.v. Higden. Mr. Kingsford does not think that 'Randle Heggenett,' the author of the *Chester Plays*, can be identified with Higden. But 'Higden,' which occurs in Rogers's list of Mayors, is an earlier form in the tradition than 'Heggenett.'

[2] Ormerod, *Hist. of Cheshire* (ed. Helsby), iii. 651; Morris, 315.

Corpus Christi.' The Saddlers' charter of 1471 similarly speaks of their 'paginae luminis et ludi corporis Christi [1].' It will be observed that the play is here called a Corpus Christi play. The term 'Whitson Playe' first occurs in a record of 1520 [2], but there is no doubt that during the sixteenth century the regular season for the performances was Whitsuntide. As the 'White Book' (†1544) still speaks of 'pagyns in play of Corpus Xρi [3],' it is possible that a cyclical play was so called, whether actually given on Corpus Christi day or not. It is also, I think, possible that the Chester plays may have been transferred from Corpus Christi to Whitsuntide in order to avoid clashing with the procession, without quite losing their old name; and this may be what is meant by the statement on the cover of MS. 'H' of the plays that they were 'playd openly . . . in the Whitsun Weeke' in 1447. It was in 1426 that a question as to the clashing of procession and plays arose in York (cf. p. 400).

Nearly all the extant notices of the plays belong to the sixteenth century. Originally annual, they became occasional at the Reformation. They can be traced in 1546, 1551, 1554, 1561, 1567 (at Christmas), 1568, 1569, 1572, and 1575. The two last performances aroused considerable opposition. In 1572 Mayor John Hankey 'would needs have the playes go forward, against the wills of the Bishops of Canterbury, York and Chester.' Apparently an inhibition was sent by Archbishop Grindal; 'but it came too late.' In 1575, under Mayor Sir John Savage, the plays were subjected to revision, and such of them as were thought suitable given 'at the cost of the inhabitants' on Sunday, Monday, Tuesday, and Wednesday after Midsummer. This performance was 'to the great dislike of many, because the playe was in on parte of the Citty.' It was also in direct contravention of inhibitions from the Archbishop and the Earl of Huntingdon. As a result both Hankey and Savage were cited before the Privy Council, but the aldermen and common council took the responsibility upon themselves, and apparently nothing further came of the matter [4].

Probably 1575 was the last year in which the plays were given as a whole. A performance in 1600 has been alleged [5], but this date is probably taken from the heading of the Banns in MS. 'h' of the plays, which runs:—

[1] Morris, 316. The Painters and Glaziers' charter is quoted as calling them 'tyme out of minde one brotherhood for the . . . plaie of the Shepperds' Wach,' but no date is given.

[2] Ibid.

[3] *Harl. MS.* 2150, f. 85 b.

[4] Morris, 318; Furnivall, xxv; *Hist. MSS.* viii. 1. 363, 366.

[5] Pennant, *Wales*, i. 145.

'The reading of the banes, 1600.
The banes which are reade Beefore the beginning of the playes of Chester 1600.
4 June 1600.'

Doubtless 1600 is the date of the transcript, as it is repeated after the signature to several of the plays. It is quite possible that this manuscript was made in view of an intended performance. George Bellin, the scribe, seems to have been of a Chester family. But if so, the intention was frustrated, for the annalists declare that Henry Hardware, mayor in 1600 'would not suffer any Playes.'.. It is to be noted also that David Rogers, whose *Breauarye* was completed in 1609 and certainly contains matter subsequent to the death of his father in 1595, states that 1575 was the last time the plays were played[1].

Mode of Performance.

The Banns were proclaimed on St. George's day by the city crier, with whom rode the Stewards of each craft. The Mayor's proclamation against disturbers of the peace was read upon the Roodee. The plays themselves lasted through the first three week-days of Whitsuntide. Nine were given on the Monday, nine on the Tuesday, and seven on the Wednesday. The first station was at the Abbey gates, the next by the pentice at the high cross before the Mayor, others in Watergate Street, Bridge Street, and so on to Eastgate Street. Scaffolds and stages were put up to accommodate the spectators, and in 1528 a law-suit is recorded about the right to a 'mansion, Rowme, or Place for the Whydson plaies.' Rogers describes the 'pagiente' or 'cariage' as

'a highe place made like a howse with ij rowmes, being open on ye tope: the lower rowme they apparrelled & dressed them selues; and in the higher rowme they played; and they stood vpon 6 wheeles [*Harl.* 1944. It is "4 wheeles" in *Harl.* 1948].'

The term 'pageant' is used at Chester both for the vehicle and for the play performed on it; but, contrary to the custom elsewhere, more usually for the latter. The vehicle is generally called a 'carriage.' It was kept in a 'caryadghouse' and occasionally served two crafts on different days. The expenses of carriage, porters, refreshments, actors, and rehearsals fell, as shown by the extant *Accounts* of the Smiths' company, on the crafts. They were met by a levy upon each member and journeyman. Vestments were hired from the clergy; both minstrels and choristers were in request for songs and music.

[1] Furnivall, xxiii, xxviii.

The Corporation supervised the performances, questions as to the incidence of the burden upon this or that craft coming before the Pentice court. In 1575 the Smiths submitted two alternative plays for the choice of the aldermen. The authoritative copy or 'originall booke' of the plays seems to have belonged to the city. The Smiths paid for reading the 'Regenall,' 'an Rygynall' or 'orraginall.' In 1568 one 'Randall Trevor, gent.' seems to have lost the book. There is an interesting allusion to the unprofessional quality of the actors, in the copy of the later Banns preserved by Rogers. The plays are not

'contryued
In such sorte & cunninge, & by such playeres of price,
As at this day good playeres & fine wittes coulde devise,
. . . .
By Craftes men & meane men these Pageauntes are played
And to Commons and Contryemen acustomablye before.
If better men & finer heades now come, what canne be saide?
But of common and contrye playeres take thou the storye;
And if any disdaine, then open is ye doore
That lett him in to heare; packe awaye at his pleasure;
Oure playeinge is not to gett fame or treasure[1].'

Exceptional Performances.

In 1567 'Richard Dutton, mayor, kept a very worthy house for all comers all the tyme of Christmas with a Lorde of Misrule and other pastymes in this city as the Whitson Plays.'

Single plays from the cycle were similarly used for purposes of special entertainment. In 1488 was the *Assumption* before Lord Strange at the High Cross; in 1497 the *Assumption* before Prince Arthur at the Abbey gates and the High Cross; in 1515 the *Assumption* again together with the *Shepherds'* play in St. John's churchyard. In 1576, the Smiths had 'our plas' (the *Purification*) 'at Alderman Mountford's on Midsomer Eve.' Finally, in 1578, Thomas Bellin, mayor, caused the Shepherds' play 'and other triumphs' to be played at the high cross on the Roodee before the Earl of Derby, Lord Strange, and others[2].

Other plays.

The play by the 'colliges and prestys' on Corpus Christi day mentioned in the 'White Book' and in the 'Banes' preserved therein has already been noted.

[1] D. Rogers, *Breauarye,* in Furnivall, xviii; Morris, 303.
[2] Morris, 322, 353; Furnivall, xxvi.

In 1529 *King Robert of Sicily* was shown at the High Cross. This is doubtless the play on the same subject referred to in a fragmentary letter to some 'Lordshypp' among the State Papers as to be played on St. Peter's day at the cost of some of the companies. It was said to be 'not newe at thys time, but hath bin before shewen, evyn as longe agoe as the reygne of his highnes most gratious father of blyssyd memorye, and yt was penned by a godly clerke.'

In 1563 'upon the Sunday after Midsommer day, the History of *Eneas* and Queen *Dido* was play'd in the *Roods Eye*. And were set out by one *William Croston*, gent. and one Mr. *Man*, on which Triumph there was made two Forts, and shipping on the Water, besides many horsemen well armed and appointed.'

The entertainment of Lords Derby and Strange by Thomas Bellin in 1578 included a 'comedy' by the 'scollers of the freescole' at the mayor's house. Was this theatrical mayor a relative of George Bellin, the scribe of MSS. 'W' and 'h' of the Chester plays?

In 1589 *King Ebranke with all his Sons* was shown before the Earl of Derby at the High Cross[1].

The Midsummer Show.

This was doubtless in its origin a folk procession. Traditionally, it was founded in 1498 and only went in years when there were no Whitsun plays. The crafts were represented by personages out of their plays, 'the Doctors and little God' riding for the Smiths, the Devil for the Butchers, Abraham and Isaac for the Barbers, Balaam and his Ass for the Bricklayers, and so forth. It does not appear that the 'carriages' were had out. Other features of the 'Show' were four giants, an elephant and castle, an unicorn, a camel, a luce, an antelope, a dragon with six naked boys beating at it, morris-dancers, the 'Mayor's Mount' and the 'Merchants' Mount,' the latter being of the nature of a hobby-ship. In 1600, Mayor Henry Hardware, a 'godly zealous man,' would not let the 'Graull' go at Midsummer Watch, but instead a man in white armour. He suppressed also 'the divill in his fethers,' a man in woman's clothes with another devil called 'cuppes and cans,' 'god in stringes,' the dragon and the naked boys, and had the giants broken up. But next year the old customs were restored. The Midsummer Show again suffered eclipse under the Commonwealth, but was revived at the Restoration and endured until 1678[2].

[1] Morris, 322; Furnivall, xxvi; Collier, i. 112.

[2] Morris, 324; Furnivall, xxiii; Fenwick, *Hist. of Chester*, 370.

Coggeshall, Essex.

Lord Howard rewarded the players of 'Kokesale' or 'Coksale' on Dec. 26, 1481, and Dec. 25, 1482 (Appendix E, vii).

Colchester, Essex.

The Chelmsford (q.v.) wardrobe was twice hired by Colchester men during 1564–6; also by William Monnteyne of Colchester in 1566.

Coleshill, Warwickshire.

The 'lusores de Coleshille' played at Maxstoke Priory between 1422 and 1461 (Appendix E, ii).

Coventry, Warwickshire.

[*Authorities.*—The facts are taken, where no other reference is given, from T. Sharp, *A Dissertation on the Pageants or Dramatic Mysteries Anciently Performed at Coventry* (1825), and J. B. Gracie, *The Weavers' Pageant* (1836: Abbotsford Club). The latter accounts of J. O. Halliwell-Phillipps, *Outlines of the Life of Shakespeare* (ninth edition, 1890), i. 335, ii. 289, and M. D. Harris, *Life in an Old English Town*, 319, add a little. The *Leet-Book* and other municipal archives used by Sharp are described by Harris, 377; his private collection passed into that of Mr. Staunton at Longbridge House, and thence into the Shakespeare Memorial Library at Birmingham, where it was burnt in 1879. It included two craft-plays, the account-books of the Smiths, Cappers, Drapers, and Weavers, and one or two MSS. (one of which is referred to as 'Codex Hales') of a set of brief local seventeenth-century *Annales*, of which other texts are printed by Dugdale, *Hist. of Warwickshire*, i. 147, and Hearne, *Fordun's Scotichronicon*, v. 1438. Several versions of these *Annales* are amongst the manuscripts of the Coventry Corporation (cf. E. S. Hartland, *Science of Fairy Tales*, 75). On their nature, cf. C. Gross, *Bibl. of Municipal History*, xviii.]

Corpus Christi Craft-Plays.

The earliest notice is a mention of the 'domum pro le pagent pannarum' in a deed of 1392. There must therefore be an error, so far as the pageants go, in the statement of the *Annals*, under the mayoral year 1416–7, 'The pageants and Hox tuesday invented, wherein the king and nobles took great delight[1].' Henry V was more than once at Coventry as prince, in 1404 for example, and in 1411. His only recorded visit as king was in 1421, too early for Corpus Christi or even Hox Tuesday[2]. There is frequent reference to the plays in corporation and craft documents of the fifteenth century. In

[1] Sharp, 8.

[2] C. L. Kingsford, *Henry V*, 346, says that he reached Coventry alone on March 15, and joined Katharine at Leicester on March 19. Ramsay, *Y. and L.* i. 290, quoting J. E. Tyler, *Henry of Monmouth*, ii. 28, gives the same dates. The entry in the *Leet Book* (Harris, 139) brings him to Coventry on March 21 and with the queen. But this was Good Friday. If the *Leet Book* is right, he might have remained for Hox Tuesday, April 1.

1457 they were seen by Queen Margaret, who 'lodged at Richard Wodes, the grocer,' whither the corporation sent an elegant collation, including 'ij cofyns of counfetys and a pot of grene gynger.' With her were the Duke and Duchess of Buckingham, Lord and Lady Rivers, the elder and younger Lady of Shrewsbury, and 'other mony moo lordes and ladyes.' They were seen also by Richard III in 1485 and twice by Henry VII. The first occasion was on St. Peter's day (June 29) in 1486, and the second in 1493, when say the *Annals*, rather oddly (cf. p. 420), 'This yeare the King came to se the playes acted by the Gray Friers, and much commended them.' In 1520 the *Annals* record 'New playes at Corpus Christi tyde, which were greatly commended.' In 1539 the mayor of Coventry, writing to Cromwell, told him that the poor commoners were at such expense with their plays and pageants that they fared the worse all the year after [1]. In the sixteenth century the Coventry plays were probably the most famous in England. The *C. Mery Talys* (1526) has a story of a preacher, who wound up a sermon on the Creed with 'Yf you beleue not me then for a more suerte & suffycyent auctoryte go your way to Couentre and there ye shall se them all playd in Corpus Cristi playe [2].' And John Heywood, in his *Foure PP*, speaks of one who

'Oft in the play of Corpus Cristi
He had played the deuyll at Couentry [3].'

Foxe, the martyrologist, records that in 1553 John Careless, in Coventry gaol for conscience sake, was let out to play in the pageant about the city. There is some confusion here, as Careless was only in gaol in Coventry for a short time in November before he was sent to London [4].

When the *Annals* say that in 1575–6 'the Pageants on Hox Tuesday that had been laid down eight years were played again,' there is probably some confusion between 'Hox Tuesday' and 'the Pageants,' for the account-books show that the latter were played regularly, except in 1575, until 1580, when the *Annals* report them as 'again laid down.' In 1584 a different play was given (cf. *infra*), and possibly also in 1591, although the fact that the songs of the Taylors and Shearmen's pageant are dated 1591 rather suggests that after all the regular plays may have been revived that year. Some of the pageants were sold in 1586 and 1587, but the Cappers preserved

[1] Brewer, xiv (1), 77.

[2] *C. Mery Talys*, lvi (ed. Oesterley, 100).

[3] Heywood, *The Foure PP*, 831 (Manly, i. 510).

[4] Foxe, vi. 411; viii. 170; Maitland, *Essays on the Reformation*, 24.

the properties of their play in 1597, and the Weavers had still players' apparel to lend in 1607. According to the *Annals*, by 1628 the pageants had 'bine put downe many yeares since.'

The plays were given annually and in one day at the feast of Corpus Christi. Contrary to the custom of the northern towns, there were only some ten or twelve pageants, each covering a fairly wide range of incident (cf. p. 423). Nor can the performances be shown to have been repeated at more than three or four stations. 'Gosford Street,' 'Mikel' or 'Much Park Street end' and 'Newgate' are recorded, and in one of these may have been the house of Richard Wodes, where Queen Margaret lay. The Drapers only provided three 'worlds' for their pageant, and probably one was burnt at each station. According to the *Annals*, part of the charges of the plays was met by the enclosure of a piece of common land (possibly to build pageant houses upon). Otherwise they fell wholly upon the crafts, to some one of which every artisan in the town was bound to become contributory for the purpose. The principal crafts were appointed by the Leet to produce the pageants, and with each were grouped minor bodies liable only for fixed sums, varying from 3*s*. 4*d*. to 16*s*. 8*d*. In 1501 an outside craft, the Tilemakers of Stoke, is found contributing 5*s*. to a pageant. These combinations of crafts varied considerably from time to time. Within the craft the necessary funds were raised, in part at least, by special levies. Strangers taking out their freedom were sometimes called upon for a contribution. Every member of the craft paid his 'pagent pencys.' In several crafts the levy was 1*s*. Amongst the Smiths it must have been less, as they only got from 2*s*. 2*d*. to 3*s*. 4*d*. in this way, whereas the Cappers in 1562 collected 22*s*. 4*d*. In 1517 William Pisford left a scarlet and a crimson gown to the Tanners for their play, together with 3*s*. 4*d*. to each craft that found a pageant. The total cost of the Smiths' play in 1490 was £3 7*s*. 5½*d*. In 1453 we find the Smiths contracting with one Thomas Colclow to have 'the rewle of the pajaunt' for twelve years, and to produce the play for a payment of 46*s*. 8*d*. A similar contract was made in 1481. But as a rule, the crafts undertook the management themselves, and the account-books studied by Sharp afford more detailed information as to the mode of production than happens to be available for any other of the great cycles.

It is therefore worth while to give some account of the chief objects of expenditure. First of all there was the pageant itself. The name appears in every possible variety of spelling in Coventry documents. Dugdale, on the authority of eye-witnesses, describes the pageants as

'Theaters for the severall Scenes, very large and high, placed upon wheels.' Painted cloths were used 'to lap aboubt the pajent,' and there was a carved and painted top, adorned with a crest, with vanes, pencils, or streamers. On the platform of the pageant such simple scenic apparatus as a seat for Pilate, a pillar for the scourging, a 'sepulchre,' and the like, was fixed. The Weavers' pageant seems to have had an 'upper part' representing the Temple; also divisions described in the stage directions as 'the for pagand' and 'the tempull warde.' The Cappers' pageant was fitted up with a 'hell-mouth.' The Drapers also had a 'hell-mouth,' with a windlass, and fire at the mouth, and a barrel for the earthquake, and three worlds to be set afire. 'Scaffolds,' distinct from the pageant itself, were drawn round with it. These, according to Sharp, were for spectators, but they may have been supplementary stages, made necessary by the number of episodes in each play at Coventry. Certainly the action was not wholly confined to the pageant, for in the Shearmen and Taylors' play, 'Here Erode ragis in the pagond & in the strete also'; and again, 'the iij Kyngis speykyth in the strete.' The pageant was constantly in need of repairs. A pageant-house had to be built or hired for it. On the day of the feast it was cleaned, strewn with rushes; and the axle was greased with soap. Men were paid to 'drive' or 'horse' it, and the Cappers expected their journeymen to undertake this job.

The players received payments varying with the importance of their parts. The sums allowed by the Weavers in 1525 ranged from 10*d.* to 2*s.* 4*d.* Minstrels, both vocalists and instrumentalists, were also hired, and in 1573 one Fawston, evidently an artist of exceptional talent, received from the Smiths, besides 4*d.* 'for hangyng Judas,' another 4*d.* 'for Coc croyng.' The Drapers paid as much as 3*s.* 4*d.* 'for pleayng God,' and 5*s.* 'to iij whyte sollys' or 'savyd sowles,' 5*s.* 'to iij blake sollys,' or 'dampnyd sowles,' 16*d.* 'to ij wormes of conscyence,' and the like. Payments also occur for speaking the prologue, preface, or 'protestacyon.'

The corporation exercised control over the players, and in 1440 ordered under a penalty of 20*s.* 'quod Robertus Gñe et omnes alii qui ludunt in festo Corporis Christi bene et sufficienter ludant ita quod nulla impedicio fiat in aliquo ioco.' In 1443, an order forbade members of certain crafts to play in any pageant except their own without the mayor's licence.

The players required refreshment at intervals during the day, and probably the craftsmen who attended the pageant took their share. Further expenses, both for refreshment, and for the hire of a room or hall, were incurred at rehearsals. The Smiths in 1490 had their first 'reherse' in Easter week, and their second in Whitsun week.

Each craft had its own 'orygynall' or 'play-boke,' and paid for making the necessary copies, for setting or 'pricking' songs, for 'beryng of ye Orygynall' or prompting, and occasionally for bringing the text up to date. Thus the Smiths had a 'new rygenale' in 1491, and in 1573 a 'new play,' by which is apparently meant an additional scene to their existing play (cf. p. 423). The Drapers added 'the matter of the castell of Emaus' in 1540. The Weavers paid 5*s*. 'for makyng of the play boke' in 1535, and the colophon of their extant text shows it to have been 'newly translate' in that year by Robert Croo. This was a regular theatrical man of all work. The matter of the Shearmen and Taylors' play was 'nevly correcte' by him in the same year. In 1557 he got 20*s*. from the Drapers 'for makyng of the boke for the paggen.' The Smiths paid him in 1563 'for ij leves of our pley boke.' And between 1556 and 1562 he further assisted the Drapers, by playing God, mending the 'devells cottes,' supplying a hat for the Pharisee, and manufacturing the requisite 'iij worldys.'

Finally, there was the not inconsiderable cost of costumes and properties, including the gloves for the performers which figure so invariably in mediaeval balance sheets. Further details as to these and all other objects of expenditure than I have here room for will be found in the invaluable volumes of Mr. Sharp.

The Destruction of Jerusalem.

In 1584, four years after the ordinary Corpus Christi plays were laid down, the *Annals* record 'This year the new Play of the Destruction of Jerusalem was first played.' This is confirmed by the accounts of the corporation, which include a sum of £13 6*s*. 8*d*. 'paid to Mr. Smythe of Oxford the xv[th] daye of Aprill 1584 for hys paynes for writing of the tragedye.' This was one John Smythe, a scholar of the Free School in Coventry and afterwards of St. John's College, Oxford. The play was produced at considerable expense upon the pageants of the crafts, but the day of performance is not stated. From the detailed accounts of the Smiths and the Cappers, Mr. Sharp infers that it was based upon the narrative of Josephus.

In 1591, the old Corpus Christi plays seem to have been proposed for exhibition, as the MS. of the Shearmen and Taylors' songs bears the date of May 13 in that year. But on May 19 the corporation resolved 'that the destruction of Jerusalem, the Conquest of the Danes, or the historie of K[ing] E[dward] the X [Confessor], at the request of the Comons of this Cittie shal be plaied on the pagens on Midsomer daye & St. Peters daye next in this Cittie & non other playes.' The two last-named plays may have been inspired by the traditional interpretations of the Hox Tuesday custom (cf. vol. i. p. 154). Which was chosen does not appear; but some performance or other was given. Several of the crafts had by this time sold their pageants. Those who had not lent them; and all compounded for the production of a scene by the payment of a sum down. This appears to have gone to one Thomas Massey, who contracted for the production. He had already supplied properties in 1584. In 1603 he quarrelled with the corporation about certain devices shown on the visit of the Princess Elizabeth to Coventry. In 1606 he hired some acting-apparel from the Weavers' company [1].

Miscellaneous Plays.

The *Annals* record:—

1490–1. 'This year was the play of St. Katherine in the little Park.

1504–5. 'This yeare they played the play of St. Crytyan in the little parke [2].'

In 1511, one of the pageants at the entry of Henry VIII had a 'goodly Stage Play' upon it [3].

The Dyers in 1478, the Cappers in 1525, and the Drapers in 1556, 1566, and 1568 appear to have had plays at their dinners. Probably 'the Golden Fleece,' for which the Cappers paid the inevitable Robert Crowe and two others, was a play [4].

The 'lusores de Coventry' played at Maxstoke Priory between 1422 and 1461 (Appendix E, ii). 'Certain Players of Coventrye' were at court in 1530 (Appendix E, viii).

Towards the end of the sixteenth century occur notices of travelling 'players of Coventrie.' They were at Bristol and Abingdon in 1570, and at Leicester in 1569 and 1571. At Abingdon they are described as 'Mr. Smythes players of Coventree.' John Smythe, the writer of the Destruction of Jerusalem, was only seven years old in 1570. Mr. Halliwell-Phillipps would read '*the* Smythes' players [5].'

The Corpus Christi Procession.

The procession or 'Ridyng' on Corpus Christi day is first mentioned in the *Leet Book* in 1444, and in 1446 is an order 'quod le Ruydyng in festo Corporis Christi fiat prout ex antiquo tempore consueverint.'

[1] Sharp, 12, 39, 64, 75, 78; *Weavers' Play*, 21.

[2] Sharp, 9; Hearne, *Fordun's Scotichronicon*, v. 1450.

[3] Sharp, 157; Hearne, loc. cit.

[4] Sharp, 216.

[5] Sharp, 209; Halliwell-Phillipps, *Outlines*, ii. 296.

It took place early in the day after a 'breakfast.' The craft-guilds rode in it, and provided minstrels and torchbearers. The Trinity Guild seems to have borne a crucifix, and the Guild of Corpus Christi and St. Nicholas the host under a canopy. The accounts of the Smiths include the following items:—

'1476. Item ffor hors hyre to Herod, iij^{d}.

1489. Item payd for Aroddes garment peynttyng that he went a prossasyon in, xx^{d}.'

The other extant guild accounts throw no light on the presence of representatives of the plays in the procession; but the Corpus Christi guild itself provided dramatic personages.

'1501. payd for a Crown of sylver & gyld for the Mare on Corpus Christi day, xliij^{s} ix^{d}.

1539. peny bred for the appostells, vj^{d}.
beiff for the appostles, viij^{d}.
to the Marie for hir gloves and wages, ij^{s}.
the Marie to offer, j^{d}.
Kateryne & Margaret, iiij^{d}.
viij virgyns, viij^{d}.
to Gabriell for beryng the lilly, iiij^{d}.
to James & Thomas of Inde, viij^{d}.
to x other apostells, xx^{d}.

1540. for makyng the lilly, iij^{s} iiij^{d}.

1541. to Gabryel for beryng the light [lilly?] iiij^{d}.
xij torches of wax for the apostles.

1544. a new coat & a peir of hoes for Gabriell, iij^{s}. iiij.[1]'

Croxton, Norfolk (?).

See s. v. *Texts* (i), *Croxton Play, The Sacrament.*

Daventry, Northamptonshire.

The 'lusores de Daventry' played at Maxstoke Priory between 1422 and 1461 (Appendix E, ii).

Dublin, Ireland.

The version of the *Quem quaeritis* used at the Church of St. John the Evangelist in the fourteenth century is printed in Appendix R.

The Chain Book of the City contains the following memorandum, apparently entered in 1498.

Corpus Christi day a pagentis:—

'The pagentis of Corpus Christi day, made by an olde law and

[1] Sharp, 159.

confermed by a semble befor Thomas Collier, Maire of the Citte of Divelin, and Juries, Baliffes and commones, the iiiith Friday next after midsomer, the xiii. yere of the reign of King Henri the VIIth [1498]:

'Glovers: Adam and Eve, with an angill followyng berryng a swerde. Peyn, xl. *s*.

'Corvisers: Caym and Abell, with an auter and the ofference. Peyn, xl.*s*.

'Maryners, Vynters, Shipcarpynderis, and Samountakers: Noe, with his shipp, apparalid acordyng. Peyn, xl.*s*.

'Wevers: Abraham [and] Ysack, with ther auter and a lambe and ther offerance. Peyn, xl.*s*.

'Smythis, Shermen, Bakers, Sclateris, Cokis and Masonys: Pharo, with his hoste. Peyn, xl.*s*.

'Skynners, House-Carpynders, and Tanners, and Browders: for the body of the camell, and Oure Lady and hir chil[d]e well aperelid, with Joseph to lede the camell, and Moyses with the children of Israell, and the Portors to berr the camell. Peyn, xl.*s*. and Steyners and Peyntors to peynte the hede of the camell. [Peyn,] xl.*s*.

'[Goldsmy]this: The three kynges of Collynn, ridyng worshupfully, with the offerance, with a sterr afor them. Peyn, xl.*s*.

'[Hoopers]: The shep[er]dis, with an Angill syngyng Gloria in excelsis Deo. Peyn, xl.*s*.

'Corpus Christi yild: Criste in his Passioun, with three Maries, and angilis berring serges of wex in ther hands. [Peyn,] xl.*s*.

'Taylors: Pilate, with his fellaship, and his lady and his knyghtes, well beseyne. Peyn, xl.*s*.

'Barbors: An[nas] and Caiphas, well araied acordyng. [Peyn,] xl.*s*.

'Courteours: Arthure, with [his] knightes. Peyn, xl.*s*.

'Fisshers: The Twelve Apostelis. Peyn, xl.*s*.

'Marchauntes: The Prophetis. Peyn, xl.*s*.

'Bouchers: tormentours, with ther garmentis well and clenly peynted. [Peyn,] xl.*s*.

'The Maire of the Bulring and bachelers of the same: The Nine Worthies ridyng worshupfully, with ther followers accordyng. Peyn, xl.*s*.

'The Hagardmen and the husbandmen to berr the dragoun and to repaire the dragoun a Seint Georges day and Corpus Christi day. Peyn, xl.*s*.'

This list is immediately followed by a second, practically identical with it, of 'The Pagentys of Corpus Christi Processioun.'

These pageants, though the subjects are drawn from the usual Corpus Christi play-cycle (with the addition of King Arthur and the nine Worthies), appear, from their irregular order, to be only dumb-show accompaniments of a procession. In 1569 the crafts were directed to keep the same order in the Shrove Tuesday ball riding (cf. vol. i. p. 150), 'as they are appointed to go with their pageants on Corpus Christi daye by the Chayne Boke[1].'

The same intermixture of profane and sacred elements marks the late and scanty records of actual plays in Dublin.

'Tho. Fitzgerald, Earl of Kildare and Lord Lieutenant of Ireland in the year 1528, was invited to a new play every day in Christmas, Arland Usher being then mayor, and Francis Herbert and John Squire bayliffs, wherein the taylors acted the part of Adam and Eve; the shoemakers represented the story of Crispin and Crispinianus; the vintners acted Bacchus and his story; the Carpenters that of Joseph and Mary; Vulcan, and what related to him, was acted by the Smiths; and the comedy of Ceres, the goddess of corn, by the Bakers. Their stage was erected on Hoggin Green (now called College Green), and on it the priors of St. John of Jerusalem, of the blessed Trinity, and All Hallows caused two plays to be acted, the one representing the passion of our Saviour, and the other the several deaths which the apostles suffered[2].' In 1541 there were 'epulae, comoediae, et certamina ludicra' when Henry VIII was proclaimed King of Ireland. These included 'the nine Worthies.' On the return of Lord Sussex from an expedition against James MacConnell in 1557, 'the Six Worthies was played by the city[3].'

A seventeenth-century transcript of a lost leaf of the Chain Book has the following order for the St. George's day procession:—

'The Pageant of St. George's day, to be ordered and kept as hereafter followeth:

'The Mayor of the yeare before to finde the Emperour and Empress with their followers, well apparelled, that is to say, the Emperor, with two Doctors, and the Empress, with two knights, and two maydens to beare the traynes of their gownes, well apparelled, and [the Guild of] St. George to pay their wages.

[1] J. T. Gilbert, *Calendar of Ancient Records of Dublin*, i. 239; ii. 54. Cf. Davidson, 222, and in *Modern Language Notes*, vii. 339.

[2] Harris, *Hist. of Dublin*, 147; J. C. Walker, *Hist. Essay on the Irish Stage* (*Trans. Roy. Irish Acad.* ii (1788), 2. 75), from MS. of Robert Ware.

[3] Walker, loc. cit.; Sir James Ware, *Annales Rerum Hibern.* (1664), 161; *Variorum*, iii. 30, from MS. in Trin. Coll. Dublin. W. F. Dawson, *Christmas: its Origin and Associations*, 52, says that Henry II kept Christmas at Hogges in 1171 with 'miracle plays.' But I cannot find the authority for this.

'Item: Mr. Mayor for the time being to find St. George a-horseback, and the wardens to pay three shillings and four pence for his wages that day. And the Bailives for the time being to find four horses, with men upon them, well apparelled, to beare the pole-axe, the standard, and the Emperor and St. George's sword.

'Item: The elder master of the yeald to find a mayd well aparelled to lead the dragon; and the Clerk of the Market to find a good line for the dragon.

'Item: The elder warden to find St. George, with four trumpettors, and St. George's [Guild] to pay their wages.

'Item: the yonger warden to finde the king of Dele and the queene of Dele, and two knightes to lead the queene of Dele, with two maydens to beare the trayne of her goune, all wholy in black apparell, and to have St. George's chappell well hanged and apparelled to every purpose with cushins . . . russhes and other necessaries belonging for said St. George's day[1].'

Dunstable, Bedfordshire.

One Geoffrey, a Norman, was 'apud Dunestapliam, expectans scholam S. Albani sibi repromissam; ubi quendam ludum de S. Katerina (quem Miracula vulgariter appellamus) fecit; ad quae decoranda petiit a Sacrista S. Albani, ut sibi capae chorales accommodarentur, et obtinuit.' Unfortunately the 'capae' were burnt. This must have been early in the twelfth century, as Geoffrey in grief became a monk, and was Abbot of St. Albans by 1119[2].

Edinburgh, Scotland.

The civic records show traces of municipal plays in 1554, but it is not clear that they were miracle-plays proper or of long standing. Sir David Lyndsay's *Satyre of the Thrie Estaitis* was played in the Greenside between 1550 and 1559 (cf. p. 442). On June 15, 1554, a payment was made to Sir William Makdougall, 'maister of werk,' for those 'that furneist the grayth to the convoy of the moris to the Abbay and of the play maid that samyn day the tent day of Junii instant.' Makdougall was to deliver to the dean of guild the 'handscenye [ensign] and canves specifiit in the said tikkit to be kepit to the behuif of the town.' Sums were also paid this summer for 'the playing place' or 'the play field now biggand in the Grenesid.'

[1] Gilbert, op. cit. i. 242.

[2] Matthew Paris, *Gesta Abbat. S. Albani*, ap. H. T. Riley, *Gesta Abbatum S. Albani* (R. S.), i. 73; Bulaeus, *Historia Universitatis Parisiensis*, ii. 226; Collier, i. 13.

On Oct. 12 Walter Bynnyng was paid for 'the making of the play graith' and for painting the 'handsenye' and 'playariss facis.' He was to 'mak the play geir vnderwrittin furthcumand to the town, quhen thai haif ado thairwith, quhilkis he has now ressauit; viz. viij play hattis, ane kingis crown, ane myter, ane fulis hude, ane septour, ane pair angell wingis, twa angell hair, ane chaplet of tryvmphe.'

On Dec. 28 'the prouest, baillies and counsale findis it necessar and expedient that the litill farsche and play maid be William Lauder be playit afoir the Quenis grace [1].' I trace a note of regret for the doubtful morals and certain expense of the entertainments which the presence in Edinburgh of the newly-made Regent, Mary of Lorraine, imposed upon the burghers.

Easterford, Essex.

Lord Howard rewarded the players of 'Esterforde' on Jan. 7, 1482 (Appendix E, vii). This place is now known as Kelvedon.

Folkestone, Kent.

Folkestone players were at New Romney in 1474, and at Lydd in 1479.

Foston, Leicestershire.

In 1561 the players of 'Fosson' borrowed 'serten stufe' from the churchwardens of St. Martin's, Leicester [2].

Fyfield, Oxfordshire.

See s. v. Shipton.

Garboldisham, Norfolk.

'Garblesham game' was at Harling (q. v.) in 1457.

Great Chart, Kent.

'Chart' players were at New Romney in 1489.

Hadleigh, Essex.

Lord Howard rewarded the 'Plaiers of Hadley' on Dec. 27, 1481 (Appendix E, vii).

Halstead, Essex.

There was a play in the church in 1529 [3].

Ham Street, Kent.

Ham players were at Lydd in 1454.

[1] J. D. Marwick, *Records of Edinburgh* (Scottish Burghs Record Soc.), ii. 193 sqq.

[2] Kelly, 19.

[3] Pearson, ii. 413.

Hanningfield, Essex.

'John Walker of Hanfild' hired the Chelmsford (q.v.) wardrobe in 1572.

Harling, Norfolk.

In 1452 the wardens paid for the 'original of an Interlude pleyed at the Cherch gate.' In 1457 payments were made for 'Lopham game,' and 'Garblesham game,' in 1463 for 'Kenningale game,' in 1467 to the 'Kenyngale players[1].'

Hascombe, Surrey.

Amongst the *Loseley MSS.* is a deposition of 157⅞:

'Coram me Henr. Goringe, ar. xij^o^ die Januar. 1578. George Longherst and John Mill ex^d^ sayeth, that on Sondaye last they were together at widow Michelles house, in the parish of Hascombe, and there delyvered their mares to kepe till they came agayne, and sayde that they wold goo to Hascombe Churche, to a kynge playe wch then was there. And sayeth y^t^ they went thither and there contynued about an houre, at which tyme the sonne was then downe[2].'

The date suggests a performance on Jan. 6. Evidently a May 'kynge playe' is out of the question; but a Twelfth Night King, or a 'Stella' belated in the afternoon, are both possible.

Hereford, Herefordshire.

On April 30, 1440, John Hauler and John Pewte sued Thomas Sporyour in the city court 'de placito detencionis unius libri de lusionibus, prec. ii*s*. iiij*d*.[3]'

The Register of the Corporation for 1503 contains a list of

'The paiants for the procession of Corpus Christi:

Furst, Glovers. Adam, Eve, *Cayne and Abell* (erased).

Eldest seriant. Cayne, Abell, and Moysey, Aron.

Carpenters. Noye ship.

Chaundelers. Abram, Isack, Moysey cum iiii^or^ pueris.

Skynners. Jesse.

Flacchers. Salutacõn of our Lady.

Vynteners. Nativite of our Lord.

Taillours. The iii Kings of Colen.

The belman. The purificacõn of our Lady, with Symyon.

[1] L. G. Bolingbroke, *Pre-Eliz. Plays and Players in Norfolk* (*Norfolk Archaeology*, xi. 338).

[2] *N. and Q.* xii. 210; Kelly, 68.

[3] *Hist. MSS.* xiii. 4. 300.

Drapers. The . . . (*blank*) deitours, goyng with the good Lord.

Sadlers. Fleme Jordan.

Cardeners. The castell of Israell.

Walkers. The good Lord ridyng on an asse ("judging at an assize," in Johnson!) with xii Appostelles.

The tanners. The story of Shore Thursday.

Bochours. The takyng of our Lord.

The eldest seriant. The tormentyng of our Lord with iiii tormentoures, with the lamentac̄on of our Lady [and Seynt John the evaungelist: *faintly added by another hand*].

[Cappers. Portacio crucis usque montem Oilverii: *added.*]

Dyers. Iesus pendens in cruce [*altered by the second hand from* Portacio crucis et Iohanne evangelista portante Mariam].

Smythes. Longys with his knyghtes.

The eldest seriant. Maria and Iohannes evangelista (*interlined*).

Barbours. Joseth Abarmathia.

Dyers. Sepultura Christi.

The eldest seriant. Tres Mariae.

Porters. Milites armati custodes sepulcri.

Mercers. Pilate, Cayfes, Annas, and Mahounde. [*This last name has been partly erased.*]

Bakers. Knyghtes in harnes.

Journeymen cappers. Seynt Keterina with tres (?) tormentors [1].'

At a law day held on Dec. 10, 1548, it was agreed that the crafts who were 'bound by the grantes of their corporacions yerely to bring forthe and set forward dyvers pageaunttes of ancient history in the processions of the cytey upon the day and fest of Corpus Xpi, which now is and are omitted and surceased' should instead make an annual payment towards the expense of repairing walls, causeways, &c.[2] The 1503 list seems to concern a dumb-show only, and it cannot be positively assumed that the *lusiones* of 1440 were a Corpus Christi play.

In 1706 a labourer went through the city in the week before Easter, being Passion week, clothed in a long coat with a large periwig, with a great multitude following him, sitting upon an ass, to the derision of our Saviour Jesus Christ's riding into Jerusalem, to the great scandal of the Christian religion, to the contempt of our Lord and his doctrine, and to the ill and pernicious example of others [3].

[1] *Hist. MSS.* xiii. 4. 288.
[2] R. Johnson, *Ancient Customs of Hereford* (ed. 2. 1882), 119.
[3] *Hist. MSS.* xiii. 4. 352.

Herne, Kent.

Herne players were at New Romney in 1429.

Heybridge, Essex.

The churchwardens' accounts for 1532 show a play, with 'a fool' and 'pagent players,' apparently in the church [1].

High Easter, Essex.

High Easter men hired the Chelmsford (q. v.) wardrobe in 1570–2.

High Halden, Kent.

'Haldene' players were at New Romney in 1499.

Holbeach, Lincolnshire.

In 1548 the churchwardens paid v^{s} viij^{d} for the 'costs of the iij kyngs of Coloyne [2].'

Hull, Yorkshire.

The accounts of the Trinity House, a guild of master mariners and pilots, contain entries concerning a play of Noah.

'1483. To the minstrels, vj^{d}.
To Noah and his wife, j^{s} vj^{d}.
To Robert Brown playing God, vj^{d}.
To the Ship-child, j^{d}.
To a shipwright for clinking Noah's ship, one day, vij^{d}.
22 kids for shoring Noah's ship, ij^{d}.
To a man clearing away the snow, j^{d}.
Straw, for Noah and his children, ij^{d}.
Mass, bellman, torches, minstrels, garland, &c., vj^{s}.
For mending the ship, ij^{d}.
To Noah for playing, j^{s}.
To straw and grease for wheels, $\frac{1}{4}$^{d}.
To the waits for going about with the ship, vj^{d}.

1494. To Thomas Sawyr playing God, x^{d}.
To Jenkin Smith playing Noah, j^{s}.
To Noah's wife, viij^{d}.
The clerk and his children, j^{s} vj^{d}.
To the players of Barton, viij^{d}.
For a gallon of wine, viij^{d}.
For three skins for Noah's coat, making it, and a rope to hang the ship in the kirk, vij^{s}.

[1] Nichols, *Extracts from Churchwardens' Accounts*, 175.
[2] W. Sandys, *Christmas Carols*, xc.

To dighting and gilding St. John's head, painting two tabernacles, beautifying the boat and over the table, vij^{s} ij^{d}.
Making Noah's ship, v^{li} viij^{s}.
Two wrights a day and a half, j^{s} vj^{d}.
A halfer (rope) 4 stone weight, iiij^{s} viij^{d}.
Rigging Noah's ship, viij^{d}.'

Hadley, the historian of Hull, extracts these items 'from the expences on Plough-day,' and says, 'This being a maritime society, it was celebrated by a procession adapted to the circumstance[1].' There are continental parallels for ship-processions at spring feasts (vol. i. p. 121); but evidently that at Hull had been assimilated, perhaps under the influence of Beverley, to a miracle-play or pageant. A recent writer, apparently from some source other than Hadley, says that the entries in the accounts run from before 1421 to 1529. Amongst his additional extracts are:—

'A payr of new mytens to Noye, iiij^{d}.
Amending Noye Pyleh, iiij^{d}.
Nicholas Helpby for wryt^{g} the pley, vij^{d}.
A rope to hyng the shipp in ye kyrk, ij^{d}.
Takyng down shype and hyngyng up agayn, ij^{s}.
Wyn when the shype went about, ij^{d}.
1421. New shype, v^{li} viij^{s} iiij^{d} [2].'

Hythe, Kent.

Hythe players were at New Romney in 1399 and at Lydd in 1467.

Idbury, Oxfordshire.

See s. v. Shipton.

Ipswich, Suffolk.

In 1325 the former Guild Merchant was reconstituted as a Guild of Corpus Christi. The Constitution provides for a procession, on Corpus Christi day, unless it is hindered 'pro qualitate temporis[3].'

The notices in the seventeenth-century Annals of the town point to a play as well as a procession[4]. The Guild included all the burgesses;

[1] G. Hadley, *Hist. of Kingston upon Hull* (1788), 823.
[2] W. Andrews, *Historic Yorkshire*, 43; *Curiosities of the Church*, 19.
[3] J. Wodderspoon, *Memorials of the Ancient Town of Ipswich* (1850), 161; *Hist. MSS.* ix. 1. 245.
[4] Nathaniel Bacon, *The Annalls of Ipswich*, 1654 (ed. W. H. Richardson, 1884), 102 and *passim*. Some additional notices are in *Hist. MSS.* ix. 1. 241 sqq.

each paying 16*d.* a year and attending the dinner on Corpus Christi day.

In 1443 the common marsh was devised 'to maintaine and repaire the pageants of the Guilde.'

In 1445 J. Causton was admitted burgess on condition of maintaining for seven years 'the ornaments belonging to Corpus X[i] pageant and the stages, receiving the Charges thereof from the farmers of the Common Marshe and the Portmen's medow, as the Bayliffs for the time being shall think meete.' Arrears were paid to J. Caldwell for his charge of 'Corpus Chr. pageant.'

In 1491 an order was made, laying down, 'Howe euery occupacion of craftsmen schuld order themselves in the goyng with their pageantes in the procession of Corpus Christi.' The list closes with the 'Friers Carmelites,' 'Friers Minors,' and 'Friers Prechors.' The subjects of the pageants are unfortunately not given. The pageant cost 45*s.* 1*d.*

In 1492 'areres of y[e] Pageant' were paid, and 'kepers of the Ornaments and utensiles of Corpus Christi appointed.'

In 1493, 1494, 1495, 1496 orders were made for the provision of the 'pageant.' In 1495 there was a grant of £3 11. 0 for it. In 1496 it was 'at the charge of such as have been used.'

In 1502 'Corpus Christi pageant shall hereafter be observed, and a convenient artificer shall be intertained to that end, and shall have 40*s.*' Each Portman was to pay 1*s.* 4*d.*, each of the 'twenty-four' 8*d.*; the other 6*s.* 8*d.* to be levied. 'Noe Bayliff shall interrupt or hinder the pageant, unless by order of the great court or uppon special cause.' Collectors for the pageant were chosen.

In 1504 the 'collectors for the play of Corpus Christi' were 'to make a free burgess for their expences at Corpus Christi play.' These collectors are again mentioned in 1505 and 1506, and in the latter year 'ornaments' and 'stageing for Corpus Christi play.'

In 1509 all inhabitants are to have 'their Tabernas and attendance at the ffeast of Corpus Christi' and 'everyone shall hold by the order of their procession, according to the Constitutions.'

In 1511 a contribution is ordered to a pageant of St. George, and the Corpus Christi dinner and pageant are laid aside.

From 1513 to 1519 the play is ordered to be laid aside in every year except 1517. In 1520 it 'shall hold this yere,' and the pageant is ordered to be ready. It is laid aside in 1521 until further order, and the master of the pageant called 'the shipp' is to have the same ready under forfeiture of £10. It is 'deferred' in 1522 and 'laid aside for ever' in 1531.

Probably it was never revived. But there is an order for the procession with the Sacrament in 1540, and in 1542 this had its 'pageants' to which each householder was rated at 1*d.*

In 1552 the guild is held on the Sunday after Trinity Sunday, and similar meetings continue until 1644.

On a possible performance of Bale's *King John* at the visit of Elizabeth to Ipswich in 1561 see *Texts* (iii), s. v. *Bale.*

Ixworth, Suffolk.

Thetford Priory made a payment 'in regard to Ixworth play,' in 1507–8 (Appendix E, iii).

Kelvedon, Essex.

See s.v. Easterford.

Kendal, Westmoreland.

The 'Boke of Record,' a municipal register begun at the incorporation in 1575, refers to the Corpus Christi play by the crafts as established at that date. On Feb. 14, 1575, the corporation forbade feasts of more than twelve guests;

'Such lyke . . . as have bene comonlye used at . . . metyings of men off Occupacyons aboute orders for their severall pagiands off Corpus xpi playe . . . exceptyd and reserved.'

An order 'ffor the playe' of Sept. 22, 1586, forbade the alderman to give permission for the acting of the play in any year without the consent of his brethren [1].'

The plays lasted into the seventeenth century. Thomas Heywood says in 1612, that, 'to this day,' Kendall holds the privilege of its fairs and other charters by yearly stage-plays [2]. And Weever, about 1631, speaks of—

'Corpus Christi play in my countrey, which I have seene acted at Preston, and Lancaster, and last of all at Kendall, in the beginning of the raigne of King James; for which the Townesmen were sore troubled; and upon good reasons the Play finally supprest, not onely there, but in all other Townes of the Kingdome [3].'

In the MS. life of the Puritan vicar of Rotherham, John Shaw, is a description of how he spoke to an old man at Cartmel of salvation by Christ:—

'Oh Sir,' said he, 'I think I heard of that man you speak of once in a play at Kendall, called Corpus Christ's play, where there was a man

[1] R. S. Ferguson, *A Boke of Record . . . of Kirkbie Kendall* (Cumb. and Westm. Arch. and Ant. Soc.), 91, 136.

[2] See s. v. Manningtree.

[3] Weever, *Funeral Monuments*, 405.

on a tree, and blood ran down, &c. And afterwards he professed he could not remember that he ever heard of salvation by Jesus, but in that play [1].'

KENNINGHALL, NORFOLK.

'Kenningale game' was at Harling (q. v.) in 1463, and the 'Kenyngale players' in 1467.

KILKENNY, IRELAND.

John Bale, in his description of his brief episcopate of Ossory, gives an account of the proclamation of Queen Mary, at Kilkenny, on August 20, 1553, 'The yonge men, in the Forenone, played a Tragedye of God's Promyses in the olde Lawe, at the Market Crosse, with Organe, Plainges, and Songes very aptely. In the Afternone agayne they played a Commedie of Sanct Johan Baptistes Preachinges, of Christes Baptisynge, and of his Temptacion in the Wildernesse, to the small contentacion of the Prestes and other Papistes there [2].'

These plays are extant; cf. *Texts* (iii), s. v. *Bale.*

KING'S LYNN, NORFOLK.

There was a Corpus Christi guild as early as 1400, and the Tailors' *Ordinances* of 1449 require them to take part in the Corpus Christi procession; but I do not find evidence of regular annual plays. The Chamberlains' Accounts for 1385, however, include:—

'iij^s iiij^d to certain players, playing an interlude on Corpus Christi day.'

'iij^s iiij^d paid by the Mayor's gift to persons playing the interlude of St. Thomas the Martyr.'

And those for 1462—

'iij^s paid for two flagons of red wine, spent in the house of Arnulph Tixonye, by the Mayor and most of his brethren, being there to see a certain play at the Feast of Corpus Christi.' In the same year the Skinners and Sailors 'of the town' received rewards 'for their labour about the procession of Corpus Christi this year [3].'

In 1409–10 Lady de Beaufort came to see a play [4].

See also s. v. MIDDLETON.

KINGSTON-ON-THAMES, SURREY.

On May 20, 1505, Henry VII made a payment

'To the Players of Kingeston toward the bilding of the churche steple, in almasse, iij^s iiij^d [5].'

[1] I. Disraeli, *Curiosities of Literature*, Second Series, iii. 343.

[2] Bale, *Vocacyon to Ossory* (1553), in *Harleian Miscellany* (ed. 1745), vi. 402; (ed. 1808), i. 345.

[3] *Hist. MSS.* xi. 3. 165, 223, 224. The original documents appear to be in Latin.

[4] Harrod, *King's Lynn Records*, 87.

[5] Cf. Appendix E (viii).

The churchwardens' accounts for 1505–6 include

'That we, Adam Backhous and Harry Nycol, amountyd of a play, 4li.'

A few later items relate to plays at Easter.

'1513–4. For thred for the resurrection, jd.
For 3 yards of dorneck for a player's cote, and the makyng, xvd.

1520–1. Paid for a skin of parchment and gunpowder for the play on Ester-day, viijd.
For bred and ale for them that made the stage and other thinges belonginge to the play, js ijd.

1565. Recd. of the players of the stage at Easter, js ijd ob.[1]'

Lancaster.

A Corpus Christi play was acted within the lifetime of Weever, who was born 1576, and wrote 1631[2].

Lanchire (?), Essex.

'Somers of Lanchire' hired the Chelmsford (q.v.) wardrobe in 1566. But I can find no such place.

Langley, Oxfordshire.

See s. v. Shipton.

Lavenham, Suffolk.

The Earl of Surrey rewarded the players of 'Lanam' on Jan. 8, 1492 (Appendix E, vii).

Leconfield, Yorkshire.

The list of customary rewards given by the fifth Earl of Northumberland to his servants, drawn up †1522, includes:—

'Them of his Lordschipes Chapell if they doo play the Play of the Nativite uppon Cristynmes-Day in the mornynge in my Lords Chapell befor his Lordship, xxs.

... Them of his Lordship Chappell and other, if they doo play the play of Resurrection upon Esturday in the morning in my Lords Chapell, xxs[3].'

Leeds, Yorkshire.

Ten Brink, ii. 256, says that Leeds formed a centre 'for the art of the cyclic plays, which were represented yearly'; and Ward, i. 55,

[1] Lysons, *Environs of London*, i. 229.

[2] See s. v. Kendal.

[3] Percy, *N.H.B.* 343, 345.

that at Leeds 'the religious drama was assiduously cultivated by the citizens.' I cannot find any authority for this, and can only suggest that it is a misapprehension of an entry in the *Catalogue* of Ralph Thoresby's manuscripts appended to his *Ducatus Leodensis* (1715), 517. This was copied by Sharp, 141. But it refers to the *York Plays*, then in Thoresby's possession.

Leicester.

The Hall book of the Corporation contains the following entries:—

1477, March 26. 'The pleyers the which pleed the passion play the yere next afore brought yne a byll the whiche was of serten devties of mony and whed^{r} the passion shulbe put to crafts to be bounden or nay. And at y^{t} tyme the seid pleyers gaff to the pachents y^{r} mony which that thei had getten yn playng of the seid play euer fore to that day and all y^{r} Rayments w^{h} al oth^{r} maner of stuff y^{t} they had at that tyme. And at the same Common Halle be the advyse of all the Comons was chosen thies persones after named for to have the gydyng and Rule of the said play' [19 persons with 2 'bedalls' named][1].

1495, Friday after xij^{te} day. 'Y^{t} ys ordent agreyt stabelechyd & acte for the comon well of the towne and of seche guds as ys yn a store hows in the Setterday marcat y^{t} ys to say wodde tymber and vdyr playyng germands yf ther be ony her hys chosyn to be ouersears thereof' [6 names][2].

It is not clear on what day the Passion play took place. There were great processions on Whit Monday from the churches of St. Martin and St. Mary to that of St. Margaret, and in these the Twelve Apostles figured[3].

The accounts of the same churches show plays apparently distinct from the Passion play.

St. Mary's.

1491. Paid to the Players on New-year's day at even in the church, vj^{d}.

1499. Paid for a play in the church, in Dominica infra Octavam Epiphaniae, ij^{s}.

1504. Paid for mending the garment of Jesus and the cross painting, j^{s} iij^{d}.

Paid for a pound of hemp to mend the angels heads, iiij^{d}.

Paid for linen cloth for the angels heads, and Jesus hoose, making in all, ix^{d}.

[1] Kelly, 27, 187. M. Bateson, *Records of Leicester*, ii. 297; J. Nichols, *History of Leicestershire*, iv. i. App. 378, 9.

[2] Kelly, 188.

[3] Kelly, 7.

1507. Paid for a pound of hemp for the heads of the angels, iij^{d}.
Paid for painting the wings and scaff, &c., viij^{d} [1].

These entries suggest a *Quem quaeritis*, but perhaps only a puppet-show.

St. Martin's.

1492. Paid to the players on New-year's day at even in the church, vj^{d}.

1546–7. P^{d}. for makynge of a sworde & payntynge of the same for Harroode.

1555–6. P^{d}. to the iij shepperds at Whytsontyde, vj^{d}.

1559–60. P^{d}. to ye plears for ther paynes.

1561. R^{d}. for serten stufe lent to the players of Fosson [2].

In 1551 the Corporation came not to a feast 'because of the play that was in the church[3].'

Lichfield, Staffordshire.

The Cathedral Statutes of Bishop Hugh de Nonant (1188–98) provide for the *Pastores* at Christmas and the *Quem quaeritis* and *Peregrini* at Easter.

'Item in nocte Natalis representacio pastorum fieri consueuit et in diluculo Paschae representacio Resurreccionis dominicae et representacio peregrinorum die lunae in septimana Paschae sicut in libris super hijs ac alijs compositis continetur.'

Similarly in the account of the *officium* of the *Succentor* it is provided:

'Et prouidere debet quod representacio pastorum in nocte Natalis domini et miraculorum in nocte Paschae et die lunae in Pascha congrue et honorifice fiant [4].'

Lincoln.

About 1244 Bishop Grosseteste names 'miracula' amongst other 'ludi' which the archdeacons, so far as possible, are to exterminate in the diocese [5].

Chapter *computi* for 1406, 1452, and 1531 include entries of payments, 'In serothecis emptis pro Maria et Angelo et Prophetis ex consuetudine in Aurora Natalis Dñi hoc anno [6].'

'In 1420 tithes to the amount of 8^{s} 8^{d} were assigned to Thomas Chamberleyn for getting up a spectacle or pageant (" cuiusdam ex-

[1] Kelly, 14, 16.

[2] Kelly, 15, 18, 19, 20; T. North, *Accounts of Churchwardens of St. Martin's*, 2, 21, 74, 86, 87.

[3] Kelly, 193.

[4] *Lincoln Statutes*, ii. 15, 23.

[5] Cf. vol. i. p. 91.

[6] Wordsworth, 126, and in *Lincoln Statutes*, ii. lv. The entry given for 1452 in the latter omits 'et Prophetis.'

cellentis visus") called *Rubum quem viderat* at Christmas . . . An anthem sung at Lauds on New Year's day . . . begins thus[1]' (cf. *Sarum Breviary*, ccxciii). Was this spectacle a Moses play forming part of, or detached from, an *Ordo Prophetarum*?

A set of local annals (1361–1515) compiled in the sixteenth century records the following plays:—

1397–8. Ludus de Pater Noster lvi anno.
1410–11. Ludus Pater Noster.
1424–5. Ludus Pater Noster.
1441–2. Ludus Sancti Laurentii.
1447–8. Ludus Sanctae Susannae.
1452–3. Ludus de Kyng Robert of Cesill.
1455–6. Ludus de Sancta Clara.
1456–7. Ludus de Pater Noster.
1471–2. Ludus Corporis Christi.
1473–4. Ludus de Corporis Christi.

Canon Rock, apparently quoting the same document, also mentions a 'Ludus de Sancto Iacobo[2].'

On Dec. 13, 1521, the Corporation 'agreed that Paternoster Play shall be played this year[3].'

In 1478–80 the Chapter *Curialitates* include 'In commun' canonicorum existent' ad videndum ludum Corporis Christi in camera Iohannis Sharpe infra clausum, 17s 11d[4].'

But the Corpus Christi play, although so called, would appear not to have been played upon Corpus Christi day, but to be identical with the *visus* or 'sights' of St. Anne's day (July 26). These are mentioned almost yearly in the city minute-books of the early sixteenth century, and appear to have been cyclic and processional. They certainly included Noah's Ship, the Three Kings of Cologne, the Ascension, and the Coronation of the Virgin. The Corporation ordered them to be played; the mayor and the 'graceman,' or chief officer of the guild of Saint Anne, directed them; the guild priest gave his assistance in the preparations. In 1517 Sir Robert Denyer was appointed on condition of doing this. Garments were often borrowed from the priory and the local magnates. In 1521 Lady Powys lent a gown for one of the Maries, and the other had a crimson gown of velvet belonging to the guild. Each craft was bound under penalty to provide a pageant. In 1540 some of the crafts had broken their

[1] Wordsworth, 126.
[2] A. F. Leach, in *Furnivall Miscellany*, 223; Rock, ii. 430.
[3] Leach, loc. cit. 224.
[4] Wordsworth, 139.

pageants and were ordered to restore them. In the same year a large door was made at the late school-house that the pageants might be sent in, and 4*d.* was charged for housing every pageant, 'and Noy schippe 12d.' In 1547 the valuables of the procession were sold, but the 'gear' (i.e. the theatrical properties) still existed in 1569. During the Marian reaction in 1554 and 1555 'it was ordered that St. Anne's Gild with Corpus Christi Play shall be brought forth and played this year[1].'

The friendly relations of the Cathedral Chapter to the civic play are noteworthy. In 1469 the chapter paid the expenses of the *visus* of the Assumption given on St. Anne's day in the nave of the church. In 1483 it was similarly agreed to have 'Ludum, sive Serimonium, de Coronatione, sive Assumptione, beatae Mariae, prout consuetum fuerat, in navi dictae Ecclesiae.' This was to be played and shown in the procession to be made by the citizens on St. Anne's day. Apparently the crafts played the earlier plays of the cycle during the progress of the St. Anne's procession through the streets, and the Chapter gave the Assumption as a finale to the whole in the cathedral itself. But their interest extended beyond their own *visus.* In 1488 Robert Clarke received an appointment, because 'he is so ingenious in the show and play called the Ascension, given every year on St. Anne's Day[2].'

Under Elizabeth a new play appears. In 1564 the Corporation ordered 'that a standing [i.e. non-processional?] play of some story of the Bible shall be played two days this summertime.' The subject chosen was Tobias, and the place the Broadgate. Some of the properties, e.g. 'Hell mouth, with a nether chap,' were possibly the old 'gear' of St. Anne's guild. In 1567 'the stage-play of the story of Toby' was again played at Whitsuntide[3].

Little Baddow, Essex.

Little Baddow men hired the Chelmsford (q.v.) wardrobe during 1564–6.

London.

William Fitzstephen (†1170–82), in a description of London prefatory to his *Vita* of St. Thomas à Becket, says:—

'Lundonia pro spectaculis theatralibus, pro ludis scenicis, ludos habet

[1] Leach, loc. cit. 224; *Lincoln Statutes,* ii. ccliv; *Hist. MSS.* xiv. 8. 25.

[2] Wordsworth, 141; Leach, loc. cit. 223, from *Chapter Act Book,* A. 31, f. 18; *Shaks. Soc. Papers,* iii. 40, from copy of same document in *Harl. MS,* 6954, p. 152. The latter has 'Seremonium' (for Ceremonium). Mr. Leach reads 'Sermonium' and translates 'speech.'

[3] Leach, loc. cit. 227; *Gentleman's Magazine,* liv. 103.

sanctiores, representationes miraculorum quae sancti confessores operati sunt, seu representationes passionum quibus claruit constantia martyrum[1].'

Nothing more is heard of plays in London until 1378, when the scholars of St. Paul's petitioned Richard II,

'to prohibit some unexpert people from representing the History of the Old Testament, to the great prejudice of the said Clergy, who have been at great expence in order to represent it publickly at Christmas[2].'

The chronicler Malvern records that in 1384,—

'Vicesimo nono die Augusti clerici Londoniae apud Skynnereswelle fecerunt quendam ludum valde sumptuosum, duravitque quinque diebus[3].'

In 1391 Malvern again records,—

'Item xviij° die Iulii clerici Londonienses fecerunt ludum satis curiosum apud Skynnereswell per dies quatuor duraturum, in quo tam vetus quam novum testamentum oculariter ludendo monstrabant[4].'

In 1393, according to the *London Chronicle*, 'was the pley of seynt Katerine[5].'

Other chronicles record a play in 1409:—

'This yere was the play at Skynners Welle, whiche endured Wednesday, Thorsday, Friday, and on Soneday it was ended[6].'

The accounts of the royal wardrobe show that a scaffold of timber was built for the King (Henry IV), prince, barons, knights, and ladies on this occasion, and that the play showed,—

'how God created Heaven and Earth out of nothing, and how he created Adam and so on to the Day of Judgment[7].'

Finally, the Grey Friars Chronicle mentions a yet longer play in 1411:—

[1] J. C. Robertson, *Materials for the Hist. of Becket* (R. S.), iii. 9.

[2] Dodsley, *Collection of Old Plays* (1744), i. xii. I cannot trace the original authority.

[3] Malvern, *Continuator* to Higden's *Polychronicon* (ed. J. R. Lumby in R.S.), ix. 47.

[4] Malvern, loc. cit. ix. 259. Probably this is the play for which the Issue Roll of the Exchequer for Easter—Michaelmas, 1391 (F. Devon, *Issues of the Exchequer, Hen. III–Hen. VI*, 244), records on July 11, 1391, a payment 'to the Clerkes of the Parish Churches and to divers other clerkes of the City of London, in money paid to them in discharge of £10 which the Lord and King commanded to be paid them of his gift on account of the play of the Passion of our Lord and the Creation of the World by them performed at Skynner Well, after the Feast of Bartholomew last past.' But the dates do not quite agree, and there may have been a play at Bartholomew-tide 1390 as well as that of July, 1391.

[5] *London Chronicle*, 80.

[6] *London Chronicle*, 91. The *Cott. MS.* reads 'Clerkenwelle' for the 'Skynners Welle' of the *Harl. MS. Gregory's Chronicle* (*Hist. Coll. of a Citizen of London*, Camden Soc.), 105, also mentions 'the grette playe at Skynners Welle' in 1409.

[7] J. H. Wylie, *Hist. of Henry IV*, iv. 213.

'This year beganne a gret pley from the begynnyng of the worlde at the skynners' welle, that lastyd vij dayes contynually; and there ware the moste parte of the lordes and gentylles of Ynglond[1].'

The performers in most, if not all, of this group of plays were the clerks in minor orders who naturally abounded in London. The Guild of St. Nicholas of Parish Clerks had existed since 1233. In 1442 they received a charter, which refers to 'diversis charitatis et pietatis operibus per ipsos annuatim exhibitis et inventis[2].' These *opera* possibly include the plays, which may have become annual between 1411 and 1442. They seem to have been given at various times of year, and hard by the well, variously described as Skinners Well or Clerkenwell. The Priory of St. Bartholomew is not far, and the plays may have had some connexion, at one time or another, with the famous Bartholomew Fair[3]. It was probably the double name of the well that led Stowe to say that 'the skinners of London held there certain plays yearly, played of Holy Scripture[4].'

There is another gap of a century in the history of these greater London plays. But on July 20, 1498, Henry VII rewarded 'the pleyers of London' (Appendix E, viii), and of 1508 the annalist of Henry VII, Bernard Andrew, says:—

'Spectacula vero natalis divi Iohannis vespere longe praeclarissima hoc anno ostensa fuerunt, quemadmodum superioris mensis huiusque aliquot festis diebus pone Christi ecclesiam circa urbis pomaria divinae recitatae fuere historiae[5].'

Some of the London churches had their own plays, as may be seen from their churchwardens' accounts. Those of St. Margaret's, Southwark, have the following entries:—

'1444–5. Peid for a play vpon Seynt Lucy day [Dec. 13], and for a pley vpon Seynt Margrete day [July 20], xiij^{s} iiij^{d}.

1445–6. [Similar entry.]

1447–8. Also peid for a pley vpon Seynt Margrete day, vij^{s}.

1449–50. Item, peyd vpon Seynt Lucy day to the Clerkes for a play, vj^{s} viij^{d}.

1450–1. [Similar entry.]

1451–2. Fyrste, peyd to the Pleyrs vpon Seynt Margretes day, vij^{s}.

[1] J. G. Nichols, *Grey Friars Chronicle* (Camden Soc.), 12; R. Howlett, *Monumenta Franciscana* (R.S.), ii. 164.

[2] J. Christie, *Some Account of Parish Clerks*, 24, 71.

[3] H. Morley, *Memoirs of Bartholomew Fair*, 15.

[4] Stowe, *Survey*, 7.

[5] Andrew, *Annales Henr. VII* (R.S.), 121.

Also peyd for hyryng of Germentes xiiij^{d}.

1453-7 and 1459 [a play on St. Margaret's day in each year [1]].'

Towards the end of Henry VIII's reign the Revels office was able to borrow 'frames for pageants' from the wardens of St. Sepulchre's [2].

Probably the guild of Parish Clerks made it a profession to supply such church plays as these for a regular fee. They were employed also at the feasts of the city guilds. The Brewers, for instance, had plays in 1425 and 1433, and in 1435 paid '4 clerkis of London, for a play [3].' The Carpenters paid iiij^{s} iiij^{d} for a play in 1490 [4]. London players occasionally performed before Henry VII. Besides 'the players of London' in 1498, he rewarded in 1501 the players at 'Myles ende [5].'

Attempts were made to revive religious plays during the Marian reaction. On June 7, 1557, 'be-gane a stage play at the Grey freers of the Passyon of Cryst [6].' On St. Olave's day, July 29, in the same year 'was the church holiday in Silver street; and at eight of the clock at night began a stage play of a goodly matter, that continued until xij at mydnyght, and then they mad an end with a good song [7].'

The last such play in London was 'the acting of Christ's Passion at Elie house in Holborne when Gundemore [Gondomar] lay there, on Good-Friday at night, at which there were thousands present [8].' This would be between 1613 and 1622.

Midsummer Watch.

A 'marching watch' was kept on the eves of Midsummer and SS. Peter and Paul (June 29) until 1538, and revived, for one year only, in 1548. Some 2,000 men went in armour; lamps and bonfires were lit in the streets, and 'every man's door shadowed with green birch, long fennel, St. John's wort; orpine, white lilies and such like, garnished upon with garlands of beautiful flowers.' It seems to have been customary for the guilds to which the Lord Mayor and Sheriffs for the year belonged to furnish pageants. Stowe says that 'where the mayor had besides his giant three pageants, each of the sheriffs had besides their giants but two pageants, each their morris dance.' In

[1] Collier, in *Shakesp. Soc. Papers*, iii. 40. The 'pagents' on a roll of vellum belonging to the Holy Trinity Guild in St. Botolph's, Bishopsgate (†1463), were probably only paintings with descriptive verses (Hone, 81).

[2] Kempe, 71. The date given, Shrovetide, 38 Hen. VIII, must be wrong, as the king died before Shrovetide (Feb. 20-2) in the thirty-eighth year of his reign.

[3] Herbert, *Hist. of Livery Companies*, i. 80.

[4] E. B. Jupp, *Hist. of Carpenters' Company*, 198.

[5] Collier, i. 51.

[6] Machyn, 138.

[7] Machyn, 145.

[8] Prynne, 117.

1505 the Grocers had 'a pageant for the maire [Sir John Wyngar] at Midsomer.' In 1510 Henry VIII, disguised as a groom, came to see the Midsummer Watch, and on St. Peter's eve came openly with the queen. There were 'diverse goodlie shewes, as had beene accustomed.' In 1522 the Drapers resolved 'that there shall be no Mydsom^r pageant becaus there was so many pageants redy standyng for the Emperors coming into London,' and 'for divers considerations' to 'surcease the said pageants and find xxx men in harness instead.' But later they decided to 'renew all the old pageants for the house; including our newe pageant of the Goldyn Flees for the mayr against mydsom^r; also the gyant, lord Moryspyks, and a morys daunce, as was used the last year.' The account-books mention Lord Moryspyks or 'Marlingspikes,' and a 'king of the Moors,' with a 'stage' and 'wyld fire.' In 1523, the King of Denmark being in London, the Drapers allowed the Sheriff two pageants, 'but to be no precedent hereafter.' They paid 'for garnyshyng and newe repayring of th' Assumpcion, and also for making a new pageant of St. Ursula.' The King of Denmark was duly brought to see the watch. In 1524 they again had a pageant, the nature of which is not specified [1].

Lopham, Norfolk.

'Lopham game' was at Harling (q.v.) in 1457.

Louth, Lincolnshire.

An inventory of documents in the rood-loft in 1516 includes the 'hole Regenall of corpus xri play.' In 1558 the corporation paid for a play 'in the markit-stede on corpus xri day.'

Lydd, Kent.

The town accounts show a play of St. George on July 4, 1456, and payment to the 'bane cryars' of 'our play' in 1468. In 1422 the Lydd players acted at New Romney, and in 1490 the chaplain of the guild of St. George at New Romney went to see a play at Lydd, with a view to reproducing it. Between 1429 and 1490 the New Romney players acted often at Lydd, and also players of Ruckinge (1431), Wytesham (1441), Ham (1454), Hythe (1467), Folkestone (1479), Rye (1480), Stone (1490). Unnamed players were in the high street in 1485 [3].

Lyneham, Oxfordshire.

See s. v. Shipton.

[1] Stowe, *Annales*, 489; *Survey*, 38; Herbert, i. 197, 454; Brand-Ellis, i. 166.

[2] R. W. Goulding, *Louth Records*.

[3] *Hist. MSS.* v. 517.

MALDEN, ESSEX.

The Chelmsford (q. v.) play was shown at Malden in 1562.

MANNINGTREE, ESSEX.

John Manningham, of the Middle Temple, wrote in his Diary, on Feb. 8, 1602, 'The towne of Manitree in Essex holds by stage plays [1].' So Heywood, in his *Apology for Actors* (1612), 'To this day there be townes that hold the priviledge of their fairs and other charters by yearly stage-plays, as at Manningtree in Suffolke, Kendall in the North, and others [2].' There are further allusions to these plays in T. Nash, *The Choosing of Valentines*,

'a play of strange moralitie,
Showen by bachelrie of Manning-tree,
Whereto the countrie franklins flock-meale swarme [3]';

and in Dekker, *Seven Deadly Sins of London* (1607), 'Cruelty has got another part to play; it is acted like the old morals at Manning-tree [4].'

MAXSTOKE, WARWICKSHIRE.

The accounts of Maxstoke Priory (a house of Augustinian canons) for 1430 include, 'pro ientaculis puerorum eleemosynae exeuntium ad aulam in castro ut ibi ludum peragerent in die Purificationis, xiv[d]. Unde nihil a domini [Clinton] thesaurario, quia saepius hoc anno ministralli castri fecerunt ministralsiam in aula conventus et Prioris ad festa plurima sine ullo regardo [5].'

MIDDLETON, NORFOLK.

In 1444 the corporation of Lynn (q. v.) showed a play with Mary and Gabriel before Lord Scales [6].

MILDENHALL, SUFFOLK.

Thetford Priory made a payment to 'the play of Mydenale' in 1503-4 (Appendix E, iii).

MILE END, MIDDLESEX.

Henry VII rewarded 'the Pleyers at Myles End' on Aug. 6, 1501 (Appendix E, viii).

MILTON, OXFORDSHIRE.

See s. v. SHIPTON.

MOREBATH, DEVONSHIRE.

The churchwardens' accounts record an Easter play at some date between 1520 and 1574 [7].

[1] *Manningham's Diary* (Camden Soc.), 130.
[2] Heywood, *Apology for Actors* (Shakespeare Soc.), 61.
[3] Quoted in *Variorum*, xvi. 295.
[4] Dekker's *Plays* (ed. Pearson).
[5] Hazlitt-Warton, iii. 312.
[6] Harrod, *King's Lynn Records*, 88.
[7] W. Hobhouse, *Churchwardens' Accounts* (Somerset Record Soc.), 209.

Nayland, Essex.

Richard More, of Nayland, hired the Chelmsford (q.v.) wardrobe in 1566.

Newcastle-on-Tyne, Northumberland.

The craft-plays on Corpus Christi day are mentioned in several fifteenth-century ordinaries, the earliest being that of the Coopers in $142\frac{6}{7}$. The last years in which performances can be proved to have been given are 1561 and 1562. Ordinaries dated from 1578 to 1589 stipulate for a performance by the crafts 'whensoever the generall plaies of the town of Newcastle, antiently called the Corpus Christi plays, shall be plaied,' or the like. The determination of this point rested with the Corporation. The Goldsmiths drew up an 'invoic of all the players apperell pertainyng to' them in $159\frac{8}{9}$. The cost of the plays fell on the crafts, who took fixed contributions from their members. The Taylors in 1536 required iij[d] from each hireling, and vij[d] from each newly admitted member. The Fullers and Dyers paid 9*s.* in 1561 for 'the play lettine' to four persons.

The mentions of 'bearers of the care and baneres' of them 'that wated of the paient' and of 'the carynge of the trowt and wyn about the town' seem to show that the plays were processional. On the other hand the one extant play (cf. p. 424) ends with a remark of the *Diabolus* to 'All that is gathered in this stead.' Perhaps the pageants first took part in the Corpus Christi procession proper and afterwards gathered in a field. The Mercers' ordinary of 1480 shows that the procession was 'by vij in morning,' and the plays were certainly in the evening, for it was deposed in a law-suit at Durham in 1569 that Sir Robert Brandling of Newcastle said on Corpus Christi day, 1562, that 'he would after his dinner draw his will, and after the plays would send for his consell, and make it up' (*Norfolk Archaeology,* iii. 18).

For the list of plays, so far as it can be recovered, see p. 424. The ordinary of the Goldsmiths (1536) requires their play (Kynges of Coleyn) to be given at their feast[1].

New Romney, Kent.

There are many notices of a play in the town accounts between 1428 and 1560. In 1456 the wardens of the play of the *Resurrection* are mentioned. In 1463 the jurats paid Agnes Ford 6*s.* 8*d.* 'for the

[1] F. Holthausen, *Das Noahspiel von N. upon T.* (1897), 11; H. Bourne, *Hist. of N.* (1736), 139; J. Brand, *Hist. of N.* (1789), ii. 369; E. Mackenzie, *Hist. of N.* (1827), ii. 664, 707; F. W. Dendy, *Newcastle Gilds* (Surtees Soc.), i. 4; ii. 161, 164, 171.

play of the Interlude of our *Lord's Passion.*' From 1474 the banns of the play are mentioned. In 1477 the play was on Whit-Tuesday. In 1518 the Lord Warden of the Cinque Ports forbade the play, but it was revived elaborately in 1560. The accounts mention the purchase of copes and vestures from the corporation of Lydd, and refer to 'a fool,' 'the Cytye of Samarye,' 'our last play,' 'the iij^th^ play,' 'the iiij^th^ play,' and the 'bane cryers.' No crafts are mentioned: perhaps the play was produced by the corporation itself. The performances may have been on Crockhill or Crockley Green. 'Playstool' is a common name for a bit of land in Kent. Performances were often given in other towns: see s.v. Lydd. The play seems to have been only a *Passion* and *Resurrection* play, and not a complete cycle. 'Le Playboke' is mentioned from 1516. It is in an Elizabethan inventory of town records. A second play of *St. George* was probably started in 1490 when a chaplain of the guild of St. George went to see the Lydd *St. George* play, with a view to reproducing it. In 1497 the chaplains received the profits of the play. Players from the following towns are found acting at New Romney: Hythe (1399), Lydd (1422), Wittersham (1426, they 'shewed th' interlude'), Herne (1429), Ruckinge (1430), Folkestone (1474), Appledore (1488), Chart (1489), Rye (1489), Wye (1491), Brookland (1494), Halden (1499), Bethersden (1508)[1].

Northampton, Northamptonshire.

Brotanek (*Anglia*, xxi. 21) conjectures that the *Abraham and Isaac* of the Dublin MS. may come from Northampton (cf. p. 427), and hints at an explanation of the 'N. towne' in the prologue to the *Ludus Coventriae* as 'N[orthampton] towne' (cf. p. 421).

But the only allusion even remotely suggesting miracle-plays that I can find in the printed civic records is in 1581, in which year some interrogatories as to St. George's Hall contain a deposition by an old man to the effect that he had known the hall fifty years, and that the mayor and chamberlains had been wont to lay therein pageants, &c.[2]

Norwich, Norfolk.

Whitsun Plays.

J. Whetley writes from Norwich on Corpus Christi even (May 20), 1478, to Sir John Paston in London, of a visit of Lord Suffolk to Hellesden, 'at hys beyng ther that daye ther was never no man that

[1] W. A. Scott-Robertson, *The Passion Play and Interludes at New Romney* (*Archaeologia Cantiana*, xiii. 216); *Hist. MSS.* v. 533; *Arch. Cantiana*, xvii. 28.

[2] C. A. Markham and J. C. Cox, *Northampton Borough Records*, ii. 184.

playd Herrod in Corpus Crysty play better and more agreable to hys pageaunt than he dud[1].'

I do not know whether it is fair to infer from this that in 1478 the Norwich plays were not at Whitsuntide, but at Corpus Christi; but this would account for J. Whetley's trope.

On Sept. 21, 1527, the guild of St. Luke, composed of painters, braziers, plumbers, &c., made a presentment to the Assembly of the town that,—

'where of longtime paste the said Guylde of Seynt Luke yerly till nowe hath ben used to be kept and holden within the citie aforesaid upon the Mundaye in pentecoste weke at which daye and the daye next ensuyng many and divers disgisyngs and pageaunts, as well of the lieffs and martyrdoms of divers and many hooly Saynts, as also many other light and feyned figurs and picturs of other persones and bests; the sight of which disgisings and pageaunts, as well yerly on the said Mondaye in pentecoste weke in the time of procession then goyng about a grett circuitte of the forsaid citie, as yerly the Tuysday in the same weke [serving] the lord named the Lord of Misrule at Tumlond within the same citie, hath ben and yet is sore coveted, specially by the people of the countre.'

The presentment goes on to show that much resort and profit have accrued to the city, but all the cost has fallen on the guild, which 'is almost fully decayed'; and urges an order,—

'that every occupacion wythyn the seyd Citye maye yerly at the said procession upon the Mondaye in Pentecost weke sette forth one pageaunt.'

It was agreed that each craft should play,—

'one such pageaunt as shalbe assigned and appoynted by Master Mair and his brethern aldermen, as more playnly appereth in a boke thereof made.

In the same hand is a list of crafts and plays (cf. p. 425)[2].

Some extracts made in the eighteenth century from the, now lost, books of the Grocers' Company, contain (*a*) two versions of their play on *The Fall*, dating from 1533 and 1565 respectively (cf. p. 425), and (*b*) various notices of the same from the Assembly Book.

The latter begin in 1534, when '4 Surveyors of yᵉ Pageant' with a 'Bedell' were chosen, and an assessment of 22*s.* 10*d.* made for the pageant and the Corpus Christi procession. The expenses include, besides repairs to the pageant, fees to actors, refreshments, &c.,—

[1] *Paston Letters*, iii. 227.

[2] H. Harrod, *Particulars concerning Early Norwich Pageants* (*Norfolk Archaeology*, iii. 3).

'It. to Sr Stephen Prowet for makyng of a newe ballet, 12^{d}.

House ferme for ye Pageant, 2^{s}.'

The pageant went in 1535 and 1536. In 1537 it 'went not at Wytsontyde,' but went in October 'in ye Processyon for ye Byrthe of Prynce Edward.' From 1538 to 1546 it went, the assessment for pageant and procession being about 20*s*. to 30*s*. As to 1547 the record is not clear. Then there is a gap in the extracts, and from 1556 onwards the 'Gryffon,' 'Angell,' and 'Pendon' of the Corpus Christi procession, with flowers, grocery, and fruit 'to garnish ye tre wth,' &c., appear alone in the accounts. In 1559 was 'no solemnite' at all. In 1563 it was agreed that the pageant should be 'preparyd ageynst ye daye of Mr Davy his takyng of his charge of ye Mayralltye,' with a 'devyce' to be prepared by the surveyors at a cost of 6*s*. 8*d*. The play cannot have quite lapsed, for in 1565 a new version was written (cf. p. 425). It was apparently contemplated that it might be played either alone or in a cycle. To the same year belongs the following

'*Inventory of ye p'ticulars appartaynyng to ye Company of ye Grocers, a.d. 1565.*

A Pageant, y^{t} is to saye, a Howse of Waynskott paynted and buylded on a Carte w^{t} fowre whelys.

A square topp to sett over ye sayde Howse.

A Gryffon, gylte, w^{t} a fane to sette on ye sayde toppe.

A bygger Iron fane to sett on ye ende of ye Pageante.

iiij^{xx} iij small Fanes belongyng to ye same Pageante.

A Rybbe colleryd Red.

A cote & hosen w^{t} a bagg & capp for dolo^{r}, steyned.

2 cotes & a payre hosen for Eve, stayned.

A cote & hosen for Adam, Steyned.

A cote w^{t} hosen & tayle for ye serpente, steyned, w^{t} a w^{t} heare.

A cote of yellow buckram w^{t} ye Grocers' arms for ye Pendon bearer.

An Angell's Cote & over hoses of Apis Skynns.

3 paynted clothes to hang abowte ye Pageant.

A face & heare for ye Father.

2 hearys for Adam & Eve.

4 head stallis of brode Inkle wth knopps & tassells.

6 Horsse Clothes, stayned, w^{t} knopps & tassells.

Item, Weights, &c.'

There is a final memorandum that in 1570 the pageant was broken to pieces for six years 'howse ferm' due. There had been no 'semblye nor metynge' of the Company for eight years. The pageant had stood for six years in a 'Gate howse,' and then 'at ye Black Fryers brydge in open strete,' where it became 'so weather beaten, y^t ye cheife parte was rotton[1].'

Processions.

There were three notable annual processions at Norwich.

(*a*) The *Corpus Christi* Procession, in which the crafts were held to take part in 1489, and which appears, as above stated, in the Grocers' records until 1558. They seem to have been represented by the 'griffon' from the top of their pageant, a banner with their arms, a crowned angel, and an emblematic 'tree' of fruit and grocery (possibly the 'tree of knowledge')[2].

(*b*) The Procession of the Guild of *S. Thomas à Becket* on the day of his Translation (July 7) to his chapel in the wood. Here interludes were played[3].

(*c*) The Riding of the Guild of *St. George* on his day (April 23). This dates from at least 1408, and a good many details as to it are preserved[4].

NUNEATON, WARWICKSHIRE.

The 'lusores de Eaton' played at Maxstoke Priory between 1422 and 1461 (Appendix E, ii).

OXFORD, OXFORDSHIRE.

The following extracts from the Bursars' *computi* of Magdalen College point to a *Quem quaeritis* of the longer type, with the 'Noli me tangere' episode.

1486–7. 'pro factura sepulturae erga pascham. xij^d.'

1506–7. 'pro scriptura lusi' of St. Mary Magdalen. x^d.'

[There were further payments in connexion with this play, and for music.]

1509–10. 'pro pane, cibo et aliis datis pueris ludentibus in die Paschae . . . $xvij^d$ ob.'

1514–5. 'pro carnibus consumptis in capella tribus noctibus ante Pascha et in tempore Nativitatis. ij^s.'

1518–9. 'pro tinctura et factura tunicae eius qui ageret partem Christi et pro crinibus mulieribus. ij^s vj^d.'

1536–7. 'pro carbonibus consumptis in sacrario per custodes sepulchri, et per pueros in festis hiemalibus.'

[Repeated in other years.]

[1] R. Fitch, *Norwich Pageants: The Grocers' Play*, in *Norfolk Archaeology*, v. 8, and separately.

[2] Fitch, op. cit.; Blomfield, *Hist. of Norfolk*, iii. 176.

[3] Blomfield, iv. 426.

[4] Cf. vol. i. p. 222.

A chapel inventory of 1495 includes 'unum frontale . . . et unum dorsale cum quibus solet sepulcrum ornari.'

The same accounts (cf. p. 248) show items for plays in the hall at various seasons, and for the Boy Bishop at Christmas [1].

The churchwardens of St. Peter's in the East kept between 1444 and 1600 a stock of players' garments, and let them out on hire [2].

PENRHYN, CORNWALL.

See *Texts* (i), *Cornish Plays, Origo Mundi.*

PERRANZABULO, CORNWALL.

The earliest historical notice of plays in Cornwall is by Richard Carew in 1602 :—

'The Guary miracle, in English, a miracle-play, is a kinde of Enterlude, compiled in *Cornish* out of some Scripture history, with that grossenes which accompanied the Romanes *vetus Comoedia.* For representing it they raise an earthen Amphitheatre in some open field, hauing the Diameter of his enclosed playne some 40 or 50 foot. The Country people flock from all sides, many miles off, to hear and see it: for they haue therein, deuils and deuices, to delight as well the eye as the eare; the players conne not their parts without booke, but are prompted by one called the Ordinary, who followeth at their back with the book in his hand, and telleth them softly what they must pronounce aloud.'

Whereupon Carew has a story of a 'pleasant conceyted gentleman' who raised laughter by repeating aloud all the Ordinary's asides to himself.

One Mr. Scawen (†1660) describes the Guirremears as—

'solemnized not without shew of devotion in open and spacious downs, of great capacity, encompassed about with earthen banks, and in some part stonework of largeness to contain thousands, the shapes of which remain in many places to this day, though the use of them long since gone.'

Bp. Nicholson, writing in 1700, says that the plays were :—

'called Guirimir, which Mr Llhuyd supposes a corruption of Guarimirkle, and in the Cornish dialect to signify a miraculous play or interlude. They were composed for begetting in the common people a right notion of the Scriptures, and were acted in the memory of some not long since deceased.'

The eighteenth-century antiquary, Borlase, identifies the places in

[1] Cf. Appendix E (v).

[2] W. Hobhouse, *Churchwardens' Accounts* (Somerset Record Soc.), 232.

which the miracle-plays were given with those known as 'rounds,' or, in Cornish, *plân an guare*. Of these he describes and figures two. That of St. Just was of stone, 126 feet in diameter, with seven rows of seats inside. It was much decayed when Norris wrote in 1859. That of Perranzabulo, or Piran-sand, was of earth, 130 feet in diameter, with a curious pit in the centre, joined to the outer ring by a narrow trench. Borlase thought that this was used for a Hell[1]. It was more likely filled with water for Noah's ship to float upon.

The *Ordinalia* printed by Mr. Norris take the Cornish plays back to at least the fourteenth, if not the thirteenth century. The circular diagrams in the manuscript exactly fall in with the round *plân an guare* described by Borlase and others. They show a ring of eight *loci* or *sedes* (cf. p. 83), for which the terms used in the stage-directions are *pulpita* or *tenti*, with an open circular space in the middle, which the stage-directions call the *platea*. The action is partly at the *pulpita*, partly in the *platea*. A new character often marks his appearance by strutting about his *pulpitum*, or perhaps around the ring—*Hic pompabit Abraham*, &c.

In the English stage-directions to the later (before 1611) *Creation of the World*, the *platea* becomes the *playne*, and for *pulpitum* the term *room* is used. The manager of the play is the 'conveyour.' Some of the directions are curious and minute. At the opening, 'The father must be in a clowde, and when he speakethe of heaven let yᵉ levys open.' Within is a 'trone,' which Lucifer tries to ascend. After the fight, 'Lucifer voydeth & goeth downe to hell apareled fowle wᵗʰ fyre about hem turning to hell and every degre of devylls of lether & spirytis on cordis runing into yᵉ playne and so remayne ther.' Meanwhile are got ready 'Adam and Eva aparlet in whytt lether in a place apoynted by the conveyour & not to be sene tyll they be called & thei knell & ryse.' Paradise has 'ii fayre trees in yt' and a 'fowntaine' and 'fyne flowers,' which appear suddenly. Similarly, a little later, 'Let fyshe of dyuers sortis apeare & serten beastis as oxen kyne shepe & such like.' Lucifer incarnates as 'a fyne serpent made wᵗʰ a virgyn face & yolowe heare vpon her head.' Presently comes the warning, 'ffig leaves redy to cover ther members,' and at the expulsion, 'The garmentis of skynnes to be geven to adam and eva by the angell. Receave the garmentis. Let them depart out of paradice and adam and eva following them. Let them put on the garmentis and shewe a spyndell and a dystaff.' The Cain and Abel scene requires 'a

[1] Norris, ii. 452; E. H. Pedler in Norris, ii. 507; Carew, *Survey of Cornwall*; D. Gilbert, *History of Cornwall*; Borlase, *Antiquities of Cornwall* (ed. 2), 207; *Nat. Hist. of Cornwall*, 295; T. F. Ordish, *Early London Theatres*, 15.

chawbone' ('Cain's jawbone, that did the first murder'). Seth is led to Paradise and 'Ther he vyseth all thingis, and seeth ij trees and in the one tree sytteth mary the virgyn & in her lappe her son jesus in the tope of the tree of lyf, and in the other tree ye serpent wch caused Eva to eat the appell.' When Adam dies, his soul is taken 'to lymbo,' and he is buried 'in a fayre tombe wth som churche songis at hys buryall.' The Noah scene requires 'tooles and tymber redy, wth planckis to make the arcke, a beam a mallet a calkyn yre[n] ropes mass[t]es pyche and tarr.' Presently 'let rayne appeare' and 'a raven & a culver ready.' When the flood ends, 'An alter redy veary fayre,' at which 'som good church songes' are sung, and 'a Rayne bowe to appeare.' Like the earlier plays, this ends with a call on the minstrels to pipe for a dance.

A study of the place names in the *Ordinalia* led Mr. Pedler to suggest that they probably belonged to the neighbourhood of Penrhyn, and may have been composed at the collegiate house of Glasney. The St. Meriasek play is assigned by Mr. Stokes to Camborne, of which that saint was patron. It ends with an invocation of St. Meriasek, St. Mary of Camborne, and the Apostles.

Preston, Lancashire.

A Corpus Christi play was acted within the lifetime of Weever, who was born 1576 and wrote 1631[1].

I find no trace of plays at the meetings of the Guild Merchant, although there was always a great procession, which from 1762 or earlier included such allegorical figures as Adam and Eve for the Tailors, Vulcan for the Smiths, &c.[2]

Reading, Berkshire.

The churchwardens' accounts of St. Lawrence's record 'a gaderyng of a stage-play' in 1498.

In 1507 a play of *Adam and Eve* was held on 'the Sonday afore Bartylmastyde' 'in the Forbury.' There was a 'schapfold,' but 'pagentts' were also used. A Corpus Christi procession is also mentioned in 1509, 1512, and 1539.

In 1512 also was the 'play of Kayme,' and in 1515, 'Cayme's pageaunt' in the market-place.

On May 1, 1499, and again in 1539, was the *Kings of Cologne*. This was distinct, no doubt, from the 'king play,' with its 'tree,' 'king

[1] See s. v. Kendal.

[2] W. A. Abram, *Memorials of the Preston Guilds*, 18, 21, 61, 99.

game,' or 'kyng ale,' which took place at Whitsuntide (cf. vol. i. p. 173). But the date, May 1 (for which cf. Abingdon), is curious for a miracle-play, and must have been influenced by the folk feast.

A payment for 'rosyn to the resurrecyon pley' (possibly for making a blaze: cf. p. 23, note 5) occurs in 1507, and in 1533–5 payments to 'Mr Laborne' 'for reforming the Resurrecon pley,' and 'for a boke' of it.

In 1508 was a 'pageaunt of the Passion on Easter Monday[1].'

Ruckinge, Kent.

Ruckinge players were at New Romney in 1430, and Lydd in 1431.

Rye, Sussex.

Rye players were at Lydd in 1480, and at New Romney in 1489.

Sabsford (?), Essex.

'Sabsforde men' hired the Chelmsford (q. v.) wardrobe in 1562, 1563, and 1566. But I can find no such place.

Saffron Walden, Essex.

'Men of Waldyne' hired the Chelmsford (q. v.) wardrobe during 1564–6.

St. Just, Cornwall.

See s. v. Perranzabulo.

Salisbury, Wiltshire.

A cathedral inventory of 1222 includes:—

'Coronae ij de latone ad representationes faciendas.'

These latten 'coronae' may, I suppose, have been either crowns for the Magi, or 'stellae[2].'

The churchwardens' accounts of St. Edmund's for 1461 include an item 'for all apparel and furniture of players at the Corpus Christi[3].'

Shelfhanger, Norfolk.

Thetford Priory made a payment 'in regard to Schelfanger play' in 1507–8 (Appendix E, iii).

[1] C. Kerry, *History of St. Lawrence, Reading*, 233. Extracts only from the accounts are given; a full transcript would probably yield more information.

[2] W. H. R. Jones, *Vetus Registrum Sarisburiense* (R.S.), ii. 129.

[3] *Cal. State Papers, Dom. Addl.* (1580–1625), 101.

Shipton, Oxfordshire.

It was decided († 1220–28), as part of an award concerning the rights of collation to the churches of Shipton and Bricklesworth, both being prebends in Sarum cathedral, as follows:—

'Actiones autem, si quae competant, in villa de Fifhide et de Idebire cedant canonico de Brikeleswrth. Actiones vero, si quae competant, in villa de Mideltone et de Langele, cedant canonico de Schiptone. Emolumentum vero actionum, si quae competant, in villa de Linham aequaliter inter se dividant[1].'

The editor of the *Sarum Charters* can only explain *actiones* as 'plays.' Ducange gives the word in the sense of *spectacula*.

All the places named, Fyfield, Idbury, Milton, Langley, and Lyneham, are in Wychwood, and may have formed in the thirteenth century, if they do not all now, part of the parish of Shipton-under-Wychwood.

Shrewsbury, Shropshire.

The civic orders and accounts refer occasionally to plays. The first on record was given before Prince Arthur in 1495. In 1516 the abbot of Shrewsbury, in 1533 the bishop of Exeter, and in 1542 the royal commissioners were present. The subject in 1516 was the martyrdoms of Saints Feliciana and Sabina. In 1518 it was the Three Kings of Cologne. In 1510, 1518, 1533, 1553, and 1556 the performances were at Whitsuntide. The bailiffs, according to a notice in 1556, 'set forward' the plays, and the 'lusores' belonging to the town, who are mentioned in 1527 and 1549, were perhaps the performers. The locality was, in 1542, the churchyard of St. Chad's. In 1495, 1516, and 1533 it was the quarry outside the walls, where it is stated in 1570 that 'the plases have bin accustomyd to be usyd[2].' Here there were traces of a seated amphitheatre as late as 1779[3]. Thomas Ashton became master of the free school in 1561, and he produced plays in the quarry. Elizabeth was to have been at his *Julian the Apostate* in 1565, but came too late. In 1567 he gave the *Passion of Christ*[4]. An undated list of Costs for the Play includes 'a desert's (*disard's*) hed and berd,' 'vi dossen belles' for a morris, 'gonne poudo^r' and other attractions for a devil[5].

Shrewsbury Show.

The craft-guilds took part in the Corpus Christi procession, and

[1] Jones and Macray, *Salisbury Charters* (R.S.), xi, 102.
[2] Cf. Appendix E (vi).
[3] Phillips, *Hist. of Shrewsbury*, 201.
[4] Phillips, 201.
[5] Owen and Blakeway, *Hist. of Shrewsbury*, i. 328.

the guild of Mercers inflicted a penalty of 12*d.* on brethren who on that feast should 'happen to ride or goe to Coventre Faire or elleswhere out of the town of Shrewesburye to by or sell[1].' Until about 1880 Shrewsbury Show was held on the Monday after Corpus Christi day. The crafts had tableaux which, after the Reformation at least, were emblematic rather than religious[2]; thus—

Tailors. Adam and Eve or Elizabeth.
Shearmen. St. Blasius or Edward IV.
Skinners and Glovers. King of Morocco.
Smiths. Vulcan.
Painters. Rubens.
Bricklayers. King Henry VIII.
Shoemakers. SS. Crispin and Crispinian.
Barbers. St. Katharine.
Bakers. Venus and Ceres.

SLEAFORD, LINCOLNSHIRE.

The accounts of the guild of Holy Trinity for 1480 include:—

'It. payd for the Ryginall of ye play for ye Ascencon & the wrytyng of spechys & payntyng of a garmet for god, iij^{s}. viij^{d}.[3]'

Miss Toulmin Smith finds in the same accounts for 1477, a 'kyngyng,' i. e. *Three Kings of Cologne* on Corpus Christi day[4]; but I read the entry:—

'It. payd for the ryngyng of ye same day, ij^{d}.'

Oliver, the historian of the guild, reads 'hymnall' for 'Ryginall' in the 1480 entry. He also asserts that there was a regular Corpus Christi play by the crafts. This seems improbable in a place of the size of Sleaford, and in fact Oliver's elaborate description is entirely based upon data from elsewhere, especially the *Gubernacio Ludi* of Beverley (cf. p. 340)[5].

STAPLEFORD, ESSEX.

'Men of Starford' hired the Chelmsford (q.v.) wardrobe during 1564–6. I find no Starford, but a Stapleford Tawney and a Stapleford Abbots in Essex.

STOKE BY NAYLAND, ESSEX.

Sir John Howard 'ȝafe to the pleyeres of Stoke, ij^{s}' on Jan. 12, 1466.

Lord Howard 'paid to the pleirs of Turton Strete xx^{d}' on Aug. 29,

[1] *Shropshire Arch. Soc. Trans.* viii. 273.

[2] F. A. Hibbert, *Influence and Development of English Craft Guilds* (1891), 113.

[3] *Add. MS.* 28,533, ff. 1^{v}, 2. *Computi* from 1477 to 1545 are in this MS.; but most of them are very summary.

[4] *York Plays*, lxv.

[5] G. Oliver, *Hist. of Holy Trinity Guild at Sleaford* (1837), 50, 68, 73, 82.

1481. Thorington is still the name given to part of Stoke. There is also an independent township so named in Essex.

On May 22, 1482, Lord Howard 'yaff to the cherche on Whitson Monday at the pley x^{s}.'

On Jan. 2, 1491, the Earl of Surrey paid iij^{s} $iiij^{d}$ 'in reward to the panget' [? pageant][1].

Stone, Kent.

Stone players were at Lydd in 1490.

Tewkesbury, Gloucestershire.

The churchwardens' accounts in 1578 mention payments for 'the players' geers, six sheep-skins for Christ's garments'; and an inventory of 1585 includes 'eight heads of hair for the Apostles, and ten beards, and a face or vizier for the Devil[2].'

Tintinhull, Somerset.

The churchwardens' accounts for 1451–2 include a receipt:—
'de incremento unius ludi vocati Christmasse play[3].'

Wakefield, Yorkshire.

See *Texts* (i), *Towneley Plays*.

Wimborne Minster, Dorsetshire.

Players of 'Wymborne Minster' were rewarded by Henry VII on Jan. 1, 1494 (Appendix E, viii).

Winchester, Hampshire.

The early use of the *Quem quaeritis* in the liturgy of the cathedral served by the Benedictines of St. Swithin's Priory has been fully discussed in Chapter xviii and Appendix O.

In 1486, Henry VII was entertained at dinner on a Sunday in the castle with a performance of *Christi descensus ad inferos* by the 'pueri eleemosynarii' of the monasteries of St. Swithin's and Hyde[4].

Windsor, Berks.

On May 24, 1416, Henry V invested the Emperor Sigismund with the Garter, the annual feast being deferred from April 23 for that purpose. Mr. John Payne Collier says, 'A chronicle in the Cottonian

[1] Cf. Appendix E (vii).

[2] Collier, ii. 67.

[3] Hobhouse, 184.

[4] Hazlitt-Warton, iii. 163, from *Register* of St. Swithin's. This is amongst the *Wulvesey MSS.*, now in the possession of the Ecclesiastical Commissioners (*York Plays*, lxv). The date is given as 1487 by Hazlitt-Warton, but the visit is said to be that 'on occasion of the birth of Prince Arthur,' which took place in the autumn of 1486.

collection gives a description of a performance before him and Henry V, on the incidents of the life of St. George. The representation seems to have been divided into three parts, and to have been accomplished by certain artificial contrivances, exhibiting, first, "the armyng of Seint George, and an Angel doyng on his spores [spurs]"; secondly, "Seint George riding and fightyng with the dragon, with his spere in his hand"; and, thirdly, "a castel, and Seint George and the Kynges daughter ledyng the lambe in at the castel gates." Here we have clearly the outline of the history of St. George of Cappadocia, which often formed the subject of a miracle-play; but whether, in this instance, it was accompanied with dialogue, or was (as is most probable) merely a splendid dumb show, assisted by temporary erections of castles, &c., we are not informed.' This performance is accepted from Collier, i. 29, by Ward, i. 50, Pollard, xx, and other distinguished writers. They ought to have known him better. The authority he quotes, *Cotton. MS. Calig. B. II*, is wrong. But in *Cotton. MS. Julius B. I*, one of the MSS. of the *London Chronicle*, is the following passage, 'And the first sotelte was our lady armyng seint George, and an angel doyng on his spores; the ij[de] sotelte was seint George ridyng and fightyng with the dragon, with his spere in his hand; the iij[de] sotelte was a castel, and seint George, and the kynges doughter ledynge the lambe in at the castel gates. And all these sotelties were served to the emperor, and to the kyng, and no ferther: and other lordes were served with other sotelties after theire degrees[1].' The representation, then, was in cake or marchpane. The term 'soteltie' is surely not uncommon[2]. But it has led a French scholar into another curious mistake. According to M. E. Picot 'La sotelty paraît n'avoir été qu'une simple farce, comme la sotternie néerlandaise[3].' A mumming by Lydgate in 1429–30 seems to have introduced a 'miracle' of St. Clotilda and the Holy Ampulla (cf. vol. i. p. 397).

Witham, Essex.

'Barnaby Riche of Witham' hired the Chelmsford (q. v.) wardrobe in 1566.

Wittersham, Kent.

Wittersham players were at New Romney in 1426 and Lydd in 1441.

Woodham Walter, Essex.

'Mrs. Higham of Woodham Walter' hired the Chelmsford (q.v.) wardrobe in 1570–2.

[1] *London Chronicle*, 159.

[2] Cf. e.g. *Durham Accounts*, i. 95, 101, 105 'Soteltez . . . Sutiltez . . . Suttelties erga Natale.'

[3] E. Picot, in *Romania*, vii. 245.

Woodkirk, Yorkshire.

See *Texts*, (i) *Towneley Plays*.

Worcester, Worcestershire.

A cathedral inventory of 1576 includes:—

'players gere

A gowne of freres gyrdles. A woman's gowne. A Ks cloke of Tysshew. A Jerkyn and a payer of breches. A lytill cloke of tysshew. A gowne of silk. A Jerkyn of greene, 2 cappes, and the devils apparell[1].'

There was a Corpus Christi play, mentioned in 1467 and 1559. It consisted of five pageants, maintained by the crafts, and was held yearly, if the corporation so decided. In 1584 a lease of the 'vacant place where the pagantes do stand' was granted for building, and there was a building known as the 'Pageant House' until 1738[2].

Wrexham, Denbighshire.

The corporation of Shrewsbury saw a play by 'quibusdam interlusoribus de Wrexam' in 1540 (Appendix E, vi).

Writtle, Essex.

'Parker of Writtell' twice hired the Chelmsford (q. v.) wardrobe during 1570–2. See also p. 184, n. 2.

Wycombe, Buckinghamshire.

Henry VII rewarded players of Wycombe on Dec. 31, 1494 (Appendix E, viii).

Wye, Kent.

Wye players were at New Romney in 1491.

Wymondham, Norfolk.

An account of the 'husbands for the wache and play of Wymondham,' made up to June, 1538, includes payments for 'the play,' 'devyls shoes,' 'the giant,' a man 'in armour,' 'the revels and dances[3].' It was at this play on July 1, 1549, that Kett's rebellion broke out. According to Alexander Neville, the 'ludi ac spectacula . . . antiquitus ita instituta' lasted two days and nights; according to Holinshed, 'one day and one night at least[4].'

[1] *Hist. MSS.* xiv. 8, 187.

[2] Halliwell-Phillipps, i. 342; Toulmin Smith, *Ordinances of Worcester* in *English Guilds*, 385, 407 (E. E. T. S.).

[3] *Norfolk Archaeology*, ix. 145; xi. 346.

[4] A. Nevyllus, *De furoribus Norfolciensium Ketto Duce* (1575), i. 18; Holinshed (1587), iii. 1028.

YARMOUTH, NORFOLK.

The churchwardens' accounts of St. Nicholas's contain items between 1462 and 1512 for 'making a new star,' 'leading the star,' 'a new balk line to the star and ryving the same star.' In 1473 and 1486 are mentioned plays on Corpus Christi day; in 1489, a play at Bartholomew tide; in 1493, a game played on Christmas day[1].

YORK, YORKSHIRE.

[*Authorities.*—The chief are R. Davies, *Municipal Records of the City of York* (1843); L. Toulmin Smith, *York Plays* (1885). From one or other of these all statements below, of which the authority is not given, are taken. The municipal documents used are enumerated in *York Plays*, ix. The earliest date from 1371. F. Drake, *Eboracum* (1736); R. H. Skaife, *Guild of Corpus Christi* (Surtees Soc.); H. T. Riley, in *Hist. MSS. Comm.* i. 109; M. Sellers, *City of York in the Sixteenth Century*, in *Eng. Hist. Rev.* ix. 275; and some craft-guild documents in *Archaeological Review*, i. 221; *Antiquary*, xi. 107; xxii. 266; xxiii. 27, may also be consulted.]

Liturgical Plays.

The traditional *Statutes* of York Cathedral, supposed to date in their present form from about 1255, provide for the *Pastores* and the *Stella*.

'Item inueniet [thesaurarius] stellas cum omnibus ad illas pertinentibus, praeter cirpos, quos inueniet Episcopus Puerorum futurorum [? fatuorum], vnam in nocte natalis Domini pro pastoribus, et ij^as in nocte Epiphaniae, si debeat fieri presentacio iij^um regum[2].'

Corpus Christi Plays.

The first mention is in 1378, when part of a fine levied on the Bakers is assigned 'a la pagine des ditz Pestours de corpore cristi.' In 1394 a civic order required all the pageants to play in the places 'antiquitus assignatis,' in accordance with the proclamation, and under penalty of a fine. In 1397 Richard II was present to view the plays. In 1415 the town clerk, Roger Burton, entered in the *Liber Memorandorum* a copy of the *Ordo paginarum ludi Corporis Christi*, which was a schedule of the crafts and their plays, together with the *Proclamacio ludi corporis cristi facienda in vigilia corporis cristi*. At this date the plays were given *annuatim*. About 1440 the existing manuscript of the plays was probably written. It was a 'register,' drawn up from the 'regynalls' or 'origenalls' in the possession of the several crafts, and kept by the city[3]. Halfway

[1] L. G. Bolingbroke, in *Norfolk Archaeology*, xi. 334.

[2] *Lincoln Statutes*, ii. 98; cf. *Use of Sarum*, i. xxii*.

[3] Cf. p. 409.

through the sixteenth century performances become irregular. In 1535 the Creed play, in 1558 the Paternoster play was given instead. In 1548 'certen pagyauntes . . . that is to say, the deyng of our lady, the assumption of our lady, and the coronacion of our lady,' were cast out. In 1550 and 1552 the play was suppressed on account of the plague, half the 'pageant silver' in 1552 being given to the sick. In 1562 the corporation attempted in vain to defer it to St. Barnabas day. In 1564, 1565, and 1566 it was not given, on account of war and sickness. In 1568 there was a dispute as to whether it should be played, and it was ordered that it must be 'perused and otherwaise amended' first. In 1569 it was given on Whit-Tuesday. It then seems to have lain dormant until 1579, when the Council made an order that it should be played but 'first the booke shalbe caried to my Lord Archebisshop [Edwin Sandys] and Mr. Deane [Mathew Hutton] to correcte, if that my Lord Archebisshop doo well like theron.' Various notes upon the 'register,' addressed to a 'Doctor,' and indicating that this or that play had been revised, were probably written at this time. In 1580 the citizens petitioned for the play, and the mayor replied that the request would be considered. There is no proof that any performance took place after this date; although the Bakers were still choosing 'pageant-masters' in 1656[1].

The ordering of the plays about 1415 was as follows: Yearly in the first or second week in Lent, the town clerk copied the 'sedulae paginarum' from the *Ordo* in the *Liber Memorandorum* and delivered it to the crafts 'per vj servientes maioris ad clavam.' On the eve of Corpus Christi a proclamation of mayor and sheriffs forbade 'distorbaunce of the kynges pees, and ye play, or hynderyng of ye processioun of Corpore Christi.' It went on to direct that the pageants must be played at the assigned places, that the men of the crafts are to come forth in customary array and manner, 'careynge tapers of ye pagentz,' that there shall be provided 'good players, well arayed and openly spekyng,' and that all shall be ready to start 'at the mydhowre betwix iiijth and vth of the cloke in the mornynge, and then all oyer pageantz fast followyng ilk one after oyer as yer course is, without tarieng.' Fines are imposed for any neglect or failure. At this date the play and the Corpus Christi procession were on the same day. In 1426 it is recorded that a Franciscan preacher, William Melton, while commending the play, 'affirmando quod bonus erat in se et laudabilis valde,' urged that it should be put on the day

[1] *York Plays*, xxxv, xli; *Arch. Review*, i. 221.

before Corpus Christi, so as not to interfere with the ecclesiastical feast[1]. This seems to have been agreed to, but the arrangement did not last. The procession was under the management of a Corpus Christi guild, founded in 1408, and the statutes of this guild dated in 1477 show that it was then the procession which was displaced, falling on the Friday after Corpus Christi day[2].

Thus the plays were essentially the affair of the whole community, and the control of them by the mayor and council may be further illustrated. In 1476 the council made an order regulating the choice of actors, and laid down—

'That yerely in the tyme of lentyn there shall be called afore the maire for the tyme beyng iiij of the moste connyng discrete and able players within this Citie, to serche, here, and examen all the plaiers and plaies and pagentes thrughoute all the artificers belonging to Corpus X^ti^ Plaie. And all suche as thay shall fynde sufficiant in personne and connyng, to the honour of the Citie and worship of the saide Craftes, for to admitte and able; and all other insufficiant personnes, either in connyng, voice, or personne to discharge, ammove, and avoide. And that no plaier that shall plaie in the saide Corpus X^ti^ plaie be conducte and reteyned to plaie but twise on the day of the saide playe; and that he or thay so plaing plaie not ouere twise the saide day, vpon payne of xl^s^ to forfet vnto the chaumbre as often tymes as he or thay shall be founden defautie in the same.'

By 'twise' is probably meant 'in two distinct pageants'; for each pageant repeated its performance at several stations. In 1394 these stations were 'antiquitus assignatis.' In 1399 the commons petitioned the council to the effect that 'le juer et les pagentz de la jour de corpore cristi' were not properly performed on account of the number of stations, and these were limited to twelve. In later years there were from twelve to sixteen, and from 1417 the corporation made a profit by letting to prominent citizens the right to have stations opposite their houses. A list of 'Leases for Corpuscrysty Play' in 1554, for instance, shows twelve stations bringing in from xiij^d^ to iij^s^ iiij^d^ each, while nothing was charged for the places 'at the Trinitie yaits where the clerke kepys the register,' 'at the comon Hall to my Lord Maior and his bredren,' 'at Mr. Bekwyth's at

[1] Drake, *Eboracum*, App. xxix; Davies, 243; *York Plays*, xxxiv. Melton is called 'sacrae paginae professor,' which Drake and many light-hearted scholars after him, down to A. W. Ward (ed. 2, 1899), i. 53, translate 'professor of holy pageantry.' The 'sacred page,' however, is the Bible, and the title = S.T.P., or D.D.

[2] Davies, 245.

Hosyerlane end, where as my Lady Mayres and her systers lay' and 'uppon the Payment.'

Outward signs of the civic control were the 'vexilla ludi cum armis civitatis,' which were set up at the stations by order of the mayor on Corpus Christi eve. Apparently the city claimed also to put its mark on the pageants themselves, for in an agreement of 1422 merging the pageants of the Shoemakers, Tilemakers, Hayresters, and Millers it was declared, 'quod nulla quatuor artium praedictarum ponet aliqua signa, arma, vel insignia super paginam praedictam, nisi tantum arma huius honorabilis civitatis.' But the more important crafts, who had a pageant to themselves, may not have been subject to this restriction.

Although the corporation profited from the 'dimissio locorum ludi Corporis Christi,' they did not meet many of the expenses. They paid for the services of the minstrels employed, and for refreshments for themselves and for important visitors to the town. They occasionally helped out the resources of a poor craft. The following extract from the Chamberlains' accounts for 1397 seems to be quite exceptional:—

'Expens' in festo de Corpore Xp' i.

Item: pro steyning de iiij^{or} pannos ad opus paginae, iiij^{s}.

Et pro pictura paginae, ij^{s}.

Et pro vexillo novo cum apparatu, xij^{s} ij^{d}.

Et in portacione et reportacione meremii ad barras coram Rege, ij^{s} j^{d}.

Et pro xx fursperres ad barras praedictas coram Rege, v^{s} x^{d}.

Et pro xix sapplynges emptis de Iohanne de Craven pro barris praedictis, vj^{s} viij^{d}.

Et viij portitoribus ducentibus et moventibus paginam, v^{s} iiij^{d}.

Et Ianitori Sanctae Trinitatis pro pagina hospitanda, iiij^{d}.

Et ludentibus, iiij^{d}.

Et ministrallis in festo de Corpore Xp'i, xiij^{s} iiij^{d}.

Et in pane, cervisiis, vino, et carnibus, et focalibus pro maiore et probis hominibus in die ad ludum, xviij^{s} viij^{d}.

Et in ministrallis domini Regis ac aliorum dominorum supervenientibus, vij^{li} vij^{s} iiij^{d}.

Et ministris camerae in albo panno et rubeo pro adventu Regis, lviij^{s} x^{d}.'

Certainly the corporation did not themselves provide a 'pagina' in 1415 or later years. I think that in 1397 they prepared one for some allegorical performance of welcome, distinct from the play itself, to Richard II. The king was evidently placed at the gate of Trinity Priory, where was the first station as late as 1569.

But the bulk of the cost fell upon the crafts. They had to build, repair, decorate, and draw the pageant (Latin, *pagina*; English, *pagiaunt*, *paiaunt*, *pachent*, *pagende*, *pagyant*, *padgin*, *padgion*, *paidgion*, *padzhand*, &c., &c.). They had to house it in one of the 'pageant howses' which until recently gave a name to 'Pageant green,' and for each of which a yearly rent of xij^{d} seems to have been the usual charge. They had also doubtless to provide dress and refresh the actors; and some of their members were bound personally to conduct the pageant on its journey. The fully organized craft-guilds appointed annual 'pageant-masters,' and met the ordinary charges by a levy of 'pageant-silver' upon each member according to his status. The amounts varied from 1*d.* to 8*d.*, and were supplemented by the proceeds of fines and payments on admissions and on setting up shop. Smaller guilds were often grouped together, and produced one pageant amongst three or four of them. Even the unincorporated trades did not escape. In 1483 four Innholders undertook the responsibility of producing a pageant for eight years on condition of a fixed payment of 4*d.* from each innholder in the city. Exceptional expenses were sometimes met in exceptional ways. The Mercers gave free admission into their fraternity to one Thomas Drawswerd, on condition that he should 'mak the Pagiant of the Dome . . . of newe substanciale for vij marks and the old pageant.' In 1501 the Cartwrights made four new wheels to a pageant, and were thereupon discharged from further charges for 6*d.* a year. Evidently the obligation of producing a pageant was considered an onerous one, and as trades rose and fell in York, the incidence of it upon this or that trade or trades was frequently altered. All such rearrangements came before the civic authorities, and many of them are upon record. Naturally they involved some corresponding revision, piecing together, or splitting up of plays (cf. p. 412). I only find one example of a play produced by any other body than a craft. The Hospital of St. Leonard produced the play of the Purification in 1415, but had ceased to do so some time before 1477. It is to be noted that in 1561 the Minstrels took their place with the other crafts, and became responsible for the Herod play [2].

Pater-Noster Play.

Wyclif in his *De Officio Pastorali*, cap. 15 (1378), says that,—

'herfore freris han tauȝt in Englond þe Paternoster in Engliȝcsh tunge, as men seyen in þe pleye of Yorke [3].'

[1] *Antiquary*, xxiii. 29.

[2] *York Plays*, xxi, 125; *E.H.R.* ix. 285.

[3] Wyclif, *English Works*, ed. Mathew (E. E. T. S.), 429.

The reference here is to a performance distinct from the Corpus Christi play. The preamble to a return of the ordinances and so forth of the guild 'Orationis Domini,' made in 1389, states that

'Once upon a time, a Play setting forth the goodness of the Lord's Prayer was played in the city of York; in which play all manner of vices and sins were held up to scorn, and the virtues were held up to praise.'

The guild was formed to perpetuate this play, and the members were bound to produce it and accompany it through the streets. In 1389 they had no possessions beyond the properties of the play and a chest. A *computus* of the guild for 1399 contains an entry of an old debt of 2*s*. 2*d*., owed by John Downom and his wife for entrance fee:—

'Sed dictus Iohannes dicit se expendisse in diuersis expensis circa ludum Accidiae ex parte Ric. Walker ij^{s} j^{d}, ideo de praedicto petit allocari[1].'

It would appear that by 1488 the guild had been converted to or absorbed in a guild of the Holy Trinity, which was moreover the craft-guild of the Merchants or Mercers. Certainly in that year this guild chose four pageant-masters to bring forth the Paternoster play. They were to bring in the pageants 'within iiij days next after Corpus Christi Day[2].' In 1488 the Paternoster play was presumably a variant for the usual Corpus Christi plays. It was similarly played on Corpus Christi day in 1558. The management was in the hands of one of the few unsuppressed guilds, that of St. Anthony; but the corporation gathered 'pageant silver' from the crafts and met the charges. A 'bayn,' or messenger, rode to proclaim the play on St. George's day, and another on Whit Monday. Another performance took place on Corpus Christi day (now called 'Thursday next after Trinitie Sonday'), 1572. The book was 'perused, amended and corrected.' Nevertheless, on July 30 the council sent a 'trewe copie' of it, at his request, to the Archbishop [Grindal] of York, and although in 1575 they sent a deputation to urge him to appoint a commission to reform 'all suche the play bookes as perteyne this cittie now in his grace's custodie,' there is no proof that his grace complied.

Creed Play.

As already stated, the guild of Corpus Christi had nothing to do with the regular craft-plays. But in 1446, William Revetor, a chantry priest and warden of the guild, bequeathed to it a 'ludus incompara-

[1] *York Plays*, xxix; Toulmin, *English Gilds* (E. E. T. S.), 137.
[2] *Antiquary*, xxii. 265.

bilis' called the 'Crede play,' to be performed every tenth year 'in variis locis dictae civitatis.' An inventory of 1465 includes:—

'Liber vocatus Originale continens Articulos Fidei Catholicae in lingua anglicana, nuper scriptum, appreciatum x[li].

Et alius liber inveteratus de eodem ludo, c[s].

Et alius liber de eodem anglice vocatus *Crede Play* continens xxij quaternos.'

There were also many banners and properties, amongst which

'Et xij rotulae nuper scriptae cum articulis fidei catholicae, apprec' iij[s] iiij[d].

Et una clavis pro sancto Petro cum ij peciis unius tunicae depictae, apprec' xij[d].

Et x diademata pro Xp'o et apostolis cum una larva et aliis novem cheverons, vj[s].'

Various performances of the Creed play are recorded. In 1483 it was given on Sunday, September 7, before Richard III, by order of the Council, 'apon the cost of the most onest men of every parish in thys Cite.' From 1495 decennial performances can be traced, generally about Lammas (August 1), and 'at the common hall.' In 1535 the Corpus Christi play proper was omitted, and the crafts contributed 'pageant silver' to the Creed play at Lammas. But they refused to give way to it again in 1545. The guild was suppressed in 1547, and the 'original or regestre' passed into the hands of the hospital of St. Thomas. In 1562 the corporation proposed the Creed play as a possible alternative for 'th' ystories of the old and new testament' on St. Barnabas day; and in 1568 they again designed to replace the regular Corpus Christi play by it. But first they submitted it to the Dean of York, Matthew Hutton, who, in a letter still extant, advised that—

'thogh it was plawsible to yeares ago, and wold now also of the ignorant sort be well liked, yet now in this happie time of the gospell, I knowe the learned will mislike it, and how the state will beare with it, I knowe not.'

Consequently the book was 'delyveryd in agayn,' and no more is heard of it.

Mr. Davies suggests that the play probably fell into twelve scenes, in each of which one of the apostles figured. If so, there is perhaps an allusion to a performance of it in a letter of Henry VIII to the justices of York in which he speaks of a riot which took place—

'at the acting of a religious interlude of St. Thomas the Apostle made in the said city on the 23rd of August now last past . . . owing to the seditious conduct of certain papists who took a part in preparing for the said interlude.'

He requires them to imprison any who in 'performing interludes which are founded on any portions of the Old or New Testament' use language tending to a breach of the peace[1].

St. George Riding.

In April, 1554, the Council made an order for 'Seynt George to be brought forth and ryde as hath been accustomed,' and the following items in the accounts show that the personages in the procession were much the same as at Dublin (q. v.):—

'to the waites for rydyng and playing before St. George and the play.'

'to the porters for beryng of the pagyant, the dragon and St. Xp'ofer.'

'to the King and Quene [of Dele] that playd.'

'to the May [the Maid].'

'to John Stamper for playing St. George[2].'

Midsummer Show.

As the regular plays waned, the 'show' or 'watch' of armed men on Midsummer eve became important. There is an ordinance for it in 1581. In 1584 it took place in the morning, and in the afternoon John Grafton, a schoolmaster, gave at seven stations a play with 'certaine compiled speaches,' for which the council allowed him to have 'a pageant frame.' Apparently the Baker's pageant was repaired for the purpose. In 1585 Grafton borrowed the pageants of the Skinners, Cooks, Tailors, Innholders, Bakers, and Dyers, and gave another play. Grafton's account for 1585 mentions 'the hearse,' 'the angell,' 'the Queene's crowne,' 'the childe one of the furyes bare.' He got iij^{s}, vj^{s}, viij^{d} for his pains[3].

[1] Halliwell, *Letters of the Kings of England*, i. 354, from a Latin original in the *Bodl. Rawlinson MSS.*

[2] Davies, 263.

[3] Davies, 273; *Arch. Review*, i. 221.

X

TEXTS OF MEDIAEVAL PLAYS AND EARLY TUDOR INTERLUDES

I. MIRACLE-PLAYS.

Chester Plays.

Manuscripts.

(i) Hg. †1475–1500. *Hengwrt MS.* 229, in the library of Mr. Wynne of Peniarth, containing Play xxiv (*Antichrist*) only. Probably a prompter's copy, as some one has 'doubled it up and carried it about in his pocket, used it with hot hands, and faded its ink.'

(ii) D. 1591. *Devonshire MS.*, in the library of the Duke of Devonshire, written by 'Edward Gregorie, a scholar of Bunbury.'

(iii) W. 1592. *Brit. Mus. Addl. MS.* 10,305. Signed at the end of each play 'George Bellin.'

(iv) h. 1600. *Brit. Mus. Harl. MS.* 2013, also signed after some of the plays by 'George Bellin' or 'Billinges.' A verse proclamation or 'banes' is prefixed, and on a separate leaf a copy of the prose proclamation made by the clerk of the pentice in 1544 (cf. p. 349) with a note, in another hand.

(v) B. 1604. *Bodl. MS.* 175, written by 'Gulielmus Bedford,' with an incomplete copy of the 'banes.'

(vi) H. 1607. *Brit. Mus. Harl. MS.* 2124, in two hands, the second being that of 'Jacobus Miller.' An historical note, dated 1628, is on the cover.

(vii) M. MS. in Manchester Free Library, containing fragment of Play xix (*Resurrection*) only.

[The MSS. D, W, h, B are derived from a common source, best represented by B. MS. H varies a good deal from this group, and is the better text. MS. Hg is probably related to H.]

Editions.

(a) 1818. Plays iii, x (*Noah*, *Innocents*) and Banes; J. H. Markland, for Roxburghe Club (No. 11).

(b) 1836. Play xxiv (*Antichrist*); J. P. Collier, *Five Miracle-Plays.*

(c) 1838. Plays iii, xxiv (*Noah*, *Antichrist*); W. Marriott, *English Miracle-Plays.*

(d) 1843–7, 1853. Cycle; Thomas Wright, from MS. W, for Shakespeare Society.

(e) 1883. Part of Play xix (*Resurrection*), from MS. M, in *Manchester Guardian*, for May 19, 1883.

(f) 1890. Plays iii, part of iv (*Noah, Isaac*); Pollard, 8.

(g) 1893–. Cycle (vol. i with Introduction, Banes and Plays i–xiii only issued by 1902); H. Deimling, from MS. H (with collation), for E. E. T. S. (Extra Series, lxii).

(h) 1897. Plays v, xxiv (*Prophetae, Antichrist*); Manly, i. 66, 170, from (g) and MS. Hg respectively.

[F. J. Furnivall, *Digby Plays*, xx, prints eighteen additional lines to the Banns as given by Deimling from MSS. h, B. These are from a copy in Rogers's *Breviary of Chester* (cf. p. 350), *Harl. MS.* 1944. A distinct and earlier (pre-Reformation) Banns is printed by Morris, 307, from *Harl. MS.* 2150 (cited in error as 2050), which is a copy of the White Book of the Pentice belonging to the City of Chester.]

The Cycle.

The list of 'pagyns in play of Corpus Xρi' contained in the 'White Book of the Pentice' (*Harl. MS.* 2150, f. 85 b), and given apparently from this source, by Rogers (Furnivall, xxi), makes them twenty-five in number, as follows :—

i. The fallinge of Lucifer.
ii. The creation of ye worlde.
iii. Noah & his shipp.
iv. Abraham & Isacke.
v. Kinge Balack & Balaam with Moyses.
vi. Natiuytie of our Lord.
vii. The shepperdes offeringe.
viii. Kinge Harrald & ye mounte victoriall.
ix. Ye 3 Kinges of Collen.
x. The destroyeinge of the Childeren by Herod.
xi. Purification of our Ladye.
xii. The pinackle, with ye woman of Canan.
xiii. The risinge of Lazarus from death to liffe.
xiv. The cominge of Christe to Ierusalem.
xv. Christs maundy with his desiples.
xvi. The scourginge of Christe.
xvii. The Crusifienge of Christ.
xviii. The harrowinge of hell.
xix. The Resurrection.
xx. The Castle of Emaus & the Apostles.
xxi. The Ascention of Christe.
xxii. Whitsonday ye makeinge of the Creede.
xxiii. Prophetes before ye day of Dome.
xxiv. Antecriste.
xxv. Domes Daye.

The list of plays contained in the pre-Reformation Banns is the same as this, with one exception. Instead of twenty-five plays it has twenty-six. After *Wyt Sonday* is inserted the play 'of our lady thassumpcon,' to be brought forth by 'the worshipfull wyves of this towne.' This play of *The Assumption* was given in 1477, and as a separate performance in 1488, 1497, and 1515 (Morris, 308, 322, 323). Doubtless it was dropped, as at York, out of Protestantism. The post-Reformation Banns and the extant MSS. of the cycle have it not. Further, they reduce the twenty-five plays of the 'White Book' list to twenty-four, by merging the plays of the *Scourging* and *Crucifixion* into one. In MSS. B, W, h, the junction is plainly apparent (see Deimling, i. ix; Wright, ii. 50). In MS. H there is no break (Deimling, i. xxiv).

Literary Relations.

Wright, i. xiv, and Hohlfeld, in *Anglia*, xi. 223, call attention to the parallels between the Chester plays and the French *Mystère du Viel Testament* and to the occurrence in them of scraps and fragments of French speech. The chief of these are put into the mouths of Octavian, the *Magi*, Herod, and Pilate, and may have been thought appropriate to kings and lordings. They may also point to translation from French originals. Davidson, 254, suggests that the earliest performances at Chester were in Anglo-Norman, and points to the tradition of MS. H (cf. p. 351) as confirming this. There are slight traces of influence upon some of the Chester plays by the York cycle (Hohlfeld, loc. cit. 260; Davidson, 287). Hohlfeld, in *M.L.N.* v. 222, regards Chester play iv as derived from a common original with the Brome *Abraham and Isaac*. H. Ungemacht, *Die Quellen der fünf ersten Chester Plays*, discusses the relation of the plays to the Brome play and the French *mystères*, and also to the *Vulgate*, the Fathers, Josephus, and the *Cursor Mundi*.

York Plays.

Manuscripts.

(i) *Brit. Mus. Addl. MS.* 35,290, recently *Ashburnham MS.* 137, fully described by L. T. Smith, *York Plays*, xiii. The MS. dates from about 1430–40, and appears to be a 'register' or transcript made for the corporation of the 'origenalls' in the hands of the crafts. In 1554 the 'register' was kept by the clerk at the gates of the dissolved Holy Trinity Priory. After the plays ceased to be performed it got into the hands of the Fairfaxes of Denton. In 1695 it belonged to Henry Fairfax, and its ownership can be traced thence to the present day.

(ii) *Sykes MS.* in possession of the York Philosophical Society, fully described in *York Plays*, 455. This is of the early sixteenth century. It contains only the Scriveners' play, of 'The Incredulity of Thomas,' is not a copy from the Ashburnham MS., and may be an 'origenall,' or a transcript for the prompter's use. It has a cover with a flap, and has been folded lengthwise, as if for the pocket.

Editions.

(a) 1797. Play xlii (*Incredulity of Thomas*), from *Sykes MS.*, in J. Croft, *Excerpta Antiqua*, 105.

(b) 1859. Play xlii (*Incredulity of Thomas*), from *Sykes MS.*, ed. J. P. Collier, in *Camden Miscellany*, vol. iv.

(c) 1885. Cycle, from *Ashburnham MS.*, in L. Toulmin Smith, *York Plays.*

(d) 1890. Play i (*Creation and the Fall of Lucifer*), from *York Plays*, in Pollard, 1.

(e) 1897. Plays xxxviii, xlviii (*Resurrection, Judgment Day*), from *York Plays*, in Manly, i. 153, 198.

The Cycle.

The subjects of the forty-eight plays and one fragment contained in the *Ashburnham MS.* are as follows:—

i. *The Barkers.* The Creation, Fall of Lucifer.
ii. *Playsterers.* The Creation to the Fifth Day.
iii. *Cardmakers.* God creates Adam and Eve.
iv. *Fullers.* Adam and Eve in the Garden of Eden.
v. *Cowpers.* Man's disobedience and Fall.
vi. *Armourers.* Adam and Eve driven from Eden.
vii. *Glovers.* Sacrificium Cayme et Abell.
viii. *Shipwrites.* Building of the Ark.
ix. *Fysshers and Marynars.* Noah and the Flood.
x. *Parchmyners and Bokebynders.* Abraham's Sacrifice.
xi. *The Hoseers.* The Israelites in Egypt, the Ten Plagues, and Passage of the Red Sea.
xii. *Spicers.* Annunciation, and visit of Elizabeth to Mary.
xiii. *Pewtereres and Foundours.* Joseph's trouble about Mary.
xiv. *Tille-thekers.* Journey to Bethlehem: Birth of Jesus.
xv. *Chaundelers.* The Angels and the Shepherds.
xvi. *Masonns.* Coming of the three Kings to Herod.
xvii. *Goldsmyths.* Coming of the three Kings, the Adoration.
xviii. *Marchallis.* Flight into Egypt.

xix. *Gyrdillers and Naylers.* Massacre of the Innocents.
xx. *Sporiers and Lorimers.* Christ with the Doctors in the Temple.
xxi. *Barbours.* Baptism of Jesus.
xxii. *Smythis.* Temptation of Jesus.
xxiii. *Coriours.* The Transfiguration.
xxiv. *Cappemakers.* Woman taken in Adultery. Raising of Lazarus.
xxv. *Skynners.* Entry into Jerusalem.
xxvi. *Cutteleres.* Conspiracy to take Jesus.
xxvii. *Baxteres.* The Last Supper.
xxviii. *Cordewaners.* The Agony and Betrayal.
xxix. *Bowers and Flecchers.* Peter denies Jesus: Jesus examined by Caiaphas.
xxx. *Tapiterers and Couchers.* Dream of Pilate's Wife: Jesus before Pilate.
xxxi. *Lytsteres.* Trial before Herod.
xxxii. *Cokis and Waterlederes.* Second accusation before Pilate: Remorse of Judas: Purchase of Field of Blood.
xxxiii. *Tyllemakers.* Second trial continued: Judgment on Jesus.
xxxiv. *Shermen.* Christ led up to Calvary.
xxxv. *Pynneres and Paynters.* Crucifixio Christi.
xxxvi. *Bocheres.* Mortificacio Christi.
xxxvii. *Sadilleres.* Harrowing of Hell.
xxxviii. *Carpenteres.* Resurrection: Fright of the Jews.
xxxix. *Wyne-drawers.* Jesus appears to Mary Magdalen after the Resurrection.
xl. *The Sledmen.* Travellers to Emmaus.
xli. *Hatmakers, Masons, and Laborers.* Purification of Mary: Simeon and Anna prophesy.
xlii. *Escreueneres.* Incredulity of Thomas.
xliii. *Tailoures.* The Ascension.
xliv. *Potteres.* Descent of the Holy Spirit.
xlv. *Draperes.* The Death of Mary.
xlvi. *Wefferes.* Appearance of our Lady to Thomas.
xlvii. *Osteleres.* Assumption and Coronation of the Virgin.
xlviii. *Merceres.* The Judgement Day.
(Fragment.) *Inholders.* Coronation of our Lady.

The majority of these plays were entered in the register about 1440. The fragment of a later play on *The Coronation of Our Lady* was added at the end of the fifteenth century. It was doubtless intended to supersede xlvii. *Adam and Eve in the Garden of Eden* (iv) and *The Purification of Mary, Simeon and Anna prophesy* (xli) were inserted in 1558. The former is probably of the same date as the rest; the latter is thought by the editor to be later. It is misplaced both in the MS. and the printed text. It should follow xvii, but there was no room for it in the MS. Some notes, probably written when the plays were submitted to the Dean of York in 1579, state that xii, xviii, xxi, xxviii had been rewritten since the register was compiled.

The register does not represent quite all the plays ever performed at York. Spaces are left for *The Marriage at Cana* and *Christ in the House of Simon the Leper*, which were never written in; and the corporation archives refer to a play of *Fergus* or *Portacio Corporis Mariae*, which came between xlv and xlvi and was 'laid apart' in 1485; and to a scene of *Suspencio Iudae*, which was in 1422 an episode of xxxiii. In other respects the contents of the register agree substantially with the fifty-one plays of the *Ordo paginarum* entered by the Town Clerk in the *Liber Memorandorum* in 1415[1] and with the fifty-seven plays of a second *Ordo* of uncertain date which comes a little later in the same *Liber*[2]. The three lists show some variations in the grouping of the subject-matter into pageants, due to the constant shifting of responsibility amongst the crafts.

Literary Relations.

Davidson, 252 sqq., attempts to trace the growth of the York plays out of a parent cycle, from which the Towneley and Coventry plays borrowed. The biblical and apocryphal sources are discussed by L. Toulmin Smith, *York Plays*, xlvii; A. R. Hohlfeld, in *Anglia*, xi. 285; P. Kamann, *Die Quellen der York-Spiele*, in *Anglia*, x. 189; F. Holthausen, in *Arch. f. d. Studium d. neueren Sprachen und Litteratur*, lxxxv. 425; lxxxvi. 280; W. A. Craigie, in *Furnivall Miscellany*, 52. I have not been able to see O. Herrtrich, *Studien zu den York Plays* (Breslau Diss. 1886). There are textual studies by F. Holthausen as above, and in *Philologische Studien* (Sievers-Festgabe), 1896; E. Kölbing, in *Englische Studien*, xvi. 279; xx. 179; J. Hall, in *Eng. Stud.* ix. 448; Zupitza, in *Deutsche Litteraturzeitung*, vi. 1304; K. Luick, in *Anglia*, xxii. 384.

Towneley Plays.

Manuscript.

Written in the second half of the fifteenth century, formerly in the

[1] Printed in *York Plays*, xix.

[2] Printed in Davies, 233.

library of Towneley Hall, long in the possession of Mr. Quaritch, the bookseller, and now in that of Major Coates, of Ewell, Surrey. There are thirty-two plays in all, but twenty-six leaves are missing.

Editions.

(a) 1822. Play xxx (*Iudicium*); F. Douce, for Roxburghe Club (*Publications*, No. 16).

(b) 1836. Play xiii (*Secunda Pastorum*); J. P. Collier, in *Five Miracle-Plays*.

(c) 1836. Complete cycle; for *Surtees Soc.* (It is uncertain whether the editor was J. Raine, J. Hunter, or J. S. Stevenson.)

(d) 1838. Plays viii, xiii, xxiii, xxv, xxx (*Pharao, Secunda Pastorum, Crucifixio, Extractio Animarum ab Inferno, Iudicium*); W. Marriott, *English Miracle-Plays*.

(e) 1867. Play iii (*Processus Noe cum filiis*), E. Mätzner, *Altenglische Sprachproben*, 360.

(f) 1875. Play ii (*Mactacio Abel*); T. Valke, *Der Tod des Abel* (Leipzig).

(g) 1885. Plays viii, xviii, xxv, xxvi, xxx (*Pharao, Pagina Doctorum, Extraccio Animarum, Resurreccio Domini, Iudicium*); L. Toulmin Smith, *York Plays*, 68, 158, 372, 397, 501 (not quite in full, for comparison with corresponding York plays).

(h) 1890. Play xiii (*Secunda Pastorum*), abridged; Pollard, 31.

(i) 1897. Cycle, G. England and A. W. Pollard, for E.E.T.S. (Extra Series, lxxi).

(k) 1897. Plays iii, v, vi, xiii (*Processus Noe, Isaac, Iacob, Secunda Pastorum*) from (i); Manly, i. 13, 58, 94.

The Cycle.

There are thirty-two extant plays, as follows:—

i. The Creation (The Barkers, Wakefeld).
ii. Mactacio Abel (The Glovers).
iii. Processus Noe cum filiis (Wakefeld).
iv. Abraham (incomplete).
v. [Isaac].
vi. Iacob.
vii. Processus Prophetarum (incomplete).
viii. Pharao (the Litsters or Dyers).
ix. Cesar Augustus.
x. Annunciacio.
xi. Salutacio Elezabeth.
xii. Una pagina Pastorum (Prima).
xiii. Alia eorundem (Secunda).
xiv. Oblacio Magorum.
xv. Fugacio Iosep & Mariae in Egyptum.

xvi. Magnus Herodes.
xvii. Purificacio Mariae (incomplete at end).
xviii. Pagina Doctorum (incomplete at beginning).
xix. Iohannes Baptista.
xx. Conspiracio (et Capcio).
xxi. Coliphizacio.
xxii. Fflagellacio.
xxiii. Processus Crucis (et Crucifixio).
xxiv. Processus Talentorum.
xxv. Extraccio Animarum.
xxvi. Resurreccio Domini.
xxvii. Peregrini (the Fishers).
xxviii. Thomas Indiae (et Resurreccio Domini).
xxix. Ascencio Domini (incomplete).
xxx. Iudicium.
xxxi. Lazarus.
xxxii. Suspencio Iudae (incomplete).

Plays xxxi and xxxii (a fragment) are obviously misplaced. The former should come between xix and xx; the latter, which is added to the MS. in an early sixteenth-century hand, between xxii and xxiii. Probably two plays at least are lost. Twelve leaves are missing after Play i, and twelve more after Play xxix. These doubtless contained plays of *The Fall* and *Pentecost*.

Literary Relations.

The Towneley Cycle is a composite one (Ten Brink, ii. 257; iii. 274; Davidson, 253; England-Pollard, xxi). Mr. Pollard distinguishes three fairly well-marked strata, and this classification is probably not exhaustive. There are (a) a group of plays of the ordinary didactico-religious type; (b) a group derived from the York plays in an earlier form than the extant text; (c) a group written by a single writer of marked power and a bold sense of humour. The plays of this group include iii, xii, xiii, xiv, xxi, and are, for literary quality, the pick of the vernacular religious drama. Mr. Pollard considers the cycle practically complete by about 1420. The horned female headdress (xxx. 269) which led the Surtees editor to put the composition in 1388, is found in miniatures of the later date. The relation of the cycle to that of York is also studied by Davidson, 271 sqq., and A. R. Hohlfeld, in *Anglia*, xi. 253, 285. Ten Brink, ii. 244; iii. 274, thinks that a much earlier (late thirteenth century) play is preserved in Plays v and vi (*Isaac* and *Iacob*). I agree with Mr. Pollard that this conjecture lacks proof.

A. Ebert has a study, *Die englischen Mysterien, mit besonderer Berücksichtigung der Townley-Sammlung*, in *Jahrbuch f. rom. u. engl. Lit.* i. 44, 131. The folk-lore incident of the *Secunda Pastorum* is supplied with parallels by E. Kölbing, in England-Pollard, xxxi, and by H. A. Eaton, in *M.L.N.* xiv. 265, from *The Merry Tales of Gotham* (H. Oesterley, *A Hundred Merry Tales* (1526), No. xxiv; Hazlitt, *Shakespeare's Jest-Books*, iii. 4). There is an allusion to the 'foles of Gotham,' in Play xii. 180. J. Hugienen, in *M.L.N.* xiv. 255, finds in Play iv. 49 an adaptation of the French *Viel Testament*, 9511.

The Locality.

Douce described the manuscript for the sale of Towneley MSS. in 1814 as supposed to have 'belonged to the Abbey of Widkirk, near Wakefield, in the county of York.' In his Roxburghe Club edition of the *Iudicium* he substitutes the name of the Abbey of Whalley, near Towneley Hall. How far either of these statements or conjectures rests upon Towneley family tradition is unknown. Widkirk is merely another form (cf. Prof. Skeat, in *Athenæum* for Dec. 2, 1893) of Woodkirk, also called West Ardsley, a small place four miles north of Wakefield. There was not, strictly speaking, an abbey at Woodkirk, but a small cell of Augustinian canons, dependent upon the great house of St. Oswald at Nostel.

The MS. itself seems to bear witness to a connexion of the plays with the crafts of Wakefield. Play i is headed 'Assit Principio, Sancta Maria, Meo. Wakefeld.' In the margin of Play ii is written 'Glover Pag.' in a later hand. Play iii is headed 'Processus Noe cum filiis. Wakefeld.' In the margin of Play viii is 'Litsters Pagonn' in a later hand, and further down, in a third hand, is 'lyster play.' Under the title of Play xxvii is 'fysher pagent' in a later hand. Further in Play xiii is a mention of 'Horbury Shroges,' Horbury being a village two or three miles from Wakefield, and a 'crokyd thorne' which may be a 'Shepherd's Thorn' near Horbury in Mapplewell. These indications are spread over the three groups of plays distinguished by Mr. Pollard, and certainly suggest that the whole cycle belonged to the Wakefield crafts. On the other hand, I find no hint of any plays in the local histories of Wakefield. The evidence for a connexion with Wakefield is strengthened by M. H. Peacock, *The Wakefield Mysteries*, in *Anglia*, xxiv. 509, from which it appears that there are places called Thornhill and Thornes to the E. and W. respectively of Horbury. Play ii, line 367 'bery me in gudeboure at the quarell hede' points to Goodybower Close in Wakefield, which once had a quarry. Play xxiv, line 155 'from this towne vnto lyn' suggests at least a borrowing from East Anglia.

Perhaps we may combine the data of the manuscript and of tradition by supposing that the plays were acted by the crafts of Wakefield, not in the town at Corpus Christi or Whitsuntide, but at one of the great fairs which the canons of Nostel held under charter at Woodkirk about the feasts of the Assumption (Aug. 15) and the Nativity (Sept. 8) of the Virgin. These fairs, run into one continuous horse fair, and known from a local family of Legh, as Lee fair, lasted until quite recently [1].

LUDUS COVENTRIAE.

Manuscript.

Brit. Mus. Cotton MS. Vespasian D. viii. Forty-two plays, the last incomplete. On f. 100ᵛ is the date 1468. At the beginning is written 'Robert Hegge, Dunelmensis' and before the twenty-ninth play 'Ego R. H. Dunelmensis, Possideo: Ου κτησις αλλα χρησις.' On the fly-leaf, in an Elizabethan hand, is 'The plaie called Corpus Christi,' and in the hand of Cotton's librarian, Richard James, 'Contenta Novi Testamenti scenice expressa et actitata olim per monachos sive fratres mendicantes: vulgo dicitur hic liber Ludus Coventriae, sive ludus Corporis Christi: scribitur metris Anglicanis.' The following account was given by a later librarian, Dr. Smith, in his printed catalogue (1696) of the Cottonian MSS.: 'A collection of plays, in Old English metre: h.e. Dramata sacra, in quibus exhibentur historiae veteris & N. Testamenti, introductis quasi in scenam personis illic memoratis quas secum invicem colloquentes pro ingenio finget Poeta. Videntur olim coram populo, sive ad instruendum sive ad placendum, a Fratribus mendicantibus representata.'

Editions.

(a) 1830. Plays i–v (*Fall of Lucifer, Days of Creation and Fall of Adam, Cain and Abel, Noah's Flood, Abraham and Isaac*) in Dugdale, *Monasticon Anglicanum* (ed. 2). vi, pt. 3, 1534.

(b) 1836. Play x (*Betrothal of Mary*), Collier, *Five Miracle-Plays.*

(c) 1838. Plays xii, xiv (*Doubt of Joseph, Trial of Mary*), William Marriott, *English Miracle-Plays.*

(d) 1841. Cycle: J. O. Halliwell[-Phillipps] for Shakespeare Society.

(e) 1890. Play xi (*Annunciation*), Pollard, 44.

(f) 1897. Plays iv, xi (*Noah's Flood, Annunciation*), Manly, i. 31, 82.

(g) A new edition of the complete cycle is promised in the 'Extra Series' of the Early English Text Society.

[1] W. Andrews, *Yorkshire in Olden Times*, 105, 146.

The Cycle.

The text is not definitely divided up into plays in the MS., although some such indication as an *Explicit* occasionally helps. Probably the following division is correct. Halliwell's is clearly wrong, but for convenience of reference I give his numbers in brackets.

i. Fall of Lucifer (Halliwell, i).
ii. Days of Creation. Fall of Adam (H. i, ii).
iii. Cain and Abel (H. iii).
iv. Noah's Flood (H. iv).
v. Abraham and Isaac (H. v).
vi. Moses (H. vi).
vii. Prophets (H. vii).

Then a prologue by Contemplacio, promising a 'matere' of 'the modyr of mercy' from her conception to the meeting with Elizabeth, and a 'conclusyon.'

viii. Joachim and Anna (H. viii).
ix. Mary in the Temple (H. ix).
x. Betrothal of Mary (H. x).
xi. Annunciation (H. xi).

Opens with scene between Contemplacio, Virtutes, Pater, Veritas, Misericordia, Iusticia, Pax, Filius.

xii. Doubt of Joseph (H. xii).
xiii. Visit to Elizabeth (H. xiii).

This group of plays closes with the promised 'conclusyon,' namely 'Ave regina coelorum,' and Contemplacio disappears.

xiv. Trial of Mary (H. xiv).
xv. Nativity (H. xv).
xvi. *Pastores* (H. xvi).
xvii. *Magi* (H. xvii).
xviii. Purification (H. xviii).
xix. Slaughter of Innocents (H. xix).
xx. Death of Herod (H. xix).
xxi. Dispute in Temple (H. xx).
xxii. Baptism (H. xxi).
xxiii. Temptation (H. xxii).
xxiv. Woman Taken in Adultery (H. xxiii).
xxv. Lazarus (H. xxiv).
xxvi. Conspiracy of Jews (H. xxv).
xxvii. Entry into Jerusalem (H. xxvi).
xxviii. Last Supper (H. xxvii).
xxix. Mount of Olives (H. xxviii).

Another group of scenes begins. Contemplacio, called in the stage direction 'an exposytour, in doctorys wede,' reappears; and after a procession has 'enteryd into the place, and the Herowdys taken his schaffalde and Pylat and Annas and Cayphas here schaffaldys,' says:—

'Be the leve and soferauns of allemythty God,
We intendyn to procede the matere that we lefte the last ȝere;
. . . .

The last ȝere we shewyd here how oure Lord for love of man
Cam to the cety of Jherusalem mekely his deth to take;
And how he made his mawndé.

. . . .

Now wold we procede, how he was browth than
Beforn Annas and Cayphas, and sythe beforn Pylate:
And so forth in his passyon how mekely he toke it for man.'

This group does not well bear splitting up into plays. The action is continuous, although it takes place now at one scaffold, now at another.

xxx. Herod desires to see Christ. Trial before Caiaphas (H. xxix, xxx).
xxxi. Death of Judas, Christ before Pilate and Herod (H. xxx).
xxxii. Pilate's Wife's Dream. The Condemnation (H. xxxi, xxxii).
xxxiii. Crucifixion (H. xxxii, xxxiii).
xxxiv. Longinus. Burial of Christ (H. xxxiv).
xxxv. Harrowing of Hell. Resurrection (H. xxxv).

Here, possibly, the group ends. Then follow:—

xxxvi. *Quem quaeritis* (H. xxxvi).
xxxvii. *Hortulanus* (H. xxxvii).
xxxviii. *Peregrini* (H. xxxviii).
xxxix. Incredulity of Thomas (H. xxxviii).
xl. Ascension (H. xxxix).
xli. Pentecost (H. xl).
xlii. Assumption of Virgin (H. xli).

The Assumption play, according to Halliwell, is inserted in a hand of the time of Henry VIII.

xliii. Doomsday (H. xlii).

A few lines appear to be missing at the end.

In dividing the plays, I have been helped by a prologue which is put in the mouths of three *Vexillatores*. Says *Primus*:—

'We purpose us pertly stylle in this prese,
The pepyl to plese with pleys full glad.
Now lystenyth us, lovely, bothe more and lesse,
Gentyllys and ȝemanry of goodly lyff lad,
This tyde.'

The *Vexillatores* then take turns to describe the 'ffyrst pagent,' 'secunde pagent,' and so on, up to 'the xl^ti pagent.' This should be 'xlii,' but by a slip two numbers are used twice. The prologue ends:—

'A Sunday next, yf that we may,
At vj of the belle we gynne oure play,
In N. towne, wherfore we pray,
That God now be ȝoure spede. *Amen.*'

The prologue so far agrees with the plays that it must have been written for them; but it was not written for them as they stand. It gives some of the incidents, especially of the trial scenes, in a different order from the text. Plays viii, xiii, xviii, xxvi, and xlii are omitted altogether. Of these xlii is a late interpolation in the text; but the fact that the numbers viii and xiii are skipped over in the enumeration, although the order in which the *Vexillatores* speak proceeds regularly, shows that the prologue is later in date than the text, and contemplates the omission of existing plays.

The Problem.

The exact nature of the *Ludus Coventriae* is a nice literary point. It is much doubted whether they have anything to do with Coventry at all. Cotton's librarians regarded them as Coventry plays, acted not by craft-guilds, but by monks or begging friars. But what was their authority? The earliest possessor of the MS. who can be traced is Robert Hegge, a Durham man by birth, and a Fellow of C. C. C., Oxford. Hegge died in 1629, and probably the MS. then passed into Sir Robert Cotton's collection through Richard James, who happened to be also a C. C. C. man, and was in the habit of picking up finds for Cotton in Oxford[1]. The note on the MS. may represent a tradition as to its origin gathered by James from Hegge.

With this note should be compared the following passage in Dugdale's *History of Warwickshire*, referring to the house of Franciscans or Grey Friars at Coventry:—

'Before the suppression of the monasteries, this city was very famous for the *Pageants* that were play'd therein, upon *Corpus-Christi*-day; which occasioning very great confluence of people thither from far and near, was of no small benefit thereto; which *Pageants* being acted with mighty state and reverence by the Friers of this House, had Theaters for the severall Scenes, very large and high, placed upon wheels, and drawn to all the eminent parts of the City, for the better advantage of Spectators: And contain'd the story of the New-Testament, composed into Old English Rithme, as appeareth by an antient MS. intituled *Ludus Corporis Christi* or *Ludus Coventriae*' [*in bibl.* Cotton, *sub effigie Vesp*. D. 9].

'I have been told by some old people, who in their younger years were eye-witnesses of these Pageants so acted, that the yearly con-

[1] *D. N. B.* s.v. Hegge. *Poems of Richard James* (ed. Grosart, xxii); T. Fowler, *Hist. of C. C. C.* 175, 183, 394.

fluence of people to see that shew was extraordinary great, and yielded no small advantage to this City[1].'

Dugdale, it is to be observed, has the MS. as one of his authorities, but he goes further than the librarians by ascribing the plays to a particular house of friars. Unfortunately his account will not hold water. He was born in 1605, and educated for five years in Coventry. Now there could have been no plays performed by the Grey Friars after 1538, for they were suppressed in that year. But the craft-plays survived, with great *éclat*, until 1580, and it is manifest that it is these plays which his informants described to him. They were acted on Corpus Christi day, obviously leaving no room for Grey Friars plays on the same day. The craft-plays seem to have been confined to the history of the New Testament (cf. p. 423), but the *Ludus Coventriae* is not. There is, however, a not very trustworthy bit of evidence which makes it just possible that the Grey Friars did act, not at Corpus Christi, but at Whitsuntide. This is the statement of the Coventry *Annals* that in 1492–3, Henry VII came to see the plays acted by the Grey Friars[2]. But the *Annals* only date from the seventeenth century, and they are not trustworthy (cf. p. 358) as to the history of the plays. I incline to think that the Grey Friars connexion is an Oxford guess of Hegge or his friends, which has found its way alike into the accounts of Richard James and Dugdale, and into the *Annals*. But is the connexion of the plays with Coventry also part of the guess, inspired by the fact that the Coventry mysteries, and these alone, obtained literary notice in the sixteenth century? Or have we Coventry guild-plays to deal with? The *Ludus Coventriae* is quite distinct from the two extant Coventry plays (p. 422); but those are of the sixteenth century, and appear to represent a recension in 1535 of 'new plays' produced, according to the *Annals*, in 1520 (p. 358). So far as this goes, the *Ludus Coventriae* might be the

[1] Dugdale, *Hist. of W.* (1656), 116. A not materially different version, from Dugdale's MSS., is given by Sharp, *Dissertation*, 218. Nor does Sharp, in the account of the Grey Friars in his *Hist. and Antiq. of Coventry* (1817), add any information as to their plays.

[2] Hearne, *Fordun's Scotichronicon*, v. 1493 (from MS. of *Annals*, penes Thomas Jesson of Ch. Ch.) 'This yeare the King came to se the playes acted by the Gray Friers and much commended them.' The mayoral list in this text of the *Annals* goes to 1675. It is probably another that Sharp, *Diss.* 5, quotes as making the same statement and describes as 'not older than the *beginning* of Charles I's reign.' He does not give the full entry. Is it the basis of Mr. Fretton's addition to the 1871 ed. of Sharp's *Hist. and Antiq. of Cov.* 202 '1492. Henry 7th and his Queen saw the Plays at Whitsuntide'? Can 'by the Gray Friers' mean 'at a station by the convent'? In the Carpenters' accounts for 1453 is an item 'for the mynstrell at the frer[s].' This, says Sharp, *Diss.* 213, relates to the craft's annual dinner held at the White Friars. There is no other possible allusion to friars' plays in Mr. Sharp's extracts.

discarded fifteenth-century cycle of the Coventry crafts. Ten Brink points out certain features in the *Ludus* which seem, from the Cappers' accounts extracted by Sharp, to have existed also at Coventry [1]. On the other hand, the Coventry plays, unlike the *Ludus*, seem to have been confined to the New Testament. The *Ludus* does not give those opportunities for showing off artisanship which are characteristic of other craft-cycles [2]. And, strongest of all, while the Coventry plays were processional, a study of the *Ludus* will make it quite clear that it was intended for a stationary performance. The 'pagents' contemplated by the prologue can only be episodes artificially distinguished in a practically continuous action. Often there is no well-marked break between pageant and pageant. The same personages appear and reappear in more than one; and the whole performance evidently takes place in and around a 'place' or *locus interludii* (Halliwell, 44) upon which are situated various 'scaffolds' or 'stages [3],' a heaven, a hell, a temple, a *sepulchrum*, and so forth. The *navis* for Noah is practicable, and can come and go.

If the plays are not from Coventry, can they be located elsewhere? They have been ascribed to Durham, but merely, I think, because Robert Hegge was 'Dunelmensis.' Mr. Pollard follows Ten Brink in assigning their dialect and scribal peculiarities to the North-East Midlands, and in ascribing them to a strolling company [4]. They regard 'N. towne' in the prologue as a common form (N = 'nomen,' as in the Church Catechism and Marriage Service). As to the dialect I offer no opinion; I am sorry not to have been able to see M. Kramer, *Sprache und Heimath der Coventry-Plays*. But I do not think that the strolling company is proved. The *vexillatores* may be merely proclaimers of banns sent round the villages hard by the town where the play was given. And 'N.' may be an abbreviation for a definite town name. Northampton (q.v.) has been suggested; but would not scan. Norwich (q.v.) would; and these might conceivably be a cycle played by the guild of St. Luke at Norwich before the crafts took the responsibility for the Whitsun plays from it. But the elaborate treatment of the legends of the Virgin suggests a performance, like that of the Lincoln plays, and of the *Massacre of the Innocents* in the *Digby MS.*, on St. Anne's day (July 26). It is to be

[1] Ten Brink, iii. 276; Sharp, 45.

[2] Hohlfeld, in *Anglia*, xi. 228.

[3] The term 'pageant' is once used in the stage-directions (Halliwell, 132) 'Hic intrabit pagentum de purgatione Mariae et Joseph.'

[4] Ten Brink, ii. 283; Pollard, xxxvii. Hohlfeld (*Anglia*, xi. 228) combines two theories by suggesting that the Coventry Grey Friars were driven by the popularity of the rival craft-plays to travel.

observed that both these examples are in the E. Midland area to which philologists assign the text of the *Ludus Coventriae*.

Literary Relations.

Ten Brink, ii. 283, calls attention to the composite character of the cycle, in which groups of various origin are placed side by side without much attempt at imposing a literary unity upon them. He thinks, however, that all the plays received their form in the same part of England, and considers the dialect to be that of the North-East Midlands. In a note (iii. 276) he finds an analogy in the treatment of certain themes between the *Ludus Coventriae* and the Coventry plays proper. Davidson, 259, thinks that the author might have been 'connected with one of the great religious houses of the Fen District.' Hohlfeld (*Anglia*, xi. 219) has some interesting remarks on the cycle. It may be observed that Plays xxx–xxxv in my grouping are evidently taken from a cycle of which only a part was given in each year. The *Purification and Presentation in the Temple* of the Digby MS. affords a parallel example. Possibly Plays viii–xiii in which, as in Plays xxx–xxxv, Contemplacio appears, have the same source.

COVENTRY PLAYS.

[See also account of *Ludus Coventriae*.]

Manuscripts.

A copy, probably the 'original' of the Shearmen and Tailors' play, was in the possession of Thomas Sharp. It is described in a colophon as 'T[h]ys matter nevly correcte by Robert Croo the xiiijth day of marche fenysschid in the yere of owre lorde god MCCCCC & xxxiiij^{te} [$153\frac{4}{5}$].' At the end are three songs, with the date 1591. A similar copy of the Weavers' play 'nevly translate be Robert Croo in the yere of oure Lorde God Mlv^{c} xxxiiij^{te} . . . yendide the seycond day of Marche in yere above sayde,' was 'unexpectedly discovered in 1832,' and a transcript made by Sharp. This also has songs at the end, but no date. The collections of Sharp passed into the Staunton collection at Longbridge House, and thence into the Shakespeare Memorial Library at Birmingham, where they were burnt in 1879.

Editions.

(a) 1817. *Shearmen and Tailors' Play.* Thos. Sharp in a series, separately paged, of *Illustrative Papers of the History and Antiquities of the City of Coventry.* [Reprinted 1871 under editorship of W. G. Fretton.]

(b) 1825. *Shearmen and Tailors' Play.* Reprinted from (a) by Thomas Sharp, with full illustrative matter, in *A Dissertation on the Coventry Mysteries*, 83.

(c) 1836. *Weavers' Play.* J. B. Gracie for the Abbotsford Club.

(d) 1838. *Shearmen and Tailors' Play.* William Marriott, *English Miracle-Plays.*

(e) 1897. *Shearmen and Tailors' Play.* Manly, i. 120, from (b).

(f) 1902. *Weavers' Play.* Edited from (c) by F. Holthausen, in *Anglia*, xxv. 209.

(g) 1903. *Shearmen and Tailors' Play.* A. W. Pollard, in *Fifteenth Century Prose and Verse* (*English Garner*), 245.

(h) Both plays are being edited by H. Craig for the E. E. T. S.

The Cycle.

The *Shearmen and Tailors' Play* has a prologue by 'Isaye the profet.' Then follow in order, the Annunciation, the Doubt of Joseph, the Journey to Bethlehem, the Nativity and Shepherds, a dialogue of two 'Profettis,' Herod and the Magi, the Flight to Egypt, the Massacre of the Innocents. The *Weavers' Play* must have followed next in the cycle. It opens with a dialogue of two '*Profetae.*' Then come the Presentation in the Temple and the Dispute with the Elders. The subjects of four of the other plays can be pretty clearly identified. The Smiths' accounts show them to have played the Trial and Crucifixion, to which was added in 1573 the 'new play' of the Death of Judas; the Descent from the Cross passed through various hands from the Pinners and Needlers in 1414 to the Coopers in 1547; the Cappers' accounts point to the Resurrection, Harrowing of Hell, and *Quem quaeritis*, with from 1540 the 'Castell of Emaus'; and those of the Drapers to Doomsday. It is difficult to say how many plays remain unidentified. The crafts were grouped and regrouped, and the total number of plays may have varied. But it would seem that besides the crafts already named, the Mercers, Whittawers, Girdlers, Cardmakers, and Tanners were playing in the middle of the fifteenth century. The 'jest' quoted on p. 358 points to a Pentecost play with the 'xij Articles of the Creed,' similar to that of Chester. It is noticeable that no Old Testament play can be established at Coventry.

Literary Relations.

These plays, of which the *Weavers' Play* was, until recently, difficult to procure, have been but little studied. Two communications by C. Davidson and A. R. Hohlfeld in *Modern Language Notes*, vii. 184,

308, call attention to the fact that the larger part of the dialogue in the *Dispute in the Temple* scene is practically the same as that common to the York, Towneley, and Chester plays (cf. *York Plays*, 158, and A. R. Hohlfeld in *Anglia*, xi. 260),

Newcastle-upon-Tyne.

Manuscript.

The Shipwrights' Play of *Noah's Ark* was in the hands of its first editor, Henry Bourne; but is not known to be now preserved (Holthausen, 32).

Editions.

(a) 1736. *Noah's Ark; or, The Shipwrights' Ancient Play or Dirge;* in H. Bourne, *Hist. of Newcastle*, 139.

(b) 1789. Reprint of (a) in J. Brand, *Hist. of Newcastle*, ii. 373.

(c) 1825. Reprint of (a) in T. Sharp, *Dissertation on Coventry Mysteries*, 223.

(d) 1897. F. Holthausen, in *Göteborg's Högskola's Ärsskrift*, and separately.

(e) 1899. R. Brotanek, in *Anglia*, xxi. 165.

Both (d) and (e) are founded on Bourne's text; but Brotanek has endeavoured to restore what he considers to have been the probable MS. text. This he dates, conjecturally, at about 1425–50.

The Cycle.

The Shipwrights' play deals with the Making of the Ark, but stops short of the Deluge. The personages are Deus, Angelus, Diabolus, Noah, Uxor Noah. The subjects of most of the plays of the other crafts can be recovered, as follows:—

Creation of Adam.	Baptism.
Noah's Ark.	Last Supper.
Offering of Isaac.	Bearing of Cross.
Israel in Egypt.	Burial of Christ.
Kings of Cologne.	Descent into Hell.
Flight into Egypt.	Burial of Our Lady.

Of these, two, the Creation of Adam and the Flight into Egypt, were maintained, in 1454, by one craft, the Bricklayers and Plasterers. The Merchant Adventurers, in 1552, paid for 'fyve playes, whereof the towne must pay for the ostmen playe.' There are six guilds whose plays are not known; so that the total number may have been as many as twenty-three[1].

[1] Holthausen, 16.

The accounts of the Merchant Adventurers also include in 1554 and 1558 charges in and about 'Hoggmaygowyk' or 'Hogmagoge[1].' I do not think, with Holthausen, that this was one of the Corpus Christi plays. I think it was a spring or summer folk-feast. One of the London 'giants' is Gogmagog.

Norwich.

Manuscript.

The extracts, made early in the seventeenth century from the Grocers' Book, and in the possession (1856) of Mr. Fitch, included two versions of the play of the *Fall.* The first was copied into the Book in 1533. It is headed *The Story of ye Creacon of Eve, w^t ye expellyng of Adam & Eve out of Paradyce.* It ends with a 'dullfull song,' perhaps the 'newe ballet' paid for in 1534 (cf. p. 388). It appears to have a *lacuna.* The second version is 'newely renvid & accordynge unto ye Skrypture, begon thys yere A^o 1565. A^o 7 Eliz.' It is quite a new text. It is provided with two speeches by a Prolocutor, one to be used 'when ye Grocers Pageant is played w^t owte eny other goenge befor y^t,' the other for use 'yf ther goeth eny other Pageants before y^t.' The former speaks of the 'Pageants apparellyd in Wittson dayes' that 'lately be fallen into decayes.'

Editions.

(a) 1856. Robert Fitch in *Norfolk Archaeology*, v. 8, and separately.
(b) 1897. Manly, i. 1, from (a).

The Cycle.

The Grocers' play begins in both versions with the creation of Eve. The first ends with the expulsion from Paradise. The *dramatis personae* are *Pater*, *Adam*, *Eva*, *Serpens*. In the second is added an *Angel*, and after the expulsion Adam and Eve depart 'to ye nether parte of ye Pageants,' are threatened by *Dolor* and *Myserye*, and comforted by the *Holy Ghost.*

A list, dating probably from 1527, makes it possible to complete the outline of the cycle[2]:—

Creation off the world.
Paradyse [*Grocers' play*].
Helle Carte.
Abell & Cain.
Noyse Shipp.
Abraham & Isaak.
Moises & Aaron, with the Children of Israel & Pharo with his Knyghts.
Conflict off David and Golias.

[1] F. W. Denby, *Newcastle Gilds* (Surtees Soc.), ii. 165, 168.
[2] *Norfolk Archaeology*, iii. 3.

The Birth off Christ with Shepherds and iij Kyngs of Colen.
The Baptysme of Criste.
The Resurrection.
The Holy Gost.

Abraham and Isaac (Dublin MS.).

Manuscript.

Trinity College, Dublin, MS. D. iv. 18, f. 16v. In the same hand are a list of mayors and bailiffs of North[ampton] up to 1458 and a brief chronicle, in which N[orthampton] recurs.

Editions.

(a) 1836. J. P. Collier, in *Five Miracle-Plays.*
(b) 1899. R. Brotanek, in *Anglia*, xxi. 21.

Literary Relations.

The play has probably no connexion with Dublin, beyond the fact that the MS. is there. Brotanek conjectures from the character of the MS. that it belongs to Northampton (cf. p. 386). The dialect appears to be South Midland of about the first half of the fifteenth century, and the text to be based on the corresponding play (xi) in the *Viel Testament* (Julleville, *Les Myst.* ii. 363).

Abraham and Isaac (Brome MS.).

Manuscript.

'The Book of Brome,' a commonplace book of 1470–80 in the possession of Sir Edward Kerrison of Brome Manor, Norfolk.

Editions.

(a) 1884. L. T. Smith, in *Anglia*, vii. 316.
(b) 1886. L. T. Smith, in *A Commonplace Book of the Fifteenth Century.*
(c) 1887. W. Rye, in *Norfolk Antiquarian Miscellany*, iii. 1.
(d) 1897. Manly, i. 41, from (a) and (b).

Literary Relations.

The play is 465 lines long. There is an epilogue by a *Doctor*, but no title or prologue, and nothing to show that it was, or was not, part of a cycle. The text is probably derived from a common source with that of the corresponding Chester play: cf. Pollard, 185; A. R. Hohlfeld, in *M. L. N.* v. 222.

F. Holthausen has some critical notes on the text in *Anglia*, xiii. 361.

CROXTON PLAY: THE SACRAMENT.

Manuscript.

Trinity College, Dublin, MS. F. 4. 20, of the latter half of the fifteenth century.

Editions.

(a) 1861. Whitley Stokes, in *Transactions of Philological Society*, 1860–1 (Appendix).
(b) 1897. Manly, i. 239.

There is a prologue by two *Vexillatores*, ending—

'And y^t place yow, thys gaderyng that here y^s,
At Croxston on Monday y^t shall be sen;
To see the conclusyon of this lytell processe
Hertely welcum shall yow bene.
. . . .
Now, mynstrell, blow vp with a mery stevyn!'

Then comes a title: 'Here after foloweth the Play of the Conversyon of Ser Jonathas the Jewe by Myracle of the Blyssed Sacrament.' The play is 927 lines long, with occasional lines in Latin. It ends with a *Te Deum*. The colophon runs: 'Thus endyth the Play of the Blyssyd Sacrament, whyche myracle was don in the forest of Aragon, in the famous cite Eraclea, the yere of ower Lord God M^lcccc.lxi, to whom be honower. Amen!' This account of the event on which the play is founded is confirmed by ll. 56–60 of the prologue. The date of composition cannot therefore be earlier than 1461, and probably is not much later. After the colophon is a list of the *dramatis personae*, who are twelve in all, and the note 'IX may play it at ease,' signed 'R.C.' The name Croxton is common to places in Norfolk, Cambridgeshire, Leicestershire, and other counties. Further identification may perhaps be helped by ll. 540–1—

'Inquyre to the Colkote, for ther ys hys loggyng,
A lytylle besyde Babwelle Mylle.'

The stage-directions imply a 'place,' with 'stages' for the chief players, a 'tabyll,' and a 'chyrche' (ll. 149, 288, 305, 445).

F. Holthausen has some textual criticism on the play in *Englische Studien*, xvi. 150, and *Anglia*, xv. 198.

SHREWSBURY FRAGMENTS.

On these, which are transitional between the liturgical play and the miracle-play proper, cf. p. 90.

Digby Plays.

[*Authorities.*—The best edition is that of Dr. Furnivall. The careful study by K. Schmidt, published partly as a Berlin dissertation (1884), partly in *Anglia*, viii (1885), 371, should be consulted.]

Manuscript.

Bodleian Digby MS. 133. The dramatic contents of this composite manuscript are as follows:—(i) f. 37. *The Conversion of St. Paul.* This is written in a single hand, except that a second has inserted on f. 45 a scene between two devils, Belial and Mercury. At the end (f. 50v), is 'ffinis conuercionis sancti pauli.' There is a prologue, headed *Poeta,* against which has been written in a later hand 'Myles Blomefylde.' Schmidt, *Diss.* 6, identifies a Miles Blomefylde as a monk of Bury born in 1525. (ii) f. 95. *St. Mary Magdalen,* written in the second hand of (i). At the beginning are the initials M. B.; at the end (f. 145) 'Explycit oreginale de sancta Maria magdalena.' (iii) f. 146. *Massacre of Innocents* and *Purification,* written in the first hand of (i). At the beginning is 'candelmes day & the kyllynge of the children of Israell, anno domini 1512'; at the end 'Anno domini Millesimo, cccccxij,' and after a list of 'The Namys of the Pleyers' the entry 'Ihon Parfre ded wryte thys booke.' None of these notes seem to be in the hand of the text. (iv) f. 158. Fragment of morality of *Mind, Will, and Understanding,* found complete in the *Macro MS.* (cf. p. 437), in a hand apparently distinct from those of (i), (ii), (iii). This also has 'M. B.' at the beginning.—The texts in the MS. are probably early sixteenth-century copies of late fifteenth-century plays. There is nothing to show that Parfre or Blomfield was concerned in the authorship. They may have been the copyists. If Blomfield was really the monk of Bury born in 1525, he was probably only an owner of the MS.

Editions.

(a) 1773. *Massacre of Innocents,* in T. Hawkins, *Origin of the English Drama.*

(b) 1835. *Massacre of Innocents, Conversion of St. Paul, St. Mary Magdalen,* in T. Sharp, *Ancient Mysteries from the Digby Manuscripts* (Abbotsford Club).

(c) 1838. *Massacre of Innocents,* in W. Marriott, *English Miracle-Plays.*

(d) 1882. Complete series in F. J. Furnivall, *The Digby Mysteries* (New Shakspere Soc., reprinted in 1896 for E. E. T. S.).

(e) 1890. *St. Mary Magdalen* (part only), from (d), in Pollard, 49.

(f) 1897. *Conversion of St. Paul,* from (d), in Manly, i. 215.

The Plays.

The plays appear to have been accidentally brought together in one MS., and should be treated separately for the purposes of literary history.

A. *Conversion of St. Paul.*

Schmidt, *Diss.* 28, assigns this to an East Midland author, and a Southern scribe. The play opens with a prologue by the *Poeta* who speaks of 'owr processe.' In the first scene or 'station,' Saul starts for Damascus and 'rydyth forth with hys seruantes a-bout the place & owt of the place.' There is a 'conclusyon' by the 'Poeta—si placet,'—

> 'ffynally of this stacon we mak a conclusyon,
> besechyng thys audyens to folow and succede
> with all your delygens this generall processyon.'

After a stage-direction 'ffinis Istius stacionis, et altera sequitur,' the *Poeta* introduces another 'prosses,'—

> 'Here shalbe brefly shewyd with all our besynes
> At thys pagent saynt poullys conuercyon.'

This scene takes place outside and in Damascus. There is a tempest, and 'godhed spekyth in heuyn.' Saul meets Ananias, and 'thys stacion' is concluded by the *Poeta,* and 'ffinis istius secunde stacionis et sequitur tarcia.'

Again the *Poeta* calls on the audience 'To vnderstond thys pagent at thys lytyll stacion.' Saul returns to Jerusalem, preaches and plans to escape over the wall in a basket. Here the later hand inserted the devil scene. The *Poeta* has his 'Conclusyo,' which ends :—

> 'Thys lytyll pagent thus conclud we
> as we can, lackyng lytturall scyens;
> besechyng yow all of hye and low degre,
> owr sympylnes to hold excusyd, and lycens,
> That of Retoryk haue non intellygens;
> Commyttyng yow all to owr lord Ihesus,
> To whoys lawd ye syng,—Exultet celum laudibus.'

The play, but for the devil scene, follows closely the biblical narrative. It was probably written for a small village, and for scene had a *platea,* and two *loca,* for Damascus and Jerusalem (with possibly a third for heaven). The audience moved with the actors from one 'station' or 'pageant' to the other, and back again. A later hand has inserted marginal directions for a 'Daunce' at various points in the speeches of the *Poeta.*

B. *St. Mary Magdalen.*

Schmidt, *Anglia*, viii. 385, assigns this to a West Midland author and Kentish scribe. Furnivall, 53, thinks the dialect East Midland. The plot covers the whole legendary life of the Magdalen, as it appears in the *Golden Legend*. The characters are very numerous, and include Satan and other devils, with allegorical figures such as the 'Kyngs of the World and the Flesch' and the 'Seven Dedly Synnes.' The action is not in any way divided in the manuscript, and implies an elaborate stationary *mise en scène* with various *loca*. These include the 'castell of Maudleyn' or Magdalum, thrones for the *Imperator*, who opens the play by calling for silence, Herod and Pilate, 'a stage, and Helle ondyr-neth that stage' for 'the prynse of dylles,' Jerusalem with a 'place,' an 'erbyr' or arbour, a tavern, the 'howse of symont leprovs,' a *sepulchrum* for Lazarus, and another for the *Quem quaeritis* and *Hortulanus* scenes which are introduced, a palace for the King of 'Marcylle' (Marseilles), a heathen temple, a 'hevyne' able to open, a lodge for the Magdalen in Marcylle, another castle, a rock, and a wilderness. There is also a practicable ship which goes to and from Marcylle (l. 1395 'Here xall entyre a shyp with a mery song'; l. 1445 'Her goth the shep owt of the place'; l. 1717 'Ett tunc navis venit in placeam'; l. 1797 'tunc remigat a montem'; l. 1879 'et tunc navis venit adcirca plateam'; l. 1915 'et tunc remigant a monte'; l. 1923 'Here goth the shep owȝt ofe the place'). The play ends with a *Te Deum*; but the following lines, added after the *Explicit*, suggest that the author had readers as well as spectators in mind:—

'yff Ony thyng Amysse be,
blame connyng, and nat me:
I desyer the redars to be my frynd,
yff ther be ony amysse, that to amend.'

C. *Massacre of the Innocents.*

Assigned by Schmidt, *Diss.* 18, to a Midland author and Southern scribe. Against the title of the play has been written, in a hand identified as that of the chronicler Stowe, 'the vij booke.' Evidently the play was one of a series, spread over successive years, and given on Saint Anne's day (July 26). This is shown by the opening speech of a *Poeta*, from which I extract:—

'This solenne fest to be had in remembraunce
Of blissed seynt Anne moder to our lady,
. . . .
The last yeer we shewid you in this place

how the shepherdes of Cristes birth made letificacion,
And thre kynges that came fro ther Cuntrees be grace
To worshipe Iesu, with enteer deuocion;
And now we purpose with hooll affeccion
To procede in oure mater as we can,
And to shew you of our ladies purificacion
That she made in the temple, as the vsage was than.
. . . .
ffrendes, this processe we purpose to pley as we can
before you all, here in your presens,
To the honour of god, our lady, & seynt Anne,
besechyng you to geve vs peseable Audiens.
And ye menstrallis, doth your diligens,
& ye virgynes, shewe summe sport & plesure,
These people to solas, & to do god reuerens,
As ye be appoynted; doth your besy cure!
¶ Et tripident.'

The action includes the Wrath of Herod, with a comic knight, Watkin, the Flight into Egypt, the Massacre of the Innocents, the Death of Herod, the Purification. The stage-directions mention a 'place' and a 'tempill.' In the latter are the virgins, who 'tripident' with Anne at the end. The *Poeta* excuses the 'rude eloquens' and 'sympyll cunnyng' of his company, promises 'the disputacion of the doctours' for next year, and calls on the minstrels and virgins for a final dance.

D. *Morality of Wisdom.*

See *Texts* (ii), s. v. *Macro Morals*.

Burial and Resurrection.

Manuscript.

Bodleian MS. e Museo, 160, f. 140. Furnivall, vii. 166, asserts that this once formed part of the *Digby MS.* 133, but offers no proof. The copy seems to date from the early fifteenth century. After the *Explicit*, in a later hand, is 'written by me . . .'; unfortunately the name is torn off. Lines here and there in the earlier part of the piece have been crossed out.

Editions.

(a) 1843. Wright and Halliwell, *Reliquiae Antiquae*, ii. 124.

(b) 1882. F. J. Furnivall, *The Digby Plays*, 171 (New Shakspere Soc., reprinted 1896 for E. E. T. S.).

See study by K. Schmidt in *Anglia*, viii. 393.

The Play.

Schmidt assigns the play to a writer whose dialect was a mixture of Northern and East Midland forms; Morris to a Northern author and West Midland scribe. Ten Brink, ii. 287, also thinks it to be Northern, and to date from 1430–60. Apparently the author set out to write, not a drama, but a narrative poem, mainly in dialogue. The first fifteen lines are headed 'The prologe of this treyte or meditatione off the buryalle of Criste & mowrnynge therat,' and contain a request to 'Rede this treyte.' The first 419 lines have a few narrative phrases introducing the speeches, such as 'Said Maudleyn,' 'Said Joseph.' At this point the writer seems to have stopped these, crossed out such as he had already written, and inserted in the margin of his second page,—

'This is a play to be playede, on part on gudfriday after-none, & the other part opon Esterday after the resurrectione, In the morowe, but at the begynnynge ar certene lynes [the prologue] which must not be saide if it be plaiede, which (. . . *a line cut off*).'

The Good Friday scene is an elaborate *planctus*. It is opened by Joseph of Arimathea, and the three Maries. Then comes Nicodemus, and the body of Christ is taken from the cross. The Virgin Mary enters with St. John, and the *planctus* is resumed. The body is laid in the sepulchre, and the scene is closed with—

'Thus her endes the most holy
Beriall of the body of Crist Iesu.'

The Easter morning scene begins with—

'Her begynnes his resurrection
On pashe daye at Morn.'

It contains a *Quem quaeritis*, a scene of lamentation between Peter, Andrew, and John, a *Hortulanus*, with a second apparition to all three Maries. They sing the first part of the *Victimae paschali*, 'in canti-fracto vel saltem in pallinodio,' and the Apostles come in for the dialogue part. Then the tidings are announced, and Peter and John visit the sepulchre; after which, 'Tunc cantant omnes simul *Scimus Christum* vell aliam sequentiam aut ympnum de resurrectione.'

Unidentified Plays.

(i) C. Hastings, *Le Théâtre Français et Anglais*, 167, says:—

'Il existe, en plus des quatre cycles de Mystères dont nous avons parlé dans les chapitres précédents, une cinquième collection (manu-scrit), propriété d'un simple particulier, M. Nicholls.'

(ii) W. C. Hazlitt, *Manual for the Collector and Amateur of Old English Plays*, 274, says:—

'Mr. F. S. Ellis told me (Dec. 10, 1864) that a gentleman at Leipsic then had a fragment of a large sheet on which was printed in types formed from a block and of a very large size an English Miracle-Play. In its perfect state it seems to have been intended to attach to a church door or any other suitable place.'

Cornwall.

i. *Origo Mundi: Passio Domini: Resurrexio Domini.*

Manuscripts.

(i) *Bodl. MS.* 791. Fifteenth century, with some alterations and additional stage-directions in a later hand. The text is Cornish, not earlier in date than the fourteenth century. Mr. Pedler (Norris, ii. 506) puts it, not very convincingly, at the end of the thirteenth.

(ii) *Bodl. MS.* 28,556. Seventeenth-century copy of (i), with an English translation of the larger part of the text by John Keigwyn, of Mousehole, 1695.

Edition.

1859. In Edwin Norris, *The Ancient Cornish Drama*, from (i), with modern translation by the editor.

Analysis.

The text forms three dramas, intended, as the closing words of the first two show, for performance on three consecutive days. At the end of each is a diagram of the disposition of the *pulpita* or *tenti* (cf. p. 391) for the day. The action on each day is continuous, but for the sake of comparison I divide it into scenes. These are sometimes indicated by a *Hic incipit* or similar formula.

(1) *Hic Incipit Ordinale de Origine Mundi.*

Fall of Lucifer (line 48).
Creation and Fall of Man (1–437).
Cain and Abel (438–633).
Seth in Paradise, and Death of Adam (634–916).
Noah and the Flood (917–1258).
Abraham and Isaac (1259–1394).
Moses and the Exodus (1395–1708).
Moses in the Wilderness (1709–1898).
David and the Rods (1899–2104).
David and Bathsheba (2105–2376).
Building of the Temple (2377–2628).
Prophecy of Maximilla (2629–2778).
Bridge over Cedron (2779–2824).

The diagram gives *Celum*, *Tortores*, *Infernum*, *Rex Pharao*, *Rex Dauid*, *Rex Sal[omon]*, *Abraham*, *Ortus*.

(2) *Hic Incipit Passio Domini Nostri Jhesu Christi.*

Temptation (1–172).
Entry into Jerusalem (173–330).
Cleansing of the Temple (331–392).
Healing of Bartimaeus (393–454).
Jesus in House of Simon the Leper (455–552).
Conspiracy of Jews (533–584).
Treachery of Judas (585–616).
Last Supper (617–930).
Gethsemane (931–1200).
Jesus before Caiaphas (1200–1504).
Remorse and Death of Judas (1505–1566).
Jesus before Pilate (1567–1616).
Jesus before Herod (1617–1816).
Condemnation (1817–2533), including—
Dream of Pilate's Wife (1907–1968, 2193–2212).
Cross brought from Cedron (2534–2584).
Bearing of the Cross (2585–2662).
Crucifixion (2663–2840).
Casting of Lots (2841–2860).
Death of Jesus (2861–3098), including—
Planctus Mariae (2925–2954).
Longinus (3003–3030).
Harrowing of Hell (3031–3078).
Descent from Cross (3099–3201).
Burial (3202–3216).

The diagram gives *Celum*, *Tortores*, *Doctores*, *Pilatus*, *Herodes*, *Princeps Annas*, *Cayaphas*, *Centurio*.

(3) *Hic Incipit Ordinale de Resurrexione Domini Nostri Jhesu Christi.*

Release of Joseph and Nicodemus (1–96, 307–334, 625–662).
Harrowing of Hell, resumed (97–306).
Setting of Watch (335–422).
Resurrection (423–678).
Quem quaeritis (679–834).
Hortulanus (835–892).
Incredulity of Thomas (893–1230, 1345–1586).
Peregrini (1231–1344).
Death of Pilate (1587–2360), including—
Veronica and Tiberius 1587–2360).
Ascension (2361–2630).

The diagram gives *Celum*, *Tortores*, *Infernum*, *Pilatus*, *Imperator*, *Josep Abar[imat]*, *Nichodemus*, *Milites*.

At the end of (1) and (3) the minstrels are directed to pipe for a dance.

Locality.

Mr. Norris prints an opinion of Mr. Pedler that the place-names suggest the neighbourhood of Penrhyn, and that the plays may have been composed in the collegiate house, hard by, of Glasney.

ii. *Creation of the World.*

Manuscripts.

(i) *Bodl.* 219, with colophon 'Heare endeth the Creacion of the worlde wth noyes flude wryten by William Jordan: the xii^th^ of August, 1611.' The text is Cornish, with English stage-directions containing forms earlier than 1611.

(ii) *Bodl.* 31,504 (MS. Corn. C. 1). Copy of (i), with English translation by John Keigwyn, 1693, written by 'H. Usticke.'

iii) *Harl.* 1867. Similar copy of (i), with Keigwyn's translation.

(iv) MS. belonging (in 1864) to J. C. Hotten the bookseller, containing also a copy of the narrative *Passion* or *Mount Calvary.*

Editions.

(a) 1827. *The Creation of the World, with Noah's Flood.* Edited from (iii) by Davies Gilbert (with Keigwyn's translation).

(b) 1864. *Gwreans an Bys. The Creation of the World.* Edited from (i), with a [new] translation by Whitley Stokes, as appendix to *Transactions of Philological Society* (1863).

The Play.

The text is headed 'The first daie [of] ye playe' and ends with a direction to minstrels to pipe for dancing, and an invitation to return on the morrow to see the Redemption. It is, therefore, probably unfinished. It appears to be based, with certain additions, on the *Origo Mundi.* It is continuous, but may be divided as follows:—

Creation and Fall of Lucifer (1–334).
Temptation and Fall (335–1055).
Cain and Abel. Birth of Seth (1056–1430).
Death of Cain (1431–1726).
Visit of Seth to Paradise (1727–1964).
Death of Adam (1965–2093).
Seth and Enoch (2094–2210).
Noah's Flood (2211–2530).

iii. *St. Meriasek.*

Manuscript.

In *Hengwrt MSS.* of Mr. Wynne at Peniarth. Cornish *Ordinale de Vita Sancti Mereadoci Episcopi et Confessoris*, written by 'dominus Hadton' in 1504. At the end is a circular diagram.

Edition.

1872. *Beunans Meriasek: The Life of Saint Meriasek.* Edited and translated by Whitley Stokes.

Locality.

Mr. Stokes suggests Camborne, of which place St. Meriasek was patron. The play invokes St. Meriasek and St. Mary of Camborne at the close.

II. POPULAR MORALITIES.

The Pride of Life.

Manuscript.

Written in two hands of the first half of the fifteenth century on blank spaces of a *Computus* of Holy Trinity Priory, Dublin, for 1343, preserved in the Irish Record Office, Dublin (Christ Church collection).

Editions.

1891. J. Mills in *Proceedings of Royal Soc. of Antiquaries of Ireland.*

1898. Brandl, 2.

Cf. H. Morley, *English Writers*, vii. 1730.

The play was probably written early in the fifteenth century. The dialect is that of the South of England, not far from London, modified by Northern scribes.

Only a fragment (502 ll.) is preserved, but a prologue gives the plot. There is no title; but '[A mens]ke gam schal gyn & ende' (l. 7), and '[Of Kyng of] lif I wol ȝou telle' (l. 17). The extant characters are *Rex Vivus*, *Primus Miles Fortitudo*, *Secundus Miles Sanitas*, *Regina*, *Nuntius Mirth*, *Episcopus*. The King rejoices with Mirth and his soldiers, and Queen and Bishop vainly call on him to repent. Later in the play Death and Life strove for the King, and Death took him. He was claimed by the 'ffendis,' but 'oure lady mylde' prayed to have him.

The play was out of doors (l. 10); the King had a *tentorium* which could be closed (l. 306); the Bishop sat on his 'se' (*sedes*); and so probably with the other actors, except Mirth, who perhaps came in 'oure þe lake' (l. 269); cf. Brandl, xix.

Macro Morals.

Manuscripts.

(a) *Macro MS.*, formerly in the possession of Mr. Cox Macro, now in that of Mr. Gurney, of Keswick Hall, Norfolk. The MS. appears from a gloss in *Mankind* (l. 674; cf. Brandl, xxvi), naming King Edward, to have been written during the reign of Edward IV (1461–1483). At the end of two of the plays is the name of Hyngham, a monk, to whom the MS. belonged.

(b) *Digby MS.* 133, on which cf. p. 428, has on f. 158 the first 754 lines of *Mind, Will, and Understanding*. The handwriting is said to be the same as that of the *Macro MS.* (Collier, ii. 207).

[A complete edition of the three moralities of the *Macro MS.* has long been contemplated by the E. E. T. S.]

i. *The Castle of Perseverance.*

Edition. 1890. Pollard, 64 (408 lines only).

Pollard dates the play not later than the middle of the reign of Henry VI. It contains about 3,500 lines.

The subject is the struggle of good and bad qualities for *Humanum Genus*. On the one side are *Malus Angelus* and *Mundus*, *Belial*, and *Caro*, aided by the Seven Deadly Sins and *Voluptas*, *Stultitia*, *Detractio*: on the other *Bonus Angelus*, with *Confessio*, *Schrift*, *Penitencia*, and the Six Divine Graces. Amongst other episodes *Humanum Genus* is besieged in the *Castle of Perseverance*. At the end *Misericordia*, *Iustitia*, *Pax*, *Veritas*, dispute in heaven, and *Pater sedens in trono* inclines to mercy.

The indications of *mise en scène* are very valuable. On the first leaf of the MS. is a diagram of the playing place, reproduced by Sharp, 23. There is a large circle with a double circumference, in which is written, 'This is the watyr a bowte the place, if any dyche may be mad ther it schal be pleyed; or ellys that it be stronglye barryd al a bowte: & lete nowth ower many stytelerys be withinne the plase.' Within the circle is a rude representation of a castle, and above, 'This is the castel of perseveranse that stondyth in the myddys of the place; but lete no men sytte ther for lettynge of syt, for ther schal be the best of all.' Beneath the castle is a small bed, with the legend, 'Mankynde is bed schal be under the castel, & ther schal the sowle lye under the bed tyl he schal ryse & pleye.' At the side is a further direction, 'Coveytyse cepbord schal be at the ende of the castel, be the beddys feet.' Outside the circle are written five directions for scaffolds, 'Sowth, Caro skaffold — West, Mundus skaffold — Northe, Belial skaffold—North Est, Coveytyse skaffold—Est, deus skaffold.' At the foot of the page are some notes for costume: '& he that schal pley belyal, loke that he have gunne powder brennyng in pypys in his hands and in his ers, and in his ars whanne he gothe to batayle. The iiij dowters schul be clad in mentelys, Mercy in wyth, rythwysnesse in red al togedyr, Trewthe in sad grene, & Pes al in blake, and they schul pleye in the place al to gedyr tyl they brynge up the sowle.'

There is a prologue by two *vexillatores*, who declare—

> 'These percell in propyrtes we spose us to playe,
> This day sevenenyt before you in syth,
> At N on the grene in ryal aray.'

They add that they will 'be onward be underne of the day' (9 a.m.).

ii. *Mind, Will, and Understanding.*

Editions.

1835. T. Sharp, *Ancient Mysteries* (Abbotsford Club, 754 lines from *Digby MS.*).

1837. W. B. D. D. Turnbull (Abbotsford Club, the rest from *Macro MS.*).

1882. F. J. Furnivall, *Digby Plays*, 139 (754 lines only).

Lucifer seduces Mind, Will, and Understanding. These are the three parts of Anima, who enters with devils running from under her skirts. Everlasting Wisdom effects a re-conversion. There are a number of mute persons attendant on the chief characters, whose coming and going, 'dysgysyde,' create scenic effects, as in a masque. There are minstrels and a hornpipe, songs and dances. At one point Lucifer snatches up 'a shrewde boy' (perhaps from the audience), and carries him off. An allusion to the Holborn quest suggests a London origin, but Schmidt (*Anglia*, viii. 390) thinks the dialect to be that of the north border of the West Midlands.

iii. *Mankind.*

Editions.

1897. Manly, i. 315.

1898. Brandl, 37.

The text is 901 lines long. A list of place-names (l. 491) makes it probable that it belongs to the borders of Norfolk and Cambridgeshire.

Mercy and Mischief, the latter helped by Nought, New Gyse, Nowadays, and the devil Titivillus, essay in turns to win the soul of Mankind.

The scene is divided. Part represents a tavern, of which Titivillus is host; part a 'deambulatorye' outside. A reference to the spectators (l. 29) runs, 'O ȝe souerens, þat sytt, and ȝe brotherne, þat stonde ryghte wppe': cf. Brandl, xxxii.

The Summoning of Everyman.

Editions.

[1509–1530.] Richard Pynson (fragment in B. M.).

[1509–1530.] Richard Pynson (fragment in Bodl.).

[1521–1537.] John Skot. 'Here begynneth a treatyse how the hye fader of heuen sendeth dethe to somon euery creature to come and gyue a counte of theyr lyues in this Worlde, and is in maner of a morall playe' (B.M. and Huth Library).

[1529–1537.] John Skot (in St. Paul's Churchyard).

There are modern editions by Hawkins (1773, vol. i), Gödeke (1865), Hazlitt-Dodsley (1874, vol. i), Pollard (1890, part only, and in full in *Fifteenth Century Prose and Verse*, 1903), H. Logeman, *Elckerlijk and Everyman* (1892), F. Sidgwick (1902). Another is announced in a series edited by I. Gollancz.

There are about 900 lines. Pollard, 202, assigns the text to the end of the fifteenth century; Ten Brink, ii. 302, to the reign of Edward IV. Prof. H. Logeman, *Elckerlijk* (1892), argues the play to be an English version of the closely similar Dutch *Elckerlijk*, attributed to Petrus Dorlandus of Diest, but K. H. de Raaf, *Spyeghel der Salicheyt van Elckerlijk* (1897), would invert the relation: cf. Brandl, xiv. The characters are Messenger, God, Death, Everyman, Fellowship, Kindred, Goods, Good Deeds, Knowledge, Confession, Beauty, Strength, Discretion, Five Wits, Angel, Doctor. The Messenger prologizes. God sends Death for Everyman, who finds that no one will accompany him save Good Deeds. The Doctor epilogizes. There are no indications of the *mise en scène*, except that there was a central scaffold for the 'House of Salvation' (Gödeke, 174, 200, cf. Brandl, xx).

The World and the Child.

Editions.

An Oxford bookseller, John Dorne, had a copy of 'mundus, a play' in 1520[1].

1522. Wynkyn de Worde. 'Here begynneth a propre newe Interlude of the Worlde and the chylde, otherwyse called (Mundus & Infans) . . .'

1523. Wynkyn de Worde.

There are a reprint by Lord Althorp (Roxburghe Club, 1817) and modern editions in Hazlitt-Dodsley, vol. i; Manly, i. 353.

[1] *Collectanea* (Oxf. Hist. Soc.), i. 130.

The *dramatis personae* are Mundus or the World, Infans or Dalliance or Wanton or Love-Lust and Liking or Manhood or Shame or Age or Repentance, Conscience, Folly, Perseverance. The representative of Man in various ages is alternately won over to good and evil. There are 979 lines. Collier, ii. 224; Pollard, li, assign the play to the reign of Henry VII; Brandl, xlii, thinks that the use of the *Narrenmotif* points to a date of composition not long before that of publication. Mundus says, 'Here I sette semely in se' (l. 22), and Manhood 'Here in this sete sytte I' (l. 285).

JOHN SKELTON. (*Magnificence.*)

Skelton was born, probably in Norfolk, about 1460. He studied at Cambridge and acquired fame as a scholar. Both universities honoured him with the degree of *poeta laureatus*. He was tutor to Henry VIII as a boy, and became rector of Diss in Norfolk. But he died in sanctuary at Westminster (1529), driven there on account of his bitter satires against Wolsey. In his *Garland of Laurell* (pr. 1523), a late work, he has a list of his writings, including—

> 'Of Vertu also the souerayne enterlude:
> . . . .
> His commedy, Achademios callyd by name:
> . . . .
> And of Soueraynte a noble pamphelet;
> And of Magnyfycence a notable mater.'

Bale, *Scriptores*, i. 652, ascribes to him *Comoediam de uirtute*, Lib. 1; *De magnificentia comoediam*, Lib. 1; *Theatrales ludos*, Lib. 1; *De bono ordine comoediam*, Lib. 1. *Magnificence* is, however, his only extant play.

Warton (Hazlitt-Warton, iii. 287) describes a piece shown him by William Collins, the poet, at Chichester, about 1759. He says:—

'It is the Nigramansir, a morall *Enterlude* and a pithie, written by Maister Skelton laureate, and plaid before the King and other estatys at Woodstoke on Palme Sunday. It was printed by Wynkyn de Worde in a thin quarto, in the year 1504. It must have been presented before Henry VII, at the royal manor or palace at Woodstock in Oxfordshire, now destroyed. The characters are a Necromancer or conjurer, the devil, a notary public, Simony, and Philargyria or Avarice. It is partly a satire on some abuses in the church . . . The story, or plot, is the trial of Simony and Avarice.'

Warton proceeds to describe the action at some length. Nothing further is known of the play. Ritson, *Bibliographia Poetica*, 106, said 'it is utterly incredible that the *Nigramansir* . . . ever existed,' and Mr. H. E. D. Blakiston (*Eng. Hist. Rev.* for April, 1896) has called attention to several cases in which Warton showed *mala fides* as a literary historian. In another place (iii. 310) Warton incidentally calls the piece 'Skelton's *The Trial of Simonie*.' E. G. Duff, *Hand Lists of English Printers*, Part i, knows of no extant copy.

Magnificence.

Editions.

[1529–1533.] John Rastell. 'Magnyfycence, a goodly interlude and a mery, deuysed and made by mayster Skelton, poet laureate, late deceasyd.' Folio.

1533. John Rastell. Quarto.

1821. J. Littledale (Roxburghe Club).

1843. A. Dyce, *Poetical Works of Skelton*, i. 225.

1890. Pollard, 106 (extract).

The characters are Felicity, Liberty, Measure, Magnificence, Fancy, Counterfeit Countenance, Crafty Countenance, Cloked Collusion, Courtly Abusion, Folly, Adversity, Poverty, Despair, Mischief, Good Hope, Redress, Sad Circumspection, Perseverance. The plot shows Magnificence brought low by evil counsellors, and restored by good ones. The players come in and out of 'the place.' There are 2,596 lines. The play was written later than 1515, as a reference to the liberality of the dead Louis of France (l. 283) must intend Louis XII who died in that year, not the niggard Louis XI.

Sir David Lyndsay. (*Ane Satyre of the Thrie Estaitis.*)

Sir David Lyndsay 'of the Mount' in Fifeshire was born in 1490. By 1511 he was employed in the royal household, first as an actor or musician, then as 'Keeper of the Kingis Grace's person.' In 1529 he became Lyon King at Arms, a post which included the charge of court entertainments. His satire did not spare the church, and he seems to have been in sympathy with Knox and other reformers, but he did not so far commit himself as to endanger his office, which he held until his death in 1555.

The Thrie Estaitis.

Performances.

(i) *Jan.* 6, 1540, *Linlithgow,* before James V. This performance, the first of which there is any satisfactory evidence, was described by Sir W. Eure in a letter to Cromwell (Ellis, *Original Letters,* 3rd Series,

iii. 275; Brewer-Gairdner, xv. 36), enclosing a 'Copie of the Nootes of the Interluyde.' The version seems to have been different from that now extant. 'Solaice' figured as the presenter. Eure mentions the 'scaffald' and 'the interluyds of the Play.' He adds that, as a result, James V admonished the Bishops to reform their ways.

(ii) *June* 7 (*Whit-Tuesday*), 1552, *Cupar of Fife*. The Bannatyne MS. (see below) has the 'Proclamation maid at Cowpar of Fyffe, upon the Castell-hill, 7 June, beginning at seven.' This was therefore the extant version. The year is fixed by an incidental reference to the day (June 7) as Whit-Tuesday.

(iii) 1554 (?), *Edinburgh*. Henry Charteris, in his preface to Lyndsay's *Warkis* of 1568 (Laing, iii. 231), says of the 'makar's' relations to the clergy, 'Sic ane spring he gaif thame in the Play, playit besyde Edinburgh, in presence of the Quene Regent, and ane greit part of the Nobilitie, with ane exceding greit nowmer of pepill, lestand fra ix houris afoir none till vj houris at evin.' The Bannatyne MS. gives the play as 'maid in the Grenesyd besyd Edinburgh,' and 'in anno 155- 3eiris.' Cf. Appendix W, p. 366.

Editions.

(*a*) 1602. Robert Charteris. 'Ane satyre of the thrie estaits, in commendation of vertew in vituperation of vyce. Maid be Sir Dauid Lindesay of the Mont, alias, Lyon King of Armes.'

Diligence, as presenter, summons the three estates before Rex Humanitas. Many 'Vycis' and other allegorical personages appear before the Rex on his 'royall sait.' In ll. 1288–1411 comes the first interlude (although the term is not used in the text) of 'The Sowtar and Tailor.' At l. 1931 is the 'End of the First Part of the Satyre,' with the direction, 'Now sall the Pepill mak collatioun: then beginnis the Interlude: the Kings, Bischops, and principal Players being out of their seats.' This interlude introduces the Pauper, Pardoner, Sowtar, and others. Part ii begins at l. 2298. At l. 4283, 'Heir sall enter Folie,' and at l. 4483, 'Heir sall Folie begin his Sermon, as followis.' The theme is, of course, *Stultorum numerus infinitus*, and at the close the preacher names recipients of his 'Follie Hattis or Hudes' (cf. ch. xvi). At l. 4629, the people are finally dismissed to dance and drink, Diligence calling on a minstrel.

(*b*) † 1568. Bannatyne MS. (ed. Hunterian Club, 1873–1896, Part iv).

George Bannatyne included in his collection of pieces by the Scots 'makaris' (*a*) the 'Proclamation' at Cupar of Fife (see above), (*b*) a preliminary interlude, not in Charteris's edition, of a Cottar, an Auld Man and his Wife, a 'Fuill,' &c.; (*c*) seven extracts from the play, headed, 'Heir begynnis Schir Dauid Lyndsay Play maid in the Grenesyd besyd Edinburgh, quhilk I writtin bot schortly be Interludis, levand the grave mater thereof, becaws the samyne abuse is weill reformit in Scotland, praysit be God, quhairthrow I omittit that principall mater and writtin only Sertane mirry Interludis thairof verry pleasand, begynnyng at the first part of the Play.'

1869. F. Hall, *Works of Lindsay*, Pt. iv (E. E. T. S. o. s. 37).

1879. D. Laing, *Works of Lindsay*, vol. ii.

[Other editions are enumerated by Laing, iii. 259. There is an analysis of the play in T. F. Henderson, *Scottish Vernacular Literature*, 219.]

III. TUDOR MAKERS OF INTERLUDES.

Henry Medwall.

Medwall was chaplain to John Morton, cardinal and Archbishop of Canterbury (1486–1500), who is probably the 'my lord' of *Nature*, i. 1438. Besides *Nature*, he wrote an interlude 'of the fyndyng of Troth, who was carried away by ygnoraunce and ypocresy,' played by the King's players before Henry VIII at Richmond on Jan. 6, 1514. The 'foolys part' was the best, but the play was too long to please the King (cf. p. 201). See also s. v. *Lucrece* (p. 458).

Nature.

Editions.

[1530–4.] William Rastell. 'A goodly interlude of Nature compyled by mayster Henry Medwall,' &c.

1898. Brandl, 73.

There are two 'partes' of the 'processe' (i. 1434). The first (1439 ll.) has Mundus, Worldly Affection, Man, Nature, Innocency, Reason, Sensuality, Privy Council, Pride, a Boy, Shamefastness. In the second (1421 ll.), on a different day, some of these recur, with Bodily Lust, Wrath, Envy, Sloth, Gluttony, Humility, Charity, Abstinence, Liberality, Chastity, Good Occupation, and Patience. The personages come in and out at 'dorys' (i. 728) and sit down on 'stole' or 'chayr.' There was also a fire (ii. 518 sqq.). Probably the scene was in a room. At the end 'they syng some goodly ballet.'

John Heywood.

John Heywood was born either in London or at North Mimms in Hertfordshire, about 1497. He is claimed as a member of Broadgates

Hall, afterwards Pembroke College, Oxford. From about 1515 he was employed at Court; in 1519 he is called a 'singer,' later a 'player at virginals,' and finally he was master of a company of children, possibly the singing-school of St. Paul's. His advancement with Henry VIII and the Princess Mary is ascribed to Sir Thomas More, whose kinsman he became. More's sister Elizabeth married John Rastell, lawyer and printer. John Heywood's wife was their granddaughter, Elizabeth. It may be added that their daughter, another Elizabeth, was the mother of John Donne. Heywood took More's line in Church matters, but conformed to the Act of Supremacy. He was in high favour under Mary, and at her death retired to Malines. He was alive in 1577, but dead in 1587.

Heywood's extant interludes are all early work; although Bale, writing in 1557 (*Scriptores*, ed. 2, ii. 110), only ascribes to him *De Aura, comoediam; De Amore, tragoediam; De quadruplici P.* The *Pardoner and Friar*, which mentions Leo X as alive, must be before 1521. *Love* and the *Four Ps* may be about as early: the rest may belong to the following decade (Brandl, li). In 1538 Heywood showed a play of children before Mary (Madden, 62). In 1539, Wolsey paid him for a masque of Arthur's Knights, or Divine Providence, at court (Brewer, xiv. (2) 782). In 1553 he set out a play of children at court (*Loseley MSS.* 89). At Mary's coronation he sat in a pageant under a vine against the school in St. Paul's Churchyard and made speeches (Holinshed (1808), iv. 6).

See W. Swododa, *J. Heywood als Dramatiker* (1888).

Plays.

i. *The Pardoner and the Friar.*

Editions.

1533. Wyllyam Rastell. 'A mery Play betwene the pardoner and the frere, the curate and neybour Pratte.'

There are modern editions in F. J. Child, *Four Old Plays* (1848); Hazlitt-Dodsley, vol. i; Pollard, 114 (extract).

The scene of the action is supposed to be a church. About 1,000 lines. The date of composition was under Leo X (1513–1521).

ii. *Love.*

Editions.

1533. William Rastell. 'A play of loue, A newe and mery enterlude concerning pleasure and payne in loue, made by Ihon̄ Heywood.'

[Unique copy in Magd. Coll., Camb. See Greg, *Plays*, 143.]

[1546–1586.] John Waley.

[Unique copy, without title-page, in Bodl., bound with *Weather* and *Four Ps*. (Bodl. 4°, P. 33, Jur.). Copies of these three plays, with one now lost, of 'Old Custom,' are mentioned in an inventory of the effects of John, Earl of Warwick, 1545–1550 (*Hist. MSS.* ii. 102).]

1898. Brandl, 159.

Little more than a series of disputations between Lover Loved, Lover not Loved, Loved not Loving, and No Lover nor Loved. There are 1,573 lines. Towards the end, 'Here the vyse cometh in ronnynge sodenly aboute the place among the audiens with a hye copyn tank on his hed full of squybs fyred.'

iii. *Four Ps.*

Editions.

[1541–1547.] William Myddleton. 'The playe called the foure P. P. A newe and very mery enterlude of A palmer. A pardoner. A poticary. A pedler. Made by Iohn Heewood.'

[1549–1569.] William Copland.

1569. John Allde.

There are modern editions in W. Scott, *Ancient British Drama*, vol. i (1810): Hazlitt-Dodsley, vol. i; Manly, i. 483.

[Copyright, with that of *Love* and *Weather* transferred, Jan. 15, 1582, from late Sampson Awdeley to John Charlwood (Arber, ii. 405). The *Four Pees* is mentioned with other early plays in *Sir Thomas More* (Shakes. Soc. 1844).]

There are no indications of *mise en scène*. There are 1,236 lines.

iv. *Weather.*

Editions.

1533. William Rastell. 'The Play of the wether. A new and very mery enterlude of all maner wethers made by Iohn̄ Heywood.'

[1564–1576.] Anthony Kytson.

1898. Brandl, 211. 1903. Gayley, 19.

The characters are Jupiter, Merry Report, 'the vyce,' Gentleman, Merchant, Ranger, Water Miller, Wind Miller, Gentlewoman, Launder, A Boy ('the lest that can play'). All in turn petition different weather from Jupiter. The piece is 1,255 lines long. Jupiter has his 'thron' (l. 179).

v. *John, Tib and Sir John.*

Editions.

153¾. William Rastell. 'A mery play between Iohan Iohan the husbande, Tyb his wyfe and Syr Ihān the preest.'

1819. Chiswick Press. 1898. Brandl, 259. 1903. Gayley, 61.

The action proceeds in the 'place' (l. 667), which represents Johan's house with a fire (ll. 399, 460). The door of the priest's chamber is also visible (ll. 316, 673). There are 680 lines.

vi. *Witty and Witless.*

Manuscript.

Harl. MS. 367.

Edition.

1846. F. W. Fairholt (Percy Soc.). 'A dialogue concerning witty and witless.'

Thomas Hacket entered the 'pleye of wytles' on S. R. in 1560–1 (Arber, i. 154). This piece is a mere dialogued *débat* or *estrif.*

vii. *Gentleness and Nobility.*

[1516–1533.] John Rastell. 'Of Gentylnes and Nobylyte. A dyaloge ... compilid in maner of an enterlude with diuers toys and gestis addyt therto to make mery pastyme and disport.'

1829. J. H. Burn.

This resembles *Witty and Witless* in character. It is only conjecturally assigned to Heywood. The copy in the British Museum of Rastell's edition (C. 40, i. 16) has a mounted woodcut portrait with the initials I. H., but I do not know whether that really belongs to it.

John Bale.

[*Authorities.*—Collier, i. 123; ii. 159; Ward, i. 173; Lives of Bale in *D. N. B.* (article by Mandell Creighton) and Cooper, *Athenae Cantabrigienses*; his own works, especially *Illustrium Maioris Britanniae Scriptorum Catalogus* (1548, ed. 2, 1557–9, i. 704) and *Vocacyon to Ossory* (*Harl. Miscellany*, ed. 1808, i. 328); editions of plays named below, especially that of Schröer.]

John Bale was born in 1495 at Cove, near Dunwich, in Suffolk. He was placed as a boy in the Carmelite convent of Norwich, thence went to that of Holn, or Holm, in Northumberland, and finally to Jesus College, Cambridge. He took orders, but was converted to Protestantism by Lord Wentworth, and married a 'faithful Dorothy.' He became vicar of Thorndon, in Suffolk, and earned the protection of Thomas Cromwell *ob editas comoedias*. Cromwell's accounts (Brewer, xiv. 2. 337) show payments to him for plays on Sept. 8, 1538, at St. Stephen's, Canterbury, and on Jan. 31, 1539. At his patron's fall in 1540 he fled to Germany, and joined vigorously in polemic. In his *Epistel Exhortatorye of an Inglyshe Christian* (1544), written under the pseudonym of Henry Stalbridge, he says: 'None leave ye unvexed and untrobled—no, not so much as the poore minstrels, and players of enterludes, but ye are doing with them. So long as they played lyes, and sange baudy songes, blasphemed God, and corrupted men's consciences, ye never blamed them, but were verye well contented. But sens they persuaded the people to worship theyr Lorde God aryght, accordyng to hys holie lawes and not yours, and to acknoledge Jesus Chryst for their onely redeemer and saviour, without your lowsie legerdemains, ye never were pleased with them.' He returned in 1547, and in 1548 printed in his *Scriptores* the following list of his 'in idiomate materno, comedias sub vario metrorum genere.'

1. 'Lib. 14. Vitam D. Ioannis Baptistae.
2. Com. 1. de Christo duodenni.
3. Com. 2. de baptismo & tentatione.
4. Com. 1. de Lazaro resuscitato.
5. Com. 1. de consilio pontificum.
6. Com. 1. de Simone leproso.
7. Com. 1. de coena Domini & pedum lotione.
8. Com. 2. de passione Christi.
9. Com. 2. de sepultura & resurrectione.
10. Lib. 2. super utroque regis coniugio.
11. Lib. 2. de sectis Papisticis.
12. Lib. 2. erga Momos et Zoilos.
13. Lib. 2. Proditiones Papistarum.
14. Lib. 1. contra adulterantes Dei verbum.
15. Lib. 2. *de Ioanne Anglorum rege.*
16. Lib. 1. de imposturis Thomae Becketi.
17. Lib. 1. *de magnis Dei promissionibus.*
18. Lib. 1. *de predicatione Ioannis.*
19. Lib. 1. *de Christi tentatione.*
20. Lib. 1. *Corruptiones legum divinarum.*
21. Lib. 1. Amoris imaginem.
22. Lib. 4. Pammachii tragoedias transtuli.'

As Bale gives a Latin translation of the opening words of each piece, his five extant plays can be identified with those I have italicized. It is to be noted that Nos. 18 and 19 have the same subject as No. 3, which seems to form part of a complete Passion cycle (Nos. 2–9).

In 1547 Bale was made rector of Bishopstoke, Hants, in 1551 of Swaffham, Norfolk, and in 1553 Bishop of Ossory, in Ireland. On the day of the proclamation of Queen Mary he had some of his plays performed at the market-cross of Kilkenny (cf. p. 374). But he had to take refuge at Basle, and on the accession of Elizabeth found himself too old to resume his see, and retired on a prebend in Canterbury Cathedral, where he died in 1563.

Plays.

i. *God's Promises.*

Editions.

(i) 1577. 'A Tragedye or enterlude manyfestyng the chefe promyses of God vnto man by all ages in the olde lawe, from the fall of Adam to the incarnacyon of the lorde Jesus Christ. Compyled by John Bale, An. Do. 1538, and now fyrst imprynted 1577. [List of characters.] *Iohn Charlwood for Stephen Peele,* 1577.'

(ii) n.d. [Another edition]. 'Compyled by Johan Bale, Anno Domini M.D.XVXXXVIII.' *B. L.*

(iii) 1874. Hazlitt-Dodsley, i. 277 (and in all earlier editions of Dodsley, from 1744).

A prologue by *Baleus prolocutor* is followed by seven 'Actes,' in which *Adam, Noah, Abraham, Moses, David, Esaias, Iohannes Baptista* discourse in turn with *Pater Coelestis.* Each Act ends with one of the pre-Christmas antiphons known as the seven Oes (cf. vol. i. p. 344), to be sung by a 'Chorus cum organis' in Latin or English. *Baleus Prolocutor* epilogizes, ending 'More of thys matter conclude hereafter we shall.' This play is practically a *Prophetae.*

ii. *John Baptist.*

Editions.

(i) n.d. 'A Brefe Comedy or Enterlude of Johan Baptystes preachynge in the Wyldernesse; openynge the craftye assaultes of the hypocrytes, with the gloryouse Baptyme of the Lorde Jesus Christ. Compyled by Johan Bale, Anno M.D.XXXVIII.'

(ii) 1744. *Harleian Miscellany,* i. 97.

Praefatio by *Baleus Prolocutor.* Then *Incipit Comoedia.* Bale has a final speech. The *Interlocutores* are *Pater Coelestis, Ioannes Baptista, Publicanus, Pharisaeus, Iesus Christus, Turba vulgaris, Miles armatus, Sadducaeus.*

iii. *Temptation.*

Editions.

(i) n.d. 'A brefe Comedy or enterlude concernynge the temptacyon of our Lorde and sauer Iesus Christ, by Sathan in the desart. Compyled by Iohan Bale, Anno M.D.XXXVIII.'

(ii) 1870. A. B. Grosart, *Miscellanies of Fuller Worthies Library,* vol. i.

Praefatio by *Baleus Prolocutor.* Then *Incipit Comoedia.* Bale has a final speech. The other *Interlocutores* are *Iesus Christus, Satan tentator, Angelus primus, Angelus alter*. The play calls itself an 'Acte.'

[These three plays closely resemble each other. They were all written at Thorndon in 1538, and are markedly Protestant in tone. They were also all performed at Kilkenny, on Aug. 20, 1553.]

iv. *Three Laws.*

Editions.

(i) n.d. A Comedy concernynge thre lawes, of nature, Moses, and Christ, corrupted by the Sodomytes Pharysees and Papystes. Compyled by Johan Bale. Anno M.D.XXXVIII.

Colophon: Thus endeth thys Comedy [&c.]. Compyled by Johan Bale. Anno M.D. XXXVIII, and lately inprented per Nicolaum Bamburgensem.

(ii) 1562. Edition by Thomas Colwell.

(iii) A. Schröer, in *Anglia*, v. 137.

The play may have been written in 1538, but the allusions (ll. 2073, 2080) to King Edward and the Lord Protector show that it was revised after 1547. It is not, like (i), (ii), and (iii), a miracle-play, but a morality, and its Protestantism is far more advanced and polemical than theirs. It is 2,081 lines long, and has five *Actus*, with the usual *Praefatio* by *Baleus Prolocutor*. The other *Interlocutores* are *Deus pater, Natura lex, Moseh lex, Christi lex vel Euangelium, Infidelitas, Idololatria, Sodomismus, Ambitio, Auaricia, Pseudodoctrina, Hypocrisis, Vindicta Dei, Fides Christiana*. At the end is a note how 'Into fyue personages maye the partes of thys Comedy be deuyded,' and another for 'The aparellynge of the six vyces or frutes of Infydelyte.'

v. *King John.*

Manuscript.

In possession of the Duke of Devonshire, found amongst papers probably belonging to the Corporation of Ipswich. Written in two hands, of which one is believed to be Bale's.

Editions.

(i) 1838. Ed. J. P. Collier for Camden Soc.

(ii) 1890. Extract in Pollard, 146.

(iii) 1897. Manly, i. 525, from (i).

'Kynge Johan' contains 2,656 lines, but is divided into 'ij playes,' i. e. Acts. At l. 1119 is a reference to 'the seconde acte' and a 'Finit

Actus Primus.' There are nineteen personages—*Kynge Johan, Yngland, Clargy, Sedycyon, Cyvyle Order, Stevyn Langton, Commynalte, Nobylyte, Cardynall Pandulphus, Pryvat Welth, Dissimulacyon, Raymundus, Symon of Swynsett, Usurpyd Power, The Pope, Interpretour* (a presenter), *Treasor, Veryte, Imperyall Majestye*—but these are marked with brackets to show that they can be taken by nine actors. The play is strongly Protestant. It was doubtless written before 1548, as 'Lib. 2. de Ioanne Anglorum Rege' are included in Bale's *Scriptores* list of that year. Collier, i. 123, quotes a deposition as to 'an enterlude concernyng King John' performed 'in Christmas tyme [1538–9] at my Lorde of Canterbury's' which was certainly anti-Papal, and was probably Bale's. But the extant text has undergone a later revision, for the prayer at the end is for Elizabeth. Fleay, *Hist. of Stage*, 62, conjectures that it was performed upon her visit to Ipswich in August, 1561. There was probably a single stage or pageant. The characters enter and go out. At l. 1377 Sedycyon speaks 'extra locum'; at l. 785 is the phrase 'Ye may perseyve yt in pagent here this hower.'

NICHOLAS GRIMALD.

Grimald was the son of a Genoese clerk in the service of Henry VII. He migrated from Christ's College, Cambridge, to Oxford, where, after a short stay at Brasenose, he became Fellow and Lecturer first of Merton in 1540, then of Christ Church in 1547. To this period belong his Latin plays, and the bulk of his lyrics and other poems in *Tottel's Miscellany*. He was widely read in theology and scholarship, and was chosen chaplain to Bishop Ridley, for whom he did much controversial work. Under Mary in 1555 he was imprisoned, but escaped by a recantation. He was dead before 1562. Bale, *Scriptores* (1557), i. 701, ascribes to him amongst other writings:—

Archiprophetae tragoediam.
Famae comoediam.
Christum nascentem.
Christum redivivum.
Protomartyrem.
Athanasium, seu infamiam.
Troilum ex Chaucero, comoediam.

Of these the first and fourth survive; of the others some can only be conjecturally put down as plays.

†1540. *Christus Redivivus.*

Editions.

1543. Gymnicus, Cologne. Christus redivivus. Comoedia tragica, sacra et nova. Authore Nicolao Grimaoldo.

1899. J. M. Hart, in *Publications of the Modern Language Association of America*, xiv. No. 3.

The dedication is dated, 'Oxoniae, e Collegio Martonensi. Anno 1543'; but according to the account of the play given therein by the author, it was performed by the *pubes* of B.N.C. before he joined Merton.

1547. *Archipropheta.*

Manuscript.

Brit. Mus. Royal MS. 12 A. 46.

Edition.

1548. Gymnicus, Cologne. Archipropheta, Tragoedia iam recens in lucem edita. Autore Nicolao Grimoaldo.

The dedication is dated 1547. The play is divided into Acts and Scenes, and has choruses. It deals with the story of John the Baptist. Herford, 116, suggests a possible influence from the *Iohannes Decollatus* (1546) of Jakob Schöpper of Dortmund (Bahlmann, *Lat. Dr.* 93).

Nicholas Udall.

[*Authorities.*—Bale, *Scriptores* (1557), i. 717; Ward, i. 254; Pearson, ii. 413; Kempe, 63, 90; S. L. Lee, s.v. Udall in *D. N. B.*; T. Fowler, *Hist. of C.C.C.* 370; Maxwell-Lyte, *Hist. of Eton* (3rd ed. 1899), 117; J. W. Hales, *The Date of the First English Comedy*, in *Englische Studien*, xviii (1893), 408; E. Flügel, *Nicholas Udall's Dialogues and Interludes*, in *Furnivall Miscellany* (1901), 81.]

Life.

Nicholas Udall, Uvedale, Owdall, Woodall, or Yevedall, was born in Hampshire in 1505, and educated at Winchester and Corpus Christi College, Oxford, where he held an informal lectureship in 1526–8. He was an early Oxford exponent of Lutheran views. In 1532 he assisted Leland in preparing verses for the London pageants at the coronation of Anne Boleyn. From 1533–7 he was vicar of Braintree, Essex, and not improbably wrote the play of *Placidas,* alias *Sir Eustace*, recorded in 1534 in the churchwardens' accounts. But from 1534 he was also head master of Eton. Thomas Cromwell's accounts for 1538 include 'Woodall, the schoolmaster of Eton, for playing before my Lord, £5' (Brewer, xiv. 2. 334). In 1541 he left Eton, under an accusation of theft and other misbehaviour. But he found favour with Katharine Parr, Somerset, and Edward VI through literary and theological work, was made tutor to Edward Courtenay and obtained in 1551 a prebend at Windsor, and in 1553 the living of Calborne, Isle of Wight. He had not, however, so far committed himself on the Protestant side as to make it impossible to conform under Mary. He was tutor to Bishop Gardiner's household, and either in 1553 or 1554 became head master of Westminster. Here he remained to his death in 1556. A letter of Mary in 1554 states that he had 'at soondrie seasons' shown 'dialogues and enterludes' before her, and requires the Revels office to provide him with 'apparell' for his 'devises' at the coming Christmas. The Revels accounts for the year mention 'certen plaies' made by him, but the items referring to them cannot be disentangled from those for masks given at the same Christmas. Bale does not mention Udall in the 1548 edition of his *Scriptores*, but in that of 1557 he gives a list of works 'Latine et Anglice,' including 'Comoedias plures, Lib. 1,' and adds that he 'transtulit' for Katherine Parr, 'tragoediam de papatu.' When Elizabeth was at Cambridge on Aug. 8, 1564, 'an English play called Ezekias made by Mr. Udal' was given before her by King's College men (Nichols, *Progr. of Eliz.* i. 186).

Roister Doister.

Editions.

[1566–7. In this year the play was entered on the Stationers' Registers to Thomas Hacket, and to this edition the unique copy, without title-page or colophon, presented in 1818 to the Eton College library, probably belongs.]

1818. Briggs.

1821. F. Marshall.

1830. Thomas White, in *Old English Drama*, vol. i.

1847. W. D. Cooper, for Shakespeare Society.

1869. E. Arber, in *English Reprints*.

1874. Hazlitt-Dodsley, iii. 53.

1897. J. M. Manly, ii. 3 (based on Arber).

1903. E. Flügel, in C. M. Gayley, *Representative English Comedies*, 105.

The play is divided into *Actus* and *Scenae*, and is called in a prologue, which refers to Plautus and Terence, a 'comedie, or enterlude.' The prayer at the end is for a 'queene' who protects the 'Gospell.' Probably Elizabeth is meant. This, however, must be later in date than that of the play itself, which has been fixed by Prof. Hales to 1553–4, on the ground that a passage in it is quoted in the third edition (1553 or 1554) of T. Wilson's *Rule of Reason*, but not in the earlier editions of 1550–1 and 1552. Prof. Hales thinks that Udall was master of Westminster as early as 1553, and wrote it for the boys there. If Wilson's date is 1554, the play may have been one of those given at court in the Christmas of 1553.

IV. LIST OF EARLY TUDOR INTERLUDES.

Pre-Controversial Moralities.

The *dramatis personae* are all abstractions, with an occasional moral type, such as Hickscorner, or a social type, such as a Taverner.

1. †1486–1501. *Henry Medwall. Nature.*

See s. v. Medwall.

2. †1513. *Hickscorner.*

[1501–35.] W. de Worde. Hyckescorner.

[1546–86.] J. Waley.

Fragments of unidentified editions are described by Greg, *Plays*, 139. On Jan. 15, 1582, the copyright was transferred from the late Sampson Awdeley to John Charlwood (Arber, ii. 405). Modern reprints are in Hawkins, vol. i; Hazlitt-Dodsley, vol. i; Manly, vol. i. There are 1,026 lines. Ten Brink, iii. 125, dates the play at about the beginning of the sixteenth century. Collier, ii. 227, and Ward, i. 119, place it in the reign of Henry VII, whose ship, the Regent, is named. Brandl, xxviii, notes that this is spoken of (l. 356) as sunk, which occurred in 1513. This is one of the 'auncient Plays' in *Captain Cox*, cxviii.

3. †1513–29. *Youth.*

[1546–86.] J. Waley. Thēterlude of Youth.

[1549–69.] W. Copland.

Greg, *Plays*, 141, mentions a fragment of a third edition. The play is printed in Hazlitt-Dodsley, vol. ii. There are about 1,200 lines. Collier, ii. 230; Ward, i. 126; Pollard, liv, put the date in Mary's reign; Brandl, xxviii, early in that of Henry VIII. Passages are borrowed from *Hickscorner*. This is named in *Captain Cox*, cxviii.

4. †1517. *John Rastell. The Nature of the Four Elements.*

[1516–33.] John Rastell. A new interlude and a mery of the nature of the .iiii. elementȩ declarynge many proper poynts of phylosophy naturall and of dyuers strange landys and of dyuers strannge effect and causis, which interlude, if the whole matter be played, will contain the space of an hour and a half; but if you list you may leave out much of the said matter, as . . . and then it will not be past three quarters of an hour of length.

There are modern editions by Halliwell (Percy Soc. lxxiv), and in Hazlitt-Dodsley, vol. i, and extracts in Pollard, 97. There are about 900 lines. A note says 'also, yf ye lyst, ye may brynge in a Dysguysinge,' and a direction for the 'dance' or disguising shows that the stage was a 'hall.' The date is fixed by Collier, ii. 238; Ward,

i. 126; Pollard, 205, on the ground that the discovery of America is said to be 'within this twenty years' and by 'Americus' (i. e. Amerigo Vespucci, 1497). The authorship has been doubted, apparently in ignorance of the ascription of it to Rastell by Bale, *Scriptores* (1557), i. 660 'Insignis hic Cosmographus, de trium mundi partium, Asiae, Africae, et Europae descriptione, ingeniosissimam ac longissimam comoediam primum edidit, cum instrumentis & figuris, quam uocabat *Naturam naturatam. Lib.* 1. *Exuberans diuinae potentiae gratia.*' The opening words quoted by Bale translate those of the play 'Thaboundant grace of the power devyne.' Probably Rastell was also the printer, although the unique and imperfect copy (*B.M.* 643, b. 45) has only a manuscript imprint.

5. †1541–8. *John Redford. Wit and Science.*

Printed by Halliwell (Shakespeare Soc., 1848) and Manly, vol. i, from *Brit. Mus. Addl. MS.* 15,233, which is imperfect at the beginning, but has the colophon 'Thus endyth the Play of Wyt and Science, made by Master Jhon Redford.'

There are 1,059 lines. The final prayer is for the 'Kyng and Quene.' Brandl, lxxii, dates the play between 1541, when the 'gaillard,' which is mentioned, was first danced in England, and the death of Katharine Parr in 1548. It was adapted in more than one Elizabethan interlude; cf. Brandl, loc. cit.; J. Seifert, *Wit- und Science-Moralitäten* (1892); and p. 200, n. 2. Redford was at one time Master of the St. Paul's song-school. The MS. also contains songs and fragments of other moralities by him.

Pseudo-Interludes: Disputations.

6. †1521. *John Heywood. Love.*

7. †1521–31. *John Heywood. Witty and Witless.*

8. †1521–31. *John Heywood* (?). *Gentleness and Nobility.*

See s. v. Heywood.

Pseudo-Interlude: Banns.

9. †1503. *W. Dunbar. The Droichis Part of the Play.* Printed in Dunbar's *Works* (ed. J. Small, for Scottish Text Soc.), ii. 314.

One MS. is headed 'Ane Littill Interlud of the Droichis Part of the [Play]'; another, and the fuller, 'Heir followis the maner of the crying of ane playe.' Both have at the end 'Finis off the Droichis Pairt of the Play.'

There are 176 lines. The Droich (dwarf) enters to an 'amyable audiens' in Edinburgh, 'to cry a cry.' He calls himself 'Welth,' and bids

'ȝe noble merchandis ever ilkane
Address ȝow furth with bow and flane
In lusty grene lufraye,
And follow furth on Robyn Hude.'

The piece is clearly a 'banns' for a May-game; cf. vol. i. p. 174. The S. T. S. editors (i. ccxxxiii), think it was written for the reception of Princess Margaret in 1503.

Pseudo-Interlude: Translation.

10. *Necromantia.*

[1516–33.] John Rastell. Necromantia. A dialog of the poet Lucyan, for his fantesye faynyd for a mery pastyme. And furst by hym compylyd in the Greke tonge. And after translated owt of the Greke into Latyn, and now lately translated out of Laten into Englissh for the erudicion of them, which be disposyd to lerne the tongis. Inter locutores, Menippus and Philonides.

R. G. C. Proctor, in *Hand Lists of English Printers*, Pt. ii, distinguishes two editions, one certainly, the other probably, printed by Rastell. Hazlitt, *Manual*, 164, describes the translation as 'after the manner of an interlude.' The Latin and English are in parallel columns, and Collier, ii. 280, who saw a fragment in the Douce collection, thought that it was 'a modern Latin play, possibly by Rightwise.' Bale, *Scriptores* (1557), i. 656, says that More translated Lucian's '*Menippum, seu Necromantiam, Dial.* 1. *Salue atrium, domusque uesti*[*bulum*]'; but the reference is probably to the Latin version of this and other dialogues published in 1506.

Farces of Mediaeval Type.

11. †1521. *John Heywood. The Pardoner and the Friar.*
12. †1521. *John Heywood. The Four Ps.*
13. †1521–31. *John Heywood. The Weather.*
14. †1521–31. *John Heywood. John, Tib and Sir John.*

See s. v. Heywood.

Translation from Spanish.

15. *Calisto and Melibaea.*

[1516–33.] John Rastell. A new cōmodye in englysh in maner Of an enterlude ryght elygant & full of craft of rethoryk wherein is shewd & dyscrybyd as well the bewte & good propertes of women as theyr vycys & euyll cōdiciōs with a morall cōclusion & exhortacyon to vertew.

A modern reprint is in Hazlitt-Dodsley, vol. i. The *dramatis personae* are Calisto, Melibaea, Sempronio, Celestina, Parmeno. The play is a partial English version through the Italian of the Spanish *Celestina* (1492) of Fernando Rojas de Montalvan and Rodrigo Costa. A later translation is J. Mabbe, *Celestina* (1630), ed. J. Fitzmaurice Kelly in *Tudor Translations*; cf. J. G. Underhill, *Spanish Literature in the England of the Tudors*, 65, 375.

Translation from Classical Latin.

16. *Terence. Andria.*

[1516–33.] John Rastell (?). Terens in englyssh. The translacyon out of Latin into englysh of the furst comedy of tyrens callyd Andria.

Translations from Neo-Latin.

17. 1537. *Thersites.*

[1558–63.] John Tysdale. A new Enterlude called Thersytes. This Enterlude Folowynge Dothe Declare howe that the greatest boesters are not the greatest doers.

There are modern editions in J. Haslewood, *Two Interludes* (Roxburghe Club, 1820); F. J. Child, *Four Old Plays* (1848); Hazlitt-Dodsley, vol. i; also a facsimile by H. S. Ashbee (1876) and extracts in Pollard, 126. There are 915 lines. The *dramatis personae* are Thersites, Mulciber, Miles, Mater, Telemachus. Mulciber has 'a sharp sword made in the place,' and Mater 'the place which is prepared for her.' The date is fixed by a prayer for Prince Edward, born Oct. 12, 1537, and Queen Jane Seymour, who died Oct. 24, 1537. Bolte, in *Vahlen-Festschrift*, 594, says that the piece is translated from the *Thersites* of J. Ravisius Textor, printed in his *Dialogi* (1651), 239. The first edition of the *Dialogi* was in 1530 (Bahlmann, *Lat. Dr.* 31).

18. †1560. *Thomas Ingelend. The Disobedient Child.*

[Probably an Elizabethan play, but included here on account of its relation to *Thersites*.]

[1561–75.] Thomas Colwell. A pretie and Mery new Enterlude: called the Disobedient Child. Compiled by Thomas Ingelend late Student in Cambridge.

There are modern editions by Halliwell (Percy Soc. xxiii) and in Hazlitt-Dodsley, vol. ii. The closing prayer is for Elizabeth. Bolte, loc. cit., considers this a translation of the *Iuvenis, Pater, Uxor* of Ravisius Textor (*Dialogi*, 71). Brandl, lxxiii, finds in it the influence of the *Studentes* (1549) of Christopherus Stymmelius (Bahlmann, *Lat. Dr.* 98).

Farces on Classical Models.

19. †1550–3. *W. Stevenson* (?). *Gammer Gurton's Needle.*

1575. Thomas Colwell. A Ryght Pithy, Pleasaunt anp merie Comedie: Intytuled Gammer gurton's Nedle: Played on Stage, not longe ago in Christes Colledge in Cambridge. Made by Mr S. Mr of Art.

1661. Thomas Johnson.

There are modern editions in Hawkins, vol. i; W. Scott, *Ancient British Drama* (1810), vol. i; *Old English Drama* (1830), vol. i; Hazlitt-Dodsley, vol. iii; Manly, vol. ii. The latest is by H. Bradley in C. M. Gayley, *Representative English Comedies* (1903).

The play is divided into Acts and Scenes, has a prologue and a *plaudite*; but the subject is not taken from Latin comedy. It is probably identical with the *Dyccon of Bedlam* entered by Colwell on the Stationers' Register in 1562–3, since 'Diccon, the bedlem' is a character. The 1575 edition may, therefore, not have been the first. Jusserand, *Théâtre*, 181, thinks that the satire is even pre-Reformation in tone. The authorship is much in dispute. I. Reed, *Biographia Dramatica* (1782), suggested John Still, afterwards bishop of Bath and Wells, who was a M.A. of Christ's in 1565. C. H. Ross, in *Modern Language Notes*, vii (1892), no. 6, and *Anglia*, xix. 297, accepts John Bridges, afterwards bishop of Oxford, who is spoken of, but with doubtful seriousness, as the author, in *Martin Marprelate's Epistle* (1588). But Bridges' initial is not S, nor was he a Christ's man. H. Bradley, in *Athenæum* for August 6, 1898, and J. Peile, *Christ's College* (1900), 54, 73, point out that one William Stevenson, a Bachelor Fellow of Christ's, is shown by college accounts to have been in charge of plays there between 1550 and 1553. His seems to me by far the strongest claim yet made.

20. †1553–4. *Nicholas Udall. Roister Doister.*

See s. v. Udall.

21. †1553–8. *Jack Juggler.*

[1562–9.] W. Copland, A new Enterlude for Chyldren to playe, named Jacke Jugeler, both wytte, and very playsent Newly Imprentid.

According to Grosart, two leaves of another edition are bound with the Duke of Devonshire's copy.

The play was entered by Copland on the Stationers' Register in 1562–3. There are modern reprints in J. Haslewood, *Two Interludes* (Roxburghe Club, 1820); F. J. Child, *Four Old Plays* (1848); A. B. Grosart, *Fuller Worthies Library Miscellanies* (1873), vol. iv; Hazlitt-

Dodsley, vol. ii, and a facsimile by E. W. Ashbee (1876). The piece is an imitation of the *Amphitruo* of Plautus. Brandl, lxxi, assigns it to the reign of Mary on the strength of a Catholic sentiment.

Tragedy on Classical Model (?).

22. †1516–33. *Lucrece.*

A fragment of a 'Play concerning Lucretia' is attributed by R. G. C. Proctor, in *Hand Lists of English Printers* (1896), Part ii, to the press of John Rastell (1516–33). It is in the Bagford collection of fragments, *Harl. MS.* 5919, f. 20 (no. 98), and consists of two pages, containing a scene in which Publius Cornelius instructs a confidential friend with the initial B to sound the feeling of 'Lucres' towards him, and the beginning of a scene between B. and 'Lucres.' Halliwell-Phillipps, ii. 340, says that the play was written by Medwall, †1490, and gives the title as 'A godely interlude of Fulgeus, Cenatoure of Rome, Lucres his daughter, Gayus Flaminius and Publius Cornelius, of the Disputacyon of Noblenes.' The 'Fulgius and Lucrelle' of seventeenth-century play-lists (Hazlitt, *Manual*, s.v.; Greg, *Masques*, lxx, may be related to this. The heroine is not Shakespeare's Lucrece.

Latin Neo-Mysteries.

23. †1535–45. *Thomas Watson* (?). *Absolon.*

Ascham, *Scholemaster* (ed. Mayor, 1869), highly praises, together with Buchanan's *Jephthes*, the *Absolon* of Thomas Watson 'in St John's College Cambridge' which he never would publish because an anapaest sometimes stood where he thought, incorrectly, that there should have been an iambus. Watson became bishop of Lincoln. Fleay, *Biog. Chron.* ii. 267, and others ascribe the play in error to John Watson, bishop of Winchester, and speak of a manuscript at Penshurst, which, however, is not mentioned in the account of the Penshurst MSS. in *Hist. MSS.* iii. app. 227. Probably the play is identical with the *Absolon* preserved in *Brit. Mus. Stowe MS.* 957, described by G. B. Churchill and W. Keller, *Die lat. Universitäts-Dramen Englands in der Zeit der Königin Elisabeth* (*Shakespeare-Jahrbuch*, xxxiv (1898), 229). An eighteenth-century ascription on the first leaf to John Bale is of no authority. The play is of a Senecan type, with acts and scenes and a chorus. The first line was originally 'Adhuc animus vexatur excusso metu,' but in the MS., which has many corrections, 'Animus adhuc' has been substituted.

24. †1540. *Nicholas Grimald. Christus Redivivus.*

25. †1547. *Nicholas Grimald. Archipropheta.*

See s. v. Grimald.

26. †1550. *John Foxe. Christus Triumphans.*

1551. Christus triumphans, Comoedia apocalyptica. Autore Ioanne Foxo Anglo. London 1551. 8o.

1556. Oporinus, Basle.

1590. Nuremberg, Gerlach.

In 1672 and 1677 the Latin text was edited by Thomas Comber for school use. A French translation by Jacques Bienvenu appeared in 1562. There is also

1579. John and Richard Day. Christ Jesus Triumphant, A fruitefull Treatise, wherein is described the most glorious Triumph, and Conquest of Christ Iesus our Saviour ... Made to be read for spiritual comfort by Iohn Foxe, and from Latin translated intoo English by the Printer....

There are later editions of 1581 and 1607. This is generally regarded as a translation of the *Christus Triumphans*, but Greg, *Masques*, cxxiii, doubts this, and notes that 'a modern reprint [1828] in the B.M. is not dramatic.' The reprint is in fact a translation of the *De Christo Triumphante, Eiusdem Autoris Panegyricon* appended to the Basle edition of the play. But possibly it does not represent the whole of Day's work. The 1551 edition is given by Bahlmann, *Lat. Dr.* 107. According to S. L. Lee, in *D. N. B.*, it only rests on the authority of Tanner. In 1551 Foxe was tutor to the children of Lord Surrey, who had been executed some years before. In 1555 he entered the printing office of Oporinus at Basle, and in 1564 that of John Day in London. The MS. of the play is *Lansd. MS.* 1073. It is an 'Antichrist' play, written under the influence of the *Pammachius* (1538) of Thomas Kirchmaier or Naogeorgus (Bahlmann, *op. cit.* 71). A full analysis is given by Herford, 138.

Translation from Latin Neo-Moral.

27. †1530–40. *J. Palsgrave. Acolastus.*

1540. Thomas Berthelet. Ioannis Palsgravi Londoniensis, ecphrasis Anglica in comoediam Acolasti. ¶ The Comedye of Acolastus translated into oure englysshe tongue, ... Interpreted by John Palsgraue.

This is a translation of the *Acolastus* (1530) of Wilhelm de Volder, known in learning as Gnaphaeus or Fullonius, of the Hague (Bahlmann, *Lat. Dr.* 39). It is arranged for school use, with marginal notes on grammar, &c. The original play is the most important of the group dealing with the Prodigal Son motive: cf. Herford, 152.

Drama of Catholic Controversy.

28. 1553. *Respublica.*

Printed by Collier, *Illustrations of Old English Literature* (1866), vol. i, and Brandl, 281, from sixteenth-century MS. of Mr. Hudson Gurney of Keswick Hall, Norfolk, with the heading 'A merye enterlude entitled Respublica, made in the yeare of our Lorde, 1553.'

The play is divided into Acts and Scenes, and is a 'Christmas devise' (prol. 6) by 'boyes' (prol. 39). The place-names are of London. The controversial tone is Catholic, and political, rather than theological. Brandl, lviii, finds the model in Lyndsay's *Satyre*. Except for the Prologue (the Poet) all the characters are abstractions. Avarice, *alias* Policy, is 'the vice of the plaie.'

Dramas of Protestant Controversy.

29. 1538. *John Bale. God's Promises.*
30. 1538. *John Bale. John Baptist.*
31. 1538. *John Bale. The Temptation.*
32. 1538. *John Bale. The Three Laws.*
33. ? 1539, 1561. *John Bale. King John.*

See s. v. Bale.

34. †1547–53. *R. Wever. Lusty Juventus.*

[1549–69.] W. Copland. An Enterlude called lusty Iuuentus. Lyuely describing the frailtie of youth: of natur prone to vyce: by grace and good counsayll, traynable to vertue.—At end of play, 'Finis, quod R. Wever.'

[1548–86.] A. Vele.

Copyright was entered on the Stationers' Register by John King in 1560–1. There are modern reprints in Hawkins, vol. i, and Hazlitt-Dodsley, vol. ii. The characters are abstractions with the Devil, a Messenger, and Little Bess a 'Curtisane.' The prayer is for a king and his council who rule, which points to the reign of Edward VI.

35. †1547–53. *T. R. Nice Wanton.*

1560. John King. A Preaty Interlude called, Nice wanton.—At end of play, 'Finis T. R.'

There are reprints in Hazlitt-Dodsley, vol. i, and Manly, vol. i. The characters are curiously heterogeneous: Messenger, Barnabas, Ismael, Dalila, Eulalia, Iniquitie, Baily Errand, Xantippe, Worldly Shame, Daniel. Brandl, lxxii, considers the play an adaptation of the *Rebelles* (1535) of George Van Langeveldt or Macropedius, of Utrecht (Bahlmann, *Lat. Dr.* 55). The rhyme 'queenes'—'things' in the final prayer shows an original date of composition under Edward VI.

36. †1547–53. *Somebody, Avarice and Minister.*

Fragment of unidentified edition amongst papers of the reign of Edward VI in Lambeth Library, reprinted by S. R. Maitland, *List of Early Printed Books at Lambeth* (1843), 280. Brandl, lix, considers this a politico-religious interlude of the school of Lyndsay.

Protestant Controversy: Translation.

37. †1561. *Henry Cheke. Freewill.*

[1558–63.] John Tisdale. A certayne Tragedie wrytten fyrst in Italian, by F. N. B. entituled, Freewyl, and translated into Englishe, by Henry Cheeke.

The copyright of a book 'of frewil' was entered on the Stationers' Register on May 11, 1561 (Arber, i. 156). The original is the *Tragedia del Libero Arbitrio* (1546) of Francesco Nigri de Bassano. The translator cannot be, as stated in the *D. N. B.*, Henry, the son of Sir John Cheke, if the date of his birth is as there given (†1548).

Protestant Controversy: Pseudo-Interludes.

38. †1547–53. *Robin Conscience.*

Often described as an 'interlude,' but really a series of dialogues between Robin Conscience, his father Covetousness, his mother New-guise, and his sister Proud-beauty. Collier, ii. 315, describes it from a printed fragment in the Devonshire library, and inclines to ascribe it to the reign of Edward VI; cf. Herford, 55. Hazlitt, iii. 225, prints the full text from a later edition.

39. 1549. *Ponet. Bishop of Rome.*

A tragoedie or Dialoge of the uniuste usurped primacie of the Bishop of Rome. A translation by John Ponet, Bishop of Winchester, from the Italian of Bernardino Ochino (1549); cf. Bale, i. 694; Herford, 33. Among the speakers are Edward VI and Somerset.

Lost Interludes.

See s.v. Skelton for the alleged *Nigramansir* (1504).

S. Jones, *Biographia Dramatica* (1812), ii. 328, describes 'A newe Interlude of Impacyente Poverte, newlye Imprinted. M. V. L. X.' The copyright of this play, which is in the Sir Thomas More list (cf. p. 200) and that in *Captain Cox*, cxviii, was transferred on the Stationers' Register from the late Sampson Awdeley to John Charlwood on Jan. 15, 1582.

Halliwell-Phillipps, *Dictionary of Old English Plays* (1860), quoting 'Coxeter's Notes,' is the authority for 'An Interlude of Welth and Helth, full of Sport and mery Pastyme,' n. d.

SUBJECT INDEX

[THIS index is almost wholly confined to the text, and only includes the principal passages dealing with each subject. I am sorry not to have been able to prepare a local or a nominal index. The want of the former may be in part met, so far as the miracle-plays are concerned, by the topographical list of representations in Appendix W.]

THE END

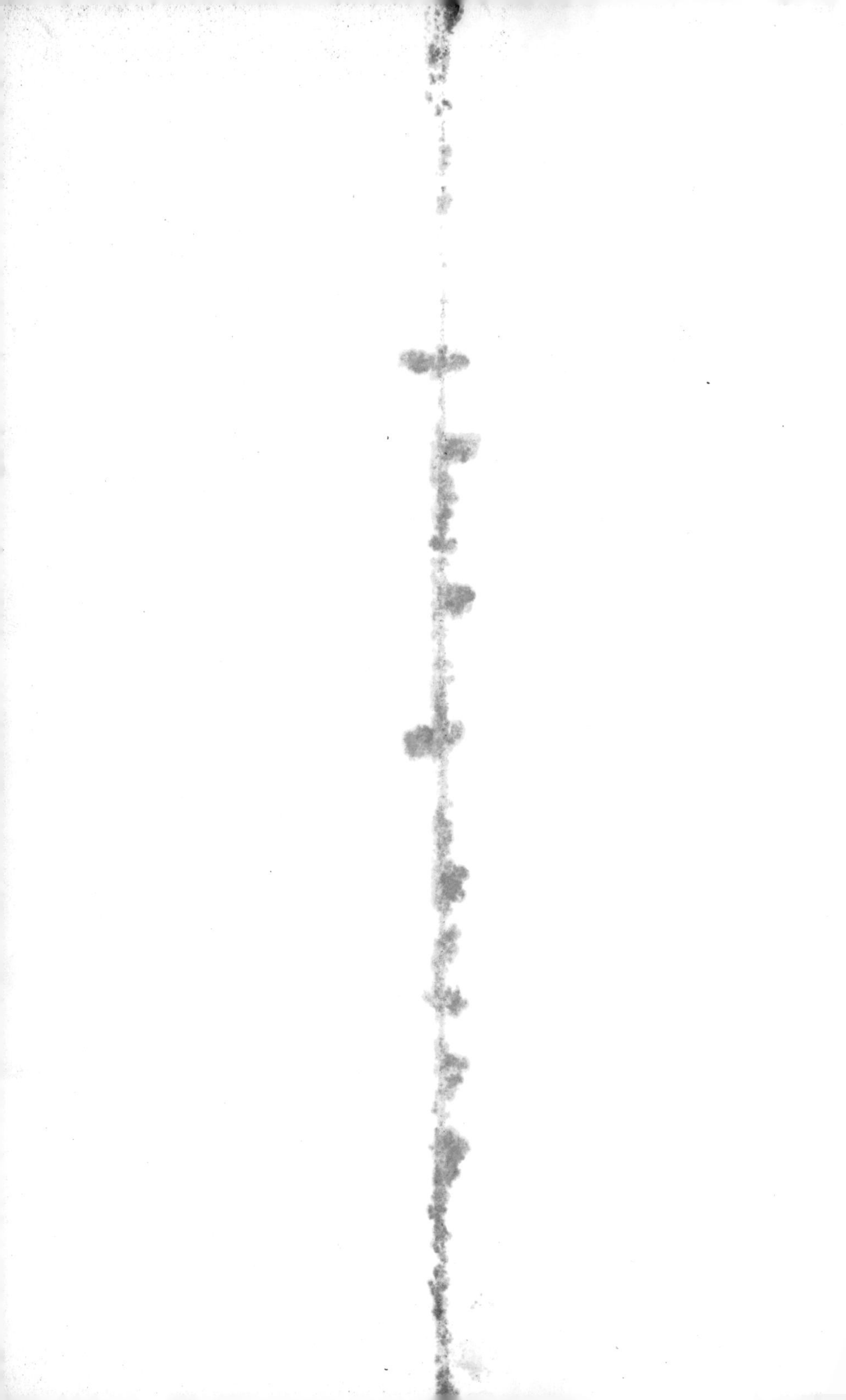